Lecture Notes in Computer Science 13600

More information about this series at https://link.springer.com/bookseries/558

Chunpeng Ge · Fuchun Guo (Eds.)

Provable and Practical Security

16th International Conference, ProvSec 2022
Nanjing, China, November 11–12, 2022
Proceedings

Springer

Editors
Chunpeng Ge
Shandong University
Jinan, China

Fuchun Guo 🆔
University of Wollongong
Wollongong, NSW, Australia

ISSN 0302-9743 ISSN 1611-3349 (electronic)
Lecture Notes in Computer Science
ISBN 978-3-031-20916-1 ISBN 978-3-031-20917-8 (eBook)
https://doi.org/10.1007/978-3-031-20917-8

This Springer imprint is published by the registered company Springer Nature Switzerland AG
The registered company address is: Gewerbestrasse 11, 6330 Cham, Switzerland

Preface

The 16th International Conference on Provable and Practical Security (ProvSec 2022) was held in an online and offline hybrid manner during November 11–12, 2022. The conference was hosted by Nanjing University of Aeronautics and Astronautics and co-organized by the Collaborative Innovation Center of Novel Software Technology and Industrialization. ProvSec is an international conference on provable security in cryptography and practical security for information systems. ProvSec is designed to be a forum for theoreticians, system and application designers, protocol developers, and practitioners to discuss and express their views on the current trends, challenges, and state-of-the-art solutions related to various issues in provable and practical security. Topics of interests include, but are not limited to, provable security for asymmetric cryptography, provable security for symmetric cryptography, provable security for physical attacks, privacy and anonymity technologies, secure cryptographic protocols and applications, security notions, approaches, and paradigms, leakage-resilient cryptography, lattice-based cryptography and post-quantum cryptography, blockchain and cryptocurrency, IoT security, cloud security, and access control.

The conference received 52 submissions. Each submission was reviewed by at least three Program Committee members or external reviewers. The Program Committee members accepted 15 full papers and four short papers to be included in the conference program. The Program Committee members also selected two best papers. These are "A Generic Construction of CCA-secure Attribute-based Encryption with Equality Test" by Kyoichi Asano, Keita Emura, Atsushi Takayasu, and Yohei Watanabe and "FolketID: A Decentralized Blockchain-based NemID Alternative against DDoS Attacks" by Wei-Yang Chiu, Weizhi Meng, Wenjuan Li, and Liming Fang.

We thank the Program Committee members and the external reviewers for their hard work in reviewing the submissions. We thank the Organizing Committee and all volunteers for their time and effort dedicated to arranging the conference.

September 2022

Chunpeng Ge
Fuchun Guo

Organization

General Co-chairs

Bing Chen   Nanjing University of Aeronautics and Astronautics, China

Zhe Liu   Nanjing University of Aeronautics and Astronautics, China

Program Co-chairs

Chunpeng Ge   Shandong University, China

Fuchun Guo   University of Wollongong, Australia

Program Committee

Elena Andreeva	TU Wien, Austria
Rishiraj Bhattacharyya	University of Birmingham, UK
Shi Bai	Florida Atlantic University, USA
Rongmao Chen	National University of Defense Technology, China
Jie Chen	East China Normal University, China
Cheng-Kang Chu	Institute for Infocomm Research, Singapore
Ting Chen	University of Electronic Science and Technology of China, China
He Debiao	Wuhan University, China
Yi Deng	Institute of Information Engineering, Chinese Academy of Sciences, China
Xiong Fan	Algorand Inc., USA
Zheng Gong	South China Normal University, China
Junqing Gong	East China Normal University, China
Swee-Huay Heng	Multimedia University, Malaysia
Qiong Huang	South China Agricultural University, China
David Jao	University of Waterloo, Canada
Peng Jiang	Beijing Institute of Technology, China
Yannan Li	University of Wollongong, Australia
Jianchang Lai	Fujian Normal University, China
Rongxing Lu	University of New Brunswick, Canada
Dongxi Liu	CSIRO, Australia
Zhen Liu	Shanghai Jiao Tong University, China

Weizhi Meng	Technical University of Denmark, Denmark
Khoa Nguyen	University of Wollongong, Australia
Somindu C. Ramanna	Indian Institute of Technology Kharagpur, India
Siwei Sun	University of Chinese Academy of Sciences, China
Daniel Slamanig	AIT Austrian Institute of Technology, Austria
Amin Sakzad	Monash University, Australia
Olivier Sanders	Orange Labs, France
Jun Shao	Zhejiang Gongshang University, China
Viet Cuong Trinh	Hong Duc University, Vietnam
Youliang Tian	Guizhou University, China
Huaqun Wang	Nanjing University of Posts and Telecommunications, China
Jinyue Xia	IBM Research Institute, USA
Haiyang Xue	The University of Hong Kong, Hong Kong
Kuo-Hui Yeh	National Dong Hwa University, Taiwan
Yong Yu	Shaanxi Normal University, China
Ren Yongjun	Nanjing University of Information Science and Technology, China
Rupeng Yang	University of Wollongong, Australia
Guomin Yang	University of Wollongong, Australia
Lei Zhang	East China Normal University, China
Jun Zhao	Nanyang Technological University, Singapore
Liehuang Zhu	Beijing Institute of Technology, China
L. F. Zhang	ShanghaiTech, China
Fangguo Zhang	Sun Yat-sen University, China
Zhen Zhao	Xidian University, China
Jiang Zhang	Institute of Software, Chinese Academy of Sciences, China
Lu Zhou	University of Aizu, Japan

Publicity Chairs

| Weizhi Meng | Technical University of Denmark, Denmark |
| Junlong Zhou | Nanjing university of Science and Technology, China |

Organizing Committee Co-chairs

| Liming Fang | Nanjing University of Aeronautics and Astronautics, China |
| Xiaozhen Lu | Nanjing University of Aeronautics and Astronautics, China |

Contents

Encryption

A Generic Construction of CCA-Secure Attribute-Based Encryption with Equality Test

Kyoichi Asano[1,2]($\boxtimes$) , Keita Emura[2] , Atsushi Takayasu[3] ,
and Yohei Watanabe[1,2]

[1] The University of Electro-Communications, 1-5-1, Chofugaoka, Chofu, Tokyo
182-8585, Japan
k.asano@uec.ac.jp
[2] National Institute of Information and Communications Technology, 4-2-1,
Nukui-Kitamachi, Koganei, Tokyo 184-8795, Japan
[3] The University of Tokyo, 7-3-1, Hongo, Bunkyo-ku, Tokyo 113-8656, Japan

Abstract. Attribute-based encryption with equality test (ABEET) is
an extension of the ordinary attribute-based encryption (ABE), where
trapdoors enable us to check whether two ciphertexts are encryptions
of the same message. Thus far, several CCA-secure ABEET schemes
have been proposed for monotone span programs satisfying selective
security under q-type assumptions. In this paper, we propose a generic
construction of CCA-secure ABEET from delegatable ABE. Specifically,
our construction is an attribute-based extension of Lee et al.'s generic
construction of identity-based encryption with equality test from hierarchical identity-based encryption. Even as far as we know, there are
various delegatable ABE schemes. Therefore, we obtain various ABEET
schemes with new properties that have not been achieved before such
as various predicates, adaptive security, standard assumptions, compact
ciphertexts/secret keys, and lattice-based constructions.

Keywords: Attribute-based encryption · Equality test ·
Chosen-ciphertext security · Generic construction

1 Introduction

1.1 Background

The notion of public key encryption with equality test (PKEET) was introduced
by Yang et al. [32]. PKEET is similar to public key encryption with keyword
search [1,12] in a multi-user setting. PKEET has multiple public/secret key pairs
$(\mathsf{pk}_1, \mathsf{sk}_1), \ldots, (\mathsf{pk}_N, \mathsf{sk}_N)$. Let ct_i and ct_j denote encryptions of plaintexts M_i
and M_j by pk_i and pk_j, respectively. As the case of the standard public key
encryption, the secret keys sk_i and sk_j can decrypt ct_i and ct_j, and recover M_i
and M_j, respectively. Moreover, PKEET has a trapdoor td to perform the equality

C. Ge and F. Guo (Eds.): ProvSec 2022, LNCS 13600, pp. 3–19, 2022.
https://doi.org/10.1007/978-3-031-20917-8_1

test. Let td_i and td_j denote trapdoors created by the secret keys sk_i and sk_j, respectively. Briefly speaking, even if the i-th user obtains the j-th trapdoor td_j, they cannot decrypt the j-th ciphertext ct_j. In contrast, any users who have trapdoors td_i and td_j can check whether ct_i and ct_j are encryptions of the same plaintexts. There are several applications of PKEET; for example, Yang et al. [32] considered outsourced databases with partitioning encrypted data where a database administrator can collect and categorize confidential data without help of message owners. Thus far, several PKEET schemes have been proposed with stronger security models, efficiency improvements, additional properties, and under various assumptions.

As a natural extension of PKEET, attribute-based encryption with equality test (ABEET) has been studied. Here, we briefly explain ABEET with a predicate $\mathsf{P} : \mathcal{X} \times \mathcal{Y} \to \{0,1\}$. ABEET has a single master public/secret key pair (mpk, msk). Let ct_i and ct_j denote encryptions of plaintexts M_i and M_j for ciphertext-attributes x_i and x_j, respectively. As the case of the standard attribute-based encryption (ABE), the secret key sk_{y_i} for key attribute y_i (resp. sk_{y_j} for y_j) can decrypt ct_i (resp. ct_j) if $\mathsf{P}(x_i, y_i) = 1$ (resp. $\mathsf{P}(x_j, y_j) = 1$) holds. Let td_{y_i} and td_{y_j} denote trapdoors created by the secret keys sk_{y_i} and sk_{y_j}, respectively. Even if the user with the key-attribute y_i obtains the trapdoor td_{y_j} of the key-attribute y_j, they cannot decrypt the ciphertext ct_{x_j} of the ciphertext-attribute x_j when $\mathsf{P}(x_j, y_i) = 0$. In contrast, any users who have trapdoors td_{y_i} and td_{y_j} can check whether ct_{x_i} and ct_{x_j} are encryptions of the same plaintexts if $\mathsf{P}(x_i, y_i) = \mathsf{P}(x_j, y_j) = 1$ holds.

The simplest case of ABEET is arguably identity-based encryption with equality test (IBEET) that has an equality predicate $\mathsf{P}_{\mathsf{IBE}} : \mathcal{V} \times \mathcal{V} \to \{0,1\}$, i.e., $\mathsf{P}_{\mathsf{IBE}}(v, v') = 1 \Leftrightarrow v = v'$. Thus far, several IBEET schemes have been proposed such as [23]. ABEET schemes for more complex monotone span programs have also been proposed [18,19,25,28] as ABE for the same predicate has been actively studied. However, ABEET research has a major drawback in the sense that progress in ABEET research is far behind that of ABE research. Although all the ABEET schemes [18,19,25,28] satisfy only selective security under q-type assumptions for monotone span programs, there are adaptively secure ABE schemes for monotone span programs under standard assumptions [9–11,16,17,24,29] and adaptively secure ABE schemes for more complex non-monotone span programs [4,20]. There are also several ABE schemes for other complex predicates such as (non-)deterministic finite automata [4,9,20,21] and circuits [13]. Although all the ABEET schemes [18,19,25,28] are pairing-based, there are lattice-based ABE schemes under the post-quantum learning with errors assumption such as [13]. Therefore, it is an important open problem to improve ABEET based on techniques of the state-of-the-art ABE schemes.

1.2   Our Contribution

To resolve the above mentioned open problem, we propose a generic construction of CCA-secure ABEET schemes from CPA-secure *delegatable* ABE schemes and cryptographic hash functions. To construct an ABEET scheme for a predicate

Table 1. Comparison among known CCA-secure ABEET schemes for complex predicates. MSP, NSP, DFA, CP, KP, ROM, and BDHE stand for monotone span program, non-monotone span program, deterministic finite automata, ciphertext-policy, key-policy, random oracle, and bilinear Diffie-Hellman exponent, respectively. The column "Compact Parameter" indicates that the content consists of the constant number of group elements.

Known scheme	Predicate	Security	Policy	Universe	Model	Complexity assumption	Compact parameter
CHH+18 [18]	MSP	selective	CP	small	ROM	q-parallel BDHE	none
CHH+19 [19]	MSP	selective	CP	small	ROM	q-parallel BDHE	none
WCH+20 [28]	MSP	selective	CP	small	Std.	q-parallel BDHE	none
LSX+21 [25]	MSP	selective	CP	large	Std.	q-1	|mpk|
Our Scheme (Base Schemes)	Predicate	Security	Policy	Universe	Model	Complexity Assumption	Compact Parameter
Scheme 1 [16,17,29]	MSP	adaptive	KP	small	Std.	k-Lin	none
Scheme 2 [3,9,26]	MSP	adaptive	KP	large	Std.	k-Lin	none
Scheme 3 [3,26]	MSP	semi-adaptive	KP	large	Std.	k-Lin	|ct|
Scheme 4 [4,11]	NSP	adaptive	KP	large	Std.	q-ratio	|mpk|
Scheme 5 [4,11]	NSP	adaptive	KP	large	Std.	q-ratio	|ct|
Scheme 6 [4,11]	NSP	adaptive	KP	large	Std.	q-ratio	|sk|
Scheme 7 [16,17,29]	MSP	adaptive	CP	small	Std.	k-Lin	none
Scheme 8 [3,9,26]	MSP	adaptive	CP	large	Std.	k-Lin	none
Scheme 9 [3,26]	NSP	semi-adaptive	CP	large	Std.	k-Lin	|ct|
Scheme 10 [4,11]	NSP	adaptive	CP	large	Std.	q-ratio	|mpk|
Scheme 11 [4,11]	NSP	adaptive	CP	large	Std.	q-ratio	|ct|
Scheme 12 [4,11]	NSP	adaptive	CP	large	Std.	q-ratio	|sk|
Scheme 13 [4,9]	DFA	adaptive	KP	large	Std.	q-ratio	|mpk|
Scheme 14 [4,9]	DFA	adaptive	CP	large	Std.	q-ratio	|mpk|

$\mathsf{P} : \mathcal{X} \times \mathcal{Y} \to \{0,1\}$, our construction uses a delegatable ABE scheme with a hierarchical structure of the depth three, where only the first level supports the predicate $\mathsf{P} : \mathcal{X} \times \mathcal{Y} \to \{0,1\}$ and the other two levels support only the equality predicate $\mathsf{P}_{\mathsf{IBE}} : \mathcal{V} \times \mathcal{V} \to \{0,1\}$. Since delegatable ABE has not been studied as much as (non-delegatable) ABE, our generic construction does not immediately provide ABEET schemes that have the same performance as all state-of-the-art ABE schemes. Nevertheless, there are several delegatable ABE schemes that enable us to obtain various more attractive ABEET schemes than known schemes [18,19,25,28]. At first, we can easily obtain selectively secure lattice-based ABEET schemes for circuits from Boneh et al.'s delegatable ABE scheme for circuits [13]. Next, we obtain several pairing-based ABEET schemes through the predicate encoding and pair encoding frameworks introduced by Wee [29] and Attrapadung [9], respectively. These frameworks are unifying methods to design ABE for a large class of predicates, where the pair encoding can handle more complex predicates than the predicate encoding. Furthermore, Ambrona et al.'s transformation [7] enables us to modify a predicate encoding scheme and a pair encoding scheme for a predicate P as a delegatable one.[1] Therefore, we can construct ABEET schemes for complex predicates captured by the predicate encoding and pair encoding frameworks. As a result, we obtain new and impressive ABEET schemes for various predicates at once.

Table 1 illustrates a comparison between CCA-secure ABEET schemes for some complex predicate including monotone span programs. All the schemes are constructed over prime-order bilinear groups. Since there are a huge number of ABE schemes through the pair encoding framework, all ABEET schemes obtained by our generic construction may not be covered in Table 1. However, 14 schemes listed in Table 1 should be sufficient for clarifying the impact of our generic construction. We briefly summarize how to obtain base ABE schemes as follows:

- Schemes 1 and 7: Instantiating predicate encoding scheme [29] with [16,17].
- Schemes 2 and 8: Instantiating pair encoding scheme [9] with [3,26].
- Scheme 3: Instantiating a pair encoding scheme [3] with [3,26].
- Scheme 9: Instantiating a pair encoding scheme [26] with [3,26].
- Schemes 4–6 and 10–12: Instantiating pair encoding schemes [11] with [4].
- Schemes 13 and 14: Instantiating pair encoding schemes [9] with [4].

Then, we explain various advantages of our results compared with known ABEET schemes for monotone span programs [18,19,25,28].

- Although all known ABEET schemes capture monotone span programs, Schemes 4–6 and 9–12 capture non-monotone span programs and Schemes 13 and 14 capture deterministic finite automata.
- Although all known ABEET schemes satisfy only selective security, Schemes 1, 2, 4–8, and 10–14 satisfy adaptive security and Schemes 3 and 9 satisfy semi-adaptive security.
- Although all known ABEET schemes except [25] support only small universe, Schemes 2–6 and 8–14 support large universe.
- Although security of all known ABEET schemes are based on q-type assumptions, security of Schemes 1–3 and 7–9 are based on the standard k-linear assumption.
- Although all known ABEET schemes do not have compact ciphertexts and secret keys, Schemes 3, 5, 9, and 11 have compact ciphertexts and Schemes 6 and 12 have compact secret keys.

Therefore, we successfully obtain several improved ABEET schemes from our generic construction. Moreover, although we only list proposed ABEET schemes for complex predicates in Table 1, our generic construction also provides various ABEET schemes for less expressive but important predicates captured by the pair encoding and the predicate encoding such as (non-zero) inner product encryption, (negated) spatial encryption, doubly spatial encryption, and arithmetic span programs.

---

[1] To be precise, Ambrona et al. provided a delegatable transformation only for predicate encoding. However, we can modify a pair encoding scheme as a delegatable one in a similar way.

1.3 Technical Overview

We explain an overview of our construction. At first, we exploit the common essence of known ABEET constructions and briefly summarize the fact that any IND-CPA secure ABE scheme for a predicate $P : \mathcal{X} \times \mathcal{Y} \rightarrow \{0,1\}$ becomes CPA-secure ABEET scheme for the same predicate by combining with cryptographic hash functions. For this purpose, we run two ABE schemes for the same predicate in parallel. Let $ABE.mpk_0$ and $ABE.mpk_1$ denote master public keys of the two ABE schemes and let H denote a cryptographic hash function. Then, we set $mpk = (ABE.mpk_0, ABE.mpk_1, H)$ as the master public key of an ABEET scheme. We encrypt a plaintext M for a ciphertext attribute $x \in \mathcal{X}$ as $ct_x = (ABE.ct_{x,0}, ABE.ct_{x,1})$, where $ABE.ct_{x,0}$ and $ABE.ct_{x,1}$ are encryptions of M and $H(M)$ for the same x computed by $ABE.mpk_0$ and $ABE.mpk_1$, respectively. We set a secret key of a key attribute $y \in \mathcal{Y}$ as $sk_y = (ABE.sk_{y,0}, ABE.sk_{y,1})$, where $ABE.sk_{y,0}$ and $ABE.sk_{y,1}$ are secret keys for the same y computed by $(ABE.mpk_0, ABE.msk_0)$ and $(ABE.mpk_1, ABE.msk_1)$, respectively. The secret key sk_y can decrypt the ciphertext ct_x if $P(x, y) = 1$ by simply decrypting the ABE ciphertext $ABE.ct_{x,0}$ with the ABE secret key $ABE.sk_{y,0}$ and recover M. We set a trapdoor for $y \in \mathcal{Y}$ as $td_y = ABE.sk_{y,1}$. Given two ciphertexts $(ct_x, ct_{x'})$ for $(x, x') \in \mathcal{X}^2$ and two trapdoors $(td_y, td_{y'})$ such that $P(x, y) = P(x', y') = 1$, we can check whether the two ciphertexts are encryptions of the same plaintexts by checking whether the decryption results of the ABE ciphertexts $ABE.ct_{x,1}$ and $ABE.ct_{x',1}$ by the trapdoors $ABE.sk_{y,1}$ and $ABE.sk_{y',1}$, respectively, have the same values.

Next, we observe that the above ABEET scheme satisfies CPA security. Briefly speaking, ABEET has to be secure against two types of adversaries called Type-I and Type-II. Let x^* denote the target ciphertext attribute. The Type-I adversary can receive trapdoors td_y such that $P(x^*, y) = 1$, while the Type-II adversary cannot receive such trapdoors. Although the Type-I adversary trivially breaks indistinguishability by definition, we can prove one-wayness against the Type-I adversary. Thus, the challenge ciphertext $ct_{x^*}^*$ is an encryption of M^* that is sampled uniformly at random from the plaintext space. The IND-CPA security of the underlying ABE scheme ensures that the first element $ABE.ct_{x^*,0}^*$ of the challenge ciphertext $ct_{x^*}^*$ does not reveal the information of M^* at all. Since the Type-I adversary has the trapdoor $td_y = ABE.sk_{y,1}$ such that $P(x^*, y) = 1$, it can recover $H(M^*)$; however, the one-wayness of the hash function H ensures that M^* cannot be recovered. In contrast, we have to prove indistinguishability against the Type-II adversary. Thus, the challenge ciphertext $ct_{x^*}^*$ is an encryption of M_{coin}^*, where the tuple (M_0^*, M_1^*) is declared by the adversary and coin $\leftarrow_\$ \{0,1\}$ is flipped by the challenger. In this case, the IND-CPA security of the underlying ABE scheme ensures that both $ABE.ct_{x^*,0}^*$ and $ABE.ct_{x^*,1}^*$ do not reveal the information of M_{coin}^* and $H(M_{coin}^*)$ at all, respectively. We note that the above construction does not provide CCA security even if the underlying ABE scheme satisfies IND-CCA security. Indeed, when the Type-II adversary receives the challenge ciphertext $ct_{x^*}^* = (ABE.ct_{x^*,0}^*, ABE.ct_{x^*,1}^*)$, it can guess the value of coin by making a decryption query on $(\mathsf{ABE.ct}_{x^*,0}, \mathsf{ABE.ct}^*_{x^*,1})$, where $\mathsf{ABE.ct}_{x^*,0}$ is the encryption of M^*_0 or M^*_1 computed by the adversary itself.

Based on the discussion so far, what we have to achieve is CCA security. For this purpose, we follow the generic construction of CCA-secure IBEET from IND-CPA secure hierarchical IBE with the depth three proposed by Lee et al. [23]. Lee et al. used the CHK transformation [15] to update the above scheme for achieving CCA security in the identity-based setting. Similarly, we use the Yamada et al.'s transformation [31], which is the attribute-based variant of the CHK transformation, to update the above CPA-secure construction for achieving CCA security in the attribute-based setting. We use a IND-CPA-secure delegatable ABE scheme with the depth three as a building block. Specifically, to construct ABEET for a predicate $\mathsf{P} : \mathcal{X} \times \mathcal{Y} \to \{0,1\}$, we use a delegatable ABE scheme for a predicate $(\mathcal{X} \times \{0,1\} \times \mathcal{V}) \times (\mathcal{Y} \times \{0,1\} \times \mathcal{V}) \to \{0,1\}$, where a secret key $\mathsf{ABE.sk}_{y,b',v'}$ can decrypt a ciphertext $\mathsf{ABE.ct}_{x,b,v}$ correctly if it holds that $\mathsf{P}(x,y) = 1 \wedge b = b' \wedge v = v'$. Here, we use the second hierarchical level $b, b' \in \{0,1\}$ to specify which of the ABE schemes in the above CPA-secure construction and the third level $v, v' \in \mathcal{V}$ to specify verification keys of the one-time signature scheme. As a result, we set a master public key, ciphertexts for $x \in \mathcal{X}$, secret keys and trapdoors for $y \in \mathcal{Y}$ of ABEET as $\mathsf{mpk} = \mathsf{ABE.mpk}$, $\mathsf{ct}_x = (\mathsf{verk}, \mathsf{ABE.ct}_{x,0,\mathsf{verk}}, \mathsf{ABE.ct}_{x,1,\mathsf{verk}}, \sigma)$, $\mathsf{sk}_y = \mathsf{ABE.sk}_y$, and $\mathsf{td}_y = \mathsf{ABE.sk}_{y,1}$, respectively, where verk is a verification key of the one-time signature scheme and σ is a signature for the message $[\mathsf{ABE.ct}_{x,0,\mathsf{verk}} \| \mathsf{ABE.ct}_{x,1,\mathsf{verk}}]$. Intuitively, the construction achieves CCA security by combining with security of the above CPA-secure construction and Yamada et al.'s technique [31].

1.4   Roadmap

In Sect. 2, we introduce notations and give some definitions. We show our generic construction of ABEET and discuss its correctness in Sect. 3. We discuss security of our construction in Sect. 4.

2   Preliminaries

Notation. Throughout the paper, λ denotes a security parameter. For an i-bit binary string $\mathsf{s}_1 \in \{0,1\}^i$ and a j-bit binary string $\mathsf{s}_2 \in \{0,1\}^j$, let $[\mathsf{s}_1 \| \mathsf{s}_2] \in \{0,1\}^{i+j}$ denote an $(i+j)$-bit concatenation of s_1 and s_2. For a finite set S, $s \leftarrow_\$ S$ denotes a sampling of an element s from S uniformly at random and let $|S|$ denotes a cardinality of S. Probablistic polynomial time is abbreviated as PPT.

2.1   Delegatable Attribute-Based Encryption

We define delegatable ABE (or simply called ABE hereafter). To make readers easier to understand, we here consider a special case of ABE, which is sufficient to describe our construction. The definition we use here differs from the general definition of ABE in the following ways:

- The hierarchical level is three, not an arbitrary number.
- The second and third levels support only the equality predicate as in identity-based encryption, where the second level and third level take elements of $\{0,1\}$ and an identity space $\mathcal{V}$, respectively.
- The Enc algorithm always takes a level-3 attribute.

Let $\mathsf{P} : \mathcal{X} \times \mathcal{Y} \to \{0,1\}$ denotes a predicate, where $\mathcal{X}$ and $\mathcal{Y}$ are attribute spaces for ciphertexts and secret keys, respectively. In our definition of ABE for a predicate P, ciphertexts $\mathsf{ABE.ct}_{x,b,v}$ and secret keys $\mathsf{ABE.sk}_{y,b',v'}$ are associated with $(x,b,v) \in \mathcal{X} \times \{0,1\} \times \mathcal{V}$ and $(y,b',v') \in \mathcal{Y} \times \{0,1\} \times \mathcal{V}$, respectively. A secret key $\mathsf{ABE.sk}_{y,b',v'}$ can decrypt a ciphertext $\mathsf{ABE.ct}_{x,b,v}$ if it holds that $\mathsf{P}(x,y) = 1 \wedge b = b' \wedge v = v'$.

Syntax. An ABE scheme Π_{ABE} for a predicate P consists of the five algorithms (ABE.Setup, ABE.KeyGen, ABE.Enc, ABE.Dec, ABE.Delegate) as follows:

ABE.Setup(1^λ) $\to$ (ABE.mpk, ABE.msk): On input the security parameter 1^λ, it outputs a master public key ABE.mpk and a master secret key ABE.msk. We assume that ABE.mpk contains a description of a plaintext space $\mathcal{M}$ that is determined only by the security parameter λ.

ABE.Enc(ABE.mpk, (x,b,v), M) $\to$ $\mathsf{ABE.ct}_{x,b,v}$: On input a master public key ABE.mpk, $(x,b,v) \in \mathcal{X} \times \{0,1\} \times \mathcal{V}$, and a plaintext $\mathsf{M} \in \mathcal{M}$, it outputs a ciphertext $\mathsf{ABE.ct}_{x,b,v}$.

ABE.KeyGen(ABE.mpk, ABE.msk, Y) $\to$ $\mathsf{ABE.sk}_Y$: On input a master public key ABE.mpk, a master secret key ABE.msk, and Y, it outputs a secret key $\mathsf{ABE.sk}_Y$, where Y is the element of $\mathcal{Y}$, $\mathcal{Y} \times \{0,1\}$ or $\mathcal{Y} \times \{0,1\} \times \mathcal{V}$.

ABE.Dec(ABE.mpk, $\mathsf{ABE.ct}_{x,b,v}$, $\mathsf{ABE.sk}_{y,b',v'}$) $\to$ M or $\perp$: On input a master public key ABE.mpk, a ciphertext $\mathsf{ABE.ct}_{x,b,v}$, and a secret key $\mathsf{ABE.sk}_{y,b',v'}$, it outputs the decryption result M if $\mathsf{P}(x,y) = 1 \wedge (b,v) = (b',v')$. Otherwise, output $\perp$.

ABE.Delegate(ABE.mpk, $\mathsf{ABE.sk}_Y$, Y') $\to$ $\mathsf{ABE.sk}_{Y'}$: On input a master public key ABE.mpk, a secret key $\mathsf{ABE.sk}_Y$ and Y', it outputs a secret key $\mathsf{ABE.sk}_{Y'}$, where Y is the element of $\mathcal{Y}$ or $\mathcal{Y} \times \{0,1\}$, Y' is the element of $\{Y\} \times \{0,1\}$ or $\{Y\} \times \{0,1\} \times \mathcal{V}$ if $Y \in \mathcal{Y}$, and Y' is the element of $\{Y\} \times \{0,1\} \times \mathcal{V}$ if $Y \in \mathcal{Y} \times \{0,1\}$.

Correctness. For all $\lambda \in \mathbb{N}$, all (ABE.mpk, ABE.msk) $\leftarrow$ ABE.Setup(1^λ), all $\mathsf{M} \in \mathcal{M}$, all $(x,y) \in \mathcal{X} \times \mathcal{Y}$ such that $\mathsf{P}(x,y) = 1$, and all $(b,v) \in \{0,1\} \times \mathcal{V}$, it is required that $\mathsf{M}' = \mathsf{M}$ holds with overwhelming probability, where $\mathsf{ABE.ct}_{x,b,v} \leftarrow$ ABE.Enc(ABE.mpk, (x,b,v), M), $\mathsf{ABE.sk}_{y,b,v} \leftarrow$ ABE.KeyGen(ABE.mpk, ABE.msk, (y,b,v)), and $\mathsf{M}' \leftarrow$ ABE.Dec(ABE.mpk, $\mathsf{ABE.ct}_{x,b,v}$, $\mathsf{ABE.sk}_{y,b,v}$). In addition, there is a correctness for ABE.Delegate, where outputs of ABE.KeyGen(ABE.mpk, ABE.msk, Y') and ABE.Delegate (ABE.mpk, ABE.KeyGen(ABE.mpk, ABE.msk, Y), Y') follow the same distribution.

Security. We consider adaptive IND-CPA security defined below. Note that the following definition is specific to the above syntax but implied by the general adaptive IND-CPA definition.

Definition 1 (Adaptive IND-CPA Security). *The adaptive IND-CPA security of an ABE scheme Π_{ABE} is defined by a game between an adversary $\mathcal{A}$ and a challenger $\mathcal{C}$ as follows:*

Init: $\mathcal{C}$ *runs* $(\mathsf{ABE.mpk}, \mathsf{ABE.msk}) \leftarrow \mathsf{ABE.Setup}(1^\lambda)$ *and gives* $\mathsf{ABE.mpk}$ *to* $\mathcal{A}$.
Phase 1: $\mathcal{A}$ *is allowed to make the following key extraction queries to* $\mathcal{C}$:
    Key extraction query: $\mathcal{A}$ *is allowed to make the query on* Y. *Upon the query,* $\mathcal{C}$ *runs* $\mathsf{ABE.sk}_Y \leftarrow \mathsf{ABE.KeyGen}(\mathsf{ABE.mpk}, \mathsf{ABE.msk}, Y)$ *and returns* $\mathsf{ABE.sk}_Y$ *to* $\mathcal{A}$, *where* Y *is the element of* $\mathcal{Y}$, $\mathcal{Y} \times \{0,1\}$ *or* $\mathcal{Y} \times \{0,1\} \times \mathcal{V}$.
Challenge query: $\mathcal{A}$ *is allowed to make the query only once. Upon* $\mathcal{A}$'s *query on* $((x^*, b^*, v^*), \mathsf{M_0}^*, \mathsf{M_1}^*) \in \mathcal{X} \times \{0,1\} \times \mathcal{V} \times \mathcal{M}^2$, *where* $\mathsf{M_0}^*$ *and* $\mathsf{M_1}^*$ *have the same length and* (x^*, b^*, v^*) *should not satisfy the following conditions for all the attributes* Y *queried on key extraction queries in Phase 1:*
    – *If* $Y = y \in \mathcal{Y}$, $\mathsf{P}(x^*, y) = 1$ *holds.*
    – *If* $Y = (y, b) \in \mathcal{Y} \times \{0,1\}$, $\mathsf{P}(x^*, y) = 1 \wedge b^* = b$ *holds.*
    – *If* $Y = (y, b, v) \in \mathcal{Y} \times \{0,1\} \times \mathcal{V}$, $\mathsf{P}(x^*, y) = 1 \wedge (b^*, v^*) = (b, v)$ *holds.*
    Then, $\mathcal{C}$ *flips a coin* $\mathsf{coin} \leftarrow_\$ \{0,1\}$ *and runs* $\mathsf{ABE.ct}^*_{x^*, b^*, v^*} \leftarrow \mathsf{ABE.Enc}(\mathsf{ABE.mpk}, (x^*, b^*, v^*), \mathsf{M}^*_{\mathsf{coin}})$. *Then,* $\mathcal{C}$ *returns* $\mathsf{ABE.ct}^*_{x^*, b^*, v^*}$ *to* $\mathcal{A}$.
Phase 2: $\mathcal{A}$ *is allowed to make key extraction queries as in Phase 1 with the following exceptions:*
    Key extraction query: *Upon* $\mathcal{A}$'s *query on* Y, Y *should not satisfy the conditions with* x^* *as we mentioned in the challenge query.*
Guess: *At the end of the game,* $\mathcal{A}$ *returns* $\mathsf{coin}' \in \{0,1\}$ *as a guess of* coin.

The adversary $\mathcal{A}$ *wins in the above game if* $\mathsf{coin} = \mathsf{coin}'$ *and the advantage is defined to*

$$\mathsf{Adv}^{\mathrm{IND\text{-}CPA}}_{\Pi_{\mathsf{ABE}}, \mathcal{A}}(\lambda) := \left| \Pr[\mathsf{coin}' = \mathsf{coin}] - \frac{1}{2} \right|.$$

If $\mathsf{Adv}^{\mathrm{IND\text{-}CPA}}_{\Pi_{\mathsf{ABE}}, \mathcal{A}}(\lambda)$ *is negligible in the security parameter* λ *for all PPT adversaries* $\mathcal{A}$, *an ABE scheme* Π_{ABE} *is said to satisfy adaptive IND-CPA security.*

Remark 1. The Definition 1 states the adaptive IND-CPA security in the sense that $\mathcal{A}$ declares the target (x^*, b^*, v^*) at the challenge query. The *selective* IND-CPA security can be defined in the same way except that $\mathcal{A}$ declares the target (x^*, b^*, v^*) before the init phase. Similarly, the *semi-adaptive* IND-CPA security can be defined in the same way except that $\mathcal{A}$ declares the target (x^*, b^*, v^*) just after the init phase.

2.2 Attribute-Based Encryption with Equality Test

Syntax. An ABEET scheme Π for a predicate $\mathsf{P} : \mathcal{X} \times \mathcal{Y} \to \{0,1\}$ consists of the following six algorithms (Setup, Enc, KeyGen, Dec, Trapdoor, Test) as follows:

Setup(1^λ) $\to$ (mpk, msk): On input the security parameter 1^λ, it outputs a master public key mpk and a master secret key msk. We assume that mpk contains a description of a plaintext space $\mathcal{M}$ that is determined only by the security parameter λ.

Enc(mpk, x, M) $\to$ ct$_x$: On input a master public key mpk, $x \in \mathcal{X}$, and a plaintext M $\in \mathcal{M}$, it outputs a ciphertext ct$_x$.

KeyGen(mpk, msk, y) $\to$ sk$_y$: On input a master public key mpk, a master secret key msk, and $y \in \mathcal{Y}$, it outputs a secret key sk$_y$.

Dec(mpk, ct$_x$, sk$_y$) $\to$ M or $\perp$: On input a master public key mpk, a ciphertext ct$_x$, and a secret key sk$_y$, it outputs the decryption result M if $P(x, y) = 1$. Otherwise, output $\perp$.

Trapdoor(mpk, sk$_y$) $\to$ td$_y$: On input a master public key mpk and a secret key sk$_y$, it outputs the trapdoor td$_y$ for $y \in \mathcal{Y}$.

Test(ct$_x$, td$_y$, ct$_{x'}$, td$_{y'}$) $\to$ 1 or 0: On input two ciphertexts ct$_x$, ct$_{x'}$ and two trapdoors td$_y$, td$_{y'}$, it outputs 1 or 0.

Correctness. We require an ABEET scheme to satisfy the following three conditions. Briefly speaking, the first condition ensures that the Dec algorithm works correctly. In contrast, the second (resp. third) conditions ensure that the Test algorithm outputs 1 (resp. 0) if ct$_x$ and ct$_{x'}$ are encryptions of the same plaintext (resp. distinct plaintexts), respectively. We consider PPT adversaries for the third condition. The three conditions are formally defined as follows:

(1) For all $\lambda \in \mathbb{N}$, all (mpk, msk) $\leftarrow$ Setup(1^λ), all M $\in \mathcal{M}$, all $x \in \mathcal{X}$ and all $y \in \mathcal{Y}$, such that $P(x, y) = 1$, it is required that M$'$ = M holds with overwhelming probability, where ct$_x$ $\leftarrow$ Enc(mpk, x, M), sk$_y$ $\leftarrow$ KeyGen(mpk, msk, y), and M$'$ $\leftarrow$ Dec(mpk, ct$_x$, sk$_y$).

(2) For all $\lambda \in \mathbb{N}$, all (mpk, msk) $\leftarrow$ Setup(1^λ), all M $\in \mathcal{M}$, all $x_0, x_1 \in \mathcal{X}$ and all $y_0, y_1 \in \mathcal{Y}$, such that $\wedge_{i \in \{0,1\}} P(x_i, y_i) = 1$, it is required that 1 $\leftarrow$ Test(ct$_{x_0}$, td$_{y_0}$, ct$_{x_1}$, td$_{y_1}$) holds with overwhelming probability, where sk$_{y_i}$ $\leftarrow$ KeyGen(mpk, msk, y_i), ct$_{x_i}$ $\leftarrow$ Enc(mpk, x_i, M), and td$_{y_i}$ $\leftarrow$ Trapdoor(mpk, sk$_{y_i}$) for $i = 0, 1$.

(3) For all $\lambda \in \mathbb{N}$, all (mpk, msk) $\leftarrow$ Setup(1^λ), all PPT adversaries $\mathcal{A}$, all $x_0, x_1 \in \mathcal{X}$ and all $y_0, y_1 \in \mathcal{Y}$, such that $\wedge_{i \in \{0,1\}} P(x_i, y_i) = 1$, it is required that

$$M_0 \neq M_1 \wedge 1 \leftarrow \text{Test}(ct_{x_0}, td_{y_0}, ct_{x_1}, td_{y_1})$$

holds with negligible probability, where $(M_0, M_1) \leftarrow \mathcal{A}(\text{mpk}, \text{msk})$, sk$_{y_i}$ $\leftarrow$ KeyGen(mpk, msk, y_i), ct$_{x_i}$ $\leftarrow$ Enc(mpk, x_i, M$_i$), and td$_{y_i}$ $\leftarrow$ Trapdoor(mpk, sk$_{y_i}$) for $i = 0, 1$.

Remark 2. In most ABEET papers, PPT adversaries do not appear in the definition of the third condition. In these works, the authors defined the third condition in the same way as the second condition except that 0 $\leftarrow$ Test(ct$_{x_0}$, td$_{y_0}$, ct$_{x_1}$, td$_{y_1}$) holds with overwhelming probability, where ct$_{x_0}$ $\leftarrow$ Enc(mpk, x_0, M$_0$) and ct$_{x_1}$ $\leftarrow$ Enc(mpk, x_1, M$_1$) such that M$_0 \neq$ M$_1$. Then, the authors proved the third condition based on the collision resistance of hash functions. However, the collision resistance itself is insufficient for proving the condition because unbounded adversaries may be able to find collisions. To this end, we modify the definition along with PPT adversaries and formally prove the condition based on the collision resistance of hash functions.

Security. For the security of ABEET, we consider two different types of adversaries. One has a trapdoor for the target attribute or not.

- Type-I adversary: This type of adversaries has trapdoors td_y such that $\mathsf{P}(x^*, y) = 1$. Therefore, the adversaries can perform the equality test with the challenge ciphertext $\mathsf{ct}^*_{x^*}$. Hence, we consider one-wayness.
- Type-II adversary: This type of adversaries has no trapdoors td_y such that $\mathsf{P}(x^*, y) = 1$. Therefore, the adversaries cannot perform the equality test with the challenge ciphertext $\mathsf{ct}^*_{x^*}$. Hence, we consider indistinguishability.

Definition 2 (Adaptive OW-CCA2 Security against Type-I Adversaries). *The adaptive OW-CCA2 security against Type-I adversaries of an ABEET scheme Π is defined by a game between an adversary $\mathcal{A}$ and a challenger $\mathcal{C}$ as follows:*

Init: *$\mathcal{C}$ runs $(\mathsf{mpk}, \mathsf{msk}) \leftarrow \mathsf{Setup}(1^\lambda)$ and gives mpk to $\mathcal{A}$.*
Phase 1: *$\mathcal{A}$ is allowed to make the following three types of queries to $\mathcal{C}$:*
  Key extraction query: *$\mathcal{A}$ is allowed to make the query on $y \in \mathcal{Y}$ to $\mathcal{C}$. Upon the query, $\mathcal{C}$ runs $\mathsf{sk}_y \leftarrow \mathsf{KeyGen}(\mathsf{mpk}, \mathsf{msk}, y)$ and returns sk_y to $\mathcal{A}$.*
  Decryption query: *$\mathcal{A}$ is allowed to make the query on (ct_x, y) to $\mathcal{C}$. Upon the query, $\mathcal{C}$ runs $\mathsf{sk}_y \leftarrow \mathsf{KeyGen}(\mathsf{mpk}, \mathsf{msk}, y)$ and $\mathsf{M} \leftarrow \mathsf{Dec}(\mathsf{mpk}, \mathsf{ct}_x, \mathsf{sk}_y)$, and returns M to $\mathcal{A}$.*
  Trapdoor query: *$\mathcal{A}$ is allowed to make the query on $y \in \mathcal{Y}$ to $\mathcal{C}$. Upon the query, $\mathcal{C}$ runs $\mathsf{sk}_y \leftarrow \mathsf{KeyGen}(\mathsf{mpk}, \mathsf{msk}, y)$ and $\mathsf{td}_y \leftarrow \mathsf{Trapdoor}(\mathsf{mpk}, \mathsf{sk}_y)$, and returns td_y to $\mathcal{C}$.*
Challenge query: *$\mathcal{A}$ is allowed to make the query only once. Upon $\mathcal{A}$'s query on $x^* \in \mathcal{X}$, x^* should not satisfy the condition $\mathsf{P}(x^*, y) = 1$ for all the attributes $y \in \mathcal{Y}$ queried on key extraction queries in Phase 1. Then, $\mathcal{C}$ chooses $\mathsf{M}^* \leftarrow_\$ \mathcal{M}$ and runs $\mathsf{ct}^*_{x^*} \leftarrow \mathsf{Enc}(\mathsf{mpk}, x^*, \mathsf{M}^*)$. Finally, $\mathcal{C}$ returns $\mathsf{ct}^*_{x^*}$ to $\mathcal{A}$.*
Phase 2: *$\mathcal{A}$ is allowed to make key extraction queries, decryption queries and trapdoor queries as in Phase 1 with the following exceptions:*
  Key extraction query: *Upon $\mathcal{A}$'s query on $y \in \mathcal{Y}$, y should not satisfy the condition $\mathsf{P}(x^*, y) = 1$.*
  Decryption query: *Upon $\mathcal{A}$'s query on (ct_x, y), $\mathsf{ct}_x = \mathsf{ct}^*_{x^*}$ does not hold.*
Guess: *At the end of the game, $\mathcal{A}$ returns $\mathsf{M}' \in \mathcal{M}$ as a guess of M^*.*

The adversary $\mathcal{A}$ wins in the above game if $\mathsf{M}^* = \mathsf{M}'$ and the advantage is defined to

$$\mathsf{Adv}^{\mathrm{OW\text{-}CCA2}}_{\Pi, \mathcal{A}}(\lambda) := \left| \Pr[\mathsf{M}^* = \mathsf{M}'] - \frac{1}{|\mathcal{M}|} \right|.$$

If $\mathsf{Adv}^{\mathrm{OW\text{-}CCA2}}_{\Pi, \mathcal{A}}(\lambda)$ is negligible in the security parameter λ for all PPT adversaries $\mathcal{A}$, an ABEET scheme Π is said to satisfy adaptive OW-CCA2 security against Type-I adversaries.

Definition 3 (Adaptive IND-CCA2 Security against Type-II Adversáries). *The adaptive IND-CCA2 security against Type-II adversaries of an* ABEET *scheme Π is defined by a game between an adversary $\mathcal{A}$ and a challenger $\mathcal{C}$ as follows:*

Init: $\mathcal{C}$ *runs* $(\mathsf{mpk}, \mathsf{msk}) \leftarrow \mathsf{Setup}(1^\lambda)$ *and gives* mpk *to* $\mathcal{A}$.
Phase 1: $\mathcal{A}$ *is allowed to make the following three types of queries to* $\mathcal{C}$:
    Key extraction query: $\mathcal{A}$ *is allowed to make the query on* $y \in \mathcal{Y}$ *to* $\mathcal{C}$. *Upon the query,* $\mathcal{C}$ *runs* $\mathsf{sk}_y \leftarrow \mathsf{KeyGen}(\mathsf{mpk}, \mathsf{msk}, y)$ *and returns* sk_y *to* $\mathcal{A}$.
    Decryption query: $\mathcal{A}$ *is allowed to make the query on* (ct_x, y) *to* $\mathcal{C}$. *Upon the query,* $\mathcal{C}$ *runs* $\mathsf{sk}_y \leftarrow \mathsf{KeyGen}(\mathsf{mpk}, \mathsf{msk}, y)$ *and* $\mathsf{M} \leftarrow \mathsf{Dec}(\mathsf{mpk}, \mathsf{ct}_x, \mathsf{sk}_y)$, *and returns* M *to* $\mathcal{A}$.
    Trapdoor query: $\mathcal{A}$ *is allowed to make the query on* $y \in \mathcal{Y}$ *to* $\mathcal{C}$. *Upon the query,* $\mathcal{C}$ *runs* $\mathsf{sk}_y \leftarrow \mathsf{KeyGen}(\mathsf{mpk}, \mathsf{msk}, y)$ *and* $\mathsf{td}_y \leftarrow \mathsf{Trapdoor}(\mathsf{mpk}, \mathsf{sk}_y)$, *and returns* td_y *to* $\mathcal{C}$.
Challenge query: $\mathcal{A}$ *is allowed to make the query only once. Upon* $\mathcal{A}$'s *query on* $(x^*, \mathsf{M}_0^*, \mathsf{M}_1^*) \in \mathcal{X} \times \mathcal{M}^2$, $|\mathsf{M}_0^*| = |\mathsf{M}_1^*|$ *holds and* x^* *should not satisfy the condition* $\mathsf{P}(x^*, y) = 1$ *for all the attributes* $y \in \mathcal{Y}$ *queried on key extraction queries and trapdoor queries in Phase 1. Then,* $\mathcal{C}$ *flips a coin* $\mathsf{coin} \leftarrow_\$ \{0, 1\}$ *and runs* $\mathsf{ct}_{x^*}^* \leftarrow \mathsf{Enc}(\mathsf{mpk}, x^*, \mathsf{M}_{\mathsf{coin}}^*)$. *Finally,* $\mathcal{C}$ *returns* $\mathsf{ct}_{x^*}^*$ *to* $\mathcal{A}$.
Phase 2: $\mathcal{A}$ *is allowed to make key extraction queries, decryption queries and trapdoor queries as in Phase 1 with the following exceptions:*
    Key extraction query: *Upon* $\mathcal{A}$'s *query on* $y \in \mathcal{Y}$, y *should not satisfy the condition* $\mathsf{P}(x^*, y) = 1$.
    Decryption query: *Upon* $\mathcal{A}$'s *query on* (ct_x, y), $\mathsf{ct}_x = \mathsf{ct}_{x^*}^*$ *does not hold.*
    Trapdoor query: *Upon* $\mathcal{A}$'s *query on* $y \in \mathcal{Y}$, y *should not satisfy the condition* $\mathsf{P}(x^*, y) = 1$.
Guess: *At the end of the game,* $\mathcal{A}$ *outputs* $\mathsf{coin}' \in \{0, 1\}$ *as a guess of* coin.

The adversary $\mathcal{A}$ wins in the above game if $\mathsf{coin} = \mathsf{coin}'$ *and the advantage is defined to*

$$\mathsf{Adv}_{\Pi,\mathcal{A}}^{\mathrm{IND\text{-}CCA2}}(\lambda) := \left| \Pr[\mathsf{coin} = \mathsf{coin}'] - \frac{1}{2} \right|.$$

If $\mathsf{Adv}_{\Pi,\mathcal{A}}^{\mathrm{IND\text{-}CCA2}}(\lambda)$ *is negligible in the security parameter λ for all PPT adversaries $\mathcal{A}$, an* ABEET *scheme Π is said to satisfy adaptive IND-CCA2 security against Type-II adversaries.*

Remark 3. As the case of ABE, we define selective security and semi-adaptive security for ABEET by following Remark 1.

3 Proposed Generic Construction

In this section, we provide a generic construction of ABEET by following the discussion in Sect. 1.3. In Sect. 3.1, we show the construction. In Sect. 3.2, we discuss the correctness.

3.1 Our Construction

In this section, we construct an ABEET scheme Π for a predicate P from an ABE scheme Π, an OTS scheme Γ and a hash function H. Here, we assume that plaintext spaces $\mathcal{M}$ of ABE and ABEET are the same. Moreover, $\mathcal{M}$ is the same as the domain of the hash function H and the range of $\mathcal{R}$ is a subset of $\mathcal{M}$.

$\mathsf{Setup}(1^\lambda) \to (\mathsf{mpk}, \mathsf{msk})$: Run
  - $(\mathsf{ABE.mpk}, \mathsf{ABE.msk}) \leftarrow \mathsf{ABE.Setup}(1^\lambda)$,
  and output $\mathsf{mpk} := (\mathsf{ABE.mpk}, \Gamma, \mathsf{H})$ and $\mathsf{msk} := \mathsf{ABE.msk}$.
$\mathsf{Enc}(\mathsf{mpk}, x, \mathsf{M}) \to \mathsf{ct}_x$: Parse $\mathsf{mpk} = (\mathsf{ABE.mpk}, \Gamma, \mathsf{H})$. Run
  - $(\mathsf{verk}, \mathsf{sigk}) \leftarrow \mathsf{Sig.Setup}(1^\lambda)$,
  - $\mathsf{ABE.ct}_{x,0,\mathsf{verk}} \leftarrow \mathsf{ABE.Enc}(\mathsf{ABE.mpk}, (x, 0, \mathsf{verk}), \mathsf{M})$,
  - $\mathsf{ABE.ct}_{x,1,\mathsf{verk}} \leftarrow \mathsf{ABE.Enc}(\mathsf{ABE.mpk}, (x, 1, \mathsf{verk}), \mathsf{H}(\mathsf{M}))$,
  - $\sigma \leftarrow \mathsf{Sig.Sign}(\mathsf{sigk}, [\mathsf{ABE.ct}_{x,0,\mathsf{verk}} \| \mathsf{ABE.ct}_{x,1,\mathsf{verk}}])$.
  Output $\mathsf{ct}_x = (\mathsf{verk}, \mathsf{ABE.ct}_{x,0,\mathsf{verk}}, \mathsf{ABE.ct}_{x,1,\mathsf{verk}}, \sigma)$.
$\mathsf{KeyGen}(\mathsf{mpk}, \mathsf{msk}, y) \to \mathsf{sk}_y$: Parse $\mathsf{mpk} = (\mathsf{ABE.mpk}, \Gamma, \mathsf{H})$ and $\mathsf{msk} = \mathsf{ABE.msk}$. Run
  - $\mathsf{ABE.sk}_y \leftarrow \mathsf{ABE.KeyGen}(\mathsf{ABE.mpk}, \mathsf{ABE.msk}, y)$.
  Output $\mathsf{sk}_y := \mathsf{ABE.sk}_y$.
$\mathsf{Dec}(\mathsf{mpk}, \mathsf{ct}_x, \mathsf{sk}_y) \to \mathsf{M} \text{ or } \bot$: Parse $\mathsf{mpk} = (\mathsf{ABE.mpk}, \Gamma, \mathsf{H})$, $\mathsf{ct}_x = (\mathsf{verk}, \mathsf{ABE.ct}_{x,0,\mathsf{verk}}, \mathsf{ABE.ct}_{x,1,\mathsf{verk}}, \sigma)$, and $\mathsf{sk}_y = \mathsf{ABE.sk}_y$. If it holds that
  - $0 \leftarrow \mathsf{Sig.Vrfy}(\mathsf{verk}, [\mathsf{ABE.ct}_{x,0,\mathsf{verk}} \| \mathsf{ABE.ct}_{x,1,\mathsf{verk}}], \sigma) \vee \mathsf{P}(x,y) = 0$,
  output $\bot$. Otherwise, run
  - $\mathsf{ABE.sk}_{y,0,\mathsf{verk}} \leftarrow \mathsf{ABE.Delegate}(\mathsf{ABE.mpk}, \mathsf{ABE.sk}_y, (y, 0, \mathsf{verk}))$,
  - $\mathsf{ABE.sk}_{y,1,\mathsf{verk}} \leftarrow \mathsf{ABE.Delegate}(\mathsf{ABE.mpk}, \mathsf{ABE.sk}_y, (y, 1, \mathsf{verk}))$,
  - $\mathsf{M} \leftarrow \mathsf{ABE.Dec}(\mathsf{ABE.mpk}, \mathsf{ABE.ct}_{x,0,\mathsf{verk}}, \mathsf{ABE.sk}_{y,0,\mathsf{verk}})$,
  - $h \leftarrow \mathsf{ABE.Dec}(\mathsf{ABE.mpk}, \mathsf{ABE.ct}_{x,1,\mathsf{verk}}, \mathsf{ABE.sk}_{y,1,\mathsf{verk}})$.
  Output M if $\mathsf{H}(\mathsf{M}) = h$ holds and $\bot$ otherwise.
$\mathsf{Trapdoor}(\mathsf{mpk}, \mathsf{sk}_y) \to \mathsf{td}_y$: Parse $\mathsf{mpk} = (\mathsf{ABE.mpk}, \Gamma, \mathsf{H})$ and $\mathsf{sk}_y = \mathsf{ABE.sk}_y$. Run
  - $\mathsf{ABE.sk}_{y,1} \leftarrow \mathsf{ABE.Delegate}(\mathsf{ABE.mpk}, \mathsf{ABE.sk}_y, (y, 1))$.
  Output $\mathsf{td}_y := \mathsf{ABE.sk}_{y,1}$.
$\mathsf{Test}(\mathsf{ct}_x, \mathsf{td}_y, \mathsf{ct}_{x'}, \mathsf{td}_{y'}) \to 1 \text{ or } 0$: Parse $\mathsf{ct}_x = (\mathsf{verk}, \mathsf{ABE.ct}_{x,0,\mathsf{verk}}, \mathsf{ABE.ct}_{x,1,\mathsf{verk}}, \sigma)$, $\mathsf{ct}_{x'} = (\mathsf{verk}', \mathsf{ABE.ct}_{x',0,\mathsf{verk}'}, \mathsf{ABE.ct}_{x',1,\mathsf{verk}'}, \sigma')$, $\mathsf{td}_y = \mathsf{ABE.sk}_{y,1}$, and $\mathsf{td}_{y'} = \mathsf{ABE.sk}_{y',1}$. If it holds that
  - $0 \leftarrow \mathsf{Sig.Vrfy}(\mathsf{verk}, [\mathsf{ABE.ct}_{x,0,\mathsf{verk}} \| \mathsf{ABE.ct}_{x,1,\mathsf{verk}}], \sigma) \vee 0 \leftarrow \mathsf{Sig.Vrfy}(\mathsf{verk}', [\mathsf{ABE.ct}_{x',0,\mathsf{verk}'} \| \mathsf{ABE.ct}_{x',1,\mathsf{verk}'}], \sigma')$,
  output 0. Otherwise, run
  - $\mathsf{ABE.sk}_{y,1,\mathsf{verk}} \leftarrow \mathsf{ABE.Delegate}(\mathsf{mpk}, \mathsf{ABE.sk}_{y,1}, (y, 1, \mathsf{verk}))$,
  - $\mathsf{ABE.sk}_{y',1,\mathsf{verk}'} \leftarrow \mathsf{ABE.Delegate}(\mathsf{mpk}, \mathsf{ABE.sk}_{y',1}, (y', 1, \mathsf{verk}'))$,
  - $h \leftarrow \mathsf{ABE.Dec}(\mathsf{mpk}, \mathsf{ABE.ct}_{x,1,\mathsf{verk}}, \mathsf{ABE.sk}_{y,1,\mathsf{verk}})$,
  - $h' \leftarrow \mathsf{ABE.Dec}(\mathsf{mpk}, \mathsf{ABE.ct}_{x',1,\mathsf{verk}'}, \mathsf{ABE.sk}_{y',1,\mathsf{verk}'})$.
  Output 1 if $h = h'$ and 0 otherwise.

3.2   Correctness

The scheme satisfies correctness. Due to the page limitation, we defer the full proof to the full version of this paper [8].

Theorem 1. *Our* ABEET *scheme* Π *satisfies correctness if the underlying* ABE *scheme* Π_{ABE} *and* OTS *scheme* Γ *satisfy correctness, and the hash function* H *satisfies collision resistance.*

Proof Sketch. If the ABE scheme Π_{ABE} and OTS scheme Γ satisfy correctness, then the Sig.Vrfy algorithm outputs 1 when running the Dec algorithm, and the ABE.Dec algorithm outputs M and h satisfying $H(M) = h$. Thus, the condition (1) holds. Similarly, if the ABE scheme Π_{ABE} and OTS scheme Γ satisfy correctness, then the Sig.Vrfy algorithm outputs 1, and the ABE.Dec algorithm outputs h and h' satisfying $h = h'$ when running the Test algorithm. Thus, the condition (2) holds. Also, if the ABE scheme Π_{ABE} satisfies correctness, it is sufficient to show that PPT adversary $\mathcal{A}$ cannot find different M_0 and M_1 satisfying $H(M_0) = H(M_1)$. If the hash function H satisfies collision resistance, $\mathcal{A}$ cannot find such M_0 and M_1, thus the condition (3) holds. Therefore, the proposed ABEET scheme is correct.

4   Security

In this section, we discuss security of our generic construction given in Sect. 3.1. Due to space limit, we defer the full proof to the full version of this paper [8].

4.1   OW-CCA2 Security Against Type-I Adversaries

Theorem 2 (OW-CCA2 Security against Type-I Adversaries). *If the underlying* ABE *scheme* Π_{ABE} *satisfies adaptive (resp. semi-adaptive, selective) CPA security,* OTS *scheme* Γ *satisfies strong unforgeability, and* H *satisfies one-wayness, then our proposed* ABEET *scheme* Π *satisfies adaptive (resp. semi-adaptive, selective) OW-CCA2 security against Type-I adversaries.*

Proof Sketch. We prove the theorem via game sequence $\mathbf{Game}_0$, $\mathbf{Game}_1$, and $\mathbf{Game}_2$. $\mathbf{Game}_0$ is the same as the original game defined in Definition 2. In $\mathbf{Game}_1$, if $\mathcal{A}$ makes decryption query $(y, \mathsf{ct}_x) = (y, (\mathsf{verk}, \mathsf{ABE.ct}_{x,0,\mathsf{verk}}, \mathsf{ABE.ct}_{x,1,\mathsf{verk}}, \sigma))$ such that

$$\mathsf{verk} = \mathsf{verk}^* \wedge \mathsf{Sig.Vrfy}(\mathsf{verk}, [\mathsf{ABE.ct}_{x,0,\mathsf{verk}} \| \mathsf{ABE.ct}_{x,1,\mathsf{verk}}], \sigma) \to 1$$
$$\wedge \, (\mathsf{ABE.ct}_{x,0,\mathsf{verk}}, \mathsf{ABE.ct}_{x,1,\mathsf{verk}}, \sigma) \neq (\mathsf{ABE.ct}^*_{x^*,0,\mathsf{verk}^*}, \mathsf{ABE.ct}^*_{x^*,1,\mathsf{verk}^*}, \sigma^*)$$

where $(\mathsf{verk}^*, \mathsf{ABE.ct}^*_{x^*,0,\mathsf{verk}^*}, \mathsf{ABE.ct}^*_{x^*,1,\mathsf{verk}^*}, \sigma^*)$ is the challenge ciphertext, then $\mathcal{C}$ aborts the game and outputs $M \leftarrow_{\$} \mathcal{M}$. In $\mathbf{Game}_2$, let $\mathsf{ABE.ct}^*_{x^*,0,\mathsf{verk}^*}$ be a ciphertext of $M \leftarrow_{\$} \mathcal{M}$ instead of M^*. We can show that $\mathbf{Game}_0$ and $\mathbf{Game}_1$ are computationally indistinguishable if the OTS scheme Γ satisfies strong unforgeability, as in the extension of the CHK transformation [15] to ABE by Yamada et al [31]. Then, if the ABE scheme Π_{ABE} satisfies adaptive CPA security, we can show that $\mathbf{Game}_1$ and $\mathbf{Game}_2$ are computationally indistinguishable.

Due to the change of $\mathbf{Game}_2$, $\mathcal{A}$ can only obtain ciphertext $\mathsf{ABE.ct}^*_{x^*,1,\mathsf{verk}^*}$ of $\mathsf{H}(\mathsf{M}^*)$ as the information of M^*. $\mathcal{A}$ who has the trapdoor td_y such that $\mathsf{P}(x^*, y) = 1$ can calculate $\mathsf{H}(\mathsf{M}^*)$. However, if the hash function H satisfies one-wayness, $\mathcal{A}$ cannot calculate M^* from $\mathsf{H}(\mathsf{M}^*)$, thus the proposed ABEET scheme satisfies one-wayness. Therefore, we can prove Theorem 2.

4.2 IND-CCA2 Security Against Type-II Adversaries

Theorem 3 (IND-CCA2 Security against Type-II Adversaries). *If the underlying* ABE *scheme* Π_{ABE} *satisfies adaptive (resp. semi-adaptive, selective) CPA security and* OTS *scheme* Γ *satisfies strong unforgeability, then our proposed* ABEET *scheme* Π *satisfies adaptive (resp. semi-adaptive, selective) IND-CCA2 security against Type-II adversaries.*

Proof Sketch. We prove the theorem via game sequence $\mathbf{Game}_0$, $\mathbf{Game}_1$, and $\mathbf{Game}_2$, which is essentially the same as in the proof of Theorem 2. Due to the change of $\mathbf{Game}_2$, $\mathcal{A}$ can only obtain the ciphertext $\mathsf{ABE.ct}^*_{x^*,1,\mathsf{verk}^*}$ of $\mathsf{H}(\mathsf{M}^*_{\mathsf{coin}^*})$ as the information of coin^*. However, unlike in Theorem 2, $\mathcal{A}$ does not have a trapdoor td_y satisfying $\mathsf{P}(x^*, y) = 1$, so $\mathsf{H}(\mathsf{M}^*_{\mathsf{coin}^*})$ cannot be obtained trivially. If the ABE scheme Π satisfies adaptive IND-CPA security, then $\mathcal{A}$ cannot identify coin^* from $\mathsf{ABE.ct}^*_{x^*,1,\mathsf{verk}^*}$, thus the proposed ABEET scheme satisfies the indistinguishability. Therefore, we can prove Theorem 3.

5   Conclusion

In this paper, we proposed a generic construction of CCA-secure ABEET from IND-CPA secure delegatable ABE with the hierarchical depth three. The construction is an attribute-based extension of Lee et al.'s generic construction of CCA-secure IBEET from IND-CPA-secure hierarchical IBE with the depth three [22]. To achieve CCA security, we used Yamada et al.'s technique [31]. Based on the predicate encoding and pair encoding frameworks [9,29] and known lattice-based delegatable ABE schemes [2,13,30], we obtain various ABEET schemes with new properties that have not been achieved so far. However, since there are no generic methods for non-delegatable ABE to satisfy the delegatability, there are several open questions. Although we obtained ABEET schemes for (non-)monotone span programs (Schemes 1–12) from ABE schemes for the same predicates in the standard model, there are more efficient schemes in the random oracle model [27]. Although we obtained the first ABEET schemes for deterministic finite automata (Schemes 13 and 14) under the q-ratio assumption, there are ABE schemes for the same predicate under the standard k-linear assumption [6,20,21] and ABE schemes for non-deterministic finite automata under the LWE assumptions [5]. Although we obtained selectively secure lattice-based ABEET schemes for circuits, there are semi-adaptively secure lattice-based ABE scheme for circuits [14]. Therefore, it is an interesting open problem to construct CCA-secure ABEET schemes with these properties.

Acknowledgments. This work is supported by JSPS KAKENHI Grant Numbers JP21H03441, JP18H05289, and JP18K11293, and MEXT Leading Initiative for Excellent Young Researchers, JST CREST JPMJCR2113, Japan.

References

1. Abdalla, M., et al.: Searchable encryption revisited: consistency properties, relation to anonymous IBE, and extensions. J. Cryptology **21**(3), 350–391 (2007). https://doi.org/10.1007/s00145-007-9006-6
2. Abdalla, M., De Caro, A., Mochetti, K.: Lattice-based hierarchical inner product encryption. In: Hevia, A., Neven, G. (eds.) LATINCRYPT 2012. LNCS, vol. 7533, pp. 121–138. Springer, Heidelberg (2012). https://doi.org/10.1007/978-3-642-33481-8_7
3. Agrawal, S., Chase, M.: A study of pair encodings: predicate encryption in prime order groups. In: Kushilevitz, E., Malkin, T. (eds.) TCC 2016. LNCS, vol. 9563, pp. 259–288. Springer, Heidelberg (2016). https://doi.org/10.1007/978-3-662-49099-0_10
4. Agrawal, S., Chase, M.: simplifying design and analysis of complex predicate encryption schemes. In: Coron, J.-S., Nielsen, J.B. (eds.) EUROCRYPT 2017. LNCS, vol. 10210, pp. 627–656. Springer, Cham (2017). https://doi.org/10.1007/978-3-319-56620-7_22
5. Agrawal, S., Maitra, M., Yamada, S.: Attribute based encryption (and more) for nondeterministic finite automata from LWE. In: Boldyreva, A., Micciancio, D. (eds.) CRYPTO 2019. LNCS, vol. 11693, pp. 765–797. Springer, Cham (2019). https://doi.org/10.1007/978-3-030-26951-7_26
6. Agrawal, S., Maitra, M., Yamada, S.: Attribute based encryption for deterministic finite automata from DLIN. In: Hofheinz, D., Rosen, A. (eds.) TCC 2019. LNCS, vol. 11892, pp. 91–117. Springer, Cham (2019). https://doi.org/10.1007/978-3-030-36033-7_4
7. Ambrona, M., Barthe, G., Schmidt, B.: Generic transformations of predicate encodings: constructions and applications. In: Katz, J., Shacham, H. (eds.) CRYPTO 2017. LNCS, vol. 10401, pp. 36–66. Springer, Cham (2017). https://doi.org/10.1007/978-3-319-63688-7_2
8. Asano, K., Emura, K., Takayasu, A., Watanabe, Y.: A generic construction of cca-secure attribute-based encryption with equality test. IACR Cryptol. ePrint Arch, p. 1371 (2021). https://eprint.iacr.org/2021/1371
9. Attrapadung, N.: Dual system encryption via doubly selective security: framework, fully secure functional encryption for regular languages, and more. In: Nguyen, P.Q., Oswald, E. (eds.) EUROCRYPT 2014. LNCS, vol. 8441, pp. 557–577. Springer, Heidelberg (2014). https://doi.org/10.1007/978-3-642-55220-5_31
10. Attrapadung, N.: Dual system encryption framework in prime-order groups via computational pair encodings. In: Cheon, J.H., Takagi, T. (eds.) ASIACRYPT 2016. LNCS, vol. 10032, pp. 591–623. Springer, Heidelberg (2016). https://doi.org/10.1007/978-3-662-53890-6_20

11. Attrapadung, N.: Unbounded dynamic predicate compositions in attribute-based encryption. In: Ishai, Y., Rijmen, V. (eds.) EUROCRYPT 2019. LNCS, vol. 11476, pp. 34–67. Springer, Cham (2019). https://doi.org/10.1007/978-3-030-17653-2_2
12. Boneh, D., Di Crescenzo, G., Ostrovsky, R., Persiano, G.: Public key encryption with keyword search. In: Cachin, C., Camenisch, J.L. (eds.) EUROCRYPT 2004. LNCS, vol. 3027, pp. 506–522. Springer, Heidelberg (2004). https://doi.org/10.1007/978-3-540-24676-3_30
13. Boneh, D., Gentry, C., Gorbunov, S., Halevi, S., Nikolaenko, V., Segev, G., Vaikuntanathan, V., Vinayagamurthy, D.: Fully key-homomorphic encryption, arithmetic circuit abe and compact garbled circuits. In: Nguyen, P.Q., Oswald, E. (eds.) EUROCRYPT 2014. LNCS, vol. 8441, pp. 533–556. Springer, Heidelberg (2014). https://doi.org/10.1007/978-3-642-55220-5_30
14. Brakerski, Z., Vaikuntanathan, V.: Circuit-abe from lwe: unbounded attributes and semi-adaptive security. In: Robshaw, M., Katz, J. (eds.) CRYPTO 2016. LNCS, vol. 9816, pp. 363–384. Springer, Heidelberg (2016). https://doi.org/10.1007/978-3-662-53015-3_13
15. Canetti, R., Halevi, S., Katz, J.: Chosen-ciphertext security from identity-based encryption. In: Cachin, C., Camenisch, J.L. (eds.) EUROCRYPT 2004. LNCS, vol. 3027, pp. 207–222. Springer, Heidelberg (2004). https://doi.org/10.1007/978-3-540-24676-3_13
16. Chen, J., Gay, R., Wee, H.: Improved dual system ABE in prime-order groups via predicate encodings. In: Oswald, E., Fischlin, M. (eds.) EUROCRYPT 2015. LNCS, vol. 9057, pp. 595–624. Springer, Heidelberg (2015). https://doi.org/10.1007/978-3-662-46803-6_20
17. Chen, J., Gong, J.: ABE with tag made easy. In: Takagi, T., Peyrin, T. (eds.) ASIACRYPT 2017. LNCS, vol. 10625, pp. 35–65. Springer, Cham (2017). https://doi.org/10.1007/978-3-319-70697-9_2
18. Cui, Y., Huang, Q., Huang, J., Li, H., Yang, G.: Outsourced ciphertext-policy attribute-based encryption with equality test. In: Guo, F., Huang, X., Yung, M. (eds.) Inscrypt 2018. LNCS, vol. 11449, pp. 448–467. Springer, Cham (2019). https://doi.org/10.1007/978-3-030-14234-6_24
19. Cui, Y., Huang, Q., Huang, J., Li, H., Yang, G.: Ciphertext-policy attribute-based encrypted data equality test and classification. Comput. J. $62(8)$, 1166–1177 (2019)
20. Gong, J., Waters, B., Wee, H.: ABE for DFA from k-Lin. In: Boldyreva, A., Micciancio, D. (eds.) CRYPTO 2019. LNCS, vol. 11693, pp. 732–764. Springer, Cham (2019). https://doi.org/10.1007/978-3-030-26951-7_25
21. Gong, J., Wee, H.: Adaptively secure ABE for DFA from k-Lin and more. In: Canteaut, A., Ishai, Y. (eds.) EUROCRYPT 2020. LNCS, vol. 12107, pp. 278–308. Springer, Cham (2020). https://doi.org/10.1007/978-3-030-45727-3_10
22. Lee, H.T., Ling, S., Seo, J.H., Wang, H.: Semi-generic construction of public key encryption and identity-based encryption with equality test. Inf. Sci. 373, 419–440 (2016)
23. Lee, H.T., Ling, S., Seo, J.H., Wang, H., Youn, T.: Public key encryption with equality test in the standard model. Inf. Sci. 516, 89–108 (2020)
24. Lewko, A., Okamoto, T., Sahai, A., Takashima, K., Waters, B.: Fully secure functional encryption: attribute-based encryption and (hierarchical) inner product encryption. In: Gilbert, H. (ed.) EUROCRYPT 2010. LNCS, vol. 6110, pp. 62–91. Springer, Heidelberg (2010). https://doi.org/10.1007/978-3-642-13190-5_4
25. Li, C., Shen, Q., Xie, Z., Feng, X., Fang, Y., Wu, Z.: Large universe CCA2 CP-ABE with equality and validity test in the standard model. Comput. J. $64(4)$, 509–533 (2021)

26. Takayasu, A.: Tag-based ABE in prime-order groups via pair encoding. Des. Codes Crypt. **89**(8), 1927–1963 (2021). https://doi.org/10.1007/s10623-021-00894-4
27. Tomida, J., Kawahara, Y., Nishimaki, R.: Fast, compact, and expressive attribute-based encryption. Des. Codes Crypt. **89**(11), 2577–2626 (2021). https://doi.org/10.1007/s10623-021-00939-8
28. Wang, Y., Cui, Y., Huang, Q., Li, H., Huang, J., Yang, G.: Attribute-based equality test over encrypted data without random oracles. IEEE Access **8**, 32891–32903 (2020)
29. Wee, H.: Dual system encryption via predicate encodings. In: Lindell, Y. (ed.) TCC 2014. LNCS, vol. 8349, pp. 616–637. Springer, Heidelberg (2014). https://doi.org/10.1007/978-3-642-54242-8_26
30. Xagawa, K.: Improved (Hierarchical) inner-product encryption from lattices. In: Kurosawa, K., Hanaoka, G. (eds.) PKC 2013. LNCS, vol. 7778, pp. 235–252. Springer, Heidelberg (2013). https://doi.org/10.1007/978-3-642-36362-7_15
31. Yamada, S., Attrapadung, N., Hanaoka, G., Kunihiro, N.: Generic constructions for chosen-ciphertext secure attribute based encryption. In: Catalano, D., Fazio, N., Gennaro, R., Nicolosi, A. (eds.) PKC 2011. LNCS, vol. 6571, pp. 71–89. Springer, Heidelberg (2011). https://doi.org/10.1007/978-3-642-19379-8_5
32. Yang, G., Tan, C.H., Huang, Q., Wong, D.S.: Probabilistic public key encryption with equality test. In: Pieprzyk, J. (ed.) CT-RSA 2010. LNCS, vol. 5985, pp. 119–131. Springer, Heidelberg (2010). https://doi.org/10.1007/978-3-642-11925-5_9

Secure-Channel Free Certificateless Searchable Public Key Authenticated Encryption with Keyword Search

Pan Yang[1], Hongbo Li[1], Jianye Huang[2], Hao Zhang[3], Man Ho Au[4], and Qiong Huang[1,5(✉)]

[1] College of Mathematics and Informatics, South China Agricultural University, Guangzhou 510642, China
pyang@stu.scau.edu.cn, {hongbo,qhuang}@scau.edu.cn
[2] School of Computing and Information Technology, University of Wollongong, Wollongong, NSW 2500, Australia
jh207@uowmail.edu.au
[3] The 5th Electronics Research Institute of the Ministry of Industry and Information Technology, Guangzhou 510610, China
sdzhh71@126.com
[4] Department of Computer Science, The University of Hong Kong, Hong Kong, China
allenau@cs.hku.hk
[5] Guangzhou Key Lab of Intelligent Agriculture, Guangzhou 510642, China

Abstract. Public-key Authenticated Encryption with Keyword Search (PAEKS) is a cryptographic primitive that can resist inside keyword guessing attack (KGA). However, most of the previously proposed PAEKS frameworks suffered from certificate management problem and key escrow problem. Inspired by the ideas of certificate-based cryptography, we propose a *secure-channel free certificateless searchable public key authenticated encryption with keyword search* (SCF-CLPAEKS) scheme which sloves the key escrow problem in identity-based cryptosystems and the cumbersome certificate problem in conventional public key cryptosystems. Our scheme achieves security against keyword guessing attacks are performed by both inside and outside adversaries. Moreover, our scheme satisfies ciphertext indistinguishability (CI), trapdoor indistinguishability (TI), and designated testability simultaneously. The comparisons indicate that our SCF-CLPAEKS scheme enjoys a better performance compared with related schemes.

Keywords: Public key authenticated encryption · Certificateless · Secure-channel free · Ciphertext indistinguishability · Trapdoor indistinguishability

1 Introduction

With the rapid development of cloud computing technology, a large amount of data has been stored in the cloud. Once the data owner loses control of the data, security and privacy issues arise in cloud storage services. Our data security cannot be guaranteed. Encrypting data is an effective way to prevent data leakage. However, it can complicate the search process. For plaintext information, traditional keyword search techniques can be used to find the desired data. However, this does not apply to encrypted data. To solve this problem, the concept of Searchable Encryption (SE) [22] has been proposed. It enables users to perform effective searches on encrypted data without revealing any information. It has various applications such as encrypted database, secure email routing, etc. Depending on how the key is used, searchable encryption is divided into symmetric searchable encryption (SSE) and public-key encryption with keyword search (PEKS) [20]. In this paper we focus on PEKS.

The workflow of PEKS is shown in Fig. 1. The sender (data owner) uploads the encrypted file data and relevant keyword ciphertexts to the cloud server, while the receiver (user) generates a trapdoor with his/her private key and sends it to the cloud server. The cloud server matches the trapdoor information sent by the user and returns the encrypted files containing the queried keyword(s) to the user.

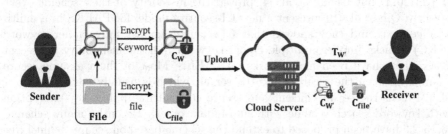

Fig. 1. The workflow of PEKS

Although many schemes tried to solve the issue of searching over ciphertexts, most existing searchable encryption schemes could not resist against *inside keyword guessing attack* (IKGA). Roughly speaking, a malicious adversary can encrypt the guessed keyword. It can calculate whether the trapdoor matches the ciphertext of the guessed keyword. The attack is feasible due to the small space of real-life keywords. To solve the issue, Huang and Li's work [11] provided ciphertext retrieval for cloud storage while defending against the inside server attacks. The approach is called *public-key authenticated encryption with keyword search* (PAEKS). The data sender in PAEKS authenticates the keyword while encrypting. The scheme solves the drawback that in traditional PEKS any user can generate encrypted keywords and the semi-trusted server has access to the test results. Recently, there are a lot of works following Huang et al.'s work [5,10,13,16,17,19]. However, most of the existing literature on PAEKS cannot avoid the problems of certificate management and key escrow. Based on this, we propose *secure-channel free certificateless searchable public key authenticated encryption with keyword search* (SCF-CLPAEKS).

1.1   Related Works

To resist inside keyword guessing attack (IKGA), Huang and Li [11] first introduced Public-key Authenticated Encryption with Keyword Search (PAEKS) in 2017 (referred as HL-PAEKS). In HL-PAEKS, the data owner encrypted a keyword using its public key and secret key, while the receiver used its secret key and public key to generate the corresponding trapdoor. The data sender in PAEKS authenticates the keyword while encrypting. Moreover, Huang et al.'s scheme can achieve ciphertext indistinguishability (CI) which ensures that no information about the underlying keyword is revealed to the cloud server. Later, Qin et al. [18] proposed trapdoor indistinguishability (TI) as a novel security concept in 2020. The trapdoor indistinguishability ensures that given two trapdoors with unknown keywords, an inside adversary cannot obtain any useful information about the keywords. At the same time, Qin et al. [18] also extended the notion of ciphertext indistinguishability and proposed the notion of multi-ciphertext indistinguishability (MCI). An attacker can roughly determine whether two tuples ciphertexts are derived from the same keyword when given two tuples ciphertexts. Multi-trapdoor indistinguishability (MTI) was proposed by Pan et al. [17] in 2021, but Cheng et al. [4] proved the insecurity of their scheme. Very recently, Qin et al. [19] present a new CI-security model for PAEKS in a multiuser context, and they showed that CI-security against fully cipher-keyword (CKC) attacks implies multiple cipher-keyword indistinguishability. In recent years, there have been many works on PAEKS. Most of them assume secure channel between the receiver and the server, which is usually costly. Wang et al. [24] constructed an efficient and secure channel free public key encryption with keyword search scheme without random oracle. Recently, many schemes [6,15,23] have been proposed to extend the scheme based on secure channel free public key encryption. However, most schemes encounter certificate management or key escrow problems.

To slove this problem, Al-Riyami et al. [1] introduced certificateless public key cryptography (CLPKC). In their proposed scheme, each user's public and private keys have two parts, KGC generated one part value and the second part generated by user-selected value. Subsequently, other improved certificateless public key searchable encryption schemes were proposed [10,27,28]. He et al. [10] present a provably secure IKGA-resistant certificateless public key authenticated encryption with keyword search technique. Lu et al. [14] constructed a concrete certificate-based searchable encryption (CBSE) scheme. Wu et al. [26] proposed a certificateless searchable public-key authenticated encryption with a designated tester for the cloud-assisted medical Internet of Things. In addition, Hassan et al. [9] proposed an efficient certificateless public key encryption scheme with authorized equality test for healthcare environments. Later, Han et al. [8] proposed a certificateless scheme that the cloud server did not act as executors of search operations, and achieved verifiability of data files. Shiraly et al. [21] constructed an efficient pairing-free scheme and proved its security in multiple-KGC security model. Wu et al. [25] proposed a channel free certificateless searchable public key authenticated encryption (dCLPAEKS) scheme.

Chenam et al. [3] proposed a primitive called a designated cloud server-based multi-user certificateless public key authenticated encryption with conjunctive keyword search (dmCLPAECKS) scheme in 2022.

1.2 Our Contributions

The main contributions of this paper are described as follows:

- We propose a notion called secure channel free certificateless searchable public key authenticated encryption with keyword search (SCF-CLPAEKS). Our scheme avoids the problems of certificate management and key escrow.
- We present security models of SCF-CLPAEKS. Under the random oracle model, it is proved that the scheme satisfies the ciphertext indistinguishability (CI), trapdoor indistinguishability (TI), and designated testability simultaneously.
- Our scheme removes the secure channel assumption between the server and the receiver which achieves security against keyword guessing attacks (KGA) performed by outside adversaries. Without knowing the private key of the designated cloud server, the attacker would not perform test algorithm even if the data receiver's trapdoor was retrieved.
- We compare our scheme with some other related schemes in terms of both computation and communication efficiency. The comparison results describe that our proposed scheme achieves the lower communication and computation overhead.

2 Preliminary

In this section, we review some background knowledge which contributes to the understanding of SCF-CLPAEKS construction and security analysis.

2.1 Bilinear Pairing

Let $\mathbb{G}$ and $\mathbb{G}_1$ be cyclic groups with the same prime order p. There is a bilinear pairing $\hat{e} : \mathbb{G} \times \mathbb{G} \rightarrow \mathbb{G}_1$ that satisfies the following properties.

- Bilinearity: For any $g_1 \in \mathbb{G}$, $g_2 \in \mathbb{G}$ and a, $b \in \mathbb{Z}_p, \hat{e}(g_1^a, g_2^b) = \hat{e}(g_1, g_2)^{ab}$.
- Non-degeneracy: For any generator $g_1 \in \mathbb{G}$, $g_2 \in \mathbb{G}, \hat{e}(g_1, g_2) \neq 1$.
- Computability: For any $g_1 \in \mathbb{G}$, $g_2 \in \mathbb{G}$ there exisits an efficient algorithm to compute $\hat{e}(g_1, g_2)$.

2.2 Hardness Assumption

Definition 1 (Computational Bilinear Diffie-Hellman problem (CBDH)). *For a symmetric bilinear pairing $\hat{e} : \mathbb{G} \times \mathbb{G} \rightarrow \mathbb{G}_1$, given $\langle g, g^a, g^b, g^c \rangle$, where a, b, $c \in \mathbb{Z}_p^*, g \in \mathbb{G}$, it is hard to compute the value $\hat{e}(g, g)^{abc}$.*

Definition 2 Decisional Bilinear Diffie-Hellman problem (DBDH) [2, 12]). *For each adversary, the algorithm can correctly distinguish* $\hat{e}(g, g)^{abc}$ *and* Z *with negligible probability* ϵ *in the probability polynomial time, namely:*

$$\mid \Pr[\mathcal{A}(g, g^a, g^b, g^c, \hat{e}(g, g)^{abc}) = 1] - \Pr[\mathcal{A}(g, g^a, g^b, g^c, Z) = 1] \mid \leqslant \epsilon$$

3   Definitions and System Model

3.1   System Model

As shown in Fig. 2, the system consists of four roles: KGC, sender, receiver, and server. The SCF-CLPAEKS scheme consists of the following algorithms:

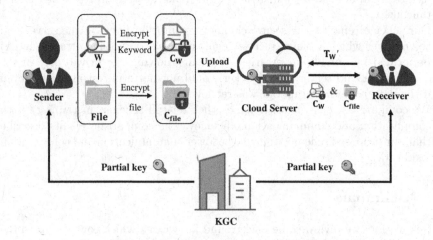

Fig. 2. The system model of CLPAEKS

- **Setup**(1^λ): It takes security parameter 1^λ as input, and generates a master public/secret key pair (mpk, msk) and global public parameter PP.
- **KeyGen$_\mathbf{v}$**(PP): It takes PP as input, and generates a public/secret key pair (pk_v, sk_v) of the server.
- **PartialKeyGen**(PP, msk, id_i): It takes PP, identity id_i as input, and KGC generates a partial private key psk_i for user (sender/receiver).
- **KeyGen$_\mathbf{usr}$**(PP, id_i, psk_i): It takes PP, identity id_i, and the user's partial private key psk_i as input, it generates the user's public/secret key pair (pk_i, sk_i) of user (sender/receiver).
- **SCF-CLPAEKS**($PP, sk_s, pk_r, pk_v, id_s, id_r, \mathbf{w}$): It takes PP, the sender's secret key sk_s and identity id_s, the receiver's public key pk_r and identity id_r, the server's public key pk_v and keyword $\mathbf{w}$ as input, it generates the ciphertext C_w.

- **Trapdoor**$(PP, pk_s, sk_r, id_s, id_r, \mathbf{w'})$: It takes PP, the sender's public key pk_s and identity id_s, the receiver's secret key sk_r and identity id_r, and search keyword $\mathbf{w}$ as input, it generates the trapdoor $T_{w'}$.
- **Test**$(PP, sk_v, C_w, T_{w'})$: It takes PP, the server's secret key sk_v, the ciphertext C_w, and trapdoor $T_{w'}$ as input, outputs 1 if $\mathbf{w'} = \mathbf{w}$ and 0 otherwise.

Correctness is defined as follows. Let $C_w \leftarrow$ SCF-CLPAEKS$(PP, sk_s, pk_r,$ $pk_v, id_s, id_r, \mathbf{w})$ and $T_{w'} \leftarrow$ Trapdoor$(PP, pk_s, sk_r, id_s, id_r, \mathbf{w'})$. If $\mathbf{w'} = \mathbf{w}$, then

$$\Pr[\text{Test}(PP, sk_v, C_w, T_{w'}) = 1] = 1.$$

3.2   Security Model

In certificateless cryptography (CL-PKC) [1], two types of attackers are available with different capabilities. Similarly, in our SCF-CLPAEKS scheme, we consider two types of adversaries. $\mathcal{A}_1$ is a type 1 adversary who lacks access to the master private key. However, $\mathcal{A}_1$ has the ability to request the public key and replace the public key as well as extract partial private keys and secret values. $\mathcal{A}_2$ is a type 2 adversary who is in possession of the master private key. $\mathcal{A}_2$ cannot issue the replace public key query, although $\mathcal{A}_2$ can issue the same queries as $\mathcal{A}_1$.

Game 1: Ciphertext indistinguishability for $\mathcal{A}_1$.

- **Setup**. The challenger $\mathcal{B}$ generates PP, the KGC public/secret key (mpk, msk) and the server's public/secret key (pk_v, sk_v). Finally, it gives (PP, mpk, pk_v, sk_v) to $\mathcal{A}_1$.
- **Phase 1**. $\mathcal{A}_1$ can adaptively query the following oracles for polynomially many times.
    - **Extract-Partial-Private-Key Query**: Given an identity id_i, $\mathcal{B}$ returns the partial private key psk_i to $\mathcal{A}_1$.
    - **Private-Key Query**: Given an identity id_i, $\mathcal{B}$ returns the secret key sk_i if the public key of the user have not been replaced by $\mathcal{A}_1$.
    - **Public-Key Query**: Given id_i, $\mathcal{B}$ returns the public key pk_i.
    - **Replace-Public-Key Query**: $\mathcal{A}_1$ can replace the public key with any value it chooses.
    - **Ciphertext Oracle** $\mathcal{O}_C$. Given a keyword $\mathbf{w}$, id_s of a sender and id_r of a receiver, the challenger $\mathcal{B}$ computes $C_w \leftarrow$ SCF-CLPAEKS$(PP, sk_s, pk_r, pk_v, id_s, id_r, \mathbf{w})$ and returns C_w to $\mathcal{A}_1$.
    - **Trapdoor Oracle** $\mathcal{O}_T$. Given a keyword $\mathbf{w'}$, id_s of a sender and id_r of a receiver, the challenger $\mathcal{B}$ computes $T_{w'} \leftarrow$ Trapdoor$(PP, pk_s, sk_r, id_s, id_r, \mathbf{w'})$ and returns $T_{w'}$ to $\mathcal{A}_1$.
- **Challenge Phase**. $\mathcal{A}_1$ randomly selects two challenge keyword $\mathbf{w}_0^*, \mathbf{w}_1^*$, id_s^* of a sender and id_r^* of a receiver, which have not been queried for phase 1. $\mathcal{B}$ chooses a random bit $\delta \in \{0,1\}$, computes $C_{w_\delta}^* \leftarrow$ SCF-CLPAEKS$(PP, sk_s, pk_r, pk_v, id_s^*, id_r^*, \mathbf{w}_\delta^*)$, and returns $C_{w_\delta}^*$ to $\mathcal{A}_1$.
- **Phase 2**. $\mathcal{A}_1$ can continue to query oracles in phase 1, with the restriction that the adversary could neither query $\mathbf{w}_0^*$ nor $\mathbf{w}_1^*$.

– **Guess Phase.** $\mathcal{A}_1$ outputs a guess bit $\delta' \in \{0, 1\}$ and wins the game if $\delta' = \delta$. The advantage of $\mathcal{A}_1$ in the game is denoted as $Adv_{\mathcal{A}_1}^{CI}(\lambda) = |\Pr[\delta = \delta'] - \frac{1}{2}|$.

Game 2: Ciphertext indistinguishability for $\mathcal{A}_2$.

– **Setup.** Same as in Game 1 expect $\mathcal{B}$ should give (PP, mpk, msk), pk_v, sk_v to the adversary $\mathcal{A}_2$.
– **Phase 1.** Same as in Game 1 expect $\mathcal{A}_2$ cannot adaptively query the Extract-Partial-Private-Key Query oracle and Replace-Public-Key Query oracle for polynomially many times.
– **Challenge Phase.** Same as in Game 1.
– **Phase 2.** The adversary $\mathcal{A}_2$ can continue to query oracles in phase 1, with the restriction that the adversary could neither query $\mathbf{w}_0^*$ nor $\mathbf{w}_1^*$.
– **Guess Phase.** The adversary $\mathcal{A}_2$ outputs a guess bit $\delta' \in \{0, 1\}$ and wins the game if $\delta' = \delta$. The advantage of $\mathcal{A}_2$ in the game is denoted as $Adv_{\mathcal{A}_2}^{CI}(\lambda) = |\Pr[\delta = \delta'] - \frac{1}{2}|$.

Game 3: Trapdoor indistinguishability for $\mathcal{A}_1$.

– **Setup.** Generate the system parameters and the server's public and private keys as in game 1, and give the system parameters and the server's private key to the adversary.
– **Phase 1.** The same as Game 1. Besides, (id_s^*, id_r^*) have not been queried for secret keys, and $\langle w_0^*, id_s^*, id_r^* \rangle$, $\langle w_1^*, id_s^*, id_r^* \rangle$ have not been submitted to trapdoor oracle nor ciphertext oracle.
– **Challenge Phase.** $\mathcal{A}_1$ randomly selects $\mathbf{w}_0^*, \mathbf{w}_1^*$ which have not been queried for phase 1. $\mathcal{B}$ chooses a random bit $\delta \in \{0, 1\}$, computes $T_{w_\delta}^*$, and returns $T_{w_\delta}^*$ to $\mathcal{A}_1$.
– **Phase 2.** $\mathcal{A}_1$ can continue to query oracles as in phase 1 with the restriction that $\mathcal{A}_1$ could neither query $\mathbf{w}_0^*$ nor $\mathbf{w}_1^*$.
– **Guess Phase.** $\mathcal{A}_1$ outputs a guess bit $\delta' \in \{0, 1\}$ and wins the game if $\delta' = \delta$. The advantage of $\mathcal{A}_1$ in the game is denoted as $Adv_{\mathcal{A}_1}^{TI}(\lambda) = |\Pr[\delta = \delta'] - \frac{1}{2}|$.

Game 4: Trapdoor indistinguishability for $\mathcal{A}_2$.

– **Setup.** Same as Game 2.
– **Phase 1.** The same as Game 2. Besides, (id_s^*, id_r^*) have not been queried for secret keys, and $\langle w_0^*, id_s^*, id_r^* \rangle$, $\langle w_1^*, id_s^*, id_r^* \rangle$ have not been submitted to Trapdoor Oracle nor Ciphertext Oracle.
– **Challenge Phase.** $\mathcal{A}_2$ randomly selects $\mathbf{w}_0^*, \mathbf{w}_1^*$ which have not been queried for phase 1. $\mathcal{B}$ chooses a random bit $\delta \in \{0, 1\}$, computes $T_{w_\delta}^*$, and returns $T_{w_\delta'}^*$ to $\mathcal{A}_2$.
– **Phase 2.** $\mathcal{A}_2$ can continue to query oracles as in phase 1, with the restriction that $\mathcal{A}_2$ could neither query $\mathbf{w}_0^*$ nor $\mathbf{w}_1^*$.
– **Guess Phase.** $\mathcal{A}_2$ outputs a guess bit $\delta' \in \{0, 1\}$ and wins the game if $\delta' = \delta$. The advantage of $\mathcal{A}_2$ in the game is denoted as $Adv_{\mathcal{A}_2}^{TI}(\lambda) = |\Pr[\delta = \delta'] - \frac{1}{2}|$.

Designated Testability. Game 5: In this game, we assume that $\mathcal{A}_1$ is an outside adversary who has access to any user's secret key. The goal of designated testability is to prevent adversaries from searching the ciphertexts while ensuring that only the designated server can.

- **Setup.** $\mathcal{B}$ generates the global public parameter PP, the KGC public/secret key (mpk, msk) and the server's public/secret key (pk_v, sk_v). Finally, it gives (PP, mpk, msk, pk_v) to $\mathcal{A}_1$.
- **Phase 1.** $\mathcal{A}_1$ can adaptively query the following oracles for polynomially many times.
  - **Private-Key Query**: Given an identity id_i, the challenger returns the secret key sk_i to $\mathcal{A}_1$ if the public key of the user should not be replaced by $\mathcal{A}_1$.
  - **Private-Key Query**: Given an identity id_i, the challenger returns the secret key sk_i to $\mathcal{A}_1$ if the public key of the user should not be replaced by $\mathcal{A}_1$.
  - **Public-Key Query**: Given an identity id_i, the challenger returns the public key pk_i.
- **Challenge Phase.** $\mathcal{A}_1$. randomly selects $\mathbf{w}_0^*, \mathbf{w}_1^*$, the id_s^* of a sender and id_r^* of a receiver, which have not been queried for phase 1. $\mathcal{B}$ chooses a random bit $\delta \in \{0, 1\}$, computes $C_{w_\delta}^*$ and returns the $C_{w_\delta}^*$ to the adversary.
- **Phase 2.** $\mathcal{A}_1$ can continue to query oracles in phase 1, with the restriction that $\mathcal{A}_1$ could neither query $\mathbf{w}_0^*$ nor $\mathbf{w}_1^*$.
- **Guess Phase.** $\mathcal{A}_1$ outputs a guess bit $\delta' \in \{0, 1\}$ and wins the game if $\delta' = \delta$. The advantage of $\mathcal{A}_1$ in the game is denoted as $Adv_{\mathcal{A}_1}^D(\lambda) = |\Pr[\delta = \delta'] - \frac{1}{2}|$.

4   Our Construction

In this section, we propose our SCF-CLPAEKS scheme that satisfies ciphertext indistinguishability, trapdoor indistinguishability, and designated testability simultaneously. The scheme is described as follows.

4.1   SCF-CLPAEKS

- **Setup(1^λ).** Given a security parameter 1^λ, this algorithm runs as follows:
  1. Select two cyclic groups $\mathbb{G}$ and $\mathbb{G}_1$ with the same prime order p, a bilinear pairing $\hat{e} : \mathbb{G} \times \mathbb{G} \to \mathbb{G}_1$, Choose three cryptographic hash functions $H : \{0, 1\}^* \to \mathbb{G}$, $H_1 : \{0, 1\}^* \times \{0, 1\}^* \to \mathbb{G}$, $H_2 : \{0, 1\}^* \times \mathbb{G}_1 \to \mathbb{Z}_p^*$.
  2. Select a random number $\alpha \in \mathbb{Z}_p^*$ as the master key msk and set $mpk = g^\alpha$, where g is an arbitrary generator of $\mathbb{G}$. Finally, it outputs $PP = (\mathbb{G}, \mathbb{G}_1, p, g, \hat{e}, H, H_1, H_2)$ and (mpk, msk).
- **KeyGen$_\mathbf{v}$(PP).** The server chooses $v \in \mathbb{Z}_p^*$ randomly, and outputs the server's public/secret key pair $(pk_v, sk_v) = (g^v, v)$.
- **PartialKeyGen(PP, id_i).** The partial private key of sender id_s, the receiver id_r are generated by KGC, it computes partial private key $psk_i = H(id_i)^\alpha$.

- **KeyGen$_{usr}$**(PP, id_i, psk_i). Upon receiving partial private key psk_i, the user selects $x_i \in \mathbb{Z}_p^*$ randomly, computes his or her public key $pk_i = g^{x_i}$ and sets the corresponding private key $sk_i = (x_i, H(id_i)^{\alpha})$.
- **SCF-CLPAEKS**$(PP, sk_s, pk_r, pk_v, id_s, id_r, w)$. Select $\beta \in \mathbb{Z}_p^*$ randomly and computes $C_1 = pk_r^{\beta}, C_2 = \hat{e}(pk_v, g^{H_2(w||\rho)})^{\beta}$, where $\rho = \hat{e}(H(id_s)^{\alpha}, H(id_r)) \cdot \hat{e}(H_1(id_s, id_r), pk_r)^{x_s}$, then outputs the ciphertext $C_w = (C_1, C_2)$.
- **Trapdoor** $(PP, pk_s, sk_r, id_s, id_r, w')$. This algorithm computes $T_{w'} = g^{H_2(w'||\rho') \cdot \frac{1}{x_r}}$, where $\rho' = \hat{e}(H(id_s), H(id_r)^{\alpha}) \cdot \hat{e}(H_1(id_s, id_r), pk_s)^{x_r}$. Then, it returns the trapdoor $T_{w'}$.
- **Test**$(PP, sk_v, C_w, T_{w'})$. This algorithm checks whether the equation holds. If it does, output 1 else 0.

$$e(C_1, T_{w'})^v = C_2$$

4.2   Correctness

$$\rho = \hat{e}(H(id_s)^{\alpha}, H(id_r)) \cdot \hat{e}(H_1(id_s, id_r), g^{x_r})^{x_s}$$
$$= \hat{e}(H(id_s), H(id_r)^{\alpha}) \cdot \hat{e}(H_1(id_s, id_r), g^{x_s})^{x_r} = \rho'$$
$$e(C_1, T_{w'})^v) = e(g^{\beta x_r}, g^{H_2(w'||\rho') \cdot \frac{1}{x_r}})^v$$
$$= e(g^v, g^{H_2(w'||\rho')})^{\beta} = e(pk_v, g^{H_2(w||\rho)})^{\beta} = C_2$$

Because $\rho = \rho'$, we have the equation $e(C_1, T_{w'})^v = C_2$ holds if $w = w'$.

5   Security Proof

In this section, we describe the security proof of SCF-CLPAEKS scheme. The proofs are described as follows.

Lemma 1. *For any polynomial-time adversary $\mathcal{A}_1$ in Game 1, $Adv_{\mathcal{A}_1}^{CI}(\lambda)$ is negligible.*

Proof. Assume $\mathcal{A}_1$ (a semi-trusted server) breaks the CI-security of our scheme with a non-negligible advantage, we use it to construct PPT algorithm B to solve the DBDH problem. Given an instance of DBDH problem $(g, g^a, g^b, g^c, Z) \in \mathbb{G}$. Algorithm $\mathcal{B}$ simulates the challenger of game.

- **Setup.** B selects $v \in \mathbb{Z}_p^*$ and set the server's public/secret key pair $(pk_v, sk_v) = (g^c, c)$. $\mathcal{B}$ outputs $PP = (\mathbb{G}, \mathbb{G}_1, p, g, \hat{e}, H, H_1, H_2, mpk = g^{\alpha})$ and $sk_v = c$ to $\mathcal{A}_1$.
- **Phase 1.** At any polynomially time, $\mathcal{A}_1$ can query the following Oracle.
  - **H-Query** Given the identity id, $\mathcal{B}$ selects a random number from $\mathbb{G}$ and returns it to $\mathcal{A}_1$ as the $H(id)$ value of id.
  - **H_1-Query.** Given a pair of identities (id_s, id_r), $\mathcal{B}$ randomly chooses an element from $\mathbb{G}$ as $H_1(id_s, id_r)$ value, and outputs it to $\mathcal{A}_1$. The rest Oracle quaries are the same as Game 1.

- H_2-**Query.** To respond to H_2 queries, $\mathcal{B}$ maintains a list of tuples $\langle w_i, u_i, b \rangle$, called H_2-list. For any H_2 query $\langle w_i, u_i \rangle \in \{0,1\}^* \times \mathbb{G}_1$, $\mathcal{B}$ first checks whether the query (w_i, u_i) already exists on the H_2-list in a tuple (w_i, u_i, b). If so, $\mathcal{B}$ responds with $H_2(w_i \parallel u_i) = b$. Otherwise, it adds the tuple (w_i, u_i, b) to the H_2-list.
- **Extract-Partial-Private-Key Query**: If $id = id_s^*$ or $id = id_r^*$, $\mathcal{B}$ outputs ω and aborts.
- **Private-Key Query**: Taking id as input, if $id \neq id_s^*$ or $id \neq id_r^*$, $\mathcal{B}$ chooses a random number γ_{id} as the secret value and returns the secret key $(g^{u_{id}}, \gamma_{id})$ to $\mathcal{A}_1$ and adds $\langle id, sk_{id} \rangle$ into L_{sk}.
- **Public-Key Query**: $\mathcal{B}$ maintains a list L_{pk}. Given an identity id, $\mathcal{B}$, computes the public key $pk_{id} = g^{\gamma_{id}}$, and then returns it to $\mathcal{A}_1$ and adds $\langle id, pk_{id} \rangle$ into L_{pk}.
- **Replace-Public-Key Query**: $\mathcal{A}_1$ can replace the public key with any value he chooses.
- **Cipherext Oracle** $\mathcal{O}_C$. Given $\mathbf{w}$. $\mathcal{B}$ selects $\beta' \in \mathbb{Z}_p^*$, and computes $C_1' = g^{x_r \beta'}, C_2' = \hat{e}(g^v, g^{H_2(w \parallel \rho')})^{\beta'}$, where $\rho' = \hat{e}(H(id_s)^\alpha, H(id_r)) \cdot \hat{e}(H_1(id_s, id_r), g^{x_r})^{x_s}$, then returns $C_w' = (C_1', C_2')$.
- **Trapdoor Oracle** $\mathcal{O}_T$. Given $\mathbf{w}'$. $\mathcal{B}$ computes $T_{w'} = g^{H_2(w' \parallel \rho')^{\frac{1}{x_r}}}$, where $\rho' = \hat{e}(H(id_s), H(id_r)^\alpha) \cdot \hat{e}(H_1(id_s, id_r), pk_s)^{x_r}$. Then returns $T_{w'}$.

- **Challenge.** $\mathcal{A}_1$ outputs $(\mathbf{w}_0^*, \mathbf{w}_1^*)$, id_s^* of a sender and id_r^* of a receiver with the restriction that $\mathbf{w}_0^*, \mathbf{w}_1^*$ have never been queried in phase 1. $\mathcal{B}$ chooses a random bit $\delta \in \{0, 1\}$, and computes $C_1^* = g^{x_r a}, C_2^* = Z$, then returns it to $\mathcal{A}_1$.
- **Phase 2.** $\mathcal{A}_1$ can continue to query Oracle, with the restriction that $\mathcal{A}_1$ could neither query $\mathbf{w}_0^*$ nor $\mathbf{w}_1^*$.
- **Guess:** Eventually, $\mathcal{A}_1$ outputs the guess δ' and wins the game if $\delta' = \delta$.

if $Z = e(g,g)^{abc}$, explain that $\mathcal{A}_1$ cannot distinguish between Z and $e(g,g)^{abc}$. If $\mathcal{B}$ guesses that the challenge identities are incorrect, $\mathcal{B}$ aborts. Denote by abt the event that $\mathcal{B}$ aborts. Assume that E denotes the occurrence of $Z = e(g,g)^{abc}$. The probability that event abt does not occur is $1/q_H \cdot (q_H - 1)$. We have that

$$Adv_B^{DBDH}(\lambda) = |\Pr_{[\delta'=\delta|abt]} \cdot \Pr_{[abt]} + \Pr_{[\delta'=\delta|\neg abt]} \cdot \Pr_{[\neg abt]} - \frac{1}{2}|$$

$$= |\frac{1}{2}(1 - \Pr_{[\neg abt]}) + (\Pr_{[\delta'=\delta|\neg abt \cap \overline{E}]} \cdot \Pr_{[E]}$$

$$+ \Pr_{[\delta'=\delta|\neg abt \cap \overline{E}]} \cdot \Pr_{[\overline{E}]}) \cdot \Pr_{[\neg abt]} - \frac{1}{2}| \qquad (1)$$

$$= \frac{1}{2}(1 - \Pr_{[\neg abt]}) + \Pr_{[\neg abt]} \cdot (\frac{1}{2}(Adv_{\mathcal{A}_1}^{CI}(\lambda) + \frac{1}{2})) - \frac{1}{2}|$$

$$= \frac{1}{2q_H \cdot (q_H - 1)} \cdot Adv_{\mathcal{A}_1}^{CI}(\lambda)$$

If $Adv_{\mathcal{A}_1}^{CI}(\lambda)$ is not negligible, then $Adv_B^{DBDH}(\lambda)$ is not negligible.

Lemma 2. *For any polynomial-time adversary A_2 in Game 2, $Adv_{A_2}^{CI}(\lambda)$ is negligible.*

Proof. Proof 2 is similar to proof 1, except that adversary A_2 is a semi-trusted KGC. Setup phase B gives $(PP, mpk, msk = \alpha)$, and the server public key $pk_v = c$ to adversary A_2. In phase 1, the adversary cannot issue partial private key and replace public key. As the same as Game 1. If $Adv_{A_2}^{CI}(\lambda)$ is not negligible, then $Adv_B^{DBDH}(\lambda)$ is not negligible.

Lemma 3. *For any polynomial-time adversary A_1 in Game 3, $Adv_{A_1}^{TI}(\lambda)$ is negligible.*

Proof. Assume A_1(a semi-trusted server) breaks the trapdoor indistinguishability of our scheme with a non-negligible advantage, we then use it to construct algorithm B to solve the DBDH assumption.

- **Setup.** B selects a random number $v \in \mathbb{Z}_p^*$ and sets the server's public/secret key pair $(pk_v, sk_v)=(g^v, v)$. B outputs $PP = (\mathbb{G}, \mathbb{G}_1, p, g, \hat{e}, H, H_1, H_2, mpk = g^a)$ and $sk_v = v$ to A_1.
- **Phase 1.** The same as Game 1. Besides, (id_s^*, id_r^*) have not been queried for secret keys, and $\langle w_0^*, id_s^*, id_r^* \rangle$, $\langle w_1^*, id_s^*, id_r^* \rangle$ have not been submitted to trapdoor oracle nor ciphertext oracle.
  - **H-Query.** To respond to H queries, B maintains a list of tuples $\langle id_i, g^{u_{id}} \rangle$, called H-list. Suppose that A_1 makes at most q_H queries. Correspond to id_s, B chooses $b \in \mathbb{Z}_p^*$, outputs $H(id) = g^b$; Correspond to id_r, B chooses $c \in \mathbb{Z}_p^*$, outputs $H(id) = g^c$.
  - **H_1-Query.** Given (id_s, id_r), B selects a random number from $\mathbb{G}$ and returns it to A_1 as the $H_1(id_s, id_r)$ value of (id_s, id_r).
  - **H_2-Query.** Given a keyword w and an element u, B randomly chooses an element from $\mathbb{G}$ as the output of $H_2(w \parallel u)$.
  - **Extract-Partial-Private-Key Query:** If $id = id_s^*$ or $id = id_r^*$, B outputs a random bit ω and aborts. Otherwise, it recovers the tuple $\langle id_i, H(id_i), u_{id} \rangle$ from List H, and returns the partial private key $psk_{id} = g^{u_{id}}$ to A_1.
  - **Privaye-Key Query:** Taking id as input, if $id \neq id_s^*$ or $id \neq id_r^*$, B chooses a random number γ_{id} as the secret value and returns the secret key $(g^{u_{id}}, \gamma_{id})$ to A_1.
  - **Public-Key Query:** Given an identity id, B computes $pk_{id} = g^{\gamma_{id}}$, and then returns it to A_1 and adds $\langle id, pk_{id} \rangle$ into L_{pk}.
  - **Replace-Public-Key Query:** A_1 can replace the public key with any value he chooses.
  - **Cipherext Oracle $\mathcal{O}_C$.** Given a keyword $\mathbf{w}$. B selects $\beta' \in \mathbb{Z}_P^*$, and computes $C_1' = g^{x_r \beta'}$, $C_2' = \hat{e}(g^v, g^{H_2(w\|\rho')})^{\beta'}$, where $\rho' = \hat{e}(H(id_s)^\alpha, H(id_r)) \cdot \hat{e}(H_1(id_s, id_r), g^{x_r})^{x_s}$, then returns $C_w' = (C_1', C_2')$ to A_1.
  - **Trapdoor Oracle $\mathcal{O}_T$.** Given keyword $\mathbf{w}'$. B computes $T_{w'} = g^{H_2(w'\|\rho')\frac{1}{x_r}}$, where $\rho' = \hat{e}(H(id_s), H(id_r)^\alpha) \cdot \hat{e}(H_1(id_s, id_r), pk_s)^{x_r}$. Then, it returns the trapdoor $T_{w'}$ to A_1.

– **Challenge**. $\mathcal{A}_1$ outputs two keywords $(\mathbf{w}_0^*, \mathbf{w}_1^*)$, id_s^* of a sender and id_r^* of a receiver. with the restriction that $\mathbf{w}_0^*, \mathbf{w}_1^*$ have never been queried in phase 1. $\mathcal{B}$ chooses $\delta \in \{0,1\}$, and computes $T_{w_\delta^*} = g^{H_2(w_\delta^* \| \rho^*)^{\frac{1}{x_r}}}$, where $\rho^* = Z \cdot \hat{e}(H_1(id_s^*, id_r^*), pk_s)^{x_r}$. Then, it returns $T_{w_\delta^*}$ to $\mathcal{A}_1$.
– **Phase 2**. $\mathcal{A}_1$ can continue to query oracle, with the restriction that $\mathcal{A}_1$ could neither query $\mathbf{w}_0^*$ nor $\mathbf{w}_1^*$.
– **Guess**: Eventually, $\mathcal{A}_1$ outputs the guess δ' and wins the game if $\delta' = \delta$.

The proof of Lemma 3 is similar to that of Lemma 1. The difference is that the simulator generates a challenge trapdoor in the challenge stage. We omitted the details of calculating the probabilities and have that

$$Adv_{\mathcal{B}}^{DBDH}(\lambda) = \frac{1}{2q_H \cdot (q_H - 1)} \cdot Adv_{\mathcal{A}_1}^{TI}(\lambda) \tag{2}$$

If $Adv_{\mathcal{A}_1}^{TI}(\lambda)$ is not negligible, then $Adv_{\mathcal{B}}^{DBDH}(\lambda)$ is not negligible.

Lemma 4. *For any polynomial-time adversary $\mathcal{A}_2$, $Adv_{\mathcal{A}_2}^{TI}(\lambda)$ is negligible.*

Proof. Proof 4 is similar to proof 2, except that adversary $\mathcal{A}_2$ is a semi-trusted KGC. Setup phase B gives $(PP, mpk, msk = \alpha)$, and the server public key $pk_v = c$ to adversary $\mathcal{A}_2$. In phase 1, $\mathcal{A}_2$ cannot issue partial private key and replace public key. $\mathcal{B}$ submitted is the challenge trapdoor in Challenge phase. As the same as Game 3. If $Adv_{\mathcal{A}_2}^{TI}(\lambda)$ is not negligible, then $Adv_{\mathcal{B}}^{DBDH}(\lambda)$ is not negligible.

Lemma 5. *For any polynomial-time adversary $\mathcal{A}_1$, $Adv_{\mathcal{A}_1}^{D}(\lambda)$ is negligible.*

Proof. Assume that $\mathcal{A}_1$ breaks the designated testability of our scheme with a non-negligible advantage, we then use it to construct PPT algorithm B to solve the DBDH problem.

– **Setup**. B outputs $PP = (\mathbb{G}, \mathbb{G}_1, p, g, \hat{e}, H, H_1, H_2, mpk = g^c)$, $pk_v = g^v$ and $msk = c$ to $\mathcal{A}_1$.
– **Phase 1**. At any polynomially time, the adversary $\mathcal{A}_1$ can query the following oracles.
  • **H-Query**. To respond to H queries, $\mathcal{B}$ maintains a list of tuples $\langle id_i, g^{u_{id}} \rangle$, called H-list. Suppose that $\mathcal{A}_1$ makes at most q_H queries. Correspond to id_s, $\mathcal{B}$ chooses $a \in \mathbb{Z}_p^*$, outputs $H(id) = g^a$; Correspond id_r, $\mathcal{B}$ chooses $b \in \mathbb{Z}_p^*$, outputs $H(id) = g^b$; Otherwise, $\mathcal{B}$ chooses a random number $u_{id} \in \mathbb{Z}_p^*$, outputs $H(id) = g^{u_{id}}$.
  • **H_1-Query**. Given (id_s, id_r), $\mathcal{B}$ selects a random number from $\mathbb{G}$ and returns it to $\mathcal{A}_1$ as the $H_1(id_s, id_r)$ value of (id_s, id_r).
  • **H_2-Query**. Given w and an element u, B randomly chooses an element from $\mathbb{G}$ as the output of $H_2(w \| u)$.
  • **Private-Key Query**: Taking id as input, if $id \neq id_s^*$ or $id \neq id_r^*$, $\mathcal{B}$ chooses a random number γ_{id} as the secret value and returns the secret key $(g^{u_{id}}, \gamma_{id})$ to $\mathcal{A}_1$.

- **Public-Key Query**: When $\mathcal{A}_2$ asks for the partial private key of the id, if $id = id_s^*$, it selects $x \in \mathbb{Z}_p^*$ and outputs $pk_{id} = g^x$, and if $id = id_r^*$, it selects $y \in \mathbb{Z}_p^*$ and outputs $pk_{id} = g^y$. Otherwise, $\mathcal{B}$ selects a random number ω and returns the private key $pk_{id} = g^\alpha$.

- **Challenge.** $\mathcal{A}_1$ outputs two keywords $(\mathbf{w}_0^*, \mathbf{w}_1^*)$, with the restriction that $\mathbf{w}_0^*, \mathbf{w}_1^*$ have never been queried in phase 1. $\mathcal{B}$ chooses $\delta \in \{0,1\}$ and $\beta \in \mathbb{Z}_p^*$, and computes $C_1^* = g^{x_r\beta}, C_2^* = \hat{e}(g^v, g^{H_2(w_\delta^* \| \rho^*)})^\beta$, where $\rho^* = Z \cdot \hat{e}(H_1(id_s^*, id_r^*), pk_r)^{x_s}$. Then returns it to $\mathcal{A}_1$.

- **Phase 2.** $\mathcal{A}_1$ can query oracle, with the restriction that the adversary could neither query $\mathbf{w}_0^*$ nor $\mathbf{w}_1^*$ as phase 1.

- **Guess:** $\mathcal{A}_1$ outputs the guess δ' and wins the game if $\delta' = \delta$.

Similarly, $Adv_B^{DBDH}(\lambda)$ is not negligible.

6   Performance Analysis

We compare our SCF-CLPAEKS framework with the previous frameworks (including HL-PAEKS [11], Qin-IPAEKS [19], SCF-PEKS [7], dCLPAEKS [26], CL-PEKS [28]). The properties of all compared frameworks are listed in Table 1. The comparison shows that our framework has better properties. Although our scheme is functionally similar to scheme [26], our scheme has more advantages in terms of computational complexity and storage cost.

Table 1. Framework comparison

Scheme	KGA[1]	CI[2]	TI[3]	CERT[4]	SCF[5]
HL-PAEKS [11]	Yes	Yes	No	No	No
Qin-IPAEKS [19]	Yes	Yes	No	No	No
SCF-PEKS [7]	Yes	No	No	No	Yes
CL-PEKS [28]	Yes	Yes	Yes	Yes	No
dCLPAEKS [26]	Yes	Yes	Yes	Yes	Yes
Our scheme	Yes	Yes	Yes	Yes	Yes

1. Resist the keyword guessing attack   2. Ciphertext indistinguishability 3. Trapdoor indistinguishability
4. Certificateless 5. Secure channel free

Next, we make a comparison with some recently proposed schemes in terms of computation and communication costs. Table 2 gives a comparison of the efficiency with schemes (dCLPAEKS [26], CL-PEKS [28]) in the encryption phase, the trapdoor phase, and the testing phase respectively. $|\mathbb{G}_1|$ and $|\mathbb{G}_2|$ are the bit length of an element in $\mathbb{G}_1$ and $\mathbb{G}_2$, respectively. The time cost of an algorithm is evaluated by the sum of all involved time-consuming operations. We have preprocessed all of the following compared scenarios. For example, ρ in our scheme is computed in the setup phase, and no additional bilinear pairing computation is required in the following encryption and trapdoor phases. The computational cost is reduced. For example, to encrypt a keyword $\mathbf{w}$, the keyword encryption algorithm in our SCF-CLPAEKS scheme needs to calculate 2 module exponentiation operations in the group, 2 general hash operations, 1 bilinear pairing operation. Thus, the time cost of the keyword encryption algorithm is $2e + h + p$. In addition, the communication cost of a keyword ciphertext/trapdoor is measured by the total number of the involved group elements and hash values. For example, a keyword ciphertext in our scheme contains 1 group element in $\mathbb{G}_1$ and 1 group element in $\mathbb{G}_2$. Thus, the bit-length of a keyword ciphertext is $|\mathbb{G}_1| + |\mathbb{G}_2|$ bits.

As shown in Table 2, Compared with the other two schemes dCLPAEKS [26], CL-PEKS [28], our scheme has great advantages. Regarding the efficiency of the encryption algorithm, our scheme is similar with the scheme [26] and more efficient than the scheme [28]. In the trapdoor algorithm, our scheme is also more efficient than the scheme [26,28]. Moreover, our scheme is more functional in assigning public and private key pairs to all three roles of the sender, receiver, and server, eliminating the assumption of a secure channel between the server and users, and having authentication capabilitie, while the scheme [28] does not have. For the communication cost, our scheme is the most space-saving in terms of ciphertext storage and trapdoor storage.

Table 2. Efficiency comparison.

Scheme	Computation complexity			Storage cost	
	Encryption	Trapdoor	Test	Ciphertext	Trapdoor
dCLPAEKS [26]	$2e + 2h + p$	$2e + h$	$2e + 2p$	$2|G_1| + |G_2|$	$2|G_1|$
CL-PEKS [28]	$2e + 2h + 2p$	$3e + h$	$e + 2p$	$2|G_1| + 2|G_2|$	$3|G_1|$
Our Scheme	$2e + h + p$	$e + h$	p	$|G_1| + |G_2|$	$|G_1|$

e: the modal exponential operation in group; h: the general hash operation; p: the bilinear pairing operation; $|G_1|$: the size of an element in group G_1; $|G_2|$: the size of an element in group G_2;

7 Conclusion and Future Work

In this paper, we proposed the notion of SCF-CLPAEKS and formalized its security definitions. Subsequently, we designed a concrete SCF-CLPAEKS scheme with authentication function, which satisfies the security against inside keyword guessing attacks. Moreover, our scheme removes the secure channel assumption between the server and the users which achieves security against outside keyword guessing attacks. Besides, our scheme avoids the problems of certificate management and key escrow. In addition, our scheme satisfies ciphertext indistinguishability, trapdoor indistinguishability and designated testability under the DBDH assumption in the random oracle model. Finally, the comparison shows that our scheme enjoys a better performance compared with the related schemes.

Acknowledgements. This work is supported by the National Natural Science Foundation of China (No. 61872152, 62272174), Major Program of Guangdong Basic and Applied Research (No. 2019B030302008), and the Science and Technology Program of Guangzhou (No. 201902010081).

References

1. Al-Riyami, S.S., Paterson, K.G.: Certificateless public key cryptography. In: Laih, C.-S. (ed.) ASIACRYPT 2003. LNCS, vol. 2894, pp. 452–473. Springer, Heidelberg (2003). https://doi.org/10.1007/978-3-540-40061-5_29
2. Boyen, X.: The uber-assumption family. In: Galbraith, S.D., Paterson, K.G. (eds.) Pairing 2008. LNCS, vol. 5209, pp. 39–56. Springer, Heidelberg (2008). https://doi.org/10.1007/978-3-540-85538-5_3
3. Chenam, V.B., Ali, S.T.: A designated cloud server-based multi-user certificateless public key authenticated encryption with conjunctive keyword search against ikga. Comput. Stan. Interfaces **81**, 103603 (2022)
4. Cheng, L., Meng, F.: Security analysis of pan et al'.s public-key authenticated encryption with keyword search achieving both multi-ciphertext and multi-trapdoor indistinguishability. J. Syst. Arch. **119**, 102248 (2021)
5. Emura, K.: Generic construction of public-key authenticated encryption with keyword search revisited: stronger security and efficient construction. In: Cryptology ePrint Archive (2022)
6. Guangbo, W., Feng, L., Liwen, F., Haicheng, L.: An efficient scf-peks without random oracle under simple assumption. Chin. J. Electron. **30**(1), 77–84 (2021)
7. Guo, L., Yau, W.-C.: Efficient secure-channel free public key encryption with keyword search for emrs in cloud storage. J. Med. Sys. **39**(2), 1–11 (2015). https://doi.org/10.1007/s10916-014-0178-y
8. Han, M., Xu, P., Xu, L., Xu, C.: Tca-peks: trusted certificateless authentication public-key encryption with keyword search scheme in cloud storage. https://doi.org/10.21203/rs.3.rs-1694526/v1
9. Hassan, A., Wang, Y., Elhabob, R., Eltayieb, N., Li, F.: An efficient certificateless public key encryption scheme with authorized equality test in healthcare environments. J. Syst. Architect. **109**, 101776 (2020)
10. He, D., Ma, M., Zeadally, S., Kumar, N., Liang, K.: Certificateless public key authenticated encryption with keyword search for industrial internet of things. IEEE Trans. Industr. Inf. **14**(8), 3618–3627 (2017)
11. Huang, Q., Li, H.: An efficient public-key searchable encryption scheme secure against inside keyword guessing attacks. Inf. Sci. **403**, 1–14 (2017)
12. Joux, A.: A one round protocol for tripartite diffie–hellman. In: Bosma, W. (ed.) ANTS 2000. LNCS, vol. 1838, pp. 385–393. Springer, Heidelberg (2000). https://doi.org/10.1007/10722028_23
13. Lu, Y., Li, J.: Lightweight public key authenticated encryption with keyword search against adaptively-chosen-targets adversaries for mobile devices. IEEE Transactions on Mobile Computing (2021)
14. Lu, Y., Li, J., Zhang, Y.: Secure channel free certificate-based searchable encryption withstanding outside and inside keyword guessing attacks. IEEE Trans. Serv. Comput. **14**, 2041–2054 (2019)

15. Ma, Y., Kazemian, H.: A secure and efficient public key authenticated encryption with multi-keywords search scheme against inside keyword guessing attack. Int. J. Cyber-Secur. Digit. Forensics **9**(2), 90–102 (2020)

16. Noroozi, M., Eslami, Z.: Public key authenticated encryption with keyword search: revisited. IET Inf. Secur. **13**(4), 336–342 (2019)

17. Pan, X., Li, F.: Public-key authenticated encryption with keyword search achieving both multi-ciphertext and multi-trapdoor indistinguishability. J. Syst. Architect. **115**, 102075 (2021)

18. Qin, B., Chen, Y., Huang, Q., Liu, X., Zheng, D.: Public-key authenticated encryption with keyword search revisited: security model and constructions. Inf. Sci. **516**, 515–528 (2020)

19. Qin, B., Cui, H., Zheng, X., Zheng, D.: Improved security model for public-key authenticated encryption with keyword search. In: Huang, Q., Yu, Yu. (eds.) ProvSec 2021. LNCS, vol. 13059, pp. 19–38. Springer, Cham (2021). https://doi.org/10.1007/978-3-030-90402-9_2

20. Shen, Z., Xue, W., Shu, J.: Survey on the research and development of searchable encryption schemes. J. Softw. **25**(4), 880–895 (2014)

21. Shiraly, D., Pakniat, N., Noroozi, M., Eslami, Z.: Pairing-free certificateless authenticated encryption with keyword search. J. Syst. Architect. **124**, 102390 (2022)

22. Song, D.X., Wagner, D., Perrig, A.: Practical techniques for searches on encrypted data. In: Proceeding 2000 IEEE Symposium on Security and Privacy. S& P 2000, pp. 44–55. IEEE (2000)

23. Wang, J., Zhao, Z., Sun, L., Zhu, Z.: Secure and efficient conjunctive keyword search scheme without secure channel. In: KSII Transactions on Internet and Information Systems (TIIS), vol. 13, no. 5, pp. 2718–2731 (2019)

24. Wang, T., Au, M.H., Wu, W.: An efficient secure channel free searchable encryption scheme with multiple keywords. In: Chen, J., Piuri, V., Su, C., Yung, M. (eds.) NSS 2016. LNCS, vol. 9955, pp. 251–265. Springer, Cham (2016). https://doi.org/10.1007/978-3-319-46298-1_17

25. Wu, B., Wang, C., Yao, H.: Security analysis and secure channel-free certificateless searchable public key authenticated encryption for a cloud-based internet of things. PLoS ONE **15**(4), e0230722 (2020)

26. Wu, L., Zhang, Y., Ma, M., Kumar, N., He, D.: Certificateless searchable public key authenticated encryption with designated tester for cloud-assisted medical Internet of Things. Ann. Telecommun. **74**(7), 423–434 (2019). https://doi.org/10.1007/s12243-018-00701-7

27. Wu, T.Y., Chen, C.M., Wang, K.H., Wu, J.M.T.: Security analysis and enhancement of a certificateless searchable public key encryption scheme for iiot environments. IEEE Access **7**, 49232–49239 (2019)

28. Yang, G., Guo, J., Han, L., Liu, X., Tian, C.: An improved secure certificateless public-key searchable encryption scheme with multi-trapdoor privacy. Peer-to-Peer Netw. Appl. **15**(1), 503–515 (2021). https://doi.org/10.1007/s12083-021-01253-9

More Efficient Verifiable Functional Encryption

Geng Wang$^{(\boxtimes)}$ ⓘ, Ming Wan ⓘ, and Dawu Gu ⓘ

School of Electronic Information and Electrical Engineering,
Shanghai Jiao Tong University, Shanghai 200240, People's Republic of China
{wanggxx,wanming,dwgu}@sjtu.edu.cn

Abstract. Functional encryption (FE for short) can be used to calculate a function output of a message when given the corresponding function key, without revealing other information about the message. However, the original FE does not guarantee the unforgeability of either ciphertexts or function keys. In 2016, Badrinarayanan et al. provide a new primitive called verifiable functional encryption (VFE for short), and give a generic transformation from FE to VFE using non-interactive witness-indistinguishable proof (NIWI proof). In their construction, each VFE ciphertext (resp. function key) consists of 4 FE ciphertexts (resp. function keys) generated from independent FE public keys (resp. secret keys) and a NIWI proof on the correctness.

In this paper, we show that there is redundancy in their construction. Concretely, we give a new construction for VFE which uses only 3 FE ciphertexts and function keys, and prove the verifiability and security of the construction. Since the NIWI proof is also simpler in our scheme, our construction may lead to an about 25% decrease in both ciphertext/key size and encryption/decryption cost.

Keywords: Functional encryption · Verifiability · Cryptographic primitive · Provable security

1 Introduction

Functional encryption (FE) was first introduced by Boneh et al. in 2011 [11], which can calculate the function output $f(m)$ given the encrypted message $\mathsf{Enc}(m)$, and leaks nothing else about the message m. Functional encryption is a mighty cryptographic primitive which can be considered as a generalization of other cryptographic primitives, such as identity-based encryption [10,28], attribute-based encryption [16,18,25], predicate encryption [17,20] and inner product encryption [1–3], and can be used to construct indistinguishability obfuscation [4].

Functional encryption is also an important method for computing on encrypted data, especially for cloud computing [21,22,24]. Using functional encryption, the cloud server can take ciphertexts as input, and outputs the required computation result as plaintext. This is different from homomorphic encryption [12,13], where the result is output as a ciphertext that requires additional decryption procedure, which limits its application.

© The Author(s), under exclusive license to Springer Nature Switzerland AG 2022
C. Ge and F. Guo (Eds.): ProvSec 2022, LNCS 13600, pp. 36–51, 2022.
https://doi.org/10.1007/978-3-031-20917-8_3

However, the security definition of FE does not guarantee unforgeability. This means that in functional encryption, we require all participants to be semi-honest (honest but curious), rather than totally dishonest. This requirement highly restricts the application scenarios for functional encryption, as we cannot always assume that the participants in cloud computing is non-adversarial.

In Asiacrypt 2016, Badrinarayanan et al. [5] proposed a new primitive called verifiable functional encryption (VFE). In a VFE scheme, both ciphertexts and function keys can be verified. The verifiability of VFE requires that: for each ciphertext ct which passes the verification, there exists a message m, such that for all function key sk_f which passes the verification, the decryption result is $f(m)$. Verifiability ensures that no dishonest encryption and/or key generation can lead to wrong decryption results, so even adversial participants cannot break the FE scheme. The authors also give a generic construction for VFE (below we call it the BGJS16 construction), using the following three cryptographic primitives:

- Non-interactive witniss indistinguishable proof (NIWI proof): If two witnesses w_1, w_2 both satisfy the relation R on instance y, then no polynomial time adversary can distinguish between a proof generated by w_1 and a proof generated by w_2. Although NIWI proof is lesser efficient than non-interactive zero-knowledge proof, NIWI proof does not require a common reference string, hence can be constructed without a trusted setup.
- Perfect binding and computationally hiding commitment: No polynomial time adversary can recover the committed message without the randomness used in the commitment. Also, different messages always commit into different commitments.
- (Non-verifiable) functional encryption with perfect correctness: A functional encryption scheme, with the restriction that the decryption always outputs the correct result $f(m)$. Otherwise, an adversary may intentionally construct an incorrect decryption to break the verifiability of the scheme.

The BGJS16 construction can also be considered as a generic transformation from FE to VFE. Since many other primitives, such as identity-based encryption (IBE), attribute-based encryption (ABE), predicate encryption (PE) and inner product encryption (IPE) can all be viewed as a special case of functional encryption, the same method can also be used to construct verifiable IBE, ABE, PE or IPE. In fact, there are already some works on verifiable IPE such as [26]. VFE can also be used to construct other primitives, such as verifiable random functions [6].

Overview of the BGJS16 Construction. Constructing a provable secure verifiable FE scheme is difficult, since reducing the security in a black-box manner means that the challenger cannot know the master secret key or randomness used in the game, while generating a NIWI proof for the correctness of ciphertexts/function keys requires all these information as witness. In their paper, the authors used a clever but complicated method to bypass those troubles.

The BGJS16 construction uses 4 independent FE master public/secret key pairs to generate 4 FE ciphertexts (say $ct_1, ..., ct_4$) and 4 FE function keys (say

$k_1, ..., k_4$), and non-interactive witness indistinguishable proof (NIWI proof) to prove the correctness of the generation. To successfully construct the hybrid argument in the security reduction which reduces the hardness of VFE to FE, they also defined a type of alternative ciphertext/function key. In an alternative ciphertext (resp. function key), it is not required that all ciphertext (resp. function key) elements are correctly generated, but only 2 out of 4 (resp. 3 out of 4) elements are correctly generated for the same message (resp. function). If an alternative ciphertext is decrypted with an alternative function key, at least 1 ciphertext element/function key element pair is correctly generated by the pigeonhole principle. We suppose that ct_i is a correct encryption of message m and k_i is a correct function key for function f.

In addition, the master public key includes a commitment of 4 FE ciphertexts $ct_1^*, ..., ct_4^*$, and the alternative ciphertext elements must be the same with them, which means that $ct_1 = ct_1^*, ..., ct_4 = ct_4^*$. In the alternative function key, it is required that the all 4 decryption results of the committed ciphertexts using the function key are the same, which means that $\mathsf{FE.Dec}(ct_1^*, k_1) = ... = \mathsf{FE.Dec}(ct_4^*, k_4)$. So if we decrypt an alternative ciphertext using an alternative function key, the all 4 decryption results equal to a decryption result with a correctly generated ciphertext/function key pair $\mathsf{FE.Dec}(ct_i, k_i) = f(m)$, hence the verifiability is satisfied. Also, they use an additional commitment to exclude the case where an alternative ciphertext is decrypted with a normal function key. If a normal ciphertext is decrypted with an alternative function key, then at least three of the decryption result is correct and the same, hence can be extracted by voting.

Our Construction. We point out that there is redundancy in the BGJS16 construction, which can let us to reduce the number of ciphertext/function key elements from 4 to 3. If we use 3 different ciphertext/function key elements, we can still use the pigeonhole principle to ensure a correctly generated ciphertext/function key pair exists as long as 2 ciphertext elements and 2 function key elements out of 3 are correctly generated. However, when reducing the number of elements from 4 to 3, we can no longer ensure that the 2 ciphertext elements encrypt the same message.

So in our construction, we use two different types of alternative ciphertexts/function keys in the security proof instead of one, and type 1 ciphertexts/function keys are similar as in BGJS16 construction. In a type 2 ciphertext, two elements in the ciphertext are correctly encrypted, but not necessarily encrypt the same message, which means that $ct_{i_1} = \mathsf{FE.Enc}(pk_{i_1}, m_0)$ and $ct_{i_2} = \mathsf{FE.Enc}(pk_{i_2}, m_1)$. We see that type 2 ciphertext cannot satisfy the verifiability property along with type 1 function keys, as the decryption result may either be $f(m_0)$ or $f(m_1)$ instead of the function output of a fixed message $f(m)$. Thus we define type 2 function keys as: two *fixed* elements of the function key (say: 1, 3) are honestly generated instead of any two of them. We assume that $i \in \{i_1, i_2\} \cap \{1, 3\}$ and ct_i is an encryption of m_b, then the verifiability is satisfied since all decryption result is the function output $f(m_b)$. Like in BGJS16, we add a commitment to exclude the case where type 2 ciphertext is decrypted using type 1 function key.

Related Works. There are also some other works related to the verifiability of functional encryption. In [27], the authors presented a VFE scheme without using NIWI, which trusted setup is done by hardware as in [15], but the verifiability of their scheme relies on hardware security, hence is much weaker. In [8], a different model of verifiability has been presented, where Setup, KeyGen and Enc are all honest, but Dec may be dishonest. We do not consider this type of model in this paper.

Organization. In Sect. 2, we give same basic notations, also formally define verifiable functional encryption and its verifiability. In Sect. 3, we give our construction and prove its verifiability. In Sect. 4, we give the security proof. Finally in Sect. 5, we draw the conclusion.

2 Preliminaries

The abbreviation p.p.t means probabilistic polynomial time. $\text{negl}(\lambda) < \lambda^{-c}$ for any constant $c > 0$ with sufficiently large λ. $x \leftarrow X$ means that x is uniformly chosen from X. $[n]$ denotes the set $\{1, 2, ..., n\}$. $\approx_c$ means that the two experiments are computationally indistinguishable.

2.1 One Message WI Proofs

In this paper, we use the same one message witness indistinguishable proofs NIWI as in [5].

Definition 1. *Let $\mathcal{R}_L$ be an NP relation, where $L := \{x | \exists w, (x, w) \in \mathcal{R}_L\}$. A pair of PPT algorithms $(\mathcal{P} : \mathcal{R} \to \{0, 1\}^*, \mathcal{V} : L \times \{0, 1\}^* \to \{0, 1\})$ is a NIWI for $\mathcal{R}_L$ if it satisfies:*

- *1. Completeness: for every $(x, w) \in \mathcal{R}_L$, $\Pr[\mathcal{V}(x, \pi) = 1 : \pi \leftarrow \mathcal{P}(x, w)] = 1$.*
- *2. (Perfect) Soundness: Proof system is said to be perfectly sound if there for every $x \notin L$ and $\pi \in 0, 1^*$: $\Pr[\mathcal{V}(x, \pi) = 1] = 0$.*
- *3. Witness indistinguishability: for any sequence $\mathcal{I} = \{(x, w_1, w_2) : w_1, w_2 \in \mathcal{R}_L(x)\}$: $\{\pi_1 : \pi_1 \leftarrow \mathcal{P}(x, w_1)\}_{(x, w_1, w_2) \in \mathcal{I}} \approx_c \{\pi_2 : \pi_2 \leftarrow \mathcal{P}(x, w_2)\}_{(x, w_1, w_2) \in \mathcal{I}}$.*

The most widely used NIWI proof in [19] is based on the decisional linear (DLIN) assumption. There are other constructions of NIWI [7,9,14] which are based on different assumptions. In all these constructions, the proof size is (at least) linear in the circuit size of relation $\mathcal{R}_L$.

2.2 Perfect Binding Commitment

Definition 2. *A commitment scheme Com is a PPT algorithm that takes as input a string x and randomness r and outputs $c \leftarrow \text{Com}(x; r)$. A perfectly binding and computationally hiding commitment scheme must satisfy the following properties:*

- *Perfectly Binding: Two different strings cannot have the same commitment. More formally, $\forall x_1 \neq x_2, r_1, r_2$, $\mathsf{Com}(x_1; r_1) \neq \mathsf{Com}(x_2; r_2)$.*
- *Computational Hiding: For all strings x_0 and x_1 (of the same length), for all non-uniform PPT adversaries $\mathcal{A}$, we have that: $|\Pr[\mathcal{A}(\mathsf{Com}(x_0)) = 1] - \Pr[\mathcal{A}(\mathsf{Com}(x_1)) = 1]| \leq \mathrm{negl}(\lambda)$.*

As it was pointed out in [5], a standard non-interactive perfectly binding and computationally hiding commitment scheme can be based on one way permutations, which size is quite small (only approximate to the length of randomness r), see [23].

2.3   Functional Encryption

Let $\mathcal{X} = \{\mathcal{X}_\lambda\}_{\lambda \in \mathbb{N}}$ and $\mathcal{Y} = \{\mathcal{Y}_\lambda\}_{\lambda \in \mathbb{N}}$ denote ensembles where each $\mathcal{X}_\lambda$ and $\mathcal{Y}_\lambda$ is a finite set. Let $\mathcal{F} = \{\mathcal{F}_\lambda\}_{\lambda \in \mathbb{N}}$ denote an ensemble where each $\mathcal{F}_\lambda$ is a finite collection of functions, and each function $f \in \mathcal{F}_\lambda$ takes as input a string $x \in \mathcal{X}_\lambda$ and outputs $f(x) \in \mathcal{Y}_\lambda$. A functional encryption scheme $\mathsf{FE} = (\mathsf{Setup}, \mathsf{Enc}, \mathsf{KeyGen}, \mathsf{Dec})$ consists of the following polynomial time algorithms:

- $\mathsf{Setup}(1^\lambda)$. The setup algorithm takes as input the security parameter λ and outputs a master public key-secret key pair $(\mathsf{MPK}, \mathsf{MSK})$.
- $\mathsf{Enc}(\mathsf{MPK}, x) \to \mathsf{CT}$. The encryption algorithm takes as input a message $x \in \mathcal{X}_\lambda$ and the master public key MPK. It outputs a ciphertext CT.
- $\mathsf{KeyGen}(\mathsf{MPK}, \mathsf{MSK}, f) \to \mathsf{SK}_f$. The key generation algorithm takes as input a function $f \in \mathcal{F}_\lambda$, the master public key MPK and the master secret key MSK. It outputs a function secret key SK_f.
- $\mathsf{Dec}(f, \mathsf{SK}_f, \mathsf{CT}) \to y$ or $\bot$. The decryption algorithm takes as input a function f, the corresponding function secret key SK_f and a ciphertext CT. It either outputs a string $y \in \mathcal{Y}_\lambda$ or $\bot$.

We say that FE has perfect correctness, if the decryption is always correct, that is, for any message x and function f, $\mathsf{MPK}, \mathsf{MSK} \leftarrow \mathsf{Setup}(1^\lambda)$, $\mathsf{CT} \leftarrow \mathsf{Enc}(\mathsf{MPK}, x)$, $\mathsf{SK}_f \leftarrow \mathsf{KeyGen}(\mathsf{MPK}, \mathsf{MSK}, f)$, $\mathsf{Dec}(f, \mathsf{SK}_f, \mathsf{CT}) = f(x)$ happens with probability 1.

We define the selective indistinguishable-based security (Sel-IND security) for FE, using the following Sel-IND interactive game.

- **Initialization**: The adversary chooses two message (m_0, m_1) of the same size (each in $\mathcal{X}_\lambda$) and hands them to the challenger.
- **Setup Phase**: The challenger runs $(\mathsf{MPK}, \mathsf{MSK}) \leftarrow \mathsf{FE.Setup}(1^\lambda)$ and then hands over the master public key MPK to the adversary.
- **Key Query Phase 1**: The adversary makes function secret key queries by submitting functions $f \in \mathcal{F}_\lambda$ under the constraint that $f(m_0) = f(m_1)$. The challenger responds by giving the adversary the corresponding function secret key $\mathsf{SK}_f \leftarrow \mathsf{FE.KeyGen}(\mathsf{MPK}, \mathsf{MSK}, f)$.

– **Challenge Phase**: The challenger selects a random bit $b \in \{0, 1\}$ and sends a ciphertext $\mathsf{CT} \leftarrow \mathsf{FE.Enc}(\mathsf{MPK}, m_b)$ to the adversary.
– **Key Query Phase 2**: The adversary may submit additional key queries $f \in \mathcal{F}_\lambda$ as long as they do not violate the constraint $f(m_0) = f(m_1)$.
– **Guess**: The adversary submits a guess b' and wins if $b' = b$. The adversary's advantage in this game is defined to be $2|\Pr[b = b'] - 1/2|$.

We say that a functional encryption scheme is Sel-IND secure, if all polynomial time adversaries have at most a negligible advantage in the Sel-IND security game.

2.4 Verifiable Functional Encryption

In this section we recall the definition of (public-key) verifiable functional encryption scheme given in [5]. A verifiable functional encryption scheme is similar to a regular functional encryption scheme with two additional algorithms (VerifyCT, VerifyK). Let $\mathcal{X}, \mathcal{Y}, \mathcal{F}$ be defined similarly as in (non-verifiable) functional encryption. Formally, VFE = (Setup, Enc, KeyGen, Dec, VerifyCT, VerifyK) consists of the following polynomial time algorithms:

– Setup(1^λ). The setup algorithm takes as input the security parameter λ and outputs a master public key-secret key pair (MPK, MSK).
– Enc(MPK, x) $\rightarrow$ CT. The encryption algorithm takes as input a message $x \in \mathcal{X}_\lambda$ and the master public key MPK. It outputs a ciphertext CT.
– KeyGen(MPK, MSK, f) $\rightarrow$ SK$_f$. The key generation algorithm takes as input a function $f \in \mathcal{F}_\lambda$, the master public key MPK and the master secret key MSK. It outputs a function secret key SK$_f$.
– Dec(MPK, f, SK$_f$, CT) $\rightarrow$ y or $\bot$. The decryption algorithm takes as input the master public key MPK, a function f, the corresponding function secret key SK$_f$ and a ciphertext CT. It either outputs a string $y \in \mathcal{Y}_\lambda$ or $\bot$. Informally speaking, MPK is given to the decryption algorithm for verification purpose.
– VerifyCT(MPK, CT) $\rightarrow$ 1/0. Takes as input the master public key MPK and a ciphertext CT. It outputs 0 or 1. Intuitively, it outputs 1 if CT was correctly generated using the master public key MPK for some message x.
– VerifyK(MPK, f, SK$_f$) $\rightarrow$ 1/0. Takes as input the master public key MPK, a function f and a function secret key SK$_f$. It outputs either 0 or 1. Intuitively, it outputs 1 if SK$_f$ was correctly generated as a function secret key for f.

The correctness and security notions of VFE are the same as standard FE. In addition, verifiability is defined for VFE as follows:

Definition 3. *A verifiable functional encryption scheme* VFE *for $\mathcal{F}$ is verifiable if, for all* MPK $\in \{0,1\}^*$*, for all* CT $\in \{0,1\}^*$*, there exists $x \in \mathcal{X}$ such that for all $f \in \mathcal{F}$ and* SK $\in \{0,1\}^*$*, if*

$$\mathsf{VerifyCT}(\mathsf{MPK}, \mathsf{CT}) = 1 \ and \ \mathsf{VerifyK}(\mathsf{MPK}, f, \mathsf{SK}) = 1$$

then

$$\Pr[\mathsf{Dec}(\mathsf{MPK}, f, \mathsf{SK}, \mathsf{CT}) = f(x)] = 1.$$

3   Our Construction

Notation: Without loss of generality, let us assume that every plaintext message is of length λ where λ denotes the security parameter of the scheme. Let (Prove, Verify) be a non-interactive witness-indistinguishable (NIWI) proof system for NP, FE = (FE.Setup, FE.Enc, FE.KeyGen, FE.Dec) be a Sel-IND secure public key functional encryption scheme, Com be a perfectly binding and computationally hiding commitment scheme. Without loss of generality, let us say Com commits to a string bit-by-bit and uses randomness of length λ to commit to a single bit. We denote the length of ciphertexts in FE by c-len = c-len(λ). Let len = 3·c-len.

Our VFE scheme VFE = (VFE.Setup, VFE.Enc, VFE.KeyGen, VFE.Dec, VFE. VerifyCT, VFE.VerifyK) is as follows:

- **Setup** VFE.Setup(1^λ):
  The setup algorithm does the following:
  - 1. For all $i \in [3]$, compute $(\mathsf{MPK}_i, \mathsf{MSK}_i) \leftarrow \mathsf{FE.Setup}(1^\lambda; s_i)$ using randomness s_i.
  - 2. Set $Z = \mathsf{Com}(0^{\mathsf{len}}; u)$, $Z_1 = \mathsf{Com}(1; u_1)$, $Z_2 = \mathsf{Com}(1; u_2)$ where u, u_1, u_2 represent the randomness used in the commitment.

  The master public key is $\mathsf{MPK} = (\{\mathsf{MPK}_i\}_{i \in [3]}, Z, Z_1, Z_2)$.
  The master secret key is $\mathsf{MSK} = (\{\mathsf{MSK}_i\}_{i \in [3]}, \{s_i\}_{i \in [3]}, u, u_1, u_2)$.

- **Encryption** VFE.Enc(MPK, m) :
  To encrypt a message m, the encryption algorithm does the following:
  - 1. For all $i \in [3]$, compute $\mathsf{CT}_i = \mathsf{FE.Enc}(\mathsf{MPK}_i, m; r_i)$.
  - 2. Compute a proof $\pi \leftarrow \mathsf{Prove}(y, w)$ for the statement that $y \in L$ using witness w where:
    $y = (\{\mathsf{CT}_i\}_{i \in [3]}, \mathsf{MPK}_{i \in [3]}, Z, Z_1, Z_2)$,
    $w = (m, 0^{|m|}, \{r_i\}_{i \in [3]}, 0, 0, 0^{|u|}, 0^{|u_1|}, 0^{|u_2|})$.

  L is defined corresponding to the relation R defined below.

  Relation R:
  Instance: $y = (\{\mathsf{CT}_i\}_{i \in [3]}, \{\mathsf{MPK}_i\}_{i \in [3]}, Z, Z_1, Z_2)$
  Witness: $w = (m, m', \{r_i\}_{i \in [3]}, i_1, i_2, u, u_1, u_2)$
  $R(y, w) = 1$ if and only if either of the following conditions hold:

  - 1. All 3 constituent ciphertexts encrypt the same message. That is,
    $\forall i \in [3], \mathsf{CT}_i = \mathsf{FE.Enc}(\mathsf{MPK}_i, m; r_i)$
    (OR)
  - 2. 2 constituent ciphertexts (corresponding to indices i_1, i_2) encrypt the message m, m', Z is a commitment to all the constituent ciphertexts and Z_1 is a commitment to 0, and either $m = m'$ or Z_2 is a commitment to 0:
    That is,
    (a) $\mathsf{CT}_{i_1} = \mathsf{FE.Enc}(\mathsf{MPK}_{i_1}, m; r_{i_1})$, $\mathsf{CT}_{i_2} = \mathsf{FE.Enc}(\mathsf{MPK}_{i_2}, m'; r_{i_2})$.
    (b) $Z = \mathsf{Com}(\{\mathsf{CT}_i\}_{i \in [3]}; u)$.
    (c) $Z_1 = \mathsf{Com}(0; u_1)$.
    (d) Either ⓐ $m = m'$ or ⓑ $Z_2 = \mathsf{Com}(0; u_2)$.

The output of the algorithm is the ciphertext $\mathsf{CT} = (\{\mathsf{CT}_i\}_{i\in[3]}, \pi)$. π is computed for statement 1 of relation R.

– **Key Generation** $\mathsf{VFE.KeyGen}(\mathsf{MPK}, \mathsf{MSK}, f)$:
To generate the function secret key K^f for a function f, the key generation algorithm does the following:

- 1. $\forall i \in [3]$, compute $\mathsf{K}_i^f = \mathsf{FE.KeyGen}(\mathsf{MSK}_i, f; r_i)$.
- 2. Compute a proof $\gamma \leftarrow \mathsf{Prove}(y, w)$ for the statement that $y \in L_1$ using witness w where:

$$y = (\{\mathsf{K}_i^f\}_{i\in[3]}, \{\mathsf{MPK}_i\}_{i\in[3]}, \mathsf{Z}, \mathsf{Z}_1, \mathsf{Z}_2),$$
$$w = (f, \{\mathsf{MSK}_i\}_{i\in[3]}, \{s_i\}_{i\in[3]}, \{r_i\}_{i\in[3]}, 0, 0, 0^{|u|}, u_1, u_2).$$

L_1 is defined corresponding to the relation R_1 defined below.

Relation R_1:
Instance: $y = (\{\mathsf{K}_i^f\}_{i\in[3]}, \{\mathsf{MPK}_i\}_{i\in[3]}, \mathsf{Z}, \mathsf{Z}_1, \mathsf{Z}_2)$
Witness: $w = (f, \{\mathsf{MSK}_i\}_{i\in[3]}, \{s_i\}_{i\in[3]}, \{r_i\}_{i\in[3]}, i_1, i_2, u, u_1, u_2)$
$R_1(y, w) = 1$ if and only if either of the following conditions hold:

- 1. Z_1 is a commitment to 1, all 3 constituent function secret keys are secret keys for the same function and are constructed using honestly generated public key-secret key pairs.
  - (a) $\forall i \in [3]$, $\mathsf{K}_i^f = \mathsf{FE.KeyGen}(\mathsf{MSK}_i, f; r_i)$.
  - (b) $\forall i \in [3]$, $(\mathsf{MPK}_i, \mathsf{MSK}_i) \leftarrow \mathsf{FE.Setup}(1^\lambda; s_i)$.
  - (c) $\mathsf{Z}_1 = \mathsf{Com}(1; u_1)$.
  - (OR)
- 2. 2 of the constituent function secret keys (corresponding to indices i_1, i_2) are keys for the same function and are constructed using honestly generated public key-secret key pairs, Z is a commitment to a set of ciphertexts CT such that each constituent ciphertext in CT when decrypted with the corresponding function secret key gives the same output, and either Z_2 is a commitment to 1 or $(i_1, i_2) = (1, 3)$. That is,
  - (a) $\forall i \in \{i_1, i_2\}$, $\mathsf{K}_i^f = \mathsf{FE.KeyGen}(\mathsf{MSK}_i, f; r_i)$.
  - (b) $\forall i \in \{i_1, i_2\}$, $(\mathsf{MPK}_i, \mathsf{MSK}_i) \leftarrow \mathsf{FE.Setup}(1^\lambda; s_i)$.
  - (c) $\mathsf{Z} = \mathsf{Com}(\{\mathsf{CT}_i\}_{i\in[3]}; u)$.
  - (d) $\exists x \in \mathcal{X}_\lambda$ such that $\forall i \in [3]$, $\mathsf{FE.Dec}(\mathsf{CT}_i, \mathsf{K}_i^f) = x$.
  - (e) Either ⓐ $\mathsf{Z}_2 = \mathsf{Com}(1; u_2)$ or ⓑ $(i_1, i_2) = (1, 3)$.

The output of the algorithm is the function secret key $\mathsf{K}^f = (\{\mathsf{K}_i^f\}_{i\in[3]}, \gamma)$. γ is computed for statement 1 of relation R_1.

– **Decryption** $\mathsf{VFE.Dec}(\mathsf{MPK}, f, \mathsf{K}^f, \mathsf{CT})$:
This algorithm decrypts the ciphertext $\mathsf{CT} = (\{\mathsf{CT}_i\}_{i\in[3]}, \pi)$ using function secret key $\mathsf{K}^f = (\{\mathsf{K}_i^f\}_{i\in[3]}, \gamma)$ in the following way:

- 1. Let $y = (\{\mathsf{CT}_i\}_{i\in[3]}, \{\mathsf{MPK}_i\}_{i\in[3]}, \mathsf{Z}, \mathsf{Z}_1, \mathsf{Z}_2)$ be the statement corresponding to proof π. If $\mathsf{Verify}(y, \pi) = 0$, then stop and output $\perp$. Else, continue to the next step.
- 2. Let $y_1 = (\{\mathsf{K}_i^f\}_{i\in[3]}, \{\mathsf{MPK}_i\}_{i\in[3]}, \mathsf{Z}, \mathsf{Z}_1, \mathsf{Z}_2)$ be the statement corresponding to proof γ. If $\mathsf{Verify}(y_1, \gamma) = 0$, then stop and output $\perp$. Else, continue to the next step.

- 3. For $i \in [3]$, compute $m_i = \mathsf{FE.Dec}(\mathsf{CT}_i, \mathsf{K}_i^f)$. If at least 2 of the m_is are equal (let us say that value is m), output m. Else, output $\perp$.
- **VerifyCT** $\mathsf{VFE.VerifyCT}(\mathsf{MPK}, \mathsf{CT})$:
  Given a ciphertext $\mathsf{CT} = (\{\mathsf{CT}_i\}_{i \in [3]}, \pi)$, this algorithm checks whether the ciphertext was generated correctly using master public key MPK. Let $y = (\{\mathsf{CT}_i\}_{i \in [3]}, \{\mathsf{MPK}_i\}_{i \in [3]}, \mathsf{Z}, \mathsf{Z}_1, \mathsf{Z}_2)$ be the statement corresponding to proof π. If $\mathsf{Verify}(y, \pi) = 1$, it outputs 1. Else, it outputs 0.
- **VerifyK** $\mathsf{VFE.VerifyK}(\mathsf{MPK}, f, \mathsf{K})$:
  Given a function f and a function secret key $\mathsf{K} = (\{\mathsf{K}_i\}_{i \in [3]}, \gamma)$, this algorithm checks whether the key was generated correctly for function f using the master secret key corresponding to master public key MPK. Let $y = (\{\mathsf{K}_i\}_{i \in [3]}, \{\mathsf{MPK}_i\}_{i \in [3]}, \mathsf{Z}, \mathsf{Z}_1, \mathsf{Z}_2)$ be the statement corresponding to proof γ. If $\mathsf{Verify}(y, \gamma) = 1$, it outputs 1. Else, it outputs 0.

Correctness follows directly from the correctness of the underlying FE scheme, correctness of the commitment scheme and the completeness of the NIWI proof system.

Comparison Between Our Construction and the BGJS16 Construction. We briefly summarize the differences between our construction and the BGJS16 construction (which are shown in red above):

- We uses 3 FE ciphertexts/function keys in each VFE ciphertext/function key instead of 4.
- In statement 2 of R and R_1, we require that 2 out of 3 elements are correctly generated. Moreover, in the relation R, we add another message m' into the witness, and let the two ciphertext elements encrypt m and m', instead of the same element m.
- We add a new commitment Z_2 into the master public key, instances of R and R_1, and its corresponding randomness u_2 into the master secret key, witnesses of R and R_1.
- We add a new condition 2(d) into statement 2 of relation R and 2(e) into statement 2 of relation R_1, which are both OR-statements. Below, we write statement 2 with the first branch in 2(d) of relation R or 2(e) of relation R_1 as statement 2ⓐ, otherwise as statement 2ⓑ.

Discussion on the Proof Size. In most NIWI proof for NP language such as [19], the proof size and verification cost is linear to the circuit size of the relation to be proved. We can see that the main cost is proving the correctness of ciphertexts/keys. Since we reduce the number of elements from 4 to 3, the size of this part is reduced by 25%. We also add some additional cost in 2(d) of relation R and 2(e) of relation R_1, mainly on opening the commitments Z_2. However, Z_2 only commits one bit, so the additional cost is much smaller compared with the correctness proof part, we can approximately assume that the size and cost of the NIWI proof is also reduced by 25%.

3.1 Verifiability

Consider any master public key MPK and any ciphertext CT = $(\{CT_i\}_{i\in[3]}, \pi)$ such that VFE.VerifyCT(MPK, CT) = 1. Now, there are two cases possible for the proof π.

– 1. Statement 1 of relation R is correct:

Therefore, there exists $m \in \mathcal{X}_\lambda$ such that $\forall i \in [3]$, $CT_i = $ FE.Enc(MPK$_i$, $m; r_i$) where r_i is a random string. Consider any function f and function secret key K = $(\{K_i\}_{i\in[3]}, \gamma)$ such that VFE.VerifyK(MPK, f, K) = 1. There are two cases possible for the proof γ.

- (a) Statement 1 of relation R_1 is correct:

Therefore, $\forall i \in [3]$, K_i is a function secret key for the same function - f. That is, $\forall i \in [3]$, $K_i = $ FE.KeyGen(MSK$_i$, $f; r'_i$) where r'_i is a random string. Thus, for all $i \in [3]$, FE.Dec(CT_i, K_i) = $f(m)$. Hence, VFE.Dec (MPK, f, K, CT) = $f(m)$.

- (b) Statement 2 of relation R_1 is correct:

Therefore, there exists 2 indices i_1, i_2 such that K_{i_1}, K_{i_2} are function secret keys for the same function - f. That is, $\forall i \in \{i_1, i_2\}$, $K_i = $ FE.KeyGen(MSK$_i$, $f; r'_i$) where r'_i is a random string. Thus, for all $i \in \{i_1, i_2\}$, FE.Dec(CT_i, K_i) = $f(m)$. Hence, VFE.Dec(MPK, f, K, CT) = $f(m)$.

– 2. Statement 2 of relation R is correct:

Therefore, $Z_1 = $ Com($0; u_1$) and $Z = $ Com($\{CT_i\}_{i\in[4]}; u$) for some random strings u, u_1. Also, there exists 2 indices i_1, i_2 and two messages $m, m' \in \mathcal{X}_\lambda$ such that for $CT_{i_1} = $ FE.Enc(MPK$_{i_1}$, $m; r_{i_1}$) and $CT_{i_2} = $ FE.Enc(MPK$_{i_2}$, $m'; r_{i_2}$) where r_{i_1}, r_{i_2} are random strings. Consider any function f and function secret key K = $(\{K_i\}_{i\in[3]}, \gamma)$ such that VFE.VerifyK(MPK, f, K) = 1. There are two cases possible for the proof γ.

- (a) Statement 1 of relation R_1 is correct:

Then, it must be the case that $Z_1 = $ Com($1; u'_1$) for some random string u'_1. However, we already know that $Z_1 = $ Com($0; u_1$) and Com is a perfectly binding commitment scheme. Thus, this scenario is impossible. That is, both VFE.VerifyCT(MPK, CT) and VFE.VerifyK(MPK, f, K) cannot be equal to 1.

- (b) Statement 2 of relation R_1 is correct:

Therefore, there exists 2 indices i'_1, i'_2 such that $K_{i'_1}, K_{i'_2}$ are function secret keys for the same function - f. That is, $\forall i \in \{i'_1, i'_2\}$, $K_i = $ FE.KeyGen(MSK$_i$, $f; r'_i$) where r'_i is a random string. Thus, by pigeonhole principle, there exists $i^* \in \{i'_1, i'_2\}$ such that $i^* \in \{i_1, i_2\}$ as well. Also, $Z = $ Com($\{CT_i\}_{i\in[3]}; u$) and $\forall i \in [3]$, FE.Dec(CT_i, K_i) is the same. We discuss the following two cases:

  - ⓐ $m = m'$. Thus for the index i^*, FE.Dec(CT_{i^*}, K_{i^*}) = $f(m)$. Then $\forall i \in [3]$, FE.Dec(CT_i, K_i) = $f(m)$. Therefore, VFE.Dec(MPK, f, K, CT) = $f(m)$.

- ⓑ $Z_2 = \mathsf{Com}(0; u_2)$. Then there must be $(i'_1, i'_2) = (1,3)$, otherwise there exists u'_2 such that $Z_2 = \mathsf{Com}(1, u'_2)$, which disobeys the perfectly binding condition of Com. If $i_1 \in \{1,3\}$, $\mathsf{FE.Dec}(\mathsf{CT}_{i_1}, \mathsf{K}_{i_1}) = f(m)$. Then $\forall i \in [3], \mathsf{FE.Dec}(\mathsf{CT}_i, \mathsf{K}_i) = f(m)$. Therefore, $\mathsf{VFE.Dec}(\mathsf{MPK}, f, \mathsf{K}, \mathsf{CT}) = f(m)$. Otherwise, there must be $i_2 \in \{1,3\}$, and $\mathsf{FE.Dec}(\mathsf{CT}_{i_2}, \mathsf{K}_{i_2}) = f(m')$. Then $\forall i \in [3], \mathsf{FE.Dec}(\mathsf{CT}_i, \mathsf{K}_i) = f(m')$. Therefore, $\mathsf{VFE.Dec}(\mathsf{MPK}, f, \mathsf{K}, \mathsf{CT}) = f(m')$.

4 Security Proof

We now prove that the proposed scheme VFE is Sel-IND secure. We will prove this via a series of hybrid experiments $H_1, ..., H_{18}$ where H_1 corresponds to the real world experiment with challenge bit $b = 0$ and H_{18} corresponds to the real world experiment with challenge bit $b = 1$. The hybrids are summarized below.

	$(\{\mathsf{CT}_i^*\}_{i\in[3]})$	π^*	$\{\mathsf{K}_i^f\}_{i\in[3]}$	γ	Z	Z_1	Z_2	Security
H_1	(m_0, m_0, m_0)	1	(f, f, f)	1	$\mathsf{Com}(0^{\mathsf{len}})$	$\mathsf{Com}(1)$	$\mathsf{Com}(1)$	-
H_2	(m_0, m_0, m_0)	1	(f, f, f)	1	$\mathsf{Com}(\{\mathsf{CT}_i^*\}_{i\in[3]})$	$\mathsf{Com}(1)$	$\mathsf{Com}(1)$	Com-Hiding
H_3	(m_0, m_0, m_0)	1	(f, f, f)	2ⓐ	$\mathsf{Com}(\{\mathsf{CT}_i^*\}_{i\in[3]})$	$\mathsf{Com}(1)$	$\mathsf{Com}(1)$	NIWI
H_4	(m_0, m_0, m_0)	1	(f, f, f)	2ⓐ	$\mathsf{Com}(\{\mathsf{CT}_i^*\}_{i\in[3]})$	$\mathsf{Com}(0)$	$\mathsf{Com}(1)$	Com-Hiding
H_5	(m_0, m_0, m_0)	2ⓐ	(f, f, f)	2ⓐ	$\mathsf{Com}(\{\mathsf{CT}_i^*\}_{i\in[3]})$	$\mathsf{Com}(0)$	$\mathsf{Com}(1)$	NIWI
H_6	(m_0, m_0, m_1)	2ⓐ	(f, f, f)	2ⓐ	$\mathsf{Com}(\{\mathsf{CT}_i^*\}_{i\in[3]})$	$\mathsf{Com}(0)$	$\mathsf{Com}(1)$	IND-secure FE
H_7	(m_0, m_0, m_1)	2ⓐ	(f, f, f)	2ⓑ	$\mathsf{Com}(\{\mathsf{CT}_i^*\}_{i\in[3]})$	$\mathsf{Com}(0)$	$\mathsf{Com}(1)$	NIWI
H_8	(m_0, m_0, m_1)	2ⓐ	(f, f, f)	2ⓑ	$\mathsf{Com}(\{\mathsf{CT}_i^*\}_{i\in[3]})$	$\mathsf{Com}(0)$	$\mathsf{Com}(0)$	Com-Hiding
H_9	(m_0, m_0, m_1)	2ⓑ	(f, f, f)	2ⓑ	$\mathsf{Com}(\{\mathsf{CT}_i^*\}_{i\in[3]})$	$\mathsf{Com}(0)$	$\mathsf{Com}(0)$	NIWI
H_{10}	(m_0, m_1, m_1)	2ⓑ	(f, f, f)	2ⓑ	$\mathsf{Com}(\{\mathsf{CT}_i^*\}_{i\in[3]})$	$\mathsf{Com}(0)$	$\mathsf{Com}(0)$	IND-secure FE
H_{11}	(m_0, m_1, m_1)	2ⓐ	(f, f, f)	2ⓑ	$\mathsf{Com}(\{\mathsf{CT}_i^*\}_{i\in[3]})$	$\mathsf{Com}(0)$	$\mathsf{Com}(0)$	NIWI
H_{12}	(m_0, m_1, m_1)	2ⓐ	(f, f, f)	2ⓑ	$\mathsf{Com}(\{\mathsf{CT}_i^*\}_{i\in[3]})$	$\mathsf{Com}(0)$	$\mathsf{Com}(1)$	Com-Hiding
H_{13}	(m_0, m_1, m_1)	2ⓐ	(f, f, f)	2ⓐ	$\mathsf{Com}(\{\mathsf{CT}_i^*\}_{i\in[3]})$	$\mathsf{Com}(0)$	$\mathsf{Com}(1)$	NIWI
H_{14}	(m_1, m_1, m_1)	2ⓐ	(f, f, f)	2ⓐ	$\mathsf{Com}(\{\mathsf{CT}_i^*\}_{i\in[3]})$	$\mathsf{Com}(0)$	$\mathsf{Com}(1)$	IND-secure FE
H_{15}	(m_1, m_1, m_1)	1	(f, f, f)	2ⓐ	$\mathsf{Com}(\{\mathsf{CT}_i^*\}_{i\in[3]})$	$\mathsf{Com}(0)$	$\mathsf{Com}(1)$	NIWI
H_{16}	(m_1, m_1, m_1)	1	(f, f, f)	2ⓐ	$\mathsf{Com}(\{\mathsf{CT}_i^*\}_{i\in[3]})$	$\mathsf{Com}(1)$	$\mathsf{Com}(1)$	Com-Hiding
H_{17}	(m_1, m_1, m_1)	1	(f, f, f)	1	$\mathsf{Com}(\{\mathsf{CT}_i^*\}_{i\in[3]})$	$\mathsf{Com}(1)$	$\mathsf{Com}(1)$	NIWI
H_{18}	(m_1, m_1, m_1)	1	(f, f, f)	1	$\mathsf{Com}(0^{\mathsf{len}})$	$\mathsf{Com}(1)$	$\mathsf{Com}(1)$	Com-Hiding

Fig. 1. Here, (m_0, m_0, m_0) indicates the messages that are encrypted to form the challenge ciphertext $\{\mathsf{CT}_i^*\}_{i\in[3]}$. Similarly for the column $\{\mathsf{K}_i^f\}_{i\in[3]}$. The column π^* (and γ) denote the statement proved by the proof in relation R (and R_1). The text in red indicates the difference from the previous hybrid. The text in blue denotes the indices used in the proofs π^* and γ. That is, the text in blue in the column $(\{\mathsf{CT}_i^*\}_{i\in[3]})$ denotes the indices used in the proof π^* and the text in blue in the column $(\{\mathsf{K}_i^f\}_{i\in[3]})$ denotes the indices used in the proof γ for every function secret key K^f corresponding to function f.

We briefly describe the hybrids below.

Hybrid H_1: This is the real experiment with challenge bit $b = 0$. The master public key is $MPK = (\{MPK_i\}_{i\in[3]}, Z, Z_1, Z_2)$ such that $Z = Com(0^{len}; u)$, $Z_1 = Com(1; u_1)$ and $Z_2 = Com(1; u_2)$ for random strings u, u_1, u_2. The challenge ciphertext is $CT^* = (\{CT_i^*\}_{i\in[3]}, \pi^*)$, where for all $i \in [4]$, $CT_i^* = FE.Enc(MPK_i, m_0; r_i)$ for some random string r_i. π^* is computed for statement 1 of relation R.

Hybrid H_2: This hybrid is identical to the previous hybrid except that Z is computed differently. $Z = Com(\{CT_i^*\}_{i\in[3]}; u)$.

Hybrid H_3: This hybrid is identical to the previous hybrid except that for every function secret key K^f, the proof γ is now computed for statement 2ⓐ of relation R_1 using indices $\{1, 2\}$ as the set of 2 indices $\{i_1, i_2\}$ in the witness. That is, the witness is $w = (f, MSK_1, MSK_2, 0^{|MSK_3|}, s_1, s_2, 0^{|s_3|}, r_1, r_2, 0^{|r_3|}, 1, 2, u, 0^{|u_1|}, u_2)$.

Hybrid H_4: This hybrid is identical to the previous hybrid except that Z_1 is computed differently. $Z_1 = Com(0; u_1)$.

Hybrid H_5: This hybrid is identical to the previous hybrid except that the proof π^* in the challenge ciphertext is now computed for statement 2ⓐ of relation R using indices $\{1, 2\}$ as the 2 indices $\{i_1, i_2\}$ in the witness. That is, the witness is $w = (m_0, m_0, r_1, r_2, 0^{|r_3|}, 1, 2, u, u_1, 0^{|u_2|})$.

Hybrid H_6: This hybrid is identical to the previous hybrid except that we change the third component CT_3^* of the challenge ciphertext to be an encryption of the challenge message m_1 (as opposed to m_0). That is, $CT_3^* = FE.Enc(MPK_3, m_1; r_3)$ for some random string r_3. Note that the proof π^* is unchanged and is still proven for statement 2ⓐ of relation R.

Hybrid H_7: This hybrid is identical to the previous hybrid except that for every function secret key K^f, the proof γ is now computed for statement 2ⓑ of relation R_1 using indices $\{1, 3\}$ as the set of 2 indices $\{i_1, i_2\}$ in the witness. That is, the witness is $w = (f, MSK_1, 0^{|MSK_2|}, MSK_3, s_1, 0^{|s_2|}, s_3, r_1, 0^{|r_2|}, r_3, 1, 3, u, 0^{|u_1|}, 0^{|u_2|})$.

Hybrid H_8: This hybrid is identical to the previous hybrid except that Z_2 is computed differently. $Z_2 = Com(0; u_2)$.

Hybrid H_9: This hybrid is identical to the previous hybrid except that the proof π^* in the challenge ciphertext is now computed for statement 2ⓑ of relation R using message m_1 and indices $\{1, 3\}$ as the 2 indices $\{i_1, i_2\}$ in the witness. That is, the witness is $w = (m_0, m_1, r_1, 0^{|r_2|}, r_3, 1, 3, u, u_1, u_2)$.

Hybrid H_{10}: This hybrid is identical to the previous hybrid except that we change the second component CT_2^* of the challenge ciphertext to be an encryption of the challenge message m_1 (as opposed to m_0). That is, $CT_2^* = FE.Enc(MPK_2, m_1; r_2)$ for some random string r_2. Note that the proof π^* is unchanged and is still proven for statement 2ⓑ of relation R.

Hybrid H_{11}: This hybrid is identical to the previous hybrid except that the proof π^* in the challenge ciphertext is now computed for statement 2ⓐ of relation R using indices $\{2, 3\}$ as the 2 indices $\{i_1, i_2\}$ in the witness. That is, the witness is $w = (m_1, m_1, 0^{|r_1|}, r_2, r_3, 2, 3, u, u_1, 0^{|u_2|})$.

Hybrid H_{12}: This hybrid is identical to the previous hybrid except that Z_2 is computed differently. $Z_2 = \mathsf{Com}(1; u_2)$.

Hybrid H_{13}: This hybrid is identical to the previous hybrid except that for every function secret key K^f, the proof γ is now computed for statement 2ⓐ of relation R_1 using indices $\{2, 3\}$ as the set of 2 indices $\{i_1, i_2\}$ in the witness. That is, the witness is $w = (f, 0^{|\mathsf{MSK}_1|}, \mathsf{MSK}_2, \mathsf{MSK}_3, 0^{|s_1|}, s_2, s_3, 0^{|r_1|}, r_2, r_3, 2, 3, u, 0^{|u_1|}, u_2)$.

Hybrid H_{14}: This hybrid is identical to the previous hybrid except that we change the first component CT_1^* of the challenge ciphertext to be an encryption of the challenge message m_1 (as opposed to m_0). That is, $\mathsf{CT}_1^* = \mathsf{FE.Enc}(\mathsf{MPK}_1, m_1; r_1)$ for some random string r_1. Note that the proof π^* is unchanged and is still proven for statement 2ⓐ of relation R.

Hybrid H_{15}: This hybrid is identical to the previous hybrid except that the proof π^* in the challenge ciphertext is now computed for statement 1 of relation R. The witness is $w = (m_1, 0^{|m_1|}, \{r_i\}_{i \in [3]}, 0, 0, 0^{|u|}, 0^{|u_1|}, 0^{|u_2|})$.

Hybrid H_{16}: This hybrid is identical to the previous hybrid except that Z_1 is computed differently. $Z_1 = \mathsf{Com}(1; u_1)$.

Hybrid H_{17}: This hybrid is identical to the previous hybrid except that for every function secret key K^f, the proof γ is now computed for statement 1 of relation R_1. The witness is $w = (f, \{\mathsf{MSK}_i\}_{i \in [3]}, \{s_i\}_{i \in [3]}, \{r_i\}_{i \in [3]}, 0, 0, 0^{|u|}, u_1, u_2)$.

Hybrid H_{18}: This hybrid is identical to the previous hybrid except that Z is computed differently. $Z = \mathsf{Com}(0^{\mathsf{len}}; u)$. This hybrid is identical to the real experiment with challenge bit $b = 1$.

The proof of indistinguishability between hybrids can be divided into three types, which rely on (1) the (computationally) hiding of Com; (2) the witness indistinguishability of NIWI proof; (3) the Sel-IND security of FE. We only prove one in each type, the others hold similarly.

Lemma 1. *Assuming that Com is a (computationally) hiding commitment scheme, the outputs of experiments H_1 and H_2 are computationally indistinguishable.*

Proof. The only difference between the two hybrids is the manner in which the commitment Z is computed. Let us consider the following adversary $\mathcal{A}_{\mathsf{Com}}$ that interacts with a challenger $\mathcal{C}$ to break the hiding of the commitment scheme. Also, internally, it acts as the challenger in the security game with an adversary $\mathcal{A}$ that tries to distinguish between H_1 and H_2. $\mathcal{A}_{\mathsf{Com}}$ executes the hybrid H_1 except that it does not generate the commitment Z on its own. Instead, after receiving the challenge messages (m_0, m_1) from $\mathcal{A}$, it computes $\mathsf{CT}^* = (\{\mathsf{CT}_i^*\}_{i \in [3]}, \pi^*)$ as an encryption of message m_0 by following the honest encryption algorithm as in H_1 and H_2. Then, it sends two strings, namely (0^{len}) and $(\{\mathsf{CT}_i^*\}_{i \in [3]})$ to the outside challenger $\mathcal{C}$. In return, $\mathcal{A}_{\mathsf{Com}}$ receives a commitment Z corresponding to either the first or the second string. It then gives this to $\mathcal{A}$. Now, whatever bit b $\mathcal{A}$ guesses, $\mathcal{A}_{\mathsf{Com}}$ forwards the same guess to the outside challenger $\mathcal{C}$. Clearly, $\mathcal{A}_{\mathsf{Com}}$ is a polynomial time algorithm and breaks the hiding property of Com unless H_1 and H_2 are computationally indistinguishable. $\square$

Lemma 2. *Assuming that* (Prove, Verify) *is a non-interactive witness indistinguishable (NIWI) proof system, the outputs of experiments* H_2 *and* H_3 *are computationally indistinguishable.*

Proof. The only difference between the two hybrids is the manner in which the proof γ is computed for each function secret key query f. In H_2, γ is computed for statement 1 of relation R_1 using the "real" witness $w = (f, \{MSK_i\}_{i \in [3]}, \{s_i\}_{i \in [3]}, \{r_i\}_{i \in [3]}, 0, 0, 0^{|u|}, u_1, u_2)$. In H_3, γ is computed for statement 2ⓐ of relation R_1 using the "trapdoor" witness $w = (f, MSK_1, MSK_2, 0^{|MSK_3|}, s_1, s_2, 0^{|s_3|}, r_1, r_2, 0^{|r_3|}, 1, 2, u, 0^{|u_1|}, u_2)$. Thus, by a standard hybrid argument, the indistinguishability of the two hybrids follows from the witness indistinguishability property of the NIWI proof system. □

Lemma 3. *Assuming that* FE *is a Sel-IND secure functional encryption scheme, the outputs of experiments* H_5 *and* H_6 *are computationally indistinguishable.*

Proof. The only difference between the two hybrids is the manner in which the challenge ciphertext is created. More specifically, in H_5, the third component of the challenge ciphertext CT_3^* is computed as an encryption of message m_0, while in H_6, CT_3^* is computed as an encryption of message m_1. Note that the proof π^* remains same in both the hybrids.

Let's consider the following adversary $\mathcal{A}_{FE}$ that interacts with a challenger $\mathcal{C}$ to break the security of the underlying FE scheme. Also, internally, it acts as the challenger in the security game with an adversary $\mathcal{A}$ that tries to distinguish between H_5 and H_6. $\mathcal{A}_{FE}$ executes the hybrid H_5 except that it does not generate the parameters (MPK_3, MSK_3) itself. It sets (MPK_3) to be the public key given by the challenger $\mathcal{C}$. After receiving the challenge messages (m_0, m_1) from $\mathcal{A}$, it forwards the pair (m_0, m_1) to the challenger $\mathcal{C}$ and receives a ciphertext CT which is either an encryption of m_0 or m_1 using public key MPK_3. $\mathcal{A}_{FE}$ sets $CT_3^* = CT$ and computes $CT^* = (\{CT_i^*\}_{i \in [3]}, \pi^*)$ as the challenge ciphertext as in H_5. Note that proof π^* is proved for statement 2ⓐ of relation R. It then sets the public parameter $Z = Com(\{CT_i^*\}_{i \in [3]}; u)$ and sends the master public key MPK and the challenge ciphertext CT^* to $\mathcal{A}$.

Now, whatever bit b $\mathcal{A}$ guesses, $\mathcal{A}_{FE}$ forwards the same guess to the outside challenger $\mathcal{C}$. Clearly, $\mathcal{A}_{FE}$ is a polynomial time algorithm and breaks the security of the functional encryption scheme FE unless H_5 and H_6 are computationally indistinguishable. □

5 Conclusion

In this paper, we present a more efficient construction for verifiable functional encryption, which reduces all costs for about 25% compared with the literature. More concretely, we improve the generic construction for verifiable functional encryption in Asiacrypt 2016, by reducing the number of FE ciphertexts (resp. FE function keys) in the VFE ciphertext (resp. function key) from 4 to 3, while only adding a (much smaller) bit commitment into the scheme. We also prove the verifiability and security of our construction using a similar method.

Acknowledgement. This work is partially supported by the National Key R&D Program of China (No. 2020YFA0712300) and the National Natural Science Foundation of China (No. 62202294).

References

1. Abdalla, M., Bourse, F., De Caro, A., Pointcheval, D.: Simple functional encryption schemes for inner products. In: Katz, J. (ed.) PKC 2015. LNCS, vol. 9020, pp. 733–751. Springer, Heidelberg (2015). https://doi.org/10.1007/978-3-662-46447-2_33
2. Agrawal, S., Libert, B., Maitra, M., Titiu, R.: Adaptive simulation security for inner product functional encryption. In: Kiayias, A., Kohlweiss, M., Wallden, P., Zikas, V. (eds.) PKC 2020. LNCS, vol. 12110, pp. 34–64. Springer, Cham (2020). https://doi.org/10.1007/978-3-030-45374-9_2
3. Agrawal, S., Libert, B., Stehlé, D.: Fully secure functional encryption for inner products, from standard assumptions. In: Robshaw, M., Katz, J. (eds.) CRYPTO 2016. LNCS, vol. 9816, pp. 333–362. Springer, Heidelberg (2016). https://doi.org/10.1007/978-3-662-53015-3_12
4. Ananth, P., Jain, A.: Indistinguishability obfuscation from compact functional encryption. In: Gennaro, R., Robshaw, M. (eds.) CRYPTO 2015. LNCS, vol. 9215, pp. 308–326. Springer, Heidelberg (2015). https://doi.org/10.1007/978-3-662-47989-6_15
5. Badrinarayanan, S., Goyal, V., Jain, A., Sahai, A.: Verifiable functional encryption. In: Cheon, J.H., Takagi, T. (eds.) ASIACRYPT 2016. LNCS, vol. 10032, pp. 557–587. Springer, Heidelberg (2016). https://doi.org/10.1007/978-3-662-53890-6_19
6. Badrinarayanan, S., Goyal, V., Jain, A., Sahai, A.: A note on VRFs from verifiable functional encryption. IACR Cryptology ePrint Archive, p. 51 (2017)
7. Barak, B., Ong, S.J., Vadhan, S.: Derandomization in cryptography. SIAM J. Comput. **37**(2), 380–400 (2007)
8. Barbosa, M., Farshim, P.: Delegatable homomorphic encryption with applications to secure outsourcing of computation. In: Dunkelman, O. (ed.) CT-RSA 2012. LNCS, vol. 7178, pp. 296–312. Springer, Heidelberg (2012). https://doi.org/10.1007/978-3-642-27954-6_19
9. Bitansky, N., Paneth, O.: ZAPs and non-interactive witness indistinguishability from indistinguishability obfuscation. In: Dodis, Y., Nielsen, J.B. (eds.) TCC 2015. LNCS, vol. 9015, pp. 401–427. Springer, Heidelberg (2015). https://doi.org/10.1007/978-3-662-46497-7_16
10. Boneh, D., Franklin, M.: Identity-based encryption from the weil pairing. In: Kilian, J. (ed.) CRYPTO 2001. LNCS, vol. 2139, pp. 213–229. Springer, Heidelberg (2001). https://doi.org/10.1007/3-540-44647-8_13
11. Boneh, D., Sahai, A., Waters, B.: Functional encryption: definitions and challenges. In: Ishai, Y. (ed.) TCC 2011. LNCS, vol. 6597, pp. 253–273. Springer, Heidelberg (2011). https://doi.org/10.1007/978-3-642-19571-6_16
12. Brakerski, Z., Gentry, C., Vaikuntanathan, V.: (Leveled) fully homomorphic encryption without bootstrapping. In Innovations in Theoretical Computer Science 2012, Cambridge, MA, USA, 8–10 January 2012, pp. 309–325. ACM (2012)
13. Cheon, J.H., Kim, A., Kim, M., Song, Y.: Homomorphic encryption for arithmetic of approximate numbers. In: Takagi, T., Peyrin, T. (eds.) ASIACRYPT 2017. LNCS, vol. 10624, pp. 409–437. Springer, Cham (2017). https://doi.org/10.1007/978-3-319-70694-8_15

14. Dwork, C., Naor, M.: Zaps and their applications. SIAM J. Comput. **36**(6), 1513–1543 (2007)
15. Fisch, B., Vinayagamurthy, D., Boneh, D., Gorbunov, S.: IRON: functional encryption using intel SGX. In: ACM-CCS 2017, pp. 765–782. ACM (2017)
16. Gorbunov, S., Vaikuntanathan, V., Wee, H.: Attribute-based encryption for circuits. In: STOC'13, pp. 545–554. ACM (2013)
17. Gorbunov, S., Vaikuntanathan, V., Wee, H.: Predicate encryption for circuits from LWE. In: Gennaro, R., Robshaw, M. (eds.) CRYPTO 2015. LNCS, vol. 9216, pp. 503–523. Springer, Heidelberg (2015). https://doi.org/10.1007/978-3-662-48000-7_25
18. Goyal, V., Pandey, O., Sahai, A., Waters, B.: Attribute-based encryption for fine-grained access control of encrypted data. In: ACM-CCS 2006, pp. 89–98. ACM (2006)
19. Groth, J., Ostrovsky, R., Sahai, A.: Non-interactive zaps and new techniques for NIZK. In: Dwork, C. (ed.) CRYPTO 2006. LNCS, vol. 4117, pp. 97–111. Springer, Heidelberg (2006). https://doi.org/10.1007/11818175_6
20. Katz, J., Sahai, A., Waters, B.: Predicate encryption supporting disjunctions, polynomial equations, and inner products. In: Smart, N. (ed.) EUROCRYPT 2008. LNCS, vol. 4965, pp. 146–162. Springer, Heidelberg (2008). https://doi.org/10.1007/978-3-540-78967-3_9
21. Kim, S., Lewi, K., Mandal, A., Montgomery, H., Roy, A., Wu, D.J.: Function-hiding inner product encryption is practical. In: Catalano, D., De Prisco, R. (eds.) SCN 2018. LNCS, vol. 11035, pp. 544–562. Springer, Cham (2018). https://doi.org/10.1007/978-3-319-98113-0_29
22. Marc, T., Stopar, M., Hartman, J., Bizjak, M., Modic, J.: Privacy-enhanced machine learning with functional encryption. In: Sako, K., Schneider, S., Ryan, P.Y.A. (eds.) ESORICS 2019. LNCS, vol. 11735, pp. 3–21. Springer, Cham (2019). https://doi.org/10.1007/978-3-030-29959-0_1
23. Naor, M., Ostrovsky, R., Venkatesan, R., Yung, M.: Perfect zero-knowledge arguments for *NP* using any one-way permutation. J. Crypt. **11**(2), 87–108 (1998). https://doi.org/10.1007/s001459900037
24. Ryffel, T., Dufour-Sans, E., Gay, R., Bach, F., Pointcheval, D.: Partially encrypted machine learning using functional encryption. CoRR, abs/1905.10214 (2019)
25. Sahai, A., Waters, B.: Fuzzy identity-based encryption. In: Cramer, R. (ed.) EUROCRYPT 2005. LNCS, vol. 3494, pp. 457–473. Springer, Heidelberg (2005). https://doi.org/10.1007/11426639_27
26. Soroush, N., Iovino, V., Rial, A., Roenne, P.B., Ryan, P.Y.A.: Verifiable inner product encryption scheme. In: Kiayias, A., Kohlweiss, M., Wallden, P., Zikas, V. (eds.) PKC 2020. LNCS, vol. 12110, pp. 65–94. Springer, Cham (2020). https://doi.org/10.1007/978-3-030-45374-9_3
27. Suzuki, T., Emura, K., Ohigashi, T., Omote, K.: Verifiable functional encryption using intel SGX. In: Huang, Q., Yu, Yu. (eds.) ProvSec 2021. LNCS, vol. 13059, pp. 215–240. Springer, Cham (2021). https://doi.org/10.1007/978-3-030-90402-9_12
28. Waters, B.: Efficient identity-based encryption without random oracles. In: Cramer, R. (ed.) EUROCRYPT 2005. LNCS, vol. 3494, pp. 114–127. Springer, Heidelberg (2005). https://doi.org/10.1007/11426639_7

Subverting Deniability

Marcel Armour$^{(\boxtimes)}$ and Elizabeth A. Quaglia

Royal Holloway, University of London, Egham, UK
{marcel.armour.2017,Elizabeth.Quaglia}@rhul.ac.uk

Abstract. Deniable public-key encryption (DPKE) is a cryptographic primitive that allows the sender of an encrypted message to later claim that they sent a different message. DPKE's threat model assumes powerful adversaries who can coerce users to reveal plaintexts; it is thus reasonable to consider other advanced capabilities, such as being able to subvert algorithms in a so-called Algorithm Substitution Attack (ASA). ASAs have been considered against a number of primitives including digital signatures, symmetric encryption and pseudo-random generators. However, public-key encryption has presented a less fruitful target, as the sender's only secrets are plaintexts and ASA techniques generally do not provide sufficient bandwidth to leak these.

In this article, we give a formal model of ASAs against DPKE, and argue that subversion attacks against DPKE schemes present an attractive opportunity for an adversary. Our results strengthen the security model for DPKE and highlight the necessity of considering subversion in the design of practical schemes.

Keywords: Cryptography · Deniable encryption · Algorithm Substitution Attacks

1 Introduction

Deniable public-key encryption (DPKE) is a primitive that allows a sender to successfully lie about which plaintext message was originally encrypted. In particular, suppose that Alice encrypts a plaintext m under some public key, using randomness r, to give ciphertext c which she sends to Bob. At some point in the future – perhaps Bob falls under suspicion – Alice is coerced to reveal the message she encrypted, together with the randomness she used. DPKE allows Alice to claim that she sent m^*, by providing r^* such that $\mathsf{enc}(m^*, r^*) = \mathsf{enc}(m, r)$. Beyond its immediate use case, deniable encryption finds applications in electronic voting, where deniability allows voters to cast their ballots without coercion and prevents vote-buying, as well as in secure multiparty computation.

An extended version of this article is available at https://pure.royalholloway.ac.uk/portal/files/46742531/main.pdf [3].

The research of Armour was supported by the EPSRC and the UK government as part of the Centre for Doctoral Training in Cyber Security at Royal Holloway, University of London (EP/P009301/1).

C. Ge and F. Guo (Eds.): ProvSec 2022, LNCS 13600, pp. 52–59, 2022.
https://doi.org/10.1007/978-3-031-20917-8_4

The adversarial model for deniable encryption assumes strong adversaries that can coerce individuals to reveal messages they encrypted; it is thus reasonable to consider other advanced capabilities, such as the ability to subvert algorithms. Powerful adversaries can insert unreliability into cryptography via external ('real-world') infrastructure: whether by influencing standards bodies to adopt 'backdoored' parameters, inserting exploitable errors into software implementations, or compromising supply chains to interfere with hardware. The Snowden revelations showed that this is indeed the case; see the survey by Schneier et al. [13] which provides a broad overview of cryptographic subversion, with case studies of known subversion attempts.

Prior work considering subversion has usually had the aim of exfiltrating secret keys (in the context of symmetric encryption and digital signatures). Berndt and Liśkiewicz [5] show that a generic ASA against an encryption scheme can only embed a limited number of bits per ciphertext. More concretely, they show that no universal and consistent[1] ASA is able to embed more than $\log(\kappa)$ bits of information into a single ciphertext in the random oracle model [5, Theorem 1.4], where κ is the key length of the encryption scheme. In the setting of symmetric key encryption, this is sufficient to successfully leak the secret key over multiple ciphertexts [2,4]. However, for asymmetric primitives, subverting ciphertexts to leak the encryption key makes little sense as it is public; leaking plaintext messages is not possible due to the limited bandwidth. Thus for generic ASAs against PKE, the best possible adversarial goal is to exfiltrate sufficient information to compromise confidentiality – knowledge of one bit of the underlying plaintext is sufficient for an adversary to break confidentiality in the sense of IND-CPA or IND\$[2]. But as Bellare et al. [4] argue, this is not an attractive goal for a mass surveillance adversary, who would rather recover plaintext messages.

Contributions. In this article we sketch out an argument to show that ASAs against DPKE schemes present an attractive opportunity for an adversary. We refer the reader to the extended version [3] for full details and an expanded argument. In this article, we begin by recalling notions of ASAs, including adversarial goals (undetectability and information exfiltration), and give an example of a generic ASA technique (rejection sampling). We then recall DPKE notions, including the formal definition, before applying ASA definitions to DPKE. This allows us to present our main contribution, namely a description of how an ASA against DPKE could be successfully realised to undermine deniability. In brief: an adversary who can subvert a DPKE scheme can transmit a commitment to the underlying plaintext using a subliminal channel. Later, the adversary can check the commitment against the message that the sender claims was sent.

---

[1] Here universal means that the ASA applies generically to any encryption scheme, and consistent essentially means that the ASA outputs genuine ciphertexts.

[2] Chen et al. [9] overcome these limitations by using non-generic techniques against KEM-DEM constructions to leak underlying plaintexts representing (session) keys.

Our work is the first to consider subverting deniable encryption[3], and we establish formal models of the adversarial goals as well as security notions for such an attack. In the extended version, we also consider how to mitigate ASAs against deniable encryption.

2 Notions of Subversion Attacks

We consider subversions of cryptographic schemes implementing encrypted communication between two parties. Abstractly, we consider a scheme $\Pi = (\Pi.\mathsf{gen}, \{\Pi.\mathsf{S}^{(i)}\}_{0 \leq i < n}, \Pi.\mathsf{R})$ consisting of three components: a key generation algorithm, together with a collection of $n \in \mathbb{N}_{>0}$ sender algorithms and a receiver algorithm $\Pi.\mathsf{R}$ representing decryption. We let $\Pi.\mathsf{S}^{(0)}$ represent encryption and write $\Pi.\mathsf{S} := \Pi.\mathsf{S}^{(0)}$. Our abstract treatment allows us to capture both PKE schemes and symmetric encryption (setting $k_\mathsf{S} = k_\mathsf{R}$). We give a generic syntax to the scheme Π as follows: Key generation $\Pi.\mathsf{gen}$ outputs a key pair $(k_\mathsf{S}, k_\mathsf{R}) \in \mathcal{K}_\mathsf{S} \times \mathcal{K}_\mathsf{R}$. Each sender algorithm $\Pi.\mathsf{S}^{(i)}$, for $0 \leq i < n$, has associated randomness space $\mathcal{R}^{(i)}$ together with input and output spaces $\mathcal{X}^{(i)}, \mathcal{Y}^{(i)}$ (respectively) and takes as input a sender key $k_\mathsf{S} \in \mathcal{K}_\mathsf{S}$ $x \in \mathcal{X}^{(i)}$, outputting $y \in \mathcal{Y}^{(i)}$; we write $\mathcal{X} := \mathcal{X}^{(0)}, \mathcal{Y} := \mathcal{Y}^{(0)}$. We note that $\mathcal{X} \subsetneq \mathcal{X}'$; in particular, $\perp \in \mathcal{X}' \setminus \mathcal{X}$. The receiver algorithm takes as input a receiver key $k_\mathsf{R} \in \mathcal{K}_\mathsf{R}$ and $y \in \mathcal{Y}$, outputting $x \in \mathcal{X}'$; the special symbol $\perp$ is used to indicate failure. Lastly, we foreground the randomness used during encryption in our notation by writing $y \leftarrow \Pi.\mathsf{S}(k_\mathsf{S}, x; r)$ for some randomness space $\mathcal{R}$ where we split the input space accordingly $\mathcal{X} \cong \tilde{\mathcal{X}} \times \mathcal{R}$; dropping the last input is equivalent to $r \leftarrow_\mathsf{s} \mathcal{R}$. This allows us to discuss particular values of r that arise during encryption.

Undetectable Subversion. In a nutshell, a subversion is undetectable if distinguishers with black-box access to either the original scheme or to its subverted variant cannot tell the two apart. A subversion should exhibit a dedicated functionality for the subverting party, but simultaneously be undetectable for all others. This apparent contradiction is resolved by parameterising the subverted algorithm with a secret subversion key, knowledge of which enables the extra functionality. We denote the subversion key space with $\mathcal{I}_\mathsf{S}$.

Formally: a subversion of the sender algorithm $\Pi.\mathsf{S}$ of a cryptographic scheme consists of a finite index space $\mathcal{I}_\mathsf{S}$ and a family $\mathcal{S} = \{\mathsf{S}_i\}_{i \in \mathcal{I}_\mathsf{S}}$ of algorithms such that for all $i \in \mathcal{I}_\mathsf{S}$ the algorithm $\Pi.\mathsf{S}_i$ can syntactically replace the algorithm $\Pi.\mathsf{S}$. As a security property we also require that the observable behaviour of $\Pi.\mathsf{S}$ and $\Pi.\mathsf{S}_i$ be effectively identical (for uniformly chosen $i \in \mathcal{I}_\mathsf{S}$). This is formalised via the games $\mathrm{UDS}^0, \mathrm{UDS}^1$ in Fig. 1(left). For any adversary $\mathcal{A}$ we define the advantage $\mathsf{Adv}_\Pi^{\mathrm{uds}}(\mathcal{A}) := \left|\Pr[\mathrm{UDS}^1(\mathcal{A})] - \Pr[\mathrm{UDS}^0(\mathcal{A})]\right|$ and say that family $\mathcal{S}$

---

[3] Gunn et al. [11] consider circumventing cryptographic deniability, which is similar in spirit. However, their scenario is quite different: firstly, they consider deniable communication protocols (such as Signal). Secondly, they do not consider subversion attacks – instead, their scenario is logically equivalent to compromising the receiver.

undetectably subverts algorithm $\Pi.S$ if $\mathsf{Adv}^{\mathsf{uds}}_{\mathsf{PKE}}(\mathcal{A})$ is negligibly small for all realistic $\mathcal{A}$.

Subliminal Information Exfiltration. Abstractly, the aim of an adversary is to exfiltrate some subliminal information. In the context of prior work considering symmetric encryption, this information typically represents the secret key. We formalise this goal as the MR game in Fig. 1(centre), which assumes a passive attack in which the adversary eavesdrops on communication, observing the transmitted ciphertexts. We allow the adversary some influence over sender inputs, with the aim of closely modelling real-world settings. This influence on the sender inputs x is restricted by assuming a stateful 'message sampler' algorithm MS that produces the inputs to $\Pi.S$ used throughout the game[4]. For any message sampler MS and adversary $\mathcal{A}$ we define the advantage $\mathsf{Adv}^{\mathsf{mr}}_{\Pi,\mathsf{MS}}(\mathcal{A}) := \Pr[\mathsf{MR}(\mathcal{A})]$. We say that subversion family $\mathcal{S}$ is key recovering for passive attackers if for all practical MS there exists a realistic adversary $\mathcal{A}$ such that $\mathsf{Adv}^{\mathsf{mr}}_{\Pi,\mathsf{MS}}(\mathcal{A})$ reaches a considerable value (e.g., 0.1)[5].

Game $\mathsf{UDS}^b(\mathcal{A})$	**Game** $\mathsf{MR}(\mathcal{A})$	**Proc** $\Pi.S_i(k_S, x, \mu)$
00 $i \leftarrow_{\$} \mathcal{I}_S$	00 $i \leftarrow_{\$} \mathcal{I}_S$	00 while $[t \neq \mu]$:
01 $S^0 := \Pi.S_i$	01 $(k_S, k_R) \leftarrow_{\$} \Pi.\mathsf{gen}; \sigma \leftarrow \diamond$	01 $\quad r \leftarrow_{\$} \mathcal{R}$
02 $S^1 := \Pi.S$	02 $\mu' \leftarrow \mathcal{A}^{\mathsf{Send}}(i)$	02 $\quad y \leftarrow \Pi.S_i(k_S, x; r)$
03 $b' \leftarrow \mathcal{A}^{\mathsf{Send}}$	03 stop with $[\mu' = \mu]$	03 $\quad t \leftarrow F_i(y)$
04 stop with b'		04 return y
	Oracle $\mathsf{Send}(\alpha)$	
Oracle $\mathsf{Send}(k_S, x)$	04 $(\sigma, x, \beta) \leftarrow \mathsf{MS}(\sigma, \alpha)$	**Proc** $\mathcal{A}(i)$
05 $y \leftarrow S^b(k_S, x)$	05 $y \leftarrow \Pi.S_i(k_S, x)$	05 pick any α
06 return y	06 return (y, β)	06 $(y, \beta) \leftarrow \mathsf{Send}(\alpha)$
		07 $\mu \leftarrow F_i(y)$
		08 return μ

Fig. 1. Left: Game UDS modelling sender subversion undetectability for a scheme Π. **Centre:** Game MR modelling key recoverability for passive adversaries. **Right:** rejection sampling subversion $\Pi.S_i$ of encryption algorithm $\Pi.S$ and corresponding message recovering adversary $\mathcal{A}$.

Generic Method: Rejection Sampling. As an example, we describe a generic method to embed a subliminal message μ with $|\mu| = \ell_\mu$ into ciphertexts of an encryption scheme $\Pi.S$. Essentially, when computing a ciphertext, the subverted algorithm uses rejection sampling to choose randomness that results in a ciphertext encoding the subliminal message. The subverted encryption algorithm $\Pi.S_i$ of a scheme Π is given in Fig. 1(right) together with the corresponding message

---

[4] See the extended version [3] for a complete discussion of the message sampler.

[5] Our informal notions ('realistic' and 'practical') are easily reformulated in terms of probabilistic polynomial-time (PPT) algorithms. However, given that asymptotic notions don't reflect practice particularly well, we prefer to use the informal terms.

recovery adversary $\mathcal{A}$. Subversion $\Pi.\mathsf{S}_i$ is parameterised by a large index space $\mathcal{I}$, a constant ℓ_μ and a PRF F_i. For the PRF we require that it be a family of functions $F_i \colon \mathcal{Y} \to \{0,1\}^{\ell_\mu}$ (that is: a pseudo-random mapping from the ciphertext space to the set strings of length ℓ_μ).

We note that the subverted encryption algorithm $\Pi.\mathsf{S}_i$ will resample randomness 2^{ℓ_μ} times on average. This means that longer messages result in exponentially slower running times of the algorithm; in practice, this means that the attack is limited to short messages (a few bits at most).

3   Deniable Public Key Encryption

DPKE allows a sender to lie about the messages that were encrypted. In particular, suppose that a user encrypts message m to obtain c which is sent to the recipient. DPKE allows the sender to choose a different message m^* and reveal fake randomness r^* which explains c as the encryption of m^*. Notice that this necessarily implies that the scheme cannot be perfectly correct as $\mathsf{dec}(\mathsf{enc}(m^*, r^*)) = m$. This counter-intuitive observation is resolved by noticing that for a given message m, there are 'sparse trigger' values r_i such that encrypting m with an r_i results in an incorrect ciphertext. Deniable public-key encryption schemes rely on the fact that finding such r_i should be easy with some trapdoor knowledge, and hard otherwise.

In this article we focus on non-interactive sender deniable public-key encryption, as introduced by Canetti et al. [6], who showed that a sender-deniable scheme can be used to construct receiver deniable (and thus bi-deniable) schemes. To date, no practical deniable scheme has been proposed. Either deniability is not practically achievable (a typical example is Canetti et al.'s scheme [6] whose ciphertexts grow inversely proportional to the deniability probability), or else the construction requires strong assumptions such as iO or functional encryption [7,10,12]. Recent work by Agrawal et al. [1] is promising in this regard, as their construction provides compact ciphertexts and is based on the security of Learning with Errors. Nevertheless, they require a running time that is inversely proportional to detection probability.

DPKE Definition. A DPKE scheme $\mathsf{DE} = (\mathsf{DE.gen}, \mathsf{DE.enc}, \mathsf{DE.dec}, \mathsf{DE.Fake})$ consists of a tuple of algorithms together with key spaces $\mathcal{K}_\mathsf{S}, \mathcal{K}_\mathsf{R}$, randomness space $\mathcal{R}$, a message space $\mathcal{M}$ and a ciphertext space $\mathcal{C}$.

- The key-generation algorithm $\mathsf{DE.gen}$ returns a pair $(pk, sk) \in \mathcal{K}_\mathsf{S} \times \mathcal{K}_\mathsf{R}$ consisting of a public key and a private key.
- The encryption algorithm $\mathsf{DE.enc}$ takes a public key pk, randomness $r \in \mathcal{R}$ and a message $m \in \mathcal{M}$ to produce a ciphertext $c \in \mathcal{C}$.
- The decryption algorithm $\mathsf{DE.dec}$ takes a private key sk and a ciphertext $c \in \mathcal{C}$, and outputs either a message $m \in \mathcal{M}$ or the rejection symbol $\bot \notin \mathcal{M}$.
- The faking algorithm $\mathsf{DE.Fake}$ takes public key pk, a pair of message and randomness m, r and fake message m^*, and outputs faking randomness $r^* \in \mathcal{R}$.

A scheme DE is correct and secure if the key generation, encryption and decryption algorithms considered as a PKE scheme (DE.gen, DE.enc, DE.dec) satisfy the standard notions of correctness and IND-CPA security properties of public-key encryption. We formalise the deniability of the scheme via the game INDEXP, the details of which are given in the extended paper and described briefly here. Essentially, the INDEXP game is an indistinguishability game in which a distinguisher must choose between two cases: INDEXP^0 represents the adversary's view of an honest encryption of m^*; INDEXP^1 represents the adversary's view when the sender lies about the underlying plaintext. The corresponding advantage is, for any distinguisher $\mathcal{A}$, given by

$$\text{Adv}_{\text{DE}}^{\text{indexp}}(\mathcal{A}) := \left| \Pr[\text{INDEXP}^0(\mathcal{A})] - \Pr[\text{INDEXP}^1(\mathcal{A})] \right|.$$

Formal Definition of Subverted DPKE. We note that a DPKE scheme satisfies the generic syntax introduced above in Sect. 2, with key generation algorithm $\Pi.\text{gen} = \text{DE.gen}$, sender algorithms $(\Pi.\text{S}_0, \Pi.\text{S}_1) = (\text{DE.enc}, \text{DE.Fake})$ and receiver algorithm $\Pi.\text{R} = \text{DE.dec}$. We may thus apply the generic notions of subversion and undetectability introduced in Sect. 2. In the extended version, we furthermore consider the game subINDEXP modelling the adversary's ability to compromise the deniability property of a subverted scheme.

4   Subverting DPKE

Now that we have introduced the notions of ASAs and DPKE, we are ready to discuss ASAs against DPKE. As we set out in the introduction, the idea is for the subverted DPKE scheme to commit to the actual message encrypted; this undermines the ability of the sender to later claim that they sent a different message. The most obvious approach is to subvert the scheme so that the randomness commits to the message. This way, when Alice is coerced by the adversary to reveal her message and randomness, the adversary is able to test whether this is the case. This is a feasible attack route and applies generically to any deniable encryption scheme. When Alice claims that she sent m^*, by providing r^* such that $\text{enc}(m^*, r^*) = \text{enc}(m, r)$, she would need r^* to commit to the message. This should be hard, as long as the commitment is provided by a cryptographically secure digital signature or even a MAC (with the authentication key hidden from Alice). This generic ASA applies to all DPKE schemes, as the security definition for DPKE requires Alice to produce explanatory randomness when coerced.

A second technique is to use subversion techniques (such as the rejection sampling approach given as an example in Sect. 2) to embed a subliminal channel in ciphertexts, such that the channel transmits a commitment to the message. The generic rejection sampling technique is unable to provide enough bandwidth to transmit sufficiently long signatures to prevent Alice forging the commitment, however non-generic techniques may be possible depending on the particular scheme and instantiation. Furthermore, we note that it is a feature of most proposed deniable encryption schemes that a large amount of randomness is consumed in the course of encryption, and that this randomness is sampled in chunks. This means that if the algorithms are considered in a non-black box fashion, then rejection sampling could potentially be used against each chunk of randomness resulting in a sufficiently large subliminal channel.

Lastly, there is another subversion approach that at first glance seems appealing, but which turns out to be unworkable; namely, to target the faking algorithm. A subverted faking algorithm $\mathsf{DE.Fake}_i(pk, m, r, m^*)$ could output subverted r^* which alerts the adversary to the fact that m^*, r^* are fake; for example, if r^* commits to the real message m. However, this fake randomness r^* still needs to be convincing from the point of view of the deniability of the scheme – the scheme's security properties should be maintained by the subversion, otherwise a detector playing the UDS game will be able to tell that the algorithm is subverted. In particular, r^* should satisfy $\mathsf{DE.enc}(pk, m^*, r^*) = c$. However, for a DPKE scheme there is no reason why this should hold for an arbitrary value of r^*. This approach does not seem to be workable without adding considerable structure to the subverted scheme that means it would be easily detected[6].

5   Conclusions

Deniable communication is a subtle concept and it is unclear what it should mean 'in the real world'. Intuitively, the notion is clear: deniability should allow Alice to plausibly evade incrimination when communicating. However, the adversarial model and evaluation of real world protocols claiming deniability is not agreed upon (should Alice be able to claim that she did not participant in a particular communication?). Celi and Symeonidis [8] give an overview of the current state of play and a discussion of open problems. Deniable encryption is one particular primitive whose definition is widely agreed upon in the literature and for which the applications are clear (including in e-voting, multi-party computation and to protect against coercion). The threat model for deniable encryption usually considers an adversary who is willing to coerce users; in this work we extend the model to consider adversaries who also undermine deniability by using subversion attacks. This seems a reasonable additional assumption to make of an adversary who is willing to engage in coercion. We hope that our work helps to elucidate some of the issues involved in designing deniable schemes and refine the threat model for deniable encryption.

---

[6] As an interesting aside, the approach for iO deniability schemes is to hide an encoding of the faked ciphertext within randomness; the encryption algorithm first checks whether the randomness encodes a ciphertext c and if so outputs c; if not, it proceeds to encrypt the message. The security follows from the fact that iO obfuscates the inner working of the algorithm so that it appears as a black box. This results in large, structured randomness inputs which would seem to facilitate subversion.

References

1. Agrawal, S., Goldwasser, S., Mossel, S.: Deniable fully homomorphic encryption from learning with errors. In: Malkin, T., Peikert, C. (eds.) CRYPTO 2021. LNCS, vol. 12826, pp. 641–670. Springer, Cham (2021). https://doi.org/10.1007/978-3-030-84245-1_22
2. Armour, M., Poettering, B.: Subverting decryption in AEAD. In: Albrecht, M. (ed.) IMACC 2019. LNCS, vol. 11929, pp. 22–41. Springer, Cham (2019). https://doi.org/10.1007/978-3-030-35199-1_2
3. Armour, M., Quaglia, E.A.: Subverting deniability. Royal Holloway University of London repository (2022). https://pure.royalholloway.ac.uk/portal/files/46742531/main.pdf
4. Bellare, M., Jaeger, J., Kane, D.: Mass-surveillance without the state: Strongly undetectable algorithm-substitution attacks. In: Ray, I., Li, N., Kruegel, C. (eds.) ACM CCS 2015: 22nd Conference on Computer and Communications Security, pp. 1431–1440. ACM Press (2015). https://doi.org/10.1145/2810103.2813681
5. Berndt, S., Liskiewicz, M.: Algorithm substitution attacks from a steganographic perspective. In: Thuraisingham, B.M., Evans, D., Malkin, T., Xu, D. (eds.) ACM CCS 2017: 24th Conference on Computer and Communications Security, pp. 1649–1660. ACM Press (2017). https://doi.org/10.1145/3133956.3133981
6. Canetti, R., Dwork, C., Naor, M., Ostrovsky, R.: Deniable encryption. In: Kaliski, B.S. (ed.) CRYPTO 1997. LNCS, vol. 1294, pp. 90–104. Springer, Heidelberg (1997). https://doi.org/10.1007/BFb0052229
7. Canetti, R., Park, S., Poburinnaya, O.: Fully deniable interactive encryption. In: Micciancio, D., Ristenpart, T. (eds.) CRYPTO 2020. LNCS, vol. 12170, pp. 807–835. Springer, Cham (2020). https://doi.org/10.1007/978-3-030-56784-2_27
8. Celi, S., Symeonidis, I.: The current state of denial. In: HotPETS (2020)
9. Chen, R., Huang, X., Yung, M.: Subvert KEM to break DEM: practical algorithm-substitution attacks on public-key encryption. In: Moriai, S., Wang, H. (eds.) ASIACRYPT 2020. LNCS, vol. 12492, pp. 98–128. Springer, Cham (2020). https://doi.org/10.1007/978-3-030-64834-3_4
10. De Caro, A., Iovino, V., O'Neill, A.: Deniable functional encryption. In: Cheng, C.-M., Chung, K.-M., Persiano, G., Yang, B.-Y. (eds.) PKC 2016. LNCS, vol. 9614, pp. 196–222. Springer, Heidelberg (2016). https://doi.org/10.1007/978-3-662-49384-7_8
11. Gunn, L.J., Parra, R.V., Asokan, N.: Circumventing cryptographic deniability with remote attestation. Proc. Priv. Enhancing Technol. **2019**(3), 350–369 (2019). https://doi.org/10.2478/popets-2019-0051
12. Sahai, A., Waters, B.: How to use indistinguishability obfuscation: deniable encryption, and more. In: Shmoys, D.B. (ed.) 46th Annual ACM Symposium on Theory of Computing, pp. 475–484. ACM Press (2014). https://doi.org/10.1145/2591796.2591825
13. Schneier, B., Fredrikson, M., Kohno, T., Ristenpart, T.: Surreptitiously weakening cryptographic systems. Cryptology ePrint Archive, Report 2015/097 (2015). https://eprint.iacr.org/2015/097

Epoch Confidentiality in Updatable Encryption

Jodie Knapp[✉][iD] and Elizabeth A. Quaglia[iD]

Information Security Group, Royal Holloway, University of London, Egham, UK
{jodie.knapp.2018,elizabeth.quaglia}@rhul.ac.uk

Abstract. In this paper we formalise *public-key* Updatable Encryption (PKUE), a primitive so far studied formally only in the symmetric setting. Defining UE in the public-key setting enables us to establish a new notion of security we call *epoch confidentiality* (EC) which considers the ability of an adversary to distinguish the public keys used in periods known as epochs and in turn reflects the leakage of the time in which a ciphertext was created. We propose a public-key UE construction and prove that it satisfies our new notion of security alongside a notion of ciphertext confidentiality such that efficiency is not affected by moving to the public-key setting.

1 Introduction

In recent years there has been an increase in the outsourcing of encrypted data to a potentially untrusted host. To protect the underlying data and mitigate the security risks of key compromise over a long time, several cryptographic schemes have been proposed that employ a technique called *key-rotation* which enables an entity to move existing ciphertexts from the old to the new key [13]. Trivially, a scheme can update a ciphertext by decrypting and then re-encrypting the underlying plaintext with the updated key. However, when the encrypted data has been outsourced, this is an impractical method. Either the owner must download, re-encrypt and update all ciphertexts themselves, which is computationally inefficient, or they outsource the update by sending the encryption keys to the untrusted host to perform re-encryption, which no longer ensures security [4].

The authors of [4] introduced the *updatable encryption* (UE) primitive to provide a more elegant, non-trivial solution to the above. Instead of re-encrypting a ciphertext from an old to a new key, the data owner instead generates a *token* that enables the host to convert the ciphertext to encryption under the new key (provided it is trusted to delete old tokens and ciphertexts after an update) *without* the need to decrypt. Traditionally, UE schemes have been designed in the symmetric-key setting [4–6,9,10,14] to convert ciphertexts in a periodic manner marked by set time-intervals known as *epochs* and using encryption keys

---

J. Knapp—The research of Knapp was supported by the EPSRC and the UK government as part of the Centre for Doctoral Training in Cyber Security at Royal Holloway, University of London (EP/P009301/1).

C. Ge and F. Guo (Eds.): ProvSec 2022, LNCS 13600, pp. 60–67, 2022.
https://doi.org/10.1007/978-3-031-20917-8_5

valid only for their associated epoch. The advantage of equipping an encryption scheme with an update functionality is met with the challenge of modelling security, due to the corruption capabilities of an adversary. As a consequence, the main focus of UE research has been on defining new notions of security and strengthening past notions. The complexities in ensuring security could potentially dominate important factors such as the efficiency, practicality and cost of implementation. For several reasons and with careful consideration, we will formalise a *public-key ciphertext-independent* UE scheme with *probabilistic updates*. As a consequence, we formalise and prove *replayable* chosen-ciphertext security of our construction, which has previously been shown to be the gold-standard level of security for probabilistic UE schemes [11]. We defer the reader to the extended version of this paper for an in-depth overview of the current literature, which comprehensively discusses the trade-offs between such factors and their consequences.

Contributions and Motivation. Our first major contribution in this paper is to explicitly define updatable encryption as a public-key primitive (PKUE) in Sect. 2. Notably, several symmetric UE works [9,11,13] have adopted public-key techniques, however, lifting UE to the public-key setting enables us to extend the already rigorously defined security of symmetric UE to capture notions of security only relevant in the context of public-key primitives and building blocks. We note that one can view UE as a special case of the public-key primitive known as *proxy re-encryption* (PRE) [2,7,12] and we are motivated to explore UE in the public-key setting for the same applications in which PRE schemes are utilised. However, we emphasise that UE and PRE are fundamentally different primitives in the sense of security guarantees.

Moreover, we identify a gap in previously proposed security modelling which sees us introduce a new notion of security called *epoch confidentiality* in Sect. 3. Epoch confidentiality can only be modelled in the public-key setting which further illustrates our motivation for formalising public-key UE: guaranteeing security notions specific to public-key building blocks. In more words, we simultaneously achieve confidentiality of both epochs and ciphertexts (UP-IND-EC-RCCA security) by asking an adversary to distinguish the underlying message *and* public key used in encryption that results in the given challenge ciphertext. Our definition of epoch confidentiality is inspired by and can be viewed as achieving key privacy [1] in public-key *updatable* encryption. Key privacy is especially important in UE schemes as the epoch keys have more function than keys in standard PKE schemes. Specifically, epoch keys are required in update token generation and they directly relate to the corresponding epoch in which they are used.

We argue that the notion of epoch confidentiality must be satisfied in any UE scheme in which the data owner cares about the leakage of the age of their encrypted information – e.g., from dating app profiles to individual medical records outsourced for storage. Whilst the leakage of ciphertext age has previously been discussed in [5,8], not only are their proposed schemes designed for different types of UE schemes, the ciphertext-dependent and deterministic ciphertext-independent update setting respectively, one critical oversight in both works is to consider the direct relationship the epoch keys have to ciphertext updates. For instance, epoch keys are used to derive the update token, and the inferable information from these is not captured in the ciphertext confidentiality model of both [3,5]. By contrast, our security model not only asks the adversary to distinguish the underlying message in a UE scheme but also requires the adversary to distinguish the epoch public key used to encrypt the ciphertext. Thus, the notion of epoch confidentiality fully captures the leakage of an epoch in a probabilistic ciphertext-independent update setting by modelling *both* epoch key indistinguishability and ciphertext confidentiality.

In the full version of the paper we present a concrete public-key UE scheme and prove it satisfies epoch confidentiality. Our PKUE scheme is an adaptation of an existing symmetric UE construction [11] explicitly using *updatable* public-key building blocks. In doing so, we can lift the security of the scheme from CPA-security to RCCA-security, thus demonstrating the existence of a public-key UE primitive satisfying (UP-IND-EC-RCCA) security. We conclude our work in the extended version by detailing the security analysis and discussing the efficiency of our construction.

2 · Public-Key Updatable Encryption

Notation. An updatable encryption scheme is defined by epochs of time e_i from the range of time $i = \{0, \ldots, \mathsf{max}\}$. We denote the current epoch e or use subscript notation e_i for $i \in \mathbb{N}$ if we define multiple epochs at once and in security games the challenge epoch is represented by $\tilde{e}$. To signify epoch keys the notation k_e, k_{e+1} and k^{old}, k^{new} is used interchangeably in this work, depending on whether we require explicit epoch notation or we only need to define consecutive epoch keys (similarly for update tokens Δ).

Traditional symmetric UE is for an owner outsourcing encrypted data over a long period. Time in a UE scheme is formally divided into equal periods known as epochs in which epochs are associated with distinct keys. A ciphertext is updated (re-encrypted) by a potentially untrusted host to the next epoch to provide stronger security by rotating the key used for encryption. Crucially, this update is performed by the host using an update token derived by the date owner, which is formed from the current and preceding epoch keys, such that the host is incapable of learning anything about the encrypted information. Following the discussion in the Introduction, we are motivated to formalise a public-key UE scheme which will be provided below. The key idea is to lift the definition of UE to the public-key setting by generating an epoch key consisting of a public key and a secret key component, and the update token is derived from the past epoch secret key and the current (full) epoch key.

Definition 1 (Updatable Encryption). *A public-key updatable encryption (UE) scheme for message space $\mathcal{MSP}$ consists of a set of polynomial-time algorithms (UE.Setup, UE.KG, UE.TG, UE.Enc, UE.Dec, UE.Upd), defined as follows:*

- UE.Setup$(1^\lambda) \xrightarrow{\$} pp$: The *owner* runs the *probabilistic* algorithm UE.setup on input security parameter λ, outputting public parameters pp. Whilst not made explicit, assume throughout that the security parameter (1^λ) is input into the algorithms of the scheme.
- UE.KG$(pp, e) \xrightarrow{\$} k_e$: The owner runs the probabilistic key-generation algorithm UE.KG for epoch e on input the public parameters. The output is an epoch key $k_e := (pk_e, sk_e)$ composed of public key (pk_e) and secret-key (sk_e) elements.
- UE.TG$(sk_e, k_{e+1}) \rightarrow \Delta_{e+1}$: The owner generates the update token by running the *deterministic* algorithm UE.TG on input the secret key sk_e of epoch key k_e and epoch key k_{e+1} for the proceeding epoch.
- UE.Enc$(pk_e, m) \xrightarrow{\$} C_e$: The owner runs the probabilistic algorithm UE.Enc on input a message $m \in \mathcal{MSP}$ and public key pk_e of some epoch e, outputting a ciphertext C_e.
- UE.Dec$(sk_e, C) \rightarrow \{m', \bot\}$: The owner runs the deterministic algorithm UE.Dec on input a ciphertext C and secret key sk_e for some epoch e, returning either the message m or abort $\bot$.
- UE.Upd$(\Delta_{e+1}, C_e) \xrightarrow{\$} C_{e+1}$: The *host* runs the probabilistic algorithm UE.Upd. This is run on input ciphertext C_e for epoch e, and update token Δ_{e+1} for the *next* epoch $(e+1)$, and returns as output the updated ciphertext C_{e+1}.

Informally, the correctness property ensures that fresh encryptions and updated ciphertexts should decrypt to the underlying plaintext, given the appropriate epoch key [5,11,13].

Correctness. Given security parameter λ, an updatable encryption scheme (UE) formalised in Definition 1 is correct if, for any message $m \in \mathcal{MSP}$ and for any $j \in \{1, \ldots, e\}$, $i \in \{0, \ldots, e\}$ with $e > i$, there exists a negligible function negl such that the following holds,

$$\Pr \left[\begin{array}{l} pp \xleftarrow{\$} \text{UE.Setup}(1^\lambda); k_{e_j} \xleftarrow{\$} \text{UE.KG}(pp, e_j); \\ \Delta_{e_j} \leftarrow \text{UE.TG}(sk_{e_{j-1}}, k_{e_j}); C_{e_i} \xleftarrow{\$} \text{UE.Enc}(pk_{e_i}, m); \\ \{C_{e_j} \leftarrow \text{UE.Upd}(\Delta_{e_j}, C_{e_{j-1}}) : j \in \{i+1, \cdots, \text{max}\}\} : \\ \text{UE.Dec}(sk_e, C_e) = m \end{array} \right] \geq 1 - \text{negl}(\lambda).$$

Before defining a novel security notion for PKUE, we highlight that the extended version of the paper contains the comprehensive details of *lists* and *oracles* required for security modelling in an experiment capturing post-compromise security and ciphertext unlinkability. To be exact, the latter notion of ciphertext unlinkability formalises replayable chosen-ciphertext security (UP-IND-RCCA) which assumes an adversary queries updates of *arbitrary* ciphertexts, however, they are incapable of distinguishing updated ciphertexts from the original ciphertext, despite access to prior ciphertexts and update tokens. Notably, modelling

RCCA-security/is viewed as the benchmark notion of *ciphertext-independent* UE security given update attacks in an untrusted environment, in line with the recent work of [11].

3   Epoch Confidentiality

In this section, we introduce the notion of an epoch confidential public-key UE primitive. We capture both epoch and ciphertext confidentiality in the UP-IND-EC-RCCA security notion, (Definition 2). We are motivated by the fact that ciphertext-independent UE literature has not yet captured epoch confidentiality, which we argue next is an important security property a UE scheme must satisfy. Namely, in the UE literature the number of key updates on a file indicates the age of the encrypted file (ciphertext). The authors of [3,5] independently highlighted ciphertext-age leakage to be problematic in real-world scenarios. For instance, [3] considers the setting of dating apps where the number of updates in a UE scheme would reveal how long the person has been a customer which is sensitive information. Indeed, numerous schemes proposed in the literature, such as [9], create a ciphertext expansion as time progresses which results in ciphertext length variance. The authors of [3] demonstrated how *ciphertext length* can be used to trivially infer ciphertext-age in a UE scheme.

A tentative solution given by [3] is to require the length of fresh and updated ciphertexts to be equal, a notion known as *compactness*. However, not only is compactness a strong property to ensure, it does not guarantee there will be no leakage of ciphertext age. Despite the satisfaction of traditional notions of security for UE schemes *and* ciphertext compactness, ciphertext patterns can indicate if the ciphertext is generated by fresh encryption or ciphertext update. Indeed, in [3] a simple example is given in which the last bit of the respective ciphertexts differ, and an adversary can determine whether the ciphertext was derived from an update of a pre-existing ciphertext *or* fresh encryption simply by comparing the last bits of the ciphertexts, thus leaking age information. In [3,5] the above issues are handled by modelling the computational indistinguishability between fresh ciphertexts and re-encrypted ones to prevent leakage of ciphertext-age. However, without further security modelling an adversary can still infer an epoch and consequently the age of a ciphertext by distinguishing the public component of the epoch key used in encryption, token generation and ciphertext updates.

In more words, our contribution in defining epoch confidentiality not only captures age leakage as in [3,5] but goes one step further by modelling the indistinguishability of epoch public keys. By definition, the epoch key is designed such that the update token can be derived from the current and proceeding epoch keys. Without specific conditions in security modelling, the corruption of epoch keys and update tokens in challenge-equal epochs enables an adversary to infer information about a version of the challenge ciphertext. In addition to requiring the computational indistinguishability of *ciphertexts* from encryption and update, we necessitate the computational indistinguishability of the *epoch public keys* to provide epoch confidentiality in a given UE scheme.

Security Modelling. To achieve epoch confidentiality for a public-key updatable encryption scheme as in Definition 1, an adversary should be unable to distinguish the public-key component of the epoch key under which a ciphertext has been generated. Thus, possession of distinct public keys and a challenge ciphertext should not give an adversary an advantage in determining which public key and therefore which epoch the ciphertext was encrypted under. This approach to modelling security is inspired by and similar in manner to key privacy [1], which is used to define anonymity in public-key encryption schemes (see the Appendices in the extended version of the paper).

To formalise Definition 2, we use the the security experiment given in Fig. 1 ($\mathsf{Exp}_{\mathsf{UE},\mathcal{A}}^{\mathsf{UP\text{-}IND\text{-}EC\text{-}CCA},b}(\lambda)$). The intuition is to model an indistinguishability game between the challenger and an adversary $\mathcal{A}$. Initially, the adversary is given two challenge public keys (pk_{e_0}, pk_{e_1}) and $\mathcal{A}$ proceeds to query the oracles detailed in the full version of this paper.

The extended version of the paper contains the details of the lists maintained by the challenger and oracles. We highlight an important list to epoch confidentiality, $\tilde{\mathcal{K}}$ which captures the epochs in which adversary $\mathcal{A}$ receives *challenge public keys* and this list must be checked before responding to all oracle queries, to prevent trivial wins.

In more words, the game in Fig. 1 starts by initialising the global state GS. Next, the key-generation algorithm is run twice in order to generate epoch keys $k_{e_0} = (pk_{e_0}, sk_{e_0})$ and $k_{e_1} = (pk_{e_1}, sk_{e_1})$ for distinct epochs of time e_0, e_1. The public keys (pk_{e_0}, pk_{e_1}) are then given to the adversary. The adversary can query oracles $\mathcal{O} = \{\mathcal{O}_{\mathsf{Dec}}, \mathcal{O}_{\mathsf{Upd}}, \mathcal{O}_{\mathsf{Next}}, \mathcal{O}_{\mathsf{Corrupt\text{-}Token}}, \mathcal{O}_{\mathsf{Corrupt\text{-}Key}}\}$ to output valid challenge messages $(m_0, m_1) \in \mathcal{MSP}$ required to be of the same length, alongside some state information s. Subsequently, the challenger encrypts m_b using public key pk_{e_b}, for a pre-determined bit $b \in \{0, 1\}$, sending the challenge ciphertext C to the adversary. Using this challenge ciphertext alongside the state information s and further access to previously detailed oracles, $\mathcal{A}$ guesses the bit b' and succeeds in the game if their guess corresponds to the bit b chosen before the experiment began. More formally,

Definition 2 (UP-IND-EC-RCCA-Security).

A public-key updatable encryption scheme (UE), formalised in Definition 1, satisfies UP-IND-EC-RCCA security if for any PPT adversary $\mathcal{A}$ there exists a negligible function negl such that

$$\Pr[\mathsf{Exp}_{\mathsf{UE},\mathcal{A}}^{\mathsf{UP\text{-}IND\text{-}EC\text{-}RCCA}}(\lambda) = 1] \leq 1/2 + \mathsf{negl}(\lambda).$$

Preventing Trivial Wins and Ciphertext Updates. The winning condition states that the intersection of lists $\mathcal{K}$ and $\mathcal{C}^*$ must be empty which is crucial in preventing the adversary from trivially winning in the security game and if these conditions are not met, then $\mathcal{A}$'s guess is discarded and the output is $\bot$. In more words, the challenge epoch of the experiment cannot belong to the set of epochs in which an update token has been learned or inferred, nor can there exist a

$$\mathsf{Exp}_{\mathsf{UE},\mathcal{A}}^{\mathsf{UP\text{-}IND\text{-}EC\text{-}RCCA},b}(\lambda)$$

Initialise global state

$\mathsf{GS} \xleftarrow{\$} \mathsf{Init}(1^{\lambda}); \mathsf{GS} = (pp, k_0, \Delta_0, \mathbf{S}, 0)$

$k_{e_0} \xleftarrow{\$} \mathsf{UE.KG}(pp, e_0), k_{e_1} \xleftarrow{\$} \mathsf{UE.KG}(pp, e_1)$ such that $k_{e_0} \neq k_{e_1}$, $(e_0, e_1) \notin \mathcal{K}$

$k_{e_0} := (pk_{e_0}, sk_{e_0}), k_{e_1} := (pk_{e_1}, sk_{e_1})$

Challenger sends (pk_{e_0}, pk_{e_1}) to $\mathcal{A}$;

$\tilde{\mathcal{K}} \leftarrow \{(e_0, e_1)\} \cap \tilde{\mathcal{K}}$

$(m_0, m_1, s) \xleftarrow{\$} \mathcal{A}^{\mathcal{O}}(pp, pk_{e_0}, pk_{e_1})$

Some state information s

if $|m_0| \neq |m_1| \vee \{m_0, m_1\} \notin \mathcal{MSP} \vee (m_0 = m_1)$ **then**

    return $\perp$

else

    $C \xleftarrow{\$} \mathsf{UE.Enc}(pk_{e_b}, m_b)$

    $\mathcal{M}^* \leftarrow \mathcal{M}^* \cup (m_0, m_1); \mathcal{C} \leftarrow \mathcal{C} \cup \{e\}; \tilde{e} \leftarrow \{e\}$

$b' \xleftarrow{\$} \mathcal{A}^{\mathcal{O}}(pp, C, s)$

if $(b' = b) \wedge (\mathcal{K} \cap \mathcal{C}^* = \emptyset)$ **then**

    return 1

else

    return $\perp$

Fig. 1. The security game for a UE scheme satisfying UP-IND-EC-RCCA-security, where set $\mathbf{S} = \{\tilde{\mathcal{L}}, \mathcal{M}^*, \mathcal{T}, \mathcal{K}, \tilde{\mathcal{K}}, \mathcal{C}, \mathcal{C}^*\}$ is initially empty, s defines some *state* information output by the adversary and $\mathcal{O} = \{\mathcal{O}_{\mathsf{Dec}}, \mathcal{O}_{\mathsf{Next}}, \mathcal{O}_{\mathsf{Upd}}, \mathcal{O}_{\mathsf{Corrupt\text{-}Token}}, \mathcal{O}_{\mathsf{Corrupt\text{-}Key}}\}$ is the set of oracles an adversary $\mathcal{A}$ calls.

single epoch where the adversary knows both the epoch key (public and secret key components) and the (updated) challenge-ciphertext [13]. To see this, if the adversary $\mathcal{A}$ corrupts token Δ_{e+1} in an epoch after which $\mathcal{A}$ has obtained the challenge ciphertext $\tilde{C}$ during epoch e, either by inference or via an update, then the adversary is capable of updating the ciphertext into the next epoch $(e + 1)$ [11].

Conclusions. Our first contribution in this work was re-imagining updatable encryption as a public-key primitive and modelling a public-key equivalent of a prior security notion, which we deem as a necessary security requirement of all probabilistic UE schemes. Our second major contribution was to introduce a new concept of security called epoch confidentiality. In the full version of this work we modified an existing, symmetric UE construction to the public-key setting with no impact on the cost/efficiency of the public-key version of the UE scheme and we use this concrete scheme to show the feasibility of a UE construction satisfying epoch confidentiality.

References

1. Bellare, M., Boldyreva, A., Desai, A., Pointcheval, D.: Key-privacy in public-key encryption. In: Boyd, C. (ed.) ASIACRYPT 2001. LNCS, vol. 2248, pp. 566–582. Springer, Heidelberg (2001). https://doi.org/10.1007/3-540-45682-1_33
2. Blaze, M., Bleumer, G., Strauss, M.: Divertible protocols and atomic proxy cryptography. In: Nyberg, K. (ed.) EUROCRYPT 1998. LNCS, vol. 1403, pp. 127–144. Springer, Heidelberg (1998). https://doi.org/10.1007/BFb0054122
3. Boneh, D., Eskandarian, S., Kim, S., Shih, M.: Improving speed and security in updatable encryption schemes. In: Moriai, S., Wang, H. (eds.) ASIACRYPT 2020. LNCS, vol. 12493, pp. 559–589. Springer, Cham (2020). https://doi.org/10.1007/978-3-030-64840-4_19
4. Boneh, D., Lewi, K., Montgomery, H., Raghunathan, A.: Key homomorphic PRFs and their applications. In: Canetti, R., Garay, J.A. (eds.) CRYPTO 2013. LNCS, vol. 8042, pp. 410–428. Springer, Heidelberg (2013). https://doi.org/10.1007/978-3-642-40041-4_23
5. Boyd, C., Davies. G.T., Gjøsteen, K., Jiang, Y.: Fast and secure updatable encryption†. Technical report, Cryptology ePrint Archive, Report 2019/1457, 2019. https://eprint.iacr.org/2019/1457.pdf (2020)
6. Chen, L., Li, Y., Tang, Q.: CCA updatable encryption against malicious' re-encryption attacks. In: Moriai, S., Wang, H. (eds.) ASIACRYPT 2020. LNCS, vol. 12493, pp. 590–620. Springer, Cham (2020). https://doi.org/10.1007/978-3-030-64840-4_20
7. Davidson, A., Deo, A., Lee, E., Martin, K.: Strong post-compromise secure proxy re-encryption. In: Jang-Jaccard, J., Guo, F. (eds.) ACISP 2019. LNCS, vol. 11547, pp. 58–77. Springer, Cham (2019). https://doi.org/10.1007/978-3-030-21548-4_4
8. Eaton, E., Jao, D., Komlo, C.: Towards post-quantum updatable public-key encryption via supersingular isogenies. IACR Cryptology ePrint Arch., 2020:1593 (2020)
9. Everspaugh, A., Paterson, K., Ristenpart, T., Scott, S.: Key rotation for authenticated encryption. In: Katz, J., Shacham, H. (eds.) CRYPTO 2017. LNCS, vol. 10403, pp. 98–129. Springer, Cham (2017). https://doi.org/10.1007/978-3-319-63697-9_4
10. Jiang, Y.: The direction of updatable encryption does not matter much. In: Moriai, S., Wang, H. (eds.) ASIACRYPT 2020. LNCS, vol. 12493, pp. 529–558. Springer, Cham (2020). https://doi.org/10.1007/978-3-030-64840-4_18
11. Klooß, M., Lehmann, A., Rupp, A.: (R)CCA secure updatable encryption with integrity protection. In: Ishai, Y., Rijmen, V. (eds.) EUROCRYPT 2019. LNCS, vol. 11476, pp. 68–99. Springer, Cham (2019). https://doi.org/10.1007/978-3-030-17653-2_3
12. Lee, E.: Improved security notions for proxy re-encryption to enforce access control. In: Lange, T., Dunkelman, O. (eds.) LATINCRYPT 2017. LNCS, vol. 11368, pp. 66–85. Springer, Cham (2019). https://doi.org/10.1007/978-3-030-25283-0_4
13. Lehmann, A., Tackmann, B.: Updatable encryption with post-compromise security. In: Nielsen, J.B., Rijmen, V. (eds.) EUROCRYPT 2018. LNCS, vol. 10822, pp. 685–716. Springer, Cham (2018). https://doi.org/10.1007/978-3-319-78372-7_22
14. Nishimaki, R.: The direction of updatable encryption does matter. Cryptology ePrint Archive (2021). https://doi.org/10.1007/978-3-030-97131-1_7

Lattice Based Cryptography

Simplified Server-Aided Revocable Identity-Based Encryption from Lattices

Yanhua Zhang[1]([✉]) [iD], Ximeng Liu[2] [iD], and Yupu Hu[3] [iD]

[1] Zhengzhou University of Light Industry, Zhengzhou 450001, China
yhzhang@email.zzuli.edu.cn
[2] Fuzhou University, Fuzhou 350108, China
[3] Xidian University, Xi'an 710071, China
yphu@mail.xidian.edu.cn

Abstract. As a new revocation mechanism for identity-based encryption (IBE), server-aided revocable IBE (SR-IBE), firstly proposed by Qin et al. in 2015, achieves remarkable advantages over previous identity revocation techniques. In this primitive, almost all of workloads on the users (i.e., receivers) side can be delegated to an untrusted server which does not possess any secret information, and the users can compute short-term decryption keys alone at any time period without having to communicate with either the private key generator (PKG) or server. In 2016, Nguyen et al. creatively presented the first lattice-based SR-IBE by adopting a "double encryption" mechanism to enable smooth interactions between the sender and the server, as well as between the server and the receiver, while ensuring the confidentiality of encrypted messages.

In this paper, inspired by recent work on a new treatment of the identity space and the time period space, we simplify the first construction of lattice-based SR-IBE provided by Nguyen et al., and remove some items from the public parameters and the master secret key. In particular, our scheme is more efficient by reducing the workloads of PKG, the server, the sender and the receivers, simultaneously. At the heart of our new design is a tool called "leveled ciphertexts" that enables constant ciphertexts and simplified encryptions, not linear in the length of user identities and without a burdensome double encryption technique, which serves as a more effective solution to the challenge in turning the pairing-based instantiation of SR-IBE into the world of lattice-based cryptography, and based on the hardness of learning with errors (LWE) problem, we prove that our new scheme is selectively secure in the standard model.

Keywords: Identity-based encryption · Lattices · Identity revocation · Server-aided · Leveled ciphertexts

1 Introduction

Identity-based encryption (IBE), as an advanced form of traditional public-key encryption, was firstly introduced by Shamir [20] in 1984. IBE can eliminate the dependency on public-key infrastructure and allow to utilize an arbitrary string

C. Ge and F. Guo (Eds.): ProvSec 2022, LNCS 13600, pp. 71–87, 2022.
https://doi.org/10.1007/978-3-031-20917-8_6

(e.g., email address) as public key of each system user. To address the challenge of identity revocation (e.g., the user misbehaves, or his key is lost or stolen) in the IBE setting, in 2001, Boneh and Franklin [5] firstly suggested a naive solution that the private key generator (PKG) periodically issues a new private key for each non-revoked user in each time period. Unfortunately, this solution is too impractical in a large-scale IBE system, and the PKG's workload grows linearly in the number of users N, moreover, each non-revoked user has to maintain a secret channel with PKG to periodically renew his private key.

The first scalable IBE with identity revocation or simply revocable IBE (RIBE) was set forth by Boldyreva et al. [4] in 2008, in which the binary tree (BT) based revocation method is adopted and the PKG's workload is only logarithmic in N. In particular, the time key update can be exactly executed for all the non-revoked users over a public channel. Nevertheless, when considering a practical application of RIBE, there is a serious problem in [4] that non-revoked users have to communicate with PKG regularly to download the update keys, further, to compute new short-term decryption keys. Obviously, this key updating process is bandwidth-consuming and non-ideal for users only with limited resources.

In 2016, Nguyen et al. [16] creatively presented a lattice-based SR-IBE scheme by combining an RIBE scheme [7] and a two-level hierarchical IBE (HIBE) [1] as two basic building blocks, additionally, by adopting a secure "double encryption" mechanism to enable smooth interactions between a sender and the server, as well as between the server and a receiver, while ensuring the confidentiality of encrypted messages. Nevertheless, a significant shortcoming of the first lattice-based SR-IBE [16] is a rather low efficiency: the encryptions process for a sender is sophisticated with the burdensome double encryption operations, and the bit-size of some item (i.e., c_0, a ciphertext component carrying the message m) in the final ciphertext $ct_{id,t}$ has been expanded by $k \approx 4 \log n$ times where n is the security parameter, when compared with the underlying lattice-based RIBE [7]. Simultaneously, PKG has to maintain a much more onerous state information of a perfect BT (i.e., each node of BT has to store $2k$ random vectors over $\mathbb{Z}_q^n$, not such two vectors as in [7]), in addition, for the user token and time update key generations, a preimage sampling algorithm, the main time-consuming procedure for lattice-based cryptography, needs to be repeated k times respectively (only one execution in the underlying RIBE [7]). Thus, k short sampling vectors for each node in path(id), the path from a leaf node (a user id is assigned to it) to the root node of BT, are stored by the server for each user id, and k short sampling vectors for each node in KUNodes(BT, RL, t), an algorithm which returns a covering set of nodes $Y \subseteq BT$ satisfying path(id) $\cap Y = \emptyset$ if and only if id has not been revoked, need to be downloaded by the server for each time period t. In conclusion, the first lattice-based SR-IBE [16] effectively alleviates the decryption burden of a receiver while without sacrificing security, yet at the same time, the scheme of Nguyen et al. [16] also involves more items in the system parameters, particularly, the PKG and the sender should spend more computing resources to complete their corresponding works, further, a requirement for the large storage of the server also often means more cost (e.g., the server-aided fees) to the receivers.

In this paper, inspired by recent work of Wang et al. [24] on a new treatment of the identity space and the time period space, we manage to simplify the first construction of lattice-based SR-IBE provided by Nguyen et al. [16] and present a new lattice-based SR-IBE scheme.

RELATED WORKS. The first scalable RIBE scheme was proposed by Boldyreva et al. [4] in 2008, which is creatively constructed by combining a fuzzy IBE and a complete subset (CS) methodology. Subsequently, an adaptively secure RIBE and an RIBE with DKER, both based on pairings, were proposed by Libert and Vergnaud [12] and Seo and Emura [19], respectively.

To resist quantum attacks, the first lattice-based RIBE without DKER, the first lattice-based RIBE with bounded (and unbounded) DKER and an adaptively secure RIBE in the quantum random oracle model were successfully constructed by Chen et al. [7], Takayasu et al. [23], Katsumata et al. [10], and Takayasu [22], respectively. In order to reduce the workloads and overcome the main decryption challenges for non-revoked receivers which are with limited resources, Qin et al. [17] introduced SR-IBE and presented a pairing-based instantiation. Later on, Hu et al. [9] showed a non-black-box construction of SR-IBE from the computational diffie-hellman assumption. Recently, the generic constructions of RIBE with CS (and subset difference) technique, server-aided revocable HIBE and RIBE with server-aided ciphertext evolution were respectively proposed by Ma and Lin [14], Lee [11], Liu and Sun [13], Sun et al. [21] and Zhang et al. [25].

OUR CONTRIBUTIONS AND TECHNIQUES. In this paper, we present a new construction of lattice-based SR-IBE. We inherit and extend the security and efficiency advantages of Qin et al.'s model and Nguyen et al.'s SR-IBE scheme: almost all of workloads on the receivers side are delegated to an untrusted server, which does not possess secret information and only performs correct operations and returns correct results, meanwhile, each receiver can compute a short-term decryption key alone at each time period without having to communicate with either the trusted PKG or untrusted server. Furthermore, the ciphertext component carrying m in the final ciphertext enjoys constant size the same as that in the underlying RIBE [7], thus, achieving a better ciphertext extension. In particular, the encryptions process is simpler for the sender and without a burdensome double encryption mechanism. As for the first lattice-based SR-IBE [16] and previous lattice-based RIBE [7, 10, 22, 23, 25], our construction only works for one-bit message, but a multi-bit version can be easily achieved by adopting a standard transformation technique [1, 8]. With a new treatment of the identity space and the time period space, some by-products are also obtained: our scheme has fewer items in the public parameters, BT and almost all of keys. In particular, our new scheme is provable secure under the classic learning with errors (LWE) hardness assumption. As in [16], each user's long-term private key is a trapdoor matrix, thus having a relatively large bit-size. A detailed comparison between the SR-IBE [16] and ours is shown in Table 1.

As a high level, the main design method of our new lattice-based SR-IBE is similar to the pairing-based instantiation of Qin et al. [17] and the lattice-based instantiation of Nguyen et al. [16] in the sense that we also adopt a lattice-based

Table 1. Comparison of lattice-based SR-IBE schemes.

Scheme	$\lvert pp \rvert$	$\lvert token \rvert$	$\lvert uk_t \rvert$	$\lvert tk_{id,t} \rvert$	$\lvert sk_{id} \rvert$	$\lvert dk_{id,t} \rvert$	$\lvert ct_{id,t} \rvert$	DKER
[16]	$(7nm + nk + 2n)\Delta_0$	$2mk\Delta_1$	$2mk + \Delta_2$	$4mk\Delta_0$	$4m^2\Delta_0$	$3m\Delta_0$	$(6m + k)\Delta_0$	Yes
Ours	$(4nm + 2n)\Delta_0$	$2m\Delta_1$	$m\Delta_2$	$3m\Delta_0$	$4m^2\Delta_0$	$3m\Delta_0$	$(6m + 1)\Delta_0$	Yes

Note: n is a security parameter, $N = 2^n$ is the maximum numbers of users, $k = \lceil \log q \rceil$, $\Delta_0 = \log q$, $\Delta_1 = (n + 1) \cdot \Delta_0$, and $\Delta_2 = \Delta_0 \cdot \mathcal{O}(r \log \frac{N}{r})$ where r is the number of revoked users; $\lvert \cdot \rvert$ denotes the bit-size, pp is the public parameter, $token$ is a token, uk_t is a time update key, $tk_{id,t}$ is a short-term transform key, sk_{id} is a long-term private key, $dk_{id,t}$ is a short-term decryption key and $ct_{id,t}$ is a ciphertext.

RIBE [7] and a two-level HIBE [1] as the basic building blocks. However, looking into the details of our new lattice-based SR-IBE, it is also not straightforward to pack these building blocks together. As it was discussed in [16], Qin et al. [17] addressed this problem by using a master-secret key splitting technique which currently seems not available in the lattice setting. In their lattice-based construction, Nguyen et al. [16] utilized a double encryption mechanism to resolve it, which is burdensome by involving the sophisticated encryptions operations. Instead, we adopt a new tool called "leveled ciphertexts", recently employed by Katsumata et al. [10] in the context of lattice-based RHIBE with DKER, which works as follows: each receiver is firstly issued an HIBE trapdoor (i.e., a short matrix) as long-term private key by PKG, namely, a short trapdoor matrix $\mathbf{R}_{\mathbf{A}_{id}}$ which can be used to sample a short vector $\mathbf{e}_{id,t}$ as a short-term decryption key $dk_{id,t} = \mathbf{e}_{id,t}$ for each time period independently from the previous periods. The sender encrypts a message $m \in \{0, 1\}$ under HIBE and RIBE to obtain the leveled ciphertexts of the form $ct_{id,t} = (c_0, \mathbf{c}_0, \mathbf{c}_1)$, where c_0 is an element of $\mathbb{Z}_q$ and is only the ciphertext component carrying m, and $\mathbf{c}_0$ and $\mathbf{c}_1$ are the level-0 and level-1 ciphertexts, respectively. In particular, the level-0 component $\mathbf{c}_0$ is responsible for achieving the identity revocation mechanism, and $(c_0, \mathbf{c}_0)$ can be successfully decrypted with a new output $\hat{c}_0$ by the server. The level-1 component $\mathbf{c}_1$ will help the receiver to decrypt the new ciphertext component $\hat{c}_0$ to recover the original message m.

ORGANIZATION. The organization of the paper is as follows. In Sect. 2, we review the definition of SR-IBE and some background knowledge on lattices. A simplified lattice-based SR-IBE in the standard model is described and analyzed in Sects. 3. In the final Sect. 4, we conclude our whole paper.

2   Definition and Security Model

Table 2 refers to the notations used in this paper.

2.1   Server-Aided Revocable Identity-Based Encryption

We review the definition and security model of SR-IBE, introduced by Qin et al. [17]. An SR-IBE is an extension of RIBE that supports identity revocation, and

Table 2. Notations of this paper.

Notation	Definition
$\mathbf{a}, \mathbf{A}$	Vectors, matrices
$\xleftarrow{\$}$	Sampling uniformly at random
$\|\cdot\|, \|\cdot\|_\infty$	Euclidean norm ℓ_2, infinity norm ℓ_∞
$\lceil e \rceil, \lfloor e \rceil$	The smallest integer not less than e, the integer closet to e
$\mod q$	$(-(q-1)/2, (q-1)/2]$
$\mathcal{O}, \tilde{\mathcal{O}}, \omega$	Standard asymptotic notations
$\log e$	Logarithm of e with base 2
ppt	Probabilistic polynomial-time

additionally, it delegates almost all of workloads on receivers side to an untrusted server which is normally assumed to perform correct operations and return the correct results. A trusted center firstly issues a master secret key (msk) and the public parameters (pp). The PKG then issues a long-term private key sk_{id} and a corresponding token to_{id} for each user (i.e., receivers) with an identity id and a time update key uk_t for each time period t by using msk, meanwhile, sk_{id} is sent to user id via a secret channel, yet to_{id} and uk_t are only sent to the server via a public channel. The PKG will maintain a revocation list (RL) to record all state information st on the revoked users. The server with to_{id} and uk_t can transform a ciphertext $ct_{id,t}$ for a non-revoked user id with period t into a partially decrypted cipertext $ct'_{id,t}$. Finally, the non-revoked user id recovers a message m from $ct'_{id,t}$ by utilizing a short-term decryption key $dk_{id,t}$ which is derived from his long-term private key sk_{id} and current time period t. The system model of SR-IBE is shown in Fig. 1.

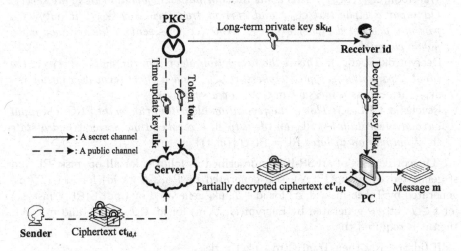

Fig. 1. System model of SR-IBE.

Definition 1. *An* SR-IBE *scheme involves 4 distinct entities:* PKG, *server, sender and receiver, associated with an identity space* $\mathcal{I}$, *a time period space* $\mathcal{T}$, *a message space* $\mathcal{M}$, *and consists of 10 polynomial-time (*pt*) algorithms:*

- Setup($1^n, N$): *This is the setup algorithm run by the* PKG. *On input a system security parameter n and the maximal number of users N, it outputs a master secret key* msk, *the public parameters* pp, *a user revocation list* RL *(initially $\emptyset$) and a state* st. *Note:* msk *is kept in secret by the* PKG, *and* pp *is made public and as an implicit input of all other algorithms.*
- PriKG(msk, id): *This is the key generation algorithm run by the* PKG. *On input a user identity* id *and the master secret key* msk, *it outputs a long-term private key* sk_{id}. *Note:* sk_{id} *is sent to the receiver via a secret channel.*
- Token(msk, id, st): *This is the token generation algorithm run by the* PKG. *On input a receiver's identity* id, *the master secret key* msk *and a state* st, *it outputs a token* to_{id} *and an updated state* st. *Note:* to_{id} *is sent to the server via a public channel.*
- UpdKG(RL, t, msk, st): *This is the key update algorithm run by the* PKG. *On input current revocation list* RL, *a time period* t, *the master secret key* msk *and a state* st, *it outputs a time update key* uk_t. *Note:* uk_t *is sent to the server via a public channel.*
- TranKG(to_{id}, uk_t): *This is the transform key generation algorithm run by the server. On input a token* to_{id}, *an update key* uk_t *(or $\perp$), it outputs a short-term transformation key* $tk_{id,t}$ *(or $\perp$ indicating that the receiver has been revoked).*
- DecKG(sk_{id}, t): *This is the decryption key generation algorithm run by the receiver* id. *On input a long-term private key* sk_{id} *and current time* t, *it outputs a short-term decryption key* $dk_{id,t}$.
- Encrypt(id, t, m): *This is the encryption algorithm run by the sender. On input a receiver's identity* id, *the encryption time period* t *and a message* m. *It outputs a ciphertext* $ct_{id,t}$.
- Transform($ct_{id,t}, tk_{id,t}$): *This is the transformation algorithm run by the server. On input a ciphertext* $ct_{id,t}$ *and current transform key* $tk_{id,t}$, *it outputs a partially decrypted ciphertext* $ct'_{id,t}$. *Note:* $ct'_{id,t}$ *is sent to the receiver via a public channel.*
- Decrypt($dk_{id,t}, ct'_{id,t}$): *This is the decryption algorithm run by the receiver. On input a partially decrypted ciphertext* $ct'_{id,t}$ *and a short-term decryption key* $dk_{id,t}$, *it outputs a message* $m \in \mathcal{M}$, *or a symbol $\perp$.*
- Revoke(id, t, RL, st): *This is the revocation algorithm run by the* PKG. *On input current revocation list* RL, *an identity* id, *a revoked time period* t *and a state* st, *it outputs an updated* $RL = RL \cup \{(id, t)\}$.

The correctness of an SR-IBE is described as follows: for all pp, msk, RL and st generated by Setup($1^n, N$), sk_{id} generated by PriKG(msk, id) for id $\in \mathcal{I}$, to_{id} generated by Token(msk, id, st) for id $\in \mathcal{I}$, uk_t generated by UpdKG(RL, t, msk, st) for t $\in \mathcal{T}$, $ct_{id',t'}$ generated by Encrypt(id', t', m) for id' $\in \mathcal{I}$, t' $\in \mathcal{T}$ and m $\in \mathcal{M}$, then it is required that:

- If (id, t) $\notin$ RL, then TranKG(to_{id}, uk_t) = $tk_{id,t}$.
- If (id = id') $\wedge$ (t = t'), then Decrypt($dk_{id,t}$, Transform($ct_{id',t'}, tk_{id,t}$)) = m.

An SR-IBE scheme is an extension of RIBE and should satisfy indistinguishability under the chosen-plaintext attack (IND-CPA) security to guarantee message hiding security. Qin et al. [17] firstly defined semantic security against adaptive-revocable-identity-time and chosen-plaintext attacks for SR-IBE. Here, as in [16], we consider selective-revocable-identity-time security (a weaker notion initially was suggested in RIBE by Boldyreva et al. [4], subsequently by Chen et al. [7], Nguyen et al. [16], Katsumata et al. [10] and Zhang et al. [25], in which an adversary $\mathcal{A}$ sends a challenge identity and time period pair $(\mathsf{id}^*, \mathsf{t}^*)$ to the challenger $\mathcal{C}$ before the execution of $\mathsf{Setup}(1^n, N)$. A slight difference is that we formalize the security with a game capturing a stronger privacy property called "indistinguishable from random" as defined in [1].

In the IND-CPA security model of SR-IBE, an attacker $\mathcal{A}$ can request the long-term private key, token, time update key, identity revocation, and short-term decryption key queries. One of the most restrictions is that if $\mathcal{A}$ has requested a long-term private key for the challenge identity id^*, then id^* must be revoked before (or at) the time update key query of the challenge time period t^*. Finally, $\mathcal{A}$'s goal is to determine that the challenge ciphertxet is completely random, or correctly encrypted on the challenge message m^* corresponding to $(\mathsf{id}^*, \mathsf{t}^*)$.

Definition 2. *The* IND-CPA *security of* SR-IBE *is described as follows:*

- Intial: *The adversary $\mathcal{A}$ declares a challenge identity and time pair $(\mathsf{id}^*, \mathsf{t}^*)$.*
- Setup: *The challenger $\mathcal{C}$ runs* $\mathsf{Setup}(1^n, N)$ *to obtain* $(\mathsf{msk}, \mathsf{pp}, \mathsf{RL}, \mathsf{st})$. *Note:* RL *is initially* $\emptyset$, $\mathcal{C}$ *keeps* msk *in secret by himself and provides* pp *to $\mathcal{A}$.*
- Query phase 1: *The query-answer between $\mathcal{A}$ and $\mathcal{C}$ is described in Table 3:*

Table 3. The query-answer between $\mathcal{A}$ and $\mathcal{C}$.

	PriKG($\cdot$)	Token($\cdot$)	UpdKG($\cdot$)	DecKG($\cdot$)	Revoke($\cdot$)
$\mathcal{A}$	id	id	RL, t	id, t	RL, id, t
$\mathcal{C}$	$\mathsf{sk_{id}}$	$\mathsf{to_{id}}$	$\mathsf{uk_t}$	$\mathsf{dk_{id,t}}$	$\mathsf{RL} = \mathsf{RL} \cup \{(\mathsf{id}, \mathsf{t})\}$

Note: the oracles share st and these queries are with some restrictions defined later.

- Challenge: *$\mathcal{A}$ submits a challenge $\mathsf{m}^* \in \mathcal{M}$. $\mathcal{C}$ firstly samples a bit $b \xleftarrow{\$} \{0, 1\}$. If $b = 0$, $\mathcal{C}$ returns a challenge ciphertext $\mathsf{ct}^*_{\mathsf{id}^*, \mathsf{t}^*}$ by running* $\mathsf{Encrypt}(\mathsf{id}^*, \mathsf{t}^*, \mathsf{m}^*)$, *otherwise, a random* $\mathsf{ct}^*_{\mathsf{id}^*, \mathsf{t}^*} \xleftarrow{\$} \mathcal{U}$.
- Query phase 2: *$\mathcal{A}$ continues to make additional queries as before with the same restrictions.*
- Guess: *$\mathcal{A}$ outputs a bit $b^* \in \{0, 1\}$, and wins if $b^* = b$.*
  In the above game, the following restrictions should be satisfied:

- UpdKG($\cdot$) *and* Revoke($\cdot$) *must be queried in a non-decreasing order of time.*
- Revoke($\cdot$) *cannot be queried at time* t *if* UpdKG($\cdot$) *has been queried at* t.
- Revoke($\cdot$) *must be queried on* id^* *at* $\mathsf{t} \leq \mathsf{t}^*$ *if* PriKG($\cdot$) *has been queried on* id^*.
- DecKG($\cdot$) *cannot be queried at* t *if* UpdKG($\cdot$) *has not been queried at* t.
- DecKG($\cdot$) *cannot be queried on* $(\mathsf{id}^*, \mathsf{t}^*)$ *if* id^* *is non-revoked at* t^*.

The advantage of $\mathcal{A}$ is defined as $\mathsf{Adv}_{\mathsf{SR\text{-}IBE},\mathcal{A}}^{\mathsf{IND\text{-}CPA}}(n) = |\Pr[b^* = b] - 1/2|$, and an SR-IBE scheme is IND-CPA secure if $\mathsf{Adv}_{\mathsf{SR\text{-}IBE},\mathcal{A}}^{\mathsf{IND\text{-}CPA}}(n)$ is negligible in the security parameter n.

2.2   Lattices

In this subsection, we recall the knowledge on integer lattices.

Definition 3. *Given* n, m, $q \geq 2$, *a random* $\mathbf{A} \in \mathbb{Z}_q^{n \times m}$, *and* $\mathbf{u} \in \mathbb{Z}_q^n$, *the* m-*dimensional* q-*ary orthogonal lattice* $\Lambda_q^\perp(\mathbf{A})$ *(and its shift* $\Lambda_q^{\mathbf{u}}(\mathbf{A})$*) is defined as:* $\Lambda_q^\perp(\mathbf{A}) = \{\mathbf{e} \in \mathbb{Z}^m \mid \mathbf{Ae} = \mathbf{0} \bmod q\}$ *and* $\Lambda_q^{\mathbf{u}}(\mathbf{A}) = \{\mathbf{e} \in \mathbb{Z}^m \mid \mathbf{Ae} = \mathbf{u} \bmod q\}$.

The discrete Gaussian over Λ with center $\mathbf{c} \in \mathbb{Z}^m$ and a parameter $s > 0$ is denoted as $\mathcal{D}_{\Lambda,s,\mathbf{c}}$, and we omit the subscript and denote it as $\mathcal{D}_{\Lambda,s}$ if $\mathbf{c} = \mathbf{0}$.

Lemma 1 ([8]). *For* $q \geq 2$, $m \geq 2n\lceil \log q \rceil$, *assume that the columns of* $\mathbf{A} \in \mathbb{Z}_q^{n \times m}$ *generate* $\mathbb{Z}_q^n$, *let* $s \geq \omega(\sqrt{\log m})$, *then the followings hold:*

1. *For* $\mathbf{e} \xleftarrow{\$} \mathcal{D}_{\mathbb{Z}^m,s}$, *the distribution of* $\mathbf{u} = \mathbf{Ae} \bmod q$ *is statistically close to uniform over* $\mathbb{Z}_q^n$.

2. *For* $\mathbf{e} \xleftarrow{\$} \mathcal{D}_{\mathbb{Z}^m,s}$, *then* $\Pr[\|\mathbf{e}\|_\infty \leq \lceil s \cdot \log m \rceil]$ *holds with a larger probability.*

A ppt trapdoor generation algorithm returning a statistically close to uniform $\mathbf{A}$ together with a low Gram-Schmidt norm basis for $\Lambda_q^\perp(\mathbf{A})$ plays a key role in lattice-based cryptography. This algorithm was firstly introduced by Ajtai [2], and two improvements were investigated in [3,15].

Lemma 2 ([2,3,15]). *Let* $n \geq 1$, $q \geq 2$, $m = 2n\lceil \log q \rceil$, *there is a* ppt *algorithm* $\mathsf{TrapGen}(q, n, m)$ *that returns* $\mathbf{A} \in \mathbb{Z}_q^{n \times m}$ *statistically close to an uniform matrix in* $\mathbb{Z}_q^{n \times m}$ *and a trapdoor* $\mathbf{R_A}$ *for* $\Lambda_q^\perp(\mathbf{A})$.

Gentry et al. [8] showed an algorithm to sample shorter vectors (or matrices) from a discrete Gaussian distribution, and an improvement was given in [15]. Meanwhile, to delegate a trapdoor for a super-lattice was given in [6].

Lemma 3 ([8,15]). *Let* $n \geq 1$, $q \geq 2$, $m = 2n\lceil \log q \rceil$, *given* $\mathbf{A} \in \mathbb{Z}_q^{n \times m}$, *a trapdoor* $\mathbf{R_A}$ *for* $\Lambda_q^\perp(\mathbf{A})$, *a parameter* $s = \omega(\sqrt{n \log q \log n})$, *and a vector* $\mathbf{u} \in \mathbb{Z}_q^n$, *there is a* ppt *algorithm* $\mathsf{SamplePre}(\mathbf{A}, \mathbf{R_A}, \mathbf{u}, s)$ *returning a shorter vector* $\mathbf{e} \in \Lambda_q^{\mathbf{u}}(\mathbf{A})$ *sampled from a distribution statistically close to* $\mathcal{D}_{\Lambda_q^{\mathbf{u}}(\mathbf{A}),s}$.

Lemma 4 ([6]). *Let* $q \geq 2$, $m = 2n\lceil \log q \rceil$, *given* $\mathbf{A} \in \mathbb{Z}_q^{n \times m}$ *who can generate* $\mathbb{Z}_q^n$, *a basis* $\mathbf{R_A} \in \mathbb{Z}^{m \times m}$ *for* $\Lambda_q^\perp(\mathbf{A})$, *a random* $\mathbf{A}' \in \mathbb{Z}_q^{n \times m'}$, *there is a deterministic algorithm* $\mathsf{ExtBasis}(\mathbf{R_A}, \mathbf{A}^* = \mathbf{A}|\mathbf{A}')$ *returning a basis* $\mathbf{R_{A^*}} \in \mathbb{Z}^{(m+m') \times (m+m')}$ *for* $\Lambda_q^\perp(\mathbf{A}^*)$, *especially,* $\mathbf{R_A}$, $\mathbf{R_{A^*}}$ *are with equal Gram-Schmidt norm. Note: this result holds for any given permutation of all columns of* $\mathbf{A}^*$.

Lemma 5 ([6]). *Let $n \geq 1$, $q \geq 2$, $m = 2n\lceil \log q \rceil$, $s \geq \|\widetilde{\mathbf{R_A}}\| \cdot \omega(\sqrt{\log n})$, $\mathbf{R_A} \in \mathbb{Z}^{m \times m}$ is a basis for $\Lambda_q^\perp(\mathbf{A})$, there is a ppt algorithm $\mathsf{RandBasis}(\mathbf{R_A}, s)$ returning a new basis $\mathbf{R'_A} \in \mathbb{Z}^{m \times m}$ and $\|\mathbf{R'_A}\| \leq s \cdot \sqrt{m}$. In particular, for two basis matrices $\mathbf{R_A}^{(1)}$ and $\mathbf{R_A}^{(2)}$ for $\Lambda_q^\perp(\mathbf{A})$, and $s \geq max\{\|\widetilde{\mathbf{R_A}^{(1)}}\|, \|\widetilde{\mathbf{R_A}^{(2)}}\|\} \cdot \omega(\sqrt{\log n})$, $\mathsf{RandBasis}(\mathbf{R_A}^{(1)}, s)$ is statistically close to $\mathsf{RandBasis}(\mathbf{R_A}^{(2)}, s)$.*

Lemma 6 ([1]). *Let $q > 2$, $m > n$, $\mathbf{A} \in \mathbb{Z}_q^{n \times m}$, $\mathbf{A'} \in \mathbb{Z}_q^{n \times m'}$, and $s > \|\widetilde{\mathbf{R_A}}\| \cdot \omega(\sqrt{\log(m + m')})$, given a trapdoor $\mathbf{R_A}$ for $\Lambda_q^\perp(\mathbf{A})$ and $\mathbf{u} \in \mathbb{Z}_q^n$, there is a ppt algorithm $\mathsf{SampleLeft}(\mathbf{A}|\mathbf{A'}, \mathbf{R_A}, \mathbf{u}, s)$ returning a shorter $\mathbf{e} \in \mathbb{Z}^{m+m'}$ sampled from a distribution statistically close to $\mathcal{D}_{\Lambda_q^\mathbf{u}(\mathbf{A}|\mathbf{A'}), s}$.*

Lemma 7 ([1]). *Let $q > 2$, $m > n$, $\mathbf{A}, \mathbf{B} \in \mathbb{Z}_q^{n \times m}$, $s > \|\widetilde{\mathbf{R_B}}\| \cdot \mathcal{O}(\sqrt{m}) \cdot \omega(\sqrt{\log m})$, given a trapdoor $\mathbf{R_B}$, a low-norm $\mathbf{R} \in \{-1, 1\}^{m \times m}$, and $\mathbf{u} \in \mathbb{Z}_q^n$, there is a ppt algorithm $\mathsf{SampleRight}(\mathbf{A}, \mathbf{B}, \mathbf{R}, \mathbf{R_B}, \mathbf{u}, s)$ returning a shorter $\mathbf{e} \in \mathbb{Z}^{2m}$ distributed statistically close to $\mathcal{D}_{\Lambda_q^\mathbf{u}(\mathbf{F}), s}$, where $\mathbf{F} = [\mathbf{A}|\mathbf{AR} + \mathbf{B}]$.*

The learning with errors (LWE) problem was firstly introduced by Regev [18].

Definition 4. *The LWE problem is defined as follows: given a random $\mathbf{s} \xleftarrow{\$} \mathbb{Z}_q^n$, a distribution χ over $\mathbb{Z}$, let $\mathcal{A}_{\mathbf{s}, \chi}$ be the distribution $(\mathbf{A}, \mathbf{A}^\top \mathbf{s} + \mathbf{e})$ where $\mathbf{A} \xleftarrow{\$} \mathbb{Z}_q^{n \times m}$, $\mathbf{e} \xleftarrow{\$} \chi^m$, and to make distinguish between $\mathcal{A}_{\mathbf{s}, \chi}$ and $\mathcal{U} \xleftarrow{\$} \mathbb{Z}_q^{n \times m} \times \mathbb{Z}_q^m$. Let $\beta \geq \sqrt{n} \cdot \omega(\log n)$, for a prime power q, given a β-bounded χ, the LWE problem is at least as hard as the shortest independent vectors problem $\mathsf{SIVP}_{\widetilde{\mathcal{O}}(nq/\beta)}$.*

An injective encoding function $\mathcal{H} : \mathbb{Z}_q^n \to \mathbb{Z}_q^{n \times n}$ is adopted for our lattice-based SR-IBE scheme. An explicit design called encoding with full-rank differences (FRD) was proposed by Agrawal et al. [1].

Definition 5. *Let $n > 1$, prime $q \geq 2$, an injective encoding function $\mathcal{H} : \mathbb{Z}_q^n \to \mathbb{Z}_q^{n \times n}$ is called FRD if:*

1. *For $\forall \mathbf{e}_1, \mathbf{e}_2 \in \mathbb{Z}_q^n$, $\mathbf{e}_1 \neq \mathbf{e}_2$, $\mathcal{H}(\mathbf{e}_1) - \mathcal{H}(\mathbf{e}_2) \in \mathbb{Z}_q^{n \times n}$ is full-rank.*
2. *$\mathcal{H}$ can be computed in a polynomial time, i.e., $\mathcal{O}(n \log q)$.*

Lemma 8 ([1]). *Let $n \geq 1$, prime $q > 2$, $m > (n+1) \log q + \omega(\log n)$, $\mathbf{A}, \mathbf{B} \xleftarrow{\$} \mathbb{Z}_q^{n \times m}$, and $\mathbf{R} \xleftarrow{\$} \{-1, 1\}^{m \times m} \bmod q$. Then, for all $\mathbf{w} \in \mathbb{Z}_q^m$, $(\mathbf{A}, \mathbf{AR}, \mathbf{R}^\top \mathbf{w})$ is statistically close to $(\mathbf{A}, \mathbf{B}, \mathbf{R}^\top \mathbf{w})$.*

3   Our Lattice-Based SR-IBE Scheme

Our lattice-based SR-IBE scheme in the standard model is a combination of a two-level lattice-based HIBE scheme [1] and a lattice-based RIBE scheme [7] via a new design tool - leveled ciphertexts. In addition, we also adopt the classical

BT revocation mechanism to alleviate the PKG's workload (a user id is viewed as a leaf node of BT and each node in BT has an identifier which is a fixed and unique string, i.e., id $= (1, id_1, id_2, \cdots, id_{\log N})$, where N is the maximal number of system users. Additionally, due to the limited space, the detailed description of KUNodes(BT,RL,t) algorithm is omitted in this paper and any interested readers please refer to [4,7,14,16,17,19,22,25]).

Additionally, as a preparation, we need to explain our treatment of identity space $\mathcal{I} \subseteq \mathbb{Z}_q^n - \{\mathbf{0}_n\}$ and time period space $\mathcal{T} \subseteq \mathbb{Z}_q^n - \{\mathbf{0}_n\}$, which was recently introduced by Wang et al. [24]. Because an identity id $= (1, id_1, \cdots, id_n) \in \mathcal{I}$, we define $\mathcal{I} = \{1\} \times \mathbb{Z}_q^{n-1}$. In addition, we define a new space $\widetilde{\mathcal{I}} = \{-1\} \times \mathbb{Z}_q^{n-1}$, which satisfies $\mathcal{I} \cap \widetilde{\mathcal{I}} = \emptyset$ and $|\mathcal{I}| = |\widetilde{\mathcal{I}}| = q^{n-1}$. Thus, there is a one-to-one correspondence between a real identity id $\in \mathcal{I}$ and a virtual identity $\widetilde{\text{id}} \in \widetilde{\mathcal{I}}$. The time period space is treated as discrete and its size is polynomial in n, i.e., $\mathcal{T} = \{0, 1, \cdots, \mathsf{t}_{\max} - 1\}$, and is encoded into the set $\{2\} \times \mathbb{Z}_q^{n-1}$.

3.1 Description of the Scheme

As in Qin et al. [17] and Nguyen et al. [16], our lattice-based SR-IBE scheme consists of 10 pt algorithms: Setup, PriKG, Token, UpdKG, TranKG, DecKG, Encrypt, Transform, Decrypt and Revoke. The algorithms are described as follows:

- Setup($1^n, N$): On input a security parameter n and the maximal number of users $N = 2^n$, set a prime modulus $q = \widetilde{\mathcal{O}}(n^3)$, a dimension $m = 2n\lceil \log q \rceil$, a Gaussian parameter $s = \widetilde{\mathcal{O}}(\sqrt{m})$ and a norm bound $\beta = \widetilde{\mathcal{O}}(\sqrt{n})$ for the distribution χ. The PKG specifies the following steps:
  1. Let the identity space $\mathcal{I} = \{1\} \times \mathbb{Z}_q^{n-1}$, time period space $\mathcal{T} = \{2\} \times \mathbb{Z}_q^{n-1}$, and message space $\mathcal{M} = \{0, 1\}$.
  2. Run TrapGen(q, n, m) to get $\mathbf{A} \in \mathbb{Z}_q^{n \times m}$ with a trapdoor $\mathbf{R_A}$.
  3. Set an FRD function $\mathcal{H} : \mathbb{Z}_q^n \to \mathbb{Z}_q^{n \times n}$ as described in Definition 5.
  4. Sample $\mathbf{A}_0, \mathbf{A}_1, \mathbf{B} \xleftarrow{\$} \mathbb{Z}_q^{n \times m}$, and $\mathbf{u} \xleftarrow{\$} \mathbb{Z}_q^n$.
  5. Set the sate st $=$ BT that BT is with at least N leaf nodes, and the initial revocation list RL $= \emptyset$.
  6. Set pp $= (\mathbf{A}, \mathbf{A}_0, \mathbf{A}_1, \mathbf{B}, \mathbf{u}, \mathcal{H})$, and the master secret key msk $= \mathbf{R_A}$.
  7. Output (pp, msk, RL, st), where msk is kept in secret by the PKG, and pp is made public and as an implicit input of all other algorithms.
- PriKG(msk, id): On input a user identity id $\in \mathcal{I}$ and the master secret key msk. The PKG specifies the following steps:
  1. Define $\mathbf{A}_{\widetilde{\text{id}}} = [\mathbf{A}|\mathbf{A}_0 + \mathcal{H}(\widetilde{\text{id}})\mathbf{B}] \in \mathbb{Z}_q^{n \times 2m}$.
  2. Run RandBasis(ExtBasis($\mathbf{R_A}, \mathbf{A}_{\widetilde{\text{id}}}$), s) to generate a trapdoor $\mathbf{R}_{\mathbf{A}_{\widetilde{\text{id}}}}$ for $\Lambda_q^\perp(\mathbf{A}_{\widetilde{\text{id}}})$.
  3. Output $\mathsf{sk}_{\text{id}} = \mathbf{R}_{\mathbf{A}_{\widetilde{\text{id}}}}$. *Note*: sk_{id} is sent to the receiver via a secret channel.
- Token(msk, id, st): On input a user identity id $\in \mathcal{I}$, the master secret key msk and a state st. The PKG specifies the following steps:

1. Set id to an unassigned leaf node of BT, and for each $\theta \in \mathsf{path}(\mathsf{id})$, if $\mathbf{u}_{1,\theta}$, $\mathbf{u}_{2,\theta}$ are undefined, then sample $\mathbf{u}_{1,\theta} \xleftarrow{\$} \mathbb{Z}_q^n$, set $\mathbf{u}_{2,\theta} = \mathbf{u} - \mathbf{u}_{1,\theta}$, and store $(\mathbf{u}_{1,\theta}, \mathbf{u}_{2,\theta})$ in node θ.
2. Define $\mathbf{A}_{\mathsf{id}} = [\mathbf{A}|\mathbf{A}_0 + \mathcal{H}(\mathsf{id})\mathbf{B}] \in \mathbb{Z}_q^{n \times 2m}$.
3. Run $\mathsf{SampleLeft}(\mathbf{A}_{\mathsf{id}}, \mathbf{R_A}, \mathbf{u}_{1,\theta}, s)$ to generate $\mathbf{e}_{\mathsf{id},\theta} \in \mathbb{Z}^{2m}$ satisfying that $\mathbf{A}_{\mathsf{id}} \cdot \mathbf{e}_{\mathsf{id},\theta} = \mathbf{u}_{1,\theta} \bmod q$.
4. Output an updated st, and $\mathsf{to}_{\mathsf{id}} = (\theta, \mathbf{e}_{\mathsf{id},\theta})_{\theta \in \mathsf{path}(\mathsf{id})}$. *Note*: $\mathsf{to}_{\mathsf{id}}$ is sent to the server via a public channel.

- $\mathsf{UpdKG}(\mathsf{RL}, \mathsf{t}, \mathsf{msk}, \mathsf{st})$: On input a period $\mathsf{t} \in \mathcal{T}$, the master secret key msk, a revocation list RL and a state st. The PKG specifies the following steps:
  1. Let $\mathbf{A}_\mathsf{t} = [\mathbf{A}|\mathbf{A}_1 + \mathcal{H}(\mathsf{t})\mathbf{B}]$, for each $\theta \in \mathsf{KUNodes}(\mathsf{BT}, \mathsf{RL}, \mathsf{t})$, retrieve $\mathbf{u}_{2,\theta}$.
  2. Run $\mathsf{SampleLeft}(\mathbf{A}_\mathsf{t}, \mathbf{R_A}, \mathbf{u}_{2,\theta}, s)$ to generate $\mathbf{e}_{\mathsf{t},\theta} \in \mathbb{Z}^{2m}$ satisfying that $\mathbf{A}_\mathsf{t} \cdot \mathbf{e}_{\mathsf{t},\theta} = \mathbf{u}_{2,\theta} = \mathbf{u} - \mathbf{u}_{1,\theta} \bmod q$.
  3. Output $\mathsf{uk}_\mathsf{t} = (\theta, \mathbf{e}_{\mathsf{t},\theta})_{\theta \in \mathsf{KUNodes}(\mathsf{BT},\mathsf{RL},\mathsf{t})}$. *Note*: uk_t is sent to the server via a public channel.

- $\mathsf{TranKG}(\mathsf{to}_{\mathsf{id}}, \mathsf{uk}_\mathsf{t}, \mathsf{t})$: On input a token $\mathsf{to}_{\mathsf{id}} = (\theta, \mathbf{e}_{\mathsf{id},\theta})_{\theta \in \mathsf{path}(\mathsf{id})}$ and an update key $\mathsf{uk}_\mathsf{t} = (\theta, \mathbf{e}_{\mathsf{t},\theta})_{\theta \in \mathsf{KUNodes}(\mathsf{BT},\mathsf{RL},\mathsf{t})}$. The server specifies the following steps:
  1. If $\mathsf{path}(\mathsf{id}) \cap \mathsf{KUNodes}(\mathsf{BT}, \mathsf{RL}, \mathsf{t}) = \emptyset$, return $\perp$ and abort.
  2. Otherwise, pick $\theta \in (\mathsf{path}(\mathsf{id}) \cap \mathsf{KUNodes}(\mathsf{BT}, \mathsf{RL}, \mathsf{t}))$ (only one θ exists).
  3. Parse $\mathbf{e}_{\mathsf{id},\theta} = \begin{bmatrix} \mathbf{e}_{\mathsf{id},\theta}^0 \\ \mathbf{e}_{\mathsf{id},\theta}^1 \end{bmatrix}$, $\mathbf{e}_{\mathsf{t},\theta} = \begin{bmatrix} \mathbf{e}_{\mathsf{t},\theta}^0 \\ \mathbf{e}_{\mathsf{t},\theta}^1 \end{bmatrix}$, where $\mathbf{e}_{\mathsf{id},\theta}^i, \mathbf{e}_{\mathsf{t},\theta}^i \in \mathbb{Z}^m$, for $i = 0, 1$.
  4. Return $\mathsf{tk}_{\mathsf{id},\mathsf{t}} = \mathbf{e}_{\mathsf{id},\mathsf{t}} = \begin{bmatrix} \mathbf{e}_{\mathsf{id},\theta}^0 + \mathbf{e}_{\mathsf{t},\theta}^0 \\ \mathbf{e}_{\mathsf{id},\theta}^1 \\ \mathbf{e}_{\mathsf{t},\theta}^1 \end{bmatrix} \in \mathbb{Z}^{3m}$.

- $\mathsf{DecKG}(\mathsf{sk}_{\mathsf{id}}, \mathsf{t})$: On input a long-term private key $\mathsf{sk}_{\mathsf{id}} = \mathbf{R}_{\mathbf{A}_{\widetilde{\mathsf{id}}}}$ and a time period t. The receiver specifies the following steps:
  1. Define $\mathbf{A}_{\widetilde{\mathsf{id}},\mathsf{t}} = [\mathbf{A}_{\widetilde{\mathsf{id}}}|\mathbf{A}_1 + \mathcal{H}(\mathsf{t})\mathbf{B}] \in \mathbb{Z}_q^{n \times 3m}$, run $\mathsf{SampleLeft}(\mathbf{A}_{\widetilde{\mathsf{id}},\mathsf{t}}, \mathbf{R}_{\mathbf{A}_{\widetilde{\mathsf{id}}}}, \mathbf{u}, s)$ to generate $\mathbf{e}_{\widetilde{\mathsf{id}},\mathsf{t}} \in \mathbb{Z}^{3m}$ satisfying that $\mathbf{A}_{\widetilde{\mathsf{id}},\mathsf{t}} \cdot \mathbf{e}_{\widetilde{\mathsf{id}},\mathsf{t}} = \mathbf{u} \bmod q$.
  2. Return $\mathsf{dk}_{\mathsf{id},\mathsf{t}} = \mathbf{e}_{\widetilde{\mathsf{id}},\mathsf{t}}$.

- $\mathsf{Encrypt}(\mathsf{id}, \mathsf{t}, \mathsf{m})$: On input a user identity $\mathsf{id} \in \mathcal{I}$, a time period $\mathsf{t} \in \mathcal{T}$ and a message $\mathsf{m} \in \{0, 1\}$. The sender specifies the following steps:
  1. Define $\mathbf{A}_{\mathsf{id},\mathsf{t}} = [\mathbf{A}|\mathbf{A}_0 + \mathcal{H}(\mathsf{id})\mathbf{B}|\mathbf{A}_1 + \mathcal{H}(\mathsf{t})\mathbf{B}]$, $\mathbf{A}_{\widetilde{\mathsf{id}},\mathsf{t}} = [\mathbf{A}|\mathbf{A}_0 + \mathcal{H}(\widetilde{\mathsf{id}})\mathbf{B}|\mathbf{A}_1 + \mathcal{H}(\mathsf{t})\mathbf{B}] \in \mathbb{Z}_q^{n \times 3m}$.
  2. Sample $\mathbf{s}_0, \mathbf{s}_1 \xleftarrow{\$} \mathbb{Z}_q^n$, $e_0 \xleftarrow{\$} \chi$, $\mathbf{e}_0, \mathbf{e}_1 \xleftarrow{\$} \chi^m$, $\mathbf{R}_{00}, \mathbf{R}_{01}, \mathbf{R}_{10}, \mathbf{R}_{11} \xleftarrow{\$} \{1, -1\}^{m \times m}$.
  3. Set $\mathbf{c}_0 = \mathbf{A}_{\mathsf{id},\mathsf{t}}^\mathrm{T} \cdot \mathbf{s}_0 + \begin{bmatrix} \mathbf{e}_0 \\ \mathbf{R}_{00}^\mathrm{T}\mathbf{e}_0 \\ \mathbf{R}_{01}^\mathrm{T}\mathbf{e}_0 \end{bmatrix} \bmod q$, $\mathbf{c}_1 = \mathbf{A}_{\widetilde{\mathsf{id}},\mathsf{t}}^\mathrm{T} \cdot \mathbf{s}_1 + \begin{bmatrix} \mathbf{e}_1 \\ \mathbf{R}_{10}^\mathrm{T}\mathbf{e}_1 \\ \mathbf{R}_{11}^\mathrm{T}\mathbf{e}_1 \end{bmatrix} \bmod q$.
  4. Compute $c_0 = \mathbf{u}^\mathrm{T} \cdot (\mathbf{s}_0 + \mathbf{s}_1) + e_0 + \mathsf{m}\lfloor \frac{q}{2} \rfloor \bmod q \in \mathbb{Z}_q$.
  5. Output $\mathsf{ct}_{\mathsf{id},\mathsf{t}} = (c_0, \mathbf{c}_0, \mathbf{c}_1) \in \mathbb{Z}_q \times (\mathbb{Z}_q^{3m})^2$.

- $\mathsf{Transform}(\mathsf{ct}_{\mathsf{id},\mathsf{t}}, \mathsf{tk}_{\mathsf{id}',\mathsf{t}'})$: On input an original ciphertext $\mathsf{ct}_{\mathsf{id},\mathsf{t}} = (c_0, \mathbf{c}_0, \mathbf{c}_1)$ and a transform key $\mathsf{tk}_{\mathsf{id}',\mathsf{t}'} = \mathbf{e}_{\mathsf{id}',\mathsf{t}'}$. The server specifies the following steps:

1. If $(\mathsf{id} \neq \mathsf{id}') \vee (\mathsf{t} \neq \mathsf{t}')$, return $\perp$ and abort.
2. Otherwise, compute $\hat{c}_0 = c_0 - \mathbf{e}_{\mathsf{id},\mathsf{t}}^{\mathrm{T}} \cdot \mathbf{c}_0 \bmod q$.
3. Output $\mathsf{ct}'_{\mathsf{id},\mathsf{t}} = (\hat{c}_0, \mathbf{c}_1) \in \mathbb{Z}_q \times \mathbb{Z}_q^{3m}$. *Note*: $\mathsf{ct}'_{\mathsf{id},\mathsf{t}}$ is sent to the receiver via a public channel.

- Decrypt($\mathsf{ct}'_{\mathsf{id},\mathsf{t}}, \mathsf{dk}_{\mathsf{id}',\mathsf{t}'}$): On input a partially decrypted ciphertext $\mathsf{ct}'_{\mathsf{id},\mathsf{t}} = (\hat{c}_0, \mathbf{c}_1)$, a decryption key $\mathsf{dk}_{\mathsf{id}',\mathsf{t}'} = \mathbf{e}_{\widetilde{\mathsf{id}}',\mathsf{t}'}$. The receiver specifies the following steps:
    1. If $(\mathsf{id} \neq \mathsf{id}') \vee (\mathsf{t} \neq \mathsf{t}')$, return $\perp$ and abort.
    2. Otherwise, compute $w_0 = \hat{c}_0 - \mathbf{e}_{\widetilde{\mathsf{id}},\mathsf{t}}^{\mathrm{T}} \cdot \mathbf{c}_1 \bmod q$.
    3. Output $\lfloor \frac{2}{q} w_0 \rceil \in \{0,1\}$.
- Revoke($\mathsf{id}, \mathsf{t}, \mathsf{RL}, \mathsf{st}$): On input current revocation list RL, a user identity id, a time period t and a state $\mathsf{st} = \mathsf{BT}$. The PKG specifies the following steps:
    1. Add $(\mathsf{id}, \mathsf{t})$ to RL for all nodes associated with id.
    2. Output an updated $\mathsf{RL} = \mathsf{RL} \cup \{(\mathsf{id}, \mathsf{t})\}$.

3.2 Analysis

In this subsection, we analysis the efficiency, correctness and security of our new lattice-based SR-IBE in the standard model.

Efficiency: The efficiency aspect of our scheme with $N = 2^n$ is as follows:

- The bit-size of public parameters pp is $(4nm + 2n) \log q = \widetilde{\mathcal{O}}(n^2)$.
- The bit-size of master secret key msk is $m^2 \log q = \widetilde{\mathcal{O}}(n^2)$.
- The bit-size of long-term private key $\mathsf{sk}_{\mathsf{id}}$ is $4m^2 \log q = \widetilde{\mathcal{O}}(n^2)$.
- The bit-size of token $\mathsf{to}_{\mathsf{id}}$ is $2m(\log N + 1) \log q = \widetilde{\mathcal{O}}(n^2)$.
- The bit-size of time update key uk_{t} is $2m \log q \cdot \mathcal{O}(r \log \frac{N}{r}) = \mathcal{O}(r \log \frac{N}{r}) \cdot \widetilde{\mathcal{O}}(n)$ where r is the number of revoked users.
- The bit-size of short-term transform key $\mathsf{tk}_{\mathsf{id},\mathsf{t}}$ is $3m \log q = \widetilde{\mathcal{O}}(n)$.
- The bit-size of ciphertext $\mathsf{ct}_{\mathsf{id},\mathsf{t}}$ is $(1 + 6m) \log q = \widetilde{\mathcal{O}}(n)$.
- The bit-size of short-term decryption key $\mathsf{dk}_{\mathsf{id},\mathsf{t}}$ is $3m \log q = \widetilde{\mathcal{O}}(n)$.

By the above analysis, though as in the first lattice-based SR-IBE [16], our new SR-IBE enjoys the same asymptotic efficiency for all items, three random matrices over $\mathbb{Z}_q^{n \times m}$ and one random matrix over $\mathbb{Z}_q^{n \times \lceil \log q \rceil}$ have been removed from pp, and only one trapdoor matrix (two in [16]) over $\mathbb{Z}^{m \times m}$ in msk. Further, only one short vector over $\mathbb{Z}^{2m}$ ($k \approx 4 \log n$ vectors in [16]) for each node $\theta \in \mathsf{path}(\mathsf{id})$ in $\mathsf{to}_{\mathsf{id}}$ or $\theta \in \mathsf{KUNodes}(\mathsf{BT}, \mathsf{RL}, \mathsf{t})$ in uk_{t}. Similarly, the size of $\mathsf{tk}_{\mathsf{id},\mathsf{t}}$ is reduced by more than k times ($4mk \log q$ in [16]). In particular, the component carrying m in our final ciphertext enjoys the same size as in the underlying RIBE [7], which is k times less than [16], and the whole encryptions process is simple and without the burdensome double encryption operations.

Correctness: If our new lattice-based SR-IBE in the standard model is operated correctly as specified, and a receiver id is not revoked at time period $\mathsf{t} \in \mathcal{T}$, then $\mathsf{tk}_{\mathsf{id},\mathsf{t}} = \mathbf{e}_{\mathsf{id},\mathsf{t}}$ satisfies $\mathbf{A}_{\mathsf{id},\mathsf{t}} \cdot \mathbf{e}_{\mathsf{id},\mathsf{t}} = \mathbf{A}_{\mathsf{id}} \cdot \mathbf{e}_{\mathsf{id},\theta} + \mathbf{A}_{\mathsf{t}} \cdot \mathbf{e}_{\mathsf{t},\theta} = \mathbf{u} \bmod q$, and $\mathsf{dk}_{\mathsf{id},\mathsf{t}} = \mathbf{e}_{\widetilde{\mathsf{id}},\mathsf{t}}$ satisfies $\mathbf{A}_{\widetilde{\mathsf{id}},\mathsf{t}} \cdot \mathbf{e}_{\widetilde{\mathsf{id}},\mathsf{t}} = \mathbf{u} \bmod q$.

- During the transformation algorithm, given a ciphertext $\mathsf{ct}_{\mathsf{id},\mathsf{t}} = (c_0, \mathbf{c}_0, \mathbf{c}_1)$, the server tries to derive a partially decrypted ciphertext $\mathsf{ct}'_{\mathsf{id},\mathsf{t}} = (\hat{c}_0, \mathbf{c}_1)$ by using $\mathsf{tk}_{\mathsf{id},\mathsf{t}} = \mathbf{e}_{\mathsf{id},\mathsf{t}}$:

$$\hat{c}_0 = c_0 - \mathbf{e}_{\mathsf{id},\mathsf{t}}^{\mathrm{T}} \mathbf{c}_0 = \mathbf{u}^{\mathrm{T}}(\mathbf{s}_0 + \mathbf{s}_1) + e_0 + \mathsf{m}\lfloor\tfrac{q}{2}\rfloor - \underbrace{(\mathbf{A}_{\mathsf{id},\mathsf{t}}\mathbf{e}_{\mathsf{id},\mathsf{t}})^{\mathrm{T}}\mathbf{s}_0}_{=\mathbf{u}^{\mathrm{T}}\mathbf{s}_0} - \mathbf{e}_{\mathsf{id},\mathsf{t}}^{\mathrm{T}}\begin{bmatrix} \mathbf{e}_0 \\ \mathbf{R}_{00}^{\mathrm{T}}\mathbf{e}_0 \\ \mathbf{R}_{01}^{\mathrm{T}}\mathbf{e}_0 \end{bmatrix}$$

$$= \mathbf{u}^{\mathrm{T}}\mathbf{s}_1 + e_0 + \mathsf{m}\lfloor\tfrac{q}{2}\rfloor - \mathbf{e}_{\mathsf{id},\mathsf{t}}^{\mathrm{T}}\begin{bmatrix} \mathbf{e}_0 \\ \mathbf{R}_{00}^{\mathrm{T}}\mathbf{e}_0 \\ \mathbf{R}_{01}^{\mathrm{T}}\mathbf{e}_0 \end{bmatrix}$$

- During the decryption algorithm, given a partially decrypted ciphertext $\mathsf{ct}'_{\mathsf{id},\mathsf{t}} = (\hat{c}_0, \mathbf{c}_1)$, the receiver id tries to derive the message m by using $\mathsf{dk}_{\mathsf{id},\mathsf{t}} = \mathbf{e}_{\widetilde{\mathsf{id}},\mathsf{t}}$:

$$w_0 = \hat{c}_0 - \mathbf{e}_{\widetilde{\mathsf{id}},\mathsf{t}}^{\mathrm{T}} \mathbf{c}_{01} = \mathbf{u}^{\mathrm{T}}\mathbf{s}_1 + e_0 + \mathsf{m}\lfloor\tfrac{q}{2}\rfloor - \mathbf{e}_{\mathsf{id},\mathsf{t}}^{\mathrm{T}}\begin{bmatrix} \mathbf{e}_0 \\ \mathbf{R}_{00}^{\mathrm{T}}\mathbf{e}_0 \\ \mathbf{R}_{01}^{\mathrm{T}}\mathbf{e}_0 \end{bmatrix} - \underbrace{(\mathbf{A}_{\widetilde{\mathsf{id}},\mathsf{t}}\mathbf{e}_{\widetilde{\mathsf{id}},\mathsf{t}})^{\mathrm{T}}\mathbf{s}_1}_{=\mathbf{u}^{\mathrm{T}}\mathbf{s}_1} - \mathbf{e}_{\widetilde{\mathsf{id}},\mathsf{t}}^{\mathrm{T}}\begin{bmatrix} \mathbf{e}_1 \\ \mathbf{R}_{10}^{\mathrm{T}}\mathbf{e}_1 \\ \mathbf{R}_{11}^{\mathrm{T}}\mathbf{e}_1 \end{bmatrix}$$

$$= \mathsf{m}\lfloor\tfrac{q}{2}\rfloor + \underbrace{e_0 - \mathbf{e}_{\mathsf{id},\mathsf{t}}^{\mathrm{T}}\begin{bmatrix} \mathbf{e}_0 \\ \mathbf{R}_{00}^{\mathrm{T}}\mathbf{e}_0 \\ \mathbf{R}_{01}^{\mathrm{T}}\mathbf{e}_0 \end{bmatrix} - \mathbf{e}_{\widetilde{\mathsf{id}},\mathsf{t}}^{\mathrm{T}}\begin{bmatrix} \mathbf{e}_1 \\ \mathbf{R}_{10}^{\mathrm{T}}\mathbf{e}_1 \\ \mathbf{R}_{11}^{\mathrm{T}}\mathbf{e}_1 \end{bmatrix}}_{\text{error}}$$

According to our parameters settings, it can be checked that error is bounded by $q/5$ (i.e., $\|\text{error}\|_\infty < q/5$), thus, we have the conclusion $\lfloor\frac{2}{q}w_0\rceil = \mathsf{m}$ with an overwhelming probability.

Security: For the IND-CPA security of our scheme, we show the following theorem.

Theorem 1. *Our new lattice-based* SR-IBE *scheme in the standard model is* IND-CPA *secure if the* LWE *assumption holds.*

Proof. We define a list of games where the first one is identical to the original IND-CPA game as in Definition 2 and show that a ppt adversary $\mathcal{A}$ has advantage zero in the last game. We show that $\mathcal{A}$ cannot distinguish between these games, and thus, $\mathcal{A}$ has negligible advantage in winning the original IND-CPA game. Let id^* be a challenge identity and t^* be a challenge time period, we consider two types of adversaries:

- Type-0: An inside adversary $\mathcal{A}_0$ (e.g., a revoked user) who queries a long-term private key on the challenge identity id^*. Thus, id^* must be revoked at $\mathsf{t} \leq \mathsf{t}^*$.
- Type-1: An outside adversary $\mathcal{A}_1$ (e.g., the server) who only queries a long-term private key on $\mathsf{id} \neq \mathsf{id}^*$. In this case, $\mathcal{A}_1$ may request a short-term decryption key on $(\mathsf{id}^*, \mathsf{t})$ where $\mathsf{t} \neq \mathsf{t}^*$.

We select a bit $ty \xleftarrow{\$} \{0,1\}$ as a guess for the different types of $\mathcal{A}$, thus, we have a probability $1/2$ to simulate the game correctly. For Type-0 adversary $\mathcal{A}_0$ or Type-1 adversary $\mathcal{A}_1$, we simulate the games as follows:

Game 0. It is the original IND-CPA game defined in Definition 2.

Game 1. We slightly change the way that $\mathcal{C}$ generates $(\mathbf{A}_0, \mathbf{A}_1, \mathbf{B})$ in pp. $\mathcal{C}$ runs TrapGen(q, n, m) to obtain $\mathbf{B}$ with a trapdoor $\mathbf{R_B}$, samples $\mathbf{R}_{00}^*, \mathbf{R}_{01}^* \xleftarrow{\$} \{1, -1\}^{m \times m}$ at the setup phase, and defines $\mathbf{A}_0 = \mathbf{A}\mathbf{R}_{00}^* - \mathcal{H}(\text{id}^*)\mathbf{B} \bmod q$, $\mathbf{A}_1 = \mathbf{A}\mathbf{R}_{01}^* - \mathcal{H}(\text{t}^*)\mathbf{B} \bmod q$. For the remainders, they are unchanged and identical to those in Game 0. Next, we show that Game 0 and 1 are indistinguishable. In Game 1, $\mathbf{R}_{00}^*$ and $\mathbf{R}_{01}^*$ are adopted only in the constructions of $\mathbf{A}_0$, $\mathbf{A}_1$, $\mathbf{R}_{00}^{*\mathrm{T}}\mathbf{e}_0$, and $\mathbf{R}_{01}^{*\mathrm{T}}\mathbf{e}_0$. According to Lemma 8, $(\mathbf{A}, \mathbf{A}\mathbf{R}_{00}^*, \mathbf{R}_{00}^{*\mathrm{T}}\mathbf{e}_0)$ and $(\mathbf{A}, \mathbf{A}\mathbf{R}_{01}^*, \mathbf{R}_{01}^{*\mathrm{T}}\mathbf{e}_0)$ are statistically close to $(\mathbf{A}, \mathbf{B}_0, \mathbf{R}_{00}^{*\mathrm{T}}\mathbf{e}_0)$ and $(\mathbf{A}, \mathbf{B}_1, \mathbf{R}_{01}^{*\mathrm{T}}\mathbf{e}_0)$, respectively, where $\mathbf{B}_0, \mathbf{B}_1 \xleftarrow{\$} \mathbb{Z}_q^{n \times m}$. In $\mathcal{A}$'s view, $\mathbf{A}\mathbf{R}_{00}^*$ and $\mathbf{A}\mathbf{R}_{01}^*$ are statistically close to uniform, and thus, $\mathbf{A}_0$ and $\mathbf{A}_1$ are close to uniform. Hence, $\mathbf{A}_0$ and $\mathbf{A}_1$ in Game 1 and 0 are indistinguishable.

Game 2: We change the way that $\mathcal{C}$ selects $(\mathbf{u}_{1,\theta}, \mathbf{u}_{2,\theta})$ for each node in BT. $\mathcal{C}$ generates short vectors for a token query for path(id^*) and a time update key query for RL and t^* as follows:

- If $ty = 0$, we simulate the game for adversary $\mathcal{A}_0$ of Type-0. $\mathbf{u}_{1,\theta}$ and $\mathbf{u}_{2,\theta}$ for each node in BT are generated as follows:
    - For $\theta \in \text{path}(\text{id}^*)$, sample $\mathbf{e}_{\text{id}^*,\theta} \xleftarrow{\$} \mathcal{D}_{\mathbb{Z}^{2m},s}$, set $\mathbf{u}_{1,\theta} = \mathbf{A}_{\text{id}^*}\mathbf{e}_{\text{id}^*,\theta} \bmod q$ and $\mathbf{u}_{2,\theta} = \mathbf{u} - \mathbf{u}_{1,\theta}$.
    - For $\theta \notin \text{path}(\text{id}^*)$, sample $\mathbf{e}_{\text{t}^*,\theta} \xleftarrow{\$} \mathcal{D}_{\mathbb{Z}^{2m},s}$, set $\mathbf{u}_{2,\theta} = \mathbf{A}_{\text{t}^*}\mathbf{e}_{\text{t}^*,\theta} \bmod q$ and $\mathbf{u}_{1,\theta} = \mathbf{u} - \mathbf{u}_{2,\theta}$.

  Because identity id^* must be revoked before (or at) the time update key query for time period t^*, we have path$(\text{id}^*) \cap$ KUNodes(BT, RL, t^*) = $\emptyset$. In addition, let $\mathbf{A}_{\widetilde{\text{id}^*}} = [\mathbf{A} | \mathbf{A}\mathbf{R}_{00}^* + (\mathcal{H}(\widetilde{\text{id}^*}) - \mathcal{H}(\text{id}^*))\mathbf{B}]$, and due to the main property of FRD, $\mathcal{H}(\widetilde{\text{id}^*}) - \mathcal{H}(\text{id}^*)$ is full-rank and $\mathbf{R_B}$ is also a trapdoor for $\Lambda_q^{\perp}((\mathcal{H}(\widetilde{\text{id}^*}) - \mathcal{H}(\text{id}^*))\mathbf{B})$, thus, $\mathcal{C}$ can respond the long-term decryption key query for id^* by running the first two steps of SampleRight$(\mathbf{A}, (\mathcal{H}(\widetilde{\text{id}^*}) - \mathcal{H}(\text{id}^*))\mathbf{B}, \mathbf{R}_{00}^*, \mathbf{R_B})$ to return a short trapdoor $\mathbf{R}_{\mathbf{A}_{\widetilde{\text{id}^*}}}$ for $\Lambda_q^{\perp}(\mathbf{A}_{\widetilde{\text{id}^*}})$. In particular, $\mathcal{C}$ should respond a token query for identity id^* with $(\theta, \mathbf{e}_{\text{id}^*,\theta})_{\theta \in \text{path}(\text{id}^*)}$, and a time update key query for time period t^* with $(\theta, \mathbf{e}_{\text{t}^*,\theta})_{\theta \in \text{KUNodes}(BT,RL,\text{t}^*)}$.

- If $ty = 1$, we simulate the game for $\mathcal{A}_1$ of Type-1, firstly sample $\mathbf{e}_{\text{t}^*,\theta} \xleftarrow{\$} \mathcal{D}_{\mathbb{Z}^{2m},s}$, and set $\mathbf{u}_{2,\theta} = \mathbf{A}_{\text{t}^*}\mathbf{e}_{\text{t}^*,\theta} \bmod q$ and $\mathbf{u}_{1,\theta} = \mathbf{u} - \mathbf{u}_{2,\theta}$. Because id^* is never queried, $\mathcal{C}$ should respond a time update key query for time period t^* with $(\theta, \mathbf{e}_{\text{t}^*,\theta})_{\theta \in \text{KUNodes}(BT,RL,\text{t}^*)}$, and a short-term decryption key by running SampleLeft$(\mathbf{A}_{\widetilde{\text{id}},\text{t}}, \mathbf{R}_{\mathbf{A}_{\widetilde{\text{id}}}}, \mathbf{u}, s)$ to return a short vector $\mathbf{e}_{\widetilde{\text{id}},\text{t}}$.

For the remainders, they are unchanged. Because $\mathbf{A}_{\text{id}^*}$ and $\mathbf{A}_{\text{t}^*}$ can be viewed as two random matrices over $\mathbb{Z}_q^{n \times 2m}$, and according to Lemma 1, $\mathbf{u}_{1,\theta}$ (or

$\mathbf{u}_{2,\theta}$) is statistically close to uniform. Hence, $\mathcal{A}$ cannot distinguish the above two types simulated by $\mathcal{C}$, and thus, we have a probability $1/2$ to simulate the game correctly. Once a correct game is simulated, Game 1 and 2 are indistinguishable.

Game 3: We redesign $\mathbf{A}$. $\mathcal{C}$ samples $\mathbf{A} \xleftarrow{\$} \mathbb{Z}_q^{n \times m}$. Let $\mathbf{A}_{\mathsf{id}} = [\mathbf{A}|\mathbf{A}\mathbf{R}_{00}^* + (\mathcal{H}(\mathsf{id}) - \mathcal{H}(\mathsf{id}^*))\mathbf{B}] \in \mathbb{Z}_q^{n \times 2m}$ and $\mathbf{A}_{\mathsf{t}} = [\mathbf{A}|\mathbf{A}\mathbf{R}_{01}^* + (\mathcal{H}(\mathsf{t}) - \mathcal{H}(\mathsf{t}^*))\mathbf{B}] \in \mathbb{Z}_q^{n \times 2m}$. Due to a main property of FRD, $\mathcal{H}(\mathsf{id}) - \mathcal{H}(\mathsf{id}^*)$ and $\mathcal{H}(\mathsf{t}) - \mathcal{H}(\mathsf{t}^*)$ are full-rank, and $\mathbf{R_B}$ is a trapdoor for $\Lambda_q^\perp((\mathcal{H}(\mathsf{id}) - \mathcal{H}(\mathsf{id}^*))\mathbf{B})$ (and $\Lambda_q^\perp((\mathcal{H}(\mathsf{t}) - \mathcal{H}(\mathsf{t}^*))\mathbf{B}))$. $\mathcal{C}$ responds a token query for any $\mathsf{id} \neq \mathsf{id}^*$ by running $\mathsf{SampleRight}(\mathbf{A}, (\mathcal{H}(\mathsf{id}) - \mathcal{H}(\mathsf{id}^*))\mathbf{B}, \mathbf{R}_{00}^*, \mathbf{R_B}, \mathbf{u}_{1,\theta}, s)$ that returns $\mathbf{e}_{\mathsf{id},\theta}$, and a time update key query for any id and $\mathsf{t} \neq \mathsf{t}^*$ by running $\mathsf{SampleRight}(\mathbf{A}, (\mathcal{H}(\mathsf{t}) - \mathcal{H}(\mathsf{t}^*))\mathbf{B}, \mathbf{R}_{01}^*, \mathbf{R_B}, \mathbf{u}_{2,\theta}, s)$ that returns $\mathbf{e}_{\mathsf{t},\theta}$. Let $\mathbf{A}_{\widetilde{\mathsf{id}}} = [\mathbf{A}|\mathbf{A}\mathbf{R}_{00}^* + (\mathcal{H}(\widetilde{\mathsf{id}}) - \mathcal{H}(\mathsf{id}^*))\mathbf{B}]$, $\mathcal{C}$ responds a long-term private key query for identity $\mathsf{id} \neq \mathsf{id}^*$ by running the first two steps of $\mathsf{SampleRight}(\mathbf{A}, (\mathcal{H}(\mathsf{id}) - \mathcal{H}(\mathsf{id}^*))\mathbf{B}, \mathbf{R}_{00}^*, \mathbf{R_B}, \mathbf{u}_{1,\theta}, s)$ that returns a short trapdoor $\mathbf{R}_{\mathbf{A}_{\widetilde{\mathsf{id}}}}$ for $\Lambda_q^\perp(\mathbf{A}_{\widetilde{\mathsf{id}}})$. Additionally, the parameter $s = \widetilde{\mathcal{O}}(\sqrt{m})$ is sufficiently large, and according to Lemmas 5 and 7, $(\mathbf{e}_{\mathsf{id},\theta}, \mathbf{R}_{\widetilde{\mathsf{id}}})$ and $\mathbf{e}_{\mathsf{t},\theta}$ are statistically close to those in Game 2. For the remainders, they are unchanged. Because $\mathbf{A}$ is statistically close to that in Game 2, $\mathcal{A}$'s advantage in Game 3 is at most negligibly different from that in Game 2.

Game 4: We redesign the partial challenge ciphertext $(c_0^*, \mathbf{c}_0^*, \mathbf{c}_1^*)$ and the remainders are unchanged. $\mathcal{C}$ samples $c_0^* \xleftarrow{\$} \mathbb{Z}_q$, $\mathbf{c}_0^*, \mathbf{c}_1^* \xleftarrow{\$} \mathbb{Z}_q^{3m}$. Because these items are random, the advantage of $\mathcal{A}$ in returning a correct message m is zero.

Next, we give a reduction from the LWE problem to show that Game 3 and 4 are computationally indistinguishable for a ppt adversary.

A reduction from LWE: Assume that there is a ppt adversary $\mathcal{A}$ distinguishing Game 3 and 4 with non-negligible advantage, then we adopt $\mathcal{A}$ to design an algorithm $\mathcal{B}$ solving the LWE problem defined in Definition 4.

Given an LWE instance, a fresh pair $(\mathbf{a}_i, b_i) \in \mathbb{Z}_q^n \times \mathbb{Z}_q$ for $i = 1, 2, \cdots, m+1$, from a sampling oracle, which is truly random $\mathcal{R}_\$ $ or noisy pseudo-random $\mathcal{R}_\mathbf{s}$ for a secret vector $\mathbf{s} \in \mathbb{Z}_q^n$, the target of $\mathcal{B}$ is to distinguish between the two oracles by utilizing $\mathcal{A}$. Due to the limited space, we omit the rest proofs of Theorem 1, if any necessary, please contact the corresponding author for the full version.

4   Conclusion

In this paper, we propose a new lattice-based SR-IBE and simplify the construction of the first lattice-based SR-IBE introduced by Nguyen et al.. A tool called "leveled ciphertexts" is adopted to enable constant ciphertext and the simplified encryptions, that is, not linear in the length of a user identity and without burdensome double encryption mechanism, which serves as a more effective solution to the challenge in turning pairing-based instantiation of SR-IBE into lattices.

Acknowledgements. The authors thank the anonymous reviewers of ProvSec 2022 for their helpful comments and this research was supported by Natural Science Foundation of Henan Province (No. 222300420371) and Key Scientific Research Projects of Colleges and Universities in Henan Province (No. 22A520047).

References

1. Agrawal, S., Boneh, D., Boyen, X.: Efficient lattice (H)IBE in the standard model. In: Gilbert, H. (ed.) EUROCRYPT 2010. LNCS, vol. 6110, pp. 553–572. Springer, Heidelberg (2010). https://doi.org/10.1007/978-3-642-13190-5_28
2. Ajtai, M.: Generating hard instances of lattice problems (Extended Abstract). In: STOC, pp. 99–108. ACM (1996) https://doi.org/10.1145/237814.237838
3. Alwen, J., Peikert, C.: Generating shorter bases for hard random lattices. Theor. Comput. Sys. **48**(3), 535–553 (2011). https://doi.org/10.1007/s00224-010-9278-3
4. Boldyreva, A., Goyal, V., Kumar, V.: Identity-based encryption with efficient revocation. In: CCS, pp. 417–426. ACM (2008). https://doi.org/10.1145/1455770.1455823
5. Boneh, D., Franklin, M.: Identity-based encryption from the weil pairing. In: Kilian, J. (ed.) CRYPTO 2001. LNCS, vol. 2139, pp. 213–229. Springer, Heidelberg (2001). https://doi.org/10.1007/3-540-44647-8_13
6. Cash, D., Hofheinz, D., Kiltz, E., Peikert, C.: Bonsai trees, or how to delegate a lattice basis. In: Gilbert, H. (ed.) EUROCRYPT 2010. LNCS, vol. 6110, pp. 523–552. Springer, Heidelberg (2010). https://doi.org/10.1007/978-3-642-13190-5_27
7. Chen, J., Lim, H.W., Ling, S., Wang, H., Nguyen, K.: Revocable identity-based encryption from lattices. In: Susilo, W., Mu, Y., Seberry, J. (eds.) ACISP 2012. LNCS, vol. 7372, pp. 390–403. Springer, Heidelberg (2012). https://doi.org/10.1007/978-3-642-31448-3_29
8. Gentry, C., Peikert, C., Vaikuntanathan, V.: Trapdoor for hard lattices and new cryptographic constructions. In: STOC, pp. 197–206. ACM (2008). https://doi.org/10.1145/1374376.1374407
9. Hu, Z., Li, S., Chen, K., et al.: Revocable identity-based encryption and server-aided revocable IBE from the computational diffie-hellman assumption. Cryptography **2**(4), 33 (2018). https://doi.org/10.3390/cryptography2040033
10. Katsumata, S., Matsuda, T., Takayasu, A.: Lattice-based revocable (Hierarchical) IBE with decryption key exposure resistance. In: Lin, D., Sako, K. (eds.) PKC 2019. LNCS, vol. 11443, pp. 441–471. Springer, Cham (2019). https://doi.org/10.1007/978-3-030-17259-6_15
11. Lee, K.: A generic construction for revocable identity-based encryption with subset difference methods. PLoS One, **15**(9), e0239053 (2020)
12. Libert, B., Vergnaud, D.: Adaptive-ID secure revocable identity-based encryption. In: Fischlin, M. (ed.) CT-RSA 2009. LNCS, vol. 5473, pp. 1–15. Springer, Heidelberg (2009). https://doi.org/10.1007/978-3-642-00862-7_1
13. Liu, Y., Sun, Y.: Generic construction of server-aided revocable hierarchical identity-based encryption. In: Wu, Y., Yung, M. (eds.) Inscrypt 2020. LNCS, vol. 12612, pp. 73–82. Springer, Cham (2021). https://doi.org/10.1007/978-3-030-71852-7_5
14. Ma, X., Lin, D.: Generic constructions of revocable identity-based encryption. In: Liu, Z., Yung, M. (eds.) Inscrypt 2019. LNCS, vol. 12020, pp. 381–396. Springer, Cham (2020). https://doi.org/10.1007/978-3-030-42921-8_22

15. Micciancio, D., Peikert, C.: Trapdoors for lattices: simpler, tighter, faster, smaller. In: Pointcheval, D., Johansson, T. (eds.) EUROCRYPT 2012. LNCS, vol. 7237, pp. 700–718. Springer, Heidelberg (2012). https://doi.org/10.1007/978-3-642-29011-4_41

16. Nguyen, K., Wang, H., Zhang, J.: Server-aided revocable identity-based encryption from lattices. In: Foresti, S., Persiano, G. (eds.) CANS 2016. LNCS, vol. 10052, pp. 107–123. Springer, Cham (2016). https://doi.org/10.1007/978-3-319-48965-0_7

17. Qin, B., Deng, R.H., Li, Y., Liu, S.: Server-aided revocable identity-based encryption. In: Pernul, G., Ryan, P.Y.A., Weippl, E. (eds.) ESORICS 2015. LNCS, vol. 9326, pp. 286–304. Springer, Cham (2015). https://doi.org/10.1007/978-3-319-24174-6_15

18. Regev, O.: On lattices, learning with errors, random linear codes, and cryptography. In: STOC, pp. 84–93. ACM (2005)

19. Seo, J.H., Emura, K.: Revocable identity-based encryption revisited: security model and construction. In: Kurosawa, K., Hanaoka, G. (eds.) PKC 2013. LNCS, vol. 7778, pp. 216–234. Springer, Heidelberg (2013). https://doi.org/10.1007/978-3-642-36362-7_14

20. Shamir, A.: Identity-based cryptosystems and signature schemes. In: Blakley, G.R., Chaum, D. (eds.) CRYPTO 1984. LNCS, vol. 196, pp. 47–53. Springer, Heidelberg (1985). https://doi.org/10.1007/3-540-39568-7_5

21. Sun, Y., Mu, Y., Susilo, W., et al.: Revocable identity-based encryption with server-aided ciphertext evolution. Theor. Comput. Sci. **2020**(815), 11–24 (2020)

22. Takayasu, A.: Adaptively secure lattice-based revocable IBE in the QROM: compact parameters, tight security, and anonymity. Des. Codes Cryptogr. (2021). https://doi.org/10.1007/s10623-021-00895-3

23. Takayasu, A., Watanabe, Y.: Lattice-based revocable identity-based encryption with bounded decryption key exposure resistance. In: Pieprzyk, J., Suriadi, S. (eds.) ACISP 2017. LNCS, vol. 10342, pp. 184–204. Springer, Cham (2017). https://doi.org/10.1007/978-3-319-60055-0_10

24. Wang, S., Zhang, J., He, J., Wang, H., Li, C.: Simplified revocable hierarchical identity-based encryption from lattices. In: Mu, Y., Deng, R.H., Huang, X. (eds.) CANS 2019. LNCS, vol. 11829, pp. 99–119. Springer, Cham (2019). https://doi.org/10.1007/978-3-030-31578-8_6

25. Zhang, Y., Liu, X., Hu, Y., Jia, H.: Revocable identity-based encryption with server-aided ciphertext evolution from lattices. In: Yu, Yu., Yung, M. (eds.) Inscrypt 2021. LNCS, vol. 13007, pp. 442–465. Springer, Cham (2021). https://doi.org/10.1007/978-3-030-88323-2_24

Lattice-Based Public Key Cryptosystems Invoking Linear Mapping Mask

Yuntao Wang[1]([☒]) [ID], Yasuhiko Ikematsu[2] [ID], and Takanori Yasuda[3] [ID]

[1] Graduate School of Engineering, Osaka University, Suita, Japan
wang@comm.eng.osaka-u.ac.jp
[2] Institute of Mathematics for Industry, Kyushu University, Fukuoka, Japan
ikematsu@imi.kyushu-u.ac.jp
[3] Institute for the Advancement of Higher Education,
Okayama University of Science, Okayama, Japan
tyasuda@ous.ac.jp

Abstract. In ProvSec 2018, Yasuda proposed a multivariate public key cryptosystem using the pq-method, whose security is based on the constrained MQ problem. Afterward, in SCIS 2020, he improved the cryptosystem by adding noise elements and simultaneously considered the cryptanalysis using the NTRU method. This improved cryptosystem is the first one combining lattice and multivariate public-key cryptosystem. In this paper, we propose three variants of Yasuda's cryptosystem. The main improvement is that we invite the linear structures instead of the multivariate quadratic polynomials. In particular, we simplify the procedure in key generation mechanism by using a linear mapping mask which produces resistance against the key-recovery attack. Furthermore, we propose a ring version that is quite efficient compared to the standard versions. Finally, we adopt the ring-LWE method instead of the original NTRU method to give a more promising cryptanalysis.

Keywords: Post-Quantum Cryptography · Lattice · Public key cryptography

1 Introduction

Nowadays, the security of modern public-key cryptographic schemes, such as RSA, ECC, DSA, ElGamal, and Diffie-Hellman key exchange, are based on number theoretic hard problems such as integer factorization problem (IFP), discrete logarithm problem (DLP) and their elliptic curve variants in certain groups, etc. With elaborately chosen parameters and implementations, the above cryptographic schemes are temporarily secure against current computing resources. However, it is known that overwhelming computing power is available by a quantum computer compared to classic computers. By coordinating with Shor's quantum algorithm [19], most of the above crypto algorithms are vulnerable to being broken in polynomial time by a sufficiently powerful quantum computer in the near future. Since the above cryptosystems are widely deployed in real-world applications (e.g., IoT, HTTPS, online banking, cryptocurrency, software, etc.), developing secure and practical next-generation cryptographic algorithms is urgent. The well-known "post-quantum cryptography" (PQC) is highly expected to withstand outstanding quantum attacks. Actually, some international standards organizations such as NIST, ISO, and IETF already started the PQC standardization projects several years ago. They mainly focus on three primitives: Public-Key Encryption algorithms (PKE), the Key Encapsulation Mechanism (KEM), and the digital signature schemes. Among the several categories, lattice-based cryptography is considered a promising contender for its robust security strength, comparative light communication cost, desirable efficiency, and excellent adaptation capabilities [1]. Indeed, three over four PKE/KEM/signature algorithms are lattice-based candidates in PQC standardization announced by NIST in 2022 [2]. Further, four PKE/KEM algorithms are selected for the fourth-round candidate finalists.

The Multivariate Public-Key Cryptography (MPKC) is also one important component in PQC, where there is one multivariate scheme among three digital signature candidates in the third-round finalists [2]. The security of MPKC is based on the hardness of solving Multivariate Quadratic polynomials (MQ) problems. On the one side, the MPKC signature scheme is efficient due to conducting in a small number field. On the other side, MPKC is generally not adaptable for PKE due to its larger key length compared to other categories. For instance, some encryption schemes such as Simple Matrix Scheme [22], EFC [21], and HFERP [13] have been proposed these years. All these cryptosystems are suffering from a common and critical shortcoming: a large number of variables are required for a relatively secure level but incur a higher cost for encryption and decryption. One method to overcome this shortcoming is constructing trapdoor one-way functions given by injective polynomial maps. However, it is observed that one can turn a polynomial map injective easily by adding a restriction on its definition range. Namely, by using a constrained polynomial map, it is easy to construct an injective trapdoor one-way function. As a result, this function can be used to construct secure MPKC encryption schemes whose security is based on the hardness of solving the constrained multivariate polynomial problem.

It is known that the key sizes or the ciphertext sizes of MPKC or lattice-based cryptography are usually larger than twice the sizes conducted in most classical public key crypto schemes in cases of AES-128 bit security. However, due to the security of the latter being based on some number of theoretical problems, the computation cost takes more than the former securely based on the algebraic problems. In ProvSec2018, Yasuda proposed a multivariate PKE using the so-called pq-method [27]. The security of pq-method is based on the difficulty of solving the constrained MQ problem which is a hard problem in MPKC. Substantially, the constrained MQ problem can be seen as a quadratic version of the Inhomogeneous Short Integer Solution (ISIS) problem in lattice theory as well. For this reason, the cryptosystem using pq-method is considered the first PKE combining lattice and MPKC. In order to reduce the size of the public key, Yasuda further improved the pq-method by inviting an error term in the encryption phase [28]. This idea is from the classical Learning with Error (LWE) problem in lattice theory which has been widely used in lattice-based cryptography [17]. The improved version of pq-method is named by pqe-method.

1.1   Motivations and Contributions

Motivations. The combination of an MPKC and lattice-based cryptography is a novel idea that may derive some benefits from the aspects of both computational cost and security: on the one side, the linear algebraic structure in lattice may provide a desirable efficiency and comparative communication cost, while cryptanalysis is challenging to handle due to a lack of thoroughgoing grasp of lattice (reduction) algorithms; on the other side, MPKC holds robust security but requires more variables resulting in relatively lower efficiency. Particularly, solving quadratic polynomials in MPKC obviously takes more effort than dealing with linear polynomials in lattice. This circumstance occurs in both mentioned above pq-method and the pqe-method, where we consider proposed methods that enjoy the lattice's fast computation and low cost and further strengthen their security from MPKC.

Contributions. We list the following contributions in this paper. Here, n is the number of variables, and p, q are moduli in the schemes.

- First, we improve the pq-method and the pqe-method by using linear structures instead of the quadratic polynomials, which we call linear-pq method and linear-pqe method, respectively. Due to different cryptanalysis, it is difficult to directly compare the keysize and ciphertext size between the improved crypto schemes and the original ones. Nevertheless, we can see the results by comparing the inside parameters used in each scheme. We summarize the parameter size and the polynomial multiplication cost in the following table.

	original pq method	linear-pq method	original pqe method	linear-pqe method
q	$O(n^4 p^6)$	$O(n^2 p^4)$	$O(n^4 p^6)$	$O(n^2 p^5)$
computational cost	$O(n^4)$	$O(n^2 \log n)$	$O(n^4)$	$O(n^2 \log n)$

- Moreover, applying a linear mapping mask at the end of key generation can strengthen the security against the key-recovery attack using the property of MPKC.
- Additionally, we propose a ring version of the linear-pqe method. As a result, the key size and computational cost are substantially reduced by a factor of $1/n$, which makes it the most efficient with the smallest key size among the three proposals.
- The security parameters are evaluated by the ring-LWE method rather than the original NTRU method.

1.2   Organization

Section 2 recalls the notations and background, including some hard problems in lattice theory and multivariate polynomial theory. In particular, the predecessor of our proposals is introduced in this section. Then, we introduce our proposed public key encryption algorithms in Sect. 3. In Sect. 4, we estimate the security parameters with respect to AES-128 bit security using the 2016 estimate which is commonly used in cryptanalysis for lattice-based cryptosystems. We also evaluate the size of keys and ciphertext, and show the practical performance of each proposal. Finally, we conclude our work in Sect. 5.

2   Preliminaries

In this section, we prepare some mathematical notations used in the paper. Then we recall the computational problems associated with lattices and multivariate polynomials. At last, we review the pq-method [27] and the pqe-method [28] proposed by Yasuda, respectively.

Notations. Let m, n and l be positive integers ($\in \mathbb{Z}_{>0}$). The set $[m]$ means $\{1, \ldots, m\}$. Denote by $\mathbb{Z}_l$ the residue ring modulo l, i.e. the elements in $\mathbb{Z}_l$ are from 0 to $l-1$. For an element $a \in \mathbb{Z}_l$, we define a list function of a by $\mathrm{lift}_l(a) \in I_l$ where $I_l := (-l/2, l/2] \cap \mathbb{Z}$. Simultaneously, we denote a finite field $\mathbb{F}_q$ with q a prime number. We represent n independent variables of $x_{i \in [n]}$ by a row vector of $\mathbf{x} = (x_1, \ldots, x_n)$. The set of polynomials with variables in $\mathbf{x}$ and coefficients in $\mathbb{F}_q$ is denoted by $\mathbb{F}_q[\mathbf{x}]$. Then, we prepare a sequence of m (upper triangular) matrices $A_1, \ldots, A_m \in \mathbb{F}_q^{n \times n}$, m row vectors $\mathbf{b}_1, \ldots, \mathbf{b}_m \in \mathbb{F}_q^n$, and m constants $c_1, \ldots, c_m \in \mathbb{F}_q$. By using the above notations, we define a quadratic polynomial system in $\mathbb{F}_q[\mathbf{x}]^m$ as $\mathcal{F}(\mathbf{x}) := \{f_i(\mathbf{x}) := \mathbf{x} A_i \mathbf{x}^T + \mathbf{b}_i \mathbf{x}^T + c_i := \sum_{j,k \in [n]} a_{ijk} x_j x_k + \sum_{j \in [n]} b_{ij} x_j + c_i \ (\mod q)\}_{i \in [m]}$. For the sake of convenience, we write its vector form by $\mathcal{F}(\mathbf{x}) = (f_1(\mathbf{x}), \ldots, f_m(\mathbf{x})) \in \mathbb{F}_q[\mathbf{x}]^m$ in this paper. Moreover, we define $\mathtt{NextPrime}(x)$ the first prime number no smaller than $x \in \mathbb{R}$.

2.1   Lattice

Lattice. A *lattice* L is generated by a *basis* B which is a set of linearly independent vectors $\mathbf{b}_1, \ldots, \mathbf{b}_n$ in $\mathbb{R}^m$: $L(\mathbf{b}_1, \ldots, \mathbf{b}_n) = \{\sum_{i=1}^n x_i \mathbf{b}_i, x_i \in \mathbb{Z}\}$. Note that in this paper we use integer lattices for convenience and we write the basis in a matrix form as $B = (\mathbf{b}_1, \ldots, \mathbf{b}_n) \in \mathbb{Z}^{m \times n}$. The integer n is the *rank* of the lattice, which equals to the *dimension* of the vector space spanned by L, i.e. $n = \dim(\mathrm{span}(L))$. It is called *full-rank* lattice when $m = n$.

The *Euclidean norm* of a lattice vector $\mathbf{v} \in \mathbb{R}^m$, also known as l_2-norm, is $\|\mathbf{v}\| := \sqrt{\mathbf{v} \cdot \mathbf{v}}$. There are at least two non-zero vectors with the same minimal Euclidean norm but contrary sign in a lattice L with basis $B = (\mathbf{b}_1, \mathbf{b}_2, \ldots, \mathbf{b}_n)$: this norm is called the *1-st successive minimum* $\lambda_1(L)$ of $L(B)$. A *shortest vector* of L is of norm $\lambda_1(L)$.

The Shortest Vector Problem. Given a basis $B = (\mathbf{b}_1, \ldots, \mathbf{b}_n)$ of a lattice L, the *Shortest Vector Problem* asks to find a non-zero shortest vector in L. SVP is NP-hard for randomized reductions.

Unique Shortest Vector Problem. The *Unique SVP Problem* (uSVP) is for a given lattice L which satisfies $\lambda_1(L) \ll \lambda_2(L)$, to find the shortest nonzero vector in L. It is called γ *Unique SVP problem* if the gap of $\lambda_2(L)/\lambda_1(L) = \gamma$ is known.

Inhomogeneous Short Integer Solution Problem. Given an integer q, a matrix $\mathbf{A} \in \mathbb{Z}_q^{n \times m}$ and a vector $\mathbf{v} \in \mathbb{Z}_q^n$, *Inhomogeneous Short Integer Solution Problem* is to compute a short vector $\mathbf{y} \in \mathcal{B}$ s.t. $\mathbf{Ay} \equiv \mathbf{v}$ (mod q), where $\mathcal{B}$ is a set of short vectors with some Euclidean norm bound.

Learning with Errors (LWE) Problem [17]. There are four parameters in the LWE problem: the number of samples $m \in \mathbb{Z}$, the length $n \in \mathbb{Z}$ of secret vector, modulo $q \in \mathbb{Z}$ and the standard deviation $\sigma \in \mathbb{R}_{>0}$ for the discrete Gaussian distribution $D_{\mathbb{Z}^n, \sigma}$. Sample a matrix $\mathbf{A} \in \mathbb{Z}_q^{m \times n}$ and a secret vector $\mathbf{s} \in \mathbb{Z}_q^n$ uniformly at random, and randomly sample a relatively small perturbation vector $\mathbf{e} \in \mathbb{Z}_q^m$ from Gaussian distribution $D_{\mathbb{Z}^n, \sigma}$, i.e. $\mathbf{e} \xleftarrow{\$} D_{\mathbb{Z}^n, \sigma}$. The LWE distribution $\varPsi$ is constructed by pairs $(\mathbf{A}, \mathbf{b} \equiv \mathbf{As} + \mathbf{e} \pmod{q}) \in (\mathbb{Z}_q^{m \times n}, \mathbb{Z}_q^m)$ sampled as above. The search *learning with errors problem* (LWE problem) is for a given pair $(\mathbf{A}, \mathbf{b})$ sampled from LWE distribution $\varPsi$, to compute the pair $(\mathbf{s}, \mathbf{e})$. The decision version of LWE problem asks to distinguish if the given pair $(\mathbf{A}, \mathbf{b})$ is sampled from LWE or uniform distribution. The proof of equivalent hardness between these two versions is given in the original LWE paper [17].

Ring Learning With Errors (Ring-LWE) Problem [14]. Let $m \geq 1$ be a power of 2 and $q \geq 2$ be an integer. Let $R_q = \mathbb{Z}_q[x]/\Phi_m(x)$, where $\Phi(x)$ is an irreducible polynomial with degree n. Let χ be a β-bounded distribution. For secret polynomial $\mathbf{s} \xleftarrow{\$} R_q$ and error polynomial $\mathbf{e} \xleftarrow{\$} \chi$, choosing $\mathbf{a} \in R_q$ uniformly at random, output $(\mathbf{a}, \mathbf{b} = \mathbf{a} \cdot \mathbf{s} + \mathbf{e}) \in (R_q, R_q)$. The search version of *ring learning with errors problem* (Ring-LWE problem) is: for $\mathbf{s} \xleftarrow{\$} R_q$, given $poly(n)$ number of samples of $(\mathbf{a}, \mathbf{b} = \mathbf{a} \cdot \mathbf{s} + \mathbf{e}) \in (R_q, R_q)$, find $\mathbf{s}$ (and $\mathbf{e}$ simultaneously).

2.2   Multivariate Public Key Cryptography (MPKC)

In this subsection, we introduce the MP/MQ problems and their constrained variants used as security bases in MPKC.

Multivariate Polynomial Problem. Given a polynomial system of $\mathcal{F}(\mathbf{x}) \in \mathbb{F}_q[\mathbf{x}]^m$ with n variables and m polynomials, the *multivariate polynomial problem* (MP problem) is to find a solution of $\mathbf{x}_0 = (x_{01}, \ldots, x_{0n}) \in \mathbb{F}_q^n$ such that $\mathcal{F}(\mathbf{x}_0) = \mathbf{0}$. The hardness of MP problem is proven to be NP-complete [11].

Constrained Multivariate Polynomial Problem [27]. Given a bound parameter $L \in \mathbb{Z}_{>0}$ and a polynomial system of $\mathcal{F}(\mathbf{x}) \in \mathbb{F}_q[\mathbf{x}]^m$ with n variables and m polynomials, the *constrained multivariate polynomial problem* (constrained-MP problem) asks to find a solution of $\mathbf{x}_0 = (x_{01}, \ldots, x_{0n}) \in I_L^n$ such that $\mathcal{F}(\mathbf{x}_0) = \mathbf{0}$.

When only quadratic polynomials are used in the MP problem (or the constrained MP problem), the problem is called the MQ problem (or the constrained MQ problem, respectively). Namely, the more specific MQ problem and constrained-MQ problem being used in multivariate public key cryptography are the versions invoking quadratic polynomials in the MP problem and Constrained-MP problem, respectively.

Common Construction of Quadratic MPKC Based on MQ Problem. Let n, m be two integers and q be a prime number. In a quadratic MPKC, the secret keys include an invertible quadratic map $F : \mathbb{F}_q^n[\mathbf{x}] \to \mathbb{F}_q^m[\mathbf{x}]$ and two affine maps of $S : \mathbb{F}_q^n[\mathbf{x}] \to \mathbb{F}_q^n[\mathbf{x}]$ and $T : \mathbb{F}_q^m[\mathbf{x}] \to \mathbb{F}_q^m[\mathbf{x}]$; the public key is bipolar structure with a composition $P = S \circ F \circ T : \mathbb{F}_q^n[\mathbf{x}] \to \mathbb{F}_q^m[\mathbf{x}]$. A plaintext $\mathbf{m} \in \mathbb{F}_q^n$ is encrypted by $\mathbf{c} = P(\mathbf{m})$; and $\mathbf{c}$ can be decrypted by $\mathbf{m} = T^{-1}(F^{-1}(S^{-1}(\mathbf{c}))$. The security of MPKC is based on the assumption that P is hard to invert without the secret keys. Matsumoto and Imai initially proposed the crypto scheme based on MP problem in EUROCRYPT'88 [15]. However, it was broken by Patarin in CRYPTO'95 [16].

2.3   MPKC Using pq-method and pqe-method

First, we recap the cryptosystem using the pq-method proposed by Yasuda in [27]. Refer to the original paper for more details of the regime constructing the multivariate polynomial trapdoor function system $G(\mathbf{x})$.

- **Key Generation:**
  Let p be an odd prime number, n be a positive integer, and l_ψ be a positive odd integer.
  1) Randomly sample a multivariate quadratic polynomial system $\Phi(\mathbf{x}) \in \mathbb{Z}[\mathbf{x}]^n$. Here $\Phi(\mathbf{x})$ mod p is (almost) injective, and its inverse can be computed efficiently.
  2) Make a quadratic multivariate polynomial system $\Psi(\mathbf{x}) \in \mathbb{Z}[\mathbf{x}]^n$ with coefficients sampled from I_{l_ψ} uniformly at random. (Note that $I_{l_\psi} = (-l_\psi/2, l_\psi/2] \cap \mathbb{Z}$)
  3) Choose a prime number q satisfying $q > 4M_\psi M_\phi$, where

$$M_\psi \geq \max_{i \in [n]} \left\{ |\psi_i(\mathbf{d})| \,\middle|\, \mathbf{d} \in I_p^n \right\},$$
$$M_\phi \geq \max_{i \in [n]} \left\{ |\phi_i(\mathbf{d})| \,\middle|\, \mathbf{d} \in I_p^n \right\}. \tag{1}$$

  4) Select a series of integers $r_1, \ldots, r_n$ in the range of (M_ϕ, q) satisfying $2M_\phi < \min_{k \in [2M_\psi]} |\text{lift}_q(r_i k)|_{i \in [n]}$. Go back to Step 3 if it failed to sample such $r_1, \ldots, r_n$. Here we denote by $\Lambda_i = \{\text{lift}_q(r_i k) | k = 0, \pm 1, \ldots, \pm M_\psi\}$.
  5) Compute $\Psi_R(\mathbf{x}) = (r_1\psi_1(\mathbf{x}), \ldots, r_n\psi_n(\mathbf{x})) \in \mathbb{Z}[\mathbf{x}]^n$, and $G(\mathbf{x}) = (g_1(\mathbf{x}), \ldots, g_n(\mathbf{x})) = (\Phi(\mathbf{x}) + \Psi_R(\mathbf{x}))$ mod $q \in \mathbb{F}_q[\mathbf{x}]^n$.

6) Randomly sample an affine transformation T on $\mathbb{F}_q^n$; randomly sample a permutation matrix S of size n.

7) Compute $F = T \circ G \circ S : \mathbb{Z}^n \to \mathbb{F}_q^n$.

   Secret key: $\Phi(\mathbf{x}) \mod p$, $\{r_i\}_{i \in [n]}$, T and S;

   Public key: p and $F(\mathbf{x})$.

- **Encryption:**

  Given a plaintext $\mathbf{m} \in I_p^n$, compute the ciphertext $\mathbf{c} = F(\mathbf{m}) \in \mathbb{F}_q^n$.

- **Decryption:**

  1) Compute $\mathbf{c}' = (c_1', \ldots, c_n') = T^{-1}(\mathbf{c})$.

  2) Find a (unique) $\lambda_i \in \Lambda_i$ such that $|\mathrm{lift}_q(c_i' - \lambda_i)| < M_\phi$ for all $i \in [n]$. Set $\tilde{c}_i = \mathrm{lift}_q(c_i' - \lambda_i) \in \mathbb{Z}$.

  3) Calculate the solution $\tilde{\mathbf{b}} \in I_p^n$ of the equations $\Phi(\mathbf{x}) \equiv (\tilde{c}_1, \ldots, \tilde{c}_n) \mod p$.

  4) Compute $\mathbf{m}' = S^{-1}(\tilde{\mathbf{b}})$ which matches with the plaintext $\mathbf{m}$.

In SCIS 2020 [28], Yasuda further improved the pq-method by adding a noise polynomial into the encryption process called pqe-method. Given a matrix $A = (a_{ij}) \in \mathbb{Z}^{n \times n}$, we set

$$M_A = \max_{i \in [n]} \{ \sum_{j=1}^{n} |a_{ij}| \}. \tag{2}$$

We show the pqe-method in the following algorithm.

- **Key Generation:**

  Let p be an odd prime number and n be a positive integer. l_ψ, l_A, l_B be positive odd integers of size close to p.

  1) Randomly sample a multivariate quadratic polynomial system $\Phi(\mathbf{x}) \in \mathbb{Z}[\mathbf{x}]^n$. Here $\Phi(\mathbf{x}) \mod p$ is (almost) injective and its inverse can be computed efficiently.

  2) Make a multivariate polynomial system $\Psi(\mathbf{x}) \in \mathbb{Z}[\mathbf{x}]^n$ with coefficients sampled from I_{l_ψ} uniformly at random.

  3) Randomly sample matrices $A \in I_{l_A}^{n \times n}$ and $B \in I_{l_B}^{n \times n}$.

  4) Compute M_ϕ, M_ψ by (1) and M_A, M_B by (2). Then compute

  $$\widetilde{M_\phi} = M_\phi + M_A \cdot \frac{l_A - 1}{2}$$
  $$\widetilde{M_\psi} = M_\psi + M_B \cdot \frac{l_B - 1}{2}.$$

  5) Choose a prime number q satisfying $q > 4\widetilde{M_\psi}\widetilde{M_\phi}$.

  6) Select a series of integers $r_1, \ldots, r_n$ in the range of $(\widetilde{M_\phi}, q)$ satisfying $2\widetilde{M_\phi} < \min_{k \in [2\widetilde{M_\psi}]} |\mathrm{lift}_q(r_i k)|_{i \in [n]}$. Here we set $\Lambda_i = \{\mathrm{lift}_q(r_i k) | k = 0, \pm 1, \ldots, \pm \widetilde{M_\psi}\}$. Return to Step 5 and choose a larger q, if it failed to sample such $r_1, \ldots, r_n$.

7) Compute $B_R(\mathbf{x}) = (r_j b_{ij})$ and $C = (pA + B_R) \mod q \in \mathbb{F}_q[\mathbf{x}]^{n \times n}$. Set $T = C^{-1}$ if C is non-singular, go back to Step 3.

8) Set $\Psi_R(\mathbf{x}) = (r_1 \psi_1(\mathbf{x}), \ldots, r_n \psi_n(\mathbf{x})) \in \mathbb{Z}[\mathbf{x}]^n$ and $G(\mathbf{x}) = (g_1(\mathbf{x}), \ldots, g_n(\mathbf{x})) = (\Phi(\mathbf{x}) + \Psi_R(\mathbf{x})) \mod q \in \mathbb{F}_q[\mathbf{x}]^n$.

9) Randomly sample a permutation matrix S of size n and compute $F = T \circ G \circ S : \mathbb{Z}^n \to \mathbb{F}_q^n$.

 Secret key: $\Phi(\mathbf{x}) \mod p$, $\{r_i\}_{i \in [n]}$, T and S;

 Public key: p and $F(\mathbf{x})$.

- **Encryption:**

  The following process encrypts a plaintext $\mathbf{m} \in I_p^n$.

  1) Randomly sample a perturbation vector $\mathbf{e} \in I_p^n$.

  2) Compute the ciphertext $\mathbf{c} = F(\mathbf{m}) + \mathbf{e} \in \mathbb{F}_q^n$.

- **Decryption:**

  1) Compute $\mathbf{c}' = (c_1', \ldots, c_n') = T^{-1}(\mathbf{c})$.

  2) Find a (unique) $\lambda_i \in \Lambda_i$ such that $|\text{lift}_q(c_i' - \lambda_i)| < \widetilde{M_\phi}$ for all $i \in [n]$. Set $\tilde{c}_i = \text{lift}_q(c_i' - \lambda_i) \in \mathbb{Z}$.

  3) Calculate the solution $\tilde{\mathbf{b}} \in I_p^n$ of the equations $\Phi(\mathbf{x}) \equiv (\tilde{c}_1, \ldots, \tilde{c}_n) \mod p$.

  4) Compute $\mathbf{m}' = S^{-1}(\tilde{\mathbf{b}})$ which matches with the plaintext $\mathbf{m}$.

By invoking a perturbation in encryption, it can shrink the secret parameter n and reduce the key length accordingly. Overall, the performance of the cryptosystem based on pqe-method is improved compared to pq-method.

The security of both pq-method and pqe-method can be reduced to the constrained MQ problem, while pqe-method can also be reduced to a lattice problem NTRU [12]. The performance can be further improved by using a linear structure instead of a quadratic system. In that case, it mainly executes as a lattice-based PKC with linear polynomial multiplication and further strengthens its security by applying some properties from MPKC.

3   Our Proposals

In this section, we propose three variants based on the pq-method and pqe-method. Note that the original algorithms are both using quadratic polynomials, while our improved cryptosystems adopt linear polynomial systems. For a positive integer p and a matrix $L \in \mathbb{Z}_p^{n \times m}$, we define $\|L\|_p := \max_{\mathbf{a} \in I_p^n}\{|\mathbf{a} \cdot L|_\infty\}$.

Linear Mapping Mask. The elements of affine isomorphisms T and S are sampled from $\mathbb{F}_q$ randomly at uniform in the bipolar structure of pq-method. As a result, the security will not be reduced if we set the S as an identity map in computing the public key P [29]. Thus, we remain only one map of T where itself is secret. We call T a linear mapping mask to preserve the secret keys from a potential key-recovery attack. In addition, eliminating S may (slightly) reduce the cost of key generation and decryption algorithms.

3.1   A Simplified Linear Version of pq-method

Firstly, we propose a variant of the pq-based public-key cryptosystem. For the sake of convenience, we call it linear-pq algorithm.

- **Key Generation:**
  Let p be a small odd prime number and n be a positive integer.
  1) Randomly sample a linear polynomial system $F(\mathbf{x}) = (f_1(\mathbf{x}),\ldots,$ $f_n(\mathbf{x})) \in \mathbb{F}_p[\mathbf{x}]^n$ where $\mathbf{x} = (x_1,\ldots,x_n)$.
  2) Set $M = \|F\|_p$, and choose integer series of $r_1,\ldots,r_n$ larger than $2M$.
  3) Randomly sample another polynomial system $H(\mathbf{x}) = (h_1(\mathbf{x}),\ldots,h_n(\mathbf{x}))$ $\in \mathbb{F}_p[\mathbf{x}]^n$ where the number of variables is $2n$, i.e. $\mathbf{x} = (x_1,\ldots,x_{2n})$.
  4) Set $L = \|H\|_p$, $r = \max\limits_{i\in[n]}\{r_i\}$ and $q = \texttt{NextPrime}(2rL + 2M)$.
  5) Randomly sample an affine transformation T on $\mathbb{F}_q^n$ such that its inverse can be computed efficiently.
  6) Set

$$G = [F \mid \mathbf{0}] + \begin{bmatrix} r_1 & & \\ & \ddots & \\ & & r_n \end{bmatrix} H.$$

  and $P = T \circ G : \mathbb{F}_q^{2n} \to \mathbb{F}_q^n$.
  Secret key: F, H, $\{r_i\}_{i\in[n]}$, T;
  Public key: p, q, P.

- **Encryption:**
  Given a plaintext $\mathbf{m} \in I_p^{2n}$, compute the ciphertext $\mathbf{c} = P(\mathbf{m}) \in \mathbb{F}_q^n$.

- **Decryption:**
  1) Compute $\mathbf{c}' = T^{-1}(\mathbf{c})$.
  2) For all $i \in [n]$, find a (unique) set of $\{\alpha_i\}$ $(-M \le \alpha_i \le M)$ and $\{\beta_i\}$ $(-L \le \beta_i \le L)$, such that $c_i' = \alpha_i + r_i\beta_i$.
  3) Calculate the solution $\mathbf{x}_0 = (x_{01},\ldots,x_{0n})$ of equations $(f_1,\ldots,f_n) = (\alpha_1,\ldots,\alpha_n)$.
  4) Substitute $\mathbf{x}_0 = (x_{01},\ldots,x_{0n})$ into $\mathbf{c}' = G(\mathbf{x})$ which remains variables of $i \in \{n+1,\ldots,2n\}$, and calculate a solution $\mathbf{x}_1 = (x_{0,n+1},\ldots,x_{0,2n})$ such that $c_i' = r_{i-n}\beta_i$. $\mathbf{m}' = (x_{01},\ldots,x_{0n},x_{0,n+1},\ldots,x_{0,2n})$ coincides with the plaintext $\mathbf{m}$.

Correctness. For the sake of convenience, we denote by $[r_j]$ $(j \in [n])$ the matrix constructed with elements in $\{r_j\}$ at Step 6 of Key Generation. In addition, we further medially separate $G = [G_1 \mid G_2]$, $H = [H_1 \mid H_2]$ and $\mathbf{m} = [\mathbf{m}_1 \mid \mathbf{m}_2]$, respectively. Now, we substitute $\mathbf{c} = P(\mathbf{m}) \in \mathbb{F}_q^n$ into $\mathbf{c}' = T^{-1}(\mathbf{c})$. $q = \texttt{NextPrime}(2rL + 2M)$ is set large enough to make sure that the elements in G will not change after the substitution, thus we can get

$\mathbf{c}' = G(\mathbf{m}) = [G_1 \mid G_2](\mathbf{m}) = [F(\mathbf{m}_1) \mid \mathbf{0}] + [r_j][H_1(\mathbf{m}_1) \mid H_2(\mathbf{m}_2)]$. Since $r_j > 2M$ and $M = \|F\|_p$, there exists only one vector of $\boldsymbol{\alpha} = (\alpha_i)$ corresponding to $F(\mathbf{m}_1) = \boldsymbol{\alpha}$. Namely, at Step 3 of Decryption, $\mathbf{x}_0 = (x_{01}, \ldots, x_{0n})$ coincides with $\mathbf{m}_1$. Then, we substitute $\mathbf{x}_0$ into $\mathbf{c}'$ which remains $c_i' = [r_j]H_2(\mathbf{x}_1)$ ($i \in \{n+1, \ldots, 2n\}$) to be recovered. Therefore, $\mathbf{x}_1 = (x_{0,n+1}, \ldots, x_{0,2n})$ corresponds to $\mathbf{m}_2$ by solving the linear functions. Finally, the message is correctly recovered by $\mathbf{m}' = (\mathbf{x}_0 \mid \mathbf{x}_1) = \mathbf{m}$.

Discussion. Now we explain the merits derived from linear-pq cryptosystem. In general, it is difficult to directly compare the improved proposal with the original one due to different security parameter evaluations. Despite this reality, we can estimate the size of $q = O(n^2 p^4)$ in the linear-pq cryptosystem, which is attributed to the design of constructing a public key with two polynomial systems where the coefficients' sizes are significantly different. This is intuitively much smaller than $q = O(n^4 p^6)$ in the pq-method.

Moreover, in the decryption of pq-method, we need to solve a quadratic polynomial system of n equations in n variables with integer coefficients. Accordingly, it requires $O(n^4)$ operations in key generation of the original pq-method by the state-of-the-art pq-TM method. Meanwhile, in the linear-pq method, the public key is designed by two linear polynomial systems. The computational cost in the key generation phase is $O(n^2 \log n)$ using the best-known Number-Theoretical Transform (NTT) algorithm for polynomial multiplications.

At the last step of key generation, the remaining T is a linear mapping mask to preserve the secret keys from a potential key-recovery attack. In addition, eliminating S may (slightly) reduce the cost of key generation and decryption algorithms.

The linear-pq method is modified obediently from the original pq-method. They are deterministic schemes, so they do not hold the security property of indistinguishability under a chosen-plaintext attack (IND-CPA). Namely, the adversary can distinguish the ciphertext c_b easily by re-encrypting the chosen plaintexts m_0 and m_1. Thus, the linear-pq method satisfies indistinguishability under onewayness attack (OW-CPA) under the hardness assumption of solving ISIS problems. (The ISIS reduction is explained in Sect. 4.1).

3.2   A Linear Polynomial Version of pqe-method

Secondly, we also propose a linear version for pqe-method, where the methodology is similar to the linear-pq algorithm. We call it linear-pqe method.

- **Key Generation**:
  Let p be an odd prime number and n be a positive integer.
  1) Sample matrices $L_{1,X}, L_{1,Y}, L_{r,X}, L_{r,Y} \in \mathbb{F}_p^{n \times n}$ randomly.
  2) Choose positive integers $M_{1,X}, M_{1,Y}, M_{r,X}, M_{r,Y}$ satisfying $\|L_{a,b}\|_p \leq M_{a,b}$ ($a \in \{1, r\}, b \in \{X, Y\}$). Set $M_1 = M_{1,X} + pM_{1,Y}$ and $M_r = M_{r,X} + M_{r,Y}$.
  3) Choose a prime number q satisfying $q > 4M_1 M_r$.

4) Select a series of integers $0 < r_1, \ldots, r_n < q$ and $k \in [2M_r]$ satisfying $2M_1 < \min_{k \in [2M_r]} |\text{lift}_q(r_i k)|_{i \in [n]}$. Return to Step 3 and choose a larger q, if it failed to sample such $r_1, \ldots, r_n$.

5) Compute

$$L_X = L_{1,X} + \begin{bmatrix} r_1 & & \\ & \ddots & \\ & & r_n \end{bmatrix} L_{r,X} \in \mathbb{Z}^{n \times n}$$

and

$$L_Y = pL_{1,Y} + \begin{bmatrix} r_1 & & \\ & \ddots & \\ & & r_n \end{bmatrix} L_{r,Y} \in \mathbb{Z}^{n \times n}.$$

Set $T = L_Y^{-1} \mod q$ if $L_Y \mod q \in \mathbb{F}_q^{n \times n}$ is non-singular, or go back to Step 1.

6) Compute $L_F = T \circ L_X \in \mathbb{F}_q^{n \times n}$ and $L_S = L_{1,X}^{-1} \mod p$.
   Secret key: L_s, $\{r_i\}_{i \in [n]}$ and L_Y;
   Public key: p, q and L_F.

- **Encryption:**
  The following process encrypts a plaintext $\mathbf{m} \in I_p^n$.
  1) Randomly sample a perturbation vector $\mathbf{e} \in I_p^n$.
  2) Compute the ciphertext $\mathbf{c} = L_F(\mathbf{m}) + \mathbf{e} \in \mathbb{F}_q^n$.

- **Decryption:**
  1) Compute $\mathbf{b} = (b_1, \ldots, b_n) = L_Y \cdot \mathbf{c}$.
  2) Find a (unique) k_i such that $|\text{lift}_q(b_i - r_i k_i)| \leq M_1$ and $|k_i| \leq M_r$ for all $i \in [n]$. Set $\hat{b}_i = \text{lift}_q(b_i - r_i k_i) \in \mathbb{Z}$.
  3) Calculate $\mathbf{u} = \hat{\mathbf{b}} \mod p \in \mathbb{F}_p^n$ and compute $\mathbf{m}' = \text{lift}_p(L_s \cdot \mathbf{u})$ which matches with the plaintext $\mathbf{m}$.

Correctness. First we take off the linear mapping mask by $\mathbf{b} = L_Y \cdot \mathbf{c} = L_Y \circ L_F(\mathbf{m}) + L_Y(\mathbf{e}) = L_Y \circ L_Y^{-1} \circ L_X(\mathbf{m}) + L_Y(\mathbf{e}) = L_X(\mathbf{m}) + L_Y(\mathbf{e}) = L_{1,X}(\mathbf{m}) + [r_i]L_{r,X}(\mathbf{m}) + pL_{1,Y}(\mathbf{e}) + [r_i]L_{r,Y}(\mathbf{e})$. Then, the computation at Step 2 in Decryption extracts items of $\hat{\mathbf{b}} = L_{1,X}(\mathbf{m}) + pL_{1,Y}(\mathbf{e})$ where the bounds of parameters ensure the items unchanged during the execution. Next, $\mathbf{u} = \hat{\mathbf{b}} \mod p \in \mathbb{F}_p^n = L_{1,X}(\mathbf{m})$ eliminates the item of $pL_{1,Y}(\mathbf{e})$. Consequently, message is correctly recovered by $\mathbf{m}' = \text{lift}_p(L_s \cdot \mathbf{u}) = \text{lift}_p(L_{1,X}^{-1} \circ L_{1,X}(\mathbf{m})) = \mathbf{m}$.

Discussion. Note that the boundary setting for q at Step 3 is because of $2M_1 \times 2M_r$ from step 4. At step 4, to make sure the decryption succeed by 100%, it requires $2M_1 < |\text{lift}_q(r_i(k_a - k_b))|$ for $-M_r \leq k_a, k_b \leq M_r$, then we get $2M_1 < \min_{k \in [2M_r]} |\text{lift}_q(r_i k)|_{i \in [n]}$ by setting $k = k_a - k_b \in [2M_r]$.

The advantages of linear-*pqe* algorithm comparing to *pqe*-method are analogous to that of the linear-*pq* method in Sect. 3.1. Due to the key construction in a linear polynomial system, a smaller modulus $q = O(n^2 p^5)$ is available versus

$q = O(n^4p^6)$ of the original pqe-method. Following the idea of pqe-method, we construct the linear mapping mask T in this scheme by computing the inverse of the secret key L_Y. It makes the computation lighter without sampling from $\mathbb{F}_q^n$ and tests its reversibility.

Furthermore, conducting the linear polynomial multiplications costs $O(n^2 \log n)$ operations which is more efficient than the $O(n^4)$ required in pqe-method. Besides, eliminating the matrix S may (slightly) speed up the composition of public key L_F in linear-pqe method.

3.3 A Ring Version of Linear-pqe Algorithm

Finally, we propose a ring version of linear-pqe algorithm, whose key size is $O(1/n)$ shorter than the other two algorithms. Thus, it derives a much better performance. We call it ring-pqe method.

We define a polynomial ring $R := \mathbb{Z}[x]/(x^n - 1)$. For a positive integer p and a polynomial $L \in R$, we define $\|L\|_p := \max_{\mathbf{a} \in I_p^n}\{|\mathbf{a} \cdot L|_\infty\}$. In this subsection, we let I_p^n represent a set of polynomials of $n - 1$ degree and coefficients lie in I_p.

- **Key Generation:**
  Let p be an odd prime number and n be a positive integer.
  1) Sample matrices $L_{1,X}, L_{1,Y}, L_{r,X}, L_{r,Y} \in R/pR$ randomly.
  2) Choose positive integers $M_{1,X}, M_{1,Y}, M_{r,X}, M_{r,Y}$ satisfying $\|L_{a,b}\|_p \leq M_{a,b}$ ($a \in \{1, r\}, b \in \{X, Y\}$). Set $M_1 = M_{1,X} + pM_{1,Y}$ and $M_r = M_{r,X} + M_{r,Y}$.
  3) Choose a prime number q satisfying $q > 4M_1M_r$.
  4) Select an integer r in $(0, q)$ which satisfies $2M_1 < \min_{k \in [2M_r]} |\text{lift}_q(rk)|_{i \in [n]}$.
     Return to Step 3 and choose a larger q, if it fails to sample such r.
  5) Compute $L_X = L_{1,X} + rL_{r,X}$ and $L_Y = pL_{1,Y} + rL_{r,Y}$ Set $T = L_Y^{-1}$ mod q if L_Y mod $q \in R/qR$ is non-singular, or go back to Step 1.
  6) Compute $L_F = T \cdot L_X \in R/qR$ and $L_S = L_{1,X}^{-1}$ mod p.
     Secret key: L_S, r and L_Y;
     Public key: p, q and L_F.

- **Encryption:**
  The following process encrypts a plaintext $\mathbf{m} \in I_p^n$.
  1) Randomly sample a perturbation vector $\mathbf{e} \in I_p^n$.
  2) Compute the ciphertext $\mathbf{c} = L_F(\mathbf{m}) + \mathbf{e} \in R/qR$.

- **Decryption:**
  1) Compute $b(\mathbf{x}) = \sum_{i=0}^{n-1} b_ix^i = L_Y \cdot \mathbf{c}$.
  2) Find a (unique) k_i such that $|\text{lift}_q(b_i - rk_i)| \leq M_1$ and $|k_i| \leq M_r$ for all $i \in [n]$. Set $\hat{b}_i = \text{lift}_q(b_i - rk_i) \in \mathbb{Z}$.
  3) Calculate $\mathbf{u} = \hat{\mathbf{b}}$ mod $p \in \mathbb{F}_p^n$ and compute $\mathbf{m}' = \text{lift}_p(L_S \cdot \mathbf{u})$ which matches with the plaintext $\mathbf{m}$.

Correctness. We omit the proof here since it is similar to what for the above linear-*pqe* method.

Discussion. The ring structure results in an overwhelming reduction on both the public key size and the secret key size, by the multiplicative factor $1/n$. Thus the ring-*pqe* crypto scheme outperforms the linear-*pqe* method. Furthermore, as the same as linear-*pqe* method, we design the linear mapping mask T in ring-*pqe* by computing from part of the secret key L_Y inside.

4   Cryptanalysis and Performance

In this section, we first evaluate proper security parameters for linear-*pq* cryptosystem, linear-*pqe* cryptosystem, and ring-*pqe* cryptosystem, respectively. We consider the security levels of AES-128 in the NIST PQC standardization project [1] that the brute force attack on AES key search requires at least 2^{143} classical computing gates. Then we show the key and ciphertext sizes with respect to the above parameters for each scheme. Finally, we show the experimental results of the three cryptosystems.

4.1   Evaluating Security Parameters and Key Size

To evaluate a proper parameter set of (n, p, q), we consider that the security of proposed cryptosystems is based on relevant lattice problems. Namely, we can see the encryption procedure of linear-*pq* $\mathbf{c} = P(\mathbf{m}) = \mathbf{m} \cdot P \in \mathbb{F}_q^n$ as an ISIS instance since the norm of $\mathbf{m} \in I_p^{2n}$ is much smaller than that of the vector in the kernel space of $L(P)$ in $\mathbb{Z}^{2n}$ computed by the Gaussian heuristic. Simultaneously, we can regard the encryption in linear-*pqe* and ring-*pqe* as dealing with the LWE instance and the Ring-LWE instance, respectively. As discussed in the above proposals, a key recovery attack is not feasible owing to the subtle linear mapping mask. Hence, we apply the message recovery attacks using the lattice method against each problem. Simultaneously, we also consider the exhaustive search for the message recovery attack.

Message Recovery Attack. Typically the LWE problem and the Ring-LWE problem can be reduced to the SVP or uSVP using Bai-Galbraith's embedding technique [7]. Indeed, the cryptanalysis for linear-*pq*, linear-*pqe* and ring-*pqe* schemes are equivalent to evaluating the hardness of SVP in $(2n+1)$-dimensional lattices with volume of $q^{(n+1)}$. Refer to [23] for a detailed application and analysis of Bai-Galbraith's embedding technique.

Moreover, the lattice algorithms are also used in cryptanalysis. One of the best-known lattice algorithms is *BKZ algorithm* [18] and its variants [6,9,25,26], which processes the given basis until being almost β-reduced. In other words, the projected lengths of each basis vector are the shortest ones in the relative β-dimensional sub-lattice. BKZ costs exponentially in the blocksize β. In 2001, Ajtai et al. proposed a sieving algorithm to solve SVP [3]. It requires a running time of $2^{0.52n+o(n)}$ in dimension n and requires exponential storage of $2^{0.2n+o(n)}$

Table 1. Parameter choice for AES-128 bit security.

Schemes	n	p	q
linear-pq	980	3	61473439 (26 bits)
linear-pqe	1022	3	133693951 (27 bits)
ring-pqe	1022	3	133693951 (27 bits)

as well. For a β-dimensional sub-lattice the cost of sieving algorithm can be estimated in $2^{0.292\beta+o(\beta)}$ operations. If we take sieving as a subroutine in the β-dimensional sub-lattices inside of an n-dimensional lattice, the total BKZ-β cost can be estimated by $8n \cdot 2^{0.292\beta+12.31}$ operations [4]. We recall the following two definitions to evaluate the performance of lattice algorithms.

(a) The *root Hermite factor* [10] is defined as:

$$\delta = \mathrm{rHF}(\mathbf{b}_1,\ldots,\mathbf{b}_n) = (\|\mathbf{b}_1\|/\mathrm{Vol}(L)^{1/n})^{1/n}.$$

The rHF of a BKZ-β reduced basis $\mathbf{B}$ of d-dimensional lattice $L(\mathbf{B})$ can be evaluated by

$$\delta = (((\pi\beta)^{1/\beta}\beta)/(2\pi e))^{\frac{1}{2(\beta-1)}}. \tag{3}$$

This is proposed and practically verified by Chen in [8].

(b) In order to estimate the hardness of LWE samples $(\mathbf{A}, \mathbf{b} \equiv \mathbf{As} + \mathbf{e} \pmod{q}) \in \mathbb{Z}_q^{m\times n} \times \mathbb{Z}_q^m$, the *2016 estimate* [5] states that if the Gaussian heuristic and the GSA hold for BKZ-β reduced basis and

$$\sqrt{\beta/d} \cdot \|(\mathbf{e}|1)\| \approx \sqrt{\beta}\sigma \leq \delta^{2\beta-d} \cdot \mathrm{Vol}(L_{(\mathbf{A},q)})^{1/d}, \tag{4}$$

then error $\mathbf{e}$ can be found by the BKZ-β reduction algorithm. It has been widely used in the cryptanalysis [24] for lattice-based cryptoschemes: given the dimension d, the modular q and the standard deviation σ of $\mathbf{e}_i$'s distribution, the 2016 estimate can output the optimal blocksize β in the attack by using Eqs. (3) (4).

Exhaustive Search
For a ciphertext $\mathbf{c}$, the complexity of finding the solution of $P(\mathbf{m}) = \mathbf{c}$ in linear-pq and $L_F(\mathbf{m}) + \mathbf{e} = \mathbf{c}$ in the ring-pq by the exhaustive search is the same of $O(p^{2n})$. In the case of using Grover's quantum search algorithm, the complexity is $O(p^n)$.

Parameter Suggestion and Key Sizes. Due to NIST's call for proposal in the PQC standardization project [1], any attack on AES-128 bit security requires at least 143 bits of classical gate operations. We evaluate the relevant parameters for AES-128 bit security in Table 1. There is no significant difference but just within one bit for the parameter sizes among different schemes.

Furthermore, we show the key sizes and ciphertext sizes in each proposed cryptosystem in Table 2. It shows that the ciphertext sizes are close to each other, while the key sizes of ring-pq are evidently $1/n$ of the other two schemes. This results in a comparatively high efficiency shown in the next section.

Table 2. The sizes of public key (pk), secret key (sk), and ciphertext (ct) for each scheme of AES-128 bit security.

Schemes	pk(kB)	sk(kB)	ct(kB)
linear-pq	6242.6	3844.8	3.1
linear-pqe	3525.1	3789.7	3.5
ring-pqe	3.5	3.7	3.5

4.2 Implementation

Table 3. The performance of each scheme with the unit of a millisecond (ms).

Schemes	KeyGen(ms)	Enc(ms)	Dec(ms)
linear-pq	21624.4	113.7	48596.6
linear-pqe	54408.5	64.1	161.9
ring-pqe	37.2	0.6	20.2

We implemented the three proposed crypto schemes in C++ language. In our implementation, we invite the number theory library (NTL) [20]. In particular, the number-theoretical transform (NTT) technique is conducted in NTL, which can speed up the polynomial multiplications over finite fields. Then we run 1,000 experiments on a computer with Intel Core i9 @ 3.6 GHz CPU, g++ version 7.4.0. We evaluate the average running time for each one in Table 3 with one decimal precision. It shows that the ring-pqe algorithm is overwhelmingly efficient compared to the other two schemes.

5   Conclusion

In this paper, we proposed three PKE algorithms based on linear-pq, linear-pqe, and ring-pqe methods, respectively. Compared to the original algorithms by Yasuda, our proposals use a much smaller modulus q and cost less by conducting linear polynomial multiplications. Besides, our schemes are secure against the key-recovery attack by invoking a linear mapping mask at the end of key generations. Furthermore, we evaluated the proper parameters for AES-128 bit security level and assessed the key size produced in our cryptosystems. In particular, the linear-pqe cryptosystem outperforms the other two algorithms regarding key size and practical efficiency.

Acknowledgement. We thank Dr. Atsushi Takayasu for his helpful comments on this work. This work was supported by JSPS KAKENHI Grant Number JP20K23322, JP21K11751, JP19K20266, JP20K03741, Japan. This work is based on the discussions at FY2019 IMI Joint Usage Research Program Short-term Joint Research "New Development of Constructing Next-Generation Cryptography via Unified Approaches of Mathematics Theory, Computation and Cryptology".

References

1. US Department of Commerce, National Institute of Standards and Technology. Post-Quantum Cryptography (2020). https://csrc.nist.gov/projects/post-quantum-cryptography/
2. PQC Standardization Process: Fourth Round Candidate Announcement (2022). https://csrc.nist.gov/News/2022/pqc-candidates-to-be-standardized-and-round-4
3. Ajtai, M., Kumar, R., Sivakumar, D.: A sieve algorithm for the shortest lattice vector problem. In: Proceedings of the Thirty-third Annual ACM Symposium on Theory of Computing, pp. 601–610 (2001)
4. Albrecht, M.R., Player, R., Scott, S.: On the concrete hardness of learning with errors. J. Math. Cryptol. **9**(3), 169–203 (2015)
5. Alkim, E., Ducas, L., Pöppelmann, T., Schwabe, P.: Post-quantum key exchange-a new hope. In: USENIX Security Symposium, pp. 327–343 (2016)
6. Aono, Y., Wang, Y., Hayashi, T., Takagi, T.: Improved progressive BKZ algorithms and their precise cost estimation by sharp simulator. In: Fischlin, M., Coron, J.-S. (eds.) EUROCRYPT 2016. LNCS, vol. 9665, pp. 789–819. Springer, Heidelberg (2016). https://doi.org/10.1007/978-3-662-49890-3_30
7. Bai, S., Galbraith, S.D.: Lattice decoding attacks on binary LWE. In: Susilo, W., Mu, Y. (eds.) ACISP 2014. LNCS, vol. 8544, pp. 322–337. Springer, Cham (2014). https://doi.org/10.1007/978-3-319-08344-5_21
8. Chen, Y.: Lattice reduction and concrete security of fully homomorphic encryption. Department Informatique, ENS, Paris, France, Ph.D. thesis (2013)
9. Chen, Y., Nguyen, P.Q.: BKZ 2.0: better lattice security estimates. In: Lee, D.H., Wang, X. (eds.) ASIACRYPT 2011. LNCS, vol. 7073, pp. 1–20. Springer, Heidelberg (2011). https://doi.org/10.1007/978-3-642-25385-0_1
10. Gama, N., Nguyen, P.Q.: Predicting lattice reduction. In: Smart, N. (ed.) EUROCRYPT 2008. LNCS, vol. 4965, pp. 31–51. Springer, Heidelberg (2008). https://doi.org/10.1007/978-3-540-78967-3_3
11. Garey, M.R., Johnson, D.S.: Computers and Intractability: A Guide to the Theory of NP-Completeness. W. H Freeman, USA (1979)
12. Hoffstein, J., Pipher, J., Silverman, J.H.: NTRU: a ring-based public key cryptosystem. In: Buhler, J.P. (ed.) ANTS 1998. LNCS, vol. 1423, pp. 267–288. Springer, Heidelberg (1998). https://doi.org/10.1007/BFb0054868
13. Ikematsu, Y., Perlner, R., Smith-Tone, D., Takagi, T., Vates, J.: HFERP - a new multivariate encryption scheme. In: Lange, T., Steinwandt, R. (eds.) PQCrypto 2018. LNCS, vol. 10786, pp. 396–416. Springer, Cham (2018). https://doi.org/10.1007/978-3-319-79063-3_19
14. Lyubashevsky, V., Peikert, C., Regev, O.: On ideal lattices and learning with errors over rings. In: Gilbert, H. (ed.) EUROCRYPT 2010. LNCS, vol. 6110, pp. 1–23. Springer, Heidelberg (2010). https://doi.org/10.1007/978-3-642-13190-5_1
15. Matsumoto, T., Imai, H.: Public quadratic polynomial-tuples for efficient signature-verification and message-encryption. In: Barstow, D., et al. (eds.) EUROCRYPT 1988. LNCS, vol. 330, pp. 419–453. Springer, Heidelberg (1988). https://doi.org/10.1007/3-540-45961-8_39
16. Patarin, J.: Cryptanalysis of the matsumoto and imai public key scheme of Eurocrypt 1988. In: Coppersmith, D. (ed.) CRYPTO 1995. LNCS, vol. 963, pp. 248–261. Springer, Heidelberg (1995). https://doi.org/10.1007/3-540-44750-4_20

17. Regev, O.: On lattices, learning with errors, random linear codes, and cryptography. In: Proceedings of the 37th Annual ACM Symposium on Theory of Computing, pp. 84–93 (2005)

18. Schnorr, C., Euchner, M.: Lattice basis reduction: improved practical algorithms and solving subset sum problems. Math. Program. **66**, 181–199 (1994). https://doi.org/10.1007/BF01581144

19. Shor, P.W.: Algorithms for quantum computation: discrete logarithms and factoring. In: 35th Annual Symposium on Foundations of Computer Science, Santa Fe, Proceeding, pp. 124–134 (1994)

20. Shoup, V.: NTL, a library for doing number theory (2017). http://www.shoup.net/ntl/

21. Szepieniec, A., Ding, J., Preneel, B.: Extension field cancellation: a new central trapdoor for multivariate quadratic systems. In: Takagi, T. (ed.) PQCrypto 2016. LNCS, vol. 9606, pp. 182–196. Springer, Cham (2016). https://doi.org/10.1007/978-3-319-29360-8_12

22. Tao, C., Diene, A., Tang, S., Ding, J.: Simple matrix scheme for encryption. In: Gaborit, P. (ed.) PQCrypto 2013. LNCS, vol. 7932, pp. 231–242. Springer, Heidelberg (2013). https://doi.org/10.1007/978-3-642-38616-9_16

23. Wang, W., Wang, Y., Takayasu, A., Takagi, T.: Estimated cost for solving generalized learning with errors problem via embedding techniques. In: Inomata, A., Yasuda, K. (eds.) IWSEC 2018. LNCS, vol. 11049, pp. 87–103. Springer, Cham (2018). https://doi.org/10.1007/978-3-319-97916-8_6

24. Wang, Y., Aono, Y., Takagi, T.: Hardness evaluation for search LWE problem using progressive BKZ simulator. IEICE Trans. **101−A**(12), 2162–2170 (2018)

25. Wang, Y., Takagi, T.: Studying lattice reduction algorithms improved by quick reordering technique. Int. J. Inf. Sec. **20**(2), 257–268 (2021). https://doi.org/10.1007/s10207-020-00501-y

26. Yamamura, K., Wang, Y., Fujisaki, E.: Improved lattice enumeration algorithms by primal and dual reordering methods. In: Park, J.H., Seo, S. (eds.) Information Security and Cryptology - ICISC 2021–24th International Conference, Seoul, South Korea, December 2021, Revised Selected Papers, volume 13218 of Lecture Notes in Computer Science, pp. 159–174. Springer (2021). https://doi.org/10.1007/978-3-031-08896-4_8

27. Yasuda, T.: Multivariate encryption schemes based on the constrained MQ problem. In: Baek, J., Susilo, W., Kim, J. (eds.) ProvSec 2018. LNCS, vol. 11192, pp. 129–146. Springer, Cham (2018). https://doi.org/10.1007/978-3-030-01446-9_8

28. Yasuda, T.: Multivariate public key system using noise. In: SCIS 2020 (2020)

29. Yasuda, T., Wang, Y., Takagi, T.: Multivariate encryption schemes based on polynomial equations over real numbers. In: Ding, J., Tillich, J.-P. (eds.) PQCrypto 2020. LNCS, vol. 12100, pp. 402–421. Springer, Cham (2020). https://doi.org/10.1007/978-3-030-44223-1_22

Batched Fully Dynamic Multi-key FHE from FHEW-Like Cryptosystems

Yuting Jiang[1]([✉])(iD), Jianghong Wei[2](iD), and Jing Pan[3](iD)

[1] State Key Laboratory of Integrated Service Networks (ISN), Xidian University,
Xi'an 710071, China
jiangyuting@foxmail.com
[2] State Key Laboratory of Mathematical Engineering and Advanced Computing,
PLA Strategic Support Force Information Engineering University, Zhengzhou 450001,
China
[3] Guangzhou Institute of Technology, Xidian University, Guanzhou 510555, China
jinglap@aliyun.com

Abstract. Multi-key fully homomorphic encryption (MKFHE) schemes
support arbitrary computations on data encrypted by different keys.
Especially, in the fully dynamic setting, any ciphertexts can be computed at any time while maintaining the compactness. In this case,
no information about the parties and the computation function need
be known before the evaluation. However, all existing constructions are
based on the learning with errors (LWE) problem or learning with rounding (LWR) problem, and thus only allow to encrypt a single bit. On the
other hand, FHEW-like cryptosystems are computation-efficient in the
sense that they can evaluate arbitrary Boolean circuits on encrypted data
followed by the boostrapping procedure. To this end, in this paper, we
propose a batched fully dynamic multi-key FHE scheme based on FHEW-
like cryptosystems. Specifically, instead of a single bit, our construction
encrypts a ring element, and thus has low amortized cost. In addition,
as a core building block of construction, we put forward a new multi-
key ring-LWE accumulator with homomorphic discrete Fourier transform
(DFT) for the boostrapping procedure, which might be of independent
interest. The theoretical analysis indicates that the amortized computation cost of generating evaluation key and storage cost achieve optimal.

Keywords: Multi-key fully homomorphic encryption · FHEW ·
Bootstrapping · Batching

1 Introduction

Traditional fully homomorphic encryption (FHE), first proposed by Gentry [18],
allows arbitrary secure computations over encrypted data without compromising
data privacy. Generally, the best-performing FHE schemes include BFV [4,17],
BGV [5], CKKS [13], FHEW [16] and TFHE [14], which are based on learning
with errors (LWE) [28] or its ring variant (RLWE) [22]. However, they are all

© The Author(s), under exclusive license to Springer Nature Switzerland AG 2022
C. Ge and F. Guo (Eds.): ProvSec 2022, LNCS 13600, pp. 105–120, 2022.
https://doi.org/10.1007/978-3-031-20917-8_8

limited by performing homomorphic operations on ciphertexts under the same key, which are not applicable to multi-user scenarios.

To perform computations on data encrypted under multiple unrelated keys, López-Alt et al. [21] introduced a new notion of multi-key fully homomorphic encryption (MKFHE), and also proposed a concrete construction based on a non-standard assumption. After that, Clear et al. [15] and Mukherjee et al. [26] constructed multi-key FHE schemes based on the standard LWE assumption. However, they focused on the single-hop setting, where all the involved parties and the function to be computed are known before the homomorphic computation.

Motivated by notion of "on-the fly" [21], in which the computations need to be performed non-interactively, arbitrarily and dynamically on data belonging to arbitrary parties, Peikert et al. [27] proposed a multi-hop MKFHE scheme. Brakerski et al. [6] presented a fully dynamic MKFHE scheme. The slight difference between multi-hop setting and fully dynamic setting is that the bound of the number of parties does not need to be known ahead of the computation time in fully dynamic setting. Chen et al. [11] put forward the first batched MKFHE in the multi-hop setting. Huang et al. [20] provided a LWR-based MKFHE in the fully dynamic setting to reduce Gaussian sampling consumption from LWE assumption.

Bootstrapping procedure [18] is a main component of FHE schemes that refreshes the ciphertexts by homomorphically computing the decryption function on the encrypted secret key under the fixed noise. In particular, FHEW-like cryptosystems, including FHEW [16] and TFHE [14], provide the fast boostrapping by using homomorphic accumulators. Chen et al. [8] presented an efficient MKFHE from TFHE, although it only supports single-bit plaintext. From above, one can observe that MKFHE from FHEW-like cryptosystems still lacks research on batch processing.

In this paper, we further investigate the problem of how to construct a batched MKFHE scheme in the fully dynamic setting to improve the efficiency.

1.1 Motivations

FHEW Vs. TFHE. Micciancio et al. [24] compared FHEW [16] with TFHE [14] in detail in terms of security assumption, secret distribution, storage overhead of bootstrapping keys, and computational overhead. Both FHEW and TFHE belong to FHEW-like cryptosystems that can evaluate arbitrary Boolean circuits on encrypted data followed by the bootstrapping procedure. In more detail, FHEW cryptosystem is based on the standard (R)LWE assumptions, while TFHE cryptosystem relies on stronger (R)LWE assumption over torus. Morever, FHEW has better performance for Gaussian secrets, while TFHE is faster for binary and ternary secrets[1]. Furthermore, FHEW has much larger bootstrapping key size than TFHE. Due to the technical similarity of FHEW

---

[1] The Homomorphic Encryption standardization document [7] supports the use of Gaussian and ternary secrets.

and TFHE, our construction mainly derives from FHEW based on standard security assumption. In the meantime, we will point out the detailed differences between the constructions from FHEW and TFHE.

Batching. Ring-based homomorphic encryption schemes have remarkable performance by packing several messages into one ciphertext and operating on them in parallel. Since the first batched FHE proposed by Smart and Vercautren [29], there are FHE schemes from BGV packing type, BFV packing type and CKKS packing type extended to the multi-key setting [9,11]. In terms of FHEW-like cryptosystems, Micciancio et al. [25] provided an amortized FHEW bootstrapping with ring packing, which has lowest amortized computational cost so far to our knowledge. Motivated by Micciancio et al.'s work [25], we try to design a batched MKFHE scheme to reduce the amortized computational cost.

Fully Dynamic. In the dream of the "on-the-fly" multiparty computation (MPC), the untrusted cloud can perform arbitrary computations on any ciphertexts at any time [21]. The parties do not know who is involved in the computation and what computation is involved until it needs to be decrypted. The desirable fully dynamic setting was first constructed by Brakerski et al. [6], but based on complicated Gentry's boostrapping technique. There are still short of fully dynamic MKFHE schemes so far. Therefore, we try to construct a more efficient MKFHE scheme in the fully dynamic setting.

1.2 Our Contributions

In this paper, we study the problem of constructing more efficient MKFHE scheme in the fully dynamic setting, and conduct the following contributions:

- We design a multi-key RLWE accumulator with homomorphic DFT for the boostrapping procedure in the multi-key setting, as the core building block of our MKFHE construction. The proposed accumulator only needs $\tilde{O}(k^2 N)^2$ polynomial multiplications, and might have the potential to be useful in the construction of other primitives.
- Based on the above accumulator and FHEW-like cryptosystems, we put forth a batced fully dynamic MKFHE scheme. Our construction naturally inherits the merits of the FHEW-like cryptosystems, and thus has low amortized computational cost. That is, the amortized storage costs and computational overhead depend only on the number of the parties involved in the evaluations and the logarithm of N, where N denotes the dimension of the RLWE problem.
- We provide a comprehensive theoretical analysis by comparing the proposed MKFHE construction with other related works, so as to demonstrate its merits. Particularly, we show our scheme supports fully dynamic, which means that homomorphic computation is not limited by the type of operation, the number of people involved in the evaluation and the time.

---

[2] k denots the number of the parties involved in the evaluation.

1.3 Roadmap

In Sect. 2, we describe some necessary preliminaries. Section 3 constructs necessary building blocks of our construction. In Sect. 4, we propose a batched fully dynamic MKFHE scheme and prove its properties. In Sect. 5, we make a theoretical analysis. In Sect. 6, we conclude this paper.

2 Preliminaries

Throughout this paper,we denote by λ denote the security parameter. For a positive integer k, we write $[k]$ denote the set $\{0, 1, \cdots, k-1\}$. Let vectors be in bold, e.g., $\boldsymbol{a}$, and matrices be in upper-case bold like $\boldsymbol{A}$. The i-th coefficient of the polynomial a is denoted as $a[i]$. The i-th entry of the vector $\boldsymbol{a}$ is denoted as $\boldsymbol{a}[i]$. Sampling x from a distribution D uniformly at random is written as $x \leftarrow D$. Finally, $\|\cdot\|_1$ denotes l_1 norm and $\|\cdot\|_\infty$ denotes l_∞ norm.

2.1 Fully Dynamic Multi-key FHE

We recall the definition of muti-key homomorphic encryption at first and state the definition of fully dynamic MKFHE followed.

Definition 1 ([9]). *A multi-key homomorphic encryption scheme* MKHE = (MKHE.Setup, MKHE.KeyGen, MKHE.Enc, MKHE.Dec, MKHE.NAND) *is a 5-tuple of efficient randomized algorithms as follows:*

- MKHE.Setup(1^λ): *On input a security parameter λ, output a public parameter pp.*
- MKHE.KeyGen(pp): *Output a pair of secret an public keys $(sk_i, pk_i)(i \in [k])$ for each party, where k is the number of parties.*
- MKHE.Enc(pp, pk_i, m): *Given a bit $m \in \{0, 1\}$, output a ciphertext ct_i of party i.*
- MKHE.Dec$(pp, \{sk_i\}_{i \in [k]}, \overline{ct})$: *Given a ciphertext $\overline{ct}$ under a sequence of secret keys $\{sk_i\}_{i \in [k]}$ of relevant parties, output a bit $m \in \{0, 1\}$:*
- MKHE.Eval$(\{pk_i\}_{i \in [k]}, \mathcal{C}, \overline{ct}_1, \overline{ct}_2)$: *Given two ciphertexts $\overline{ct}_1, \overline{ct}_2$ along with a sequence of public keys $\{pk_i\}_{i \in [k]}$ of relevant parties, and a Boolean circuit $\mathcal{C}$, output a ciphertext $\overline{ct}'$ such that $\Pr[\text{MKHE.Dec}(pp, \{sk_i\}_{i \in [k]}, \overline{ct}') \neq \mathcal{C}(m_1, m_2)] = negl(\lambda)$, where m_1 and m_2 are the plaintexts of $\overline{ct}_1$ and $\overline{ct}_2$, respectively.*

Definition 2 ([6]). *Let k be any polynomial in λ, $pp \leftarrow$ MKHE.Setup(1^λ) and $(sk_i, pk_i) \leftarrow$ MKHE.KeyGen(pp) for $i \in [k]$. Let $\overline{ct}_1, \overline{ct}_2$ be ciphertexts such that $m_j \leftarrow$ MKHE.Dec$(pp, S_j, \overline{ct}_j)$ for $j = 1, 2$, where $S_j \in \{sk_i\}_{i \in [k]}$. A multi-key homomorphic encryption is fully dynamic MKFHE if the following holds:*

$$\Pr[\text{MKHE.Dec}(pp, \{sk_i\}_{i \in [k]}, \text{MKHE.Eval}(\{pk_i\}_{i \in [k]}, \mathcal{C}, \overline{ct}_1, \overline{ct}_2))$$
$$\neq \mathcal{C}(m_1, m_2)] = negl(\lambda).$$

The scheme is compact if there exists a polynomial poly$(\cdot, \cdot)$ *such that the size of the output ciphertext is less than* poly(λ, k).

2.2   Ring-LWE Encryption

The RLWE problem first proposed by Lyubashevsky [22,23] is a ring variant of the LWE problem [28]. Let $\mathcal{R} = \mathbb{Z}[X]/(X^N + 1)$ be the $2N$th cyclotomic ring, where N is power of two. We write $\mathcal{R}_q$ for the residue ring of $\mathcal{R}$ modulo an integer q. The basic RLWE symmetric encryption is as follows:

- RLWE.Setup(1^λ): On input the security parameter λ, generate a RLWE dimension N, a ciphertext modulus q and a B-bounded discrete distribution χ in $\mathcal{R}_q$ for $B \ll q$. Return a public parameter $pp^{\mathrm{RLWE}} = (N, q, B, \chi)$.
- RLWE.KeyGen(pp^{RLWE}): Sample a RLWE secret key $s \leftarrow \chi$ uniformly at random.
- RLWE.Enc(m, s): On input a message $m \in \mathcal{R}$, sample $a \leftarrow \mathcal{R}_q$ and $e \leftarrow \chi$. Return a ciphertext $(b, a) = (as + e + qm/t \bmod q, a) \in \mathcal{R}_q^2$. We represent the ciphertext (b, a) as $\mathrm{RLWE}_s(m)$.
- RLWE.Dec($((b, a), s)$): On input the ciphertext $(b, a) = \mathrm{RLWE}_s(m)$ and the secret key s, the decryption is computing $\lfloor t(b - as)/q \rceil \bmod t = m \in \mathbb{Z}_t$, where $\lfloor \cdot \rceil$ is a function that rounds each coordinate to the closest multiple of q/t. Return the message m.

The error of a ciphertext (a, b) is $\mathrm{err}(a, b) = (b - as - qm/t) \bmod q$.

2.3   Homomorphic Accumulator

Based on the suggestion of [1], Ducas et al. [16] proposed notion of the homomorphic accumulator to efficiently refresh a (R)LWE ciphertext. The homomorphic accumulator is defined as

Definition 3 ([1]). *A homomorphic accumulator scheme* ACC=(Encryption, Initialization, Increment, SampleExtract) *is a 4-tuple of efficient algorithms as follows:*

- Encryption: *Generate some key material related to secret keys s.*
- Initialization: *On input a constant v, simply set accumulator to a noiseless encryption of v.*
- Increment: *Update the key material to the accumulator sequentially.*
- SampleExtract: *Extract a new ciphertext of msb(v) under the secret key s from the accumulator.*

Lemma 1 ([1]). *On input a ciphertext of message m to the homomorphic accumulator* ACC, *if the accumulator* ACC *is correct, then the output ciphertext is the encryption of m with fixed noise.*

2.4   A Masking Scheme for RLWE

A masking scheme is the main component of the MKFHE scheme. Clear et al. [15] proposed its abstract conception, and Mukherjee et al. [26] introduced a specific construction for GSW. Intuitively, masking scheme allows to encrypt a ring element to generate a uni-encryption. Then it allows to encrypts the randomness as the auxiliary value. Finally, we can multiply the uni-encryption to a multi-key RLWE ciphertext to expand the ciphertext. In the following, we introduce the second method of the masking scheme in [8] for RLWE, which has better storage cost and smaller noise growth.

Let $q = 2^\ell$ be a suitably large ciphertex modulus, $\mathbf{g}=(2^0, 2^1, \cdots, 2^{\ell-1})$ be the gadget vector. Any ring element $c \in \mathcal{R}_q$ can be represented as $c = \sum_j 2^j c_j$ for $j = [\ell]$, where each coefficient of polynomial c_j is binary. We write function $\mathbf{g}^{-1}(c) = (c_0, \cdots, c_\ell)$ such that $\mathbf{g}^{-1}(c) \cdot \mathbf{g} = c$. Note the ciphertext modulus q is 1 and the gadget vector $\mathbf{g} = (2^{-1}, \cdots, 2^{-\ell})$ in TFHE.

First, all parties need to complete the following parameter settings.

- MS.Setup(1^λ): On input the security parameter λ, run RLWE.Setup(1^λ) to get parameters (N, q, B, χ). Choose a common random vector $\boldsymbol{a} \in R_q^\ell$ uniformly at random. Output the public parameter $pp^{\mathrm{MS}} = (N, q, B, \chi, \boldsymbol{a})$.
- MS.KeyGen(pp^{MS}): Sample a secret $z \leftarrow \chi$ uniformly at random and an error $\boldsymbol{e} \leftarrow \chi^\ell$. Set the public key $\boldsymbol{b} = \boldsymbol{a}z + \boldsymbol{e} \bmod q \in \mathcal{R}_q^\ell$. Output $(\boldsymbol{b}, z) \in \mathcal{R}_q^{\ell+1}$.
- MS.UniEnc(μ, z): On input a message $\mu \in \mathcal{R}$, and the secret z, output the ciphertext and auxiliary information $(\boldsymbol{d}, \boldsymbol{F}) \in \mathcal{R}_q^\ell \times \mathcal{R}_q^{\ell \times 2}$ as follows:
  - Sample a random polynomial $r \leftarrow \chi$ uniformly at random and an error $\boldsymbol{e}' \leftarrow \chi^\ell$, set $\boldsymbol{d} = \boldsymbol{a} \cdot r + \mu \cdot \mathbf{g} + \boldsymbol{e}' \bmod q \in \mathcal{R}_q^\ell$.
  - Sample random polynomials $\boldsymbol{f}_1 \leftarrow \mathcal{R}_q^\ell$ and errors $\boldsymbol{e}'' \leftarrow \chi^\ell$. Output the auxiliary ciphertext $\boldsymbol{F} = [\boldsymbol{f}_0 | \boldsymbol{f}_1] \in \mathcal{R}_q^{2\ell}$, where $\boldsymbol{f}_0 = \boldsymbol{f}_1 \cdot z + r \cdot \mathbf{g} + \boldsymbol{e}'' \bmod q$.

Suppose there are k parties, multiplication between the uni-encryption $(\boldsymbol{d}_i, \boldsymbol{F}_i)$ encrypted by ith party and a multi-key RLWE ciphertext as follows:
- MS.Prod($\bar{\boldsymbol{c}}, (\boldsymbol{d}_i, \boldsymbol{F}_i), \{\boldsymbol{b}_j\}_{j \in \{1, \cdots, k\}}$): Given a multi-key RLWE ciphertext $\bar{\boldsymbol{c}} = (c_0, c_1, \cdots, c_k) \in \mathcal{R}_q^{k+1}$ and the public keys $\{\boldsymbol{b}_j\}_{j \in \{1, \cdots, k\}}$ of k parties associated to $\bar{\boldsymbol{c}}$ (set $\boldsymbol{b}_0 = -\boldsymbol{a}$), we first compute the following inner products for $0 \leq j \leq k$: $u_j = \langle \mathbf{g}^{-1}(c_j), \boldsymbol{d}_i \rangle$, $v_j = \langle \mathbf{g}^{-1}(c_j), \boldsymbol{b}_j \rangle$, $w_{j,0} = \langle \mathbf{g}^{-1}(v_j), \boldsymbol{f}_{i,0} \rangle$, $w_{j,1} = \langle \mathbf{g}^{-1}(v_j), \boldsymbol{f}_{i,1} \rangle$. Next, output the multi-key RLWE ciphertext $\bar{\boldsymbol{c}}' = (c_0', \cdots, c_k') \in \mathcal{R}_q^{k+1}$, where $c_0' = u_0 + \sum_{j=0}^k w_{j,0} \bmod q$, $c_i' = u_i + \sum_{j=0}^k w_{j,1} \bmod q$ and $c_j' = u_j$ for $j \in [k] \setminus \{i\}$.

Lemma 2 ([8]). *The output multi-key ciphertext $\bar{\boldsymbol{c}}'$ of the above masking scheme satisfies that $\langle \bar{\boldsymbol{c}}, \boldsymbol{z} \rangle \approx \mu_i \langle \boldsymbol{c}, \boldsymbol{z} \rangle$ for $\boldsymbol{z} = (1, -z_1, \cdots, -z_k)$, where μ_i is the plaintext of the i-th parity. The computation complexity is $O(k \log q)$ polynomial multiplications. Furthermore, the noise of the output ciphertext is bounded by $(k+1)BN\ell(2B+1)$.*

2.5 The Ciphertext Extension

The goal of the ciphertext extension algorithm is to convert a low dimensional ciphertext to a larger dimensional ciphertext under a new larger dimensional secret key. For any $(k'+1)$-dimensional RLWE ciphertext under concatenated the secret key $(1, -s_{1'}, \cdots, -s_{k'})$, we can simply extend to larger dimension $(k + 1)^3$ under a new secret key $(1, -s_1, \cdots, -s_k)$ in the following way. Let the RLWE ciphertext $\mathbf{c}' = (b, a_{1'}, \cdots, a_{k'}) \in \mathcal{R}_q^{k'+1}$ be an encryption corresponding to a set of parties' index $S' = (j_{1'}, \cdots, j_{k'})$. For $j \in [k]$, if $j = j_l$ for $l \in [k']$, we set $a_j = a_{j_l}$; otherwise, we set $a_j = 0$. Therefore, we can output a new ciphertext $c = (b, a_1, \cdots, a_k) \in \mathcal{R}_q^{k+1}$ satisfying $c' \cdot (1, -s_{1'}, \cdots, -s_{k'}) = c \cdot (1, -s_1, \cdots, -s_k)$.

3 Building Blocks

3.1 Multi-key-switching on Ring-LWE Ciphertexts

Let χ be a B-bounded Gaussian error distribution. The multi-key RLWE ciphertext under $\mathbf{z} = (1, -z_1, \cdots, -z_k) \in \mathcal{R}^{k+1}$ can be converted to a new secret key $\mathbf{s} = (1, -s_1, \cdots, -s_k) \in \mathcal{R}^{k+1}$ by the following method.

- RLWE.KSGen(z_i, s_i): Given RLWE secret keys $z_i, s_i \in \mathcal{R}$ of the ith party, sample random vectors $\mathbf{r}_i \leftarrow \mathcal{R}_q^\ell$ and errors $\mathbf{e}_i \leftarrow \chi^\ell$. Compute $\mathsf{KS}_i = (-\mathbf{r}_i s_i + z_i \mathbf{g} + \mathbf{e}_i \bmod q, \mathbf{r}_i) \in \mathcal{R}_q^{2\ell}$ for each party. Output the key-switching key KS_i.
- RLWE.MKSwitch$(\bar{c}, \{\mathsf{KS}_i\}_{i \in \{1, \cdots, k\}})$: Given a multi-key RLWE ciphertext $\bar{c} = (b, a_1, \cdots, a_k) \in \mathcal{R}_q^{k+1}$ and the key-switching keys $\{\mathsf{KS}_i\}_{i \in \{1, \cdots, k\}}$, compute $\bar{c}' = (b - \sum_{i=1}^k \mathbf{g}^{-1}(a_i) \cdot \mathsf{KS}_i \bmod q, \mathbf{g}^{-1}(a_1) \cdot \mathbf{r}_1, \cdots, \mathbf{g}^{-1}(a_k) \cdot \mathbf{r}_k) \in \mathcal{R}_q^{k+1}$. Output the new RLWE ciphertext $\bar{c}'$.

Correctness. The output ciphertext $\bar{c}'$ satisfies the following equation as desired:

$$\langle \bar{c}', \mathbf{s} \rangle = b - \sum_{i=1}^k \mathbf{g}^{-1}(a_i) \cdot \mathsf{KS}_i - \sum_{i=1}^k \mathbf{g}^{-1}(a_i) \mathbf{r}_i s_i$$

$$= b - \sum_{i=1}^k a_i z_i - \sum_{i=1}^k \mathbf{g}^{-1}(a_i) \mathbf{e}_i \approx \langle \bar{c}, \mathbf{z} \rangle.$$

The noise of the output ciphertext $\bar{c}'$ is bounded by $\sum_{i=1}^k \|\mathbf{g}^{-1}(a_i)\mathbf{e}_i\|_\infty \leq k\|\mathbf{g}^{-1}(a_i)\|_\infty \|\mathbf{e}_i\|_\infty$. Since the coefficient of the polynomial of $\mathbf{g}^{-1}(a_i)$ is binary, then $\|\mathbf{g}^{-1}(a_i)\|_\infty \leq \log q$. Therefore, the noise of the output ciphertext $\bar{c}'$ is less than $k \log q BN$.

Security. The ith key switching key KS_i from $\mathsf{KSKeyGen}(\mathbf{z}, \mathbf{s})$ is generated by adding $z_i \mathbf{g}$ to the RLWE samples under the secret $-s_i$. Therefore, KS_i are computationally indistinguishable from the uniform distribution over $\mathcal{R}_q^{2\ell}$ under the RLWE assumption and additional circular security assumption.

---

[3] k is always larger than k'.

3.2   Multi-key RLWE Accumulators

Ring-LWE accumulators ACC is an important implement in FHEW-like cryptosystems' bootstrapping procedure [14,16]. We extend it to multi-key setting in the following.

Let ω_{2N} be the $2N$th principal root of unity of ring $\mathcal{R}$, $a, s \in \mathcal{R}$. Motivated by homomorphic discrete Fourier transform (DFT) in [25], $as \bmod X^N + 1$ can be translated to N dot products $DFT^{-1}(\frac{1}{N} DFT(a) \cdot DFT(s))$, where $\hat{a}_i = DFT(a)_i = \sum_{j=0}^{N-1} a[j]\omega_{2N}^{ij}$ and its inverse $a[j] = DFT^{-1}(\hat{a})_j = \sum_{i=0}^{N-1} \hat{a}_i \omega_{2N}^{-ij}$. To homomorphically compute $as \bmod X^N + 1$, we exploit the following method.

- Encryption: On input the multi-secret-key $\boldsymbol{s} = (1, -s_1, \cdots, -s_k) \in \mathcal{R}^{k+1}$ and a key $z \in \mathcal{R}$, each secret value $-s_i \in \mathcal{R}$ need to be DFT to a sequence of $(\hat{s}_{i,0}, \hat{s}_{i,1}, \cdots \hat{s}_{i,N-1}) \in \mathbb{Z}_q^N$ for $i \in \{1, \cdots, k\}$. Let $\hat{s}_{i,j}$ be expressed as $\hat{s}_{i,j} = \sum_{\tau=0}^{\log q} 2^\tau \hat{s}_{i,j,\tau}$ with $\hat{s}_{i,j,\tau} \in \{0,1\}$. The secret encryption function is

$$E(\hat{s}_{i,j}) = \{(\boldsymbol{d}_{i,j,\tau}, \boldsymbol{F}_{i,j,\tau}) \leftarrow \mathsf{MK.UniEnc}(\hat{s}_{i,j,\tau}, z)\}.$$

  for $i \in \{1, \cdots, k\}, j \in [N]$ and $\tau \in [\log q]$.
- Initialization: On input a contant $v \in \mathbb{Z}_q$, usually set to $q/8$ in FHEW and $1/8$ in TFHE, simply set $\overline{ACC}_j$ to a trivial multi-key RLWE sample $\overline{ACC}_j := (v, 0, \cdots, 0) \in \mathcal{R}_q^{k+1}$.
- Increment: On input the multi-key RLWE ciphertext $\bar{\boldsymbol{c}} = (b, a_1, \cdots, a_k) \in \mathcal{R}_q^{k+1}$, secret encryption $\{(\boldsymbol{d}_{i,j,\tau}, \boldsymbol{F}_{i,j,\tau})\}_{i \in \{1, \cdots, k\}, j \in [N], \tau \in [\log q]}$, the component of the ciphertext a_i also need to be DFT to a sequence of $(\hat{a}_{i,0}, \hat{a}_{i,1}, \cdots, \hat{a}_{i,N-1}) \in \mathbb{Z}_q^N$ for $i \in \{1, \cdots, k\}$. Note that in TFHE, the a_i needs to be amplified by $2N$ times before DFT, since TFHE works over torus $\mathbb{T} = \mathbb{R} \bmod 1$. The update operation is computed by sequentially updating

$$\overline{ACC}_j \leftarrow \overline{ACC}_j + \mathsf{MK.Prod}(X^{\hat{a}_{i,j} 2^\tau} \overline{ACC}_j, (\boldsymbol{d}_{i,j,\tau}, \boldsymbol{F}_{i,j,\tau}), \{b_i\}_{i \in \{1, \cdots, k\}}).$$

- SampleExtract: On input all accumulators and the component b of the ciphertext $\bar{\boldsymbol{c}}$, we compute the DFT inversion of the accumulators on the exponential, and obtain a sequence of multi-key RLWE ciphertext ACC_j for $j \in N$. Let $ACC_j = (c'_{j,0}, \cdots, c'_{j,k}) \in \mathcal{R}_q^{k+1}$.
  - In FHEW, firstly $ACC_j \leftarrow X^{b[j]} \cdot ACC_j$. Let $\boldsymbol{c}'_{j,i}$ be the vector representation of $c'_{j,i}$ for all $i \in \{1, \cdots, k\}$. Compute $ACC_j = \boldsymbol{t}^T (\boldsymbol{c}_{j,0}, \cdots, \boldsymbol{c}_{j,k})^4$, where $\boldsymbol{t} = (-1, -1, \cdots, -1) \in \mathbb{Z}^N$. Set the first entry of $\boldsymbol{c}'_{j,0}$ to $b'_{j,0}$, the polynomial representation of $\boldsymbol{c}'_{j,i}$ to $a'_{j,i}$ for $i \in \{1, \cdots, k\}$. Compute $\bar{\boldsymbol{c}}'_j = (v, 0, \cdots, 0) + (b'_{j,0}, a'_{j,1}, \cdots, a'_{j,k})$. Output N multi-key RLWE ciphertext $\{\bar{\boldsymbol{c}}'_j\}_{j \in [N]}$.
  - In TFHE, compute $ACC_j \leftarrow X^{\lfloor 2Nb[j] \rceil} ACC_j (1 + X + \cdots + X^N) X^{\frac{N}{2}}$. Set the consterm of $c'_{j,0}$ to $b'_{j,0}$, $a'_{j,i} = c'_{j,i}$ for $i \in \{1, \cdots, k\}$. Compute $\bar{\boldsymbol{c}}'_j = (v, 0, \cdots, 0) + (b'_{j,0}, a'_{j,1}, \cdots, a'_{j,k})$. Output N multi-key RLWE ciphertext $\{\bar{\boldsymbol{c}}'_j\}_{j \in [N]}$.

---

[4] T represents a transposition.

Correctness. The homomorphic multi-key RLWE accumulator is correct by the following steps:

- Increment: Since $(d_{i,j,\tau}, F_{i,j,\tau})$ is the uni-encryption of $\hat{s}_{i,j,\tau}$, the message of accumulator $\overline{ACC}_j$ is $v \sum_{i=1}^{k} \sum_{\tau=0}^{\ell-1} X^{\hat{a}_{i,j} 2^\tau \hat{s}_{i,j,\tau}} = v X^{\sum_{i=1}^{k} \hat{a}_{i,j} \hat{s}_{i,j}}$ for $j \in [N]$ according to Lemma 2.
- SampleExtract: In FHEW, if the jth coefficient of message m of multi-key ciphertext $\bar{c}$ is 1, then $t^T \cdot v X^{\frac{q}{t} m[j]+e} = 1$. Otherwise, if $m[j] = 0$, then $t^T \cdot v Y^{\frac{q}{t} m[j]+e} = -1$. We can get that $t^T \cdot v X^{\frac{q}{t} m[j]+e} = 2m[j] - 1$. Therefore, $t^T \cdot v X^{\frac{q}{t} m[j]+e} + v = 2vm[j]$. The message of output multi-key ciphertext is $2m[j]v$.

  In TFHE, after the inverse DFT on exponential, the message of accumulator ACC_j is $v X^{\sum_{i=1}^{k} -2N a_{i,j} s_{i,j}}$. Therefore,

  $$X^{\lfloor 2Nb[j] \rceil} ACC_j (1 + X + \cdots + X^N) X^{\frac{N}{2}} \\ = v X^{2N(b[j] - \sum_{i=1}^{k} a_{i,j} s_{i,j})} (1 + X + \cdots + X^N) X^{\frac{N}{2}}. \tag{1}$$

  If the jth coefficient of message m of multi-key ciphertext $\bar{c}$ is $1/2$, then the constant of (1) is v. Otherwise, if $m[j] = 0$, the the constant of (1) is $-v$. Therefore, the message of output multi-key ciphertext is $4m[j]v$.

Noise Estimation. According to Lemma 2, each calling subroutine MK.Prod will increase the noise with maximum $(k + 1)BN\ell(2B + 1)$ since the message $\hat{s}_{i,j,\tau}$ of uni-encryption is binary. We recursively evaluate the MK.Prod $k \cdot \log q$ for each accumulator. Therefore the output of accumulator has an error bounded by $(k^2 + k)BN\ell^2(2B + 1)$.

4   Batched Fully Dynamic MKFHE from FHEW-like Cryptosystems

In this section, we describe a batched fully dynamic MKFHE scheme based on RLWE problem. The bootstrapping technique of our scheme follows the FHEW-like cryptosystmes, including FHEW [16] and TFHE [14].

4.1   The Basic Scheme

This scheme MKFHE is parameterized by a message modulus $t = 4$, a dimension N which is power-of-two, and a ciphertext modulus q such that $q|2N$.

- MKFHE. Setup(1^λ): Run MS.Setup(1^λ) to generate the parameter $pp=(N, q, B, \chi, a)$. Return the public parameters pp.
- MKFHE.KeyGen(pp): Each party independently generates its keys as follows.
  - Sample a RLWE secret key $s \leftarrow$ RLWE.Keygen(pp) for general encryption. Compute $\hat{s}_j = DFT(-s)_j$ for $j \in [N]$.

- Let $\ell = \log q$. Run $(\boldsymbol{b}, z) \leftarrow \mathsf{MS.KeyGen}(pp)$ for uni-encryption. Run $(\boldsymbol{d}_{j,\tau}, \boldsymbol{F}_{j,\tau}) \leftarrow \mathsf{MS.UniEnc}(\hat{s}_{j,\tau}, z)$ for $\tau \in [\log q]$, where $\hat{s}_{j,\tau}$ satisfies that $\hat{s}_j = \sum_{\tau=0}^{\ell} \hat{s}_{j,\tau} \cdot 2^{\tau}$. Set public key as $\mathsf{PK} = \boldsymbol{b}$, and the bootstrapping key as $\mathsf{BK} = \{\boldsymbol{d}_{j,\tau}, \boldsymbol{F}_{j,\tau}\}_{j \in [N], \tau \in [\ell]}$.
- Run $\mathsf{KS} \leftarrow \mathsf{RLWE.KSGen}(z, s)$. Set key-switching key as KS.

Return the secret key s. Publish the triple $(\mathsf{PK}, \mathsf{BK}, \mathsf{KS})$.

- $\mathsf{MKFHE.Enc}(m, s)$: On input the message $m \in \mathcal{R}_t$, of which the coefficients are binary. Run $\boldsymbol{c} \leftarrow \mathsf{RLWE.Enc}(m, s)$. Return the RLWE ciphertext $\boldsymbol{c} \in \mathcal{R}_q^2$.

The dimension of a ciphertext increases after homomorphic computations or ciphertext extension (see Sect. 2.5), a multi-key ring-LWE ciphertext $\bar{c} = (b, a_1, a_2, \cdots, a_k) \in \mathcal{R}_q^{k+1}$ corresponding to the concatenated secret key $s = (1, -s_1, -s_2, \cdots, s_k)$ can be obtained.

- $\mathsf{MKFHE.Dec}(\bar{c}, \{s_i\}_{i \in \{1, \cdots, k\}})$: On input a ciphertext $\bar{c}$, concatenate the secret key $s = (1, -s_1, \cdots, s_k)$, return the message $m = \lfloor 2(b - \sum_{i=1}^{k} a_i s_i)/q \rceil \mod 2$.
- $\mathsf{MKFHE.NAND}(\bar{c}_1, \bar{c}_2)$: On input two multi-key ciphertext $\bar{c}_0$ and $\bar{c}_1$ which are associated with k parties. Compute $\bar{c}' = (\sum_{j=0}^{N-1} \frac{5q}{8} X^j, 0, \cdots, 0) - \bar{c}_1 - \bar{c}_2 \mod q$. Return the ciphertext $\bar{c}'$.

Correctness. Let the multi-key RLWE ciphertexts $\bar{c}_\iota = (b_\iota, a_{\iota,1}, \cdots, a_{\iota,k})$ satisfy that $\langle \bar{c}_\iota, s \rangle = \frac{q}{4} m_\iota + e_\iota$ for $\iota = 1, 2$. Then,

$$\langle \bar{c}, s \rangle = \sum_{j=0}^{N-1} \frac{5q}{8} X^j - (b_1 - \sum_{i=1}^{k} a_{1,i} s_i) - (b_2 - \sum_{i=1}^{k} a_{2,i} s_i)$$

$$= \sum_{j=0}^{N-1} [\pm\frac{q}{8} - e_1[j] - e_2[j] + \frac{q}{2}(1 - m_1[j] m_2[j])] X^j.$$

Therefore, the message of the output ciphertext $\bar{c}'$ is $m' = \sum_{j=0}^{N-1}(m_1[j] \bar{\wedge} m_2[j]) X^j$ as desired. Observe that the noise of the output ciphertext $\bar{c}'$ is $\sum_{j=0}^{N-1}(\pm\frac{q}{8} - e_1[j] - e_2[j]) X^j$. Therefore, the noise is bounded by $N \cdot \frac{q}{8} \cdot 2B = \frac{q}{4} NB$.

Security. The encryption security of our scheme depends on RLWE assumption [22]. Therefore, our scheme is semantic secure under RLWE assumption. In addition, each party publishes the uni-encryption of $\hat{s}_{j,\tau}$ encrypted by z, similar to FHEW [16] and all other bootstrappable FHE schemes such as [10,12,19], we also need additional circular security.

4.2   Bootstrapping Procedure

Given a multi-key ring-LWE ciphertext $\mathsf{RLWE}_s(m) = (b, a_1, \cdots, a_k) \in \mathcal{R}_q^{k+1}$, the bootstrapping procedure constructs an encryption of m under the same key

s but with a fixed amount of noise. As in [8], we will use uni-encrytption as an intermediate encryption scheme to perform the hybrid product. The difference is that our work relies on the multi-key ring-LWE accumulator for batching and multi-setting, while Chen et al's work just supports a single-bit bootstrapping. See Algorithm 1 for the pseudo-code.

Algorithm 1. Bootstrapping procedure$(\bar{c}, \mathsf{BK}, \mathsf{KS}, \mathsf{PK}, v)$

Input: A multi-key RLWE ciphertext $\mathsf{RLWE}_s(m) = (b, a_1, \cdots, a_k)$, bootstrapping keys $\{\mathsf{BK}_i\}_{i \in \{1,\cdots,k\}}$ where $\mathsf{BK}_i = \{d_{i,j,\tau}, F_{i,j,\tau}\}_{j \in [N], \tau \in [\ell]}$ under secret z_i, key-switching keys $\{\mathsf{KS}_i\}_{i \in \{1,\cdots,k\}}$ where $\mathsf{KS}_i = \mathsf{RLWE}_{-s_i}(z_i)$, public keys $\{\mathsf{PK}_i\}_{i \in \{1,\cdots,k\}}$, a constant v

Output: N multi-key RLWE ciphertexts $\mathsf{RLWE}_s(m[j])$ where $s = (1, -s_1, \cdots, -s_k)$
1: $\hat{a}_i = DFT(a_i)$
2: **for** $j = 0$ to $N - 1$ **do**
3:     Initialize the trivial multi-key RLWE sample as $\overline{ACC}_j = (v, 0, \cdots, 0) \in \mathcal{R}_q^{k+1}$
4:     **for** $i = 1$ to k **do**
5:         **for** $\tau = 0$ to $\ell - 1$ **do**
6:             $\overline{ACC}_j \leftarrow \overline{ACC}_j + \mathsf{MS.Prod}(X^{\hat{a}_{i,j}2^\tau}ACC_j, (d_{i,j,\tau}, F_{i,j,\tau}), \mathsf{PK})$
7:         **end for**
8:     **end for**
9: **end for**
10: $\{\bar{c}'_j\}_{j \in [N]} \leftarrow \mathsf{SampleExtract}(b, \{\overline{ACC}_j\}_{j \in [N]})$
11: **return** $\{\bar{c}'_j\}_{j \in [N]}$

4.3   Analysis

Lemma 3. *Let k be the number of the parities involved in the evaluation. Assume that the noise sampled from Gaussian error distribution χ is bounded by B. The noise of the output ciphertext of the batched MKFHE is bounded by $\tilde{O}(Nk^2B^2)$.*

Proof. The noise grows according to the following steps:

- **Ciphertext extension.** In Sect. 2.4, we simply extend it to FHEW which works in $\mathcal{R}_q$, while TFHE works in torus $\mathbb{T} = \mathbb{R} \bmod 1$. As shown in [8], the noise of the output ciphertext after MK.Prod algorithm is $r_i \sum_{j=0}^k \langle g^{-1}(c_j), e_j \rangle + \langle \sum_{j=0}^k z_j g^{-1}(c_j), e'_i \rangle + \langle \sum_{j=0}^k g^{-1}(v_j), e''_i \rangle$. Therefore, its noise is bounded by $(k + 1)BN\ell(2B + 1)$.
- **Accumulation.** For each accumulator $\overline{ACC}_j$, we recursively compute the MK.Prod algorithm $k\ell$ times. Furthermore, the plaintext $\hat{s}_{i,j,\tau}$ of uni-encryption is binary. So the noise of accumulator is bounded by $(k^2 + k)BN\ell^2(2B + 1)$.
- **Multi-key Switching.** As shown in Sect. 3.1, the noise of the output ciphertext after RLWE.MKSwitch algorithm is $\sum_{i=1}^k \langle g^{-1}(a_i), e_i \rangle$. Therefore, its noise is bounded by $k\ell BN$.

In summary, the noise of the output ciphertext of our batched MKFHE scheme is bounded by $(k^2 + k)BN\ell^2(2B + 1) + k\ell BN = \tilde{O}(Nk^2B^2)$.

Lemma 4. *Let k be any polynomial in λ, $pp \leftarrow$ MKFHE.Setup(1^λ) and $(sk_i, pk_i) \leftarrow$ MKFHE.KeyGen(pp) for $i \in \{1, \cdots, k\}$. Let $\bar{c}_1, \bar{c}_2$ be the multi-key RLWE ciphertexts under the secret keys S_1, S_2, respectively. Formally, $m_j \leftarrow$ MKFHE.Dec (pp, S_ι, c_ι) for $\iota = 1, 2$, where $S_j \in \{sk_i\}_{i \in \{1, \cdots, k\}}$. Then the following holds:*

$$\text{MKHE.Dec}(pp, \{sk_i\}_{i \in [k]}, \text{MKHE.NAND}(\{pk_i\}_{i \in [k]}, \bar{c}_1, \bar{c}_2)) = m_1 \bar{\wedge} m_2. \quad (2)$$

Proof. By the correctness of the MKFHE.NAND, the multi-key ciphertext $\bar{c}'$ from MKHE.NAND($\{pk_i\}_{i \in [k]}, \bar{c}_1, \bar{c}_2$) is an encryption of $m_1 \bar{\wedge} m_2$ under secret $S_1 \cup S_2$. Since $S_1 \cup S_2 \in \{sk_i\}_{i \in \{1, \cdots, k\}}$, we can convert the ciphertext $\bar{c}'$ to a larger dimensional ciphertext under secret key $\{sk_i\}_{i \in \{1, \cdots, k\}}$ (see Sect. 2.5). Next we need to ensure successful decryption.

To ensure correct decryption, the noise of the ciphertext $\bar{c}'$ must less than $q/4$. By Lemma 3, the upper limit of noise $(k^2 + k)BN\ell^2(2B + 1) + k\ell BN < q/4$. Note that the constant B is often very small. In practice, B is usually set to 1, where the secret distribution is ternary distribution. Therefore, we can get that $6k^2N\ell^2 < q/4$, namely, $k < \frac{1}{\ell}\sqrt{\frac{q}{24N}}$. Since N, ℓ are polynomials in λ, we can guarantee that decryption is successful by choosing a sufficiently large q. Therefore, the equality (2) holds as desired.

5   Theoretical Analysis

We compare our batched fully dynamic MKFHE with other FHEW-like MKFHE, batched MKFHE and full dynamic MKFHE schemes in Table 1 and 2.

Table 1 shows the main properties comparisons. One can observe that our scheme is the only MKFHE scheme that support batching, bootstrapping and fully dynamics. Moreover, our construction naturally inherits characteristics of the comprehensible FHEW-like cryptosystems, in which we can evaluate Boolean circuits on encrypted data. Although Brakerski et al.'s scheme [6] is also fully dynamic, their work relied on Gentry's bootstrapping technique and Barrington's theorem [3], which are complex and impractical.

Table 2 shows the complexity comparisons. The MKFHE schemes of Peikert et al. [27] and Huang et al. [20] are of GSW-type, and its computation complexity depends on matrix multiplication. The matrix multiplication has complexity of $O(N^{2.37})$ for N dimension matrices [30]. Brakerski et al.'s scheme [6] performed matrix-vector multiplication and vector-vector addition, which can all be performed in poly(k, N). Moreover, [11] required expanding the ciphertext into a matrix according to the number of parties. One can observe that the amortized cost of our scheme depend only on the the number of the parites involved in the evaluations and the logarithm of N. Furthermore, our scheme has better amortized computation complexity in evaluation key generation, which just $\tilde{O}(k)$.

The sizes of evaluation key and ciphertext grow linearly with the number of the parties, so does Chen et al.'s work [9].

In summary, we first proposed a batched fully dynamic MKFHE that supports bootstrapping. Furthermore, our work has the optimal amortized computation complexity in evaluation key generation and lowest storage cost.

Table 1. Main properties comparisons.

Scheme	Assumption	Type	Batch	Bootstrap	FHE Cryptosystem
Peikert et al. [27]	LWE	Multi-hop	✗	✗	GSW
Brakerski et al. [6]	LWE	Fully dynamic	✗	✓	GSW
Chen et al. [11]	RLWE	Multi-hop	✓	✗	BGV
Chen et al. [8]	LWE	Not given[1]	✗	✓	TFHE
Chen et al. [9]	RLWE	Not given	✓	✓	BFV/CKKS
Huang et al. [20]	LWR[2]	Fully dynamic	✗	✓	GSW
This work	RLWE	Fully dynamic	✓	✓	FHEW-like

1 The authors did not explain and prove.
2 LWR denotes learning with rounding problem introduced by Banerjee et al. [2].

Table 2. Complexity comparisons. k denotes the number of parties involved in the evaluation, N is the dimension of the RLWE (or LWE) assumption. PK denotes the public keys, EvaKey denotes the evaluation (or bootstrapping) keys.

Scheme	Space			Time		
	Type	Complexity	Amortized	Type	Complexity	Amortized
Peikert et al. [27]	PK	$\tilde{O}(kN^4)$	$\tilde{O}(kN^4)$	Hom Mult	$\tilde{O}(k^{2.37}N^{2.37})$	$\tilde{O}(k^{2.37}N^{2.37})$
	Cipher	$\tilde{O}(k^2N^4)$	$\tilde{O}(k^2N^4)$			
Brakerski et al. [6]	PK	$\tilde{O}(kN^3)$	$\tilde{O}(kN^3)$	Hom NAND	$\text{poly}(k,N)$	$\text{poly}(k,N)$
	Cipher	$\tilde{O}(kN)$	$\tilde{O}(kN)$			
Chen et al. [11]	EvaKey	$\tilde{O}(k^3N)$	$\tilde{O}(k^3)$	EvaKey Gen	$\tilde{O}(k^3N)\tilde{O}(k^3N)$	$\tilde{O}(k^3)\tilde{O}(k^3)$
	Cipher	$\tilde{O}(kN)$	$\tilde{O}(k)$	Hom Mult		
Chen et al. [8]	EvaKey	$\tilde{O}(kN)$	$\tilde{O}(kN)$	EvaKey Gen	$\tilde{O}(kN)\tilde{O}(k^2N^2)$	$\tilde{O}(kN)\tilde{O}(k^2N^2)$
	Cipher	$\tilde{O}(kN)$	$\tilde{O}(kN)$	Hom NAND		
Chen et al. [9]	EvaKey	$\tilde{O}(kN)$	$\tilde{O}(kN)$	EvaKey Gen	$\tilde{O}(kN^3)\tilde{O}(k^2N)$	$\tilde{O}(kN^2)\tilde{O}(k^2)$
	Cipher	$\tilde{O}(kN)$	$\tilde{O}(k)$	Hom Mult		
Huang et al. [20]	PK	$\tilde{O}(kN^3)$	$\tilde{O}(kN^3)$	Hom Mult	$\tilde{O}(k^{2.37}N^{2.37})$	$\tilde{O}(k^{2.37}N^{2.37})$
	Cipher	$\tilde{O}(kN)$	$\tilde{O}(kN)$			
This work	EvaKey	$\tilde{O}(kN)$	$\tilde{O}(k)$	EvaKey Gen	$\tilde{O}(kN)\tilde{O}(k^2N)$	$\tilde{O}(k)\tilde{O}(k^2)$
	Cipher	$\tilde{O}(kN)$	$\tilde{O}(k)$	Hom NAND		

6   Conclusion

In this paper, motivated by the packing work of FHEW-like cryptosystems, we propose a batched multi-key FHE in fully dynamic setting. Our construction has lower amortized storage and computational overhead in evaluation key generation, when compared with other fully dynamic or multi-hop MKFHE. Morever, to obtain an efficient bootstrapping in the multi-key setting, we design a multi-key RLWE accumulator with homomorphic DFT. The accumulator only needs $\tilde{O}(k^2 N)$ polynomial multiplications. We also provide a comprehensive theoretical analysis to demonstrate its merits.

Acknowledgement. This work was supported by the National Nature Science Foundation of China under Grant 62172434.

References

1. Alperin-Sheriff, J., Peikert, C.: Faster bootstrapping with polynomial error. In: Garay, J.A., Gennaro, R. (eds.) CRYPTO 2014. LNCS, vol. 8616, pp. 297–314. Springer, Heidelberg (2014). https://doi.org/10.1007/978-3-662-44371-2_17
2. Banerjee, A., Peikert, C., Rosen, A.: Pseudorandom functions and lattices. In: Pointcheval, D., Johansson, T. (eds.) EUROCRYPT 2012. LNCS, vol. 7237, pp. 719–737. Springer, Heidelberg (2012). https://doi.org/10.1007/978-3-642-29011-4_42
3. Barrington, D.A.M.: Bounded-width polynomial-size branching programs recognize exactly those languages in nc^1. J. Comput. Syst. Sci. **38**(1), 150–164 (1989). https://doi.org/10.1016/0022-0000(89)90037-8
4. Brakerski, Z.: Fully homomorphic encryption without modulus switching from classical GapSVP. In: Safavi-Naini, R., Canetti, R. (eds.) CRYPTO 2012. LNCS, vol. 7417, pp. 868–886. Springer, Heidelberg (2012). https://doi.org/10.1007/978-3-642-32009-5_50
5. Brakerski, Z., Gentry, C., Vaikuntanathan, V.: (leveled) fully homomorphic encryption without bootstrapping. ACM Trans. Comput. Theory **6**(3), 13:1-13:36 (2014). https://doi.org/10.1145/2633600
6. Brakerski, Z., Perlman, R.: Lattice-based fully dynamic multi-key FHE with short ciphertexts. In: Robshaw, M., Katz, J. (eds.) CRYPTO 2016. LNCS, vol. 9814, pp. 190–213. Springer, Heidelberg (2016). https://doi.org/10.1007/978-3-662-53018-4_8
7. Chase, M., et al.: Security of homomorphic encryption. Technical report, HomomorphicEncryption.org, Redmond WA, USA (2017)
8. Chen, H., Chillotti, I., Song, Y.: Multi-key homomorphic encryption from TFHE. In: Galbraith, S.D., Moriai, S. (eds.) ASIACRYPT 2019. LNCS, vol. 11922, pp. 446–472. Springer, Cham (2019). https://doi.org/10.1007/978-3-030-34621-8_16
9. Chen, H., Dai, W., Kim, M., Song, Y.: Efficient multi-key homomorphic encryption with packed ciphertexts with application to oblivious neural network inference. In: Proceedings of the 2019 ACM SIGSAC Conference on Computer and Communications Security, CCS, pp. 395–412. ACM (2019). https://doi.org/10.1145/3319535.3363207

10. Chen, H., Han, K.: Homomorphic lower digits removal and improved FHE boot-strapping. In: Nielsen, J.B., Rijmen, V. (eds.) EUROCRYPT 2018. LNCS, vol. 10820, pp. 315–337. Springer, Cham (2018). https://doi.org/10.1007/978-3-319-78381-9_12

11. Chen, L., Zhang, Z., Wang, X.: Batched multi-hop multi-key FHE from Ring-LWE with compact ciphertext extension. In: Kalai, Y., Reyzin, L. (eds.) TCC 2017. LNCS, vol. 10678, pp. 597–627. Springer, Cham (2017). https://doi.org/10.1007/978-3-319-70503-3_20

12. Cheon, J.H., Han, K., Kim, A., Kim, M., Song, Y.: Bootstrapping for approximate homomorphic encryption. In: Nielsen, J.B., Rijmen, V. (eds.) EUROCRYPT 2018. LNCS, vol. 10820, pp. 360–384. Springer, Cham (2018). https://doi.org/10.1007/978-3-319-78381-9_14

13. Cheon, J.H., Kim, A., Kim, M., Song, Y.: Homomorphic encryption for arithmetic of approximate numbers. In: Takagi, T., Peyrin, T. (eds.) ASIACRYPT 2017. LNCS, vol. 10624, pp. 409–437. Springer, Cham (2017). https://doi.org/10.1007/978-3-319-70694-8_15

14. Chillotti, I., Gama, N., Georgieva, M., Izabachène, M.: Faster fully homomorphic encryption: bootstrapping in less than 0.1 seconds. In: Cheon, J.H., Takagi, T. (eds.) ASIACRYPT 2016. LNCS, vol. 10031, pp. 3–33. Springer, Heidelberg (2016). https://doi.org/10.1007/978-3-662-53887-6_1

15. Clear, M., McGoldrick, C.: Multi-identity and multi-key leveled FHE from learning with errors. In: Gennaro, R., Robshaw, M. (eds.) CRYPTO 2015. LNCS, vol. 9216, pp. 630–656. Springer, Heidelberg (2015). https://doi.org/10.1007/978-3-662-48000-7_31

16. Ducas, L., Micciancio, D.: FHEW: bootstrapping homomorphic encryption in less than a second. In: Oswald, E., Fischlin, M. (eds.) EUROCRYPT 2015. LNCS, vol. 9056, pp. 617–640. Springer, Heidelberg (2015). https://doi.org/10.1007/978-3-662-46800-5_24

17. Fan, J., Vercauteren, F.: Somewhat practical fully homomorphic encryption. IACR Cryptol. ePrint Arch. 2012, 144 (2012). http://eprint.iacr.org/2012/144

18. Gentry, C.: Fully homomorphic encryption using ideal lattices. In: Proceedings of the 41st Annual ACM Symposium on Theory of Computing, STOC 2009, pp. 169–178. ACM (2009). https://doi.org/10.1145/1536414.1536440

19. Halevi, S., Shoup, V.: Bootstrapping for HElib. In: Oswald, E., Fischlin, M. (eds.) EUROCRYPT 2015. LNCS, vol. 9056, pp. 641–670. Springer, Heidelberg (2015). https://doi.org/10.1007/978-3-662-46800-5_25

20. Huang, Y., Wu, K., Chen, M.: Fully dynamic multi-key FHE without gaussian noise. IEEE Access 9, 50639–50645 (2021). https://doi.org/10.1109/ACCESS.2021.3069214

21. López-Alt, A., Tromer, E., Vaikuntanathan, V.: On-the-fly multiparty computation on the cloud via multikey fully homomorphic encryption. In: Proceedings of the 44th Symposium on Theory of Computing Conference, STOC 2012, pp. 1219–1234. ACM (2012). https://doi.org/10.1145/2213977.2214086

22. Lyubashevsky, V., Peikert, C., Regev, O.: On ideal lattices and learning with errors over rings. In: Gilbert, H. (ed.) EUROCRYPT 2010. LNCS, vol. 6110, pp. 1–23. Springer, Heidelberg (2010). https://doi.org/10.1007/978-3-642-13190-5_1

23. Lyubashevsky, V., Peikert, C., Regev, O.: A toolkit for ring-LWE cryptography. In: Johansson, T., Nguyen, P.Q. (eds.) EUROCRYPT 2013. LNCS, vol. 7881, pp. 35–54. Springer, Heidelberg (2013). https://doi.org/10.1007/978-3-642-38348-9_3

24. Micciancio, D., Polyakov, Y.: Bootstrapping in FHEW-like cryptosystems. In: WAHC 2021: Proceedings of the 9th on Workshop on Encrypted Computing & Applied Homomorphic Cryptography, Virtual Event, pp. 17–28. WAHC@ACM (2021). https://doi.org/10.1145/3474366.3486924

25. Micciancio, D., Sorrell, J.: Ring packing and amortized FHEW bootstrapping. In: 45th International Colloquium on Automata, Languages, and Programming, ICALP 2018. LIPIcs, vol. 107, pp. 100:1–100:14. Schloss Dagstuhl - Leibniz-Zentrum für Informatik (2018). https://doi.org/10.4230/LIPIcs.ICALP.2018.100

26. Mukherjee, P., Wichs, D.: Two round multiparty computation via multi-key FHE. In: Fischlin, M., Coron, J.-S. (eds.) EUROCRYPT 2016. LNCS, vol. 9666, pp. 735–763. Springer, Heidelberg (2016). https://doi.org/10.1007/978-3-662-49896-5_26

27. Peikert, C., Shiehian, S.: Multi-key FHE from LWE, revisited. In: Hirt, M., Smith, A. (eds.) TCC 2016. LNCS, vol. 9986, pp. 217–238. Springer, Heidelberg (2016). https://doi.org/10.1007/978-3-662-53644-5_9

28. Regev, O.: On lattices, learning with errors, random linear codes, and cryptography. In: Proceedings of the 37th Annual ACM Symposium on Theory of Computing, pp. 84–93. ACM (2005), https://doi.org/10.1145/1060590.1060603

29. Smart, N.P., Vercauteren, F.: Fully homomorphic SIMD operations. Des. Codes Crypt. **71**(1), 57–81 (2012). https://doi.org/10.1007/s10623-012-9720-4

30. Williams, V.V.: Multiplying matrices faster than coppersmith-winograd. In: Proceedings of the 44th Symposium on Theory of Computing Conference, STOC, pp. 887–898. ACM (2012). https://doi.org/10.1145/2213977.2214056

Zero-Knowledge Range Arguments for Signed Fractional Numbers from Lattices

Priyanka Dutta[1]([✉])[ID], Dung Hoang Duong[1][ID], Willy Susilo[1][ID],
Kazuhide Fukushima[2][ID], and Shinsaku Kiyomoto[2][ID]

[1] Institute of Cybersecurity and Cryptology, School of Computing and Information Technology, University of Wollongong, Northfields Avenue, Wollongong, NSW 2522, Australia
pd397@uowmail.edu.au, {hduong,wsusilo}@uow.edu.au

[2] Information Security Laboratory, KDDI Research, Inc., 2-1-15 Ohara, Fujimino-shi, Saitama 356-8502, Japan
{ka-fukushima,kiyomoto}@kddi-research.jp

Abstract. Range proofs introduced by Brickell et al. at CRYPTO 1988, allow a prover to convince a verifier that the committed value belongs to an interval without revealing anything else. It has become an essential building block in various modern cryptographic protocols such as distributed ledgers, anonymous transactions, e-cash, e-voting, auction protocols, privacy-preserving certificate transparency, and many more. In this paper, we provide a zero-knowledge range argument system showing that a committed value is in a public or hidden range by constructing a zero-knowledge argument system to prove inequalities between signed fractional numbers as well as non-negative integers in the standard lattice settings. The complexity of our range arguments is only logarithmic in the size of the range. Negative numbers and fractional numbers play an important role in our everyday life, especially in financial loss, medical data, bank account balances, GPA and tax records, etc. It would be desirable to handle them in a privacy-preserving manner. Prior to this work, all the lattice-based zero-knowledge range argument systems only address a range of non-negative integers, whereas our range arguments can handle signed fractional numbers and fill an interesting research gap in the literature.

1 Introduction

Range proofs allow a prover to convince a verifier that committed value belongs to an interval without revealing anything else. It is an important primitive in the arsenal of privacy-preserving cryptographic protocols. For example, in Blockchain-based distributed ledger, requires that the transaction amount should

This work is partially supported by the Australian Research Council Linkage Project LP190100984.

be hidden to ease privacy disclosure and other problems. But, using the range proof protocol, one can still verify the legitimacy of a transaction. Efficient range proofs have recently become central components in distributed ledgers, the prime example being the recent integration of Bulletproof [5] in the cryptocurrency Monero. Range proofs also play an essential role in anonymous credentials, where users can prove that their identity or private information belongs to a certain range without revealing any other details. Furthermore, for e-voting [10,22], e-cash [11,28], confidential transaction [38], e-auctions [31] and procurement, there are many works describing direct applications of range proofs, explicitly zero-knowledge range proofs [32,35].

Currently known range proofs proceed via two distinct approaches. The first one proceeds by breaking integers into bits or small digits [3,6,9,21,23], which allows communicating a sub-logarithmic (in the range size) number of group elements in the best known constructions [6,21,23]. The second approach [4,8,22, 30] appeals to integer commitments and groups of hidden order. This approach is usually preferred for very large ranges (which often arise in applications like anonymous credentials [14], where range elements are comprised of thousands of bits) where it tends to be more efficient and it does not require the maximal range length to be known when the commitment key is chosen.

There are many efficient constructions of range proof have been proposed in various cryptographic context [7,29,34,39]. However, there is only one paper [34] considering signed fractional numbers, which is constructed in code-based settings. Negative numbers do often appear in our daily life in the forms of financial loss, bad reputation, medical data, etc., and it would be desirable to be able to handle them in a privacy-preserving manner. Moreover, these data values could be stored as fractional numbers, e.g., bank account balances, GPAs and tax records, and hence, a protocol addressing them directly in such forms would potentially be interesting. However, code-based privacy-preserving cryptographic constructions are still rather underdeveloped. On the other hand, lattice-based cryptography already facilitating the quantum-safe constructions for e-voting [2], e-cash [11,28], confidential transaction [38] and many others [13–18,37]. Hence, lattice-based zero-knowledge range arguments for signed fractional numbers are expected to facilitate ongoing research to construct quantum-safe e-voting, e-cash, confidential transactions, and many more.

Our Contributions and Overview of Techniques: In lattice-based cryptography, zero-knowledge range arguments for committed numbers are only explored for non-negative integers [7,12,29,39] and there has been no treatment for signed fractional numbers. In this paper, we aim to fill this gap in the literature by presenting the first zero-knowledge range arguments for committed signed fractional numbers based on standard lattices. It is worth mentioning that the proposed protocol has the same communication complexity, *logarithmic in range size* as in [29]. In summary, our contributions are two folds, each of which potentially yields various other applications:

- First, we build a zero-knowledge arguments of knowledge (ZKAoK) for proving inequalities between signed fractional numbers as well as non-negative integers in the standard lattice settings.
- Second, using this core argument system, we construct an efficient ZKAoK showing that a committed value is in a public or hidden range.

In order to build a zero-knowledge range argument for committed signed fractional numbers as well as non-negative integers, we depart from the lattice-based KTX commitment scheme [25]. From a very high level, we first build a zero-knowledge argument system for proving that a committed signed fractional number X satisfies inequalities $X \leq Y$ or $X < Y$, where Y is another signed fractional number that could be publicly given or committed. Then, based on these core argument systems, we obtain a range argument system for the statements "$X \in [\mu, \nu]$", "$X \in (\mu, \nu]$", "$X \in [\mu, \nu)$", "$X \in (\mu, \nu)$", where X is committed under the KTX commitment, and a, b can be publicly given or committed.

In more detail, we consider fractional numbers represented in fixed-point binary format. For $\ell > 0$ and $f \geq 0$, signed fractional numbers X is represented as $x_\ell \cdots x_0 . x_{-1} \cdots x_{-f}$, where x_ℓ is the sign bit, $x_{\ell-1}, \cdots, x_0$ are the integer bits, and $x_{-1}, \cdots, x_{-f}$ are the fractional bits. To handle the inequalities among signed fractional numbers in lattice settings, we have utilized the strategy developed by Nguyen et al. [34] for the code-based settings. At first, to build a lattice-based zero-knowledge argument system for showing that two committed signed fractional numbers X, Y, satisfy the inequality $X \leq Y$, we show via zero-knowledge that there exists $Z \geq 0$ such that $X + Z = Y$. To handle strict inequalities $X < Y$ between two committed signed fractional numbers X, Y, specifically, we show the existence of $Z \geq 0$ such that $X + Z + 1 = Y$, which we achieve by doing some additional improvement in the protocol for $X \leq Y$. If Y is public, then the inequalities such as $X \leq Y$, or $X < Y$ can be handled using a simplified version of the above protocols, where the bits representing Y are not required to be kept secret. To prove $X < Y$ for public Y, we can build a zero-knowledge argument system for $X \leq Y'$, where $Y' = Y - 2^{-f}$. By combining these zero-knowledge argument systems, we build zero-knowledge range arguments for showing that a committed value is in a public or hidden range.

2 Preliminaries

We denote the set of real numbers, rational numbers and integers by $\mathbb{R}$, $\mathbb{Q}$ and $\mathbb{Z}$ respectively. We denote column-vectors by lower-case bold letters (e.g. $\mathbf{b}$), and row-vectors are represented via transposition (e.g. $\mathbf{b}^t$). Matrix is denoted by upper-case bold letters and treated interchangeably as an ordered set of its column vectors. Let $\mathbf{I}$ and $\mathbf{0}$ denote the identity and the zero matrices respectively, where the dimension will clear from the context. A negligible function is generically denoted by $\mathsf{negl}(n)$. We say that a probability is overwhelming if it is $1 - \mathsf{negl}(n)$. The *statistical distance* between two distributions $\mathbf{X}$ and $\mathbf{Y}$ over a countable domain Ω is defined as $\frac{1}{2} \sum_{w \in \Omega} |\mathsf{Pr}[\mathbf{X} = w] - \mathsf{Pr}[\mathbf{Y} = w]|$. We say that a distribution over Ω is ϵ-far if its statistical distance from the uniform distribution is at most ϵ. We assume that all vectors are column vectors. The concatenation of matrices $\mathbf{A} \in \mathbb{Z}^{k \times i}, \mathbf{B} \in \mathbb{Z}^{k \times j}$ is denoted by $[\mathbf{A}|\mathbf{B}] \in \mathbb{Z}^{k \times (i+j)}$. The concatenation of two column vectors $\mathbf{b}_1 \in \mathbb{Z}^m, \mathbf{b}_2 \in \mathbb{Z}^n$ is denoted by $(\mathbf{b}_1 \| \mathbf{b}_2) \in \mathbb{Z}^{m+n}$. For $a, b \in \mathbb{Z}$ and $c \in \mathbb{Q}$, we let $[a, b]$ denote the set of all integers between a and b (inclusive), and let $c \cdot [a, b]$ denote the set $\{c \cdot x | x \in [a, b]\}$. For $b \in \{0, 1\}$, we denote the bit $1 - b \in \{0, 1\}$ by $\bar{b}$. For a positive integer i, we let $[i]$ be the set $\{1, \cdots, i\}$. For a finite set S, $x \xleftarrow{\$} S$ means that x is chosen uniformly at random from S. All logarithms are of base 2. The addition in $\mathbb{Z}_2$ is denoted by $\oplus$.

2.1 Lattices

A *lattice* Λ is a discrete additive subgroup of $\mathbb{R}^m$. Specially, a lattice Λ in $\mathbb{R}^m$ with a basis $\mathbf{B} = [\mathbf{b}_1 | \cdots | \mathbf{b}_n] \in \mathbb{R}^{m \times n}$, where each $\mathbf{b}_i$ is written in column form, is defined as $\Lambda := \{\sum_{i=1}^n \mathbf{b}_i x_i | x_i \in \mathbb{Z} \; \forall i \in [n]\} \subseteq \mathbb{R}^m$. We call n the rank of Λ and if $n = m$ we say that Λ is a full rank lattice. In this paper, we mainly consider full rank lattices containing $q\mathbb{Z}^m$, called q-ary lattices, which are defined as follows. Given a matrix $\mathbf{A} \in \mathbb{Z}_q^{n \times m}$ and $\mathbf{u} \in \mathbb{Z}_q^n$ $\Lambda_q(\mathbf{A}) = \{\mathbf{z} \in \mathbb{Z}^m : \exists \mathbf{s} \in \mathbb{Z}_q^n \; s.t. \; \mathbf{z} = \mathbf{A}^\top \mathbf{s} \bmod q\}; \; \Lambda_q^\perp(\mathbf{A}) = \{\mathbf{z} \in \mathbb{Z}^m : \mathbf{A}\mathbf{z} = 0 \bmod q\}$. We define $\Lambda_q^\mathbf{u}(\mathbf{A}) = \{\mathbf{z} \in \mathbb{Z}^m : \mathbf{A}\mathbf{z} = \mathbf{u} \bmod q\} = \Lambda_q^\perp(\mathbf{A}) + \mathbf{x}$ *for* $\mathbf{x} \in \Lambda_q^\mathbf{u}(\mathbf{A})$.

Vector and Matrix Norms: For a vector $\mathbf{u} \in \mathbb{Z}^m$, let $\|\mathbf{u}\|_2 = \sqrt{\sum_i |u_i|^2}$ denote its ℓ_2 norm, and $\|\mathbf{u}\|_\infty = \max_i |u_i|$ denote its infinity-norm (ℓ_∞). For a matrix $\mathbf{R} \in \mathbb{Z}^{k \times m}$, let $\|\mathbf{R}\|$ be the ℓ_2 length of the longest column of $\mathbf{R}$. $\|\mathbf{R}\|_2$ is the operator norm of $\mathbf{R}$ defined as $\|\mathbf{R}\|_2 = \sup_{\|\mathbf{x}\|=1} \|\mathbf{R}\mathbf{x}\|$, and $\|\mathbf{R}\|_\infty$ is the infinity-norm of $\mathbf{R}$ defined as $\|\mathbf{R}\|_\infty = \max_i \sum_j |r_{ij}|$.

Definition 1 ($\mathsf{SIS}_{n,m,q,\beta}^\infty$ [1,19]). Given uniformly random matrix $\mathbf{A} \in \mathbb{Z}_q^{n \times m}$, find a non-zero vector $\mathbf{x} \in \mathbb{Z}^m$ such that $\|\mathbf{x}\|_\infty \leq \beta$ and $\mathbf{A} \cdot \mathbf{x} = \mathbf{0} \bmod q$.

If $m, \beta = poly(n)$, and $q > \beta \cdot \widetilde{\mathcal{O}}(\sqrt{n})$, then the $\mathsf{SIS}_{n,m,q,\beta}^\infty$ problem is at least as hard as worst-case lattice problem SIVP_γ for some $\gamma = \beta \cdot \widetilde{\mathcal{O}}(\sqrt{nm})$. For details, see [19,33].

2.2 The KTX Commitment Scheme

In this section, we present the lattice-based commitment schemes, proposed by Kawachi, Tanaka and Xagawa (KTX) [25]. It has two flavours, one is fixed-length commitment scheme, another one is the string commitment scheme. We use the fixed-length commitment scheme to commit to secret bits, and use the string commitment scheme to design the stern-like protocols.

The KTX Commitment Scheme. Let n be the security parameter. Let $q = \mathcal{O}(\sqrt{L} \cdot n)$ be the prime modulus, and $m = n(\lceil \log_2 q \rceil + 3)$ be an integer. Also, let $L \leq poly(n)$ be the length of the committed vector.

The commitment keys of the commitment scheme is $(\mathbf{a}_0, \mathbf{a}_1, \cdots, \mathbf{a}_{L-1}, \mathbf{b}_1, \cdots, \mathbf{b}_m)$, where $\mathbf{a}_0, \cdots, \mathbf{a}_{L-1} \xleftarrow{\$} \mathbb{Z}_q^{n \times 1}$ and $\mathbf{b}_1, \cdots, \mathbf{b}_m \xleftarrow{\$} \mathbb{Z}_q^{n \times 1}$.

To commit to $(x_0, \cdots, x_{L-1}) \in \{0,1\}^L$, the commit algorithm first samples $r_1, \cdots, r_m \xleftarrow{\$} \{0,1\}$, then it outputs a commitment $\mathbf{c} = \sum_{i=0}^{L-1} \mathbf{a}_i \cdot x_i + \sum_{j=1}^m \mathbf{b}_j \cdot r_j$ mod $q \in \mathbb{Z}_q^n$.

To Open the commitment, it reveals $(x_0, \cdots, x_{L-1}) \in \{0,1\}^m$, and $r_1, \cdots, r_m \in \{0,1\}$.

Computationally Binding: If one can compute two valid openings $(x_0', \cdots, x_{L-1}', r_1', \cdots, r_m')$ and $(x_0'', \cdots, x_{L-1}'', r_1'', \cdots, r_m'')$ for the same commitment $\mathbf{c}$ such that $(x_0', \cdots, x_{L-1}') \neq (x_0'', \cdots, x_{L-1}'')$, then one can solve the $\mathsf{SIS}_{n,m+L,q,1}^\infty$ problem associated with the uniformly random matrix $[\mathbf{a}_0 | \mathbf{a}_1 | \cdots | \mathbf{a}_{L-1} | \mathbf{b}_1 | \cdots | \mathbf{b}_m] \in \mathbb{Z}_q^{n \times (m+L)}$. Thus, the scheme is computationally binding, assuming the hardness of $\mathsf{SIVP}_{\widetilde{\mathcal{O}}(\sqrt{L} \cdot n)}$.

Statistically Hiding: By the left over hash lemma [20], the distribution of a commitment $\mathbf{c}$ is statistically close to uniform over $\mathbb{Z}_q^n$. This implies that the scheme is statistically hiding.

For $L = 1$, the scheme becomes a bit commitment scheme, using a small modulus $q = \widetilde{\mathcal{O}}(n)$, rely on a weak SIVP assumption with $\gamma = \widetilde{\mathcal{O}}(n)$.

Kawachi *et al.* [25] extended the above fixed-length commitment scheme to a string commitment scheme $\mathsf{COM} : \{0,1\}^* \times \{0,1\}^m \leftarrow \mathbb{Z}_q^n$. This scheme is also statistically hiding for the given setting of parameters, and computationally binding assuming that $\mathsf{SIVP}_{\widetilde{\mathcal{O}}(n)}$ is hard.

2.3   Zero-Knowledge Argument System and Stern-Like Protocols

In this paper, we build statistical zero-knowledge argument systems, namely, interactive protocols where the zero-knowledge property holds against any cheating verifier, while the soundness property only holds against *computationally bounded* cheating provers.

Let the set of statements-witnesses $R = \{(y,w)\} \in \{0,1\}^* \times \{0,1\}^*$ be an NP relation. A two-party protocol $\langle \mathcal{P}, \mathcal{V} \rangle$ is called an interactive argument system for the relation R with soundness error e if the following two conditions hold:

- Completeness. If $(y,w) \in R$ then $\Pr[\langle \mathcal{P}(y,w), \mathcal{V}(y) \rangle = 1] = 1$.
- Soundness. If $(y,w) \notin R$ then $\forall$PPT $\widehat{\mathcal{P}}$: $\Pr[\langle \widehat{\mathcal{P}}(y,w), \mathcal{V}(y) \rangle = 1] \leq e$.

An argument system is called statistical zero-knowledge if for any $\widehat{\mathcal{V}}(y)$, there exists a PPT simulator $\mathcal{S}(y)$ producing a simulated transcript that is statistically close to the one of the real interaction between $\mathcal{P}(y,w)$ and $\widehat{\mathcal{V}}(y)$. A related notion is argument of knowledge, which requires the witness-extended emulation property. For protocols consisting of 3 moves (i.e., commit-challenge-response), witness-extended emulation is implied by special soundness, where the latter assumes that there exists a PPT extractor which takes as input a set of valid transcripts with respect to all possible values of the 'challenge' to the same 'commitment', and outputs w' such that $(y, w') \in R$.

The statistical zero-knowledge arguments of knowledge (sZKAoK) presented in this paper are Stern-type protocols [36]. Specifically, they are Σ-protocols in a more generalized sense [24]. In particular, instead of two valid transcripts, they need three valid transcripts for extraction. Using the KTX commitment scheme [25], we obtain statistical zero-knowledge argument of knowledge (ZKAoK) systems with perfect completeness, constant soundness error $2/3$. To make the soundness error negligibly small in n, the protocol needs to be repeated $\kappa = \omega(\log n)$ times.

2.4   Extending-Then-Permuting Techniques

We recall the extending-then-permuting techniques for proving in Stern's framework [36] the knowledge of a single bit x and a product of 2 secret bits $x_1 \cdot x_2$, presented in [26,27], respectively.

For any bit $b \in \{0, 1\}$, define $\bar{b} = b + 1 \mod 2$, and $\mathsf{ext}_2(b) = (\bar{b}, b) \in \{0, 1\}^2$. For any bit $c \in \{0, 1\}$, define P_c^2 be the permutation that transforms the integer vector $\mathbf{v} = (v_0, v_1) \in \mathbb{Z}^2$ into $P_c^2(\mathbf{v}) = (v_c, v_{\bar{c}}) \in \mathbb{Z}^2$. In details, for $c = 0$, P_c^2 keeps the arrangement of $\mathbf{v}$ as it is; otherwise swaps them if $c = 1$. We have,

$$\mathbf{v} = \mathsf{ext}_2(b) \iff P_c^2(\mathbf{v}) = \mathsf{ext}_2(b + c \mod 2). \tag{1}$$

As shown in [27], the equivalence (1) helps proving knowledge of a secret bit x that may appear in several correlated linear equations. To this end, one extends x to $\mathsf{ext}_2(x)$, and permutes the latter using P_c^2, where c is a uniformly random bit. Seeing the permuted vector $\mathsf{ext}_2(x + c \mod 2)$ convinces the verifier that the original vector $\mathsf{ext}_2(x)$ is well-formed – which in turn implies knowledge of some bit x – while c acts as a "one-time pad" that completely hides x.

To prove that a bit is the product $x_1 \cdot x_2$ of two secret bits, Libert et al. [26] introduced the following technique. For any 2 bits b_1, b_2, define an extension of the bit product $b_1 \cdot b_2$ as $\mathsf{ext}_4(b_1, b_2) = (\bar{b}_1 \cdot \bar{b}_2, \bar{b}_1 \cdot b_2, b_1 \cdot \bar{b}_2, b_1 \cdot b_2) \in \{0, 1\}^4$.

For any two bits $c_1, c_2 \in \{0, 1\}$, define P_{c_1, c_2}^4 be the permutation that transforms the integer vector $\mathbf{v} = (v_{0,0}, v_{0,1}, v_{1,0}, v_{1,1}) \in \mathbb{Z}^4$ into the integer vector $P_{c_1, c_2}^4(\mathbf{v}) = (v_{c_1, c_2}, v_{c_1, \bar{c}_2}, v_{\bar{c}_1, c_2}, v_{\bar{c}_1, \bar{c}_2}) \in \mathbb{Z}^4$. We have,

$$\mathbf{v} = \mathsf{ext}_4(b_1, b_2) \iff P_{c_1, c_2}^4(\mathbf{v}) = \mathsf{ext}_4(b_1 + c_1 \mod 2, b_2 + c_2 \mod 2). \tag{2}$$

As a result, to prove the well-formedness of $x_1 \cdot x_2$, one can extend it to the vector $\mathsf{ext}_4(x_1, x_2)$, permute the latter using P_{c_1, c_2}^4, where c_1, c_2 are uniformly random bits, and send the permuted vector to the verifier who should be convinced that the original vector, i.e., $\mathsf{ext}_4(x_1, x_2)$ is well-formed, while learning nothing else about x_1 and x_2, due to the randomness of c_1 and c_2.

2.5   A Treatment of Signed Fractional Numbers

In this section, we recall some results related to signed fractional numbers, presented in [34]. We consider *signed fractional numbers* represented in *fixed-point binary format*. For $\ell > 0$ and $f \geq 0$, signed fractional numbers X is represented as $x_\ell \cdots x_0.x_{-1} \cdots x_{-f}$, where x_ℓ is the sign bit, $x_{\ell-1}, \cdots, x_0$ are the integer bits, and $x_{-1}, \cdots, x_{-f}$ are the fractional bits. We define the set $\mathbf{Q}\langle \ell \bullet f \rangle$ as follows:

$$\mathbf{Q}\langle \ell \bullet f \rangle = 2^{-f} \cdot [-2^{\ell+f}, 2^{\ell+f} - 1]$$

$$= \Big\{ -2^\ell \cdot x_\ell + \sum_{i=-f}^{\ell-1} 2^i \cdot x_i \,\big|\, (x_\ell, \cdots, x_0, x_{-1}, \cdots, x_{-f}) \in \{0,1\}^{1+\ell+f} \Big\}.$$

For each element $X \in \mathbf{Q}\langle \ell \bullet f \rangle$, $\mathsf{sbin}_{\ell,f}(X)$ represents the binary vector $(x_\ell, \cdots, x_0, x_{-1}, \cdots, x_{-f}) \in \{0,1\}^{1+\ell+f}$. We write $A = \mathsf{sbin}_{\ell,f}^{-1}(\mathbf{a})$ if $\mathbf{a} = \mathsf{sbin}_{\ell,f}(A)$. So, we have $\mathbf{Q}\langle \ell \bullet f \rangle = \{\mathsf{sbin}_{\ell,f}^{-1}(\mathbf{a}) | \mathbf{a} \in \{0,1\}^{1+\ell+f}\}$. As discussed in [34], handling signed fractional numbers, mainly inequalities over $\mathbf{Q}\langle \ell \bullet f \rangle$ are not trivial, due to the signed bit, and the problems of overflows. To overcome these issues, we treat elements of $\mathbf{Q}\langle \ell \bullet f \rangle$ as elements of $\mathbf{Q}\langle (\ell + 2) \bullet f \rangle$. If $X \in \mathbf{Q}\langle \ell \bullet f \rangle$ with $\mathsf{sbin}_{\ell,f}(X) = (x_\ell, \cdots, x_0, x_{-1}, \cdots, x_{-f})$, then we have $X = -2^\ell \cdot x_\ell + \sum_{i=-f}^{\ell-1} 2^i \cdot x_i = (-2^{\ell+2} + 2^{\ell+1} + 2^\ell) \cdot x_\ell + \sum_{i=-f}^{\ell-1} 2^i \cdot x_i$, and thus $\mathsf{sbin}_{\ell+2,f}(X) = (x_\ell, x_\ell, x_\ell, x_{\ell-1}, \cdots, x_0, x_{-1}, \cdots, x_{-f}) \in \{0,1\}^{3+\ell+f}$, an element of $\mathbf{Q}\langle (\ell + 2) \bullet f \rangle$.

Definition 2 (Signed Fractional additions in Binary [34]). Let $X, Z \in \mathbf{Q}\langle (\ell + 2) \bullet f \rangle$. The sum $\mathsf{sbin}_{\ell+2,f}(X) \boxplus_{\ell+2,f} \mathsf{sbin}_{\ell+2,f}(Z)$ is a vector $\mathbf{y} = (y_{\ell+2}, \cdots, y_0, y_{-1}, \cdots, y_{-f})$ associated with a vector $\mathbf{c} = (c_{\ell+2}, \cdots, c_0, c_{-1}, \cdots, c_{-f+1})$ such that

$$c_{-f+1} = x_{-f} \cdot z_{-f}$$
$$c_i = x_{i-1} \cdot z_{i-1} \oplus y_{i-1} \cdot c_{i-1} \oplus c_{i-1}, \forall i \in [-f+2, \ell+2]$$
$$y_{-f} = x_{-f} \oplus z_{-f}$$
$$y_i = x_i \oplus z_i \oplus c_i, \forall i \in [-f+1, \ell+2].$$

The following lemma implies that, given $X, Y \in \mathbf{Q}\langle \ell \bullet f \rangle$, if we compute their sum over $\mathbf{Q}\langle (\ell + 2) \bullet f \rangle$, then we can avoid overflows. Hence, this will help us to capture the inequality $X \leq Y$ via addition.

Lemma 1 (Lemma 3, [34]). *Let $X, Y \in \mathbf{Q}\langle \ell \bullet f \rangle \subset \mathbf{Q}\langle (\ell + 2) \bullet f \rangle$. Then $X \leq Y$ if and only if $Z = Y - X \in 2^{-f} \cdot [0, 2^{1+\ell+f} - 1] \subset \mathbf{Q}\langle (\ell + 2) \bullet f \rangle$ and $\mathsf{sbin}_{\ell+2,f}(X) \boxplus_{\ell+2,f} \mathsf{sbin}_{\ell+2,f}(Z)$ does not cause an overflow. As a corollary, $\mathsf{sbin}_{\ell+2,f}(X) \boxplus_{\ell+2,f} \mathsf{sbin}_{\ell+2,f}(Z) = \mathsf{sbin}_{\ell+2,f}(Y)$; $\mathsf{sbin}_{\ell+2,f}(Z) = (0, 0, z_\ell, \cdots, z_{-f})$.*

The following Theorem 1 is about the necessary and sufficient conditions for $X \leq Y$, with $X, Y \in \mathbf{Q}\langle \ell \bullet f \rangle$, such that these conditions can be correctly and efficiently proved in zero-knowledge.

Theorem 1 (Theorem 2, [34]). *Let* $X, Y \in \mathbf{Q}\langle \ell \bullet f \rangle$, *and* $\mathsf{sbin}_{\ell,f}(X) = (x_\ell, x_{\ell-1}, \cdots, x_0, x_{-1}, \cdots, x_{-f}), \mathsf{sbin}_{\ell,f}(Y) = (y_\ell, y_{\ell-1}, \cdots, y_0, y_{-1}, \cdots, y_{-f})$. *Then,* $X \leq Y$ *if and only if there exist bits* $z_\ell, z_{\ell-1}, \cdots, z_0, z_{-1}, \cdots, z_{-f}, c_{\ell+1}, c_\ell, c_{\ell-1}, \cdots, c_0, c_{-1}, \cdots, c_{-f+1}$ *satisfying*

$$c_{-f+1} = x_{-f} \cdot z_{-f}$$
$$c_i = x_{i-1} \cdot z_{i-1} \oplus y_{i-1} \cdot c_{i-1} \oplus c_{i-1}, \forall i \in [-f+2, \ell+1]$$
$$y_{-f} = x_{-f} \oplus z_{-f}$$
$$y_i = x_i \oplus z_i \oplus c_i, \forall i \in [-f+1, \ell]$$
$$y_\ell = x_\ell \oplus c_{\ell+1}.$$

For strict inequality $X < Y$, we have the following Theorem 2.

Theorem 2 (Theorem 3, [34]). *Let* $X, Y \in \mathbf{Q}\langle \ell \bullet f \rangle$, *and* $\mathsf{sbin}_{\ell,f}(X) = (x_\ell, x_{\ell-1}, \cdots, x_0, x_{-1}, \cdots, x_{-f}), \mathsf{sbin}_{\ell,f}(Y) = (y_\ell, y_{\ell-1}, \cdots, y_0, y_{-1}, \cdots, y_{-f})$. *Then,* $X < Y$ *if and only if there exist bits* $z_\ell, z_{\ell-1}, \cdots, z_0, z_{-1}, \cdots, z_{-f}, c_{\ell+1}, c_\ell, c_{\ell-1}, \cdots, c_0, c_{-1}, \cdots, c_{-f+1}$ *satisfying*

$$c_{-f+1} = x_{-f} \cdot z_{-f} \oplus y_{-f} \oplus 1$$
$$c_i = x_{i-1} \cdot z_{i-1} \oplus y_{i-1} \cdot c_{i-1} \oplus c_{i-1}, \forall i \in [-f+2, \ell+1]$$
$$y_{-f} = x_{-f} \oplus z_{-f} \oplus 1$$
$$y_i = x_i \oplus z_i \oplus c_i, \forall i \in [-f+1, \ell]$$
$$y_\ell = x_\ell \oplus c_{\ell+1}.$$

3   Range Arguments for Signed Fractional Numbers

In this section, we build our zero-knowledge argument system for the statement that *signed fractional numbers*, committed via the lattice-based commitment scheme belong to a hidden or given range. At first, we present our protocol for proving in zero-knowledge that two committed signed fractional numbers X, Y satisfies the inequality $X \leq Y$. Next, we discuss how to derive in zero-knowledge other variants of inequalities, such as for $X \leq Y$, where Y is given; the strict inequality $X < Y$, where X, Y both are committed, or Y is given. Finally, we discuss how to derive various variants of range arguments, based on the results of Sect. 2.5 and 3.1.

3.1   Proving Inequalities Between Committed Signed Fractional Numbers

Let $\ell > 0, f \geq 0$ be integers, and let $L = (1 + \ell + f) > 0$. Let a prime $q = \mathcal{O}(\sqrt{L} \cdot n)$ and $m = n(\lceil \log q \rceil + 3)$. Consider the KTX commitment scheme with parameters n, q, m, L and commitment key $(\mathbf{a}_0, \mathbf{a}_1, \cdots, \mathbf{a}_{L-1}, \mathbf{b}_1, \cdots, \mathbf{b}_m)$, where

$\mathbf{a}_0, \cdots, \mathbf{a}_{L-1}, \mathbf{b}_1, \cdots, \mathbf{b}_m \xleftarrow{\$} \mathbb{Z}_q^{n \times 1}$. Let $X, Y \in \mathbf{Q}\langle \ell \bullet f \rangle$, whose binary representations are as $\mathbf{x} = \mathsf{sbin}_{\ell,f}(X) = (x_\ell, \cdots, x_0, x_{-1}, \cdots, x_{-f})$, $\mathbf{y} = \mathsf{sbin}_{\ell,f}(Y) = (y_\ell, \cdots, y_0, y_{-1}, \cdots, y_{-f})$. Let $\mathbf{x}, \mathbf{y}$ be committed as

$$\mathbf{c_x} = \sum_{i=0}^{L-1} \mathbf{a}_i \cdot x_{\ell-i} + \sum_{j=1}^{m} \mathbf{b}_j \cdot r_{\mathbf{x},j} \mod q \in \mathbb{Z}_q^n$$

$$\mathbf{c_y} = \sum_{i=0}^{L-1} \mathbf{a}_i \cdot y_{\ell-i} + \sum_{j=1}^{m} \mathbf{b}_j \cdot r_{\mathbf{y},j} \mod q \in \mathbb{Z}_q^n, \text{where } r_{\mathbf{x},j}, r_{\mathbf{y},j} \xleftarrow{\$} \{0,1\} \forall j \in [m].$$

$$(3)$$

Our goal is to design an argument system allowing the prover to convince the verifier in zero-knowledge that the vectors $\mathbf{x}, \mathbf{y}$ committed in $\mathbf{c_x}, \mathbf{c_y}$ satisfy $\mathsf{sbin}_{\ell,f}^{-1}(\mathbf{x}) \leq \mathsf{sbin}_{\ell,f}^{-1}(\mathbf{y})$, i.e., they represent numbers $X, Y \in \mathbf{Q}\langle \ell \bullet f \rangle$ such that $X \leq Y$. Formally, we will build a ZKAOK for the relation $R_{ineq}^{(0)}$ defined as:

$R_{ineq}^{(0)} = \{(((\mathbf{a}_0, \cdots, \mathbf{a}_{L-1}, \mathbf{b}_1, \cdots, \mathbf{b}_m), \mathbf{c_x}, \mathbf{c_y}), \mathbf{x}, \mathbf{y}, r_{\mathbf{x},1}, \cdots, r_{\mathbf{x},m}, r_{\mathbf{y},1}, \cdots, r_{\mathbf{y},m}) : \mathsf{sbin}_{\ell,f}^{-1}(\mathbf{x}) \leq \mathsf{sbin}_{\ell,f}^{-1}(\mathbf{y}) \bigwedge \mathbf{c_x} = \sum_{i=0}^{L-1} \mathbf{a}_i \cdot x_{\ell-i} + \sum_{j=1}^{m} \mathbf{b}_j \cdot r_{\mathbf{x},j} \mod q \bigwedge \mathbf{c_y} = \sum_{i=0}^{L-1} \mathbf{a}_i \cdot y_{\ell-i} + \sum_{j=1}^{m} \mathbf{b}_j \cdot r_{\mathbf{y},j} \mod q\}.$

To prove in zero knowledge that the inequality $\mathsf{sbin}_{\ell,f}^{-1}(\mathbf{x}) \leq \mathsf{sbin}_{\ell,f}^{-1}(\mathbf{y})$ holds, we will use the results of Sect. 2.5. Using Theorem 1, we can equivalently prove the existence of bits $z_\ell, \cdots, z_0, z_{-1}, \cdots, z_{-f}, c_{\ell+1}, \cdots, c_0, c_{-1}, \cdots, c_{-f+1}$ satisfying the following $2(\ell + f) + 3 = 2L + 1$ equations modulo 2:

$$c_{-f+1} \oplus x_{-f} \cdot z_{-f} = 0$$
$$c_i \oplus x_{i-1} \cdot z_{i-1} \oplus y_{i-1} \cdot c_{i-1} \oplus c_{i-1} = 0, \forall i \in [-f+2, \ell+1]$$
$$y_{-f} \oplus x_{-f} \oplus z_{-f} = 0$$
$$y_i \oplus x_i \oplus z_i \oplus c_i = 0, \forall i \in [-f+1, \ell]$$
$$y_\ell \oplus x_\ell \oplus c_{\ell+1} = 0.$$

$$(4)$$

To incorporate with above, we modify the relation $R_{ineq}^{(0)}$ into $R_{ineq}^{(1)}$ as follows:

$R_{ineq}^{(1)} = \{(((\mathbf{a}_0, \cdots, \mathbf{a}_{L-1}, \mathbf{b}_1, \cdots, \mathbf{b}_m), \mathbf{c_x}, \mathbf{c_y}), \mathbf{x}, \mathbf{y}, z_\ell, \cdots, z_0, \cdots, z_{-f}, c_{\ell+1}, \cdots, c_{-f+1}, r_{\mathbf{x},1}, \cdots, r_{\mathbf{x},m}, r_{\mathbf{y},1}, \cdots, r_{\mathbf{y},m}) : \mathsf{sbin}_{\ell,f}^{-1}(\mathbf{x}) \leq \mathsf{sbin}_{\ell,f}^{-1}(\mathbf{y}) \bigwedge \mathbf{c_x} = \sum_{i=0}^{L-1} \mathbf{a}_i \cdot x_{\ell-i} + \sum_{j=1}^{m} \mathbf{b}_j \cdot r_{\mathbf{x},j} \mod q \bigwedge \mathbf{c_y} = \sum_{i=0}^{L-1} \mathbf{a}_i \cdot y_{\ell-i} + \sum_{j=1}^{m} \mathbf{b}_j \cdot r_{\mathbf{y},j} \mod q\}.$

i.e., $R_{ineq}^{(1)} = \{(((\mathbf{a}_0, \cdots, \mathbf{a}_{L-1}, \mathbf{b}_1, \cdots, \mathbf{b}_m), \mathbf{c_x}, \mathbf{c_y}), \mathbf{x}, \mathbf{y}, z_\ell, \cdots, z_0, z_{-1}, \cdots, z_{-f}, c_{\ell+1}, \cdots, c_0, \cdots, c_{-f+1}, r_{\mathbf{x},1}, \cdots, r_{\mathbf{x},m}, r_{\mathbf{y},1}, \cdots, r_{\mathbf{y},m})$: (3) and (4)$satisfy$\}.

To handle Eqs. (3), (4) in zero-knowledge, we use the extending-then-permuting techniques of Sect. 2.4. We proceed as follows:

1. Extend $x_i \mapsto \mathbf{x}_i = \mathsf{ext}_2(x_i)$, $y_i \mapsto \mathbf{y}_i = \mathsf{ext}_2(y_i)$, $z_i \mapsto \mathbf{z}_i = \mathsf{ext}_2(z_i)$, and $c_{i+1} \mapsto \mathbf{c}_{i+1} = \mathsf{ext}_2(c_{i+1})$ respectively for each $i \in [-f, \ell]$.

2. Extend $r_{\mathbf{x},i} \mapsto \mathbf{r}_{\mathbf{x},i} = \mathsf{ext}_2(r_{\mathbf{x},i})$, $r_{\mathbf{y},i} \mapsto \mathbf{r}_{\mathbf{y},i} = \mathsf{ext}_2(r_{\mathbf{y},i})$ for each $i \in [m]$.
3. Extend $x_{i-1} \cdot z_{i-1} \mapsto \mathbf{t}_{i-1} = \mathsf{ext}_4(x_{i-1}, z_{i-1})$ for all $i \in [-f+1, \ell+1]$
   and $y_{i-1} \cdot c_{i-1} \mapsto \mathbf{g}_{i-1} = \mathsf{ext}_4(y_{i-1}, c_{i-1})$ for all $i \in [-f+2, \ell+1]$.

Let us construct $\mathbf{A}_i = [0^n | \mathbf{a}_i] \in \mathbb{Z}_q^{n \times 2} \forall i \in \{0, \cdots, L-1\}$ and $\mathbf{B}_j = [0^n | \mathbf{b}_j] \in \mathbb{Z}_q^{n \times 2} \forall j \in [m]$. Then Eqs. (3) can be rewritten as follows:

$$\mathbf{c_x} = \sum_{i=0}^{L-1} \mathbf{A}_i \cdot \mathbf{x}_{\ell-i} + \sum_{j=1}^{m} \mathbf{B}_j \cdot \mathbf{r}_{\mathbf{x},j} \mod q \in \mathbb{Z}_q^n$$

$$\mathbf{c_y} = \sum_{i=0}^{L-1} \mathbf{A}_i \cdot \mathbf{y}_{\ell-i} + \sum_{j=1}^{m} \mathbf{B}_j \cdot \mathbf{r}_{\mathbf{y},j} \mod q \in \mathbb{Z}_q^n. \tag{5}$$

Letting $\mathbf{M}_0 = [\mathbf{A}_0 | \cdots | \mathbf{A}_{L-1} | \mathbf{B}_1 | \cdots | \mathbf{B}_m] \in \mathbb{Z}_q^{n \times 2(L+m)}$, and $\mathbf{w_x} = (\mathbf{x}_\ell \| \cdots \| \mathbf{x}_{-f} \| \mathbf{r}_{\mathbf{x},1} \| \cdots \| \mathbf{r}_{\mathbf{x},m}) \in \{0,1\}^{2(L+m)}$, $\mathbf{w_y} = (\mathbf{y}_\ell \| \cdots \| \mathbf{y}_{-f} \| \mathbf{r}_{\mathbf{y},1} \| \cdots \| \mathbf{r}_{\mathbf{y},m}) \in \{0,1\}^{2(L+m)}$ respectively, the above Eqs. (5) can be written as follows:

$$\mathbf{c_x} = \mathbf{M}_0 \cdot \mathbf{w_x} \mod q \in \mathbb{Z}_q^n, \text{ and } \mathbf{c_y} = \mathbf{M}_0 \cdot \mathbf{w_y} \mod q \in \mathbb{Z}_q^n. \tag{6}$$

Letting $\mathbf{M}_1 = \begin{bmatrix} \mathbf{M}_0 & 0^{n \times 2(L+M)} \\ 0^{n \times 2(L+M)} & \mathbf{M}_0 \end{bmatrix} \in \mathbb{Z}_q^{2n \times 4(L+m)}$, $\mathbf{w}_1 = (\mathbf{w_x} \| \mathbf{w_y}) \in \{0,1\}^{4(L+m)}$, and $\mathbf{c}_1 = (\mathbf{c_x} \| \mathbf{c_y}) \in \mathbb{Z}_q^{2n}$, the above Eqs. (6) can be unified into one equations as follows:

$$\mathbf{M}_1 \cdot \mathbf{w}_1 = \mathbf{c}_1 \mod q. \tag{7}$$

Let us construct two matrices $\mathbf{H}_2 = [0|1] \in \mathbb{Z}_2^{1 \times 2}$ and $\mathbf{H}_4 = [0|0|0|1] \in \mathbb{Z}_2^{1 \times 4}$. Then Eqs. (4) can be rewritten as follows:

$$\mathbf{H}_2 \cdot \mathbf{c}_{-f+1} \oplus \mathbf{H}_4 \cdot \mathbf{t}_{-f} = 0$$
$$\mathbf{H}_2 \cdot \mathbf{c}_i \oplus \mathbf{H}_4 \cdot \mathbf{t}_{i-1} \oplus \mathbf{H}_4 \cdot \mathbf{g}_{i-1} \oplus \mathbf{H}_2 \cdot \mathbf{c}_{i-1} = 0, \forall i \in [-f+2, \ell+1]$$
$$\mathbf{H}_2 \cdot \mathbf{y}_{-f} \oplus \mathbf{H}_2 \cdot \mathbf{x}_{-f} \oplus \mathbf{H}_2 \cdot \mathbf{z}_{-f} = 0$$
$$\mathbf{H}_2 \cdot \mathbf{y}_i \oplus \mathbf{H}_2 \cdot \mathbf{x}_i \oplus \mathbf{H}_2 \cdot \mathbf{z}_i \oplus \mathbf{H}_2 \cdot \mathbf{c}_i = 0, \forall i \in [-f+1, \ell]$$
$$\mathbf{H}_2 \cdot \mathbf{y}_\ell \oplus \mathbf{H}_2 \cdot \mathbf{x}_\ell \oplus \mathbf{H}_2 \cdot \mathbf{c}_{\ell+1} = 0. \tag{8}$$

Let $\mathbf{M}_2 \in \mathbb{Z}_2^{(2L+1) \times 16L}$ be a public matrix, built from $\mathbf{H}_2, \mathbf{H}_4$, and $\mathbf{w}_2 = (\mathbf{x}_\ell \| \cdots \| \mathbf{x}_{-f} \| \mathbf{y}_\ell \| \cdots \| \mathbf{y}_{-f} \| \mathbf{z}_\ell \| \cdots \| \mathbf{z}_{-f} \| \mathbf{c}_{\ell+1} \| \cdots \| \mathbf{c}_{-f+1} \| \mathbf{t}_\ell \| \cdots \| \mathbf{t}_{-f} \| \mathbf{g}_{\ell+1} \| \cdots \| \mathbf{g}_{-f+1}) \in \{0,1\}^{16L}$. Then the above Eqs. (8) can be unified into one equations as follows:

$$\mathbf{M}_2 \cdot \mathbf{w}_2 = 0^{2L+1} \mod 2. \tag{9}$$

Let us construct a vector $\mathbf{w} = (\mathbf{w}_1 \| \mathbf{w}_2) \in \{0,1\}^{20L+4m}$, which has of the form $(\mathbf{x}_\ell \| \cdots \| \mathbf{x}_{-f} \| \mathbf{r}_{\mathbf{x},1} \| \cdots \| \mathbf{r}_{\mathbf{x},m} \| \mathbf{y}_\ell \| \cdots \| \mathbf{y}_{-f} \| \mathbf{r}_{\mathbf{y},1} \| \cdots \| \mathbf{r}_{\mathbf{y},m} \| \mathbf{x}_\ell \| \cdots \| \mathbf{x}_{-f} \| \mathbf{y}_\ell \| \cdots \| \mathbf{y}_{-f} \| \mathbf{z}_\ell \| \cdots \| \mathbf{z}_{-f} \| \mathbf{c}_{\ell+1} \| \cdots \| \mathbf{c}_{-f+1} \| \mathbf{t}_\ell \| \cdots \| \mathbf{t}_{-f} \| \mathbf{g}_{\ell+1} \| \cdots \| \mathbf{g}_{-f+1})$.

Encoding Vector $\mathsf{ENC}(\cdot)$. In the following protocol, we will work with a binary vector of length $20L + 4m$ that has a very specific constraint determined by $4L + 2m$ bits. For any vector $\mathbf{b} = (b_1, \cdots, b_L, b_{L+1}, \cdots, b_{2L}, b_{2L+1}, \cdots, b_{3L}, b_{3L+1}, \cdots, b_{4L}, \cdots, b_{4L+m}, b_{4L+m+1}, \cdots, b_{4L+2m}) \in \{0,1\}^{4L+2m}$, we denote by $\mathsf{ENC}(\mathbf{b}) \in \{0,1\}^{20L+4m}$ the vector encoding $\mathbf{b}$ as follows:

$$\mathsf{ENC}(\mathbf{b}) = \big(\mathsf{ext}_2(b_1) \| \cdots \| \mathsf{ext}_2(b_L) \| \mathsf{ext}_2(b_{4L+1}) \| \cdots \| \mathsf{ext}_2(b_{4L+m}) \| \mathsf{ext}_2(b_{L+1}) \| \cdots \| \mathsf{ext}_2(b_{2L}) \| \mathsf{ext}_2(b_{4L+m+1}) \| \cdots \| \mathsf{ext}_2(b_{4L+2m}) \| \mathsf{ext}_2(b_1) \| \cdots \| \mathsf{ext}_2(b_L) \| \cdots \| \mathsf{ext}_2(b_{2L}) \| \mathsf{ext}_2(b_{2L+1}) \| \cdots \| \mathsf{ext}_2(b_{3L}) \| \cdots \| \mathsf{ext}_2(b_{4L}) \| \mathsf{ext}_4(b_1, b_{2L+1}) \| \cdots \| \mathsf{ext}_4(b_L, b_{3L}) \| \mathsf{ext}_4(b_{L+1}, b_{3L+1}) \| \cdots \| \mathsf{ext}_4(b_{2L}, b_{4L})\big),$$ where $\mathsf{ext}_2, \mathsf{ext}_4$ are as in Sect. 2.4.

Permutations Γ. To prove in zero-knowledge of a vector that has of the form $\mathsf{ENC}(\cdot)$, we will need a specific type of permutation. We associate each $\mathbf{c} = (c_1, \cdots, c_L, c_{L+1}, \cdots, c_{2L}, \cdots, c_{3L}, c_{3L+1}, \cdots, c_{4L}, c_{4L+1}, \cdots, c_{4L+m}, c_{4L+m+1}, \cdots, c_{4L+2m}) \in \{0,1\}^{4L+2m}$ with a permutation $\Gamma_{\mathbf{c}}$. On applying $\Gamma_{\mathbf{c}}$ on $\mathsf{ENC}(\mathbf{b})$, it transforms its block as $\mathsf{ext}_2(b_i) \mapsto P_{\mathbf{c}}^2(\mathsf{ext}_2(b_i))$, $\mathsf{ext}_4(b_j, b_k) \mapsto P_{\mathbf{c}}^4(\mathsf{ext}_4(b_j, b_k))$, where $P_{\mathbf{c}}^2, P_{\mathbf{c}}^4$ are as in Sect. 2.4. Based on the observations in Eqs. (1), (2), it can be checked that the following holds. For all $\mathbf{b}, \mathbf{c} \in \{0,1\}^{4L+2m}$, and $\mathsf{ENC}(\mathbf{b}) \in \{0,1\}^{20L+4m}$,

$$\mathbf{v} = \mathsf{ENC}(\mathbf{b}) \iff \Gamma_{\mathbf{c}}(\mathbf{v}) = \mathsf{ENC}(\mathbf{b} + \mathbf{c} \mod 2). \tag{10}$$

Let us assume $\mathbf{s} = (x_\ell \| \cdots \| x_{-f} \| y_\ell \| \cdots \| y_{-f} \| z_\ell \| \cdots \| z_{-f} \| c_{\ell+1} \| \cdots \| c_{-f+1} \| r_{\mathbf{x},1} \| \cdots \| r_{\mathbf{x},m} \| r_{\mathbf{y},1} \| \cdots \| r_{\mathbf{y},m}) \in \{0,1\}^{4L+2m}$, and construct a vector $\mathbf{w} = (\mathbf{w}_1 \| \mathbf{w}_2) \in \{0,1\}^{20L+4m}$, which has of the form $(\mathbf{x}_\ell \| \cdots \| \mathbf{x}_{-f} \| \mathbf{r}_{\mathbf{x},1} \| \cdots \| \mathbf{r}_{\mathbf{x},m} \| \mathbf{y}_\ell \| \cdots \| \mathbf{y}_{-f} \| \mathbf{r}_{\mathbf{y},1} \| \cdots \| \mathbf{r}_{\mathbf{y},m} \| \mathbf{x}_\ell \| \cdots \| \mathbf{x}_{-f} \| \mathbf{y}_\ell \| \cdots \| \mathbf{y}_{-f} \| \mathbf{z}_\ell \| \cdots \| \mathbf{z}_{-f} \| \mathbf{c}_{\ell+1} \| \cdots \| \mathbf{c}_{-f+1} \| \mathbf{t}_\ell \| \cdots \| \mathbf{t}_{-f} \| \mathbf{g}_{\ell+1} \| \cdots \| \mathbf{g}_{-f+1})$. Then, by the above definitions, we have $\mathbf{w} = \mathsf{ENC}(\mathbf{s})$.

The transformation we have done so far allow us to reduce the original statement to proving knowledge of a vector $\mathbf{s} \in \{0,1\}^{4L+2m}$, such that the component vectors $\mathbf{w}_1, \mathbf{w}_2$ of $\mathbf{w} = \mathsf{ENC}(\mathbf{s})$ satisfy the equations $\mathbf{M}_1 \cdot \mathbf{w}_1 = \mathbf{c}_1 \mod q$ and $\mathbf{M}_2 \cdot \mathbf{w}_2 = \mathbf{0}^{2L+1} \mod 2$. The derived statements can be handled in Stern's framework, based on the following main ideas.

1. To prove that $\mathbf{w} = \mathsf{ENC}(\mathbf{s})$, we will use the equivalence (10). To this end, we sample a uniformly random $\mathbf{c} \in \{0,1\}^{4L+2m}$ and prove instead that $\Gamma_{\mathbf{c}}(\mathbf{w}) = \mathsf{ENC}(\mathbf{s} + \mathbf{c} \mod 2)$. Seeing this, the verifier is convinced in ZK that $\mathbf{w}$ indeed satisfies the required constraints, thanks to the randomness of $\mathbf{c}$.
2. To prove that $\mathbf{M}_1 \cdot \mathbf{w}_1 = \mathbf{c}_1 \mod q$ and $\mathbf{M}_2 \cdot \mathbf{w}_2 = \mathbf{0}^{2L+1} \mod 2$ hold, we sample $\mathbf{r}_1 \xleftarrow{\$} \mathbb{Z}_q^{4(L+m)}, \mathbf{r}_2 \xleftarrow{\$} \mathbb{Z}_2^{16L}$, and demonstrate that $\mathbf{M}_1 \cdot (\mathbf{w}_1 + \mathbf{r}_1) = \mathbf{c}_1 + \mathbf{M}_1 \cdot \mathbf{r}_1 \mod q$; $\mathbf{M}_2 \cdot (\mathbf{w}_2 + \mathbf{r}_2) = \mathbf{0}^{2L+1} + \mathbf{M}_2 \cdot \mathbf{r}_2 \mod 2$.

The interactive protocol Our interactive protocol goes as follows:

1. The public input consists of matrices $\mathbf{M}_1, \mathbf{M}_2$ and vectors $\mathbf{c}_1, \mathbf{0}^{2L+1}$, which are constructed from the original public input, as discussed above.
2. The prover's witness consists of the original secret vector $\mathbf{s} \in \{0,1\}^{4L+2m}$ and vector $\mathbf{w} = (\mathbf{w}_1 \| \mathbf{w}_2) = \mathsf{ENC}(\mathbf{s}) \in \{0,1\}^{20L+4m}$ derived from $\mathbf{s}$, as described above.

1. **Commitment** : $\mathcal{P}$ samples $\mathbf{c} \xleftarrow{\$} \{0,1\}^{4L+2m}$, $\mathbf{r}_1 \xleftarrow{\$} \mathbb{Z}_q^{4(L+m)}$, $\mathbf{r}_2 \xleftarrow{\$} \mathbb{Z}_2^{16L}$, and computes $\mathbf{r} = (\mathbf{r}_1\|\mathbf{r}_2)$, $\mathbf{z} = \mathbf{w} \boxplus \mathbf{r}$.

   Then $\mathcal{P}$ samples randomness ρ_1, ρ_2, ρ_3 for COM, and sends $CMT = (C_1, C_2, C_3)$ to $\mathcal{V}$, where

   $$C_1 = \mathsf{COM}(\mathbf{c}, \mathbf{M}_1 \cdot \mathbf{r}_1 \mod q, \mathbf{M}_2 \cdot \mathbf{r}_2 \mod 2; \rho_1)$$
   $$C_2 = \mathsf{COM}(\Gamma_{\mathbf{c}}(\mathbf{r}); \rho_2)$$
   $$C_3 = \mathsf{COM}(\Gamma_{\mathbf{c}}(\mathbf{z}); \rho_3).$$

2. **Challenge** : $\mathcal{V}$ sends a challenge $Ch \xleftarrow{\$} \{1, 2, 3\}$ to $\mathcal{P}$.

3. **Response** : $\mathcal{P}$ sends RSP computed according to Ch, as follows:
   - $Ch = 1$: $RSP = (\mathbf{c}^*, \beta, \rho_2, \rho_3)$, where $\mathbf{c}^* = \mathbf{s} + \mathbf{c} \mod 2$ and $\beta = \Gamma_{\mathbf{c}}(\mathbf{r})$.
   - $Ch = 2$: $RSP = (\mathbf{b}, \mathbf{x}, \rho_1, \rho_3)$, where $\mathbf{b} = \mathbf{c}$ and $\mathbf{x} = \mathbf{z}$.
   - $Ch = 3$: $RSP = (\mathbf{e}, \mathbf{y}, \rho_1, \rho_2)$, where $\mathbf{e} = \mathbf{c}$ and $\mathbf{y} = \mathbf{r}$.

4. **Verification** : Receiving RSP, $\mathcal{V}$ proceeds as follows:
   - $Ch = 1$: Let $\alpha = \mathsf{ENC}(\mathbf{c}^*)$. Check that $C_2 = \mathsf{COM}(\beta; \rho_2)$, $C_3 = \mathsf{COM}(\alpha \boxplus \beta; \rho_3)$.
   - $Ch = 2$: Parse $\mathbf{x} = (\mathbf{x}_1\|\mathbf{x}_2)$, where $\mathbf{x}_1 \in \mathbb{Z}_q^{4(L+m)}$, $\mathbf{x}_2 \in \mathbb{Z}_2^{16L}$, and check that $C_1 = \mathsf{COM}(\mathbf{b}, \mathbf{M}_1 \cdot \mathbf{x}_1 - \mathbf{c}_1 \mod q, \mathbf{M}_2 \cdot \mathbf{x}_2 - \mathbf{0}^{2L+1} \mod 2; \rho_1)$, $C_3 = \mathsf{COM}(\Gamma_{\mathbf{b}}(\mathbf{x}); \rho_3)$.
   - $Ch = 3$: Parse $\mathbf{y} = (\mathbf{y}_1\|\mathbf{y}_2)$, where $\mathbf{y}_1 \in \mathbb{Z}_q^{4(L+m)}$, $\mathbf{y}_2 \in \mathbb{Z}_2^{16L}$, and check that $C_1 = \mathsf{COM}(\mathbf{e}, \mathbf{M}_1 \cdot \mathbf{y}_1 \mod q, \mathbf{M}_2 \cdot \mathbf{y}_2 \mod 2; \rho_1)$, $C_2 = \mathsf{COM}(\Gamma_{\mathbf{e}}(\mathbf{y}); \rho_2)$.

   In each case, $\mathcal{V}$ outputs 1 if and only if all the conditions hold.

Fig. 1. The interactive protocol

The prover $\mathcal{P}$ and the verifier $\mathcal{V}$ interact as described in Fig. 1. The protocol uses the KTX string commitment scheme COM, which is statistically hiding and computationally binding. For simplicity of presentation, for vectors $\mathbf{w} = (\mathbf{w}_1\|\mathbf{w}_2) \in \mathbb{Z}^{20L+4m}$ and $\mathbf{r} = (\mathbf{r}_1\|\mathbf{r}_2) \in \mathbb{Z}^{20L+4m}$, we denote by $\mathbf{w} \boxplus \mathbf{r}$ the operation that computes $\mathbf{z}_1 = \mathbf{w}_1 + \mathbf{r}_1 \mod q$, $\mathbf{z}_2 = \mathbf{w}_2 + \mathbf{r}_2 \mod 2$, and outputs $(20L+4m)$-dimensional vector $\mathbf{z} = (\mathbf{z}_1\|\mathbf{z}_2)$. We note that, for all $\mathbf{c} \in \{0,1\}^{4L+2m}$, if $\alpha = \Gamma_{\mathbf{c}}(\mathbf{w})$ and $\beta = \Gamma_{\mathbf{c}}(\mathbf{r})$, then we have $\Gamma_{\mathbf{c}}(\mathbf{w} \boxplus \mathbf{r}) = \alpha \boxplus \beta$.

In the following theorem, we prove that the protocol described in Fig. 1 has perfect completeness, it is a statistical zero-knowledge argument of knowledge.

Theorem 3. *Suppose that* COM *is a statistically hiding and computationally binding string commitment. Then, the protocol described in Fig. 1 is a statistical* ZKAOK *for the considered relation, with perfect completeness, soundness error* $2/3$ *and communication cost* $\mathcal{O}(\ell + f)$.

Proof. The proof is deferred to the full version due to space constrained. $\square$

For other cases of inequalities such as $X \leq Y$, where Y is public, the above protocol will be easily applied. Moreover, it will simplify the above protocol and reduces their complexity as the number of secret bits to deal with is smaller than in the above protocol. To build zero-knowledge argument of strict inequality such as $X < Y$, where X, Y both are committed, we can simply apply the results of 2 in the above protocol. For public Y, we can interpret $X < Y$ as $X \le Y'$ for public $Y' = Y - 2^{-f}$, and we can easily build zero-knowledge argument system by applying above protocol.

3.2 Range Arguments for Signed Fractional Numbers

We now discuss how to use the argument system presented in Sect. 3.1 to derive various variants of range arguments for signed fractional numbers.

1. **Public ranges with non-strict inequalities.** We consider the problem of proving in zero-knowledge that a committed signed fractional number $X \in \mathbf{Q}\langle \ell \bullet f \rangle$ satisfies $X \in [\mu, \nu]$, i.e., $\mu \le X \le \nu$, for publicly known signed fractional numbers μ, ν. This type of range arguments is the easiest one, and we can build it based on the interactive protocol of proving inequalities of Fig. 1. Consider the lattice-based commitment scheme of Sect. 2.2 with parameters n, q, m, L as in Sect. 3.1. Let $X \in \mathbf{Q}\langle \ell \bullet f \rangle$, and $\mathbf{x} = \mathsf{sbin}_{\ell,f}(X) = (x_\ell, \cdots, x_0, x_{-1}, \cdots, x_{-f})$. Let $\mathbf{x}$ be committed as

$$\mathbf{c_x} = \sum_{i=0}^{L-1} \mathbf{a}_i \cdot x_{\ell-i} + \sum_{j=1}^{m} \mathbf{b}_j \cdot r_{\mathbf{x},j} \mod q \in \mathbb{Z}_q^n, \text{where } r_{\mathbf{x},j} \xleftarrow{\$} \{0,1\} \forall j \in [m]. \quad (11)$$

Let binary representation of μ, ν be $\boldsymbol{\mu} = \mathsf{sbin}_{\ell,f}(\mu) = (\mu_\ell, \cdots, \mu_0, \cdots, \mu_{-f})$, $\boldsymbol{\nu} = \mathsf{sbin}_{\ell,f}(\nu) = (\nu_\ell, \cdots, \nu_0, \cdots, \nu_{-f})$. Our goal is to design an argument system allowing the prover to convince the verifier in zero-knowledge that the vector $\mathbf{x}$ committed in $\mathbf{c_x}$ satisfy $\mathsf{sbin}_{\ell,f}^{-1}(\boldsymbol{\mu}) \le \mathsf{sbin}_{\ell,f}^{-1}(\mathbf{x}) \le \mathsf{sbin}_{\ell,f}^{-1}(\boldsymbol{\nu})$, i.e., $\mu \le X \le \nu$. We observe that X satisfies $\mu \le X \le \nu$ if and only if $\mathsf{sbin}_{\ell,f}^{-1}(\boldsymbol{\mu}) \le \mathsf{sbin}_{\ell,f}^{-1}(\mathbf{x})$ and $\mathsf{sbin}_{\ell,f}^{-1}(\mathbf{x}) \le \mathsf{sbin}_{\ell,f}^{-1}(\boldsymbol{\nu})$. We thus reduce the task of proving $X \in [\mu, \nu]$ to proving two inequality relations among signed-fractional numbers, which can be achieved (by running two instances) using the techniques of Sect. 3.1. In fact, inequalities $\mu \le X$ and $X \le \nu$ can be handled using the simplified version of the protocol in Sect. 3.1, where the bits representing μ, ν are not required to be kept secret.

2. **Public ranges with strict inequalities.** For the strict inequality $\mu < X < \nu$, where μ, ν are public, and X is a committed signed fractional number, we can interpret the strict inequality $\mu < X$ as non-strict inequality $\mu' \le X$ for public $\mu' = \mu + 2^{-f}$. Similarly, we can interpret the strict inequality $X < \nu$ as non-strict inequality $X \le \nu'$ for public $\nu' = \nu - 2^{-f}$. Then, we can proceed for the argument system of Public ranges with non-strict inequalities, as described above.

3. **Hidden ranges with non-strict inequalities.** For the non-strict inequality $\mu \le X \le \nu$, where μ, ν are hidden, we require to prove that $\mu \le X \le \nu$, where μ, X, ν are all committed signed fractional numbers. So, we need to prove that X satisfies $\mu \le X$ and $X \le \nu$. Such a range argument can be achieved by running two instances of the interactive protocol in Sect. 3.1.

4. **Hidden ranges with strict inequalities.** For the strict inequality $\mu < X < \nu$, where μ, ν are hidden, we require to prove that $\mu < X < \nu$, where μ, X, ν are all committed signed fractional numbers. Here, a zero-knowledge argument of strict inequality is required. Such a protocol can be obtained by results of Theorem 2 and the techniques used in Sect. 3.1.

In all cases considered above, the size of range arguments remains $\mathcal{O}(\ell + f)$, i.e., it is logarithmic in the size of range.

4   Conclusion

In this paper, we build zero-knowledge argument systems for proving inequalities between signed fractional numbers as well as non-negative integers in the standard lattice settings. Using this core argument system, we construct efficient zero-knowledge range argument systems showing that a committed value is in a public or hidden range. Our work left an open problem in building a zero-knowledge range argument for multi-dimensional arrays.

References

1. Ajtai, M.: Generating hard instances of lattice problems. In: STOC, pp. 99–108 (1996)
2. Aranha, D.F., Baum, C., Gjøsteen, K., Silde, T., Tunge, T.: Lattice-based proof of shuffle and applications to electronic voting. In: Paterson, K.G. (ed.) CT-RSA 2021. LNCS, vol. 12704, pp. 227–251. Springer, Cham (2021). https://doi.org/10.1007/978-3-030-75539-3_10
3. Bellare, M., Goldwasser, S.: Verifiable partial key escrow. In: CCS, pp. 78–91 (1997)
4. Boudot, F.: Efficient proofs that a committed number lies in an interval. In: Preneel, B. (ed.) EUROCRYPT 2000. LNCS, vol. 1807, pp. 431–444. Springer, Heidelberg (2000). https://doi.org/10.1007/3-540-45539-6_31
5. Bünz, B., Bootle, J., Boneh, D., Poelstra, A., Wuille, P., Maxwell, G.: Bulletproofs: short proofs for confidential transactions and more. In: S&P 2018, pp. 315–334. IEEE (2018)
6. Camenisch, J., Chaabouni, R., shelat, A.: Efficient protocols for set membership and range proofs. In: Pieprzyk, J. (ed.) ASIACRYPT 2008. LNCS, vol. 5350, pp. 234–252. Springer, Heidelberg (2008). https://doi.org/10.1007/978-3-540-89255-7_15
7. Couteau, G., Klooß, M., Lin, H., Reichle, M.: Efficient range proofs with transparent setup from bounded integer commitments. In: Canteaut, A., Standaert, F.-X. (eds.) EUROCRYPT 2021. LNCS, vol. 12698, pp. 247–277. Springer, Cham (2021). https://doi.org/10.1007/978-3-030-77883-5_9
8. Couteau, G., Peters, T., Pointcheval, D.: Removing the strong RSA assumption from arguments over the integers. In: Coron, J.-S., Nielsen, J.B. (eds.) EUROCRYPT 2017. LNCS, vol. 10211, pp. 321–350. Springer, Cham (2017). https://doi.org/10.1007/978-3-319-56614-6_11
9. Damgrard, I., Jurik, M.: A Generalisation, a Simplification and Some Applications of Paillier's Probabilistic Public-Key System. In: Kim, K. (ed.) PKC 2001. LNCS, vol. 1992, pp. 119–136. Springer, Heidelberg (2001). https://doi.org/10.1007/3-540-44586-2_9

10. Damgrard, I., Jurik, M., Nielsen, J.B.: A generalization of paillier's public-key system with applications to electronic voting. Int. J. Inf. Secur. 9(6), 371–385 (2010)
11. Deo, A., Libert, B., Nguyen, K., Sanders, O.: Lattice-based E-cash, revisited. In: Moriai, S., Wang, H. (eds.) ASIACRYPT 2020. LNCS, vol. 12492, pp. 318–348. Springer, Cham (2020). https://doi.org/10.1007/978-3-030-64834-3_11
12. Devevey, J., Libert, B.: Peters, TRational modular encoding in the DCR setting: non-interactive range proofs and paillier-based Naor-Yung in the standard model. In: Hanaoka, G., Shikata, J., Watanabe, Y. (eds.) PKC 2022. LNCS, vol. 13177, pp. 615–646. Springer, Cham (2022)
13. Dutta, P., Jiang, M., Duong, D.H., Susilo, W., Fukushima, K., Kiyomoto, S.: Hierarchical identity-based puncturable encryption from lattices with application to forward security. In: AsiaCCS, pp. 408–422 (2022)
14. Dutta, P., Susilo, W., Duong, D.H., Baek, J., Roy, P.S.: Identity-based unidirectional proxy re-encryption and re-signature in standard model: lattice-based constructions. J. Internet Serv. Inf. Secur. 10(4), 1–22 (2020)
15. Dutta, P., Susilo, W., Duong, D.H., Baek, J., Roy, P.S.: Identity-based unidirectional proxy re-encryption in standard model: a lattice-based construction. In: You, I. (ed.) WISA 2020. LNCS, vol. 12583, pp. 245–257. Springer, Cham (2020). https://doi.org/10.1007/978-3-030-65299-9_19
16. Dutta, P., Susilo, W., Duong, D.H., Roy, P.S.: Collusion-resistant identity-based proxy re-encryption: lattice-based constructions in standard model. Theoret. Comput. Sci. 871, 16–29 (2021)
17. Dutta, P., Susilo, W., Duong, D.H., Roy, P.S.: Puncturable identity-based encryption from lattices. In: Baek, J., Ruj, S. (eds.) ACISP 2021. LNCS, vol. 13083, pp. 571–589. Springer, Cham (2021). https://doi.org/10.1007/978-3-030-90567-5_29
18. Dutta, P., Susilo, W., Duong, D.H., Roy, P.S.: Puncturable identity-based and attribute-based encryption from lattices. Theoret. Comput. Sci. 929, 18–38 (2022)
19. Gentry, C., Peikert, C., Vaikuntanathan, V.: Trapdoors for hard lattices and new cryptographic constructions. In: STOC 2008, pp. 197–206 (2008)
20. Goldwasser, S., Kalai, Y.T., Peikert, C., Vaikuntanathan, V.: Robustness of the learning with errors assumption (2010)
21. González, A., Ráfols, C.: New techniques for non-interactive shuffle and range arguments. In: Manulis, M., Sadeghi, A.-R., Schneider, S. (eds.) ACNS 2016. LNCS, vol. 9696, pp. 427–444. Springer, Cham (2016). https://doi.org/10.1007/978-3-319-39555-5_23
22. Groth, J.: Non-interactive zero-knowledge arguments for voting. In: Ioannidis, J., Keromytis, A., Yung, M. (eds.) ACNS 2005. LNCS, vol. 3531, pp. 467–482. Springer, Heidelberg (2005). https://doi.org/10.1007/11496137_32
23. Groth, J.: Efficient zero-knowledge arguments from two-tiered homomorphic commitments. In: Lee, D.H., Wang, X. (eds.) ASIACRYPT 2011. LNCS, vol. 7073, pp. 431–448. Springer, Heidelberg (2011). https://doi.org/10.1007/978-3-642-25385-0_23
24. Jain, A., Krenn, S., Pietrzak, K., Tentes, A.: Commitments and efficient zero-knowledge proofs from learning parity with noise. In: Wang, X., Sako, K. (eds.) ASIACRYPT 2012. LNCS, vol. 7658, pp. 663–680. Springer, Heidelberg (2012). https://doi.org/10.1007/978-3-642-34961-4_40
25. Kawachi, A., Tanaka, K., Xagawa, K.: Concurrently secure identification schemes based on the worst-case hardness of lattice problems. In: Pieprzyk, J. (ed.) ASIACRYPT 2008. LNCS, vol. 5350, pp. 372–389. Springer, Heidelberg (2008). https://doi.org/10.1007/978-3-540-89255-7_23

26. Libert, B., Ling, S., Mouhartem, F., Nguyen, K., Wang, H.: Zero-knowledge arguments for matrix-vector relations and lattice-based group encryption. In: Cheon, J.H., Takagi, T. (eds.) ASIACRYPT 2016. LNCS, vol. 10032, pp. 101–131. Springer, Heidelberg (2016). https://doi.org/10.1007/978-3-662-53890-6_4

27. Libert, B., Ling, S., Nguyen, K., Wang, H.: Zero-knowledge arguments for lattice-based accumulators: logarithmic-size ring signatures and group signatures without trapdoors. In: Fischlin, M., Coron, J.-S. (eds.) EUROCRYPT 2016. LNCS, vol. 9666, pp. 1–31. Springer, Heidelberg (2016). https://doi.org/10.1007/978-3-662-49896-5_1

28. Libert, B., Ling, S., Nguyen, K., Wang, H.: Zero-knowledge arguments for lattice-based PRFs and applications to E-cash. In: Takagi, T., Peyrin, T. (eds.) ASIACRYPT 2017. LNCS, vol. 10626, pp. 304–335. Springer, Cham (2017). https://doi.org/10.1007/978-3-319-70700-6_11

29. Libert, B., Ling, S., Nguyen, K., Wang, H.: Lattice-based zero-knowledge arguments for integer relations. In: Shacham, H., Boldyreva, A. (eds.) CRYPTO 2018. LNCS, vol. 10992, pp. 700–732. Springer, Cham (2018). https://doi.org/10.1007/978-3-319-96881-0_24

30. Lipmaa, H.: On diophantine complexity and statistical zero-knowledge arguments. In: Laih, C.-S. (ed.) ASIACRYPT 2003. LNCS, vol. 2894, pp. 398–415. Springer, Heidelberg (2003). https://doi.org/10.1007/978-3-540-40061-5_26

31. Lipmaa, H., Asokan, N., Niemi, V.: Secure vickrey auctions without threshold trust. In: Blaze, M. (ed.) FC 2002. LNCS, vol. 2357, pp. 87–101. Springer, Heidelberg (2003). https://doi.org/10.1007/3-540-36504-4_7

32. Micali, S., Rabin, M.O.: Cryptography miracles, secure auctions, matching problem verification. Commun. ACM **57**(2), 85–93 (2014)

33. Micciancio, D., Peikert, C.: Hardness of SIS and LWE with small parameters. In: Canetti, R., Garay, J.A. (eds.) CRYPTO 2013. LNCS, vol. 8042, pp. 21–39. Springer, Heidelberg (2013). https://doi.org/10.1007/978-3-642-40041-4_2

34. Nguyen, K., Tang, H., Wang, H., Zeng, N.: New code-based privacy-preserving cryptographic constructions. In: Galbraith, S.D., Moriai, S. (eds.) ASIACRYPT 2019. LNCS, vol. 11922, pp. 25–55. Springer, Cham (2019). https://doi.org/10.1007/978-3-030-34621-8_2

35. Rabin, M.O., Mansour, Y., Muthukrishnan, S., Yung, M.: Strictly-black-box zero-knowledge and efficient validation of financial transactions. In: Czumaj, A., Mehlhorn, K., Pitts, A., Wattenhofer, R. (eds.) ICALP 2012. LNCS, vol. 7391, pp. 738–749. Springer, Heidelberg (2012). https://doi.org/10.1007/978-3-642-31594-7_62

36. Stern, J.: A new paradigm for public key identification. IEEE Trans. Inf. Theory **42**(6), 1757–1768 (1996)

37. Susilo, W., Dutta, P., Duong, D.H., Roy, P.S.: Lattice-based HRA-secure attribute-based proxy re-encryption in standard model. In: Bertino, E., Shulman, H., Waidner, M. (eds.) ESORICS 2021. LNCS, vol. 12973, pp. 169–191. Springer, Cham (2021). https://doi.org/10.1007/978-3-030-88428-4_9

38. Alberto Torres, W., Kuchta, V., Steinfeld, R., Sakzad, A., Liu, J.K., Cheng, J.: Lattice RingCT V2.0 with multiple input and multiple output wallets. In: Jang-Jaccard, J., Guo, F. (eds.) ACISP 2019. LNCS, vol. 11547, pp. 156–175. Springer, Cham (2019). https://doi.org/10.1007/978-3-030-21548-4_9

39. Yang, R., Au, M.H., Zhang, Z., Xu, Q., Yu, Z., Whyte, W.: Efficient lattice-based zero-knowledge arguments with standard soundness: construction and applications. In: Boldyreva, A., Micciancio, D. (eds.) CRYPTO 2019. LNCS, vol. 11692, pp. 147–175. Springer, Cham (2019). https://doi.org/10.1007/978-3-030-26948-7_6

Information Security

Fast Out-of-Band Data Integrity Monitor to Mitigate Memory Corruption Attacks

Jian Huang[1,2], Shanliang Xue[1,2], and Caiyi Wang[1,2]($\boxtimes$)

[1] Nanjing University of Aeronautics and Astronautics, Nanjing 211106, China
wangcy41@126.com
[2] Collaborative Innovation Center of Novel Software Technology and
Industrialization, Nanjing 211106, China

Abstract. Memory corruption is a root cause of software attacks. Existing defense mechanisms (e.g., DEP, ASLR, CFI, CPI/CPS, and DFI) either offer limited security guarantees or incur high performance overhead. In this paper, we designed and developed a fast out-of-band (OOB) integrity monitor dubbed FastDIM to protect both applications and kernels against memory corruption attacks with less overhead. With FastDIM, a program in question is statically hardened by a compiler module. After that, the integrity of sensitive program data such as control-flow transfers (e.g., code pointers) and security relevant non-control data (e.g., encryption keys) are automatically protected by a monitor at run time. The key differences between FastDIM and related work are in the following aspects: 1) FastDIM offers an OOB monitor that protects the programs independently rather than letting the protected programs verify themselves using inlined reference monitor (IRM); 2) FastDIM extends the concept of shadow stacks originally proposed in CFI to protect not only return addresses but also other sensitive data such as function pointers, vtable pointers, and user-annotated sensitive non-control data. Thus, the protection of FastDIM is beyond control-flow data; 3) FastDIM provides a fast communication mechanism between programs and the monitor, so that the integrity checks are performed efficiently without context switch; and 4) for a better scalability and compatibility, FastDIM does not rely on LTO and Cross-DSO to support applications with dynamically linked libraries. We implemented a Kernel version and a TrustZone version of FastDIM to protect both user programs and Linux/Android kernels. The evaluation results show that the average overhead of FastDIM is 4.4% on SPEC CPU2017 C/C++ benchmarks and around 3% on AnTuTu benchmarks.

Keywords: Memory corruption · Control-flow integrity · Data-flow integrity · Software hardening · Integrity Monitor

1 Introduction

Memory corruption is one of the most intractable vulnerabilities for programs written in low-level unsafe programming languages such as C/C++. Due to this

C. Ge and F. Guo (Eds.): ProvSec 2022, LNCS 13600, pp. 139–155, 2022.
https://doi.org/10.1007/978-3-031-20917-8_10

kind of vulnerabilities, in-memory data can be altered illegally by an attacker, leading to various attacks such as arbitrary code execution, privilege escalation, and information leak. Memory corruption attacks can be broadly classified into two categories: *control-oriented* and *data-oriented*. Control-oriented attacks target control-related data such as return addresses, function pointers, and virtual function tables. An attacker who tampers with those data may hijack the control flow of the program and execute unintended code. By contrast, data-oriented attacks target non-control-related data including syscall arguments, branch conditions, and user credentials, which are exploited to escalate privileges or bypass security checks.

Early control-oriented attacks focused on code injection, while recent attacks leveraged Return-Oriented Programming (ROP) [11] and Just-In-Time (JIT) [19] techniques to launch code-reuse attacks. In response, numerous defenses for control-flow hijacking attacks have been proposed and become increasingly practical and efficient; they include data-execution prevention (DEP), memory randomization (such as ASLR, DSR [3], randomized NOP insertion , and TASR [4]), Control-Flow Integrity (CFI) [1] and its variants surveyed in [2], and code pointer protections (such as CCFI [12] and CPS/CPI [10]).

' In this paper, we propose FastDIM, an unified out-of-band data integrity monitoring solution to protect both control-flow data and critical non-control data. To the best of our knowledge, this is the first work on enforcing the integrity of code/data pointers on both applications and OS kernels by using ARM Trust-Zone technology. Unlike traditional CFI or DFI methods, our approach does not depends on static analysis of control-flow graphs (CFGs) or data-flow graphs (DFGs) which cannot be computed accurately in practice [5]. Instead, the security code is automatically inserted into target programs to track load/store operations of sensitive memory addresses such as return addresses, function pointers, `vtable` pointers, and user-annotated non-control data. During runtime, an out-of-band monitor running in Secure World (or as a standalone kernel module if ARM TrustZone is not supported) is responsible to check the integrity of the value used by the application using its shadow copies maintained by the monitor. If any mismatch is found, memory corruption is then detected. In such a way, FastDIM can mitigate memory corruption attacks including *use-after-free* flaws, which is hardly addressed by other approaches. Note that early CFI techniques also adopt a similar idea that uses shadow stack to protect function returns, but it was omitted later for performance issues as it incurred too much overhead. In this work, we present a new architecture to speed up shadow copying and verification.

FastDIM has two major components: a compiler-based *software hardening tool* and an out-of-band *integrity monitor*. A new technique was developed to avoid link time optimization (LTO) which requires changing the system linker (e.g., using LLVM's gold linker). With this technique, our hardening tool offers modular instrumentation and supports dynamically-linked libraries, which significantly increases the compatibility and scalability to support complex applications as well as OS kernels. A shared-memory-based mechanism was developed to support fast communication between applications and the monitor. To further reduce overhead, several optimizations such as loop-invariant code motion and caching were applied . For pressure testing, FastDIM was evaluated on RIPE benchmarks and SEPC CPU2017 benchmarks. The results showed that all attacks in RIPE were successfully detected, and FastDIM incurred a geometric mean of 2.1% and a max of 27% overhead on SEPC CPU2017 C/C++ benchmarks. For real-platform testing, we instrumented a COTS Android Kitkat (kernel v3.14) running on a i.MAX.6 development board. The hardened kernel is 2.5% larger than the original one, and increases the Binder (i.e., Android's IPC) latency by 1.4% on average. AnTuTu benchmarks show a marginal 3% overall system slowdown. Source code of both the LLVM compiler and the monitor module are available in github.

In summary, we make the following contributions:

- We designed an unified out-of-band data integrity monitor to mitigate both control-flow and data-oriented attacks; previous work focused on either control- or data-oriented attacks.
- We developed a shared-memory based communication mechanism through which an out-of-band security monitor runs concurrently with target programs. This significantly reduces the monitoring overhead, at the expense of adding a small amount of security risk.
- We developed a new technique that supports compiler instrumentation without LTO to achieve better scalability and compatibility.
- We implemented and evaluated two prototypes of FastDIM (a standalone kernel module and a ARM TrustZone version) to protect both applications and operating system kernels on real-world platforms.

The rest of this paper is organized as follows. In Sect. 2, we describe the background about control-flow and data-flow attacks with several motivating examples. In Sect. 3, we present the design of FastDIM and its security guarantees. In Sect. 4, we present the evaluation of FastDIM. In Sect. 5 we review the related work, followed by conclusions in Sect. 6.

2 Background

Security researchers have focused on developing countermeasures against memory-corruption attacks for decades. We next briefly discuss two principled solutions: CFI and DFI, and their limitations, which serve as the motivation for this work.

2.1 Control-Flow Integrity

Control-Flow Integrity (CFI) is considered a principled security solution [2] towards control-oriented attacks. Google and Microsoft has integrated CFI into Clang and Visual Studio , respectively. CFI defines a set of legitimate targets for every control-flow transfer in a program and ensures that the transfer at runtime

```
1  int server() {
2      int authenticated = 0;
3      char packet[1000];
4      void (*handler) (char *);
5      while(!authenticated) {
6          readPacket(packet); //vulnerable function
7          if(Auth(packet)) {
8              authenticated = 1;
9              if (getUser(packet) == ADMIN){
10                 handler = priv;
11             }else{
12                 handler = unpriv;
13             }
14         }
15     }
16     if (authenticated == 1)
17         handler(packet);
18     ;
19 }
```

Fig. 1. An example that illustrates how non-control data can affect control flows.

cannot deviate from that set. The set is derived statically from a Control-Flow Graph (CFG) of the program. Thus, the security guarantee of CFI depends on the precision of the CFG. However, it is difficult to computing a precise CFG statically.

In addition, a CFG is stateless, which does not capture dynamic contexts. As a result, control flows may be affected by non-control data. Figure 1 presents an example (used in [2,7]). The value of the **handler** function pointer (at lines 10 and 12) depends on a branch condition (at line 9), which cannot be determined at compile time. Although this specific problem can be addressed by path-sensitive analysis [7], in general the set for a control-flow transfer has to be over-approximated; otherwise the program would not work correctly under the CFI protection.

2.2   Data-Flow Integrity

Compared to control-oriented attacks, non-control data are far more abundant than control-flow data. By corrupting some critical non-control data such as decision-making variables and cryptographic keys, attackers can escalate privileges, read and exfiltrate sensitive information, or corrupt a program's internal logic. In Fig. 1, variable **authenticated** is sensitive. By exploiting the vulnerable function at line 6, an attacker may corrupt its value and bypass the authentication check at line 16. Since data-oriented attacks do not violate stateless CFGs, they are invisible to the state-of-the-art control-flow defenses.

2.3   ARM TrustZone

The isolated execution allows a piece of code to run in a complete isolation from other codes. The execution isolation provides secrecy and integrity of both code

```
1   struct compound {
2       struct list_head list;
3
4       int (*func)(void *data);
5   }//this structure contains a function pointer
6   //and is attached to a list
7
8   int foo(){
9
10      struct compound mylist;
11      INIT_LIST_HEAD(&mylist.list);
12      struct compound *tmp;
13
14      tmp= (struct compound *)malloc(sizeof(struct compound));
15      tmp->func = &valid_func;
16      list_add(&(tmp->list), &(mylist.list));
17
18      vulnerable(tmp);//this function may free tmp from the heap
19
20      if (tmp->func)
21          tmp->func(data);
22          /*this function pointer may point to an invalid address
23          forged by attacker*/
24  }
```

Fig. 2. An example that illustrates how use-after-free vulnerabilities can evade CFI.

and data at run-time. The isolated execution is one of the desired security properties. Putting the security critical components and other software components to run in the same domain brings the potential risks that once an adversary escalates privileges, the adversary may disable the security critical components. ARM's TrustZone technology is a system-wide security solution that provides two execution domains: *Normal World* and *Secure World*. Through an isolated memory space and proper configured secure peripherals, TrustZone can securely isolate the Secure World from the Normal World. Thus, security sensitive components can run inside the Secure World with all access control policies protected by underlying hardware.

While TrustZone separates the execution domains, the between-world communication is still needed for security operations. The world switching from the Normal World to the Secure World is done usually by executing a dedicated instruction, the Secure Monitor Call (SMC) instruction, or a subset of the hardware exception mechanisms. When an SMC instruction is issued from the normal world, an ARM processor core running in the normal world will save its context into memory, flush the Memory Management Unit (MMU) and switch the execution world by changing its state. After the core enters the secure world, the core will restore its context in the secure world and start the security operations. One challenging issue to utilize this feature is that the SMC-based method will introduce excessive overhead and may greatly reduce the system execution performance, In order to improve the performance, FastDIM uses On-Chip RAM (OCRAM) as a shared memory between worlds. The OCRAM is mapped statically in the memory address space and can be accessed directly via the Advanced eXtensible Interface (AXI) bus. Unlike using regular RAM, the MMU is not needed to be consulted to access OCRAM. Using the OCRAM, run-time overhead can be greatly reduced by excluding the use of the MMU.

3   Design

FastDIM is a unified framework that enforces the integrity of sensitive in-memory data to mitigate memory corruption attacks.

3.1   Protection Targets

In this work, we only consider the following potential memory corruption targets including both control-flow data and non-control data.

- **Return addresses:** When a function gets called, the return address which is arguably the most infamous target of control-flow attacks will be stored on the stack. By corrupting the return address, an attacker can execute arbitrary code (e.g., injected code or ROP gadgets) once the function returns. Although stack canaries, ASLR, and safestack [10] have been used in practice to protect return addresses, recent work [8] shows that they can be bypassed by advanced attacks. Hence, we still include return addresses in our protection.
- **Function pointers:** Another type of control-flow transfers is function pointer, which stores the address of a function. Function pointers are widely stored on stack, heap, and other data segments. If a function pointer is compromised, an attacker can alter the control flow to an arbitrary location, when the program makes an indirect call through that function pointer.
- **Vtables pointers:** In C++, a class that defines a virtual function or derives from a class with virtual functions has a virtual function table (`vtable`) at runtime. For implementing dynamic dispatch, a `vtable` of a class is a look-up table comprised of a set of code pointers for every virtual function in the class. Although `vtables` themselves are housed in read-only memory, the pointer pointing to the base of `vtable` (a.k.a., `vptr`) is stored in writable memory regions. By overwriting the `vptr`, an attacker can hijack the control flow of the victim C++ programs.
- **User-annotated non-control data:** As illustrated in Fig. 1, non-control data can be security critical. For example, tampering with the parameters of system calls such as `setuid()`, `execute()` may lead to privilege escalation or unintended program execution; Overwriting the in-memory data read from the configuration files may result in bypassing the default access control of certain server applications. If decision-making data are compromised, an attacker can redirect the control flow of a program to unintended branches and thus bypass security checks.

3.2   System Overview

The protection of FastDIM is achieved through offline *compiler instrumentation* and runtime *out-of-band (OOB) monitoring*. As shown in Fig. 3, unprotected applications/kernels are automatically instrumented by our compiler plugin to add security checks wrapped in a support library. These hardened programs are capable of reporting the operations of protected targets to a monitor running in

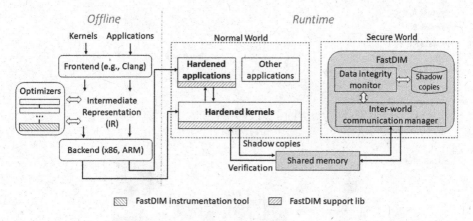

Fig. 3. An overview of FastDIM's system architecture.

Secure World. Based on the type of each operation, the monitor is responsible to perform necessary actions. In response, the monitor will terminate the corresponding program and reports a violation to users through the **proc** filesystem. In this design, the true value of each protected memory object along with its life cycle is tracked by the monitor dynamically, rather than being determined by a static set inferred from the CFG/DFG. Hence, it can significantly reduce the false errors caused by the inaccurate CFG/DFG.

3.3 Compiler-Time Instrumentation

The input of FastDIM's instrumentation tool is the source code of a program, and the output is the enhanced program with security code inserted. Particulary, the instrumentation will perform static analyze to identify all targets that need protection and their operations, and insert necessary instructions in the program to report operations associated with those targets to the monitor. The detail is discussed as follows.

Locating Targets. At this stage, we need to understand where to insert the code to report the target memory data. Different targets has different ways. The location of a *return address* object can be computed through a fixed offset from the frame pointer on the stack.

Instrumentation for Assignment. After identifying all targets, FastDIM will instrument the program with reporting capability. A few instructions will be inserted right after each assignment operation, writing a message to the shared memory so that the monitor can make a shadow copy of assigned values.

Instrumentation for Dereference. When targets are used or dereferenced somewhere in the program, the program is instrumented to notify the monitor to validate whether the data are altered illegally. Regarding non-return sensitive data such as function pointers, **vptrs**, and annotated memory objects, FastDIM

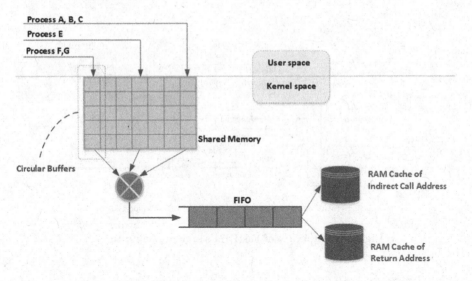

Fig. 4. Multiple ring buffers in shared memory and look-up tables in the monitor.

tracks all the `load` instructions, since those sensitive data have to be loaded into a register from memory before the use. The reporting instruction is inserted right before the `load` instruction. When a block of memory is copied from source to destination, the integrity of the source needs verification before making a new shadow copy for the assignment of the destination. For return addresses, the reporting instructions are inserted before the `ret` instructions for select functions that are not optimized. Note that no instrumentation is needed when sensitive data already in registers are used, as the data has already been checked before it is loaded into the registers.

Instrumentation for Fork and Destory. In order to prevent *use-after-free* attacks as illustrated in Fig. 2, FastDIM tracks the lifetime of each target. When a function returns, all the saved shadow copies associated with that function will be destroyed; for that, FastDIM insert a few instructions before the `ret` instruction to notify the monitor. Similarly, when a block of memory is freed on the heap, a notification message is sent to the monitor. After receiving the notification, the monitor will remove all the related shadow copies.

3.4   Runtime Integrity Monitoring

We have two monitor versions implemented in a kernel driver and in the secure world enabled by ARM TrustZone technology, respectively. Two versions have the same design principles with only differences in the implementation. For simplicity, the description of this section focuses on the kernel monitor module.

As shown in Fig. 4, a memory buffer (i.e., shared memory) is managed by the monitor, where multiple ring buffers are created to facilitate passing data from the user space to the kernel space. The shared memory is organized as a matrix of blocks and each column of the matrix stands for a ring buffer. Each element in the ring buffer contains a data structure as follows:

$$
Entity_{ring} := \begin{cases} tid, address, value, OP\_STORE, sig \\ tid, address, value, OP\_LOAD, sig \\ tid, address, \_, OP\_PUSH, sig \\ tid, address, \_, OP\_POP, sig \\ tid, \_, parent'stid, OP\_FORK, sig \\ tid, address, size, OP\_FREE, sig \end{cases}
$$

An individual ring buffer is assigned to a set of processes with the same hash of their task identifier (i.e., `tid`). When reporting an operation of sensitive data, a program process will push one of the above entities in the corresponding ring. With this design, the monitor allows multiple processes running on different CPU cores to write different ring buffers concurrently. To avoid the potential race conditions, a locking mechanism between user space and kernel space is implemented. Each entity in the ring buffer is signed by the program who write the shared memory.

There are two types of RAM caches managed by the monitor: a shadow lookup table and a shadow stack for non-return data and return addresses, respectively. Both are implemented in hash tables for O(1) search, while the detail is slightly different. Due to page limit, we only present the shadow lookup table here.

Non-return target data are stored in a dual-lookup table. As shown in the left part of Fig. 5, a hash bucket stores the task ID, the memory location of the sensitive data (referred to as data address), the value of the data, and a timestamp. When a new message is written into the shared memory by a user-space program, the kernel monitor will first determine whether the write operation is authenticated by verifying the message signature. After authentication, the monitor will compute the hash key based on the task ID and data address embedded in the message. With the key computed, the monitor will operate on a corresponding hash bucket based on the type of messages.

In order to speed up the duplication or removal of a batch of shadow copies associated to individual tasks when a task is forked or exits, we create an auxiliary `task hash table` shown in the right part of Fig. 5. In such a hash table, the key is calculated using the task ID only, and the hash bucket contains a list of references of shadow copies that have the same task ID. As a result, the removal of dead entries or the duplication of parent entries becomes an O(1) operation.

3.5   Security Analysis

One fundamental question is how the shared memory is protected against attacks. This is discussed from the consideration of malicious programs and benign but vulnerable programs separately. A malicious program attempts to corrupt the messages written by benign programs, so that the protection of benign programs will cease the effectiveness. For example, a malicious program

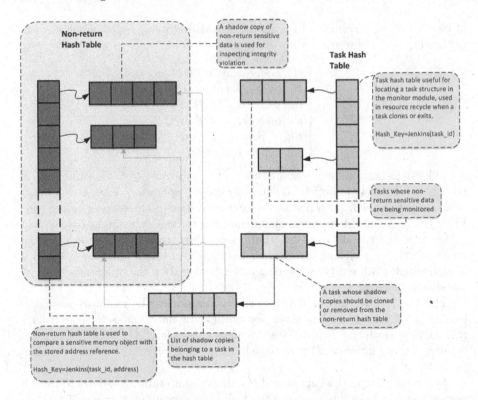

Fig. 5. Workflow of shadow lookup tables.

may write the shared memory with forged task ID and arbitrary content. In defense, FastDIM ensures that every message written to the shared memory is signed by the secret only known to the program. With the signature, what a malicious program can do is to simply replay existing messages, which only affect the efficiency of the shared memory (similar to deny of service) but not compromise the correctness of integrity checks. In order to further reduce the opportunities of DoS attacks, our future work will incorporate the access control of the protected programs, e.g., white list and limitation of writing rate.

For benign but vulnerable programs, FastDIM provides several methods to prevent an attacker from using a buffer overflow to modify the shared memory illegally. The first countermeasure provided by FastDIM is that the shared memory is randomly mapped to the address space of the program. Hence, an attacker is not easy to guess the base of the shared memory. Furthermore, the digital signature can provide enough protection against the direct access through buffer overflow. However, we do not assume that an attacker can arbitrarily read/write all readable/writable memories like debugger tools at the execution of the program.

In addition, our approach may have a risk of delayed checking by the monitor, but this is intended to reduce the runtime overhead of integrity checks. The protected programs only write a single message to the shared memory before or after each operation of sensitive data without blocking to wait the results from the monitor. Hence, the processing performed by the monitor will not negatively affect the effectiveness of the protected programs. At the cost, there are delays between the operations of sensitive data and the checking results. The situation may become worse when too many programs are writing the shared memory at the same time, while the monitor is not fast enough to consume those messages in time. However, according to experiment results on various benchmarks, the delay typically has a few instruction cycles. It can be further improved if we dedicate a CPU core or a hardware accelerator to run the monitor. In such a small time window, an attacker hardly launch an attack successfully.

4   Evaluation

To evaluate our prototype of FastDIM, we designed and performed experiments aiming to answer the following questions:

1. **Correctness (Q1).** Are intended functionalities of programs negatively affected by our protection mechanism?
2. **Effectiveness (Q2).** Can our prototype accurately detect memory-corruption attacks targeting function pointers, return addresses, `vtable` pointers, and other non-control data annotated by users?
3. **Efficiency (Q3).** How much performance overhead does FastDIM impose on programs?

4.1   Evaluation of FastDIM

FastDIM can be used to protect user-space programs thanks to its integerity monitor implemented inside an OS kernel. To evaluate it, we collected several benchmarks including RIPE benchmarks, SPEC CPU2017 C/C++ benchmarks, and several real-world applications including the Apache webserver and the TORQUE resource manager for HPC systems. These bencmarks were compiled by FastDIM's compiler tool (based on Clang/LLVM 3.9) and tested under the protection of FastDIM's integrity monitor module. RIPE and TORQUE programs contain vulnerable targets including return addresses, stack function pointers, heap function pointers, `.bss` function pointers, `.data` function pointers, and attack samples. They are evaluated aiming to answer the effectiveness question. The Apache server was used to test the efficiency of our prototype. SPEC CPU2017 has reference inputs and verification code that can be used to test whether its benchmarks generate correct output; so we use them for both efficiency and correctness evaluation.

SPEC CPU2017 (Q1 and Q3). Table 1 lists the overhead results for SPEC CPU 2017 benchmarks (the first 9 programs in the table are SPECrate Integer benchmarks and the last 6 programs are SPECrate 2017 Floating Point benchmarks). All programs were compiled by stock Clang/LLVM 3.9 and were

Table 1. Performance overhead of SEPC CPU2017 benchmarks

Programs	KLoc	Original (sec)	FastDIM (Code-Pointer-only)	FastDIM (all)
500.perlbench_r	362	488 ± 5	+21.9%	+26.8%
502.gcc_r	1304	315 ± 3	+8.9%	+14.5%
505.mcf_r	3	395 ± 6	+0.1%	+1.8%
520.omnetpp_r	134	489 ± 4	+21.3%	+32.6%
523.xalancbmk_r	520	375 ± 3	+15.3%	+29.6%
525.x264_r	96	350 ± 1	+6.2%	+10.5%
531.deepsjeng_r	10	323 ± 3	+0.7%	+0.3%
541.leela_r	21	491 ± 1	+0.9%	+8.3%
557.xz_r	33	391 ± 17	+3.3%	+3.6%
508.namd_r	8	282 ± 5	+1.4%	+1.2%
510.parest_r	427	421 ± 3	+3.1%	+19.9%
511.povray_r	170	540 ± 4	+27.4%	+27.3%
519.lbm_r	1	274 ± 3	+0.1%	+1.4%
538.imagick_r	259	556 ± 1	+0.5%	+0.2%
544.nab_r	24	457 ± 0	+0.4%	+0.4%
Geo.Mean	57	400	+2.1%	+4.4%

measured on an Ubuntu 14.04.5 machine (x86_64) with Xeon(R) CPU E5-1620 and 16GB RAM. The second column ("KLoc") of the table shows the number of thousand lines of code for each benchmark. As a baseline, we compiled the unmodified benchmarks using Clang/LLVM 3.9, with some modification to their CMake files to make benchmarks compilable with LLVM 3.9. The third column ("Original") shows the averaged time in seconds to complete the reference workload over three runs. To enable the protection of FastDIM, we modified the CMake files by setting a path to our LLVM pass (in `LVM_MODULE_PATH`) and library (in `link_directories`), as well as adjusting `CFLAGS`, `CXXFLAGS`, and `LDFLAGS`. The fourth column of the table shows the overhead of FastDIM when protecting only function pointers and `vptrs`, while the fifth column shows the overhead of FastDIM when protecting all targets.

The results show that FastDIM incurs a geometric mean of 2.1% overhead for the protection of function pointers only, and 4.4% overhead for all targets across the 15 SPEC CPU2017 benchmarks with max 32.6% overhead on `520.omnetpp_r`. Note that FastDIM (all) is sometimes slightly faster than Fast-DIM (Code-Pointer-only), that is due to the fluctuation.

RIPE Benchmark (Q2). We evaluated FastDIM using RIPE benchmark which is a synthesized C programs that includes many ways of attacks by overflowing buffer allocated on the stack, heap, in `.bss` and `.data` segments. By default, the RIPE benchmark is compiled for 32-bit machine (with -m32). We tested it on a x84_32 Ubuntu 16.04 VM. In total, there are 3840 combination of attacks, where 83 succeeded, 767 failed, and 2990 are not possible. With the protection of FastDIM, all the succeeded attacks are detected.

We annotated the CGI-BIN configuration string (CONFIG config;) in the main.h file as sensitive data, i.e., __attribute__((annotate("sensitive"))). After applying FastDIM on this program, non-control data attacks were successfully prevented.

Apache HTTP Server (Q3). We also evaluated our prototype on the Apache HTTP Server 2.4.27. As a baseline, Apache was compiled by using the original Clang/LLVM 3.9 and was tested by using the built-in ApachBench (ab) tool. On a x84 Ubuntu 14.04.5 VM (4 cores and 4G RAM), we started the compiled Apache server via the following command line:

```
apachectl -f /local-path/conf/httpd.conf
```

On the host machine (Xeon(R) CPU E5-1620 and 16GB RAM), the following command line was used to run the benchmark:

```
ab -n 5000 -c 1000 http://**.**.**.**:80/
```

This command sends 5000 HTTP GET requests, processing up to 1000 requests concurrently, to the Apache server running on the VM. The average time to process each request took about 128 milliseconds and the total transfer rate was about 1798 Kbytes per second. We then compiled the Apache server again under FastDIM (FP) and FastDIM (All) and performed the same commands. Table 2 shows the geometric mean of the results for 10 times.

Table 2. Performance results of Apache HTTP server

	Total Time (sec)	Transfer Rate (Kpbs)	Avg Conn Time (ms)	Longest Conn Time (ms)
Original	0.84	1798.43	66.69	808.69
FastDIM (FP)	0.95	1497.15	82.77	908.45
FastDIM (All)	0.97	1488.97	92.96	936.86

On average, FastDIM and TEE-FastDIM incurred 12–24% overhead and 12–39% overhead on Apache HTTP server.

4.2 Performance Evaluation of TEE-FastDIM

To evaluate FastDIM's ability to protect OS kernels, we compiledd Linux/Android kernel 3.14.38 shipped with the i.MAX.6 development board.

We applied the patches from LLVMLinux project and our own ones to make it compatible with the LLVM toolchain 3.9. On top of the kernel, a stock Android Lollipop (v5) was running. the Android binder testsuite and AnTuTu benchmarks were used for efficiency evaluation.

Keystore Vulnerability (Q2). Android contains a secure storage service called *Keystore* that is responsible for the storage of cryptographic keys and other sensitive credentials. Earlier years, researchers found a stack-based buffer overflow vulnerability that all versions of Android before 4.3 are open to attacks [9]. A stack buffer is created by the `KeyStore::getKeyForName` function located in `system/security/keystore/keystore.cpp`. In this function, the `filename` array is allocated on the stack and the input parameter `keyName` is copied into this array by calling a function. However, that function does not verify the size of the input parameter `keyName`. If the parameter is too larger that a buffer overflow will occur, overwritting the return address. The evaluation showed that TEE-FastDIM was able to detect the modification of the return address caused by this vulnerability.

Android OS (Q1 and Q3). Our instrumentation tool embeds security code into the target programs to enforce the security, thus increasing the resultant executable binary size. We compared the uncompressed Android/Linux kernel image size. These images have been verified to be compatible with both Android and Linux and runnable on the i.MAX6 platform. Overall, the security hardened kernel is 2.5% larger than the original one.

The binder mechanism is a part of Android kernel, and serves as the major Inter Process Communication (IPC) mechanism for Android. On average, FastDIM increased the binder latency by 1.4%.

Lastly, AnTuTu is a well-known benchmark tool for mobile platforms, and is widely used to evaluate the overall system performance across different hardware platforms. On average, FastDIM does not affect the overall system performance as measured by AnTuTu. The overhead of the security hardened kernel protected by FastDIM is around 3%.

5   Related Work

Control-Flow Attacks and Defenses. A significant body of work has adapted the original definition of CFI coupled with shadow stacks and developed sophisticated implementations that validate the target of a control transfers. Compact Control Flow Integrity and Randomization (CCFIR) [20] optimizes the performance of validating a transfer target by randomizing the layout of allowable transfer targets at each jump. Opaque CFI (O-CFI) [13] ensures that an attacker who can inspect the rewritten code cannot learn additional information about the targets of control jumps that are admitted as valid by the rewritten code. BinCFI [21] implements CFI without access to the program source, but only access to a stripped binary. Modular CFI [18] implements CFI for programs constructed from separate compilation units. Recent All of the above approaches enforce security defend by the results of a inaccurate static analysis.

Non-control Attacks and Defenses. Many countermeasures have been proposed to prevent data-oriented data attacks. Data-flow integrity ensures that the flow of data in a vulnerable program stays within a data-flow graph [6]. The data-flow graph is generated by static analysis, which makes the defense coarse-grained. Another type of defense mechanisms focused on enforcing memory-safety on systems. Softbound [14] has brought memory safety to un-safe C language by using bound checking with fat-pointer. CETS [15] enhanced this method by preventing memory errors. CCured [16] introduced a safe type system that statically detects the occurrence of memory error and dynamically enforces bound checking on them. However, the high performance overhead limits the adoption of these approaches. The work [17] proposed a defense mechanism that uses dynamic taint analysis to label all critical data to track the propagation of tainted data, and therefore can detect overflow attacks by identifying the integrity of tainted data. However, programs protected by this technique is too expensive to be adopted widely.

6   Conclusion

This paper describes an Out-Of-Band (OOB) integrity monitor named FastDIM to protect systems against both control-related and data-oriented memory corruption attacks. The key idea is to extend the idea of shadow stacks to protect not only code pointers but also user-annotated sensitive non-control data, and keep the integrity checks by an OOB monitor (verifier) rather than the programs themselves. A set of techniques are proposed to provide a fast shared-memory-based mechanism through which the monitor can enforce the integrity for both user applications and OS kernels. We implemented a prototype of our approach either as a loadable Linux kernel module or a integrated TEE running in Secure World. Evaluation results showed that our approach was correct, effective, and efficient. We believe that our approach makes a step toward a deterministic secure defense that are fully immune to memory corruption attacks.

Acknowledgements. We sincerely thank reviewers for their insightful feedback. This work was supported in part by NSFC Award #61972200.

References

1. Abadi, M., Budiu, M., Erlingsson, U., Ligatti, J.: Control-flow integrity. In: Proceedings of the 12th ACM Conference on Computer and Communications Security, pp. 340–353. CCS 2005, ACM, New York, NY, USA (2005)
2. Abadi, M., Budiu, M., Erlingsson, U., Ligatti, J.: Control-flow integrity principles, implementations, and applications. ACM Trans. Inf. Syst. Secur. **13**(1), 4:1-4:40 (2009)

3. Bhatkar, S., Sekar, R.: Data space randomization. In: Zamboni, D. (ed.) DIMVA 2008. LNCS, vol. 5137, pp. 1–22. Springer, Heidelberg (2008). https://doi.org/10.1007/978-3-540-70542-0_1

4. Bigelow, D., Hobson, T., Rudd, R., Streilein, W., Okhravi, H.: Timely rerandomization for mitigating memory disclosures. In: Proceedings of the 22Nd ACM SIGSAC Conference on Computer and Communications Security, pp. 268–279. CCS 2015, ACM, New York, NY, USA (2015)

5. Carlini, N., Barresi, A., Payer, M., Wagner, D., Gross, T.R.: Control-flow bending: on the effectiveness of control-flow integrity. In: 24th USENIX Security Symposium (USENIX Security 15), pp. 161–176. USENIX Association, Washington, D.C (2015)

6. Castro, M., Costa, M., Harris, T.: Securing software by enforcing data-flow integrity. In: Proceedings of the 7th Symposium on Operating Systems Design and Implementation, pp. 147–160. OSDI 2006, USENIX Association, Berkeley, CA, USA (2006)

7. Ding, R., Qian, C., Song, C., Harris, B., Kim, T., Lee, W.: Efficient protection of path-sensitive control security. In: 26th USENIX Security Symposium (USENIX Security 17), pp. 131–148. USENIX Association, Vancouver, BC (2017)

8. Goktas, E., et al.: Bypassing Clang's SafeStack for fun and profit. In: Black Hat Europe (2016)

9. Intelligence, S.: Android keystore stack buffer overflow: to keep things simple, buffers are always larger than needed (2014)

10. Kuznetsov, V., Szekeres, L., Payer, M., Candea, G., Sekar, R., Song, D.: Code-pointer integrity. In: 11th USENIX Symposium on Operating Systems Design and Implementation (OSDI 2014), pp. 147–163. USENIX Association, Broomfield, CO (2014)

11. Li, J., Wang, Z., Jiang, X., Grace, M., Bahram, S.: Defeating return-oriented rootkits with "return-less" kernels. In: Proceedings of the 5th European Conference on Computer Systems, pp. 195–208. EuroSys 2010, ACM, New York, NY, USA (2010)

12. Mashtizadeh, A.J., Bittau, A., Boneh, D., Mazières, D.: CCFI: cryptographically enforced control flow integrity. In: Proceedings of the 22Nd ACM SIGSAC Conference on Computer and Communications Security, pp. 941–951. CCS 2015, ACM, New York, NY, USA (2015)

13. Mohan, V., Larsen, P., Brunthaler, S., Hamlen, K.W., Franz, M.: Opaque control-flow integrity. In: NDSS (2015)

14. Nagarakatte, S., Zhao, J., Martin, M.M., Zdancewic, S.: SoftBound: highly compatible and complete spatial memory safety for C. In: Proceedings of ACM PLDI (2009)

15. Nagarakatte, S., Zhao, J., Martin, M.M., Zdancewic, S.: CETS: compiler enforced temporal safety for C. In: Proceedings of ISMM (2010)

16. Necula, G.C., McPeak, S., Weimer, W.: CCured: type-safe retrofitting of legacy code. In: Proceedings of ACM POPL (2002)

17. Newsome, J., Song, D.X.: Dynamic taint analysis for automatic detection, analysis, and signaturegeneration of exploits on commodity software. In: NDSS (2005)

18. Niu, B., Tan, G.: Modular control-flow integrity. SIGPLAN Not. 49(6), 577–587 (2014)

19. Snow, K.Z., Monrose, F., Davi, L., Dmitrienko, A., Liebchen, C., Sadeghi, A.R.: Just-in-time code reuse: on the effectiveness of fine-grained address space layout randomization. In: Proceedings of the 2013 IEEE Symposium on Security and Privacy, pp. 574–588. SP 2013, IEEE Computer Society, Washington, DC, USA (2013)

20. Zhang, C., et al.: Practical control flow integrity and randomization for binary executables. In: Proceedings of the 2013 IEEE Symposium on Security and Privacy, pp. 559–573. SP 2013, IEEE Computer Society, Washington, DC, USA (2013)
21. Zhang, M., Sekar, R.: Control flow integrity for cots binaries. In: Proceedings of the 22Nd USENIX Conference on Security, pp. 337–352. SEC 2013, USENIX Association, Berkeley, CA, USA (2013)

Construction of a New UAV Management System Based on UMIA Technology

Ge Zhang[1]([⊠]) [iD], Yu Geng[2] [iD], Xueman Kong[2] [iD], and Yifa Li[2] [iD]

[1] China Industrial Control Systems Cyber Emergency Response Team, Beijing, China
zhangge0957@163.com
[2] School of Cyberspace Security, Zhengzhou University, Zhengzhou, China

Abstract. With the rapid development of unmanned aerial vehicle (UAV) technology in multiple fields, there are more and more scenarios needed to complete tasks through UAV communication and collaboration, and naturally, the need for cross-domain authentication and confidential communication has been proposed. Nowadays, sensor technology and Internet of Things technology continue to develop, and UAV technology has become more and more mature, and it has become a popular industry. Due to the high-speed mobility of UAV and the variation of network environment, it is difficult for the traditional cross-domain authentication based on CA certificate to meet the needs. Because on the one hand, CA online support is difficult to guarantee, on the other hand, certificate verification will also increase the delay. Therefore, how to achieve rapid certification in the process of cooperation in different domains has become a temporary research hot topic and difficulty. Based on the newly emerged unified multi-domain identity authentication (UMIA) technology and the lightweight cryptographic algorithm, this paper proposes a new idea of constructing a UAV management system.

Keywords: Cross-domain authentication · UAV network · Lightweight cryptographic algorithm

1 Introduction

With the development of unmanned aerial vehicle (UAV) technology and related artificial intelligence and other technologies, UAVs can cooperate to complete specific tasks. Therefore, the mission field of UAVs is expanding, and the previous traditional, single communication mode has been gradually eliminated. UAVs of different companies and organizations often need to complete tasks together through task networking. For example, in the civil field, especially in disaster rescue, due to the tight time and heavy task, all civil UAVs of different brands and different models in a certain area can be uniformly deployed together to complete the rescue work together. Many tasks of rescue work, which naturally need to carry out multiple different groups, which requires a variety of UAVs can automatically identify each other in the air and group according to the requirements, so cross-domain authentication is inevitable. In the military field, especially during wars, UAVs from different companies, different models, and even different countries often need to cooperate with each other to carry out large-scale investigations or strikes on targets in the same area. At this point, authentication (especially cross-domain authentication) and confidential communication between UAVs are particularly important.

UAVs usually have the following characteristics: (1). High-speed movement performance. The high-speed motion of the UAV naturally determines that the authentication in the UAV network must have a low latency. (2). Uncertainty of the network. Due to the high-speed mobility of the UAV, the network is changing and the links are unstable. Therefore, authentication in the UAV network cannot assume fixed base station support and stable communication. (3). Low operational performance. UAVs are powered by batteries and try not to use chips with high power consumption, so it is difficult for most UAVs to have good computing performance. Therefore, the authentication scheme of UAV generally requires the use of lightweight cryptography algorithm to minimize the high power consumption caused by complex operations, and complex operations can increase the latency. (4). Uncertainty of the UAV nodes. UAVs are often in the open air network, may be other UAVs into formation, may also appear UAVs are controlled, forming malicious UAV node, and even UAVs failure (or captured in the war, shot down), may need to supplement UAVs as a new node, these factors will lead to the change of the UAV node. Therefore, the UAV also needs to consider the authentication problem in the process of node dynamic change. The key to solving the above problems is to build a UAV management system, so that the UAV in the system, whether from different security domains, can authenticate each other and communicate confidential. Certification within the same domain is easier to achieve, but cross-domain authentication is much more difficult.

The traditional way to solve the certification problem, is the international long proposed PKI technology, that is, the establishment of public key infrastructure, through the PKI/CA certificate to achieve certification [1, 2]. However, cross-domain authentication requires collaborative services by multiple CA agencies, or by multiple CA agencies (which include applications for public key certificates, issuance, management, help verification certificates, management certificate cancellation list, etc.) to meet the certificates issued by different CA can be certified to each other. This not only requires online network and bandwidth resources, but also requires high construction and maintenance costs of CA, which greatly limits the application and promotion of PKI. In particular, the high-speed mobility, network instability, and node degeneration of the UAV network itself make it difficult to rely on a fixed CA to provide certificate service, and it is even more inappropriate to use the UAV node as the CA in the air, because once the node has problems, the whole UAV network cannot achieve authentication.

Another way of authentication is the identity-based Cryptography System (IBC), proposed by the cryptographer Shamir in 1984 [3–5]. This is a special password algorithm, which "binds" the user's identity to the private key of the key generation center (KGC) to form the user's private key, which does not need the user public key, or the user's identity can be equivalent as the public key, which does not need the public key certificate. However, the IBC algorithm requires large computing resources and slow computing speed, which is a "heavyweight" cryptographic algorithm, which is not applicable to most small and medium-sized UAVs with low computing power. And it is difficult to identify different domains (and thus different KGC's that distribute private keys) to authenticate with each other. This series of limitations of IBC make it equally difficult to apply to UAV cross-domain certification.

Besides, there are no-certificate certification methods based on the lightweight national standard SM2 algorithm, such as CPK [6], FC-CPK [7], CLA [8] and so on. Although the lightweight algorithms meet the requirements, and the authentication in a single domain also has its unique advantages, but it still does not solve the cross-domain authentication. Therefore, the cross-domain authentication in the UAV network has become a hot and difficult point.

With the development of blockchain technology, people in recent years have proposed the authentication method of combining blockchain and CA, which builds blockchain nodes as infrastructure and forms a larger infrastructure together with PKI [9–12]. Supported by this infrastructure, public key certificates are incorporated into the blockchain to ensure their authenticity. The UAV network confirms the validity of the public key certificate by accessing its "nearest" (i. e., the fastest accessible node in the air) blockchain nodes. This can indeed in the UAV can access any block chain node to achieve cross-domain authentication, but on the one hand, the cost is very high, on the other hand, once the UAVs do not block chain node support (such as disaster relief fly into the block chain node was destroyed area, wartime into the enemy area, etc.), the scheme still cannot achieve cross-domain authentication.

Recently, a new cross-domain authentication (patent) technology, namely, based on Unified Multi-domain Identity Authentication (UMIA) technology [13, 14]. Then, we propose a new UAV management system construction method. This method does not rely on huge infrastructure such as PKI and blockchain, which can greatly reduce the cost; only lightweight national standard password algorithms such as SM2/3/4 can meet the lightweight requirements of UAV certification; but requires unified management at the national level, formulate several relevant standards of unified identification and certification protocol, and give a few unified parameters. In terms of management, this method does not interfere with the self-management of each domain, that is, except for the domain identification, as long as the domain identification meets the length requirements of the standard, the others are managed by each domain itself, which does not hinder the management autonomy of each domain. In terms of certification, UAVs can be authenticated directly through near-range communication (including in-domain certification and cross-domain certification, even without ground support). Due to the certificate is not used, there is no need to verify the certificate, so it can not only improve the authentication efficiency, but also reduce the authentication delay, especially if it can easily achieve cross-domain authentication. At the same time, the method is also compatible with the certificate system, which is very suitable for multi-domain UAV management.

2 UMIA Technology

2.1 Domain Management Structure in UMIA

UMIA technology consists of three parts: IMPK (Identity Map to Public Key, identifier mapping public key) technology, IBPK (Identity Bound Public Key, identifier binding public key) technology, and unified authentication protocol. IMPK refers to the identity that uniquely corresponds to a fixed public key through a specific rule; IBPK refers to the binding relationship between the public key and the identity, and the identity that also uniquely corresponds to a specific public key after binding [15]. However, unlike IMPK, IBPK can unbind and then rebind, and the identity corresponds to another specific public key through the binding relationship.

UMIA involves a root domain and multiple subdomains, but each subdomain is more independent, including its own personnel, equipment, equipment, etc. All nodes (such as domain gateway, edge gateway) and terminals in the domain key management center (DKMC), key management center (RKMC) in each domain, and the nodes and endpoints in the root domain. And the UMIA is suitable for two-layer domain management structures which can be shown as follows:

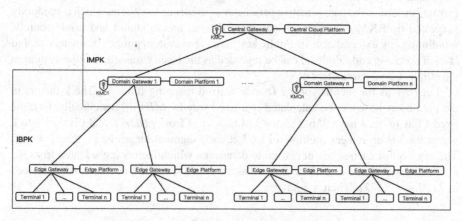

Fig. 1. Two-layer domain management structure

In Fig. 1, the top layer is the root domain, KMC * is RKMC, domain 1 to domain n is a subdomain, also called a domain, and KMC1 to KMC n is DKMC. Usually, we call all domains, namely the root domain, together with domain 1 to domain n, as a global domain. In particular, although RKMC is different from DKMC, the root domain is also equal to other domains after the domain public and private keys are distributed. The identification and public keys of all nodes and terminals within the root domain are also managed by the root domain itself. Since both nodes and terminals are considered equal to DKMC, we do not distinguish between nodes and terminals below, which is uniformly called "endpoints".

2.2 IMPK Technology

The IMPK is used in the UMIA for the management of the domain public keys. Each domain has its own domain public and private key pair, Domain i (noted as D_i) public and private keys are recorded as pk_i, sk_i, where pk_i are public parameter of the D_i. The public and private key pairs of the root domain are recorded as pk^*, sk^*.

The root domain is only responsible for defining a unified identity structure and the identity of each domain, while developing a unified authentication (encryption) protocol. The internal identity (in-domain identification) and public keys of all endpoints of each domain are managed by the domain itself. The identity of each domain is uniformly assigned by the root domain, and the length of the identity in the domain is also uniformly defined by the root domain.

The root domain manages the domain public and private keys of each domain (including the root domain itself) through the IMPK technology. Specifically:

A set of public key bases (Base consisting of PK factors, abbreviated as BPK). Let the public key base contain r public keys, noted as $BPK = \{bpk_1, \cdots, bpk_r\}$. Corresponding to the BPK is a set of private key bases (abbreviated as BSK), noted as $BSK = \{bsk_1, \cdots, bsk_r\}$, where bpk_i and bsk_i are consist a key pair, namely $bpk_i = bsk_i G$ and G is the basis point of an addition group of elliptic curves over a finite field. Private key base is the core sensitive parameter of the security system, which is randomly generated by RKMC in a secure password device, and is stored and used securely, prohibiting any external access. Public key base is the system public parameters, stored at each node and endpoint, and can be regarded as the basic parameters of the system as the elliptic curve parameters used.

Let ID_{D_i} as the identity of the $D_i.\varphi$ as a fixed mapping function, The k factors in the public key base can be calculated in a fixed way by $h(ID_{D_i})$. Specifically, take the fixed l bits (e. g., l have 256, 160, or 128 bits, etc.) from $h(ID_{D_i})$, and divide l into k segments (l is an integer multiple of k). Let each segment length be m, then $l = mk$. The low t bit of each segment is used to determine which factors are selected from the public key base, and the m-t bits are used as the coefficient, the k coefficients are nodeed as $\lambda_1, \lambda_2, \cdots, \lambda_k$. Then, we have

$$pk_i = \varphi\big(h(ID_{D_i})\big) = \sum_{j=1}^{k} \lambda_j bpk_j^i$$

Under a given public key base, the domain public key is uniquely determined and any node with a public key base is computable. The domain private key ski corresponding to the domain public key pki must be securely injected securely into the DKMC's password device to generate the public and private keys for all the nodes and endpoints that the domain governs. Generally, to accommodate the limited terminal storage space, it is recommended $r \leq 16$, so that the public key base does not exceed 1 KB.

2.3 IBPK Technology

For all endpoints within its jurisdiction, DKMC coordinates or generates public and private key pairs, i. e. the private keys of the endpoint can be generated and distributed by DKMC, or by the endpoint and DKMC [16]. When collaborative generation, the endpoint private key has only the endpoint. When the endpoint is the main user, it meets the security requirements of the electronic signature method. In the following, we describe the process by which the KMC of domain Di generates identifying private keys with the endpoint U under its jurisdiction:

Step 1: Let the identity of node U as ID_U, the U generates the private key factor usk_U by itself, and let $upk_U = usk_U G$. Then, U sends ID_U and upk_U together to the subordinate DKMC;

Step 2: The DKMC pseudorandom hsk_U was generated, and calculate that $hpk_U = hsk_U G$, $apk_U = upk_U + hpk_U$ and $isk_U = v_U * sk_i$, where,apk_U is called the accompanying public key of a U, $v_U = h_{SM3}(ID_U || apk_U || *ET_U)$, *stands for options, ET_U is the validity period of the apk_U. If the validity period is not set, then $v_U = h_{SM3}(ID_U || apk_U)$. DKMC then calculates $dsk_U = isk_U + hsk_U$, then sends encryption dsk_U,apk_U (if any) and ET_U (if any) to U, and also sends it along with (if any) to U.

Step 3: When U recive dsk_U,apk_U and ET_U, it calculates its own private key:$sk_U = dsk_U + usk_U$. Then, U need to verify that whether its private key is correct, namely, The values of $pk_U = sk_U G$ and $apk_U + v_U pk_i$ are calculated separately to determine whether they are equal: If equal, the public-private key pair is correct, if not, indicates that the dsk_U and apk_U distribution went wrong, and we need to ask for a redistribution.

When the endpoint does not need to generate part of the private key by itself (such as the distribution device or equipment that preset the private key), that is, when the private keys of the endpoint are all generated by DKMC, we can omit the Step 1 and let $upk_U = 0$ in the Step 2 directly. Then, for node U, we have that the private key $sk_U = dsk_U$, and adjugate public key $apk_U = hpk_U$.

2.4 Universal Unified Certification Agreement

Let A and B be any two endpoints (available within the same domain or in a different domain), and the unified two-way authentication protocol is as follows:

$$A \rightarrow B : \quad type_A, ID_B, M_A, ID_A, apk_A, *ET_A, S_A;$$
$$B \rightarrow A : \quad type_B, ID_A, M_B, ID_B, apk_B, *ET_B, S_B,$$

where, $A \rightarrow B : X$ stand for the message X that from A to B, $type_A$ is the protocol type specified by A (can specify the protocol is key negotiation, data encryption, authentication, authentication code type, etc.), M_A is the data from A to B that needs to be certified, S_A is an authentication code, namely a digital signature value or an HMAC value with shared secrets, and the authentication type is specified by $type_A$.

When signing, $S_A = Sig_{SM2}(sk_A, h(ID_B || M_A))$, namely the signature content contains the identification ID_B of B and data of M_A. $Sig_\psi(sk_A, h(M))$ Stand for that A signs the hash value of the message M using the signature algorithm ψ and its own private key sk_A. When the ψ is a default algorithm, we have $Sig(sk_A, h(M))$.

When A and B are in the same domain, since both A and B know the public key of the domain, the complete public key can be calculated directly by using the accompanying public key of the other party, and then the signature can be verified again. When A and B are not in the same domain, they should first use the public key of the other party domain to calculate the public key base, and then calculate the complete public key according to the other party's accompanying public key, and then verify the signature. The reason why A and B can do cross-domain authentication is that the whole domain has the same public key base. So that although A and B are not in the same domain, they can calculate the domain public key of the other domain from the public key base, so as to calculate the public key of the other party.

By the definition of $type_U$, we have that the unified authentication protocol includes key negotiation, data encryption, and certificate-based authentication. In fact, when $type_U$ as key negotiation, M_A is negotiated data, and when $type_U$ as cryphred, M_A is ciphertext. When $type_U$ as the certificate certification, pass the public key certificate without passing apk_U. Turn to the certificate-based certification module for the certificate-based certification, which is compatible with the certificate system.

3   Construction of a New UAV Management System Based on UMIA Technology

3.1   UAV Management Organizational Architecture Based on UMIA

Since UMIA technology can achieve cross-domain authentication without using certificates, it will bring great convenience to apply it to UAV management [17]. Therefore, we give the following suggestions to build the UAV organization and management system based on the UMIA in Fig. 2.

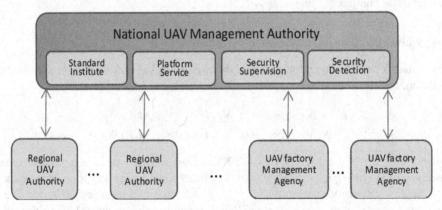

Fig. 2. The two-layer organizational architecture of UAV management

That is, in the organization and management, two layers of design, set up special management agencies at the national level, and according to the needs of the region and manufacturers, registered with the national management department to establish the independent management agencies. Its topology is shown in Fig. 3, where, the specialized agency of national UAV management should build a national UAV management cloud platform and RKMC. At the same time, according to the actual needs, the UAV registration and management domain and corresponding institutions are set up by different regions and manufacturers, and each domain has its own domain KMC, which can independently manage the UAV under its jurisdiction.

The national UAV management agency shall formulate the national UAV management policies and standards, define the unified UAV identification norms, and distribute

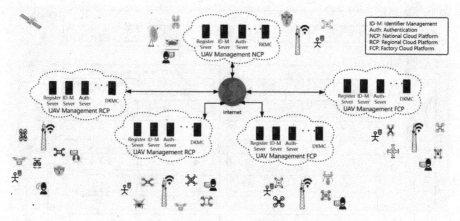

Fig. 3. UAV management architecture topology

a unique domain identification for each registration management domain.At the same time, the national UAV management agencies should also be drone regulation, including the function of drones, performance detection, for unregistered drones banned fly, etc., to ensure that each drove in a certain area or manufacturer's domain platform registration and obtain public and private key, and each drone operator should also be registered and obtain public and private key.

As the root domain, the national UAV management cloud platform is the working platform and technical support of the national UAV management agency. It not only provides domain registration services for the regional cloud platform and the manufacturer cloud platform, but more importantly, it also generates and publishes the public key base to provide domain public and private key distribution services for each domain.

Regions or manufacturers can apply to become an independent UAV management domain according to their own needs [18]. After obtaining the permission from the national UAV management agency, it can establish its own domain cloud platform to manage its UAV and provide various services such as UAV registration, key management, certification and so on.

Certainly, regional or UAV manufacturers need to apply to the national UAV management authority for the establishment of a management domain, and, after examination and approval, to obtain the unique domain identification and domain public and private keys. Then we can establish its own domain KMC and management cloud platform, implement the UAV registration management within the jurisdiction, including the registration of UAV, identification allocation, public (private) key generation, validity period management, public (private key) update, etc.

3.2 UAV Management Technology System Based on UMIA

To implement the management of UAV, the corresponding technical management system must be established. To this end, we give the following UAV management technology architecture (Table 1):

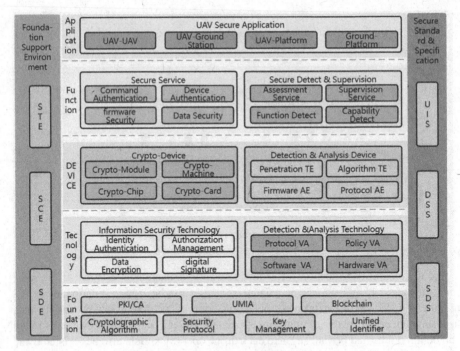

Fig. 4. UAVs management technology system

We give the Abbr. Table as follows:

Table 1. Abbr. of Fig. 4

SDE	Secure Detection Environment	SDS	Secure Detection Specification
SCE	Secure Computing Environment	DSS	Data Secure Standard
STE	Secure Transmission Environment	UIS	Unified Identifier Specification
VA	Vulnerability Analysis	AE	Analysis Equipment
TE	Testing Equipment		

4   Conclusion

The unified management and certification of UAVs across the country is not only necessary for daily management, but also can quickly organize a large number of UAVs into use in emergency situations. Based on the new UMIA technology, this paper gives a national macro architecture of unified UAV certification management for the reference of relevant departments, and also hopes for interested peers to participate in further research. Based on the architecture built by UMIA technology, this paper can realize the nationwide unified UAV authentication, data encryption and security supervision. In peacetime, between UAVs, between UAVs and ground stations, between UAVs and platforms, and between ground stations and platforms can be certified and confidential communication based on UMIA technology, and can be subject to the supervision of the regulatory authorities on any occasion. In emergency use, UAVs in each domain can directly realize intra-domain and cross-domain authentication through UMIA technology, and can accept unified deployment without temporary security configuration. Of course, there is still much work to be done to achieve this system. In management, there are many standards and norms that need to be studied and established. Technically, the session key negotiation protocol, the group session key establishment protocol, etc., are all topics for further research. In the equipment, a large number of safety equipment and testing and supervision equipment, also need to do more detailed design and development. In the future, UAV hardware will be improved, and UAVs embracing big data will become a development trend. We will conduct more in-depth research on the invisibility, intelligence and systemization of UAVs.

References

1. Kohnfelder, L.M.: Towards a practical public-key cryptosystem. Massachusetts Institute of Technology (1978)
2. Perlman, R.: An overview of PKI trust models. IEEE Netw. **13**(6), 38–43 (1999)
3. Shamir, A.: Identity-based cryptosystems and signature schemes. In: Blakley, G.R., Chaum, D. (eds.) CRYPTO 1984. LNCS, vol. 196, pp. 47–53. Springer, Heidelberg (1985). https://doi.org/10.1007/3-540-39568-7_5
4. Tsujii, S., Itoh, T.: An ID-based cryptosystem based on the discrete logarithm problem. IEEE J. Sel. Areas Commun. **7**(4), 467–473 (1989)
5. Chunlai, D., Mingzeng, H., Hongli, Z.: An authentication-based mobile ad hoc key management framework in elliptic curve domains. J. Commun. **2007**(12), 53–59 (2007). (In chinese)
6. Xianghao, N., Zhong, C.: Introduction to network security technology. Comput. Secur. **2003**(30), 76–76 (2003). (In chinese)
7. Yifa, L., Duo, C., Mengyang, X.: A flexible and configurable combined public key scheme. ICAIS2022 (In press)
8. Al-Riyami, S.S., Kenneth, G.P.: Certificateless public key cryptography. In: Laih, C.S. (ed.) ASIACRYPT 2003. Lecture Notes in Computer Science, vol. 2894, pp. 452–473. Springer, Berlin, Heidelberg (2003). https://doi.org/10.1007/978-3-540-40061-5_29
9. Yakubov, A., Shbair, W., Wallbom, A., Sanda, D.: A blockchain-based PKI management framework network operations and management symposium (2018)
10. Yuchen, W., Wenhui, Q., Lizhen, X.: Blockchain-based drone swarm security collaboration. Comput. Sci. **48**(S2), 528–532+546 (2021). (In Chinese)
11. Zhicheng, Z., Lixin, L., Zuohui, Li.: Efficient cross-domain authentication scheme based on blockchain technology. Comput. Appl. **38**(02), 316–320+326 (2018). (In Chinese)
12. Aqsa, R., et al.: Blockchain-based public key infrastructure: a transparent digital certification mechanism for secure communication. IEEE Netw. (2021)
13. Xueman, K., Mengyang, X.: Key processing method, device and system based on unified multi-domain identification (In Chinese)
14. Yifa, L., Yu, G., Xueman, K.: A cross-domain authenticated key management scheme for the internet of UAVs. In: ICAIS2022 (In press)

15. Zeng, Y., Zhang, R.: Energy-efficient UAV communication with trajectory optimization. IEEE Trans. Wireless Commun. **16**(6), 3747–3760 (2017)
16. Zeng, Y., Qingqing, W., Zhang, R.: Accessing from the sky: a tutorial on UAV communications for 5G and beyond. Proc. IEEE **107**(12), 2327–2375 (2019)
17. Zhang, G., Qingqing, W., Cui, M., Zhang, R.: Securing UAV communications via joint trajectory and power control. IEEE Trans. Wireless Commun. **18**(2), 1376–1389 (2019)
18. Zhou, X., Qingqing, W., Yan, S., et al.: UAV-enabled secure communications: joint trajectory and transmit power optimization. IEEE Trans. Veh. Technol. **68**(4), 4069–4073 (2019)

FP²-MIA: A Membership Inference Attack Free of Posterior Probability in Machine Unlearning

Zhaobo Lu[1] , Yilei Wang[1]([✉]) , Qingzhe Lv[1] , Minghao Zhao[2] ,
and Tiancai Liang[3]

[1] School of Computer Science, Qufu Normal University, Rizhao 276826, China
wang_yilei2019@qfnu.edu.com
[2] School of Computer Science and Technology, East China Normal University,
Shanghai 200062, China
[3] Institute of Artificial Intelligence and Blockchain, Guangzhou University,
Guangzhou 510700, China

Abstract. Generally speaking, machine learning is to train an ML model (original model) on a dataset to perform a certain function. But sometimes, in order to protect the data privacy of a specified user, machine unlearning requires the original model owner to delete the specified user's data in its training dataset and retrain a new model (unlearned model). However, the research of CCS'21 shows that the adversary can judge whether a data sample is deleted by comparing the prediction vectors of the original and unlearned models, thus being attacked by membership inference. To mitigate this privacy leak, CCS'21 proposes that models that only output predicted labels (*i.e.,* , cannot obtain model posterior probabilities) can effectively defend against existing attacks. However, our research shows that even machine unlearning models that only output labels have certain privacy risks. This paper proposes an inference attack that does not rely on posterior probability against machine unlearning, named FP²-MIA. Specifically, the adversary queries the original and unlearned models for candidate data samples respectively, and adds perturbations to them to change the predicted labels of the two models, and then the adversary uses the magnitude of the perturbations to distinguish whether they are deleted data samples. We conduct experiments on four datasets, MNIST, CIFAR10, CIFAR100 and STL10. The results show that member inference can be effectively inferred even when only the predicted labels are output, in which the AUC (Area Under Curve) index on the MNIST dataset is as high as 0.96.

Keywords: Membership inference attack · Label-only · Machine learning

© The Author(s), under exclusive license to Springer Nature Switzerland AG 2022
C. Ge and F. Guo (Eds.): ProvSec 2022, LNCS 13600, pp. 167–175, 2022.
https://doi.org/10.1007/978-3-031-20917-8_12

1 Introduction

1.1 Background

The right to be forgotten refers to the right of the data owner to ask the data user to delete his personal data, and the user must delete the personal data in a timely manner in this case. A lot of legislation has recently been enacted in support of the right to be forgotten, notably the European Union's General Data Protection Regulation (GDPR) [1]. Users expect the model to be able to forget certain sensitive data and its complete lineage. Therefore, some MLaaS providers (such as Google and Amazon) must comply with the law by removing certain URLs from their websites and taking necessary actions for the machine learning models they provide. MLaaS providers remove the impact of their private data on machine learning models at the user's request, a process known as machine unlearning.

Machine unlearning generates two version models before and after, one is the original model, and the other the a unlearned model formed by eliminating the influence of the specified user data on the old model on the basis of the old model. The reason for the success of existing membership inference attacks against machine unlearning [10] is the inherent overfitting property of ML models, that is, the ML model has more confidence in the data samples it has seen, and this confidence is reflected in the posterior probability of the model. superior. Existing attacks believe that the deletion of the target sample will produce differences between the two models, so the adversary judges whether x is a deleted sample by comparing the output posterior probabilities of the two models for the candidate samples. However, a major disadvantage of existing attacks is that they can be easily mitigated if the model only outputs the predicted outcome, *i.e.*, the final model decision, rather than the confidence score. We call this defense method Label-Only Defense. This is more common in real life because most users only care about the last prediction result.

1.2 Motivation and Contribution

However, existing attacker can be easily mitigated if the ML model only outputs the predicted labels, i.e. the final model decision, rather than the posterior probability. This setting is called Label-Only Exposure, and this is more common in real life because most users only care about the last prediction result. This motivates us to care about a membership inference attack based on predicted labels against machine unlearning, and to our knowledge, such attacks have not been studied so far. We show that a target machine unlearning model that only exposes labels is still vulnerable to membership inference attacks. Our intuition is that it is harder to change the predicted labels of a target model for member samples than for non-member samples. Specifically, the adversary queries the original model and the unlearned model for candidate data samples respectively, and adds perturbations to them to change the predicted labels of the two models, and then the adversary uses the amplitude of the perturbations to distinguish whether they are deleted data samples.

In general, our contributions can be summarized as the following:

1. We propose a new label-only membership inference attack, the first black-box membership inference attack against machine unlearning in the setting where the model only outputs predicted labels.
2. We conduct experiments on a range of settings and datasets. The evaluation shows that our attack performs well, especially the attack AUC on the MNIST dataset reaches 0.96.

2   Related Work

2.1   Membership Inference Attack

Member inference attack [14,19,20] is a privacy attack against machine learning models, which leaves the user's information unprotected and causes damage to the user. Membership inference attack is a privacy attack against machine learning models, which exposes users' data. Formally, given a data sample x and a trained model $\mathcal{M}$, the adversary $\mathcal{A}$ can calculate the membership state according to the additional knowledge Ω:

$$\mathcal{A}(\mathcal{M}, x, \Omega) \rightarrow \{0, 1\} \tag{1}$$

where 1 means that x belongs to the training set of $\mathcal{M}$, otherwise not.

2.2   Machine Unlearning

The concept of Machine Unlearning was first proposed by Cao *et al.* [21]. If users want to protect their private data, the institutions or organizations that have used this data before must forget this data to regain security. The process of letting machine learning systems forget is called machin unlearning. The easiest way to implement machine unlearning is to remove the target sample x from the model training set and retrain the model, which is called Scratch. Specifically, we denote the original model trained on dataset D_o as M_o, and the data to be deleted as x, then the unlearned model is retrained on dataset $D_u = D_o/x$. Retraining from scratch is relatively easy to implement. However, the size of the original dataset is too large, which can result in computational overhead of retraining too large. In order to solve the problem that the unlearned dataset D_u is too large and the overhead is too large, Bourtoule *et al.* [14] proposed a new method, namely SISA. The main idea of SISA is to divide the target training set D_o into several parts, train sub-models on each sub-training set, and then use the idea of ensemble learning to aggregate the sub-models into the final target model. When doing machine unlearning, only retrain the sub-dataset that x is on. Since it can be divided into several sub-datasets, the cost of retraining is greatly reduced.

2.3 Label-Only Defense

Unlike defense methods such as differential privacy and reducing overfitting, we move in a different direction, i.e., continue to reduce the additional knowledge available to the adversary. Most of the membership reasoning relies on the posterior probability returned by the target model, so one of the defense methods is to make this posterior probability unavailable to the adversary. In this case, the model only returns the class label to which the query sample x belongs. Formally, the labels output by the model are $c = \arg\max_c(y = c|x)$.

3 Methodology

In this section, we introduce our proposed membership inference attack.

3.1 Threat Model

We consider an adversary, given a target sample x, an original model M_o and its unlearned model M_u, the adversary's purpose is to infer whether x is unlearned from M_o. In layman's terms, the adversary's goal is to infer whether the target sample x is in D_o but not in D_u.

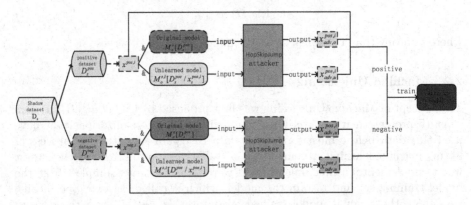

Fig. 1. Attack Model Training. Positive dataset D_s^{pos} is used to train shadow model M_o^s, and $M_u^{s,i}$ is trained on $\{D_s^{pos}/x^{pos,i}\}$. $x^{pos,i}$ and $x^{neg,i}$ belong to R^{pos} and R^{neg} respectively. The adversary adds perturbations to $x^{pos,i}$ to change the prediction of M_o^s to obtain $x_{adv,o}^{pos,i}$ and the prediction of $M_u^{s,i}$ to obtain $x_{adv,u}^{pos,i}$. Then the adversary adds perturbations to $x^{neg,i}$ to change the prediction of M_o^s to obtain $x_{adv,o}^{neg,i}$ and the prediction of $M_u^{s,i}$ to obtain $x_{adv,u}^{neg,i}$. The adversary can calculate the positive example $d_o^{pos,i}$, $d_u^{pos,i}$, $d_{o,n}^{pos,i}$ and the negative example $d_o^{neg,i}$, $d_u^{neg,i}$, $d_{o,n}^{neg,i}$ of the attack model.

Assumptions. We assume that the adversary does not know the internal structure of the model, but has black-box access to the target original model and the unlearned model, while assuming that the model only outputs predicted labels, which is more realistic than outputting posterior probabilities. To evaluate the accuracy of our attack, we will consider an adversary that tries to distinguish whether a data sample x is deleted by the original model. The adversary has a set of data points that they suspect are dropped when training a unlearned model and a local shadow dataset that can be used to train the shadow model. Although the adversary does not know the specific structure of the target model, he can use the same MLaaS service as the target model to train the shadow model.

Attack Intuition. There have been many studies [5–7,22] showing that membership leakage is directly or indirectly related to model overfitting, and our intuition also follows a general rule for the nature of overfitting. In other words, an ML model is more confident in its performance on the training set data, which can be directly reflected in the fact that the true class of the training set data has a higher posterior probability, while the other classes have a lower probability. Li *et al.* proved that members are farther from the decision boundary than non-members [10], that is, given an ML model and a set of data samples, adding random perturbations to them to change the predicted labels of the model, then the perturbations of the samples in the training set The magnitude is larger than the perturbation magnitude of the non-training set samples. We assume that these perturbations provide the approximate distance of the data points to the decision boundary. Our intuition is that if samples are removed from the original model training set, then x is a training set sample of the original model and not a training set member of the unlearned model. Similarly, the adversary adds random perturbations to the target samples x to change the predicted labels in the original model and the unlearned model, respectively, denote the new samples after adding perturbations as x_{adv}^o and x_{adv}^u, respectively, and then the adversary trains a generic binary classification with x, x_{adv}^o and x_{adv}^u which is used to judge whether it is a deleted target sample.

3.2   Attack Model Training

Since we cannot get the ground truth labels about members and non-members, the adversary needs to train a series of shadow models that mimic the behavior of M_o and M_u to obtain this information. We assume that the adversary has a local shadow dataset with the same distribution as D_o, called D_s. To train the attack model, the adversary will be split into two disjoint datasets, denoted as positive shadow dataset D_s^{pos} and negative shadow dataset D_s^{neg} respectively. D_s^{pos} is used to train the shadow original model M_o^s, a series of data points are randomly selected in D_s^{pos} to constitute $R^{pos} = \{x^{pos,1}, x^{pos,2}, \ldots, x^{pos,k}\}$, and the i-th unlearned shadow model $M_u^{s,i}$ is trained on $D_s^{pos}/x^{pos,i}$. Similarly, a series of data points in D_s^{neg} are randomly selected to constitute $R^{neg} = \{x^{neg,1}, x^{neg,2}, \ldots, x^{neg,k}\}$. The attacker adds perturbation to the sample $x^{pos,i}$, obtains the sample $x_{adv,o}^{pos,i}$ to make M_o^s change the decision result, and obtains $x_{adv,u}^{pos,i}$ to make $M_u^{s,i}$ change the decision label.

Also for the sample point $x^{neg,i}$, the adversary obtains $x_{adv,o}^{neg,i}$ and $x_{adv,u}^{neg,i}$. Finally, the adversary takes $x^{pos,i}, x_{adv,o}^{pos,i}$ and $x_{adv,u}^{pos,i}$ as the positive example of the training set of the attack model and $x^{neg,i}, x_{adv,o}^{neg,i}$ and $x_{adv,u}^{neg,i}$ as the negative example of the training set of the attack model. We show our attack model training process in Fig. 1.

4   Evaluation

In this section, we present an experimental evaluation of the attacks described above.

4.1   Experimental Setup

Test Bench. Experiments are performed using PyTorch on a workstation running Ubuntu Server 18.04 LTS, equipped with a 2.50 GHz CPU 8255C, 45G RAM, and NVIDIA RTX 3080 GPU card.

Datasets. We consider four benchmark datasets of different size and complexity, namely MNIST [2], CIFAR-10 [3], CIFAR-100 [3], STL10 [4], to conduct our experiments. Since the image sizes in STL10 are different from other datasets, we resize them to 32×32 pixels.

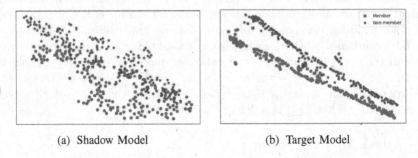

(a) Shadow Model   (b) Target Model

Fig. 2. The visualization of member and non-member boundaries for shadow model (a) and target model (b). We mapped 200 member samples and 200 nonmember samples which were randomly sampled into the transformed space and embed the three distances into the 2D space using t-distributed stochastic neighbor embedding.

Model Architecture. For the MNIST dataset, we use LeNet [13] proposed by LeCun et al. Then, for other datasets, we use widely used convolutional neural networks. In our work, we use 4 convolutional layers and 4 pooling layers to build the target model, and finally use 2 hidden layers. We train for 100 epochs and we optimize using SGD at each epoch with a learning rate equal to 0.5.

Metrics. To better evaluate our attack performance, we choose AUC (area under the ROC curve) as our evaluation metric. AUC is insensitive to whether the sampling of positive and negative samples is uniform, and is also independent of the threshold, giving a better overview of the attacker's performance. The AUC value of 0.5 is a random guess, and the closer the AUC value is to 1, the better the attack performance. AUC is widely used to evaluate the performance of various binary classification models [8,9,11].

4.2 Result

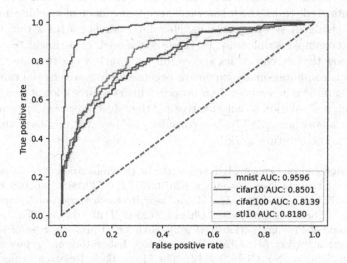

Fig. 3. ROC curves for the four datasets. The x-axis is the false positive rate FPR, and the y-axis is the true positive rate TPR.

Distribution of Distance. First, we investigate the distribution of three distances from a visual perspective. Therefore, we map the target data samples into the transformed space and embed the three distances into the 2D space using t-Distributed Stochastic Neighbor Embedding (t-SNE) [16]. We randomly sampled 400 samples (MNIST) in the target model and the shadow model, including 200 members and 200 non-members, respectively. The results are shown in Fig. 2. We can observe that the data distribution of the shadow model is similar to the target model due to the transferability between the target model and the shadow model. This shows that the shadow model can simulate the target model well, which is one of the factors for the success of our attack.

Attack AUC Performance. Figure 3 shows the performance of our attack on complex neural networks and standard image datasets. Our shadow model has the same structure as the target model, where LeNet network is used for

MNIST and our CNN network is used for CIFAR10, CIFAR100 and STL10. Our attack performance is excellent, the best case can achieve an AUC of 0.95 on the MNIST dataset, and even the worst case has an AUC of 0.81 on the CIFAR100 dataset. The reason why MNIST outperforms other datasets is the highest degree of overfitting, which is consistent with the results of previous studies [15,18].

5 Conclusion

In this paper, we study the impact of Label-only Defense on privacy leakage in machine unlearning scenarios. Our research shows that even if the model only outputs predictions, the privacy leakage phenomenon of machine unlearning cannot be changed. We propose a membership inference a ttack that can infer whether an example is unlearned by the target model. Experiments on four real datasets show that we can attack successfully in a variety of situations. However, our attack is computationally expensive because finding adversarial examples of the target sample is an enumeration process which requires a lot of computation. In addition, our solution is not effective for the latest proposed more advanced unlearning algorithms [12,17]. We consider the recently proposed unlearning algorithm into our future work.

Acknowledgements. This study is supported by the Foundation of National Natural Science Foundation of China (Grant No.: 62072273, 72111530206, 619-62009, 61873117, 61832012, 61771231, 61771289); The Major Basic Research Project of Natural Science Foundation of Shandong Province of China (ZR20-19ZD10); Natural Science Foundation of Shandong Province (ZR2019MF062); Shandong University Science and Technology Program Project (J18A326); Guan-gxi Key Laboratory of Cryptography and Information Security (No: GCIS20-2112); The Major Basic Research Project of Natural Science Foundation of Shandong Province of China (ZR2018ZC0438); Major Scientific and Technological Special Project of Guizhou Province (20183001), Foundation of Guizhou Provincial Key Laboratory of Public Big Data (No. 2019BD-KFJJ009), Talent project of Guizhou Big Data Academy. Guizhou Provincial Key Laboratory of Public Big Data. ([2018]01).

References

1. https://gdpr-info.eu/
2. http://yann.lecun.com/exdb/mnist/
3. https://www.cs.toronto.edu/~kriz/cifar.html/
4. https://cs.stanford.edu/~acoates/stl10/
5. Bourtoule, L., et al.: Machine unlearning. In: 2021 IEEE Symposium on Security and Privacy (SP), pp. 141–159. IEEE (2021)
6. Cao, Y., Yang, J.: Towards making systems forget with machine unlearning. In: 2015 IEEE Symposium on Security and Privacy, pp. 463–480. IEEE (2015)
7. Chen, M., Zhang, Z., Wang, T., Backes, M., Humbert, M., Zhang, Y.: When machine unlearning jeopardizes privacy. In: Proceedings of the 2021 ACM SIGSAC Conference on Computer and Communications Security, pp. 896–911 (2021)

8. Fredrikson, M., Lantz, E., Jha, S., Lin, S., Page, D., Ristenpart, T.: Privacy in pharmacogenetics: an {End-to-End} case study of personalized warfarin dosing. In: 23rd USENIX Security Symposium (USENIX Security 14), pp. 17–32 (2014)

9. Hagestedt, I., et al.: MBeacon: privacy-preserving beacons for DNA methylation data (2019)

10. He, Y., Rahimian, S., Schiele, B., Fritz, M.: Segmentations-leak: membership inference attacks and defenses in semantic image segmentation. In: Vedaldi, A., Bischof, H., Brox, T., Frahm, J.-M. (eds.) ECCV 2020. LNCS, vol. 12368, pp. 519–535. Springer, Cham (2020). https://doi.org/10.1007/978-3-030-58592-1_31

11. Jia, J., Salem, A., Backes, M., Zhang, Y., Gong, N.Z.: Memguard: defending against black-box membership inference attacks via adversarial examples. In: Proceedings of the 2019 ACM SIGSAC Conference on Computer and Communications Security, pp. 259–274 (2019)

12. Kim, J., Woo, S.S.: Efficient two-stage model retraining for machine unlearning. In: Proceedings of the IEEE/CVF Conference on Computer Vision and Pattern Recognition, pp. 4361–4369 (2022)

13. LeCun, Y., Bottou, L., Bengio, Y., Haffner, P.: Gradient-based learning applied to document recognition. Proc. IEEE **86**(11), 2278–2324 (1998)

14. Li, Z., Zhang, Y.: Membership leakage in label-only exposures. In: Proceedings of the 2021 ACM SIGSAC Conference on Computer and Communications Security, pp. 880–895 (2021)

15. Long, Y., et al.: Understanding membership inferences on well-generalized learning models. arXiv preprint arXiv:1802.04889 (2018)

16. Van der Maaten, L., Hinton, G.: Visualizing data using t-SNE. J. Mach. Learn. Res. **9**(11) (2008)

17. Mehta, R., Pal, S., Singh, V., Ravi, S.N.: Deep unlearning via randomized conditionally independent hessians. In: Proceedings of the IEEE/CVF Conference on Computer Vision and Pattern Recognition, pp. 10422–10431 (2022)

18. Nasr, M., Shokri, R., Houmansadr, A.: Comprehensive privacy analysis of deep learning: passive and active white-box inference attacks against centralized and federated learning. In: 2019 IEEE Symposium on Security and Privacy (SP), pp. 739–753. IEEE (2019)

19. Salem, A., Zhang, Y., Humbert, M., Berrang, P., Fritz, M., Backes, M.: ML-leaks: model and data independent membership inference attacks and defenses on machine learning models. arXiv preprint arXiv:1806.01246 (2018)

20. Shokri, R., Stronati, M., Song, C., Shmatikov, V.: Membership inference attacks against machine learning models. In: 2017 IEEE Symposium on Security and Privacy (SP), pp. 3–18. IEEE (2017)

21. Song, C., Ristenpart, T., Shmatikov, V.: Machine learning models that remember too much. In: Proceedings of the 2017 ACM SIGSAC Conference on Computer and Communications Security, pp. 587–601 (2017)

22. Yeom, S., Giacomelli, I., Fredrikson, M., Jha, S.: Privacy risk in machine learning: analyzing the connection to overfitting. In: 2018 IEEE 31st Computer Security Foundations Symposium (CSF), pp. 268–282. IEEE (2018)

Practical Federated Learning for Samples with Different IDs

Yu Li⬤, Junzuo Lai$^{(\boxtimes)}$⬤, Xiaowei Yuan⬤, and Beibei Song⬤

College of Information Science and Technology, Jinan University, Guangzhou, China
`laijunzuo@gmail.com`

Abstract. Federated learning is widely used in various fields, it usually consists of sample alignment phase and training phase, where sample alignment is the first phase. For example, in horizontal federated learning, if the databases of parties contain some identical samples, then parties could use sample alignment to remove these duplicate samples before training, and in vertical federated learning, parties are required to use sample alignment to put the samples of the same user on the same row of both databases before training. Meanwhile, the current sample alignment schemes in federated learning are almost ID-based, and they assume the two participants have the same ID. Consider that these schemes cannot deal with the sample alignment problem for samples with different IDs, we present a sample alignment scheme that allows two participants with different IDs to align their samples. Our sample alignment scheme is based on Oblivious Programmable PRF (OPPRF), which doesn't have much public key operation. After aligning the samples utilizing our scheme, the two participants could accomplish a variety of secure two-party machine learning tasks. In this paper, we design the privacy-preserving logistic regression training scheme using additive homomorphic encryption, thus achieving the whole federated logistic regression process.

We implement our sample alignment scheme to verify the efficiency, and the experiments show that our sample alignment scheme only requires 216 s when the set sizes of sender and receiver are 2^{24} and 2^{20}. Besides, we conduct experiments to verify the feasibility of our logistic regression training scheme.

Keywords: Privacy-preserving · Sample alignment · Logistic regression · Federated learning

1 Introduction

With the development of big data, people pay more attention to the privacy and security of data, which brings new challenges to traditional data processing in machine learning. In the field of machine learning, training a model requires a large amount of data. However, different types of data are distributed in different institutions, and the amount of data also depends on the size of the institutions.

C. Ge and F. Guo (Eds.): ProvSec 2022, LNCS 13600, pp. 176–195, 2022.
https://doi.org/10.1007/978-3-031-20917-8_13

The data owned by these institutions may be independent or overlapped. Traditional machine learning contains many algorithms, such as logistic regression [1], statistical analysis [2], gradient descent [3], linear regression [4], data mining [5], etc. It usually uses a centralized method to train models, which requires the training to be concentrated on the same server. With the improvement of laws and regulations related to personal information and data security, such as the General Data Protection Regulations (GDPR) [6] implemented by the European Union and the Cyber Security Law of the People's Republic of China, users' private data has been better protected. Accordingly, it's becoming more difficult to collect data from different institutions to train models. Data exists in the form of data islands, and it is impossible to exchange data between different institutions, which greatly reduces the circulation and availability of data. Consequently, federated learning (FL) [7–9] comes into being.

Federated learning can effectively protect the local private data and break down the data barriers between different institutions. Federated learning has been deployed in an increasing number of applications such as mobile platforms, healthcare, and industrial engineering [10,11]. It can help those institutions to train a model collaboratively without revealing their own data. As a distributed machine learning framework, Federated learning is similar to the combination of secure multi-party computation (MPC) [12,13] and distributed machine learning [14,15]. In the process of federated learning, different data owners have complete autonomy over their local data. Data can only be used locally, and the data owners will not exchange information in plaintext form. All data owners train and update the model to complete the learning purpose jointly, and the parameters of the obtained model are distributed among all the participants.

According to the distribution of data, federated learning can be divided into horizontal federated learning, vertical federated learning and federated transfer learning. Horizontal federated learning is suitable for situations, where the user features of participants' datasets overlap a lot and the user samples overlap little. For example, in the datasets of two medical examination centers, both datasets contain the features such as height, weight, blood pressure, and heart rate, but user samples rarely overlap, horizontal federated learning increases the number of user samples. Vertical federated learning is suitable for datasets with little overlap in user features but a lot of overlap in user samples, such as bank and e-commerce, which provide customers with different services so that they have different aspects of features, but the customers they serve have a large overlap, vertical federated learning increases the feature dimension of the training data. Federated transfer learning is applied to the datasets that both the user samples and user features rarely overlap, such as the datasets of banks and supermarkets in different regions. Our work mainly considers the scenario of vertical federated learning, which requires sample alignment. Horizontal federated learning rarely needs sample alignment since the samples usually overlap little.

Motivation. In vertical federated learning, it requires sample alignment before training, while there are many sample alignment solutions, they still cannot meet the requirement of the real-life scenario, consider the setting where two participants have different IDs, and want to cooperatively train a model. For example, these online social platforms, such as Facebook and Weibo, usually push information that users may be interested in based on the information they have clicked on, some of them require an e-mail or a phone number to create a new account, but some platforms require a phone number to receive message verification code, hence users must use phone numbers to register on them. Now, if Facebook and Weibo need to train a model for pushing information to users, but people register on Facebook using e-mail, and use the phone number to register on Weibo. Then before training, they need to align their samples. But the current sample alignment schemes cannot solve the sample alignment problem for such setting.

Our Contributions. Under the framework of vertical federated learning, aimed at the above setting, we provide a sample alignment solution, the main idea is to let a third party, who has a huge amount of data, to help two participants to align their samples. Later, we construct the privacy-preserving logistic regression training scheme using additive homomorphic encryption, hence achieving the whole federated logistic regression process. To sum up, our contributions are as follows.

1. We first consider the setting, where two parties don't have the same ID in federated learning, and design a sample alignment scheme for such setting based on Oblivious Programmable PRF (OPPRF).
2. We construct the secure logistic regression training scheme using additive homomorphic encryption, thus accomplishing the whole federated logistic regression process.
3. We implement the sample alignment scheme, and the experiments show that our sample alignment scheme is efficient. We also conduct experiments of our logistic regression scheme over vertically distributed datasets.

Organizations We discuss related works in Sect. 2, and discuss the preliminaries in Sect. 3, Sect. 4 shows the problem statement, we describe our scheme in Sect. 5, Sect. 6 gives the security analysis and Sect. 7 shows the experiment evaluation. Finally, we conclude the paper in Sect. 8.

2 Related Works

Federated learning can be regarded as privacy-preserving distributed machine learning. Much research has been devoted to this area, there are various privacy-preserving methods in federated learning, such as homomorphic encryption [16], secret sharing [17], Yao's garbled circuits [18], differential privacy [19] and private set intersection [20]. Among them, private set intersection is mostly used to protect the sample information in the sample alignment phase, and the rest methods are almost used to protect the private information in the training phase.

Secret sharing distributes a secret among a group of participants, none of them knows the secret, and each participant cannot recover the secret alone, but they can work together to recover the secret. Homomorphic encryption allows the user to add or multiply two ciphertexts without decryption, then the decrypted value is the same as adding or multiplying the corresponding plaintext. Homomorphic encryption is divided into partial homomorphic encryption and fully homomorphic encryption (FHE). Partial homomorphic encryption only supports additive homomorphism or multiplicative homomorphism, such as ElGamal cryptosystem [21], Goldwasser-Micai cryptosystem [22], Paillier cryptosystem [23], etc. Fully Homomorphic encryption can support both additive and multiplicative homomorphism, such as the BGV scheme [24], the BFV scheme [25,26], etc. Yao's garbled circuits were first proposed to solve the millionaire problem, then it was used to construct the general secure two-party protocol. Differential privacy can be used to prevent differential attack, which makes it impossible to distinguish whether a special sample is in the database by adding some noise to the result, moreover, the noise has little effect on the statistical result. Our work is based on additive homomorphic encryption scheme.

Cheng et al. [27] implemented a lossless federated learning framework over vertically partitioned data called SecureBoost, which uses additive homomorphic encryption to protect the private information in the training process, and their results show their framework is as accurate as other non-privacy-preserving approaches. Hardy et al. [28] also proposed a privacy-preserving federated learning on vertically partitioned data, they first used entity resolution to find the common users, then adopted additive homomorphic encryption to achieve the secure training phase with the help of the third party, they implemented the federated logistic regression, and the results show that their federated logistic regression can scale to millions of rows in the order of hours. Nikolaenko et al. [29] presented a privacy-preserving ridge regression system based on homomorphic encryption and Yao's garbled circuit, they pointed out that the combination of homomorphic encryption and Yao's garbled circuit has better performance than either method alone, concretely, they used homomorphic encryption to handle the linear part of the computation and Yao garbled circuits for the non-linear part. Sanil et al. [30] designed a secure linear regression in vertical federated learning setting, they used secret sharing to protect the data, and the regression coefficients are shared among the data owners. Geyer et al. [31] considered the setting, where a trusted party helps multiple clients to train the model, they pointed out that the client is vulnerable to differential attacks when it makes contributions during the training, then they used differential privacy to solve this problem, and finally hid the client's whole datasets and achieved the trade-off between privacy and accuracy.

In the sample alignment phase, the current alignment schemes require the samples in the datasets with the same ID. Most works use private set intersection to achieve the sample alignment. PSI can help the participants to get the intersection of their sets, and not reveal their elements beyond the intersection. The federated learning framework Fate [32] uses the PSI protocol based on RSA encryption and hash to align the samples, Liu et al. [33] applied asymmetrical PSI protocol based on Pohlig-hellman to achieve the sample alignment in the asymmetrical vertical federated learning setting. Besides, there are various PSI protocols can be used to align the samples, such as the PSI protocol based on Oblivious Transfer (OT), Diffie-Hellman (DH), Circuit and FHE. The OT-based PSI [34–37] is the fastest one when the set size is large, but it has more communication overhead. On the contrary, the DH-based PSI [38–40] is suitable for small sets, it has the lower communication overhead, but more computation overhead. The Circuit-based PSI [41,42] occupies a larger memory as the set size increases, but it can be easily merged into the following secure computation protocols and compute arbitrary functions of the intersection. Huang et al. [41] proved that the performance of PSI protocol based on garbled circuits is competitive with the best-known custom PSI protocols. Chen et al. [43] proposed an FHE-based PSI, which can be used to get the intersection of two unequal sets and achieve a low communication overhead, they tested the running time when the item length is 32 bits, as the item length increases, the encryption would have a large negative impact on performance.

These related works [27,28,30,33] in the vertical federated learning setting either did not take into account the sample alignment or didn't consider that the sample alignment problem when the IDs of the same user in different databases may be different. Moreover, the current PSI protocols cannot directly be applied to solve the above sample alignment problem. Thus, we use OPPRF [44] to construct the sample alignment scheme, which can help two databases with different IDs to align the samples. We also construct the training scheme using additive homomorphic encryption, hence accomplishing the whole federated learning process.

3   Preliminaries

3.1   Oblivious, Programmable PRF

Oblivious, Programmable PRF (OPPRF) was first introduced to construct multi-party PSI protocol by Kolesnikov et al. [44] in 2017, it is a combination of Oblivious PRF (OPRF) and Programmable PRF (PPRF), thus we first review OPRF and PPRF.

Oblivious PRF. OPRF is a two-party secure computation protocol, in which sender and receiver jointly compute the pseudo-random function F, where sender inputs k, receiver inputs $\{q_1, \cdots, q_m\}$ and obtains $\{F(k, q_1), \cdots, F(k, q_m)\}$. In the end, sender knows nothing about the inputs of receiver and receiver knows nothing about k.

Programmable PRF. Different from PRF, PPRF means that the output of PRF is programmed according to a point set, it consists of the following algorithms:

1. KeyGen $(1^\kappa, \mathcal{P}) \rightarrow (k, \text{hint})$: Inputs a security parameter κ and a point set $\mathcal{P} = \{(x_i, y_i), i \in n\}$, where all the values x_i are distinct and $x_i, y_i \in \{0,1\}^\kappa$. Outputs a PRF key k and public, auxiliary information hint.
2. $F(k, \text{hint}, x) \rightarrow y$: Computes the PRF on input x, gives output $y \in \{0,1\}^\kappa$.

Definition 1 *(Correctness). A programmable PRF satisfies correctness if for all $(x,y) \in \mathcal{P}$,*

$$\Pr\left[KeyGen(1^\kappa, \mathcal{P}) \rightarrow (k, hint) : F(k, hint, x) = y \right] = 1$$

As for security, given the following experiments:

$\text{Exp}^{\mathcal{A}}(\mathcal{P}, \mathcal{Q}, \kappa)$:
1. for each $x_i \in X$, choose random $y_i \leftarrow \{0,1\}^\kappa$
2. $(k, \text{hint}) \leftarrow \text{Key Gen}(1^\kappa, \{(x_i, y_i) \mid x_i \in X\})$
3. return $\mathcal{A}(\text{hint}, \{F(k, \text{hint}, q) \mid q \in \mathcal{Q}\})$

Definition 2 *(Security). A Programmable PRF is (n, m)-secure if, for distinct point sets $\mathcal{P}_1$, $\mathcal{P}_2$, and query set $\mathcal{Q}$, $|\mathcal{P}_1| = |\mathcal{P}_2| = n$, $|\mathcal{Q}| = m$, and all polynomial-time adversaries $\mathcal{A}$, such that,*

$$\left| \Pr\left[\text{Exp}^{\mathcal{A}}(\mathcal{P}_1, \mathcal{Q}, \kappa)\right] - \Pr\left[\text{Exp}^{\mathcal{A}}(\mathcal{P}_2, \mathcal{Q}, \kappa)\right] \right| \leq \text{negl}(\kappa)$$

In other words, if the values y_i are uniformly random, then for any two sets $\mathcal{P}_1$, $\mathcal{P}_2$, it is difficult to tell which point set is programmed, that is, when given the hint and m outputs of the PRF, the output of programming $\mathcal{P}_1$ is computationally indistinguishable from the output of programming $\mathcal{P}_2$.

Oblivious Programmable PRF. Different from OPRF, OPPRF allows the sender to program the output of the PRF, and it also gives the "hint" to the receiver. Namely, sender inputs $\mathcal{P} = \{(x_1, y_1), \cdots, (x_n, y_n)\}$ and receiver inputs $\{q_1, \cdots, q_m\}$, finally, receiver obtains hint and $\{F(k, hint, q_1), \cdots, F(k, hint, q_m)\}$.

Kolesnikov et al. uses three different ways to instantiate the OPPRF protocol in [44], such as Polynomial, Bloom Filters and Table, their experiments show that the table-based construction is the fastest one, therefore, in this paper, we use the table-based OPPRF.

In table-based OPPRF, the input of sender is a point set $\mathcal{P} = \{(x_i, y_i), i \in n\}$, the input of receiver is a query q, then the table-based OPPRF consists of the following five steps:

Step 1: Sender and receiver invoke an Oblivious PRF, in which sender inputs k, receiver inputs q and receives $F(k, q)$.
Step 2: For $x_i, i \in n$, sender computes $\{F(k, x_1), F(k, x_2), .., F(k, x_n)\}$. Then sender samples a nonce v, until all $\{H(F(k, x_i)||v)\}$ are different.
Step 3: For $i \in [n]$, sender first computes $h_i = H(F(k, x_i)||v)$, next sets $T_{h_i} = F(k, x_i) \oplus y_i$.

Step 4: Sender fills random values into locations except for $\{h_i, i \in [n]\}$, then sends the table T and hint v to receiver.

Step 5: Receiver computes $h = H(F(k, x) \| v)$, and outputs $T_h \oplus F(k, q)$.

It is shown in [44] that the table-based OPPRF satisfies the correctness and security. For correctness, it's clear that for $x_i \in \mathcal{P}$, $T_h \oplus F(k, x_i) = F(k, x_i) \oplus y_i \oplus F(k, x_i)$. For security, it can be observed that the table T itself is uniformly distributed when the y_i values are uniformly distributed.

3.2   Simple Hashing

Simple hashing consists of a two-dimension hash table $T_{b \times m}$ and k hash functions $h_1, h_2, ..., h_k$. Each location $T_i, i \in [b]$ can be seen as a bin, then the table includes b bins $B_1, B_2, .., B_b$, each bin can hold more than one element, namely m. To insert an item x, it computes $h_1(x), h_2(x), ..., h_k(x)$ using k hash functions, then maps it into k bins $B_{h_1}(x), B_{h_2}(x), ..., B_{h_k}(x)$. When given b bins, k hash function and n items, the bin size can be computed using ball-to-bin analysis. Pinkas et al. [34] point out that the probability of "n balls are mapped at random to b bins, and the most occupied bin has at least l balls" is as Eq. 1.

$$Pr(\exists bin \quad with \geq l \quad balls) \leq b(\frac{en}{bl})^l \tag{1}$$

3.3   Cuckoo Hashing

Cuckoo hashing was first proposed by Pagh et al. [45], which was used to resolve the hash collision. Later, Kirsch et al. [46] proposed a variant of Cuckoo hashing with a stash. In their Cuckoo hashing scheme, it involves k hash functions $h_1, h_2, .., h_k$, a stash S and b bins $B_1, B_2, .., B_b$. For n items $x_1, x_2, ..., x_n$, each item x_i is stored in one of the bins $\{B_{h_1(x_i)}, B_{h_2(x_i)}, .., B_{h_k(x_i)}\}$ or the stash. Each bin stores no more than one element, and the stash can hold many elements. To insert an item x, it first checks whether all the bins $\{B_{h_i(x)}, i \in [k]\}$ are occupied, if not, then x will be placed in one of these empty bins $B_{h_i(x)}$, otherwise select a random $\{B_{h_i(x)}, i \in [k]\}$ and remove the current old item to place this new item, then the old item is recursively inserted in the same way. After a fixed number of iterations, if there is still no bins to place the old item, then it is placed into stash S.

3.4   Paillier Encryption

In this paper, we adopt the Paillier encryption, which is a well-known partial homomorphic encryption scheme, it usually consists of key generation algorithm **keyGen**, encryption algorithm **Enc** and decryption algorithm **Dec**. We detail the three algorithms as follows.

1. **keyGen**$(\lambda) \rightarrow (pk, sk)$
2. **Enc**$(m, pk) \rightarrow (c)$
3. **Dec**$(c, sk) \rightarrow (m)$

Paillier encryption has the additive homomorphism property, let $[\![u]\!]$ denote the ciphertext of plaintext u, $\oplus$ denote homomorphic addition, $\odot$ denote multiplying a ciphertext by a plaintext, then for any plaintexts u and v, it supports the following two operations:

$$[\![u]\!] \oplus [\![v]\!] = [\![u + v]\!], u \odot [\![v]\!] = [\![u \cdot v]\!]$$

3.5 Gradient Descent

Gradient descent is widely applied to optimize neural networks, it aims to minimize the loss function by updating the parameters. In this paper, we use the gradient descent algorithm to train a logistic regression model and adopt Taylor series expansion to obtain the approximations of the logistic loss function. For example, using second-order Taylor series expansion, the approximation to the logistic loss function is written as

$$\mathcal{L}(\boldsymbol{\theta}) = \frac{1}{n} \sum_{i=1}^{n} log2 - \frac{1}{2} y_i \boldsymbol{\theta}^T \mathbf{x}_i + \frac{1}{8} (\boldsymbol{\theta}^T \mathbf{x}_i)^2$$

and the gradient is written as:

$$\frac{\partial \mathcal{L}(\boldsymbol{\theta})}{\partial \boldsymbol{\theta}} = \frac{1}{n} \sum_{i=1}^{n} (\frac{1}{4} \boldsymbol{\theta}^T \mathbf{x}_i - \frac{1}{2} y_i) \mathbf{x}_i$$

then the parameters can be updated using $\boldsymbol{\theta} \leftarrow \boldsymbol{\theta} - \eta \frac{\partial \mathcal{L}(\boldsymbol{\theta})}{\partial \boldsymbol{\theta}}$, η is the learning rate.

4   Problem Statement

4.1 Setting

People have different identifiers on different occasions. For example, students have student numbers, employees have employee numbers. For another example, some apps require an e-mail to register, some require a phone number, and some require the ID card number. Moreover, people may have multiple e-mail accounts and use different email accounts to sign in different apps. If these apps want to cooperatively train a model, the first step is to align their samples, but these current sample alignment schemes are not suitable for this setting. Figure 1 shows the setting where the databases of party A and B hold the samples with different IDs, and C holds both IDs.

Party A holds the ID **Tel** and party B holds the ID **E-mail**, they have partial features respectively, and party A has the label. Party A and B want to securely train a logistic regression model, then they need to align their samples, while the database of party C has both ID **Tel** and ID **E-mail**, party A and B need party C as the coordinator to help them align the samples. After the sample alignment, party A and B could train the model together.

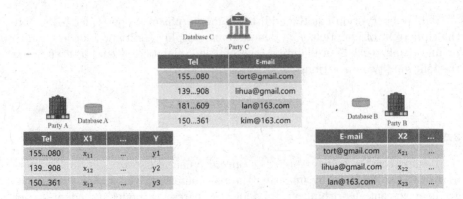

Fig. 1. Samples with different IDs.

4.2 Threat Model

In the above setting, we consider that A, B and C are honest-but-curious. They follow the protocol execution, but try to get as much information as possible. Specially, in the sample alignment phase, C honestly helps A and B to align their samples, meanwhile, C is inquisitive about the sample information of A and B, A and B is also curious about the sample information of C. A and B want to know the sample information about each other during their interaction. In the training phase, A and B wonder to know the information of training datasets about each other. C honestly helps A and B decrypt the messages, but attempts to learn more information about these messages.

4.3 Design Goal

According to the above analysis of the threat model, we aim to protect the private information in the sample alignment and the training phase, thus achieving the secure federated learning, our design goals are as follows.

Protect the Privacy of Sample. Parties need to exchange the sample information to align the samples, the disclosure of samples may cause a great loss to the parties, thus the parties cannot exchange the sample information in plaintext form, we need to hide the sample information while aligning the samples.

Protect the Privacy of Training Dataset. Due to the definition of federated learning, parties can't directly exchange raw data, which may reveal sensitive information. Instead, parties exchange the intermediate results to obtain the gradient, thus updating the model, but the adversary may infer the gradient from the intermediate results, there are various gradient based attacks [47–49], the adversary can derive the original training dataset from the gradient, thus the intermediate results cannot be exchanged directly, and the gradient during the training should be protected.

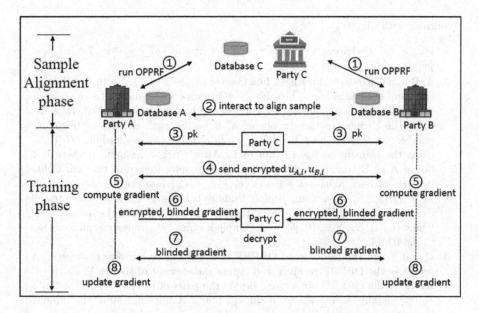

Fig. 2. Architecture of our vertical federated learning for samples with different IDs.

5   The Protocol Description

Our whole protocol consists of sample alignment phase and training phase. Figure 2 depicts the architecture of our vertical federated learning for samples with different IDs. Our protocol is described in the following.

5.1   Sample Alignment Phase

Before training, C will help A and B to align their samples, we describe the protocol in Fig. 3 and 4. The sizes of set E and P are balanced, namely, they are of the same order of magnitude.

Input: A inputs e-mail set $E = \{e_1, e_2, \cdots, e_{m_1}\}$, B inputs telephone number set $P = \{p_1, p_2, \cdots, p_{m_2}\}$, C inputs set $EP = \{(e'_1, p'_1), (e'_2, p'_2), \cdots, (e'_n, p'_n)\}$, and $e_i, p_i, e'_i, p'_i \in \{0, 1\}^\sigma$, σ is public, κ is the computational security parameter, and λ is the statistical security parameter.
Output: A outputs S_a, B outputs S_b.

(continued...)

Fig. 3. The sample alignment protocol.

(continue with Fig. 3)

1. For $j \in [n]$, C chooses a random r_j, then computes $\{y_j = p'_j \oplus r_j, j \in [n]\}$ and $\{x_j = e'_j \oplus r_j, j \in [n]\}$.

2. A, B and C agree on three hash functions $h_1, h_2, h_3 : \{0,1\}^\sigma \to \{0,1\}^{\lambda+\log_2(n)}$, the number of bins b and bin size β. A hashes each element of e-mail set E into b bins $B_a[1], B_a[2]..., B_a[b]$ using Cuckoo hashing in section 3.3, $B_a[i]$ denotes the element in the ith bin of A. B hashes each element of telephone number set P into b bins $B_b[1], B_b[2]..., B_b[b]$ using Cuckoo hashing, $B_b[i]$ denotes the element in the ith bin of B. After Cuckoo hashing, if there is a bin of A or B that is empty, then place a dummy item into the bin. C has two sets of bins, it hashes n items $\{e'_1, e'_2, \cdots, e'_n\}$ into the first set of b bins $B_{c_1}[1], B_{c_1}[2]..., B_{c_1}[b]$ using Simple hashing in section 3.2. $B_{c_1}[i]$ denotes all elements in the ith bin, C hashes n items $\{p'_1, p'_2, \cdots, p'_n\}$ into the second set of b bins $B_{c_2}[1], B_{c_2}[2]..., B_{c_2}[b]$ using Simple hashing. $B_{c_2}[i]$ denotes all elements in the ith bin.

3. C and A run the table-based OPPRF protocol bin-by-bin. For each bin i, A serves as the OPPRF receiver and inputs the element of the ith bin $B_a[i]$, C serves as the OPPRF sender and inputs the pairs of the ith bin $\{(e'_l, y_l)|e'_l \in B_{c_1}[i]\}$, finally A receives y'_i, if the ith bin of A does not store the dummy item, A can compute $B_a[i] \oplus y'_i$.

4. C and B run the table-based OPPRF protocol bin-by-bin. For each bin i, B serves as the OPPRF receiver and inputs the element of the ith bin $B_b[i]$, C serves as the OPPRF sender and inputs the pairs of the ith bin $\{(p'_l, x_l)|p'_l \in B_{c_2}[i]\}$, finally B receives x'_i, if the ith bin of B does not store the dummy item, B can compute $B_b[i] \oplus x'_i$.

5. For B, let $K_B = \{(B_b[j] \oplus x'_j), j \in m_2\}$, then B sends K_B to A.

6. For A, let $K_A = \{(B_a[j] \oplus y'_j), j \in m_1\}$. For each $K_A[j] \in K_A$, A checks whether $K_A[j] \in K_B$, if it is, then put item $B_a[j]$ into the intersection set S_a and put $K_A[j]$ into K'_A. Finally, A sends K'_A to B.

7. For each $K_B[k] \in K_B$, B checks whether $K_B[k] \in K'_A$, if $K_B[k] = K'_A[j]$, then put item $B_b[k]$ into row j of set S_b. Finally, B holds intersection set S_b.

Fig. 4. The sample alignment protocol (continued).

In the sample alignment protocol, we use OPPRF to align the samples of A and B with the help of C. In the end, if the e-mail e_i and telephone number p_i belong to the same person, then e_i and p_i will be the same row of S_a and S_b respectively, which is also the aim of step 7. Besides, we set the bit-length of the hash value to $\lambda + \log_2(n)$, which ensures the probability that a non-intersection item is falsely put into the intersection is $2^{-\lambda}$.

We also give an instantiation of our sample alignment scheme in Fig. 6. It can be divided into three parts: Hashing, OPPRF, and Alignment. Firstly, A, B and C hash the elements into 2 bins, the first bin of A contains e_1, the second contains e_3. Similarly, so do the bins of B and C. Then, A and C, B and C perform OPPRF for each corresponding pair of bins, A and B input the element in that bin, C inputs the relevant key-value pairs in that bin. Finally, A and B exchange the blinded set to align the samples. It can be seen that A and B get one intersection element, namely A holds e_3, and B holds p_3, and they are both in the first row.

5.2 Training Phase

In most real-life applications that focus on timeliness, federated learning with coordinator is more valuable. In this paper, we use a coordinator to help the parties train the model, the coordinator can be the party C in the sample alignment phase or other trusted third party. Besides, we use the Paillier encryption scheme to protect the private information in the training process.

Suppose that A and B have permuted their datasets after running the sample alignment phase, and their datasets have both n samples, the secure logistic regression training process is shown in Fig. 5.

Input: A inputs dataset $\mathbf{X}_A = (\mathbf{x}_{A,1}, \mathbf{x}_{A,2}, \cdots, \mathbf{x}_{A,n})$, and each sample $\mathbf{x}_{A,i}$ has d_A feature values. B inputs dataset $\mathbf{X}_B = ((\mathbf{x}_{B,1}, y_1), (\mathbf{x}_{B,2}, y_2), \cdots, (\mathbf{x}_{B,n}, y_n))$, each $\mathbf{x}_{B,i}$ has d_B feature values, and its corresponding label is y_i, A initializes the d_A-dimensional weight column vector $\boldsymbol{\theta}_A$. B initializes the d_B-dimensional weight column vector $\boldsymbol{\theta}_B$, A and B agree on the learning rate η and the approximation to the logistic loss function $\mathcal{L}(\boldsymbol{\theta}) = \frac{1}{n}\sum_{i=1}^{n} log2 - \frac{1}{2}y_i\boldsymbol{\theta}^T\mathbf{x}_i + \frac{1}{8}(\boldsymbol{\theta}^T\mathbf{x}_i)^2$, where $\mathbf{x}_i = \mathbf{x}_{A,i}|\mathbf{x}_{B,i}$ and $\boldsymbol{\theta}^T = \boldsymbol{\theta}_A^T|\boldsymbol{\theta}_B^T$.
Output: A outputs $\boldsymbol{\theta}_A$, B outputs $\boldsymbol{\theta}_B$.

1. C generates key pair (pk, sk) using **KeyGen** algorithm of Paillier encryption scheme, and sends pk to A and B.
2. For $i = 1, 2, \cdots, n$, A and B do the following:
   (a) A computes $u_{A,i} = \frac{1}{4}\boldsymbol{\theta}_A^T\mathbf{x}_{A,i}$, then uses pk to encrypt it and gets the ciphertext $[\![u_{A,i}]\!]$, finally sends them to B.
   (b) B computes $u_{B,i} = \frac{1}{4}\boldsymbol{\theta}_B^T\mathbf{x}_{B,i} - \frac{1}{2}y_i$, then uses pk to encrypt it and gets the ciphertext $[\![u_{B,i}]\!]$, finally sends them to A.
   (c) A and B compute $[\![u_i]\!] = [\![u_{A,i}]\!] \oplus [\![u_{B,i}]\!]$. A computes $[\![u_i]\!] \odot x_{A,i}$, B computes $[\![u_i]\!] \odot x_{B,i}$.
3. A computes $[\![\frac{\partial\mathcal{L}(\boldsymbol{\theta})}{\partial\boldsymbol{\theta}_A}]\!] = \frac{1}{n} \odot [\oplus_{i=1}^{n}([\![u_i]\!] \odot \mathbf{x}_{A,i})]$, then randomly chooses R_A and computes $[\![W_A]\!] = [\![\frac{\partial\mathcal{L}(\boldsymbol{\theta})}{\partial\boldsymbol{\theta}_A}]\!] \odot R_A$, finally sends it to C.
4. B computes $[\![\frac{\partial\mathcal{L}(\boldsymbol{\theta})}{\partial\boldsymbol{\theta}_B}]\!] = \frac{1}{n} \odot [\oplus_{i=1}^{n}([\![u_i]\!] \odot \mathbf{x}_{B,i})]$, then randomly chooses R_B and computes $[\![W_B]\!] = [\![\frac{\partial\mathcal{L}(\boldsymbol{\theta})}{\partial\boldsymbol{\theta}_B}]\!] \odot R_B$, finally sends them to C.
5. C decrypts them using sk to get W_A and W_B, and sends them to A and B accordingly.
6. A computes $\frac{\partial\mathcal{L}(\boldsymbol{\theta})}{\partial\boldsymbol{\theta}_A} = W_A \cdot \frac{1}{R_A}$ and updates the weight by computing $\boldsymbol{\theta}_A = \boldsymbol{\theta}_A - \eta\frac{\partial\mathcal{L}(\boldsymbol{\theta})}{\partial\boldsymbol{\theta}_A}$.
7. B computes $\frac{\partial\mathcal{L}(\boldsymbol{\theta})}{\partial\boldsymbol{\theta}_B} = W_B \cdot \frac{1}{R_B}$ and updates the weight by computing $\boldsymbol{\theta}_B = \boldsymbol{\theta}_B - \eta\frac{\partial\mathcal{L}(\boldsymbol{\theta})}{\partial\boldsymbol{\theta}_B}$.
   Repeat step 2 to step 7 until $\mathcal{L}(\boldsymbol{\theta})$ doesn't decrease for a while or reaches the max iterations

---

Fig. 5. The training protocol.

6　Security Analysis

We consider the semi-honest security of our scheme and give the security proof below.

Definition 3. $f = (f_A, f_B, f_C)$ *is a polynomial function, and protocol Π computes f. A, B and C compute $f(E, P, EP, \mathbf{X}_A, \mathbf{X}_B)$ using Π. E, P and EP are respectively the ID set of A, B and C, $\mathbf{X}_A$ and $\mathbf{X}_B$ are the permuted datasets after sample alignment. We think protocol Π is secure in the semi-honest model if there exist probabilistic polynomial-time simulators $\mathbf{Sim}_A$, $\mathbf{Sim}_B$, and $\mathbf{Sim}_C$, such that,*

$$\mathbf{Sim}_A(E, \mathbf{X}_A, f(E, P, EP, \mathbf{X}_A, \mathbf{X}_B)) \stackrel{c}{\equiv} \mathbf{view}_A^{\Pi}(E, P, EP, \mathbf{X}_A, \mathbf{X}_B)$$

$$\mathbf{Sim}_B(P, \mathbf{X}_B, f(E, P, EP, \mathbf{X}_A, \mathbf{X}_B)) \stackrel{c}{\equiv} \mathbf{view}_B^{\Pi}(E, P, EP, \mathbf{X}_A, \mathbf{X}_B)$$

$$\mathbf{Sim}_C(EP, f(E, P, EP, \mathbf{X}_A, \mathbf{X}_B)) \stackrel{c}{\equiv} \mathbf{view}_C^{\Pi}(E, P, EP, \mathbf{X}_A, \mathbf{X}_B)$$

where $\mathbf{view}_A^{\Pi}$, $\mathbf{view}_B^{\Pi}$, and $\mathbf{view}_C^{\Pi}$ denote the information, that adversaries can derive from A, B and C. $\stackrel{c}{\equiv}$ denotes computational indistinguishability.

Theorem 1. *The sample alignment protocol in Sect. 5.1 is secure in the semi-honest model.*

Proof. A and B run table-based OPPRF with C and get the OPPRF output respectively, since the x_i and y_i values are uniformly distributed, they cannot distinguish whether the output is a programmed output or a random value, which is guaranteed by OPPRF. B sends K_B to A, those values in K_B are all blinded by different random values, A sends the blinded version of intersection K'_A to B. Those values pass between A and B are all randomly distributed. The view of A is $\mathbf{view}_A^{\Pi} = (E, S_a, y'_i, K_A, K_B)$, we construct a simulator $\mathbf{Sim}_A$ to simulate the corrupted A, and sketch the simulation of $\mathbf{Sim}_A$. $\mathbf{Sim}_A$ obtains $\hat{y'_i}$ and computes $\hat{K}_A$ using each element and the corresponding $\hat{y'_i}$. Then $\mathbf{Sim}_A$ gets $\hat{K}_B$ and computes $\hat{S}_a$ using $\hat{K}_B$ and $\hat{K}_A$, finally, $\mathbf{Sim}_A$ outputs $\mathbf{Sim}_A(E) = (E, \hat{S}_a, \hat{y'_i}, \hat{K}_A, \hat{K}_B)$.

A cannot distinguish y'_i from $\hat{y'_i}$ due to the security of OPPRF. As all the items in K_A, $\hat{K}_A$, K_B, $\hat{K}_B$ are all blinded by random values, thus the distributions of K_B and $\hat{K}_B$, K_A and $\hat{K}_A$ are all indistinguishable. Thus, for A, the distribution of $(E, \hat{S}_a, \hat{y'_i}, \hat{K}_A, \hat{K}_B)$ and (E, S_a, y'_i, K_A, K_B) is indistinguishable, which means the view generated by the simulator is indistinguishable from the view in the real execution, that is, $\mathbf{Sim}_A(E) \stackrel{c}{\equiv} \mathbf{view}_A^{\Pi}$. Similarly, for B, $\mathbf{Sim}_B(P) = (P, \hat{S}_b, \hat{x'_i}, \hat{K}'_A)$, $\mathbf{Sim}_B(P) \stackrel{c}{\equiv} \mathbf{view}_B^{\Pi}$.

For C, the view of C is $\mathbf{view}_C^{\Pi} = (EP, x_i, y_i)$, we construct a simulator $\mathbf{Sim}_C$ to simulate the corrupted C. $\mathbf{Sim}_C$ computes $\hat{x}_i$ and $\hat{y}_i$, and outputs $\mathbf{Sim}_C(EP) = (EP, \hat{x}_i, \hat{y}_i)$. Since x_i, $\hat{x}_i$, y_i, $\hat{y}_i$ are all blinded by random elements, thus A cannot distinguish x_i from $\hat{x}_i$, y_i from $\hat{y}_i$, $\mathbf{Sim}_C(EP) \stackrel{c}{\equiv} \mathbf{view}_C^{\Pi}$ holds.

Theorem 2. *The training protocol in Sect. 5.2 is secure in the semi-honest model.*

Proof. If the Paillier encryption is semantically secure, we can construct $\mathbf{Sim}_A$, $\mathbf{Sim}_B$ and $\mathbf{Sim}_C$ to simulate the view of A, B and C in the real execution of the training phase, we discuss them respectively.

View of A and B. A and B do not know sk, all the messages pass between A and B are encrypted. The message sent to C are all blinded by random values. The view of A is $\mathbf{view}_A^\Pi = (\mathbf{X}_A, \boldsymbol{\theta}_A, [\![u_i]\!], [\![\frac{\partial \mathcal{L}(\boldsymbol{\theta})}{\partial \boldsymbol{\theta}_A}]\!], [\![W_A]\!], \frac{\partial \mathcal{L}(\boldsymbol{\theta})}{\partial \boldsymbol{\theta}_A}, W_A)$. Suppose that A is corrupted, we sketch the simulation of $\mathbf{Sim}_A$. $\mathbf{Sim}_A$ computes $[\![\hat{u}_i]\!]$ and $[\![\frac{\partial \hat{\mathcal{L}}(\boldsymbol{\theta})}{\partial \boldsymbol{\theta}_A}]\!]$, then randomly chooses $\hat{R}_A$ and computes $[\![\hat{W}_A]\!]$ by multiplying $[\![\frac{\partial \hat{\mathcal{L}}(\boldsymbol{\theta})}{\partial \boldsymbol{\theta}_A}]\!]$ by $\hat{R}_A$, later, $\mathbf{Sim}_A$ computes $\frac{\partial \hat{\mathcal{L}}(\boldsymbol{\theta})}{\partial \boldsymbol{\theta}_A} = \hat{W}_A \cdot \frac{1}{\hat{R}_A}$ and updates $\hat{\boldsymbol{\theta}}_A$. Finally, $\mathbf{Sim}_A$ outputs $\mathbf{Sim}_A(\mathbf{X}_A) = (\mathbf{X}_A, \hat{\boldsymbol{\theta}}_A, [\![\hat{u}_i]\!], [\![\frac{\partial \hat{\mathcal{L}}(\boldsymbol{\theta})}{\partial \boldsymbol{\theta}_A}]\!], [\![\hat{W}_A]\!], \frac{\partial \hat{\mathcal{L}}(\boldsymbol{\theta})}{\partial \boldsymbol{\theta}_A}, \hat{W}_A)$.

Without sk, A cannot distinguish $[\![u_i]\!], [\![\frac{\partial \mathcal{L}(\boldsymbol{\theta})}{\partial \boldsymbol{\theta}_A}]\!], [\![W_A]\!]$ from $[\![\hat{u}_i]\!], [\![\frac{\partial \hat{\mathcal{L}}(\boldsymbol{\theta})}{\partial \boldsymbol{\theta}_A}]\!], [\![\hat{W}_A]\!]$ due to the semantic security of Paillier encryption. Since R_A and $\hat{R}_A$ are randomly chosen in the same way, thus A cannot distinguish $\frac{\partial \mathcal{L}(\boldsymbol{\theta})}{\partial \boldsymbol{\theta}_A}, W_A$ from $\frac{\partial \hat{\mathcal{L}}(\boldsymbol{\theta})}{\partial \boldsymbol{\theta}_A}, \hat{W}_A$. From the view of A, the distribution of $(\mathbf{X}_A, \boldsymbol{\theta}_A, [\![u_i]\!], [\![\frac{\partial \mathcal{L}(\boldsymbol{\theta})}{\partial \boldsymbol{\theta}_A}]\!], [\![W_A]\!], \frac{\partial \mathcal{L}(\boldsymbol{\theta})}{\partial \boldsymbol{\theta}_A}, W_A)$ and $(\mathbf{X}_A, \hat{\boldsymbol{\theta}}_A, [\![\hat{u}_i]\!], [\![\frac{\partial \hat{\mathcal{L}}(\boldsymbol{\theta})}{\partial \boldsymbol{\theta}_A}]\!], [\![\hat{W}_A]\!], \frac{\partial \hat{\mathcal{L}}(\boldsymbol{\theta})}{\partial \boldsymbol{\theta}_A}, \hat{W}_A)$ is indistinguishable, thus $\mathbf{Sim}_A(\mathbf{X}_A) \stackrel{c}{=} \mathbf{view}_A^\Pi$ holds. Similarly, $\mathbf{Sim}_B(\mathbf{X}_B) = (\mathbf{X}_B, \hat{\boldsymbol{\theta}}_B, [\![\hat{u}_i]\!], [\![\frac{\partial \hat{\mathcal{L}}(\boldsymbol{\theta})}{\partial \boldsymbol{\theta}_B}]\!], [\![\hat{W}_B]\!], [\![\frac{\partial \hat{\mathcal{L}}(\boldsymbol{\theta})}{\partial \boldsymbol{\theta}_B}]\!], [\![\hat{W}_B]\!])$, $\mathbf{Sim}_B(\mathbf{X}_B) \stackrel{c}{=} \mathbf{view}_B^\Pi$.

View of C. All the message sent by A and B are blinded by random elements. The view of C is $\mathbf{view}_C^\Pi = ([\![W_A]\!], [\![W_B]\!], W_A, W_B)$. Suppose that C is corrupted, we sketch the simulation of $\mathbf{Sim}_C$. $\mathbf{Sim}_C$ obtains $[\![\hat{W}_A]\!]$, $[\![\hat{W}_B]\!]$ and decrypts them to get $\hat{W}_A$ and $\hat{W}_B$, finally outputs $\mathbf{Sim}_C = ([\![\hat{W}_A]\!], [\![\hat{W}_B]\!], \hat{W}_A, \hat{W}_B)$.

Since the above values are all blinded by random values, the distribution of $([\![\hat{W}_A]\!], [\![\hat{W}_B]\!], \hat{W}_A, \hat{W}_B)$ and $([\![W_A]\!], [\![W_B]\!], W_A, W_B)$ is indistinguishable, thus, $\mathbf{Sim}_C \stackrel{c}{=} \mathbf{view}_C^\Pi$ holds.

7 Experiment Evaluation

7.1 Hash Parameters Analysis

In our scheme, we use hash-to-bin to improve efficiency. A and B act as OPPRF receivers, they use Cuckoo hashing to hash each element into bins. C acts as OPPRF sender, and uses Simple hashing to hash each element into bins. The hashing parameters of Cuckoo hashing and Simple hashing are chosen as follows.

Simple Hashing Parameters. The Simple hashing involves four parameters: the number of elements of party C n, the number of hash functions k, the number of bins b, and the bin size β. We let $k = 3$, now we have to determine b and β.

Our approach is to determine β first, then we use Eq. 1 to get b. The concrete process of determining β is as follows:

After hashing each element into bins, for each bin, the OPPRF sender and the OPPRF receiver will run a table-based OPPRF. By the second step of table-based OPPRF, sender needs to sample a nonce v to make all $\{H(F_k(x_i)\|v), i \in [N]\}$ distinct, N is the number of elements stored in that bin. Kolesnikov et al. [44] point out that for a random v, the probability of "all $H(F_k(x_i)\|v), i \in [N]$ are distinct" is as Eq. 2, m denotes the output length of $H(\cdot)$, and the expected number of sampling a proper v is $1/Pr_{unique}$. Sampling v requires computing τN hash functions, where τ is the number of choosing v.

$$Pr_{unique} = \prod_{i=1}^{N-1} (1 - \frac{i}{2^m}) \tag{2}$$

The table size is 2^m and the bin size $\beta = 2^m$, then we can analyze m to get the bin size β. When m is too small, the bin size is small, then each bin stores fewer elements, therefore it needs more bins to store elements, we observed that as the number of bins increases, sender needs to send more tables, then the communication cost is increasing. When m is too large, it requires fewer bins to store elements, each bin can store more elements, then the Pr_{unique} is little, the expected number of sampling v will be more, which will increase the computation cost. Therefore, we need to choose a proper m to get a compromise between communication cost and computation cost. When $n \in \{2^{24}, 2^{25}, 2^{26}, 2^{27}\}$, we run a number of experiments to get the proper m. In all set sizes, we observed that the sample alignment scheme is the fastest one when $m = 6$, and can achieve the balance between communication cost and computation cost, then we set $m = 6$, thus obtaining the bin size $\beta = 2^m$, then we evaluate Eq. 1 with set size n, bin size β and number of the hash functions k to get the number of the bins $b = \zeta n$ when the hashing failure probability is 2^{-30} and 2^{-40}. The concrete parameters are depicted in Table 1.

Table 1. The concrete ζ with different set sizes for hashing failure probability 2^{-30} and 2^{-40}.

Hashing failure	2^{-30}				2^{-40}			
n	2^{24}	2^{25}	2^{26}	2^{27}	2^{24}	2^{25}	2^{26}	2^{27}
ζ	0.23	0.23	0.23	0.24	0.25	0.26	0.26	0.26

What's more, when hashing $n = 2^{24}$ elements into $0.25n$ bins, we observed that more than half of the bins store no more than 12 elements, thus the expected number of sampling v is only 3.

Cuckoo Hashing Parameter. In the above analysis, we have fixed the bin size β and the number of bins b. Party A and B hold m_1, m_2 elements respectively.

Now, we analyze the Cuckoo hashing parameters. In our scheme, consider that the stash will cause an extra expensive cost, hence we avoid using stash. Pinkas et al. [34] point out that Cuckoo hashing with no stash performs badly when the number of hash functions $k = 2$, however, if k is too large, for Simple hashing, it will need more bins or a larger bin to store elements. Hence, we fix the number of hash functions to 3. What's more, Pinkas et al. [34] analyze the minimum number of bins $b_{min} = \epsilon_{min} m_1$, such that the hashing process succeeds with no stash except for negligible probability, and reach the conclusion that the hashing failure probability is below 2^{-30} when $\epsilon_{min} = 1.20$, and the hashing failure probability is below 2^{-40} when $\epsilon_{min} = 1.27$. Moreover, in our experiments, we let $m_1 = m_2$, and $m_1, m_2 \in \{2^{19}, 2^{20}\}$, which satisfies the actual small business user scale. Besides, we have determined the number of bins ζn according to the analysis of Simple hashing, $\zeta \in [0.23, 0.26], n \in [2^{24}, 2^{27}]$. It's oblivious that $(\zeta n)/m_1 > \epsilon_{min} = 1.27$, thus when hashing m_1 elements into ζn bins without stash, the hashing failure probability is negligible.

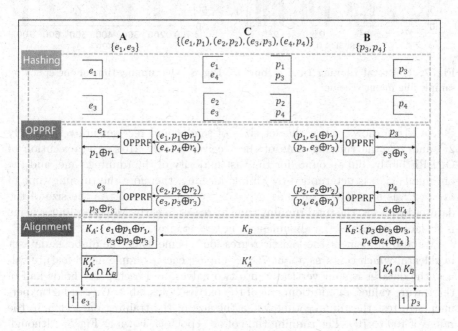

Fig. 6. An instantiation of the sample alignment scheme.

7.2 Experiment Result

To verify the efficiency of our scheme, we run experiments on a Server with 2 20-core Intel Xeon CPU 5218R @2.1GHz and 256 GB of RAM, the operating system is Ubuntu 20.04. In the training phase, we use the library that implements the paillier homomorphic encryption [50], it supports the arithmetic operations with floating point numbers. In the sample alignment phase, the length of each element σ is 128 bits, the statistical security parameter λ is 40 and the computational security parameter κ is 128. We test the running time of our sample alignment scheme with set sizes $n \in \{2^{24}, 2^{25}, 2^{26}, 2^{27}\}$ of C(Sender) and set sizes $m_1, m_2 \in \{2^{19}, 2^{20}\}$ of A and B(Receiver). The total process consists of offline phase and online phase, the offline phase consists of the operation that is independent with the input, such as the base OT used in OPRF. The results are shown as Fig. 7, which are the average of 5 trials.

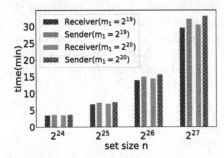
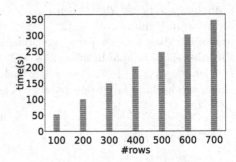

Fig. 7. The total running time of our sample alignment scheme

Fig. 8. The running time of one epoch.

As Fig. 7 shows, when the set sizes of sender and receiver are respectively 2^{24} and 2^{20}, the running time of the receiver is only 216 s. The execution of OPPRF bin by bin accounts for the vast majority of the running time, and the bin number ζn is determined by Simple hashing, therefore the running time of $m_1 = 2^{19}$ is almost the same as $m_1 = 2^{20}$ when n is fixed. As the size of the dataset increases, the total running time increases linearly. Moreover, our scheme is scalable, it enables the alignment of larger set sizes.

We also implement the logistic regression scheme using the diabetes dataset in sklearn, which contains about 768 examples, each example has 8 feature values, the dataset is split vertically into two halves, and each party holds half of the feature values, in addition, one of the parties holds label. We conduct experiments to test the running time when the size of the training dataset is in the range of 100 to 700. The running time of one epoch is shown as Fig. 8. Although training a model using hundreds of data requires hundreds of seconds, once a model has been trained, it can be used to make multiple predictions, therefore, we think timeliness is not a primary concern in the training phase.

8   Conclusions

In this paper, we consider how to align the samples when the databases of two participants don't have the same ID in federated learning. Aimed at vertical federated learning, we construct a sample alignment scheme using OPPRF, when the set size of sender and receiver is 2^{24} and 2^{20}, the running time is 216 s. Besides, we design the secure logistic regression training scheme using additive homomorphic encryption and conduct experiments to verify its feasibility.

Acknowledgements. This paper was supported by the National Natural Science Foundation of China (Nos. 61922036, U2001205), National Key Research and Development Program of China (No. 2019YFE0123600), Major Program of Guangdong Basic and Applied Basic Research Foundation (No. 2019B030302008), Science and Technology Project of Guangzhou City (No. 201707010320), and TESTBED2 (No. H2020-MSCA-RISE-2019).

References

1. Wu, S., Teruya, T., Kawamoto, J., Sakuma, J., Kikuchi, H.: Privacy-preservation for stochastic gradient descent application to secure logistic regression. In: The 27th Annual Conference of the Japanese Society for Artificial Intelligence, vol. 27, pp. 1–4 (2013)
2. Du, W., Atallah, M.J.: Privacy-preserving cooperative statistical analysis. In: Seventeenth Annual Computer Security Applications Conference, pp. 102–110. IEEE (2001)
3. Wan, L., Ng, W.K., Han, S., Lee, V.C.: Privacy-preservation for gradient descent methods. In: Proceedings of the 13th ACM SIGKDD International Conference on Knowledge Discovery and Data Mining, pp. 775–783 (2007)
4. Gascón, A., et al.: Secure linear regression on vertically partitioned datasets. IACR Cryptol. ePrint Arch. **2016**, 892 (2016)
5. Vaidya, J., Clifton, C.: Privacy preserving association rule mining in vertically partitioned data. In: Proceedings of the Eighth ACM SIGKDD International Conference on Knowledge Discovery and Data Mining, pp. 639–644 (2002)
6. Voigt, P., Von dem Bussche, A.: The EU general data protection regulation (GDPR). A Practical Guide, 1st Ed., Cham: Springer International Publishing **10**(3152676), 10–5555 (2017)
7. Konečnỳ, J., McMahan, H.B., Ramage, D., Richtárik, P.: Federated optimization: Distributed machine learning for on-device intelligence. arXiv preprint arXiv:1610.02527 (2016)
8. Konečnỳ, J., McMahan, H.B., Yu, F.X., Richtárik, P., Suresh, A.T., Bacon, D.: Federated learning: strategies for improving communication efficiency. arXiv preprint arXiv:1610.05492 (2016)
9. McMahan, H.B., Moore, E., Ramage, D., y Arcas, B.A.: Federated learning of deep networks using model averaging. arXiv preprint arXiv:1602.05629 2 (2016)
10. Li, L., Fan, Y., Tse, M., Lin, K.Y.: A review of applications in federated learning. Comput. Ind. Eng. **149**, 106854 (2020)
11. Yang, Q., Liu, Y., Chen, T., Tong, Y.: Federated machine learning: concept and applications. ACM Trans. Intell. Syste. Technol. (TIST) **10**(2), 1–19 (2019)
12. Goldreich, O.: Secure multi-party computation. Manuscript Preliminary version **78**, 110 (1998)
13. Evans, D., Kolesnikov, V., Rosulek, M., et al.: A pragmatic introduction to secure multi-party computation. Found. Trends® Priv. Secur. **2**(2–3), 70–246 (2018)
14. Peteiro-Barral, D., Guijarro-Berdiñas, B.: A survey of methods for distributed machine learning. Prog. Artif. Intell. **2**(1), 1–11 (2013). https://doi.org/10.1007/s13748-012-0035-5

15. Verbraeken, J., Wolting, M., Katzy, J., Kloppenburg, J., Verbelen, T., Rellermeyer, J.S.: A survey on distributed machine learning. ACM Comput. Surv. (CSUR) **53**(2), 1–33 (2020)

16. Rivest, R.L., Adleman, L., Dertouzos, M.L., et al.: On data banks and privacy homomorphisms. Found. Secure Comput. **4**(11), 169–180 (1978)

17. Shamir, A.: How to share a secret. Commun. ACM **22**(11), 612–613 (1979)

18. Yao, A.C.: Protocols for secure computations. In: 23rd Annual Symposium on Foundations of Computer Science (sfcs 1982), pp. 160–164. IEEE (1982)

19. Dwork, C., Roth, A., et al.: The algorithmic foundations of differential privacy. Found. Trends® Theor. Comput. Sci. **9**(3–4), 211–407 (2014)

20. Freedman, M.J., Nissim, K., Pinkas, B.: Efficient private matching and set intersection. In: Cachin, C., Camenisch, J.L. (eds.) EUROCRYPT 2004. LNCS, vol. 3027, pp. 1–19. Springer, Heidelberg (2004). https://doi.org/10.1007/978-3-540-24676-3_1

21. ElGamal, T.: A public key cryptosystem and a signature scheme based on discrete logarithms. IEEE Trans. Inf. Theory **31**(4), 469–472 (1985)

22. Goldwasser, S., Micali, S.: Probabilistic encryption & how to play mental poker keeping secret all partial information. In: Providing sound foundations for cryptography: on the work of Shafi Goldwasser and Silvio Micali, pp. 173–201 (2019)

23. Paillier, P.: Public-key cryptosystems based on composite degree residuosity classes. In: Stern, J. (ed.) EUROCRYPT 1999. LNCS, vol. 1592, pp. 223–238. Springer, Heidelberg (1999). https://doi.org/10.1007/3-540-48910-X_16

24. Brakerski, Z., Gentry, C., Vaikuntanathan, V.: (Leveled) fully homomorphic encryption without bootstrapping. ACM Trans. Comput. Theory (TOCT) **6**(3), 1–36 (2014)

25. Brakerski, Z.: Fully homomorphic encryption without modulus switching from classical GapSVP. In: Safavi-Naini, R., Canetti, R. (eds.) CRYPTO 2012. LNCS, vol. 7417, pp. 868–886. Springer, Heidelberg (2012). https://doi.org/10.1007/978-3-642-32009-5_50

26. Fan, J., Vercauteren, F.: Somewhat practical fully homomorphic encryption. Cryptology ePrint Archive (2012)

27. Cheng, K., et al.: Secureboost: a lossless federated learning framework. IEEE Intell. Syst. **36**(6), 87–98 (2021)

28. Hardy, S., et al.: Private federated learning on vertically partitioned data via entity resolution and additively homomorphic encryption. arXiv preprint arXiv:1711.10677 (2017)

29. Nikolaenko, V., Weinsberg, U., Ioannidis, S., Joye, M., Boneh, D., Taft, N.: Privacy-preserving ridge regression on hundreds of millions of records. In: 2013 IEEE Symposium on Security and Privacy, pp. 334–348. IEEE (2013)

30. Sanil, A.P., Karr, A.F., Lin, X., Reiter, J.P.: Privacy preserving regression modelling via distributed computation. In: Proceedings of the Tenth ACM SIGKDD International Conference on Knowledge Discovery and Data Mining, pp. 677–682 (2004)

31. Geyer, R.C., Klein, T., Nabi, M.: Differentially private federated learning: a client level perspective. arXiv preprint arXiv:1712.07557 (2017)

32. FATE: An Industrial Grade Federated Learning Framework. https://fate.fedai.org/

33. Liu, Y., Zhang, X., Wang, L.: Asymmetrical vertical federated learning. arXiv preprint arXiv:2004.07427 (2020)

34. Pinkas, B., Schneider, T., Zohner, M.: Scalable private set intersection based on OT extension. ACM Trans. Priv. Secur. (TOPS) **21**(2), 1–35 (2018)

35. Kolesnikov, V., Kumaresan, R., Rosulek, M., Trieu, N.: Efficient batched oblivious PRF with applications to private set intersection. In: Proceedings of the 2016 ACM SIGSAC Conference on Computer and Communications Security, pp. 818–829 (2016)
36. Pinkas, B., Rosulek, M., Trieu, N., Yanai, A.: SpOT-light: lightweight private set intersection from sparse OT extension. In: Boldyreva, A., Micciancio, D. (eds.) CRYPTO 2019. LNCS, vol. 11694, pp. 401–431. Springer, Cham (2019). https://doi.org/10.1007/978-3-030-26954-8_13
37. Chase, M., Miao, P.: Private set intersection in the internet setting from lightweight oblivious PRF. In: Micciancio, D., Ristenpart, T. (eds.) CRYPTO 2020. LNCS, vol. 12172, pp. 34–63. Springer, Cham (2020). https://doi.org/10.1007/978-3-030-56877-1_2
38. Meadows, C.: A more efficient cryptographic matchmaking protocol for use in the absence of a continuously available third party. In: 1986 IEEE Symposium on Security and Privacy, pp. 134–134. IEEE (1986)
39. De Cristofaro, E., Kim, J., Tsudik, G.: Linear-complexity private set intersection protocols secure in malicious model. In: Abe, M. (ed.) ASIACRYPT 2010. LNCS, vol. 6477, pp. 213–231. Springer, Heidelberg (2010). https://doi.org/10.1007/978-3-642-17373-8_13
40. Rosulek, M., Trieu, N.: Compact and malicious private set intersection for small sets. In: Proceedings of the 2021 ACM SIGSAC Conference on Computer and Communications Security, pp. 1166–1181 (2021)
41. Huang, Y., Evans, D., Katz, J.: Private set intersection: are garbled circuits better than custom protocols? In: NDSS (2012)
42. Pinkas, B., Schneider, T., Tkachenko, O., Yanai, A.: Efficient circuit-based PSI with linear communication. In: Ishai, Y., Rijmen, V. (eds.) EUROCRYPT 2019. LNCS, vol. 11478, pp. 122–153. Springer, Cham (2019). https://doi.org/10.1007/978-3-030-17659-4_5
43. Chen, H., Laine, K., Rindal, P.: Fast private set intersection from homomorphic encryption. In: Proceedings of the 2017 ACM SIGSAC Conference on Computer and Communications Security, pp. 1243–1255 (2017)
44. Kolesnikov, V., Matania, N., Pinkas, B., Rosulek, M., Trieu, N.: Practical multi-party private set intersection from symmetric-key techniques. In: Proceedings of the 2017 ACM SIGSAC Conference on Computer and Communications Security, pp. 1257–1272 (2017)
45. Pagh, R., Rodler, F.F.: Cuckoo hashing. J. Algorithms **51**(2), 122–144 (2004)
46. Kirsch, A., Mitzenmacher, M., Wieder, U.: More robust hashing: cuckoo hashing with a stash. SIAM J. Comput. **39**(4), 1543–1561 (2010)
47. Zhu, L., Liu, Z., Han, S.: Deep leakage from gradients. In: Advances in Neural Information Processing Systems, vol. 32 (2019)
48. Fredrikson, M., Jha, S., Ristenpart, T.: Model inversion attacks that exploit confidence information and basic countermeasures. In: Proceedings of the 22nd ACM SIGSAC Conference on Computer and Communications Security, pp. 1322–1333 (2015)
49. Shokri, R., Stronati, M., Song, C., Shmatikov, V.: Membership inference attacks against machine learning models. In: 2017 IEEE Symposium on Security and Privacy (SP), pp. 3–18. IEEE (2017)
50. A Python 3 library implementing the Paillier Partially Homomorphic Encryption. https://github.com/data61/python-paillier

Blockchain

Reinforcement-Mining: Protecting Reward in Selfish Mining

Zhaojie Wang[1] , Willy Susilo[2](✉) , Jianan Guo[1] , Yilei Wang[1] ,
and Minghao Zhao[3]

[1] School of Computer Science, Qufu Normal University, Rizhao, China
wang_yilei2019@qfnu.edu.cn
[2] School of Computing and Information Technology, University of Wollongong,
Wollongong, Australia
wsusilo@uow.edu.au
[3] School of Data Science and Engineering, East China Normal University,
Shanghai, China

Abstract. Selfish mining is notorious for receiving additional rewards disproportionate to the attacker's mining power in Proof-of-Work (PoW) consensus-based blockchain, e.g., Bitcoin. Unfair reward distribution may cause partial honest miners to quit blockchain mining, which will seriously weaken the security of the PoW blockchain since the security is guaranteed by strong mining power. Various efforts have been proposed to alleviate this problem, but are generally expensive to implement, e.g., upgrading the blockchain backbone protocol. In this work, we propose a method, named Reinforcement-Mining, to protect honest miners' mining rewards to mitigate the harm of selfish mining. The key insight of Reinforcement-Mining is to employ a deep reinforcement learning framework to choose the optimal policy for honest miners to protect their rewards when the blockchain suffers from a selfish mining attack. Experiments on mining reward and chain quality property are conducted respectively. The analysis of experiment results demonstrates that our approach moderates the unfair reward distribution of selfish mining and improves the chain quality property of the blockchain. The proposed method may be still far from practical application, however, it provides a new perspective for defense against selfish mining.

Keywords: Blockchain · Selfish mining · Mining reward

1 Introduction

The selfish mining attack, proposed in [4], is an adversarial mining strategy that enables the attacker, so-called the selfish miner, to get additional reward by leveraging the blockchain incentive mechanism. Unlike honest miners who always follow the public chain, the selfish miner does not broadcast newly mined blocks immediately, but withholds it to maintain a private chain in its local view.

C. Ge and F. Guo (Eds.): ProvSec 2022, LNCS 13600, pp. 199–209, 2022.
https://doi.org/10.1007/978-3-031-20917-8_14

When receiving a new block from an honest miner, the selfish miner strategically releases a number of blocks in the private chain. According to the longest public chain rule in Bitcoin, the released blocks invalidate the new block of the honest miner, thus wasting the mining power of the honest network. To incentivize block mining, miners receive a block reward, *i.e.*, an amount of cryptocurrency, for every block they mine and successfully append to the longest public chain. Ideally, the received block reward of a miner is proportional to the fraction of its mining power to the entire network. However, some honest mienrs waste power without receiving block rewards since some honest blocks are invalid due to selfish mining. Stated differently, the rewards belonging to those honest miners are lost, while the selfish miner gets this part of the rewards. This unfair reward distribution deviates from the incentive mechanism of Bitcoin and may induce other participants to be selfish. Moreover, the unfair reward distribution may cause honest miners to drop out of mining or transfer mining power to other blockchain networks. The decline in mining power will severely weaken the security of the Bitcoin network since it is secured by requiring lots of mining power to participate in the PoW consensus. Poor security also opens up opportunities for other attacks, *e.g.*, double-spend attacks. Hence, efforts must be made to mitigate the impact of selfish mining attacks.

Several schemes are proposed to alleviate the selfish mining attack. These schemes mainly focus on two points: (1) Upgrading the backbone protocol to eliminate the attack motivation [10,19,22]. (2) Employing detection methods to detect the potential attack [3,17,20]. The former measure can effectively curb the selfish mining attack, but the implementation cost is large. The latter can only report the presence of attacks, and additional measures are required to protect the rewards of honest nodes.

In this work, we propose the Reinforcement-Mining, a solution for using deep reinforcement learning (DRL) to counteract the selfish mining attack. Reinforcement-Mining is designed to protect honest miners rewards without modifying the Bitcoin protocol, reducing the damage of selfish mining. Concretely, a selfish miner is embedded in the environment construction to simulate a selfish mining attack on the Bitcoin blockchain. We then initialize a deep Q-network (DQN) to interact with the environment. During the interaction, the DQN chooses an action in the light of the current environment state and submits it to the environment, then collects the feedback information of the environment. The above state, action, and feedback will be organized as training data, also known as experience, which is used to train the DQN. The trained DQN will be applied to resist selfish mining, *i.e.*, choosing the optimal mining action for non-malicious miners to reduce their losses when faced with a selfish mining attack. We summarize the contributions of this work below.

- We present Reinforcement-Mining as a solution for shielding Bitcoin miners against the selfish mining attack. Reinforcement-Mining mainly involves the environment construction and DQN training. In particular, we construct a Bitcoin selfish mining environment and define the representation of the environment state. Based on the constructed environment, a DQN is instantiated and trained to choose the optimal mining action for the miner.

- We apply Reinforcement-Mining to an instantiated environment to evaluate its performance, mainly concerning reward distribution and the chain quality property. Reward analysis demonstrates that Reinforcement-Mining can alleviate the issue of unfair reward distribution. Especially, it reduces the reward share of the selfish miner and protects the rewards of other miners. Moreover, that the application of Reinforcement-Mining improves the chain quality property of the blockchain. Particularly, Reinforcement-Mining improves the chain quality property by about 0.02 even if the selfish miner owns a big power, *e.g.*, $\alpha = 0.4$.

Roadmap of this Paper. The rest of the paper is organized as follows. Section 2 gives the background on the selfish mining attack. In Sect. 3, we present the details of Reinforcement-Mining, including the necessary assumptions, environment construction, and training of the deep Q-network. In Sect. 4, the experiment results and discussion of the proposed method are given. Some prior works on blockchain security related to our work are presented in Sect. 5. Finally, we conclude this work in Sect. 6.

2   Selfish Mining

The selfish mining attack [4,5] departs from the Bitcoin backbone protocol, allowing the attacker to collect additional block reward during mining process. Loosely speaking, instead of broadcasting the newly mined block immediately, the selfish miner withholds it to build a private chain. The private chain gives the selfish miner an advantage of mining the next block before other miners. The selfish miner tirelessly and secretly mines on the private chain to extend its length. Once an honest miner finds a new block, the selfish miner leverages blocks on the private chain to carry out the attack to invalidate the honest miner's block.

We briefly illustrate the process of this attack with a simple example. Suppose the selfish miner withholds a block with height b_h on his private chain, see (1) in Fig. 1, he can take the lead to mine block b_{h+1} on it, while others are mining the block with height b_h since they do not aware of the existence of withheld block b_h. Then, we list the possible cases:

- Case 1: If the selfish miner finds the block b_{h+1} before others, he withholds it and continues to mine the next block to extend the private chain.
- Case 2: If an honest miner finds the block with height b_h, denoted as b'_h, before the selfish miner finds block b_{h+1}. The selfish miner publishes his private chain to fork the blockchain, see (2) in Fig. 1. Next, two subcases will occur:
  - Subcase 1: One miner (either the selfish miner or others) finds the block b_{h+1} on b_h, see (3) in Fig. 1. Then, the two blocks (b_h and b_{h+1}) become valid and their miners are rewarded. However, the honest miner who finds the block b'_h suffers a loss.

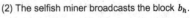

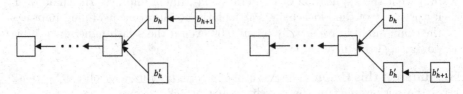

(1) The selfish miner withholds the block b_h to build a private chain.

(2) The selfish miner broadcasts the block b_h.

(3) The selfish miner mines the next block first.

(4) One honest miner mines the next block first.

Fig. 1. A simple example for the selfish mining attack. The shaded block represents the unpublished block in the private chain.

- Subcase 2: An honest miner finds the next block on b'_h, denoted as b'_{h+1}, see (4) in Fig. 1. Note that the selfish miner does not mine on the b'_h since he endeavors to make his block b_h valid. The blocks b'_h and b'_{h+1} are valid and their miners are rewarded. Hence, the selfish miner fails to attack the blockchain and loses the reward of block b_h.

3   Reinforcement-Mining

The key insight of Reinforcement-Mining is that honest nodes use deep reinforcement learning to choose the optimal action against the selfish miner during mining process, as illustrated in Fig. 2. Overall, we construct an environment to model the Bitcoin blockchain subject to the selfish mining attack. Then, the agent (a honest miner that wants to seek reward protection) interacts with the environment. Specifically, he observes an environment state and transmits it to an activated deep Q-network (DQN), which gives a suggested action. The environment performs the action, then transfers to a new state and returns a reward as feedback. During continuous interaction, the agent collects and organizes the interaction data as *experience* for DQN training. Below we describe the details of our method.

3.1   Assumptions

We first explain some concepts and assumptions to better describe the details of Reinforcement-Mining.

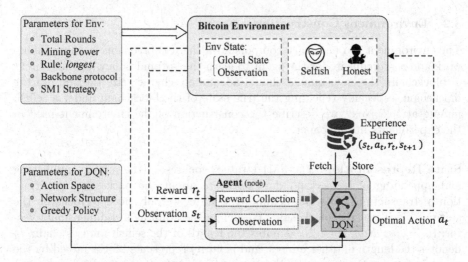

Fig. 2. The workflow for Reinforcement-Mining. "Env" represents the environment with built-in the selfish miner and honest miners. "Mining power" includes the adversarial power (α) and agent's power (β), then the total power for all other honest miners is $1 - \alpha - \beta$. "Backbone protocol" indicates the Bitcoin core protocol. "Rule" denotes the Bitcoin longest chain rule, unsurprisingly.

1. **Miners.** In Bitcoin, nodes that participate in the consensus process to maintain the blockchain are usually called miners, in our study, they consist of a selfish miner and a group of honest miners. Honest miners follow the Bitcoin core protocol, which can be modeled by the Bitcoin ideal world functionality [16]. The selfish miner, however, behaves maliciously and follows the selfish mining strategy presented in [4], abbreviated as SM1.

2. **Hash Power.** Hash power denotes the ability of a miner to perform hash calculations. Stated differently, it represents the probability of a miner finding a new block in the Proof-of-Work (PoW) consensus mechanism. As in prior works [4,5], we normalize the hash power of the whole network to 1. Then, we set the hash power of the selfish miner to $\alpha \in [0, 0.49]$, and the power of all honest miners to be $1 - \alpha$.

3. **Round.** In each round, all Miners compete to mine a new block according to its hash power. Whenever a new block is found and appended to the chain, we call this round the end, and the next round of mining begins.

4. **Rewards.** The miner who successfully appends a block on the longest public chain (also called the main chain) receives a block reward, i.e., 6.25 coins on July 12 2022. For simplicity, we normalize the block reward to 1 for ease of description and analysis. In particular, we calculate a miner's reward by cumulating its block reward in one experimental episode. In fact, the above reward is generally called the *absolute reward*. While in the selfish mining setting, we focus on the *relative reward*, that is, the miner's share of the total network reward.

3.2   Environment Construction

The environment is a necessary component in the reinforcement learning framework and a prerequisite for the agent to learn the optimal policy. In the context of blockchain, the environment should adequately characterize the state of the blockchain, especially reflecting the true state of the blockchain under a selfish mining attack. Next, we describe the construction of the environment used in the experiments in this paper.

State Representation. The SM1 strategy focuses on the mining, publishing and appending of blocks and does not care about the packaging, confirmation of transactions, so when defining the state, we only need to focus on the state of blocks on the blockchain. We define the state as a 4-dimensional vector: $(l_a, l_h, pending, fork)$, l_a denotes the length of the selfish miner's chain, l_h denotes the length of other miners, and $pending$ represents blocks mined by the agent but not yet consensus. The element $fork \in \{normal, forking, catch\,up\}$ represents the forking state of the blockchain, $normal$ means no fork on the blockchain, $forking$ means a fork with two equal length branches, and $catch\,up$ means that the selfish miner withholds some blocks on its chain. Another concern is that the state observed by the agent from the environment may not be consistent with the actual blockchain state, since blocks withheld by the selfish miner are not visible to the agent. In order to solve this problem, we divide the environment state into *global state* and *observed state*, where *global state* represents the complete blockchain state and *observed state* denotes the observed state by the agent.

The Agent's Actions. We list the actions that the agent can choose when interacting with the environment. For the agent, although it is not allowed to withhold blocks, it can freely control the mining and appending of blocks. Based on this point of view, we define the action space as:

- *mine*: The agent mines the new block on the top of the blockchain. This action is always available.
- $follow_a$: The agent follows the first branch of a fork. This action is allowed when the blockchain is forking.
- $follow_b$: The agent follows another branch of the fork. This action is also allowed when the blockchain is forking.

3.3   Deep Q-Network Training

In this work, we utilize a deep Q-network (DQN) [9] to choose an optimal action for the agent during the interaction. Our goal is to train a suitable DQN to help the agent fight against the selfish miner in blockchain mining. We first instantiate a fully connected neural network, and then let the network interact with the given environment. The training of the network is achieved during continuous interaction. Concretely, whenever the network receives a state, it chooses an action to submit to the environment, which feeds back a corresponding reward along with a new blockchain state.

We store those interaction data (the observed state, a chosen action, the reward, and the updated state) into a buffer as experience for the network training. The network randomly fetches a batch of experience for training when the buffer is full. Particularly, we apply the back propagation algorithm to update the network parameters.

4   Experiment Results

To verify the feasibility of Reinforcement-Mining, we conduct experiments and analyze the results. The experiments are programed by Python programming language(version 3.6.8). In particular, we use Pytorch (version 1.10.2) [13] to implement the deep Q-network that chooses the optimal action for the agent. We collect data and final results from code execution for the analysis, which is presented below.

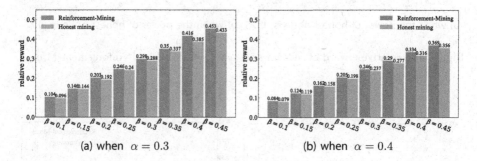

(a) when $\alpha = 0.3$ (b) when $\alpha = 0.4$

Fig. 3. Reinforcement-Mining can increase the mining node's relative reward when a selfish miner exists.

Relative Reward. In the context of selfish mining, the most important metric is the distribution of rewards between parties. Figure 3 presents the comparison of the miner's relative reward when adopting Reinforcement-Mining and honest mining. It can be seen that in the presence of selfish mining, Reinforcement-Mining can increase the relative reward of the honest miner. For instance, when the selfish miner's power $\alpha = 0.3$ ($\alpha = 0.4$), by adopting Reinforcement-Mining, the relative reward of the honest miner can be increased by about 4.75% (4.3%), on average. This indicates that Reinforcement-Mining evaluates the expected reward for each candidate action when making action chosen. The actions with higher risk will be evaded when an attack occurs to reduce reward losses. However, the increment of mienr's reward is limited since the premise that no malicious actions can be made. In addition, from the data, it can be seen that the effect of Reinforcement-Mining on reward boosting is inversely proportional to the power of the selfish miner.

We also evaluate the impact of Reinforcement-Mining on the relative reward of the selfish miner. The relative reward of the selfish miner is reduced by applying Reinforcement-Mining during the mining process, as illustrated in Fig. 4. For example, a honest miner (with power 0.25) adopts Reinforcement-Mining against the selfish mining, the selfish miner (power $\alpha = 0.3$) loses the relative reward of 0.02 (see Fig. 4a). One possible reason is that the optimal action chosen for honest miner by the deep Q-network adds the failures of the selfish mining attack, especially when the blockchain is forking.

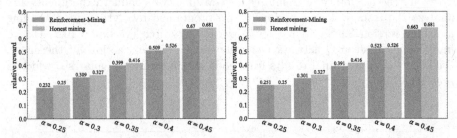

(a) when the power of honest node is 0.25 (b) when the power of honest node is 0.35

Fig. 4. The relative reward of selfish miner can be reduced by Reinforcement-Mining.

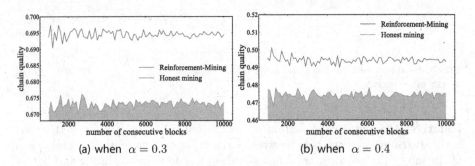

(a) when $\alpha = 0.3$ (b) when $\alpha = 0.4$

Fig. 5. Reinforcement-Mining improves the chain quality property in Bitcoin selfish mining context.

Chain Quality Property. The chain quality property Q_{cq} (usually with parameters $\mu \in \mathbb{R}$ and $l \in \mathbb{N}$) denotes that, for any l consecutive blocks in the blockchain maintained by any honest miner, the ratio of honest blocks is at least μ [1,7,8,15].

One symptom of the selfish mining attack is that it leads to a decrease in the chain quality property Q_{cq} of the blockchain. We further perform experiments to evaluate the impact of Reinforcement-Mining on chain quality, and the results are illustrated in Fig. 5. Comparing Fig. 5a and 5b, the stronger the mining power of selfish miner, the lower the chain quality, unsurprisingly. Reinforcement-Mining, however, can always improve the chain quality property, even if the selfish miner has a strong power. For instance, by applying Reinforcement-Mining, the chain quality is improved by about 0.02 on average when $\alpha = 0.4$. This proves that, from another aspect, Reinforcement-Mining reduces the number of blocks mined by the attacker on the main chain. In other words, it plays a positive role in improving the security of the blockchain.

5 Related Work

The selfish mining attack [4] was first proposed to broken the Proof-of-Work consensus protocol. Since then, a large number of attack schemes and models have been sought to refine ecological mining security [5, 14, 18]. Liu et al. [12] analyzed the mining strategy in the case of multiple attackers. Gao et al. [6] discussed the situation in which the attacker dynamically adjusts its mining power, and proposed a new attack strategy, named Bribery Selfish Mining, combined with the bribery attack [2]. Given to enforcement of mining security, all sorts of schemes or techniques have been proposed to detect and against the selfish mining attack. Ethan Heilman [10] presented Freshness Preferred to against selfish mining with unforgeable timestamps. Solat et al. [19] further considered the situation where an adversary withholds a block for longer than a preset time interval and proposed ZeroBlock, which is rejected by all honest nodes. A strategy based deep reinforcement learning called SquirRL is recently proposed to identify blockchain attack strategies under multiple selfish miners [11]. Zhang [21] presented insightful mining to counteract selfish mining, infiltrating an undercover miner into the selfish pool, whereby the insightful pool could acquire the number of its hidden blocks.

6 Conclusion

The selfish mining attack undermines the fairness of the Bitcoin blockchain ecosystem, especially for the distribution of mining rewards. To solve this, we propose a method, named Reinforcement-Mining, that utilizes deep reinforcement learning to protect the mining rewards of honest miners from selfish mining. We conduct an environment that models the Bitcoin blockchain, specifically embedding a selfish miner into the environment. In the environment construction, we specify the state representation to denote the blockchain state and the action space supplied for the honest miner, i.e., the agent. Then, we train a Deep Q-Network to interact with the environment and choose the optimal action for the agent. Experiment results and analysis demonstrate Reinforcement-Mining can protect the rewards of honest miners in the presence of selfish mining. Additionally, this method can improve the chain quality property of the blockchain which is decreased due to selfish mining. This work, however, has a certain limitation, namely, the improvement of rewards and chain quality is limited. This is because the optional actions of honest miners are constrained, i.e. no action can violate Bitcoin's protocol. In future work, we will refine and extend the proposed method to improve its performance.

References

1. Badertscher, C., Maurer, U., Tschudi, D., Zikas, V.: Bitcoin as a transaction ledger: a composable treatment. In: Katz, J., Shacham, H. (eds.) CRYPTO 2017. LNCS, vol. 10401, pp. 324–356. Springer, Cham (2017). https://doi.org/10.1007/978-3-319-63688-7_11
2. Bonneau, J., Felten, E.W., Goldfeder, S., Kroll, J.A., Narayanan, A.: Why buy when you can rent? bribery attacks on bitcoin consensus (2016)
3. Chicarino, V., Albuquerque, C., Jesus, E., Rocha, A.: On the detection of selfish mining and stalker attacks in blockchain networks. Ann. Telecommun. **75**(3), 143–152 (2020). https://doi.org/10.1007/s12243-019-00746-2
4. Eyal, I., Sirer, E.G.: Majority is not enough: bitcoin mining is vulnerable. In: Christin, N., Safavi-Naini, R. (eds.) FC 2014. LNCS, vol. 8437, pp. 436–454. Springer, Heidelberg (2014). https://doi.org/10.1007/978-3-662-45472-5_28
5. Feng, C., Niu, J.: Selfish mining in ethereum. In: 2019 IEEE 39th International Conference on Distributed Computing Systems (ICDCS), pp. 1306–1316. IEEE (2019)
6. Gao, S., Li, Z., Peng, Z., Xiao, B.: Power adjusting and bribery racing: Novel mining attacks in the bitcoin system. In: Proceedings of the 2019 ACM SIGSAC Conference on Computer and Communications Security, pp. 833–850 (2019)
7. Garay, J., Kiayias, A., Leonardos, N.: The bitcoin backbone protocol: analysis and applications. In: Oswald, E., Fischlin, M. (eds.) EUROCRYPT 2015. LNCS, vol. 9057, pp. 281–310. Springer, Heidelberg (2015). https://doi.org/10.1007/978-3-662-46803-6_10
8. Graf, M., Rausch, D., Ronge, V., Egger, C., Küsters, R., Schröder, D.: A security framework for distributed ledgers. In: Proceedings of the 2021 ACM SIGSAC Conference on Computer and Communications Security, pp. 1043–1064 (2021)
9. Guo, J., Wang, Y., An, H., Liu, M., Zhang, Y., Li, C.: IIDQN: an incentive improved DQN algorithm in EBSN recommender system. Secur. Commun. Netw. 2022 (2022)
10. Heilman, E.: One weird trick to stop selfish miners: fresh bitcoins, a solution for the honest miner (poster abstract). In: Böhme, R., Brenner, M., Moore, T., Smith, M. (eds.) FC 2014. LNCS, vol. 8438, pp. 161–162. Springer, Heidelberg (2014). https://doi.org/10.1007/978-3-662-44774-1_12
11. Hou, C., et al.: SquirRL: automating attack analysis on blockchain incentive mechanisms with deep reinforcement learning. arXiv preprint arXiv:1912.01798 (2019)
12. Liu, H., Ruan, N., Du, R., Jia, W.: On the strategy and behavior of bitcoin mining with n-attackers. In: Proceedings of the 2018 on Asia Conference on Computer and Communications Security, pp. 357–368 (2018)
13. Paszke, A., et al.: Pytorch: an imperative style, high-performance deep learning library. In: Advances in neural information processing systems, vol. 32 (2019)
14. Ritz, F., Zugenmaier, A.: The impact of uncle rewards on selfish mining in ethereum. In: 2018 IEEE European Symposium on Security and Privacy Workshops (EuroS&PW), pp. 50–57. IEEE (2018)

15. Saad, M., Anwar, A., Ravi, S., Mohaisen, D.: Revisiting nakamoto consensus in asynchronous networks: a comprehensive analysis of bitcoin safety and chainquality. In: Proceedings of the 2021 ACM SIGSAC Conference on Computer and Communications Security, pp. 988–1005 (2021)
16. Saad, M., Chen, S., Mohaisen, D.: Syncattack: double-spending in bitcoin without mining power. In: 2021 ACM SIGSAC Conference on Computer and Communications Security, pp. 1668–1685 (2021)
17. Saad, M., Njilla, L., Kamhoua, C., Mohaisen, A.: Countering selfish mining in blockchains. In: 2019 International Conference on Computing, Networking and Communications (ICNC), pp. 360–364. IEEE (2019)
18. Sapirshtein, A., Sompolinsky, Y., Zohar, A.: Optimal selfish mining strategies in bitcoin. In: Grossklags, J., Preneel, B. (eds.) FC 2016. LNCS, vol. 9603, pp. 515–532. Springer, Heidelberg (2017). https://doi.org/10.1007/978-3-662-54970-4_30
19. Solat, S., Potop-Butucaru, M.: Brief announcement: ZeroBlock: timestamp-free prevention of block-withholding attack in bitcoin. In: Spirakis, P., Tsigas, P. (eds.) SSS 2017. LNCS, vol. 10616, pp. 356–360. Springer, Cham (2017). https://doi.org/10.1007/978-3-319-69084-1_25
20. Wang, Z., Lv, Q., Lu, Z., Wang, Y., Yue, S.: ForkDec: accurate detection for selfish mining attacks. Secur. Commun. Netw. **2021** (2021)
21. Zhang, M., Li, Y., Li, J., Kong, C., Deng, X.: Insightful mining equilibria. arXiv preprint arXiv:2202.08466 (2022)
22. Zhang, R., Preneel, B.: Publish or perish: a backward-compatible defense against selfish mining in bitcoin. In: Handschuh, H. (ed.) CT-RSA 2017. LNCS, vol. 10159, pp. 277–292. Springer, Cham (2017). https://doi.org/10.1007/978-3-319-52153-4_16

FolketID: A Decentralized Blockchain-Based NemID Alternative Against DDoS Attacks

Wei-Yang Chiu[1] , Weizhi Meng[1(✉)] , Wenjuan Li[2] , and Liming Fang[1]

[1] SPTAGE Lab, DTU Compute, Technical University of Denmark,
Kongens Lyngby, Denmark
weme@dtu.dk
[2] Department of Electronic and Information Engineering,
The Hong Kong Polytechnic University, Hong Kong, China

Abstract. Electronic Identity (eID) is a solution toward solving the identity problem when deploying e-Government. Such solution should not only be secure, but also have to be robust enough under adversarial conditions. In Denmark, NemID is a digital eID used to log into public websites, for online banking and many digital services. However, it suffers from some security threats such as Distributed Denial of Service (DDoS) attack. In 2013, a tremendous DDoS attack over NemID caused chaos in Danish society, people found themselves out-of-reach to many services. Focused on this threat, we develop FolketID, a blockchain-based NemID alternative against DDoS attacks. The DDoS mitigation is achieved by not only utilizing its powerful data distribution ability, but also exploiting the economy system in blockchain. It particularly takes use of the transaction fees to effectively prevent DDoS attacks. In the evaluation, our experimental results demonstrate the viability and effectiveness of FolketID in defeating DDoS attacks.

Keywords: Blockchain technology · DDoS attack · e-Government · Identity management · NemID

1 Introduction

Currently, many organizations are deploying and investing their IT infrastructure, either self-built or outsourced. Such trend is also applied to governments, with the purpose of enhancing the reachability of government services. Thus the term *e-Government* is coined. It has been figured out that e-Government had changed the way of people interacting with the government – it is about building a partnership between governments and citizens [1]. Electronic identity (eID) is an essential solution to solve the identity problem for e-Government. It is a type of digital media, hardware, or proof to display a user's identity when accessing different types of services online [2].

C. Ge and F. Guo (Eds.): ProvSec 2022, LNCS 13600, pp. 210–227, 2022.
https://doi.org/10.1007/978-3-031-20917-8_15

Many governments have their own solutions toward the nationally recognized eID [3]. Different eID systems usually have different functionalities, from as simple as personal identification and service authentication to digital signature and single-sign-on service [4,5]. For instance, Denmark has one capable eID system, named as NemID (or EasyID). NemID has been well-integrated into Danish society, allowing to access most online governmental services in Denmark. NemID is also serving as a secure national single-sign-on service for many private sectors, especially financial services and banks [6].

Motivation. Such system shows the well-integration and cooperation between the government and the private sectors. Though NemID brings an easy-to-use interface for both users and service providers, the robustness of the system has been threatened in practical usage. On 11 April of 2013, NemID suffered from a DDoS attack [11]. The service went down, which caused huge chaos in Danish society. People found themselves unable to access online governmental services and was locked out from accessing their online banking service. Although the company, Nets, who is responsible for developing and maintaining NemID, took instant responses and several countermeasures, which was finally able to make the system up and running within few hours. The incident has woken up some private sectors that integrating their online services with NemID should have an alternative emergency access method when NemID is not reachable [9]. People has started questioning the reliability and the availability of NemID.

According to the Deloitte's report [8], Danish public data systems such as NemID are highly centralized, which have several advantages and disadvantages. The government finds it reachable for collecting data, and citizens find it convenient to use. However, it makes these systems tied up together and difficult to withstand a single point of failure issue. The recently released MitID [10] in Denmark also suffers the same issue due to a similar architecture.

Contributions. To enhance NemID against DDoS attacks, upgrading the IT infrastructure can be a feasible and effective way in a short-term, but it would not solve the issue fundamentally. This is because DDoS attacks have become more complex and higher in traffic volume. In this case, decentralizing the service into different nodes can be a feasible solution, making more rooms on the limited IT infrastructure, and at the same time, ensuring the services would not be brought down due to the issue of single point of failure. Motivated by the recent development of blockchain technology, in this work, we design *FolketID* (The Folk's ID), a blockchain-based NemID alternative against DDoS attacks. Our contributions can be summarized as below.

- Our proposed FolketID can provide similar services as NemID and replace its underlying storage system. It can defeat DDoS attacks by creating an ecology of usage allowance in blockchain.
- In the evaluation, we test the system performance under flooding attacks, including flooding login requests and flooding data requests, in addition to a malicious service point. The experimental results demonstrate the viability and the effectiveness of FolketID.

It is worth noting that in our FolketID, the local session management and the access control management are similar to the NemID system, which are not the focus in our design and discussion scope.

Paper Organization. In Sect. 2, we briefly introduce the background on NemID, and present related work on decentralized services and DDoS attacks. Section 3 details the design of our proposed FolketID system. Section 4 evaluates the system performance under DDoS attacks and malicious eID service point. Finally, we discuss the open challenges and limitations in Sect. 5, and conclude our work in Sect. 6.

2   Background and Related Work

2.1   NemID - The Danish eID

NemID, which is now in transition to a more secure and easy-to-use system of MitID [10], is an eID system where each Danish citizen can obtain from governmental offices and banks in Denmark. The binding between the NemID and the CPR Number (the Danish social security number), is presumably done manually, since such operation requires to have a personal appointment [7]. Different from issuing a digital certificate that is bound with media token (e.g., chip card), the operation requires users to provide their preferred username as login credential. Temporary password will be issued in the first time, but users can change it later after logging into the system successfully.

Users, who have applied for NemID successfully, will receive a code card that contains a series of code pairs, consisting of a 4-digit challenge and a corresponding 6-digit answer, as shown in Fig. 1(b). When using NemID to log into a service, the system will challenge users with one of the 4-digit challenges listed on the code card. Users have to search the correct answer and input to the system, as shown in Fig. 1(a). If a code pair has been used successfully, it will never be reused. If the NemID system notices any users are close to running out of code pairs, it will notify the authority to send a new code card.

This is how NemID represents itself to most users. Meanwhile, some smart methods of authentication are provided, such as using a NemID smartphone client or a NemID CodeFile. From the users' perspective, NemID works differently from other eID systems, which may require a chip card or any form of token media. According to Digitaliseringsstyrelsen [22], NemID is based on public key infrastructure. The only difference is that the users' private keys are all managed centralized [23], unlike other solutions in which private keys are on the full responsibility of the users, which are stored on different media.

However, if the central server that manages the private keys is compromised, the whole system can collapse instantly. A report from Deloitte [8] has already pointed out that many public government information-services in Denmark are under such risks, since many of them are highly centralized. This motivates our work towards the design of a decentralized solution.

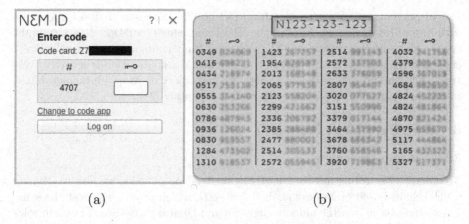

Fig. 1. (a) NemID challenge (b) Code card

2.2 Related Work

Blockchain technology has been applied in many domains, such as data management [12,15], intrusion detection [17] and smart city [13,14]. In the literature, using blockchain to mitigate DDoS attacks is not new (e.g., blockchain-based DDoS defence [18–20]), it is usually applied on network infrastructures rather than services. Generally, blockchain is a decentralized datastore that utilizes a consensus algorithm to ensure every participant following the agreed version of the chain, which provides the characteristics of "immutable once-write available-everywhere". Smart contract further provides the ability to construct complex data structures with permission control. Thus, the combination of these two has become an important solution for network infrastructures to share strategies and security policies [24].

For example, placing SDN strategy, such as flow information, onto the chain for every SDN-enabled switch to follow. Assume putting it into a large telecom operator that has many switches around nation – once the strategy has been deployed, all switches can all dump the malicious data flow together, which can effectively suppress unwanted traffic flows. Another case is to utilize blockchain to prevent cyber-attacks in smart grid, by allowing all entities to have the data, without the hassle and blockage during the communication [25].

However, what we have to notice is that these services rely more on "reading data" more than "writing data". For SDN, it is usually the controller that has to do the rule writing, in which most of the network participants only retrieve data. Blockchain is known for its reputation on writing bandwidth, hence we may find that blockchain has kind of ability to defeat DDoS attacks, especially on data retrieving. While performing a DDoS attack on blockchain network to prevent others from data retrieving, the attacker can only flood every known participant, which is impossible in many cases. If such applications require constant data writing, blockchain might perform worse than other known solutions when defending against DDoS attacks. However, it does not mean there are no way of preventing – for example, Javaid *et al.* [26] proposed that since a transaction requires one's own fund in the Ethereum wallet, a DDoS attacker might use up all the fund eventually. Thus, the gas-limit configuration can effectively control transactions that require over it – hence, if a transaction is severely oversized than the normal packet, the network can reject it. More blockchain-based solutions against DDoS attacks can refer to a survey [21].

3   Our Proposed FolketID

3.1   System Overview

To enhance the robustness of NemID against DDoS attacks, we aim to develop a blockchain-based eID system called *FolketID*, which provides almost the same functionalities as NemID: namely, Sign-On and Digital Signature. The main roles are defined as follows.

- FolketID: This is the main entity of the whole system, which manages all login sessions and maintains the bounding between entities and identifiers, including a list of registered accounts.
- Service Providers: These are entities that help implement FolketID as the login solution for end users.
- End Users: These are users who use FolketID to log into demanded governmental services.

Each role holds its own keypair. Figure 2 shows the system overview of FolketID, including data entities.

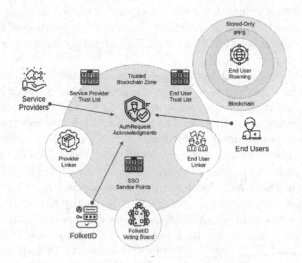

Fig. 2. System and entity overview of FolketID

Overall, there are three main entities, two sub-entities, and one special smart contract.

- eID Service Point: The data entity is a hash map that takes an entity's address as input, and the query result as output. If the query address is a properly registered eID service point, it will return true; otherwise false.
- Service Provider Trust List: It shares the same design as above. If the query address is a properly registered Service Provider, it will return true; otherwise false.
- End User Trust List: It shares the same design as above. If the query address is a properly registered End User, it will return true; otherwise false.
- Provider Linker: This is one sub-entity with the capability to authenticate whether the corresponding identifier is relevant to the claimed entity. Hence, the user should be prompt to input both the CVR (Danish equivalent of VAT Number) and blockchain wallet address. If the bounding between the identifier and the entity exists, it will return true; otherwise false.
- End User Linker: This is one sub-entity that shares a similar design and application as the Provider Linker. Thus, the user should input both CPR (Danish equivalent of Social Security Number) and blockchain wallet address. If the bounding pair exists, it will return true; otherwise false.
- eID Service Point Voting Board: This is a special smart contract that forces all eID service points into the involvement of critical decisions. When adding or removing an existing eID service point, at least 3/4 of all the eID service points must be acknowledged. Otherwise, the action will never be taken. This is to prevent any tampered eID service points from having the power to manipulate the whole system.

Parties that belong to the service provider group do not have extra data entities, except for their own key pair. The followings are the secret information that will be maintained by users.

- Username and Password: It contains an AES key to encrypt the IPFS location [16] toward the user's private key.
- PIN: A password that encrypts the user's private key.
- The End User Roaming Profile: The main disadvantage of utilizing blockchain technology is that all users must be able to keep a copy of their private key on the device in which they would like to use to access the blockchain-based services. It may become an issue when it comes to portability. To make it similar to a traditional NemID login, we put the encrypted IPFS location-information toward the private key onto the blockchain, while the encrypted private key is floated on IPFS, as shown in Fig. 3.

Finally, the data entity can involve three parties such as end user, service provider, and eID service point:

- AuthRequest Acknowledgement: This is the data entity that will be initiated by end user first, along with the service provider's wallet address being proposed. The authRequest entity will return a UUID (*Universal Unique Identifier*) as the identifier of such authRequest. Users need to provide this UUID to the service provider. Then service providers will follow the UUID and

User Roaming Profile		
Data Entities	**private** *address* owner	The creator of this roaming profile.
	private *string* encUserAddress	The user's private key location on IPFS, encrypted with user's username and password with AES encryption.

Constructor	(*string* eUA) {
	    owner = msg.sender();
	    encUserAddress = eUA;
	}
		When the smart contract is created, it will set the owner as the message sender (The creator)

Functions	**public** destroy() <u>ownerOnly</u>	Invalidate this user roaming profile.

Modifiers	<u>ownerOnly</u> {
	    require(owner = msg.sender();
	    —'
	}
		To check whether the transaction sender is stated in the owner. If the sender is not the same as owner, it will terminate the function.

Fig. 3. Data entity of user roaming profile

check whether the user's wallet address is properly registered in FolketID. If the user is properly registered, the service provider will provide session information encrypted with the user's public key, alongside with its signature. The eID service point acknowledges the existence of **authRequest**, and checks the address of both parties and the signature provided by the service provider. If these data attributes are normal, the eID service point will formally acknowledge it. Finally, the user will grab all the information, verify and accept the session. During the transaction, if any anomalies are found, the **authRequest** will be left incomplete and terminated early.

Data Encryption. As every verified participant can have a partial or full copy of the chain, data encryption is required in FolketID if we would like to ensure that a piece of data can be solely accessed by particular users. At this stage, similar to NemID, our FolketID also uses asymmetric cryptography as our encryption and decryption solution. However, we still have to build a mechanism that is close to a Public Key Infrastructure (PKI); otherwise, we may lose the capability of differentiating the outsider and the legitimate user, turning the system from convergence to divergence.

To address the issue, our FolketID builds up a trust list, which acts like a certification authority and validation authority in PKI. Only the FolketID service point can maintain the data, while the others can only send a query to check whether a user is properly registered. Originally, we plan to implement the trust list as a normal dynamic array. However, it allows everyone to instantly have an overview of all properly registered users in the system, which is not ideal. Instead, we change the implementation from normal array to hash map. Hence in order to have a full view of the hash map, the only way is to dump everything out from the blockchain and piece them up bit by bit. This will greatly increase the cost for attackers.

3.2   Platform Selection

If we allow everyone to serve the network, which means the network may be placed in a dangerous balance - DDoS attackers can slow down the network by sending a tremendous amount of transactions, while at the same time, serving the network to continuously gain quotas. In this case, we should adopt a blockchain system in which only a set of limited members can mine or complete transactions. There are some available options:

- Ethereum with Clique: Clique is a Proof-of-Authority consensus algorithm that works similarly to Byzantine Fault Tolerance (BFT). In such network, only assigned nodes can serve the network. Others, who would like to put a transaction onto the network, must send the transactions to these assigned nodes with transaction fees accordingly.
- Hyperledger Fabric: There are three major roles in the network: *the Client* that sends transactions, *the Peer* that maintains and generates blocks, and *the Orderer* that ensures the broadcast of information. Only the node that has been assigned as Peer can serve the network [27].

However, Hyperledger Fabric does not come with a transaction-fee mechanism like Ethereum does. Anodola *et al.* [28] figured out that it is possible for several clients to flood the Orderer with transaction, which would compromise the availability. *As a result, our FolketID adopts Ethereum with Clique in this work.*

3.3   The DDoS Protection

Different from many existing studies, our main idea against DDoS attacks is based on the transaction fee. As a blockchain network requires every participant to guard its integrity, and relies on the computing resources of miners, who can confirm and pack transactions into block. It is then reasonable for someone to pay fees to the network, who would like to have the transaction completed. That is, the more transactions made, the more fees have to pay. Hence, the wallet will be emptied eventually if a user keeps transacting.

To maintain a quick and responsive system, we utilized Clique as the consensus algorithm for the system. A system that runs Clique requires to have a list of nodes (either pre-defined or later-added under authorization) that are authorized to serve the network. These nodes are named "Sealers". Only them can validate transactions and complete them into blocks within the network. In our system, servers that run the eID service points are selected as sealers, as they are the one that can serve the network, eventually all crypto-coins will be back to their wallet if they do not distribute any of them later. This allows us to create an ecosystem that works the same as the current NemID implementation.

In NemID:

- User is given a code card that contains hundreds of code pairs.

- If any authorization action is performed, one of the code pairs is invalidated, no matter whether the authentication is a success or not.
- User needs to order a new card from NemID to continue using this system.

In ForketID:

- User is given a few amount of currency from eID service point.
- If any authorization action is performed, some of the currency is deducted.
- User needs to request for more currency from the eID service point.

However, there are two important differences that make ForketID more robust than the current NemID:

- *Request for Authorization requires users to deposit their allowance:* Users can still send authorization request to the current NemID system, even are running out of code pairs. Servers still have to handle the request anyway, though nothing can be performed. However, in our ForketID system, an empty allowance makes users not able to go anywhere, because sending request for authorization requires deposit of allowance before it can be sent. Attackers cannot generate any transactions to the network, and servers do not need to handle anything.
- *Easier to detect DDoS attack:* In the current NemID system, if one consumes up their code pairs too fast, we can accurately state that the attacker is abusing one's identity. However, we cannot say that the user is performing a DDoS. However, if one uses up their allowance too fast in ForketID, we can accurately state that the attacker is not only abusing one's identity, but also trying to sabotage the system. In our system, the attack can be stopped through eID authority by not giving further currency to the suspicious account. However, in the NemID system, it is impossible to stop an attack by not giving user the NemID code card.

It is worth nothing that we treat the currency (coins) in our ForketID network only as a token of "Network usage allowance" rather than regarding it as "real money" in the traditional sense of economy. **That is, the money is not real money we can spend in our daily life, but is a kind of usage quotas that users can use the network service.**

On the whole, such design eliminates leachers and attackers out naturally: that is, it makes the currency in the wallet more like usage quotas of this network. If users are using up their currency much faster than a normal user would reach, eID service points can stop the user by refusing the request of giving the user more currency. The attack will eventually die down as soon as the attacking account ran out of money.

3.4   Critical Steps

After understanding how the whole system works, we introduce the main work-flow of several critical steps as follows.

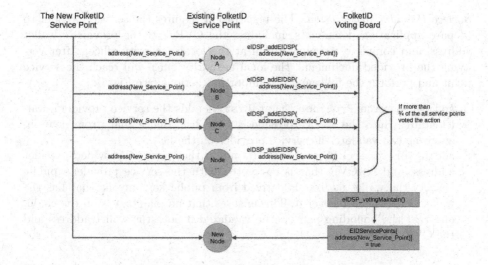

Fig. 4. The workflow of eID service point registration

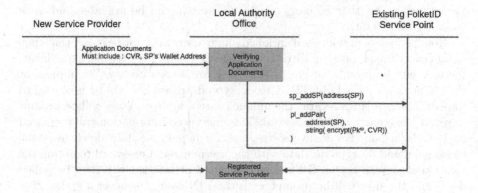

Fig. 5. Workflow of service provider registration

eID Service Point Registration. Fig. 4 describes the additional eID service point registration after the very first eID service point has been registered. This is because the first eID service point in the system will automatically become the eID service point.

It is worth noting that FolketID aims to provide a bockchain-based DDoS resistant scheme over NemID, we thus assume that the eID service points are reachable by authorities. Hence, it is reasonable when a new eID service point is added, most of the IT administrators will be notified. This can ensure that not only all administrators are aware of such event, but also increasing the difficulty for attackers when adding or removing an existing eID service point.

Service Provider Registration. The registration requires the service provider to prepare application documents, including the CVR and the provider's wallet address, and complete the registration at the local authority office. After verifying the provided documents, the local authority office will reach the service point and perform the following two important actions (see Fig. 5):

- `Adding Service Provider Trust List`: It adds the service provider's wallet address into the service provider's trust list. Hence that, from now on, everyone can validate the service provider on the list.
- `Adding Provider Linker List`: It adds the service provider's wallet address, and its CVR that is encrypted with the service provider's public key. As the wallet address is derived from public key, anyone that has the wallet address can recover it. This ensures that no plaintext is on the chain, and that the bounding pair can be validated if both the wallet address and the CVR are on hand.

End User Registration. The registration is very similar to the registration steps of a service provider. However, there is a big difference between them regarding the system usage: that is, users expect the system can be available and work whenever they want.

However, as we previously mentioned, many users may not be aware that they should carry the private key with them. To make the user experience more fluent, the user will be prompt to give a PIN code to the private key. We implement the system with AES-128-CTR. This encrypted private key will be uploaded to the IPFS. When IPFS returns the unique content address, users will be prompt to setup a username and a password. This encrypted information will be placed on the blockchain. For login process, users will pull the data down from the blockchain, and decrypt the data with the username and password to obtain the location of private key on IPFS. The encrypted private key will then be pulled down and the user will be prompt with the PIN code, whenever a transaction requires the private key.

User Session. When a user requires to login to a service provider and obtain its desired services, it has to obtain the public key of the service provider from its frontend. From the public key that is given, the user can then generate the corresponding address of the public key. This needs to consult FolketID, aiming to ensure that such service provider is properly registered.

If the user could not find the corresponding address registered in FolketID, it can terminate the login session at once. If everything is correct, it will acknowledge the service provider what public key the user is taking. The service provider will then turn around and check whether such user is properly registered.

If everything is correct, the service provider will order an empty `authRequest` form, with a set of UUID corresponding to the `authRequest`. This UUID will then be sent back to the end user, which can be utilized in a later phase. Service Provider will start generating session information at the same time. After the session information is generated, the following three parties will be involved:

- **Service Provider**: This party will firstly setup three records: the address of end user that requests `authRequest`, the session information encrypted with the user's public key, and, as verification, the encrypted session data signed with the user's private key.
- **eID Service Point**: This party will check three entities: the address of the involved end user, the address of involved service provider, and the signature provided by the service provider. If both involved addresses are correctly registered in FolketID, the eID service point will use its private key to sign the encrypted user information session, as acknowledgment. Otherwise, the eID service point will refuse to sign – hence `authRequest` will never be completed.
- **End User**: Finally, the end user will pull down two signatures, two addresses, and the encrypted session information. It will check whether both the proposed eID service point and the service provider are registered in FolketID. If nothing goes wrong, it will decrypt the user session information, and provide a copy of such encrypted information with service provider's public key. This allows the service providers to ensure that both sides receive the correct user session information.

4   Evaluation and Results

This section introduces the environmental configurations, and tests our FolketID under several malicious conditions.

4.1   System and Environmental Setup

To investigate the performance of our FolketID, we built up a test-bed using a mobile workstation, with the settings including both hardware and software, as shown in Table 1 and Table 2. In particular, in the evaluation, we configured two eID service points, one service provider, and several end users. Table 3 summarizes the settings for the blockchain network, including chain & network ID, consensus algorithm and initial gas limit.

Table 1. Host computer setup

Hardware		Software	
Item	Config.	Item	Version
CPU	Intel Xeon E-2286M @ 2.4GHz x 8	Hypervisor	Oracle VirtualBox 6.1.32
Memory	128 GB ECC DDR4-2666	Host OS	Fedora 36
Storage	1TB NVMe SSD		

Table 2. Virtual machine settings

VM Resources		Software	
Item	Config.	Item	Version
CPU	Intel Xeon E-2286M @ 2.4GHz x2	Hypervisor	Oracle VirtualBox 6.1.32
Memory	4GB	Guest OS	Ubuntu 22.04 LTS
Storage	32GB	Blockchain Platform	Ethereum 1.10.16
Network	Virtual Network 1G	Contract Platform	Solidity/EVM

Table 3. Private blockchain settings

Blockchain Configuration			
Item	Config.	Item	Version
Chain & Network ID	40000	Initial Difficulties	0×100
Initial Gas Limit	0×8000000	Consensus Algorithm	Clique (BFT-Like/PoA)

4.2 The DDoS Flooding Attack

In 2013, the DDoS attack was made by flooding incredible amount of traffic toward NemID, especially login requests and information queries, which have not been completed afterward. To evaluate the performance of FolketID against DDoS attacks, we considered two types of attacks: the tremendous amount of login requests, and the tremendous amount of information queries.

Flooding Login Requests. To simulate this attack, we started from a small amount of login requests as our goal: that is, 10,000 login requests sent from a set of user accounts. It is quickly found that the end user would not have enough ETH to support further transactions. This is because when users are trying to login, it requires to order both `authRequset` and `UUID` to continue, with an estimated cost around 35,000 gas unit. For the current design, we generously estimated that a user can perform 500 login trials in FolketID every month, and each operation demands around 30,000 gas for end users. In the end, the login flooding attempt from a single node stopped at around 400 trials, which was far from the targeted 10,000 login trials.

Then we increased the number of malicious users to 10, but the transaction counts were still far from 10,000 login trials. When more transactions needed to be completed on the Ethereum network, the gas price gets increased. This means that each transaction becomes more costly than before. We found that the attempt ended up with around 4,200 trials, which were still far from 10,000 login trials. Based on the obtained result, we estimated that, in our condition, there is a need for at least 25 different end-user accounts and used up all their allowance in the wallet to reach 10,000 login trials.

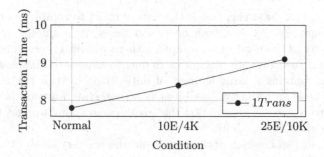

Fig. 6. AuthRequest ordering speed under different conditions

During the NemID DDoS case in 2013, only few persons would cause login attempts greater than 10,000. In the comparison, our FolketID system requires at least 25 different end-users to attack the system at the same time. Figure 6 shows the authRequest ordering speed under different conditions. In a normal authRequest ordering speed, our system can complete the task in around 7.8 ms. When 10 users send 4000 transactions, our system can complete the task in around 8.4 ms. Then when 25 users send 10000 transactions, our system can complete the task in around 9.1 ms. That means normal users will probably not even notice the time difference. The result indicates the effectiveness of our FolketID system against flooding login requests.

Flooding Data Requests. We also performed the flooding data request attack, by sending requests to provide data. However, it does not make sense in a blockchain-based system, as data should be accessed from the local copy of the chain. With more requests sent, it may flood the client to perform more local I/O operation. The network performance remains unaffected.

4.3   Malicious eID Service Point

We further considered a malicious eID service point, which may launch a smart-contract attack to create something that is similar or even copied and deployed from the original source code. Thus the involved party could not tell which one is genuine. The situation is critical for many blockchain-enabled systems: if the participants can be fooled, the integrity of the system can be crumbled.

A malicious eID service point can recreate the system as long as it has the source-code copy of smart contracts. In our proposed FolketID, we have several countermeasures:

– **Protecting the source code of main entities**: People may still argue that this achievement can be reached by decompiling the binary code of the main entity. However, it can slow down the time for cyber-attackers to interpret and recreate a similar system.

- The `Gas Limit Barrier`: Gas is the unit of effort to complete a transaction in Ethereum Blockchain. If an operation takes some amount of computational power of the network to complete, there will be a represented gas unit. In short, if such operation requires frequent changes to the chain, or such operation contains a large amount of data to pack, then the required gas unit will raise accordingly. Gas Limit is a protection function in Ethereum, in order to reject any transaction that requires an amount of gas that would be higher than the gas limit.

  As the contract creation of these main entities are very costly (i.e., 2,319,695 gas units for deploying the maximum entity, in which the cost is about 70–110 times higher than an averaged normal transaction), it is impossible to have one operation that requires such huge amount of gas. As long as the main entity of the system is deployed, an updated configuration file will be distributed to all participants in the network through software update, which can deliberately limit the possibility of recreating the system. This means that even existing a malicious eID service point attempts to re-create another similar system, the other eID service point(s) with updated configuration file will reject to complete the transactions.

- The `Integrity of Client Software`: A hash or signature of the client software must be presented; otherwise, the software will refuse to run. This can ensure that the hard-coded contract addresses in the program would not be changed easily.

5   Discussion and Limitation

Our system is still developed at an early stage, and the DDoS attacks are the main focus. There are still some open challenges that should be addressed in our future work.

- `Scalability`: The scalability of blockchain networks is always the top concern. Unfortunately, due to the resource limitations, our host machine with hypervisor can only handle a maximum of 30 nodes running simultaneously. Under this configuration, two nodes are working as the mining machines of the whole network. The performance remains great, even with another 25 machines that send out a total of 10,000 transactions. This is an important topic in the second stage of our work.

- `Longevity`: The Longevity of the system is another topic that we have not discussed in this work. Currently, blockchain is an append-only data storage. Hence that, the cost of maintaining the system will go higher, with the transactions accumulated. Though both Ethereum and Hyperledger provide options to archive ancient chain data, it does not mean that we can discard the data - it still requires one ancient node to hold the whole chain. To address such issue, we can create a new chain and migrate the active data to the new chain. However, this action can be quite vulnerable, especially many breaches can occur during the process. This is because such kind of node can alter whatever data placed onto the new chain.

– **Protocol Security**: For system implementation, we cannot closely look into how the NemID system works due to the non-disclosure agreement. The most we can do is to imitate the functionality that NemID has. However, NemID is a centralized and web-based system, hence that communications are mostly situated on TCP/IP and mutable storage. It has a tremendous advantage over blockchain: that is, the ability to remove data. When we move to a blockchain-based system – FolketID, we have to closely inspect what kind of data should be on-chain and what should be not. As whatever data on chain is unremovable, it may create a double-sided sword situation - the balance between privacy, security, and data integrity. This is an open challenge and one important topic in our future work.

6 Concluding Remarks

Electronic Identity is an undeniable trend as we are moving forward to a digital era, where government should optimize their services' reachability and usability. Denmark, compared to many other European countries, has a comprehensive eID system called NemID, which has been integrated with almost all citizens' life. However, the NemID was brought down by a DDoS attack in 2013, causing a nation-wide chaos. This is because of its highly centralized IT infrastructure and insufficient reaction plan. In some way, it makes sense that Denmark has a highly centralized IT infrastructure in its governmental network. It provides an easy access for both the government agents and citizens to reach services in one place, but this structure also makes it vulnerable to various attacks.

In this work, we developed FolketID, a blockchain-based NemID alternative by situating the whole NemID service into a decentralized network. To defeat DDoS attacks, we implemented a kind of control where the administrators can assign miners; others who are not assigned cannot mine. We also introduced the system's ecology of usage allowance - if users are not willing to serve the network, they will use up the allowance eventually. This creates a system similar to NemID's code card, and provides a method for system maintainers to notice the issue quickly, especially someone consume their allowance too fast. In the evaluation, we explore the performance of FolketID against DDoS attacks. The experimental results indicated that our system is effective against DDoS attacks, including flooding login requests and flooding data requests. The attackers were instantly stopped, due to the lack of transaction fees to complete a login trial. Also, our FolketID was found to be robust under malicious eID service points.

Acknowledgments. This work was partially supported by H2020 CyberSec4Europe and H2020 DataVaults.

References

1. Silcock, R.: What is e-Government. Parliam. Aff. **54**(1), 88–101 (2001)
2. Arora, S.: National e-ID card schemes: a European overview. Inf. Secur. Tech. Rep. **13**, 46–53 (2008)
3. National IDs Around the World – Interactive map — World Privacy Forum. https://www.worldprivacyforum.org/2021/10/national-ids-and-biometrics/
4. Gronlund, A.: Electronic identity management in Sweden: governance of a market approach. Identity Inf. Soc. **3**, 195–211 (2010). https://doi.org/10.1007/s12394-010-0043-1
5. Rissanen, T.: Electronic identity in Finland: ID cards vs. bank IDs. Identity Inf. Soc. **3**, 175–194 (2010). https://doi.org/10.1007/s12394-010-0049-8
6. National Identity and Signing. https://en.digst.dk/digitisation/eid
7. NemID.   https://lifeindenmark.borger.dk/apps-and-digital-services/nemid. Accessed 1 Apr 2022
8. The future market for cybersecurity in Denmark. https://innovationsfonden.dk/sites/default/files/2018-07/thefuturemarketforcybersecurityindenmark.pdf. Accessed 15 Apr 2022)
9. UPDATE: NemID system running again following attack. https://wikimili.com/en/NemID. Accessed 1 May 2022
10. MitID: A stronger and safer digital Denmark. https://penneo.com/blog/nemid-to-mitid/. Accessed 18 Apr 2022
11. DDoS attack on NemID costs 4 months probation. https://www.version2.dk/artikel/ddos-angreb-mod-nemid-koster-4-maaneders-betinget-faengsel. Accessed 1 May 2022
12. Chiu, W.Y., Meng, W., Jensen, C.D.: My data, my control: a secure data sharing and access scheme over blockchain. J. Inf. Secur. Appl. **63**, 103020 (2021)
13. Chiu, W.Y., Meng, W.: EdgeTC - A PBFT blockchain-based ETC scheme for smart cities. Peer-to-Peer Netw. Appl. **14**, 2874–2886 (2021). https://doi.org/10.1007/s12083-021-01119-0
14. Chiu, W.Y., Meng, W.: Towards decentralized bicycle insurance system based on blockchain. The 36th ACM/SIGAPP Symposium on Applied Computing (ACM SAC), pp. 249–256 (2021)
15. Chiu, W.-Y., Meng, W., Jensen, C.D.: NoPKI - a point-to-point trusted third party service based on blockchain consensus algorithm. In: Xu, G., Liang, K., Su, C. (eds.) FCS 2020. CCIS, vol. 1286, pp. 197–214. Springer, Singapore (2020). https://doi.org/10.1007/978-981-15-9739-8_16
16. IPFS Powers the Distributed Web. https://ipfs.io/
17. Meng, W., Li, W., Zhou, J.: Enhancing the security of blockchain-based software defined networking through trust-based traffic fusion and filtration. Inf. Fusion **70**, 60–71 (2021)
18. Houda, Z.A.E., Hafid, A., Khoukhi, L.: Co-IoT: a Collaborative DDoS Mitigation Scheme in IoT environment based on blockchain using SDN. In: Proceedings of GLOBECOM, pp. 1–6 (2019)
19. Rodrigues, B., Stiller, B.: The cooperative DDoS signaling based on a blockchain-based system. In: Proceedings of IM, pp. 760–765 (2021)
20. Guo, W., Xu, J., Pei, Y., Yin, L., Jiang, C.: LDBT: a lightweight DDoS attack tracing scheme based on blockchain. In: Proceedings of ICC Workshops, pp. 1–6 (2021)

21. Shah, Z., Ullah, I., Li, H., Levula, A., Khurshid, K.: Blockchain based solutions to mitigate distributed denial of service (DDoS) attacks in the internet of things (IoT): a survey. Sensors **22**(3), 1094 (2022)

22. Teknologien Bag NemID. https://digst.dk/it-loesninger/nemid/om-loesningen/teknik/. Accessed 1 Apr 2022

23. Sikkerheden Bag NemID. https://digst.dk/it-loesninger/nemid/om-loesningen/sikkerheden-bag-nemid/. Accessed 2 Apr 2022

24. Wani, S., Imthiyas, M., Almohamedh, H., Alhamed, K., Almotairi, S., Gulzar, Y.: Distributed denial of service (DDoS) mitigation using blockchain - a comprehensive insight. Symmetry **13**(2), 227 (2021)

25. Singh, K., Choube, S.: Using blockchain against cyber attacks on smart grids. In: Proceedings of SCEECS, pp. 1–8 (2018)

26. Javaid, U., Siang, A., Aman, M:, Sikdar, B.: Mitigating IoT device based DDoS attacks using blockchain Cry'Block 2018. In: Proceedings of Cryptocurrencies and Blockchains for Distributed Systems, pp. 71–76 (2018)

27. Peers - Hyperledger-Fabricdosc Mater Documentation. https://hyperledger-fabric.readthedocs.io/en/release-2.2/peers/peers.html. Accessed 22 Apr 2022

28. Andola, N., Manas Gogoi, R., Venkatesan, S., Verman, S.: Vulnerabilities on hyperledger fabric. Pervasive Mob. Comput. **59** (2019)

Secure Collaboration Between Consortiums in Permissioned Blockchains

Juzheng Huang[1], Qiang Tang[2], Chunhua Su[3], and Na Ruan[1]($\boxtimes$)

[1] Shanghai Jiaotong University, Shanghai, China
ctoast@sjtu.edu.cn, naruan@cs.sjtu.edu.cn
[2] The University of Sydney, Sydney, Australia
qiang.tang@sydney.edu.au
[3] University of Aizu, Aizuwakamatsu, Japan
chsu@u-aizu.ac.jp

Abstract. Secure collaboration between consortiums is imperative for the distributed applications deployed on distinct permissioned blockchains or consortium blockchains to provide superior services. The collaboration can be realized by cross-chain transactions processed by cross-chain protocol. The previous two-phase commit and two-phase locking cross-chain protocol are unable to be applied in the scenario where the consortium can be malicious. In this work, we propose the ledger framework of the multiple consortium blockchain systems including the global cross-chain ledger. The cross-chain ledger establishes the order relationship between cross-chain sub-transactions defined in the cross-chain protocol and adopts the hierarchical Byzantine fault-tolerant consensus to tolerate malicious consortiums. We also give two instances of the framework. Based on the cross-chain ledger, we propose the revoke operation in the two-phase commit and two-phase locking cross-chain protocol. We also make the protocol secure in the presence of malicious consortiums and prove its security. Finally, we conduct comprehensive experiments to characterize the performance of the two instances and the cross-chain protocol. The experimental results reveal the efficiency of our scheme even in the presence of malicious consortiums.

Keywords: Permissioned blockchain · Cross-chain transaction · Protocol

1 Introduction

Permissioned blockchain or consortium blockchain is the blockchain system maintained by authorized nodes and characterized by high performance and confidentiality [13]. It is the resilient system that provides data processing in the presence of byzantine behaviors [9]. Permissioned blockchain turns out to be the best fit for distributed applications to solve trust issues.

To further extend the application in permissioned blockchain, the collaboration between consortiums is essential. Application is usually on their blockchain maintained by a consortium for the sake of performance and confidentiality. The superior service [3] requires interoperability between applications. Consortia that maintain distinct distributed applications need to collaborate by cross-chain transactions [3] to provide interoperability.

The existing cross-chain solution has difficulty being directly applied in multiple consortium blockchains systems where consortium can be malicious. The solutions from permissionless blockchain [8,10] are usually designed for asset transfer and are not general enough. Some previous work in permissioned blockchain or sharding systems support cross-chain transactions but have difficulty dealing with contention [3,9] or depend on specifics data model [2]. The most promising solution is using the two-phase commit(2PC) and two-phase locking(2PL) protocol [7,9], which can be applied in any data model. But the protocol requires that each blockchain is maintained by a pre-determined fault-tolerant cluster.

We find that the assumption that all consortiums are fault-tolerant is difficult to hold in some applications of consortium blockchain. An example is the use case of the supply chain [3]. It involves five consortiums: supplier, manufacturer, buyer, carrier, and middleman. Each consortium internally uses blockchain to handle the internal transaction but they also need to collaborate with other consortiums by the cross-chain transaction. In such a scenario, a conflict of interest exists between these consortiums. They are adversarial to each other and we can not simply assume that they will always behave honestly.

Some additional mechanisms should be in combination with the original two-phase commit and two-phase locking cross-chain protocol to enhance its security in the presence of a malicious consortium. It faces the challenge that the solution should be general enough so that it can be instantiated to satisfy the need of distributed applications with different data models and consensus requirements. And the security of the solution should be proven.

In this work, we propose a solution that uses the global cross-chain ledger to enhance the security of the two-phase commit and two-phase locking cross-chain protocol. We first introduce a ledger framework for multiple consortium blockchain systems. We show that our framework is general and give two instances of our framework. The first one is instantiated to the solution of CAPER [3]. The second one uses the directed acyclic graph to improve performance. Then, based on the ledger framework, we make the two-phase commit and two-phase locking cross-chain protocol support revoke operation and can work in the presence of malicious consortiums. Our contributions to this work are listed as follows:

- We introduce the ledger framework of the multiple consortium blockchain systems including the global cross-chain ledger. The cross-chain ledger can establish order relationships of cross-chain sub-transactions and tolerate the existence of malicious consortiums. We instantiate the framework with two instances.

- Based on the framework, we enhance the security of traditional two-phase commit and two-phase locking cross-chain protocol. We prove that the protocol is secure even in the presence of malicious consortiums.
- We conduct comprehensive experiments to characterize the performance of the two instances and the cross-chain protocol.

2   Background

2.1   Two-Phase Commit Cross-Chain Protocol

The two-phase commit and two-phase locking cross-chain protocol, which we abbreviate as the two-phase commit cross-chain protocol in this work, is discussed in previous work and proved to be the correct and general cross-chain protocol [2,7,9]. There exists a coordinator which is usually also a fault-tolerant consortium in the system to coordinate the transaction processing. The whole process can be generally summarized as follow: the coordinator first sends the prepare message including the cross-chain transaction to all concerned consortiums. Each concerned consortium reaches a consensus on whether to vote commit for the transaction, acquire the locks, and send the result to the coordinator. If the coordinator finds that all concerned consortiums vote commit for the transaction, it sends the commit message to the concerned consortium to finalize the transaction. Otherwise, it sends the abort message to abort the transaction.

The original two-phase commit cross-chain protocol is no longer secure where the participant may behave maliciously. For example, the coordinator in the protocol can send conflicted cross-chain messages to different consortiums.

2.2   Consensus Protocol

In this section, we give brief introductions to the PBFT consensus and hashgraph consensus used in our system.

PBFT is the traditional consensus algorithm used in many consortium blockchain systems. Informally, to reach a consensus, the leader first broadcasts the pre-prepare message. Upon receiving the pre-prepare message, the node broadcasts prepare the message. Upon receiving a matching prepare messages from more than two-thirds of the nodes, the node broadcast the commit message. Upon receiving matching commit messages from more than two-thirds of the nodes, the consensus is reached.

Hashgraph [5] is a directed acyclic graph based blockchain consensus. In the hashgraph, each event (i.e. block) has two hash references. The references point to the last event on the node's chain and also point to the event from the synchronized neighbor chain [5].

The hashgraph uses complex virtual voting to achieve consensus. We give an intuitive introduction here. Event Y can be seen by the other event X if there is a directed reference path from X to Y. When there are paths from X to Y passing through more than two-thirds of members, it is defined that X can *strongly see*

Y. The relationship of strongly seeing can be considered as virtual voting. Then the event can be committed by going through the three-stage voting procedure like the traditional BFT consensus.

3 Ledger Framework

In this section, we first introduce the model definition of our scheme. Then we give the ledger framework of multiple consortium blockchain systems including a global cross-chain ledger. Finally, we give two instances and discuss safety and liveness.

3.1 System Model and Security Definition

In our system model, there exist multiple consortiums $C = \{C_1, C_2...C_n\}$. Each consortium contain a set of nodes $C_i = \{n_1^i, n_2^i...\}$. The consortiums are disjoint sets, meaning $C_i \cap C_j = \emptyset$ where $i \neq j$. Each consortium C_i maintains a blockchain ledger L_i independently and a global cross-chain ledger L_g. For simplicity and without loss of generality, we assume each block consists of a single transaction and do not distinguish the concept of block and transaction. And we assume that the order of transactions in the ledger is captured by the sequence number.

The node n^i in C_i can directly read the state of ledger L_i. However, to obtain information about other ledgers, nodes need to communicate with other consortiums that maintain the ledger. In our system, the nodes initiate cluster-sending protocols that are defined in Byshard [9] to finish such a communication process. Informally, the cluster-sending protocol rules that when consortium C_i sends messages to consortium C_j, the nodes in consortium C_i reach consensus on the message they send, and the nodes in consortium C_j receive $f + 1$ matching message if there are f malicious nodes in consortium C_i.

In our model, we define two levels of behavior. The first level is the node level. A node can be honest or malicious. The malicious node behaves arbitrarily to prevent the agreement within its consortium while the honest node strictly obeys its consensus protocol to reach the agreement within the consortium. We assume that each consortium C_i has at most $\lfloor \frac{|C_i|-1}{3} \rfloor$ malicious nodes. That is, let security assumption A_i for C_i become $|C_i| \geq 3f_i + 1$ where f_i is the number of byzantine nodes in C_i. Then $\forall C_i \in C, A_i$ for C_i is satisfied.

The second level is the consortium level. In our model, we assume that the consortiums have conflicts of interest during cooperation and do not trust each other. The consortium may reach an agreement internally to cheat the other consortiums by cluster-sending. Therefore we distinguish the behavior of malicious consortium and honest consortium. The malicious consortium behaves arbitrarily to prevent the agreement among the consortiums(e.g. whether to commit the cross-chain transaction). The honest consortium strictly obeys the protocols and rules defined in the system to reach an agreement among the consortiums. We assume that there are at most $\lfloor \frac{|C|-1}{3} \rfloor$ malicious consortiums. That is, let security A_g become $|C| \geq 3|C_f| + 1$ where $C_f = \{C_i|C_i \in C, C_i \text{ is malicious.}\}$. Then A_g is satisfied.

Note that the two levels of behavior are totally independent. It means that even if all the nodes are honest, the consortium may still reach the agreement to behave maliciously [3].

The nodes in the blockchain system reach an agreement on the decision or sequence by the consensus algorithm. According to the definition of safety and liveness in [1,9], we give the following security definition for a consensus algorithm.

Definition 1 *(Security of consensus algorithm.) The consensus algorithm is secure if the properties of safety and liveness are satisfied.*

- *Safety. The honest nodes in the honest consortium running the consensus algorithm agree on the transactions and their order in the ledgers.*
- *Liveness. The transaction proposed by the honest nodes in the honest consortium running the consensus algorithm will eventually be ordered in ledgers.*

The transactions in the model are of two types: internal or cross-chain. The internal transaction only accesses the state of one ledger and can be directly executed by the consortium it belongs to. The cross-chain transaction accesses the state of multiple ledgers.

For simplicity and without loss of generality, We assume that the cross-chain transaction is divided into several cross-chain sub-transactions executing the operations defined in the cross-chain protocol(e.g. vote, commit, abort operation in two-phase commit cross-chain protocol). And the cross-chain protocol is also responsible to orchestrate and execute these cross-chain sub-transaction [9].

3.2   Description of the Framework

We expect the framework to support both internal transactions and cross-chain transactions. The ledger in the framework should provide the following properties: (1)It should order the transactions that are initiated by a consortium including the internal transactions and cross-chain sub-transactions. (2)It should order all the cross-chain sub-transactions.

The second property is necessary so that the node can execute the cross-chain sub-transaction one by one and deterministically know whether to commit or abort the cross-chain transaction by predefined protocol. It is essential, especially in the case where a malicious consortium may send wrong or conflicted sub-transactions to confuse the other consortium.

In the framework, each consortium C_i is supposed to maintain its ledger L_i and the global cross-chain ledger L_g. Figure 1 shows the logical relationship between ledgers in the framework. The white block represents the internal transaction. The grey block represents the cross-chain sub-transaction. All the internal transactions and cross-chain sub-transactions proposed by consortium C_i are sequenced in L_i to establish an order relationship. Besides all the cross-chain sub-transactions are also sequenced in L_g to establish an order relationship.

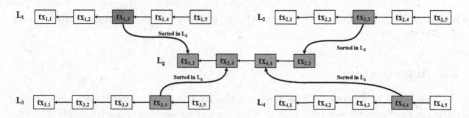

Fig. 1. The logical ledgers in the framework. $tx_{i,j}$ represents the jth transaction proposed by consortium C_i. The white block represents the internal transaction while the grey one is the cross-chain sub-transaction.

The nodes agree on the ledger state by the consensus algorithm. We consider the consensus algorithm as the black box denoted as BFT to sequence the transactions. We denote the consensus algorithm for L_i as BFT_i and the consensus algorithm for L_g as BFT_g. The BFT_i is supposed to output the transaction tx and its sequence number h_i in L_i. The BFT_g is supposed to output the transaction tx and its sequence number h_g in L_g. The implementation of BFT run by node r provides the local transactions set $BFT.\bar{b}_r$, the primitive procedure $BFT.input(b)$ and notification $BFT.output()$ [6]. The nodes adopt the Algorithm 1 to process transactions.

Algorithm 1. Processing transaction

1: r←the node that initiates the algorithms
2: i←the index of the consortium that the node belongs to

3: **upon** received $< REQ, tx >$ **then**
4:     **if** should be sequenced in L_i **then**
5:         $BFT_i.input(< BFT_i.\bar{b}_r, tx >)$
6:     **if** should be sequenced in L_g **then**
7:         $BFT_g.input(< BFT_g.\bar{b}_r, tx >)$

8: **upon** $BFT_i.output()$ **then**
9:     tx, h_i ←newly committed transaction and its sequence number from $BFT_i.\bar{b}_r$
10:     $L_i \leftarrow$ update ledger with tx, h_i

11: **upon** $BFT_g.output()$ **then**
12:     tx, h_g ←newly committed transaction and its sequence number from $BFT_i.\bar{b}_r$
13:     $L_g \leftarrow$ update ledger with tx, h_g

As shown in Algorithm 1, Upon the receipt of the transaction, the node decides whether to sequence it on L_i or L_g. The decision rules are defined by the concrete collaboration protocol or cross-chain protocol. If the transaction should be sequenced, the node passes the transaction to the input of BFT. Upon the output of BFT, the node obtains the committed transaction and its sequence number. Then it appends the transaction according to its sequence number into the ledger.

3.3 Instantiation

We give two instances of the framework. In these two instances, we assume each consortium C_i uses PBFT as its internal consensus algorithm BFT_i. The different part between the instances is L_g and BFT_g.

Instance 1. The direct implementation is to use an independent L_g maintains by all consortiums to store cross-chain sub-transactions. The first one of the instances comes from this direct implementation but merges the L_g into the consortium's own ledger, which actually is the solution of CAPER [3]. Under such a ledger, it is possible to use BFT_g to obtain both the sequence number of transactions in L_i and L_g and it ensures the data integration.

As shown in Fig. 2(a), the internal transaction is the white block and the cross-chain sub-transaction is the grey one. Each consortium C_i maintains a blockchain ledger L_i that chains cross-chain sub-transactions and internal transactions proposed by C_i. All the cross-chain sub-transactions proposed by different consortiums also chain together to form the L_g.

The node initiates the PBFT to reach an agreement on the order of internal transactions. For cross-chain sub-transaction, the node assigns its sequence number in L_i and in L_g and then initiated the BFT_g to reach agreement on the order of cross-chain sub-transaction in L_i and L_g simultaneously. The BFT_g is the hierarchical PBFT consensus in CAPER [3]. The detail of this hierarchical consensus and the proof of its safety and liveness are introduced in CAPER [3]. Intuitively it is the PBFT algorithm on the consortium level which considers each consortium as the node in the original algorithm.

Instance 2. We also give another instance that uses directed acyclic graph based blockchain technology. It is based on the hashgraph consensus algorithm [5]. In this instance, we instantiate the L_g as hashgraph and BFT_g as hierarchical hashgraph consensus algorithm.

As shown in Fig. 2(b), each consortium C_i maintain a blockchain ledger L_i chaining internal transactions and cross-chain sub-transactions proposed by C_i. All the cross-chain sub-transactions form a hashgraph-style ledger. The node initiates the PBFT to reach an agreement on the order of internal transactions. The order of transactions in L_g is established by BFT_g, which we present in Algorithm 2.

Intuitively it is the hashgraph algorithm on the consortium level. Here in Algorithm 1, we use the interface provided by the BFT model introduced before.

In Algorithm 1, the node frequently receives the sync message from other consortiums by cluster-sending. Upon receiving sync messages, the node updates $BFT_g.\bar{b}_r$ which is in the form of hashgraph. Then the leader node picks a new transaction tx from input. It also find two reference H_{C_1} and H_{C_2} to reference

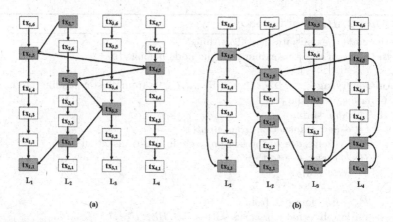

Fig. 2. Two kinds of instances of ledger. $tx_{i,j}$ represents the jth transaction proposed by consortium C_i. The white block represents the internal transaction while the grey one is the cross-chain sub-transaction. The arrow represents the order relationship between transactions like the hash pointer.

its previous cross-chain sub-transaction and reference the tx in sync messages. Then the node assigns the timestamp and randomly chooses a consortium. It initiate the internal consensus BFT_i within its consortium to reach agreement on $< tx', H_{C_1}, H_{C_2}, t, c_{from}, c_{to} >$. Upon the agreement is reached, the node append the tx' into the $BFT_g.\bar{b}_r$. It then determines the committed transactions in $\bar{b}_r$ by the reference relationship according to the hashgraph virtual voting. Then the node sends the notification for the committed transaction. Finally, it syncs with the C_{to} by cluster-sending.

We then proof the safety and liveness of the hashgraph based BFT_g.

Theorem 1. *The BFT_g of instance 2 achieves safety and liveness when A_g is satisfied.*

Proof. The consortium C_i reaches agreement on the sync message by its internal consensus BFT_i and then sends it by cluster-sending. If C_i is an honest consortium that obeys the consensus protocol, it will always send the correct sync message to other consortiums because of the safety and liveness of BFT_i. According to assumption A_g, the number of malicious consortiums that may send incorrect sync messages is at most $\lfloor \frac{|C|-1}{3} \rfloor$. By the safety and liveness of the hashgraph algorithm, the BFT_g of instance 2 achieves safety and liveness.

Instance 2 attempts to solve the problem of high network complexity faced by instance 1. The network complexity of instance 1 is rather high, especially in our scenario where cluster-sending protocol brings extra network communication. It performs poorly to handle a large amount of cross-chain transactions as shown in our later experiment. Therefore, we introduce directed acyclic graph based blockchain technology to reduce network burden and allow multiple consortiums to process cross-chain sub-transaction in parallel. We choose hashgraph because

Algorithm 2. BFT_g of Instance 2

1: r←the node that initiates the algorithms
2: i←the index of the consortium that the node belongs to

3: **upon receiving** $< tx, H_{C_1}, H_{C_2}, t, C_{from}, C_{to} >$ from cluster-sending **then**
4:    update $\bar{b}_r$ with the tx
5:    **if** $isLeader$ **then**
6:       $tx\prime$ ←new transaction from input()
7:       H_{C_1} ←reference to the last cross-chain sub-transaction
8:       H_{C_2} ←reference to the tx
9:       $t \leftarrow timestamp$
10:      $C_{from} \leftarrow C_i$
11:      C_{to} ←random one from C
12:      initiate internal consensus with $< tx\prime, H_{C_1}, H_{C_2}, t, C_{from}, C_{to} >$

13: **upon achieving** internal agreement on $< tx, H_{C_1}, H_{C_2}, t, C_{from}, C_{to} >$ **then**
14:    update $BFT_g.\bar{b}_r$ with the tx
15:    determine the committed transactions in $\bar{b}_r$.
16:    call output() to send notification
17:    multicast $< tx\prime, H_{C_1}, H_{C_2}, t, C_{from}, C_{to} >$ to C_{to} by cluster-sending

---

its parallel typologies [15] is suitable for multiple consortium blockchain systems and it has prove [5] for its security.

4   Secure Cross-Chain Protocol

In this section, We first give the description of our secure cross-chain protocol built on top of our ledger framework. We show that the protocol is derived from the two-phase commit cross-chain protocol but it is more secure and supports revocation. Then we prove its security and correctness.

4.1   Protocol Description

We adopt the cross-chain transaction model introduced in [9] to make our protocol support any data model in the blockchain. The cross-chain transaction τ can be expressed like $\tau = (Con^\tau, Mod^\tau)$ where Con^τ is the set of constraints. Mod^τ is set of modifications. $Con^\tau(L_i)$ is to denote the constraints of τ in ledger L_i. $Mod^\tau(L_i)$ is to denote the constraints of τ in ledger L_i. Then we have $Con^\tau = Con^\tau(L_1) \cup Con^\tau(L_2) \cup ... \cup Con^\tau(L_n)$ and $Mod^\tau = Mod^\tau(L_1) \cup Mod^\tau(L_2) \cup ... \cup Mod^\tau(L_n)$. And it is obvious that $Con^\tau(L_i) \cap Con^\tau(L_j) = \emptyset$ and $Mod^\tau(L_i) \cap Mod^\tau(L_j) = \emptyset$ where $i\prime = j$. Therefore, the execution of a cross-chain transaction can be divided into several steps that are independently done on corresponding ledgers to check constraints and modify the state.

Our protocol provides vote-step, commit-step, and abort-step like the traditional two-phase commit and two-phase locking protocol. We adopt the definition of these steps in [9] with lock-based execution to give a general protocol. And we also give the definition of revoke-step additionally provided by our protocol:

- **Vote-step** Vote-step verifies the constraints of transactions τ and yield commit vote $Vot_{c,\tau,L}$ or abort vote $Vot_{a,\tau,L}$. If the vote commits, the step makes a local change like modifying local data and acquiring locks in ledger L. If the vote aborts, nothing will happen to the ledger state.
- **Commit-step** Commit-step $Com_{\tau,S}$ finalize τ when it is committed. The operations in the step include modifying data and releasing locks obtained during a preceding vote-step in ledger L.
- **Abort-step** Abort-step $Abo_{tx,S}$ roll back τ when it is aborted. The operations in the step include rolling back local change and releasing locks obtained during a preceding vote-step in ledger L.
- **Revoke-step** revoke-step $Rev_{tx,S}$ revoke the preceding commit vote and replace it with a abort vote for τ. The operations in the step include rolling back local change and releasing locks obtained during a preceding vote-step in ledger L.

For the consortium C_i with $Con^\tau(L_i) \neq \emptyset$, the consortium has to do vote-step for the transaction τ. It also may be required to do abort-step or commit-step or revoke-step to release locks, modify data or roll back change. For the consortium C_i where $Mod^\tau(L_i) \neq \emptyset$, the consortium has to do commit-step for the transaction τ.

As is shown in our model introduced in Sect. 3.1, without loss of generality, these protocol steps can be executed through the cross-chain sub-transaction which is denoted as $tx(step)$. The consortium ledger L_i keep track of the state of specific state object like UTXO, and account balance, depending on the data and state model that the consortium adopt. The cross-chain ledger L_g keeps track of the state of the cross-chain transaction.

We next show how to process a cross-chain transaction τ. For cross-chain transaction τ we define the consortium C_i as concerned consortium if $Con^\tau(L_i) \neq \emptyset$ or $Mod^\tau(L_i) \neq \emptyset$.

Initial Broadcast. The user sends the cross-chain transaction τ to all of the concerned consortiums.

Process Vote. Upon Receiving the τ or seeing the other consortium C_j sequenced $tx(Vot_{c,\tau,L_j})$ in cross-chain ledger L_g, nodes in consortium C_i with $Con^\tau(L_i) \neq \emptyset$ sequence τ in L_i. Then, the nodes in the consortium can have the same consistent decision on whether to commit or abort the τ according to the validation rules. If the decision is to commit, it sequence the $tx(Vot_{c,\tau,L_i})$ in cross-chain ledger L_g. Otherwise, it sequences $tx(Vot_{a,\tau,L_i})$ in L_g. Note that the τ sequenced in L_i logically represent the $tx(vote\text{-}step)$ and correspond to the

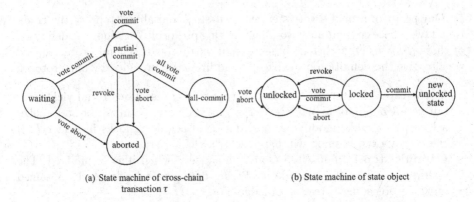

(a) State machine of cross-chain
transaction τ

(b) State machine of state object

Fig. 3. State machine for cross-chain transaction τ and state object.

$tx(vote\text{-}step)$ sequenced in L_g. Therefore we use $tx(vote\text{-}step)$ to represent the τ sequenced in L_i later in this work.

Generally, The validation rules for τ include checking whether the corresponding signatures are valid, whether the constraints in $Con^\tau(L_i)$ are satisfied, and whether the related ledger state objects are unlocked. The rules can be easily instantiated by the specific cross-chain scenarios where the constraint and modifications in our cross-chain model are instantiated.

Figure 3 shows the state machine of cross-chain transaction τ and state object. The initial state of the related state object in L_i is unlocked. The initial state of the cross-chain transaction in L_g is the waiting state. The $tx(Vot_{c,\tau,L_i})$ in L_i will turn related state object into locked state While the $tx(Vot_{a,\tau,L_i})$ do nothing. For L_g, $tx(Vot_{c,\tau,L_i})$ turn the state of τ from waiting state to the partial-commit state or from partial-commit state to partial-commit state. If all the concerned consortium vote commit for the τ and $tx(Vot_{c,\tau,L_i})$ is the last sub-transaction to vote commit, it will turn the state from the partial-commit state to the all-commit state. Instead, $tx(Vot_{a,\tau,L_i})$ turn the state of τ from waiting state to the aborted state or from partial-commit state to aborted state.

Process Revoke. Nodes are allowed to propose $tx(revoke\text{-}step)$ to revoke the previous commit vote if some conditions are triggered. The condition can be the timeout for τ or the coming of revoke request from the client. First, $tx(Rev_{\tau,L_i})$ is sequenced in the L_g by node in C_i. The revoke sub-transaction is valid if the state of τ is partial-commit state and the consortium C_i has proposed $tx(Vot_{c,\tau,L_i})$ before. If the $tx(Rev_{\tau,L_i})$ in L_g is valid, the consortium C_i sequenced the $tx(Rev_{\tau,L_i})$ in its own ledger L_i to roll back previous change and release locks.

Process Commit. Upon all the consortium with $Con^\tau(L) \neq \emptyset$ voting commit for the τ, which make the state of τ become all-commit state, the consortiums with $Con^\tau(L) \neq \emptyset$ and the consortiums with $Mod^\tau(L) \neq \emptyset$ can finally commit the τ. The consortium C_i will sequence the $tx(Com_{\tau,L_i})$ in L_g, which is valid if the state of τ is all-commit state and $Con^\tau(L) \neq \emptyset$ or $Mod^\tau(L) \neq \emptyset$. Then C_i sequenced $tx(Com_{\tau,L_i})$ in its own ledger L_i to finalize τ and release locks.

Process Abort. Upon one of the consortium with $Con^\tau(L) \neq \emptyset$ voting abort or revoking for the τ, which make the state of τ become abort state, the consortiums with $Con^\tau(L) \neq \emptyset$ require to abort the τ. The consortium C_i sequence the $tx(Abo_{\tau,L_i})$ in L_g, which is valid if the state of τ is aborted state and $Con^\tau(L) \neq \emptyset$. Then C_i sequenced $tx(Abo_{\tau,L_i})$ in its own ledger L_i to roll back modifications and release locks.

4.2 Security of the Cross-Chain Protocol.

We first introduce the security definition for the cross-chain protocol in [2] while we do not require the assumption that all consortium is honest.

Definition 2 *(Security of cross-chain protocol.) The cross-chain protocol is secure if the properties of liveness, consistency, and validity are satisfied.*

- *Liveness. The cross-chain transaction that is proposed to at least one honest node in the honest concerned consortium will eventually result in either being committed or aborted by honest consortiums.*
- *Consistency. For the transactions that concurrently access the ledger state of honest consortiums and have conflictions, at most one of them will be committed.*
- *Validity. The transaction may only be committed if it is valid according to the ledger state of honest consortiums.*

We then prove that the protocol has the properties of liveness, consistency and validity.

Theorem 2. *The cross-chain protocol has the property of liveness.*

Proof. When the cross-chain transaction τ is proposed to the honest node in the honest concerned consortium C_i, the node initiates the vote process. Because of the safety and liveness guaranteed by BFT_i, τ is sequenced in L_i and the consistent decision to commit or abort the τ is made by the honest node in C_i. Then either the $tx(Vot_{c,\tau,L_i})$ or $tx(Vot_{a,\tau,L_i})$ is sequenced in L_g because of the safety and liveness guaranteed by BFT_g. If $tx(Vot_{a,\tau,L_i})$ is sequenced, the τ is aborted. If $tx(Vot_{c,\tau,L_i})$ is sequenced, then the other honest consortiums will initiate the vote process. Similar to the process we just described, these honest consortiums vote commit or abort and sequence the $tx(vote\text{-}step)$ in L_g. If one of these consortiums votes abort for τ, then the τ is aborted.

If the honest consortiums all vote commit, the malicious consortium C_j corrupted by adversary can have following behaviors: (1) propose a valid $tx(Vot_{c,\tau,L_j})$ or $tx(Vot_{a,\tau,L_j})$. (2) propose both $tx(Vot_{c,\tau,L_j})$ and $tx(Vot_{a,\tau,L_j})$.

(3) propose valid $tx(Vot_{c,\tau,L_j})$ and then propose $tx(Rev_{\tau,L_j})$. (4) does not propose or delay proposing any valid concerned sub-transaction. In case 1, the τ becomes committed or aborted. In case 2, these two conflicted sub-transactions will be consistently sorted in L_g and the preceding one become valid. Therefore the state of τ becomes committed or aborted finally. In case 3, $tx(Vot_{c,\tau,L_j})$ and the $tx(Rev_{\tau,L_j})$ will be consistently sorted with the other sub-transactions containing commit vote in L_g. If the $tx(Rev_{\tau,L_j})$ precede the last sub-transactions containing commit vote, the $tx(Rev_{\tau,L_j})$ become valid and τ is aborted. Otherwise, τ is committed. In case 4, the other honest consortiums can propose revoke sub-transaction in the case of timeout and then the τ becomes aborted.

Therefore, τ eventually results in either being committed or aborted in L_g. The honest nodes in the honest consortium can propose either $tx(commit\text{-}step)$ or $tx(abort\text{-}step)$ according to the state of τ in L_g and eventually τ result in either being committed or aborted for these honest nodes.

Theorem 3. *The cross-chain protocol has the property of consistency.*

Proof. Without loss of generality, assume that there are two conflicting transactions τ_1 and τ_2 which both access the ledger state of honest consortium C_i and have conflictions. τ_1 is received by C_i first and then C_i sequence τ_1, lock the concerned state in L_i and sequence $tx(Vot_{c,\tau_1,L_i})$ in L_g. The lock will not be released until the protocol concludes. If τ_2 is processed by C_i before the protocol concludes, it will be aborted because of validation rules. When C_i committing the τ_1, the $tx(Com_{\tau,L_i})$ proposed by C_i not only release the lock, but also finalize the state change. If τ_2 is processed by C_i after τ_1 is committed, it is also aborted because the state it access if already change(e.g., The UTXO spent by τ_2 is already spent by τ_1). Therefore it is impossible to both commit two conflicting transactions that access the ledger state of honest consortiums.

Theorem 4. *The cross-chain protocol has the property of Validity.*

Proof. The transaction τ is committed if valid $tx(Com_{\tau,L})$ is proposed by consortium proposed in L_g. The $tx(Com_{\tau,L})$ is valid only if all the concerned consortiums vote commit for τ and sequence $tx(Vot_{c,\tau,L})$ in L_g. When the honest consortium C_i receives the τ from a client, it sequences it in the L_i. Then according to the ledger state of L_i, the consortium C_i decides the validity of τ including the satisfaction of the constraints in $Con^\tau(L_i)$, the unlocking of all the concerned state objects, and so on. The honest node in C_i will have the consistent and correct decision on the validity of τ because of the safety and liveness of BFT_i. Only if the τ is valid, the honest nodes will decide to vote commit for it and sequence the vote in L_g. The vote is unable to be forged by malicious nodes because BFT_g uses a cluster-sending process that requires the agreement of honest nodes. And by the safety and liveness of BFT_g, the vote will consistently be agreed by other honest consortiums. Therefore, the invalid transaction is impossible to collect the commit vote of C_i. The transaction may only be committed if it is valid according to the ledger state of honest consortiums.

The malicious consortiums can choose to do malicious behaviors like voting commit for conflicting transactions. However, these malicious behaviors are auditable. The properties above imply that the malicious consortiums are unable to prevent the agreement on the cross-chain transaction. The agreement can be used to settle disputes during the collaboration between consortiums.

5 Experiment

In this section, we conduct two evaluation experiments to characterize the performance of our scheme. The first one evaluates the two kinds of instances of our ledger framework. The second one evaluates our cross-chain protocol.

5.1 Evaluation for Framework Instance

We use the ns-3 network simulator to evaluate the instances. We implement the internal and hierarchical consensus protocols of the instances in ns-3. We run experiments with 16 consortiums, each of which contains 4 nodes connected by the switch. The bandwidth is set to be 100MBps and the network latency between nodes is 10ms. We adjust the percentage of cross-chain sub-transaction p_{cross} and transaction arrival rate r_{tx} and show the average throughput and latency in the multiple consortium blockchain systems.

Figure 4 shows the result of throughput and an average latency of a transaction. It can be observed that instance 1 performs better than instance 2 when the p_{cross} is low or when the r_{tx} is small. The reason is that instance 2 requires the generations of new cross-chain sub-transactions to reach cross-chain consensus due to the characteristics of hashgraph consensus. Therefore the low p_{cross} and small r_{tx} lead to low performance.

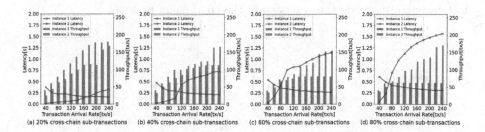

Fig. 4. Throughput and latency measurement.

Increasing the p_{cross} and r_{tx}, instance 2 outperform instance 1. Though the PBFT-like algorithm can adopt the out-of-order processing of transaction [9] to improve performance, the transactions still have to be processed one by one in the final commit. The $O(N^2)$ network complexity makes the commitment of cross-chain transactions slow, which also blocks the internal transactions. Therefore the performance of instance 1 degrades quickly. Besides, the high p_{cross} and large r_{tx} can accelerate the agreement reached in hashgraph consensus in instance 2. Therefore instance 2 performs better than instance 1 in such an environment.

5.2 Evaluation for Cross-Chain Protocol

In this evaluation, we evaluate and compare our cross-chain protocol and original two-phase commit and two-phase locking cross-chain protocol(2PC protocol for short). The evaluations adopt the experiments scheme and parameters in ByShard [9] which comprehensively simulates the 2PC cross-chain protocol.

We run experiments with 16 consortiums. Each consortium is supposed to process 500 transactions including internal transactions and cross-chain transactions. We adopt the account-transfer model. Each cross-chain transaction affects 4 consortium ledgers and has constraints and modifications on 2 accounts for each ledger. The accounts affected by the transaction are chosen randomly. We make our protocol run on instance 1. We set the message delay between nodes as 10ms. The consensus decision by PBFT is 30ms and the consensus decision by hierarchical PBFT is 90ms. Each consortium can make 1000 decisions per second. The timeout for cross-chain transactions in our protocol is set to be 190 ms after which the consortium will do a revoke-step to revoke the transaction. We also adopt the wake-up strategy. When the transaction visits the locked accounts, the transaction will be aborted and placed in the wake queue. After the concerned account is unlocked, the node will wake up and re-propose the transaction in the wake queue.

The parameters we adjust include the percentage of cross-chain transaction p_{cross} and the number of accounts an. Besides, to simulate the message delay caused by network partition or the malicious consortium, we also adjust another parameter dp, which represents the probability of a delay event. If the delay event happened, one of the consortiums processing the cross-chain transaction will delay 500 ms to do the vote-step in the cross-chain protocol.

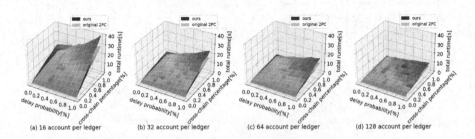

Fig. 5. Total time measurement.

Figure 5 shows the result of the total time to finish all the transactions. It can be observed that the high p_{cross} degrades the performance because of the relatively complex steps of the cross-chain protocols. When the dp is small, the

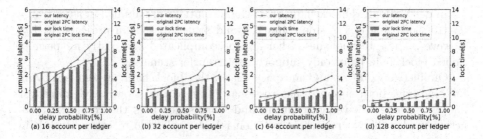

Fig. 6. Cumulative latency and lock time measurement.

original 2PC protocol takes less time to finalize the transactions because it does not need to do cross-chain consensus. However, with the increase of dp, our protocol outperforms the original 2PC protocol because the consortium in our protocol can choose to timely revoke the cross-transaction and release the lock on accounts. Then the other transaction accessing the related accounts can be committed in time.

Another interesting phenomenon is that the increase in the number of accounts make our protocol perform better than the original 2PC protocol in more situation. The reason may be that a large number of accounts lead to a large number of combinations of accounts. After the consortium does the revoke step, the released accounts are more likely to be combined with the other unlocked accounts and then trigger the wake-up of the transaction that accesses these unlocked accounts in the wait queue. Then these transactions can be committed in time.

Figure 6 shows the result of the cumulative latency of all transactions and the lock time of all accounts. Here we set the p_{cross} is 50% and adjust the dp. It can be observed that the increase in the number of accounts reduces the cumulative latency and the lock time because the contention between transactions decreases. The increase of dp causes a quick increase in the lock time of the original 2PC protocol but does not influence much on the lock time of our protocol because the consortium can timely revoke transactions and release the lock. For the same reason, our protocol reaches lower cumulative latency than the original 2PC protocol if dp is high.

From the experiments shown above, we can conclude that our scheme can have better performance than the original 2PC cross-chain protocol in the worse environment where network congestion happened or messages may be delayed or suppressed by the malicious consortium. The experiments support our previous statement that the scheme can work in the presence of malicious consortiums.

6   Related Work

The cross-chain solution is well-studied by researchers to support cross-chain transfer, sharding, and distributed applications in recent years.

In permissionless blockchain, cross-chain solutions are applied in asset transfer [10], sharding [2,11], side chain [14] and some cross-chain projects [12,16]. However, These technologies either are too complicated and costly for permissioned blockchain [3] or only support asset-transfer scenarios.

Omniledger [11] and Chainspace [2] is the blockchain system achieving full sharding, both support the cross-shard transaction. However, Omniledger adopts the client-driven mechanism and Chainspace uses the complex transaction model. Their cross-chain solution is not applicable to other blockchain systems.

AHL [7] and ByShard [9] introduce 2PC and 2PL cross-chain protocols to ensure the atomicity and isolation of cross-chain transactions. These protocols require pre-determined fault-tolerant clusters.

The solution of CAPER [3] introduces a directed acyclic graph permissioned blockchain that supports both internal and cross-application transactions. However, CAPER cannot support complex cross-chain transactions because it lacks the cross-chain protocol to ensure the atomicity and isolation of cross-chain transactions.

Sharper [4] and Pyramid [1] use the cross-chain consensus to commit the cross-chain transaction in a single consensus round. However, these works require the coordinated nodes concurrently exist in multiple consortiums or require blockchain-level lock [9].

7 Conclusion

In this work, we propose the cross-chain scheme for permissioned blockchain where the consortium may be malicious. We introduce the ledger framework containing a cross-chain ledger for multiple consortium blockchain systems and give two instances. We also introduce the cross-chain protocol which is built on top of our framework and derived from the two-phase commit and two-phase locking cross-chain protocols. We prove the security of the protocol in the presence of malicious consortiums. The experiment characterizes the performance of our scheme and shows that the scheme performs well even with malicious consortiums.

References

1. Adelson, E.H., Anderson, C.H., Bergen, J.R., Burt, P.J., Ogden, J.M.: Pyramid methods in image processing. RCA Eng. **29**(6), 33–41 (1984)
2. Al-Bassam, M., Sonnino, A., Bano, S., Hrycyszyn, D., Danezis, G.: Chainspace: a sharded smart contracts platform. arXiv preprint arXiv:1708.03778 (2017)
3. Amiri, M.J., Agrawal, D., Abbadi, A.E.: Caper: a cross-application permissioned blockchain. Proc. VLDB Endowment **12**(11), 1385–1398 (2019)
4. Amiri, M.J., Agrawal, D., El Abbadi, A.: Sharper: sharding permissioned blockchains over network clusters. In: Proceedings of the 2021 International Conference on Management of Data, pp. 76–88 (2021)

5. Baird, L.: The swirlds hashgraph consensus algorithm: fair, fast, byzantine fault tolerance. Swirlds Tech Reports SWIRLDS-TR-2016-01, Technical Report (2016)
6. Bonomi, S., Del Pozzo, A., García-Pérez, Á., Tucci-Piergiovanni, S.: Sok: achieving state machine replication in blockchains based on repeated consensus. arXiv preprint arXiv:2105.13732 (2021)
7. Dang, H., Dinh, T.T.A., Loghin, D., Chang, E.C., Lin, Q., Ooi, B.C.: Towards scaling blockchain systems via sharding. In: Proceedings of the 2019 International Conference on Management of Data, pp. 123–140 (2019)
8. Gaži, P., Kiayias, A., Zindros, D.: Proof-of-stake sidechains. In: 2019 IEEE Symposium on Security and Privacy (SP), pp. 139–156. IEEE (2019)
9. Hellings, J., Sadoghi, M.: Byshard: sharding in a byzantine environment. Proc. VLDB Endow. **14**(11), 2230–2243 (2021)
10. Herlihy, M.: Atomic cross-chain swaps. In: Proceedings of the 2018 ACM Symposium on Principles of Distributed Computing, pp. 245–254 (2018)
11. Kokoris-Kogias, E., Jovanovic, P., Gasser, L., Gailly, N., Syta, E., Ford, B.: Omniledger: a secure, scale-out, decentralized ledger via sharding. In: 2018 IEEE Symposium on Security and Privacy (SP), pp. 583–598. IEEE (2018)
12. Kwon, J., Buchman, E.: Cosmos: a network of distributed ledgers (2016). https://cosmos.network/whitepaper
13. Marvin, R.: Blockchain: The invisible technology that's changing the world. PC MAG Australia. ZiffDavis, LLC. Archived from the original on 25 (2017)
14. Poon, J., Dryja, T.: The bitcoin lightning network: scalable off-chain instant payments (2016)
15. Wang, Q., Yu, J., Chen, S., Xiang, Y.: Sok: diving into dag-based blockchain systems. arXiv preprint arXiv:2012.06128 (2020)
16. Wood, G.: Polkadot: vision for a heterogeneous multi-chain framework. White Paper 21 (2016)

Foundations

(Public) Verifiability for Composable Protocols Without Adaptivity or Zero-Knowledge

Carsten Baum[1], Bernardo David[2]([envelope]), and Rafael Dowsley[3]

[1] Aarhus University, Aarhus, Denmark
cbaum@cs.au.dk
[2] IT University Copenhagen, Copenhagen, Denmark
beda@itu.dk
[3] Monash University, Melbourne, Australia
rafael.dowsley@monash.edu

Abstract. The Universal Composability (UC) framework (FOCS '01) is the current standard for proving security of cryptographic protocols under composition. It allows to reason about complex protocol structures in a bottom-up fashion: any building block that is UC-secure can be composed arbitrarily with any other UC-secure construction while retaining their security guarantees. Unfortunately, some protocol properties such as the verifiability of outputs require excessively strong tools to achieve in UC. In particular, "obviously secure" constructions cannot directly be shown to be UC-secure, and verifiability of building blocks does not easily carry over to verifiability of the composed construction. In this work, we study Non-Interactive (Public) Verifiability of UC protocols, *i.e.* under which conditions a verifier can ascertain that a party obtained a specific output from the protocol. The verifier may have been part of the protocol execution or not, as in the case of public verifiability. We consider a setting used in a number of applications where it is ok to reveal the input of the party whose output gets verified and analyze under which conditions such verifiability can generically be achieved using "cheap" cryptographic primitives. That is, we avoid having to rely on adaptively secure primitives or heavy computational tools such as NIZKs. As Non-Interactive Public Verifiability is crucial when composing protocols with a public ledger, our approach can be beneficial when designing these with provably composable security and efficiency in mind.

1 Introduction

Universal Composability (UC) [14] is currently the most popular framework for designing and proving security of cryptographic protocols under arbitrary com-

Funded by the European Research Council (ERC) under the European Unions' Horizon 2020 program under grant agreement No 669255 (MPCPRO).

Supported by the Concordium Foundation and by the Independent Research Fund Denmark grants number 9040-00399B (TrA²C), number 9131-00075B (PUMA) and number 0165-00079B (Foundations of Privacy Preserving and Accountable Decentralized Protocols).

C. Ge and F. Guo (Eds.): ProvSec 2022, LNCS 13600, pp. 249–272, 2022.
https://doi.org/10.1007/978-3-031-20917-8_17

position. It allows one to prove that a protocol remains secure even in complex scenarios consisting of multiple nested protocol executions. The benefit of UC is that, as a formal framework, it allows to discuss the different aspects of an interactive protocol with mathematical precision. But in practice, one often sees that protocol security is argued on a very high level only. This is partially due to the complexity of fully expressing (and then proving) a protocol in UC, but also because achieving provable (UC) security sometimes requires additional, seemingly unnecessary protocol steps or assumptions.

One such case is that of (public) verifiability, which is the focus of this work. A verifiable protocol allows each protocol participant $\mathcal{P}_i$ to check if another party $\mathcal{P}_j$ in the end of the protocol obtained a certain claimed output (or that it aborted). A publicly verifiable protocol has this property even for external verifiers that did not take part in the protocol itself. Public verifiability is particularly important in the setting of decentralized systems and public ledgers (*e.g.* blockchains [24,27,28,32,35]), where new parties can join an ongoing protocol execution on-the-fly after verifying that their view of the protocol is valid. It also plays a central role in a recent line of research [2,5,11,33] on secure multiparty computation (MPC) protocols that rely on a public ledger to achieve fairness (*i.e.* ensuring either all parties obtain the protocol output or nobody does, including the adversary) by penalizing cheating parties, circumventing fundamental impossibility results [25]. Protocol verifiability also finds applications in MPC protocols that have identifiable abort such as [8,9,30], where all parties in the protocol either agree on the output or agree on the set of cheaters. Furthermore, public verifiability is an intrinsic property of randomness beacons [22,23] and a central component of provably secure Proof-of-Stake blockchain protocols [5,24,33]. However, most of these works achieve (public) verifiability by relying on heavy tools such as non-interactive zero knowledge proof systems and strong assumptions such as adaptive security of the underlying protocols.

1.1   The Problems of Achieving (Public) Verifiability in UC

Consider a UC functionality $\mathcal{F}$ which has one round of inputs by the parties $\mathcal{P} = \{\mathcal{P}_1, \ldots, \mathcal{P}_n\}$, computes outputs based on the inputs and in the end sends these outputs to each $\mathcal{P}_i$. In this work, we are interested in adding verifiability to $\mathcal{F}$ to obtain an extended functionality $\mathcal{F}^{\mathsf{V}}$. This functionality $\mathcal{F}^{\mathsf{V}}$ performs the same operations as $\mathcal{F}$, but it additionally allows verifiers to confirm that certain inputs were provided by a party $\mathcal{P}_i$ to $\mathcal{F}^{\mathsf{V}}$ to perform these operations and that certain outputs of these operations were given to $\mathcal{P}_i$ from $\mathcal{F}^{\mathsf{V}}$. Moreover, we want to obtain a protocol Π^{V} realizing $\mathcal{F}^{\mathsf{V}}$ from an existing protocol Π that realized $\mathcal{F}$. More concretely, we are interested in compiling a UC-secure protocol Π into a UC-secure counterpart Π^{V} that has (public) verifiability.

The (intuitive) first step is to construct Π^{V} where each party commits to its inputs and randomness. The parties then run Π using the committed input and randomness, exchanging exchange authenticated messages. This approach assumes that we are okay with revealing the inputs after Π is completed in case cheating is suspected, which we will discuss in more detail. Intuitively, this yields a simple verification procedure: each party can use the committed inputs and randomness of all other parties to re-execute Π in its head and compare the resulting messages to the authenticated protocol transcript. Any external verifier could do the same based on the commitments and an authenticated transcript of Π. Unfortunately, using this simple approach leads to adaptivity problems when trying to prove $\Pi^\vee$ secure: in the security proof, the simulation must have been performed without knowing the actual inputs to the functionality. But afterwards, these inputs become known to the verifier so the simulator must be able to explain the whole transcript of Π in terms of the previously unknown inputs, requiring adaptive security of Π to begin with. Similar issues have been observed before (e.g. [30]). This means that any such $\Pi^\vee$ would be quite inefficient, since adaptive protocols Π are often significantly less efficient than their counterparts with static security.

Consider, as an example, a 2PC protocol Π_{2PC} with active security based on Garbled Circuits (GCs) such as [18,34]. Protocol Π_{2PC} is executed by a sender $\mathcal{P}_1$ and a receiver $\mathcal{P}_2$ (where only $\mathcal{P}_2$ obtains output) as follows: (1) $\mathcal{P}_1$ generates multiple GCs together with input keys for each circuit. $\mathcal{P}_1$ commits to the GCs and their input keys. It inputs the input keys belonging to $\mathcal{P}_2$ into an Oblivious Transfer (OT) functionality $\mathcal{F}_{OT}$; (2) $\mathcal{P}_2$ uses $\mathcal{F}_{OT}$ to obtain its input keys; (3) $\mathcal{P}_1$ decommits the GCs and its own input keys; (4) $\mathcal{P}_2$ evaluates the GCs. Both parties run a consistency check showing that most GCs were correctly generated and that their input keys are consistent. The security proof of Π_{2PC} (for static security) usually consists of simulators for a corrupted sender ($\mathcal{S}_1$) and receiver ($\mathcal{S}_2$). $\mathcal{S}_1$ sends random inputs to $\mathcal{F}_{OT}$, extracts the inputs of $\mathcal{P}_1$ and then checks that the GCs were generated correctly by the malicious $\mathcal{P}_1$. For $\mathcal{S}_2$ the standard strategy is to first extract the input x_2 of the malicious $\mathcal{P}_2$ using $\mathcal{F}_{OT}$, then to obtain the output y from the functionality $\mathcal{F}_{2PC}$, to choose a random input $\tilde{x}_1$ and finally to simulate GCs such that they output y for the input keys of $\tilde{x}_1, x_2$. In order to make Π_{2PC} verifiable (with respect to revealing inputs and outputs), let $\mathcal{F}_{2PC}^\vee$ release the real input x_1 of $\mathcal{P}_1$ after the computation finished. But in $\mathcal{S}_2$ we generated the GCs such that for the dummy input $\tilde{x}_1$ it outputs y, so the garbling may not even be a correct garbling of the given circuit. There might not exist randomness to explain the output of $\mathcal{S}_2$ consistently with x_1, unless Π_{2PC} was an adaptively secure protocol.

This seems counter-intuitive: beyond the technical reason to allow (UC) simulation of verifiability, we see no explanation why only adaptively secure protocols should be verifiable when following the aforementioned compilation steps.

1.2   Our Contributions

In this work, we show how to compile a large class of statically UC-secure protocols into publicly verifiable versions that allow a party to non-interactively prove that it obtained a certain output by revealing its input. We focus on a setting where at least one party is assumed to be honest, and where the compiled protocol was already maliciously secure to begin with. While revealing an input is a caveat, this flavor of (public) verifiability is sufficient for a number of applications (*e.g.* [5,7,23]) and allows us to circumvent the need for expensive generic zero knowledge proofs and adaptive security (as needed in [30,33]). We introduce a compiler relying only on commitments and "joint authentication" functionalities that can be realized with cheap public-key primitives.

Our approach is compatible with protocols realizing non-reactive functionalities such as OT, Commitments or Secure Function Evaluation. We describe a standard wrapper for any such functionality to equip it with the interfaces necessary for non-interactive verification, allowing external verifiers to register and to perform verification. This wrapper is designed to amalgamate the reactive nature of UC with non-interactivity and might be of independent interest. Extending the results to reactive functionalities is an interesting open problem.

When is Revealing Inputs for Verification Justifiable? Although our focus on revealing inputs might seem very restrictive, there is a quite substantial set of protocols where it can be applied. As a starting point, our techniques can be used to instantiate preprocessing for UC-secure MPC with Identifiable Abort without adaptive assumptions [9,30]. Our approach also applies when one wants to publicly and randomly sample from a distribution and identify cheaters who disturbed the process. For example, our results have already been used as an essential tool in follow-up work constructing UC randomness beacons [23]. A third application is to bootstrap MPC without output verifiability to MPC with output verifiability *without revealing of inputs*. Here, each physical party $\mathcal{P}_i$ in the protocol Π_{MPC} runs two virtual parties $\mathcal{P}_i^C, \mathcal{P}_i^V$. It will give $\mathcal{P}_i^C$ the actual input x (while $\mathcal{P}_i^V$ has no input), and both parties obtain the same output y from Π_{MPC}. Now, in order to convince a verifier that $\mathcal{P}_i$ had y as output, it can "sacrifice" $\mathcal{P}_i^V$ and reveal its randomness for verification. Observe that this requires Π_{MPC} to be secure against a dishonest majority of parties. A fourth application lies in achieving cheater identification in the output phase of MPC protocols, which is a prequisite for obtaining MPC with monetary fairness such as [2,5,11,33]. For example, using our techniques, it is possible to construct the publicly verifiable building blocks of the output phase of Insured MPC [5] and related applications [7] since the inputs of the output phase with cheater identification are supposed to be revealed anyway. In [5] the authors had to individually redefine each functionality with respect to verifiability and reprove the security of each protocol involved. Using our techniques, we show in the full version [6] that this tedious task can be avoided and that the same result can be obtained by inspecting the primitives used in their protocol and verifying that the protocols fulfill the requirements of our compiler.

Shortcomings of Other Approaches. In case adaptive security is required, it is well-known that adaptively secure protocols usually have larger computation or communication overheads (or stronger assumptions) than their statically secure counterparts. For example, Yao's Garbling Scheme and optimizations thereof are highly efficient with static security (e.g. [38]) but achieve similar performance with adaptive security only for NC1-circuits [31] (unless one relies on Random Oracles [10]). When implementing Π_{2PC}, one would also additionally have to realize an adaptively UC-secure $\mathcal{F}_{OT}$, which is also cheaper with static instead of adaptive security. This is also true when OT-extension is used [20,21].

Previous works such as [33] obtain public verifiability, even without revealing inputs and without adaptive protocols, by using generic UC-NIZKs. They follow the GMW paradigm [29] where each party would prove in every protocol step of Π that it created all messages correctly, given all previous messages as well as commitments to inputs and randomness. To the best of our knowledge, no work that uses UC-NIZKs to achieve verifiability estimated concrete parameters for their constructions. This is because the UC-NIZKs, in addition to proving the protocol steps, also have to use the code of the cryptographic primitives in a white-box way. That also means that UC-NIZKs cannot be applied if the compiled protocol Π uses Random Oracles, which are popular in efficient protocols.

Another solution for verifiability, which also does not require an adaptive protocol and that works in the case that Π is an MPC protocol, is to i) let Π commit to the output of y_i of each $\mathcal{P}_i$ by running a commit algorithm for a non-interactive commitment scheme inside Π; ii) output all these commitments to all parties, which sign them and broadcast the signed commitments to each other; and iii) reveal outputs and commitment openings to the respective parties. Obviously, this does not generalize to arbitrary protocols Π, whereas our approach does. Additionally, in this approach one needs to evaluate the commitment algorithm white-box in MPC. Evaluating cryptographic primitives inside MPC can be costly, in particular if the MPC protocol is defined over a ring where the commitment algorithm has a large circuit. This also rules out cheap Random Oracle-based commitments.

Efficiency. The only overheads in relation to the original protocol required by our compiler are a simple commitment (*e.g.* based on a random oracle) on the input/randomness of each party and the subsequent joint authentication of this commitment as well as of subsequent messages. If messages are exchanged over public channels, this joint authentication be done by requiring each party to compute multisignatures on the messages exchanged in each round and then combining these signatures into a single multisignature, saving on space. If messages are exchanged over private channels, there is an extra overhead of computing 2 modular exponentiations and transmitting a string of security parameter size per message, which is needed for our private joint authentication scheme. The verification procedure requires the verifier to re-execute the protocol on the jointly authenticated transcript of the protocol using a party's opened input/randomness. While this seems expensive, notice that executing the protocol's next message function is strictly cheaper than verifying a NIZK showing that every message in the transcript is correctly computed according to this function, which is required by previous schemes and that would also add the overhead of having each party compute such a NIZK for every message they send.

1.3   Our Techniques

We construct a compiler that generically achieves public verifiability for protocols with one round of input followed by multiple computation and output rounds as formalized in Sect. 2. For this, we start with an observation similar to [30], namely that by fixing the inputs, randomness and messages in a protocol Π we can get guarantees about the outputs. This is because fixing the inputs, randomness and received messages essentially fixes the view of a party, as the messages generated and sent by a party are deterministic given all of these other values. Our compiler creates a protocol Π^V that fixes parties' input and randomness pairs by having parties commit to these pairs and authenticate the messages exchanged between parties in such a way that an external party can verify such committed/authenticated items after the fact. This idea of fixing messages for the purpose of public verifiability is not new, and other works that focus on it such as [3,33] have taken a similar route. However, fixing all messages exchanged in the original protocol Π is costly and might be overkill for some protocols. We explore this concept in the notion of *transcript non-malleability* as defined in Sect. 3. There, we formalize the intuition that we might not need that all exchanged messages are fixed in some protocols: *e.g.* an adversary that is allowed to replace messages exchanged between dishonest parties possibly does not have enough leverage to forge a consistent transcript for a different output.

Proving Security in UC: It might seem obvious that Π^V, i.e. a version of Π with all of its inputs and messages fixed, is publicly verifiable and implements $\mathcal{F}^V$. Unfortunately, as we outlined above, a construction of a simulator $\mathcal{S}^V$ in the proof of security needs to assume that Π is adaptively secure. In Sect. 3.1 we address this by using *input-aware simulators* (or *über simulators*) $\mathcal{S}^U$. These are special simulators which can be parameterized with the inputs for the simulated honest parties, generating transcripts consistent with these inputs but indistinguishable from the transcripts of $\mathcal{S}$. We then embed an über simulator of a protocol Π into the publicly verifiable functionality $\mathcal{F}^V$. This delegates the simulation of Π to the internal über simulator of $\mathcal{F}^V$ – whereas in our naive approach, $\mathcal{S}^V$ had to simulate Π itself. Since we let $\mathcal{F}^V$ only release the transcripts that $\mathcal{S}^U$ generates, this does not leak any additional information to the adversary. Moreover, $\mathcal{S}^U$ now also extracts the inputs of the dishonest parties.

Getting Über Simulators (Almost) for Free: Following our example with Π_{2PC} from Sect. 1.1, $\mathcal{S}_1$ for a corrupted sender uses a random input to $\mathcal{F}_{OT}$ and otherwise follows Π_{2PC}. Towards constructing $\mathcal{S}_1^U$, observe that as $\mathcal{F}_{OT}$ by its own UC-security hides the input of $\mathcal{P}_2$, running $\mathcal{S}_1$ inside $\mathcal{F}_{2PC}^V$ using real inputs of $\mathcal{P}_2$ is indistinguishable and we can use such a modified $\mathcal{S}_1$ as $\mathcal{S}_1^U$. Conversely, we can also construct $\mathcal{S}_2^U$, which runs Π_{2PC} based on the input x_1 that it obtains. By the UC-security of Π_{2PC}, the distribution of $\mathcal{S}_2^U$ will be indistinguishable from $\mathcal{S}_2$. As can be seen from this example, an efficient über simulator must not be artificial or strong, but could be quite simply obtained from either the existing protocol or existing $\mathcal{S}$. Its requirement also differs from requiring adaptivity of Π_{2PC}: $\mathcal{S}_2^U$ still only requires Π_{2PC} to be statically secure. In fact, this strategy for constructing an über simulator works for any protocols that simulate their online phase in the security proof using "artificial" fixed inputs and otherwise run the protocol honestly while they are able to extract inputs (*e.g.* MPC protocols such as [26, 36]). Hence, we can directly make a large class of protocols verifiable. This is discussed further in the full version [6].

How to Realize Transcript Non-malleability. Besides fixing inputs and randomness, in order to construct compilers from Π to Π^V we need to fix the transcript of Π. For this, we have parties in Π^V use what we call "joint authentication" (defined in Sect. 4). Joint Authentication works for both public and private messages. In the public case, joint authentication is achieved by having all parties sign a message sent by one of them. In the private case, we essentially allow parties to authenticate commitments to private messages that are only opened to the rightful receivers. Later on, any party who received that private message (*i.e.* the opening of the commitment to the message) can publicly prove that it obtained a certain message that was jointly authenticated by all parties involved in Π^V. More importantly, joint authentication does not perform any communication itself but provides authentication tokens that can be verified in a non-interactive manner. In our example with Π_{2PC}, this means that both $\mathcal{P}_1, \mathcal{P}_2$ initially commit to their inputs and randomness and then sign all exchanged messages (checking that each message is signed by its sender).

Putting Things Together. We use the techniques described above to compile any protocol Π that fits one of our transcript non-malleability definitions and UC-realizes a functionality $\mathcal{F}$ in the $\mathcal{F}_1, \ldots, \mathcal{F}_n$-hybrid model into a protocol Π^V that UC-realizes a publicly verifiable $\mathcal{F}^V$ in the $\mathcal{F}_1^V, \ldots, \mathcal{F}_n^V$-hybrid model (*i.e.* assuming that the setup functionalities can also be made publicly verifiable). Moreover, if a global functionality is used as setup, it must allow all parties to make the same queries and obtain the same answers, so that the verification procedure can be performed. Our compilation technique has two main components: 1. commit to and authenticate each party's input and randomness pairs of Π (fixing input and randomness pairs); 2. execute Π and use public/secret joint authentication to jointly authenticate each exchanged protocol message (fixing the transcript). These steps achieve two goals: allowing parties to publicly and non-interactively show that they have a certain input/randomness pair and transcript, making Π transcript non-malleable, since the adversary cannot lie about its input, randomness or view of the transcript. In order to realize the public verifiability interface of $\mathcal{F}^V$, we have a party open its input and randomness pair as well as its view of the transcript, which could not have been forged, allowing the verifier to execute an honest party's steps as in Π to verify that a given output is obtained. When proving security of this compiler, we delegate the simulation of the original steps of Π to an über simulator $\mathcal{S}^U$ for Π embedded in $\mathcal{F}^V$. This guarantees that the transcript of $\mathcal{S}$'s simulated execution of Π^V is consistent with honest parties' inputs if they activate public verification and reveal their input. To compile our example GC protocol, we now combine all of the aforementioned steps and additionally assume that $\mathcal{F}_{OT}$ as well as the commitment-functionality are already verifiable. By the compiler theorem, the resulting protocol is verifiable according to our definition. In the full version [6] we give a detailed example by easily achieving verifiability in [5].

1.4   Related Work

Despite being very general, UC has seen many extensions such as e.g. UC with joint state [19] or Global UC [16], aiming at capturing protocols that use global ideal setups. Verifiability for several kinds of protocols has been approached from different perspectives, such as cheater identification [8,30], verifiability of MPC [4,37], incoercible secure computation [1], secure computation on public ledgers [2,11,33], and improved definitions for widely used primitives [12,13]. Another solution to solve the adaptivity requirement was presented in [9], but their approach only works for functionalities without input. A different notion of verifiability was put forward in publicly verifiable covert 2PC protocols such as [3] and its follow-up works, where parties can show that the other party has cheated. Here, both the 2PC protocol and therefore also the verifiability guarantee only hold against covert adversaries, while we focus on the malicious setting. To the best of our knowledge, no previous work has considered a generic definition of non-interactive public verifiability for malicious adversaries in the UC framework nor a black-box compiler for achieving such a notion *without* requiring adaptive security of the underlying protocol or ZK proof systems.

2   Preliminaries

We denote the security parameter by κ. The set $\{1, \ldots, n\}$ is denoted by $[n]$ while we write $[n]_i$ to mean $[n] \setminus \{i\}$. We denote by $\mathsf{negl}(x)$ the set of negligible functions in x and abbreviate *probabilistic polynomial time* as PPT. We write $\{0,1\}^{\mathsf{poly}(\kappa)}$ to denote a set of bit-strings of polynomial length in κ.

Secure Protocols. A protocol Π run by n parties (which we denote as $\mathcal{P} = \{\mathcal{P}_1, \ldots, \mathcal{P}_n\}$) consists of the algorithms $\mathsf{nmes}, \mathsf{out}$ and additional parameters: the number of parties n, the setup resources $\mathcal{F}_1, \ldots, \mathcal{F}_r$, the number of output rounds G, the number of rounds H_τ to obtain each output $\tau \in [G]$ as well as the communication and output model. We assume that external system parameters $s \in \{0,1\}^{\mathsf{poly}(\kappa)}$ are fixed for the protocol. Each party $\mathcal{P}_i$ uses their input $x_i \in \mathcal{X}$ as well as randomness $r_i \in \{0,1\}^{\mathsf{poly}(\kappa)}$ for the actual protocol. Formally, Π is described in Fig. 1 with algorithms nmes and out defined as follows:

nmes is a deterministic polynomial-time (DPT) algorithm which on input the party number i, protocol input $x_i \in \mathcal{X}$, randomness $r_i \in \{0,1\}^{\mathsf{poly}(\kappa)}$, auxiliary input $s \in \{0,1\}^{\mathsf{poly}(\kappa)}$, output round $\tau \in [G]$, round number $\rho \in [H_\tau]$ and previous messages $\mathcal{M}_{.,i}$ from parties and $\mathcal{N}_{.,i}$ from resources outputs $\{\mathsf{m}_{i,j}^{(\tau,\rho)}\}_{j \in [n]_i}, \{\mathsf{mres}_{i,q}^{(\tau,\rho)}\}_{q \in [r]}$.

out is a DPT algorithm which on input the party number i, the protocol input $x_i \in \mathcal{X}$, randomness $r_i \in \{0,1\}^{\mathsf{poly}(\kappa)}$, auxiliary input $s \in \{0,1\}^{\mathsf{poly}(\kappa)}$, output round $\tau \in [G]$, a set of messages $\mathcal{M}_{.,i}$ from parties and $\mathcal{N}_{.,i}$ from resources outputs $y_i^{(\tau)}$ which is either an output value or $\perp$. The values x_i, r_i might not be necessary in every protocol, so out might run without these.

Algorithm nmes generates two different types of messages: 1. m-messages, which are used for communication *among parties*; 2. mres-messages, which are exchanged *between a party and a functionality*. Therefore, each mres-message consists of an interface $(\mathbf{Input}_i, \mathbf{Compute}^{(\tau)}, \mathbf{Output}_i^{(\tau)})$ with whom the party wants to communicate as well as the actual payload. Each message that is an output of nmes may either be an actual string or a symbol $\perp$, meaning that no message is sent to a party/functionality in this round. We write $\mathsf{m}_{i,j}$ whenever we mean that a message was sent from party $\mathcal{P}_i$ to $\mathcal{P}_j$. Similarly, we write $\mathsf{mres}_{i,q}$ when the message was sent from $\mathcal{P}_i$ to $\mathcal{F}_q$ and $\mathsf{mres}_{q,i}$ when sent from $\mathcal{F}_q$ to $\mathcal{P}_i$. We denote messages received by party $\mathcal{P}_i$ from another party as $\mathcal{M}_{.,i}$ and those sent by $\mathcal{P}_i$ to another party as $\mathcal{M}_{i,.}$. We write $\mathcal{N}_{.,i}$ for all messages that $\mathcal{P}_i$ received from resources while $\mathcal{N}_{i,.}$ denotes messages which $\mathcal{P}_i$ sent to resources.

Each $\mathcal{P}_i$ has input $x_i \in \mathcal{X}$ as well as common public input $s \in \{0,1\}^{\mathsf{poly}(\kappa)}$.

$\mathbf{Input}_i$: Party $\mathcal{P}_i$ samples $r_i \xleftarrow{\$} \{0,1\}^{\mathsf{poly}(\kappa)}$ uniformly at random. Let $\mathcal{M}_{.,i}, \mathcal{N}_{.,i} \leftarrow \emptyset$.

$\mathbf{Compute}^{(\tau)}$: Let $\tau \in [G]$. Then each party $\mathcal{P}_i$ for $\rho \in [H_\tau]$ does the following:

1. Locally compute

$$\left(\{\mathsf{m}_{i,j}^{(\tau,\rho)}\}_{j \in [n]_i}, \{\mathsf{mres}_{i,q}^{(\tau,\rho)}\}_{q \in [r]} \right) \leftarrow \mathsf{nmes}(i, x_i, r_i, s, \tau, \rho, \mathcal{M}_{.,i}, \mathcal{N}_{.,i}).$$

2. For each $j \in [n]_i$ send $\mathsf{m}_{i,j}^{(\tau,\rho)}$ to $\mathcal{P}_j$. For each $q \in [r]$ send $\mathsf{mres}_{i,q}^{(\tau,\rho)}$ to $\mathcal{F}_q$.

3. For each $j \in [n]_i$ get $\mathsf{m}_{j,i}^{(\tau,\rho)}$ from each $\mathcal{P}_j$ and $\mathsf{mres}_{q,i}^{(\tau,\rho)}$ from each $\mathcal{F}_q$ for $q \in [r]$.

4. Set $\mathcal{M}_{.,i} \leftarrow \mathcal{M}_{.,i} \cup \{\mathsf{m}_{j,i}^{(\tau,\rho)}\}_{j \in [n]_i}$ and $\mathcal{N}_{.,i} \leftarrow \mathcal{N}_{.,i} \cup \{\mathsf{mres}_{q,i}^{(\tau,\rho)}\}_{q \in [r]}$.

$\mathbf{Output}_i^{(\tau)}$: Party $\mathcal{P}_i$ computes and outputs $y_i^{(\tau)} \leftarrow \mathsf{out}(i, x_i, r_i, s, \tau, \mathcal{M}_{.,i}, \mathcal{N}_{.,i})$.

Fig. 1. The generic protocol Π.

Communication and Output Model: We do not restrict how messages are exchanged, except that their length is polynomial in κ. If messages are sent through point-to-point secure channels, then we call this *private communication*. If parties instead send the same message to all other parties, then we consider this as *broadcast communication*. Parties may arbitrarily mix private and broadcast communication. We do not restrict the output $y_i^{(\tau)}$ which each party obtains in the end of the computation, meaning that all the $y_i^{(\tau)}$ might be different.

Universal Composition of Secure Protocols. In this work we use the (Global) Universal Composability or (G)UC model [14, 16] for analyzing security. We focus on dishonest-majority protocols as e.g. honest-majority protocols can have all parties vote on the result (if broadcast is available). Protocols are run by interactive Turing Machines (iTMs) which we call *parties*. We assume that each party $\mathcal{P}_i$ in Π runs in PPT in the implicit security parameter κ. The PPT *adversary* $\mathcal{A}$ will be able to corrupt k out of the n parties, denoted as $I \subset \mathcal{P}$. We opt for the static corruption model where the parties are corrupted from the beginning, as this is what most efficient protocols currently are developed for. Parties can exchange messages with each other and also with PPT resources, also called *ideal functionalities*. To simplify notation we assume that the messages between parties are sent over secure channels.

We start with protocols that are already UC-secure, but not verifiable. For this, we assume that the ideal functionality $\mathcal{F}$ of a protocol Π follows the pattern described in Fig. 2: following Fig. 1 we consider protocols with one input and G output rounds. This is general enough to e.g. model commitment schemes. At the same time, our setting is not strong enough to permit reactive computations which inherently make the notation a lot more complex.

Functionality $\mathcal{F}$ has common public input $s \in \{0,1\}^{\mathsf{poly}(\kappa)}$ and interacts with a set $\mathcal{P}$ of n parties and an ideal adversary $\mathcal{S}$. Upon initialization, $\mathcal{S}$ is allowed to corrupt a set $I \subset \mathcal{P}$ of k parties where $k < n$. Each of $\mathcal{F}$'s interfaces falls into one of 3 different categories for providing inputs as well as running the G evaluation and output steps.

Input$_i$: On input (INPUT, sid, x_i) by $\mathcal{P}_i$ and (INPUT, sid) by all other parties store $x_i \in \mathcal{X}$ locally and send (INPUT, sid, i) to all parties. Every further message to this interface is discarded and once set, x_i may not be altered anymore.

Compute$^{(\tau)}$: On input (COMPUTE, sid, τ) by a set of parties $J_\tau \subseteq \mathcal{P}$ as well as $\mathcal{S}$ perform a computation based on s as well as the current state of the functionality. The computation is to be specified in concrete implementations of this functionality. The last two steps of this interface are fixed and as follows:
  1. Set some values $\mathbf{y}_1^{(\tau)}, \cdots, \mathbf{y}_n^{(\tau)}$. Only this interface is allowed to alter these.
  2. Send (COMPUTE, sid, τ) to every party in J_τ.
Every further call to **Compute$^{(\tau)}$** is ignored. Every call to this interface before all **Input$_i$** are finished is ignored, as well as when **Compute$^{(\tau-1)}$** has not finished yet.

Output$_i^{(\tau)}$: On input (OUTPUT, sid, τ) by $\mathcal{P}_i$ where $\tau \in [G]$ and if $\mathbf{y}_i^{(\tau)}$ was set send (OUTPUT, $sid, \tau, \mathbf{y}_i^{(\tau)}$) to $\mathcal{P}_i$.

Fig. 2. The generic functionality $\mathcal{F}$.

It is not necessary that all of the interfaces which $\mathcal{F}$ provides are used for an application. For example in the case of coin tossing, no party $\mathcal{P}_i$ ever has to call **Input$_i$**. While **Input$_i$**, **Output$_i^{(\tau)}$** are fixed in their semantics, the application may freely vary how **Compute$^{(\tau)}$** may act upon the inputs or generate outputs.

The only constraint is that for each of the $\tau \in [G]$ rounds, $\mathbf{Compute}^{(\tau)}$ sets output values $(\mathbf{y}_1^{(\tau)}, \ldots, \mathbf{y}_n^{(\tau)})$.

As usual, we define security with respect to a PPT iTM $\mathcal{Z}$ called *environment*. The environment provides inputs to and receives outputs from the parties $\mathcal{P}$. Furthermore, the adversary $\mathcal{A}$ will corrupt parties $I \subset \mathcal{P}$ in the name of $\mathcal{Z}$ and gain full control over I. To define security, let $\Pi \circ \mathcal{A}$ be the distribution of the output of $\mathcal{Z}$ when interacting with $\mathcal{A}$ in a real protocol instance Π. Furthermore, let $\mathcal{S}$ denote an *ideal world adversary* and $\mathcal{F} \circ \mathcal{S}$ be the distribution of the output of $\mathcal{Z}$ when interacting with parties which run with $\mathcal{F}$ instead of Π and where $\mathcal{S}$ takes care of adversarial behavior.

Definition 1 (Secure Protocol). *We say that Π securely implements $\mathcal{F}$ if for every PPT iTM $\mathcal{A}$ that maliciously corrupts at most k parties there exists a PPT iTM $\mathcal{S}$ (with black-box access to $\mathcal{A}$) such that no PPT environment $\mathcal{Z}$ can distinguish $\Pi \circ \mathcal{A}$ from $\mathcal{F} \circ \mathcal{S}$ with non-negligible probability in κ.*

In our (public and secret) Join Authentication protocols we use the standard functionalities for digital signatures $\mathcal{F}_{\mathsf{Sig}}$ [15] and for key registration functionality $\mathcal{F}_{\mathsf{Reg}}$ [17]. Moreover, to simplify our compiler description, we use an authenticated bulletin board functionality $\mathcal{F}_{\mathsf{BB}}$ described in the full version [6].

2.1 Verifiable Functionalities

We extend the functionality $\mathcal{F}$ from Sect. 2 to provide a notion of non-interactive verification using a functionality wrapper $\mathcal{F}^{\mathsf{V}}$ described in Fig. 3. For this, we assume that there are additional parties $\mathcal{V}_i$ which can partake in the verification. These, as well as regular protocol parties, can register at runtime to be verifiers of the computation using a special interface **Register Verifier**. Once they are registered, these verifiers are allowed to check the validity of outputs for parties that have initiated verification at any point. We keep track of this using the set of verifiers $\mathcal{V}$ (which is initially empty) inside the functionality. For values whose output has been provided using the interface $\mathbf{Output}_i^{(\tau)}$ (that we inherit from the definition of $\mathcal{F}$ of Sect. 2) we allow the parties $\mathcal{P}$ to use an interface called **Activate Verification** to enable everyone in $\mathcal{V}$ to check their outputs via the interface **Verify**$_i$. The modifications to **Input**$_i$ and the new interface $\mathbf{NMF}_{\mathcal{S}^{\mathsf{u}}}$ are related to the über simulators discussed in Appendix 3.2.

Notice that, in our constructions, a verifier $\mathcal{V}_i \in \mathcal{V}$ can perform verification with help from data obtained in two different ways: 1. receiving verification data from another verifier $\mathcal{V}_j \in \mathcal{V}$ or a party $\mathcal{P}_i \in \mathcal{P}$; 2. reading verification data from publicly available resource such as $\mathcal{F}_{\mathsf{BB}}$. In case $\mathcal{V}_i$ obtains verification data from another party in $\mathcal{V} \cup \mathcal{P}$, that party might be corrupted, allowing the ideal adversary $\mathcal{S}$ to interfere (*i.e.* providing corrupted verification data or not answering at all). When $\mathcal{V}_i$ obtains verification data from a setup resource that is untamperable by the adversary, $\mathcal{S}$ has no influence on the verification process. To model these cases, $\mathcal{F}^{\mathsf{V}}$ might implement only **Register Verifier (public)** or only **Register Verifier (private)**, respectively. We do not require $\mathcal{F}^{\mathsf{V}}$ to

The functionality wrapper $\mathcal{F}^V[\mathcal{F}]$ adds the interfaces below to a generic functionality $\mathcal{F}$ defined as in Figure 2, still allowing direct access to $\mathcal{F}$. $\mathcal{F}^V$ is parameterized by an über simulator $\mathcal{S}^U$ executed internally (as discussed in Appendix 3.2) and maintains binary variables verification-active, verify-1, ..., verify-n that are initially 0 and used to keep track of the verifiable outputs. Apart from the set of parties $\mathcal{P}$ and ideal adversary $\mathcal{S}$ defined in $\mathcal{F}$, $\mathcal{F}^V$ interacts with verifiers $\mathcal{V}_i \in \mathcal{V}$.

Register Verifier (private): Upon receiving (REGISTER, sid) from $\mathcal{V}_i$:
- If verification-active $= 1$ send (REGISTER, sid, $\mathcal{V}_i$) to $\mathcal{S}$. If $\mathcal{S}$ answers with (REGISTER, sid, $\mathcal{V}_i$, ok), set $\mathcal{V} \leftarrow \mathcal{V} \cup \mathcal{V}_i$ and return (REGISTERED, sid) to $\mathcal{V}_i$.
- If verification-active $= 0$ return (VERIFICATION-INACTIVE, sid) to $\mathcal{V}_i$.

Register Verifier (public): Upon receiving (REGISTER, sid) from $\mathcal{V}_i$:
- If verification-active $= 1$ set $\mathcal{V} \leftarrow \mathcal{V} \cup \mathcal{V}_i$ and return (REGISTERED, sid) to $\mathcal{V}_i$.
- If verification-active $= 0$ return (VERIFICATION-INACTIVE, sid) to $\mathcal{V}_i$.

Activate Verification: Upon receiving (ACTIVATE-VERIFICATION, sid, open-i, open-input-i) from each $\mathcal{P}_i$ and if **Compute**$^{(1)}$, ..., **Compute**$^{(G)}$ succeeded:
1. Let $Y \leftarrow \{j \in [n] \mid$ open-j $= 1 \wedge$ verify-j $= 0\}$. If $Y = \emptyset$ then return.
2. Set verification-active $\leftarrow 1$ (if it is not set already) and deactivate the interfaces **Compute**$^{(\tau)}$ for all $\tau \in [G]$.
3. If open-input-i $= 1$, then set $z_i = x_i$; otherwise $z_i = \bot$.
4. Send (ACTIVATING-VERIFICATION, sid, Y, $\{z_j, \mathbf{y}_j^{(\tau)}\}_{j \in Y, \tau \in [G]}$) to $\mathcal{S}$. If $\mathcal{P}_i$ is honest, append its randomness R_i (obtained from $\mathcal{S}^U$) to this message.
5. Upon receiving (ACTIVATING-VERIFICATION, sid, ok) from $\mathcal{S}$ set verify-j $\leftarrow 1$ for each $j \in Y$. Then return (VERIFICATION-ACTIVATED, sid, Y, $\{z_j, \mathbf{y}_j^{(\tau)}\}_{j \in Y, \tau \in [G]}$) to all parties in $\mathcal{P}$.

Verify$_j$: Upon receiving (VERIFY, sid, j, a, $b^{(1)}$, ..., $b^{(G)}$) from $\mathcal{V}_i$ where $\mathcal{V}_i \in \mathcal{V}$ and $\mathcal{P}_j \in \mathcal{P}$ do the following:
- if verify-j $= 1$ then compute the set $B \leftarrow \{\tau \in [G] \mid b^{(\tau)} \neq \mathbf{y}_j^{(\tau)}\}$. If $a = z_j$, then set $f \leftarrow 1$; otherwise $f \leftarrow 0$. Return (VERIFY, sid, j, f, B) to $\mathcal{V}_i$.
- If verify-j $= 0$ then send (CANNOT-VERIFY, sid, j) to $\mathcal{V}_i$.

Input$_i$: On input (INPUT, sid, x_i) by $\mathcal{P}_i$ and (INPUT, sid) by all other parties, forward (INPUT, sid, x_i) to $\mathcal{F}$ and also forward responses from $\mathcal{F}$ to $\mathcal{P}_i$. Finally, after receiving (INPUT, sid, x_i) from all $\mathcal{P}_i$, $i \in \overline{I}$ (i.e. all honest parties), initialize $\mathcal{S}^U$ parameterizing it with $\mathcal{F}$'s randomness tape and with x_i for all honest $\mathcal{P}_i$.

NMF$_{\mathcal{S}^U}$: Upon input (NEXTMSGP, sid, j, τ, ρ, $\{\mathtt{m}_{i,j}\}_{i \in I}$) where $j \in \overline{I}$ or (NEXTMSGF, sid, q, τ, ρ, $\mathtt{mres}_{i,q}$) where $i \in I$ and $q \in [r]$ by $\mathcal{S}$, send the respective message to $\mathcal{S}^U$. Forward all messages between $\mathcal{S}^U$ and $\mathcal{F}$, so that $\mathcal{S}^U$ mediates interaction between $\mathcal{F}$ and $\mathcal{S}$, also delivering extracted adversarial inputs to $\mathcal{F}$. Finally, after $\mathcal{S}^U$ outputs a response (NEXTMSGP, sid, j, τ, $\rho + 1$, $\{\mathtt{m}_{j,i}\}_{i \in I}$) or (NEXTMSGF, sid, q, τ, $\rho + 1$, $\mathtt{mres}_{q,i}$), forward it to $\mathcal{S}$.

Fig. 3. The Functionality wrapper $\mathcal{F}^V[\mathcal{F}]$. The modifications to interface **Input$_i$** and the new interface **NMF$_{\mathcal{S}^U}$** are discussed in Appendix 3.2.

implement both of these interfaces simultaneously, and thus define the properties of $\mathcal{F}^V$ according to which of them is present:

- A functionality which implements the interface **Register Verifier (public)** is said to have *Public Verifier Registration*. We say that it has *Private Verifier Registration* if it implements **Register Verifier (private)**
- A functionality which implements the interfaces **Activate Verification** and **Verify**$_j$ and which has *Verifier Registration* is called Non-Interactively Verifiable (*NIV*). If it has *Public Verifier Registration* then it is *Publicly Verifiable*, if it has *Private Verifier Registration* it is *Privately Verifiable*

3   Verifiable Protocols

We now present our definitions of non-interactively verifiable protocols. For this, we will first sketch a classification for the robustness of a protocol to attacks on its "inherent" verifiability. Then, we define properties that are necessary to achieve simulation-based security for our approach to verifiability.

Our approach to verification (as outlined in Sect. 1.3) is to leverage properties for verifiability that are already built into a protocol Π. As the verifier can only rely on the protocol transcript, consider how such a transcript comes into existence: we first run an instance of Π with an adversary $\mathcal{A}$. Afterwards, the adversary may change parts of the protocol transcript in order to trigger faulty behavior in the outputs of parties. If the adversary cannot trigger erroneous behavior this way, then this means that we can establish correctness of an output of such a protocol by using the messages of its transcript, some opened inputs and randomness as well as some additional properties of $\Pi = (\text{nmes}, \text{out})$.

Transcript Validity: If our verification relies on the transcript of Π, then a transcript is incorrect if messages that a party $\mathcal{P}_i$ claims to have sent were not received by receiving party $\mathcal{P}_j$, if messages to and from a NIV functionality $\mathcal{F}^V$ were not actually sent or received by $\mathcal{P}_i$ or if, in case a party $\mathcal{P}_i$ reveals its inputs x_i and randomness r_i, the messages $\mathcal{P}_i$ claims to have sent are inconsistent with x_i, r_i when considering nmes and the remaining transcript. We formalize this as *Transcript Validity* in the full version [6].

Transcript Non-Malleability: Tampering of an adversary with the transcript can be ok unless it leads to two self-consistent protocol transcripts with outputs $\widehat{y}_i^{(\tau)} \neq y_i^{(\tau)}$ for some $\mathcal{P}_i$ such that both $\widehat{y}_i^{(\tau)}, y_i^{(\tau)} \neq \bot$. To prevent this, transcript validity is a necessary, but not a sufficient condition. For example, if no messages or inputs or randomness of any party are fixed, then $\mathcal{A}$ could easily generate two correctly distributed transcripts for different outputs that fulfill this definition using the standard UC simulator of Π. We now describe a security game that constrains $\mathcal{A}$ beyond transcript validity:

1. $\mathcal{A}$ runs the protocol with a challenger $\mathcal{C}$, which simulates honest parties whose inputs and randomness $\mathcal{A}$ does not know, generating a transcript τ.

2. The adversary will obtain some additional potentially secret information of the honest parties from $\mathcal{C}$, upon which it outputs two valid protocol transcripts Π_0, Π_1.

3. $\mathcal{A}$ wins if Π_0, Π_1 coincide in certain parts with τ, while the outputs of some party $\mathcal{P}_i$ are different and not $\bot$.

We want to cover a diverse range of protocols which might come with different guarantees. We consider scenarios regarding: (1) whether the dishonest parties can change their inputs and randomness after the execution (parameter ν); (2) what is the set of parties RIR that will reveal their input and randomness later; and (3) which protocol messages the adversary can replace when he attempts to break the verifiability by presenting a fake transcript (parameter μ).

The parameters ν, RIR have the following impact: if $\nu = \mathsf{ncir}$ then the dishonest parties *are not committed* to the input and randomness in the beginning of the execution. Anything that is revealed from parties in $I \cap \mathsf{RIR}$ might be altered by the adversary. If instead $\nu = \mathsf{cir}$ then all parties *are committed* to the input and randomness in the beginning of the execution and the adversary cannot alter x_i, r_i revealed for verification by honest or dishonest parties from RIR. For μ we give the adversary the following choices:

$\mu = \mathsf{ncmes}$: $\mathcal{A}$ can replace all messages *by all parties*.
$\mu = \mathsf{chsmes}$: $\mathcal{A}$ can replace messages *from corrupted senders*.
$\mu = \mathsf{chmes}$: $\mathcal{A}$ can replace messages exchanged *between corrupted parties*.
$\mu = \mathsf{cmes}$: $\mathcal{A}$ cannot replace *any message*.

The full definition of *Transcript Non-Malleability* is given in the full version [6].

3.1   Simulating Verifiable Protocols: Input-Aware Simulation

Most simulators $\mathcal{S}$ for UC secure protocols Π work by executing an internal copy of the adversary $\mathcal{A}$ towards which they simulate interactions with simulated honest parties and ideal functionalities in the hybrid model where Π is defined. In general, $\mathcal{S}$ receives no external advice and generates random inputs for simulated honest parties and simulated ideal functionality responses with the aid of a random input tape, from which it samples all necessary values. However, a crucial point for our approach is being able to parameterize the operation of simulators for protocols being compiled, as well as giving them external input on how queries to simulated functionalities should be answered.

We need simulators with such properties in order to obtain publicly verifiable versions of existing protocols without requiring them to be adaptively secure as explained in Sect. 1.1. Basically, in the publicly verifiable version of a protocol, we wish to embed a special simulator into the publicly verifiable functionality that it realizes. This allows to "delegate" the simulation of the compiled protocol, while the simulator for the publicly verifiable version handles the machinery needed to obtain public verifiability. This simplifies the security analysis of publicly verifiable versions of existing UC-secure protocols, since only the added machinery for public verifiability must be analysed.

Über Simulator $\mathcal{S}^{U}$: We now introduce the notion of an *über simulator* for a UC-secure protocol Π realizing a functionality $\mathcal{F}$. We denote über simulators as $\mathcal{S}^{U}$, while we denote by $\mathcal{S}$ the original simulator used in the original UC proof. Basically, an über simulator $\mathcal{S}^{U}$ takes the inputs to be used by simulated honest parties, as well as the randomess of the functionality, as an external parameter, and uses these in interactions with the adversary. It furthermore outputs (through a special tape) the randomness used by these simulated parties. Instead of interacting with an internal copy of the adversary, an über simulator interacts with an *external* copy. Moreover, an über simulator allows for responses to queries to simulated functionalities to be given externally. Otherwise, $\mathcal{S}^{U}$ operates like a regular simulator, *e.g.* extracting corrupted partis' inputs.

In the case of a probabilistic functionality $\mathcal{F}$, the über simulator $\mathcal{S}^{U}$ also receives the randomness tape used by $\mathcal{F}$. $\mathcal{S}^{U}$ uses this tape to determine the random values that will be sampled by $\mathcal{F}$, simulating an execution compatible with such values and with the inputs from honest parties (if they have any).

Most existing simulators for protocols realizing the vast majority of natural UC functionalities can be trivially modified to obtain an über simulator which we explain in the full version [6]. This is because they basically execute the protocol as an honest party would, except that they use random inputs and leverage the setup to equivocate the output in the simulated execution. Departing from such a simulator, an über simulator can be constructed by allowing the simulated honest party inputs to be obtained externally, rather than generated randomly.

Syntax of Über Simulator $\mathcal{S}^{U}$: Let $\mathcal{S}^{U}$ be a PPT iTM with the same input and output tapes as a regular simulator $\mathcal{S}$ plus additional ones as defined below:

- **Input tapes:** a tape for the input from the environment $\mathcal{Z}$, a tape for messages from an ideal functionality $\mathcal{F}$, a tape for inputs for the simulated honest parties, a tape for messages from a copy of an adversary $\mathcal{A}$ (either connected to $\mathcal{A}$ or to $\mathcal{F}^{V}$'s **NMF**$_{\mathcal{S}^{U}}$ interface) and a tape for messages from the global ideal functionalities in the hybrid model where Π is defined. If $\mathcal{F}$ is probabilistic, $\mathcal{S}^{U}$ also receives $\mathcal{F}$'s random tape.
- **Output tapes:** tapes for output to $\mathcal{Z}$, tapes for messages to $\mathcal{F}, \mathcal{A}$, tapes for messages for the global ideal functionalities in the hybrid model where Π is defined as well as a special "control output tape" that outputs the randomness used by simulated honest parties.

For any PPT iTM $\mathcal{S}^{U}$ with the input and output tapes defined above, we then say that $\mathcal{S}^{U}$ is an über simulator if it has the properties of *simulation- and execution-consistency*, which are described in Definitions 2 and 3 below. Simulation consistency says that any regular ideal world execution of $\mathcal{F}$ with $\mathcal{S}$ is indistinguishable from an execution of $\mathcal{F}$ with $\mathcal{S}^{U}$ where $\mathcal{S}^{U}$ operates as $\mathcal{S}$ does (*i.e.* with direct access to a copy of the adversary $\mathcal{A}$ and the global setup) but is parameterized by the dummy honest party inputs instead of choosing simulated honest party inputs at random. Formally, simulation consistency is as follows:

Definition 2 (Simulation Consistency). *Let Π be a protocol UC-realizing functionality $\mathcal{F}$ using ideal functionalities $\mathcal{F}_1, \ldots, \mathcal{F}_r$ as setup and let $\mathcal{S}$ be the* *simulator of $\mathcal{F}$'s proof. We say that the PPT iTM $\mathcal{S}^{U}$ is Simulation-consistent for $(\Pi, \mathcal{F}, \mathcal{S})$ if these distributions are indistinguishable for all PPT iTM $\mathcal{Z}$:*

1. *$\mathcal{F} \circ \mathcal{S}$: The distribution of outputs of $\mathcal{Z}$ in an ideal execution of $\mathcal{F}$ and $\mathcal{S}$ executing an internal copy of adversary $\mathcal{A}$ and potentially a set of global functionalities.*
2. *$\mathcal{F} \circ \mathcal{S}^{U}$: The distribution of outputs of $\mathcal{Z}$ in an ideal execution of $\mathcal{F}$ with $\mathcal{S}^{U}$, where $\mathcal{S}^{U}$'s corresponding input/output tapes are connected directly to a copy of $\mathcal{A}$ and to global setup functionalities (instead of $\mathcal{F}^{V}$'s $\mathbf{NMF}_{\mathcal{S}^{U}}$ interface). $\mathcal{S}^{U}$'s tapes for simulated honest party inputs are initialized with the same inputs that are provided by the dummy honest parties to $\mathcal{F}$ and $\mathcal{S}^{U}$ is given a uniformly random tape.*

$\mathcal{Z}$ gives inputs to all parties as in the standard UC simulation experiment but only has access to the same input/output tapes of $\mathcal{S}^{U}$ that it can access for $\mathcal{S}$.

We remark that $\mathcal{S}^{U}$ does not have two explicitly different modes of operations depending on whether it is executed inside $\mathcal{F}^{V}$ or in the experiment of Definition 2. In both scenarios, $\mathcal{S}^{U}$ has the same input/output tapes and access to $\mathcal{F}$'s interfaces, with the sole differences being its input/output tapes for a copy of the adversary being either directly connected to the adversary in the experiment of Definition 2 or to $\mathcal{F}^{V}$'s $\mathbf{NMF}_{\mathcal{S}^{U}}$ interface and its input/output tapes for global setup functionalities being connected to these functionalities in the experiment of Definition 2 or to $\mathcal{F}^{V}$'s $\mathbf{NMF}_{\mathcal{S}^{U}}$ interface. This observation is important when arguing why $\mathcal{S}^{U}$ does not give $\mathcal{F}^{V}$'s ideal adversary (*i.e.* $\mathcal{F}^{V}$'s simulator) any undue advantage by, *e.g.*, leaking information about honest parties' inputs.

Execution consistency states that the randomness for simulated honest parties output by an über simulator $\mathcal{S}^{U}$ parameterized with the same inputs as the real honest parties must be consistent with the randomness of a real protocol execution. We use the following formal definition:

Definition 3 (Execution Consistency). *Let Π be a UC-secure implementation of the functionality $\mathcal{F}$ in the $\mathcal{F}_1, \ldots, \mathcal{F}_r$-hybrid model and let $\mathcal{S}$ be the simulator of the proof. We say that the PPT iTM $\mathcal{S}^{U}$ is Execution-consistent for $(\Pi, \mathcal{F}, \mathcal{S})$ if for all PPT iTM $\mathcal{Z}$ and PPT iTM $\mathcal{A}$ the following distributions are indistinguishable:*

1. *The distribution of outputs of $\mathcal{Z}$ in a real execution of Π with adversary $\mathcal{A}$ and honest parties $\mathcal{P}_1, \ldots, \mathcal{P}_k$ whose input and randomness pairs are (x_{h_1}, R_{h_1}), $\ldots, (x_{h_k}, R_{h_k})$ in the $\mathcal{F}_1, \ldots, \mathcal{F}_r$-hybrid model. The tuple of honest party randomness $(R_{h_1}, \ldots, R_{h_k})$ is output by $\mathcal{S}^{U}$ after an execution with $\mathcal{F}$ where $\mathcal{S}^{U}$ interacts with a copy of $\mathcal{A}$ and $\mathcal{S}^{U}$'s tapes for simulated honest party inputs are initialized with the same honest party inputs $(x_{h_1}, \ldots, x_{h_k})$ as those given to $\mathcal{P}_1, \ldots, \mathcal{P}_k$.*
2. *The distribution of outputs of $\mathcal{Z}$ in a real execution of Π with adversary $\mathcal{A}$ and honest parties $\mathcal{P}_1, \ldots, \mathcal{P}_k$ with inputs $(x_{h_1}, \ldots, x_{h_k})$ in the $\mathcal{F}_1, \ldots, \mathcal{F}_r$-hybrid model where honest party randomness is sampled by $\mathcal{Z}$.*

$\mathcal{Z}$ gives inputs to all parties in both the ideal and real executions as in the standard UC simulation experiment, the difference being that in 1. honest party randomness is provided by $\mathcal{S}^{U}$ and in 2. it is sampled by $\mathcal{Z}$.

For any PPT iTM $\mathcal{S}^{U}$ with the input and output tapes defined above we then say that $\mathcal{S}^{U}$ is an über simulator if it is simulation- and execution-consistent. We summarize this in the full version [6].

Über Simulators with Global Setup: In order to argue that $\mathcal{S}^{U}$ does not leak any information on honest parties' inputs through $\mathcal{F}^{V}$'s $\mathbf{NMF}_{\mathcal{S}^v}$ interface, we will restrict the class of global functionalities that can be used as setup in compiled protocols. Intuitively, we require that all global functionalities used by a protocol with a global simulator provide all parties with access to the same interface and answers queries from all parties with the same answer (e.g. in a global random oracle). This is necessary both for practical and technical reasons: 1-(practical) the verification procedure of our compiler needs the same access to global setup as the party who activated verification and revealed its input/randomness; 2-(technical) $\mathcal{S}^{U}$ must not be able to distinguish whether it is operating within $\mathcal{F}^{V}$ or within the experiment of Definition 2. In order to achieve these goals, we introduce the notion of Admissible Global Setup in Definition 4 and restrict our compiler to work only on protocols with Admissible Global Setup.

Definition 4 (Admissible Global Setup). *A global ideal functionality $\mathcal{G}$ is admissible if:*

- *All parties $\mathcal{P}_i \in \mathcal{P}$ have access to the same interfaces (i.e. all parties can send the same queries to $\mathcal{G}$).*
- *For all of $\mathcal{G}$'s interfaces, for all possible queries Q, there exists a single response R such that, upon receiving a query Q_j from any party $\mathcal{P}_i \in \mathcal{P}$, $\mathcal{G}$ returns R.*

3.2   Functionalities $\mathcal{F}^{V}$ with Embedded Über Simulator $\mathcal{S}^{U}$

We now outline how an über simulator $\mathcal{S}^{U}$ (Definition in the full version [6]) for the protocol Π will be used with a functionality $\mathcal{F}^{V}$. Note that $\mathcal{S}^{U}$ is internally executed by the functionality wrapper $\mathcal{F}^{V}$ presented in Fig. 3, which can be accessed by an ideal adversary (i.e. $\mathcal{F}^{V}$'s Simulator) interacting with $\mathcal{F}^{V}$ through interfaces $\mathbf{Input}_i$ and $\mathbf{NMF}_{\mathcal{S}^v}$. Moreover, $\mathcal{F}^{V}$ allows $\mathcal{S}^{U}$ to query admissible global setup functionalities $\mathcal{F}_1, \ldots, \mathcal{F}_n$ (according to Definition 4) on behalf of honest parties.

The internal $\mathcal{S}^{U}$ executed by $\mathcal{F}^{V}$ takes care of simulating the original protocol Π that realizes $\mathcal{F}$ being compiled into a publicly verifiable protocol Π^{V} that realizes $\mathcal{F}^{V}[\mathcal{F}]$, while the external $\mathcal{S}^{V}$ interacting with $\mathcal{F}^{V}$ will take care of simulating the additional protocol steps and building blocks used in obtaining public verifiability in Π^{V}. In order to do so, $\mathcal{F}^{V}$ will parameterize $\mathcal{S}^{U}$ with the inputs of all honest parties $\mathcal{P}_i$, which are received through interface $\mathbf{Input}_i$, as well as the randomness of $\mathcal{F}$ if the functionality is probabilistic. As the execution progresses, $\mathcal{S}^{\mathsf{V}}$ executes the compiled protocol Π^{V} with an internal copy $\mathcal{A}$ of the adversary and extracts the messages of the original protocol Π from this execution, forwarding these messages to $\mathcal{S}^{\mathsf{U}}$ through the interface $\mathbf{NMF}_{\mathcal{S}^{\mathsf{U}}}$. Moreover, $\mathcal{S}^{\mathsf{V}}$ will provide answers to queries to setup functionalities from $\mathcal{A}$ as instructed by $\mathcal{S}^{\mathsf{U}}$ also through interface $\mathbf{NMF}_{\mathcal{S}^{\mathsf{U}}}$. All the while, queries from honest parties simulated by $\mathcal{S}^{\mathsf{U}}$ to setup functionalities are directly forwarded back and forth by $\mathcal{F}^{\mathsf{V}}$. If verification is ever activated by an honest party $\mathcal{P}_i$ (and $\mathcal{P}_i \in \mathsf{RIR}$), $\mathcal{F}^{\mathsf{V}}$ not only leaks that party's input to $\mathcal{S}^{\mathsf{V}}$ but also leaks that party's randomness R_{h_i} in the simulated execution with $\mathcal{S}^{\mathsf{U}}$ (provided by $\mathcal{S}^{\mathsf{U}}$). As we discuss in Sect. 5, this will allow $\mathcal{S}^{\mathsf{V}}$ to simulate verification, since it now has both a valid transcript of an execution of Π^{V} with $\mathcal{A}$ and a matching input and randomness pair that matches that transcript (provided by $\mathcal{F}^{\mathsf{V}}$ with the help of $\mathcal{S}^{\mathsf{U}}$).

We remark that this strategy does not give the simulator $\mathcal{S}^{\mathsf{V}}$ any extra power in simulating an execution of the compiled protocol Π^{V} towards $\mathcal{A}$ other than the power the simulator $\mathcal{S}$ for the original protocol Π already has. We will establish that the access to $\mathcal{S}^{\mathsf{U}}$ given by $\mathcal{F}^{\mathsf{V}}$ to $\mathcal{S}^{\mathsf{V}}$ does not allow it to obtain any information about the inputs of honest parties. Notice that in an execution with admissible global setup (according to Definition 4), the only difference between $\mathcal{S}^{\mathsf{U}}$'s execution within $\mathcal{F}^{\mathsf{V}}$ and $\mathcal{S}^{\mathsf{U}}$'s execution in the experiment of Definition 2 is that, when it is executed within $\mathcal{F}^{\mathsf{V}}$, its input/output tapes for a copy of the adversary are connected to $\mathcal{S}^{\mathsf{U}}$ via the $\mathbf{NMF}_{\mathcal{S}^{\mathsf{U}}}$ interface. Hence, the only way $\mathcal{S}^{\mathsf{U}}$ can detect that it is being executed within $\mathcal{F}^{\mathsf{V}}$ and leak any undue information is via its interaction via the adversary input/output tapes. However, the definition in the full version [6] establishes that this interaction is indistinguishable from that of the original simulator $\mathcal{S}$ for protocol Π. Since Π is UC-secure, an execution of $\mathcal{F}$ with $\mathcal{S}$ does not leak any information about the simulated parties' inputs (i.e. inputs randomly picked by $\mathcal{S}$), which would trivially allow $\mathcal{Z}$ to distinguish an execution of $\mathcal{F}$ with $\mathcal{S}$ from a real world execution of Π with $\mathcal{A}$. Thus, by the definition of an über simulator in the full version [6] and the UC security of Π, $\mathcal{S}^{\mathsf{U}}$ does not leak any information about honest party inputs to $\mathcal{S}^{\mathsf{V}}$ via interface $\mathbf{NMF}_{\mathcal{S}^{\mathsf{U}}}$ when executed within $\mathcal{F}^{\mathsf{V}}$.

4   Joint Authentication Functionalities

We now define authentication functionalities that serve as building blocks for our compiler. These functionalities allow for a set of parties to jointly authenticate messages but do *not* deliver these messages themselves. Later on, a verifier can check that a given message has indeed been authenticated by a given set of parties, meaning that they have received this message through a channel and agree on it. More interestingly, we extend this functionality to allow for joint authentication of *private* messages that are only known in encrypted form.

As opposed to classical point-to-point or broadcast authenticated channels, our functionalities do not deliver messages to the receiving parties and consequently do not ensure consensus. These functionalities come into play in our compiler later as they allow for verifiers to check that all parties who executed a protocol agree on the transcript (that might contain private messages) regardless of how the messages in the transcript have been obtained. Having the parties agree on which messages have been sent limits the adversary's power to generate an alternative transcript aiming at forging a proof that the protocol reached a different outcome, i.e. our notion of *transcript non-malleability*.

Public Joint Authentication: First, consider the simple case of authenticating public messages (known by all parties participating in the joint authentication procedure). Here, the *sender* starts by providing a message and *ssid* pair to the functionality and joint authentication is achieved after each of the other parties sends the same pair to the functionality. This can be implemented by a simple protocol where all parties sign each message received from each other party in each round, sending the resulting signatures to all other parties. A message is considered authenticated if it is signed by all parties. Notice that this protocol does not ensure consensus and can easily fail if a single party does not provide a valid signature on a single message, which an adversary corrupting any party (or the network) can always cause (this is captured in the functionality). Functionality $\mathcal{F}_{\mathsf{PJAuth}}$ is described in the full version [6].

Secret Joint Authentication: We further define a functionality $\mathcal{F}_{\mathsf{SJAuth}}$ (described inthe full version [6]). This functionality works similarly to $\mathcal{F}_{\mathsf{PJAuth}}$, allowing parties to jointly authenticate messages received through private channels to which they have access. However, it also allows for *bureaucrat* parties who observe the encrypted communication (but do not see plaintext messages) over the private channel to jointly authenticate a *committed* version of these plaintext messages. If a private message is revealed by its sender (or one of its receivers), $\mathcal{F}_{\mathsf{SJAuth}}$ allows third parties (including the bureaucrats) to verify that this message is indeed the one that was authenticated.

In order to capture the different actions of each party it interacts with, $\mathcal{F}_{\mathsf{SJAuth}}$ is parameterized by the following (sets of) parties: a sender $\mathcal{P}_{\mathsf{snd}}$ that can input messages to be jointly authenticated; a set of parties $\mathcal{P}$ who receive input messages from $\mathcal{P}_{\mathsf{snd}}$ and jointly authenticate them; a set of bureaucrats $\mathcal{B}$ who jointly authenticate that $\mathcal{P}_{\mathsf{snd}}$ has sent a certain (unknown to them) committed message to $\mathcal{P}$. $\mathcal{F}_{\mathsf{SJAuth}}$, like $\mathcal{F}_{\mathsf{PJAuth}}$, does not aid in sending messages, notifications about sent messages nor joint authentication information to any party. The responsibility for sending messages lies with $\mathcal{P}_{\mathsf{snd}}$, while $\mathcal{P}_{\mathsf{snd}}$ or $\mathcal{P}_i \in \mathcal{P}$ can notify other parties that plaintext verification is possible.

We realize $\mathcal{F}_{\mathsf{SJAuth}}$ with a signature scheme and a certified encryption scheme with plaintext verification, *i.e.* an encryption scheme with two properties: (1) all parties' public keys are registered in a PKI, making sure that encrypted messages can only be opened by the intended receiver; (2) Both encrypting and decrypting parties can generate publicly verifiable proofs that a certain message was contained in a given ciphertext. The private channel itself is realized by encrypting messages under the encryption scheme, while joint authentication is achieved by having all parties in $\mathcal{P}$ (including the sender) and bureaucrats in $\mathcal{B}$ sign the resulting ciphertext. To prove that a certain message was indeed contained in the ciphertext, the receiver(s) recovers the plaintext message and a proof of plaintext validity from the ciphertext and sends those to the verifier(s). Finally, a verifier first checks that the message was indeed contained in a previously sent ciphertext and that this ciphertext has been signed by all parties in $\mathcal{P}$ and $\mathcal{B}$. This construction and a concrete realization are described in the full version [6].

Authenticating Inputs and Randomness: To provide an authentication of inputs and randomness we adapt the functionality $\mathcal{F}_{\mathsf{SJAuth}}$, as the desired capabilities are like a message authentication without a receiver. In the full version [6] we present a functionality $\mathcal{F}_{\mathsf{IRAuth}}$ that implements this.

5   Compilation for Input-Revealing Protocols

We now sketch how to compile protocols from Sect. 2 into non-interactively verifiable counterparts. As we focus on protocols according to the definition in the full version [6] there are 8 combinations of parameters (ν, μ) for (ν, RIR, μ)-transcript non-malleable protocols to consider. Furthermore we might either have public or private verifier registration, which in total yields 16 different definitions. To avoid redundancy we now outline how to get the respective verifiability in each setting. We simplify notation by just using a single verifier $\mathcal{V}$.

Assume a (ν, RIR, μ)-transcript non-malleable protocol Π that UC realizes the functionality $\mathcal{F}$ in the (global) $\mathcal{F}_1, \ldots, \mathcal{F}_r$-hybrid model with über simulator $\mathcal{S}^{\mathsf{U}}$ for $(\Pi, \mathcal{F}, \mathcal{S})$. Then compilation works as follows:

1. We describe how to construct a protocol Π^{V} by modifying Π with access to a signature functionality $\mathcal{F}_{\mathsf{Sig}}$, a key registration functionality $\mathcal{F}_{\mathsf{Reg}}$ and authentication functionalities $\mathcal{F}_{\mathsf{PJAuth}}, \mathcal{F}_{\mathsf{SJAuth}}, \mathcal{F}_{\mathsf{IRAuth}}$. We will furthermore require that we can replace the hybrid functionalities $\mathcal{F}_1, \ldots, \mathcal{F}_r$ used in Π with verifiable counterparts $\mathcal{F}_1^{\mathsf{V}}, \ldots, \mathcal{F}_r^{\mathsf{V}}$.
2. In Appendix 3.2 we show how Π^{V} UC-realizes $\mathcal{F}^{\mathsf{V}}[\mathcal{F}]$ in the $\mathcal{F}_1^{\mathsf{V}}, \ldots, \mathcal{F}_r^{\mathsf{V}}$-hybrid by constructing a simulator $\mathcal{S}^{\mathsf{V}}$.

Protocol Compilation - The Big Picture. In order to verify we let the verifier $\mathcal{V}$ simulate each such party whose output shall be checked and which participated in an instance of Π. This check is done locally, based on the inputs, randomness and messages related to such a party (and/or other parties) which $\mathcal{V}$ obtains for this process. In case of public verifier registration we assume that a bulletin board is available which holds the protocol transcript, whereas in case of private registration the verifier contacts one of the protocol parties to obtain a transcript which it can then verify non-interactively. We want to stress that the Bulletin Board which may contain the protocol transcript *does not have to be used to exchange messages during the actual protocol run.*

In Π we assume that messages can either be exchanged secretly between two parties or via a broadcast channel. Furthermore, parties may send messages to hybrid functionalities or receive them from these. An adversary may be able to replace certain parts of the protocol transcript. As long as we assume that a protocol is (ν, RIR, μ)-transcript non-malleable and constrain his ability to maul the protocol transcript to those parts permitted by the definition, the overall construction achieves verifiability. We now explain, on a high level, the modifications to Π for the different values of μ, ν:

$\mu = \mathsf{ncmes}$: The adversary can replace all messages by any party at his will, and messages are just exchanged as in Π.

$\mu = \mathsf{chsmes}$: Before the protocol begins, each $\mathcal{P}_i$ generates a signing key with $\mathcal{F}_{\mathsf{Sig}}$ and registers its signing key with $\mathcal{F}_{\mathsf{Reg}}$. Whenever $\mathcal{P}_i$ sends a message $\mathsf{m}_{i,j}$ to $\mathcal{P}_j$ it uses $\mathcal{F}_{\mathsf{Sig}}$ to authenticate $\mathsf{m}_{i,j}$ with a signature $\sigma_{i,j}$. $\mathcal{V}$ will later be able to verify exactly those messages that were sent by honest parties, as $\mathcal{A}$ can fake messages and signatures sent by dishonest parties.

$\mu = \mathsf{chmes}$: Each message that is either sent or received by an honest party must remain unaltered. Each party will do the same as for $\mu = \mathsf{chsmes}$, but whenever $\mathcal{P}_i$ receives a message $\mathsf{m}_{j,i}$ from $\mathcal{P}_j$ then it uses $\mathcal{F}_{\mathsf{Sig}}$ to authenticate $\mathsf{m}_{j,i}$ with a signature $\sigma_{j,i}$. Now $\mathcal{V}$ can establish for each message of the protocol if both sender and receiver signed the same message. $\mathcal{A}$ can only alter messages that were both sent and received by dishonest parties.

$\mu = \mathsf{cmes}$: Here dishonest parties cannot replace their messages before verification. To achieve this, we use $\mathcal{F}_{\mathsf{SJAuth}}, \mathcal{F}_{\mathsf{PJAuth}}$ as defined in Sect. 4 which the parties now use to register their private message exchange. These functionalities can then be used by $\mathcal{V}$ to validate the transcript.

$\nu = \mathsf{ncir}$: Based on each $\mathcal{P}_i$ setting up a key with $\mathcal{F}_{\mathsf{Sig}}$ and registering it with $\mathcal{F}_{\mathsf{Reg}}$ let each party sign both its input x_i and its randomness r_i using $\mathcal{F}_{\mathsf{Sig}}$ before sending it in **Activate Verification**. $\mathcal{V}$ now only accepts such signed values which it can verify via $\mathcal{F}_{\mathsf{Sig}}$. $\mathcal{A}$ can replace the pairs (x_j, r_j) of dishonest parties $\mathcal{P}_j$ by generating different signatures.

$\nu = \mathsf{cir}$: The parties use $\mathcal{F}_{\mathsf{IRAuth}}$ to authenticate their inputs and randomness. $\mathcal{V}$ uses $\mathcal{F}_{\mathsf{IRAuth}}$ to check validity of the revealed x_i, r_i which it obtained.

Hybrid Functionalities: Replace the hybrid functionalities $\mathcal{F}_1, \ldots, \mathcal{F}_r$ with NIV counterparts, i.e. with functionalities $\mathcal{F}_1^{\mathsf{V}}, \ldots, \mathcal{F}_r^{\mathsf{V}}$ that have the same interfaces as defined in Sect. 2.1. To achieve public verifiability each such $\mathcal{F}_q^{\mathsf{V}}$ must also be publicly verifiable. If a global functionality is used as setup, it must be admissible according to Definition 4, so that the verification procedure can re-execute the protocol. For any such $\mathcal{F}_q^{\mathsf{V}}$, $\mathcal{V}$ can establish if a message $\mathsf{mres}_{q,i}$ was indeed sent to $\mathcal{P}_i$ or not. If $\mathcal{F}_q^{\mathsf{V}}$ does also reveal inputs, it can also test if $\mathsf{mres}_{i,q}$ as claimed to be sent by $\mathcal{P}_i$ was indeed received by the functionality.

Public Verifiability Compiler. The basic idea is to turn any (ν, RIR, μ)-transcript non-malleable protocol into a $(\mathsf{cir}, \mathsf{RIR}, \mu)$-transcript non-malleable protocol by forcing the adversary to commit to all the corrupted parties' randomness and inputs, and then turn it into a $(\mathsf{cir}, \mathsf{RIR}, \mathsf{cmes})$-transcript non-malleable protocol by forcing the adversary to commit to all messages. While this might be overkill for some protocols, we focus on the worst case scenario of compiling (ncir, RIR, ncmes)-transcript non-malleable protocols, since it is the most challenging. After making a protocol (cir, RIR, cmes)-transcript non-malleable, the protocol execution becomes deterministic and can be verified upon revealing of the randomness, input and transcript of any party that activates the verification. All the verifier has to do is to execute the protocol's next message function on these randomness and input taking received messages from the transcript. We present a detailed description of this compiler and a formal theorem statement together with its proof in the full version [6].

References

1. Alwen, J., Ostrovsky, R., Zhou, H.-S., Zikas, V.: Incoercible multi-party computation and universally composable receipt-free voting. In: Gennaro, R., Robshaw, M. (eds.) CRYPTO 2015. LNCS, vol. 9216, pp. 763–780. Springer, Heidelberg (2015). https://doi.org/10.1007/978-3-662-48000-7_37
2. Andrychowicz, M., Dziembowski, S., Malinowski, D., Mazurek, L.: Secure multi-party computations on bitcoin. In: 2014 IEEE Symposium on Security and Privacy, pp. 443–458. IEEE Computer Society Press, May 2014
3. Asharov, G., Orlandi, C.: Calling out cheaters: covert security with public verifiability. In: Wang, X., Sako, K. (eds.) ASIACRYPT 2012. LNCS, vol. 7658, pp. 681–698. Springer, Heidelberg (2012). https://doi.org/10.1007/978-3-642-34961-4_41
4. Baum, C., Damgård, I., Orlandi, C.: Publicly auditable secure multi-party computation. In: Abdalla, M., De Prisco, R. (eds.) SCN 2014. LNCS, vol. 8642, pp. 175–196. Springer, Cham (2014). https://doi.org/10.1007/978-3-319-10879-7_11
5. Baum, C., David, B., Dowsley, R.: Insured MPC: efficient secure computation with financial penalties. In: Bonneau, J., Heninger, N. (eds.) FC 2020. LNCS, vol. 12059, pp. 404–420. Springer, Cham (2020). https://doi.org/10.1007/978-3-030-51280-4_22
6. Baum, C., David, B., Dowsley, R.: (Public) verifiability for composable protocols without adaptivity or zero-knowledge. Cryptology ePrint Archive, Paper 2020/207 (2020). https://eprint.iacr.org/2020/207
7. Baum, C., David, B., Frederiksen, T.K.: P2DEX: privacy-preserving decentralized cryptocurrency exchange. In: Sako, K., Tippenhauer, N.O. (eds.) ACNS 2021. LNCS, vol. 12726, pp. 163–194. Springer, Cham (2021). https://doi.org/10.1007/978-3-030-78372-3_7
8. Baum, C., Orsini, E., Scholl, P.: Efficient secure multiparty computation with identifiable abort. In: Hirt, M., Smith, A. (eds.) TCC 2016. LNCS, vol. 9985, pp. 461–490. Springer, Heidelberg (2016). https://doi.org/10.1007/978-3-662-53641-4_18
9. Baum, C., Orsini, E., Scholl, P., Soria-Vazquez, E.: Efficient constant-round MPC with identifiable abort and public verifiability. In: Micciancio, D., Ristenpart, T. (eds.) CRYPTO 2020. LNCS, vol. 12171, pp. 562–592. Springer, Cham (2020). https://doi.org/10.1007/978-3-030-56880-1_20
10. Bellare, M., Hoang, V.T., Rogaway, P.: Adaptively secure garbling with applications to one-time programs and secure outsourcing. In: Wang, X., Sako, K. (eds.) ASIACRYPT 2012. LNCS, vol. 7658, pp. 134–153. Springer, Heidelberg (2012). https://doi.org/10.1007/978-3-642-34961-4_10

11. Bentov, I., Kumaresan, R.: How to use bitcoin to design fair protocols. In: Garay, J.A., Gennaro, R. (eds.) CRYPTO 2014. LNCS, vol. 8617, pp. 421–439. Springer, Heidelberg (2014). https://doi.org/10.1007/978-3-662-44381-1_24

12. Camenisch, J., Dubovitskaya, M., Rial, A.: UC commitments for modular protocol design and applications to revocation and attribute tokens. In: Robshaw, M., Katz, J. (eds.) CRYPTO 2016. LNCS, vol. 9816, pp. 208–239. Springer, Heidelberg (2016). https://doi.org/10.1007/978-3-662-53015-3_8

13. Camenisch, J., Lehmann, A., Neven, G., Samelin, K.: UC-secure non-interactive public-key encryption. In: IEEE CSF 2017 (2017)

14. Canetti, R.: Universally composable security: a new paradigm for cryptographic protocols. In: 42nd FOCS, pp. 136–145. IEEE Computer Society Press, October 2001

15. Canetti, R.: Universally composable signature, certification, and authentication. In: CSFW 2004 (2004)

16. Canetti, R., Dodis, Y., Pass, R., Walfish, S.: Universally composable security with global setup. In: Vadhan, S.P. (ed.) TCC 2007. LNCS, vol. 4392, pp. 61–85. Springer, Heidelberg (2007). https://doi.org/10.1007/978-3-540-70936-7_4

17. Canetti, R., Herzog, J.: Universally composable symbolic analysis of mutual authentication and key-exchange protocols. In: Halevi, S., Rabin, T. (eds.) TCC 2006. LNCS, vol. 3876, pp. 380–403. Springer, Heidelberg (2006). https://doi.org/10.1007/11681878_20

18. Canetti, R., Jain, A., Scafuro, A.: Practical UC security with a global random oracle. In: Ahn, G.-J., Yung, M., Li, N. (eds.) ACM CCS 2014, pp. 597–608. ACM Press, November 2014

19. Canetti, R., Rabin, T.: Universal composition with joint state. In: Boneh, D. (ed.) CRYPTO 2003. LNCS, vol. 2729, pp. 265–281. Springer, Heidelberg (2003). https://doi.org/10.1007/978-3-540-45146-4_16

20. Canetti, R., Sarkar, P., Wang, X.: Blazing fast OT for three-round UC OT extension. In: Kiayias, A., Kohlweiss, M., Wallden, P., Zikas, V. (eds.) PKC 2020. LNCS, vol. 12111, pp. 299–327. Springer, Cham (2020). https://doi.org/10.1007/978-3-030-45388-6_11

21. Canetti, R., Sarkar, P., Wang, X.: Efficient and round-optimal oblivious transfer and commitment with adaptive security. In: Moriai, S., Wang, H. (eds.) ASIACRYPT 2020. LNCS, vol. 12493, pp. 277–308. Springer, Cham (2020). https://doi.org/10.1007/978-3-030-64840-4_10

22. Cascudo, I., David, B.: SCRAPE: scalable randomness attested by public entities. In: Gollmann, D., Miyaji, A., Kikuchi, H. (eds.) ACNS 2017. LNCS, vol. 10355, pp. 537–556. Springer, Cham (2017). https://doi.org/10.1007/978-3-319-61204-1_27

23. Cascudo, I., David, B.: ALBATROSS: publicly AttestabLe BATched randomness based on secret sharing. In: Moriai, S., Wang, H. (eds.) ASIACRYPT 2020. LNCS, vol. 12493, pp. 311–341. Springer, Cham (2020). https://doi.org/10.1007/978-3-030-64840-4_11

24. Chen, J., Micali, S.: Algorand: a secure and efficient distributed ledger. Theor. Comput. Sci. **777**, 155–183 (2019)

25. Cleve, R.: Limits on the security of coin flips when half the processors are faulty (extended abstract). In: 18th ACM STOC, pp. 364–369. ACM Press, May 1986

26. Damgård, I., Pastro, V., Smart, N., Zakarias, S.: Multiparty computation from somewhat homomorphic encryption. In: Safavi-Naini, R., Canetti, R. (eds.) CRYPTO 2012. LNCS, vol. 7417, pp. 643–662. Springer, Heidelberg (2012). https://doi.org/10.1007/978-3-642-32009-5_38

27. David, B., Gaži, P., Kiayias, A., Russell, A.: Ouroboros praos: an adaptively-secure, semi-synchronous proof-of-stake blockchain. In: Nielsen, J.B., Rijmen, V. (eds.) EUROCRYPT 2018. LNCS, vol. 10821, pp. 66–98. Springer, Cham (2018). https://doi.org/10.1007/978-3-319-78375-8_3

28. Garay, J., Kiayias, A., Leonardos, N.: The bitcoin backbone protocol: analysis and applications. In: Oswald, E., Fischlin, M. (eds.) EUROCRYPT 2015. LNCS, vol. 9057, pp. 281–310. Springer, Heidelberg (2015). https://doi.org/10.1007/978-3-662-46803-6_10

29. Goldreich, O., Micali, S., Wigderson, A.: How to play any mental game or a completeness theorem for protocols with honest majority. In: Aho, A. (ed.) 19th ACM STOC, pp. 218–229. ACM Press, May 1987

30. Ishai, Y., Ostrovsky, R., Zikas, V.: Secure multi-party computation with identifiable abort. In: Garay, J.A., Gennaro, R. (eds.) CRYPTO 2014. LNCS, vol. 8617, pp. 369–386. Springer, Heidelberg (2014). https://doi.org/10.1007/978-3-662-44381-1_21

31. Jafargholi, Z., Oechsner, S.: Adaptive security of practical garbling schemes. In: Bhargavan, K., Oswald, E., Prabhakaran, M. (eds.) INDOCRYPT 2020. LNCS, vol. 12578, pp. 741–762. Springer, Cham (2020). https://doi.org/10.1007/978-3-030-65277-7_33

32. Kiayias, A., Russell, A., David, B., Oliynykov, R.: Ouroboros: a provably secure proof-of-stake blockchain protocol. In: Katz, J., Shacham, H. (eds.) CRYPTO 2017. LNCS, vol. 10401, pp. 357–388. Springer, Cham (2017). https://doi.org/10.1007/978-3-319-63688-7_12

33. Kiayias, A., Zhou, H.-S., Zikas, V.: Fair and robust multi-party computation using a global transaction ledger. In: Fischlin, M., Coron, J.-S. (eds.) EUROCRYPT 2016. LNCS, vol. 9666, pp. 705–734. Springer, Heidelberg (2016). https://doi.org/10.1007/978-3-662-49896-5_25

34. Lindell, Y., Pinkas, B.: Secure two-party computation via cut-and-choose oblivious transfer. J. Cryptol. 25(4), 680–722 (2012)

35. Nakamoto, S.: Bitcoin: a peer-to-peer electronic cash system (2008)

36. Nielsen, J.B., Nordholt, P.S., Orlandi, C., Burra, S.S.: A new approach to practical active-secure two-party computation. In: Safavi-Naini, R., Canetti, R. (eds.) CRYPTO 2012. LNCS, vol. 7417, pp. 681–700. Springer, Heidelberg (2012). https://doi.org/10.1007/978-3-642-32009-5_40

37. Schoenmakers, B., Veeningen, M.: Universally verifiable multiparty computation from threshold homomorphic cryptosystems. In: Malkin, T., Kolesnikov, V., Lewko, A.B., Polychronakis, M. (eds.) ACNS 2015. LNCS, vol. 9092, pp. 3–22. Springer, Cham (2015). https://doi.org/10.1007/978-3-319-28166-7_1

38. Zahur, S., Rosulek, M., Evans, D.: Two halves make a whole - reducing data transfer in garbled circuits using half gates. In: Oswald, E., Fischlin, M. (eds.) EUROCRYPT 2015. LNCS, vol. 9057, pp. 220–250. Springer, Heidelberg (2015). https://doi.org/10.1007/978-3-662-46803-6_8

Practical Non-malleable Codes from Symmetric-Key Primitives in 2-Split-State Model

Anit Kumar Ghosal[✉] [ID], Satrajit Ghosh[ID], and Dipanwita Roychowdhury[ID]

Department of Computer Science and Engineering, IIT Kharagpur, Kharagpur, India
anit.ghosal@gmail.com

Abstract. Non-malleable codes (NMC) are introduced as a relaxation of error correcting codes to protect message against tampering attacks. It is guaranteed that a message encoded with non-malleable codes, if tampered by some classes of tampering functions, produces either completely unrelated message or the original message, when tampering has no effect. Kiayias et al. [19] have proposed a NMC construction based on leakage resilient authenticated encryption (AE) and 1-more extractable hash function. They obtain a codeword of length $|m| + 18n$ in *common reference string* (CRS) model. In this paper, we propose a construction of computationally secure non-malleable code in 2-split-state model from an *authenticated encryption* scheme with close to optimal codeword length $|m| + 2n$. Specifically we use an AE based on triple M-DES and CBC-MAC. The security of our NMC reduces to related-key and pseudorandom permutation security of the underlying block cipher under leakage, and also to the unforgeability of the CBC-MAC under leakage.

Keywords: Authenticated encryption · Block cipher · Leakage resilient CBC-MAC · Non-malleable code · 2-split-state model

1 Introduction

In this era of digital revolution it is often required to store highly sensitive information into various devices. Crypto devices that are used in embedded applications, store the secret key in conjunction with the cryptographic algorithm as a part of hardware implementation. Physical attacks on crypto hardware modules exploit the weaknesses of implementation mechanisms. One of the active classes of physical attack is the tampering attack which can be performed by viruses, malwares or adversaries with fault injection capabilities. Fault attack is an active class of physical attack where an adversary injects some faults during runtime of cryptographic algorithms [4]. The goal of an adversary is to extract a valid key by analysing faulty and fault free outputs. A number of research methodology have also been explored to protect cryptographic schemes from tampering attacks [5,10,11,13,15].

Non-malleable code, introduced by Dziembowski et al. [9], is used as one of the important tools of tamper-resilient cryptography. Instead of storing secret message in clear form, one may store the encoded version of secret message using non-malleable code. During cryptographic computation, decoding is performed to retrieve clear message. Any tampering on the encoded secret message, changes the output in an independent way from the original one. Let k be the secret message we store using non-malleable code as Encode(k). An adversary uses tampering function f on the encoded message. Non-malleability property guarantees that Decode(f(Encode(k))) is either k, when tampering has no effect, or k', which is computationally independent of k, in case of successful tampering. In the ideal case, non-malleability should be achieved for arbitrary classes of tampering functions but this does not hold in general. One of the widely used tampering function class is 2-split-state class where tampering occurs in two parts of the memory $\mathcal{M}_L$ and $\mathcal{M}_R$ respectively. Codeword is divided into two halves and stored in $\mathcal{M}_L$, $\mathcal{M}_R$. Two independent tampering functions $f = \{f_1(\mathcal{M}_L), f_2(\mathcal{M}_R)\}$ modify the left and right half of the memory in an arbitrary and independent way.

NMC are broadly categorized into information-theoretic [14] and computational [20] constructions. In [16], information theoretic non-malleable codes with codeword size $\mathcal{O}((|m| + n)^7 \log^7(|m| + n))$ is proposed, where m is the message size and n denotes the security parameter. Subsequently, a better version with respect to the codeword size is achieved in [17]. Liu et al. [12] show a construction of NMC in computational settings from public key primitives [8] and robust NIZK [2]. Combining the idea of [16] and [20], NMC of size $|m| + \mathcal{O}(n^7)$ is proposed and later, it is further reduced to $|m| + \mathcal{O}(n^2)$ [7,8,12,20]. NMC can also be developed using symmetric-key primitives like block ciphers, authenticated encryption schemes etc. Kiayias et al. [19] use one-time leakage-resilient AE along with l-*more* extractable hash function to build an NMC with close to optimal codeword length $|m| + 18n$. However, they prove their scheme to be secure under not so standard *knowledge of exponent* assumption (KEA) in the CRS model. In practical scenario, it is difficult to manage such CRS based setup. Later, in [21] authors propose a non-malleable code with optimal codeword length $|m| + 2n$ in 2-split-state model based on related-key secure block cipher with no CRS based trusted setup.

Our Contribution. In this work, we propose a computationally secure non-malleable code with close to optimal codeword size of $1.5|m| + 2n$ in 2-split-state model from an AE scheme, specifically using encrypt then MAC approach. We do not need any trusted setup assumption like CRS in our construction. Our instantiation is based on triple M-DES [1] and leakage resilient CBC-MAC [18].

In [19], the authors observe that an NMC of size $|m| + \mathcal{O}(n^7)$ can be obtained from AE using the results of [16] and [20]. Later, they propose an NMC of size $|m| + 18n$ from AE in the CRS model. Unfortunately, their construction uses *knowledge of exponent* (KEA) assumption, which is not that standard [6]. In this scenario our result gives a construction which uses an AE scheme and obtains

Table 1. Comparison of multi-bit NMC in the 2-split-state model [19]. The message length is denoted by $|m|$ and n represents security parameter. In the table IT stands for *information-theoretic*, Comp. stands for *computational*, AE stands for *authenticated encryption* and LR stands for *leakage-resilient*.

Scheme	Codeword length	Model	Assumption
[16]	$\mathcal{O}((|m|+n)^7 \log^7(|m|+n))$	IT	–
[17]	$\mathcal{O}(max(|m|,n))$	IT	–
[16] + [20]	$|m| + \mathcal{O}(n^7)$	Comp.	AE
[7]+ [8]+ [12]+ [20]	$|m| + \mathcal{O}(n^2)$	Comp., CRS	LR PKE + robust NIZK
[19]	$|m| + 18n$	Comp., CRS	one-time LR AE + KEA
[21]	$|m| + 2n$	Comp.	PRP with leakage + Fixed related-key
This work	$\mathcal{O}(|m| + 2n)$	Comp.	Related-key + PRP with leakage + LR CBC-MAC unforgeability [1]

[1]It is an encrypt then MAC AE scheme. Block cipher of the underlying AE should satisfy related-key security, PRP security under leakage and MAC should be unforgeable under leakage.

an NMC with close to optimal codeword length. As a proof of concept, we also implement our NMC in software platform.

In Table 1, we compare our result with existing multi-bit non-malleable codes in 2-split-state model by extending the comparison table from [19].

Comparison with [21]. The first computational NMC with optimal codeword length is proposed in [21], where the authors use related-key secure block ciphers in their construction. In this work, we show that it is also possible to construct an NMC using a specific AE scheme with close to optimal codeword length. Note that it is not clear whether one can achieve the same codeword length using other AE schemes.

2   Preliminaries

Basic Notations. Let $\mathcal{M}_L$, $\mathcal{M}_R$ be the left and right half of memory in 2-split-state model where the actual codeword is stored. f_L and f_R are two functions tampering on $\mathcal{M}_L$ and $\mathcal{M}_R$ respectively. $\mathcal{K}$ denotes the key-space. $k \xleftarrow{\$} \mathcal{K}$ implies that the key k is sampled uniformly at random from $\mathcal{K}$. $\mathcal{M}$, $\mathcal{C}$ and n denote the message set, codeword set and security parameter respectively. $m \in \mathcal{M}$ and $c \in \mathcal{C}$ denote the particular message and codeword. m is further divided into small chunks as m_1, m_2 etc. Two different messages are denoted by m^1, m^2.

2.1   Non-malleable Codes

A non-malleable code (NMC) is an encoding scheme which consists of two algorithms (Encode, Decode), where:

- Encode : $\mathcal{K} \times \mathcal{M} \to \mathcal{C}$: Encoding algorithm takes input a $m \in \mathcal{M}$ and key $k \in \mathcal{K}$, with $|m| \geq n$ and $|k| \geq n$. It outputs codeword $c = c_L || c_R$, where $c_L \in \{0,1\}^{\mathcal{M}_L}$ resides in $\mathcal{M}_L$ and $c_R \in \{0,1\}^{\mathcal{M}_R}$ resides in $\mathcal{M}_R$.

– Decode : $\{0,1\}^{\mathcal{M}_L} \times \{0,1\}^{\mathcal{M}_R} \rightarrow \mathcal{M}$: Decoding algorithm takes codeword $c = c_L \| c_R$ and outputs $m \in \mathcal{M}$.

For correctness, we require that $\mathsf{Decode}(\mathsf{Encode}_k(m)) = m$, $\forall m \in \mathcal{M}$ and $\forall k \in \mathcal{K}$, happens with probability one.

Strong Non-malleability. *Let $\mathcal{F}$ be a family of tampering functions. For each $f = (f_L, f_R) \in \mathcal{F}$ and $m \in \mathcal{M}$, we define the tampering experiment:*

$$\mathbf{Tamper}_{NMC}^f = \left\{ \begin{array}{l} c \leftarrow \mathsf{Encode}_k(m), c = \{\mathcal{M}_L, \mathcal{M}_R\} \\ \{\mathcal{M}'_L, \mathcal{M}'_R\} = \{f_L(\mathcal{M}_L), f_R(\mathcal{M}_R)\} \\ c' = \{\mathcal{M}'_L, \mathcal{M}'_R\}, m' = \mathsf{Decode}(c') \\ output : same^*, if\ c' = c; else\ m'. \end{array} \right\},$$

where randomness comes from the encoding algorithm.

A coding scheme $(\mathsf{Encode}, \mathsf{Decode})$ is strongly non-malleable with respect to tampering function family $\mathcal{F}$ if for each $f = (f_L, f_R) \in \mathcal{F}$, an adversary cannot distinguish the tampered decoding of two chosen messages m^1 and m^2, apart from the case when the tampering has no effect. For a more formal definition we refer the readers to [21].

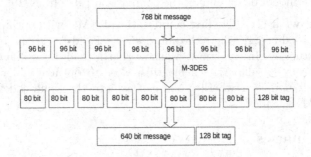

Fig. 1. Memory Layout of 768 bit encoding in $\mathcal{M}_R$.

3   Code Construction

Message m is encoded as $\mathsf{Encode}_k(m) = \mathcal{M}_L \| \mathcal{M}_R$. $\mathcal{M}_L$ stores set of keys and some states that enable decoding; We denote that by $\{k\}$, thus $\mathcal{M}_L = \{k\}$. $\mathcal{M}_R = \{\mathfrak{E}_k(m), \mathsf{tag}\}$, where $\mathfrak{E}$ is a block cipher and tag is generated using leakage resilient CBC-MAC [18]. The keys for the block cipher and the leakage resilient CBC-MAC are stored in $\mathcal{M}_L$. $\mathsf{Decode}(c_L \| c_R)$, extracts the keys from c_L, checks whether tag in c_R is valid; If valid then decrypts $\mathfrak{E}_k(m)$ to obtain the message m. In our instantiation we use an encrypt then MAC scheme, which uses a M-3DES block cipher and CBC-MAC with leakage. The codeword length of our NMC is almost $|m| + 2n$. Note that we also have to store intermediate states of size $m/2$ in order to enable decoding, thus the total codeword length is $1.5|m| + 2n$.

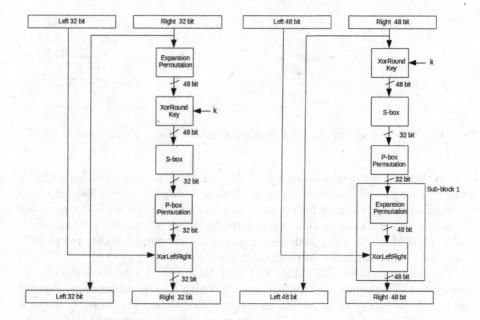

Fig. 2. DES and M-DES algorithm execution.

We prove our construction to be secure when the underlying block cipher and CBC-MAC satisfies the following properties:

1. The block cipher is related-key secure with respect to any single related-key function [21] that can deal with output-predictable functions.
2. When limited bits from the keyspace are leaked, quality of the output produced by the block cipher degrades gracefully in standard pseudo-random permutation (PRP) security notion [21].
3. Tag generated by the CBC-MAC algorithm is unforgeable under leakage [18]

We refer the readers to [5,18,21] for formal definitions of the required security properties.

Concrete Instantiation. We build the codeword using an encrypt then MAC AE scheme. We instantiate the AE with triple M-DES [1], denoted as M-3DES and leakage resilient CBC-MAC [18]. Figure 2 describes DES and M-DES execution. We use M-DES function three times to construct M-3DES.

Encoding. To encode a 768 bit message m (Fig. 1), we first divide it into small chunks m_1 to m_8 of 96 bits. Each 96 bit message is encrypted using M-3DES algorithm and it produces 80 bit message. The idea is that in the last round of M-3DES we don't run Sub-block 1 (see Fig. 3), and store $48 + 32$ bits, 80-bits in $\mathcal{M}_R$. For correct decoding we also need the left 48-bits of M-3DES from the previous round; That is stored in $\mathcal{M}_L$ as temp-state along with the other keys.

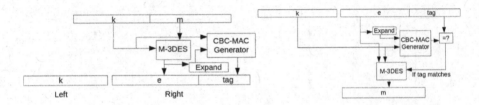

Fig. 3. Encoding and Decoding of non-malleable codes in 2-split-state model.

In this way, encoded message of 640 bit (8×80) is generated and the 128 bit tag for that 640 bit message is generated using leakage resilient CBC-MAC. To generate the tag, each 80 bit encoded message is expanded with our proposed *expansion permutation* in Table 2 which produces 128 bit output. Let the output of a single M-3DES be e_1 and the expanded 128 bit output is denoted as e_1^{128}. Similarly, other expanded M-3DES outputs are e_2^{128}, e_3^{128}, e_4^{128}, e_5^{128}, e_6^{128}, e_7^{128}, e_8^{128}. Leakage resilient CBC-MAC [18] takes these $\{e_i^{128}\}$ with the key k_{MAC} to generate 128 bit secure tag which is appended with the 640 bit message. Figure 1 shows the memory layout of $\mathcal{M}_R$ in 2-split-state model. $\mathcal{M}_R$ stores e, which is $\mathfrak{E}_k(m)$ and tag ($|\mathfrak{E}_k(m)| = 640$ bit and $|\text{tag}| = 128$ bit) as depicted in Fig. 3.

Left part of the memory $\mathcal{M}_L$ stores a set of keys $\{k_{DES}\|k_{MAC}\|\text{temp-state}\}$, where k_{DES} is the key for M-3DES, k_{MAC} is the key for leakage resilient CBC-MAC and temp-state is intermediate state that is used to decode the codeword, as explained earlier. Finally we get the codeword $\mathcal{M}_L\|\mathcal{M}_R$, where $\mathcal{M}_L = \{k_{DES}\|k_{MAC}\|\text{temp-state}\}$ and $\mathcal{M}_R = \{\mathfrak{E}_k(m), \text{tag}\}$.

Decoding. Figure 3 shows the decoding procedure. First the decoding procedure extracts k_{MAC} from $\mathcal{M}_L$ and uses that to verify whether the tag is a valid MAC on $\mathfrak{E}_k(m)$; If not, it returns $\perp$. Otherwise, it extracts k_{DES} from $\mathcal{M}_L$ and runs the decryption procedure to obtain m.

Expansion Permutation. Table 2 describes 80 bit to 128 bit expansion permutation. It contains 16 rows and 8 columns in total. The value of each cell comes from the bit position of 80 bit data generated by M-3DES. The working principle of the proposed permutation is the following: Let 80 bit output of a single M-3DES be stored into a register R_1. The final 128 bit output of the permutation is stored into the register R_2. The 1st bit of R_2 is generated by AND-ing of 55th bit and 16th bit of R_1, accordingly the entry of $(1,1)$ position of the table is 55&&16. Similarly, the 2nd bit of R_2 comes from 1st bit of R_1 and so on. In this way, we are generating all the bits of R_2.

Correctness and Security. We prove our construction to be secure if the underlying block cipher is related key secure and PRP secure, and if the CBC-MAC is unforgeable under leakage. For full proof of correctness and security we refer the readers to the full version of the paper.

Table 2. 80 bit to 128 bit expansion permutation.

55 && 16	1	2	3	4	5	6	7 && 8
5 && 6	7	8	9	10	11	12	13 &&14
11 && 12	13	14	15	16	17	18	19 && 20
17 && 18	19	20	21	22	23	24	25 && 26
23 && 24	25	26	27	28	29	30	31 && 32
29 && 30	31	32	33	34	35	36	37 && 38
35 && 36	37	38	39	40	41	42	43 && 44
41 && 42	43	44	45	46	47	48	49 && 50
47 && 48	49	50	51	52	53	54	55 && 56
53 && 54	55	56	57	58	59	60	61 && 62
59 && 60	61	62	63	64	65	66	67 && 68
65 && 66	67	68	69	70	71	72	73 && 74
71 && 72	73	74	75	76	77	78	79 && 80
77 && 78	79	80	11	52	63	34	65 && 76
63 && 64	65	76	27	18	39	69	61 && 72
39 && 69	61	72	53	44	55	16	1 && 2

Performance. We have also implemented our non-malleable code in software platform using C++ (g++ 9.4 compiler) in a computer with Intel Core i3 processor. AES-128 [3] is used as the underlying block cipher in the leakage resilient CBC-MAC. With our proof of concept implementation, to generate the codeword, it takes 75 ms wall clock time.

4 Conclusion

We propose a concrete NMC with nearly optimal codeword length from an AE scheme. In general it is not known how to construct an optimal computational NMC from any AE scheme. Our result shows that even in that case, it is possible to achieve better codeword length if we consider specific concrete instantiations.

References

1. Shamir, A.: Differential cryptanalysis of DES-like cryptosystems. J. Cryptol. 4(1), 3–72 (1991)
2. De Santis, A., Di Crescenzo, G., Ostrovsky, R., Persiano, G., Sahai, A.: Robust non-interactive zero knowledge. In: Kilian, J. (ed.) CRYPTO 2001. LNCS, vol. 2139, pp. 566–598. Springer, Heidelberg (2001). https://doi.org/10.1007/3-540-44647-8_33
3. Joan, D., Vincent, R.: The Design of Rijndael. Springer, New York (2002). https://doi.org/10.1007/978-3-662-60769-5

4. Skorobogatov, S.P., Anderson, R.J.: Optical fault induction attacks. In: Kaliski, B.S., Koç, K., Paar, C. (eds.) CHES 2002. LNCS, vol. 2523, pp. 2–12. Springer, Heidelberg (2003). https://doi.org/10.1007/3-540-36400-5_2

5. Bellare, M., Kohno, T.: A theoretical treatment of related-key attacks: RKA-PRPs, RKA-PRFs, and applications. In: Biham, E. (ed.) EUROCRYPT 2003. LNCS, vol. 2656, pp. 491–506. Springer, Heidelberg (2003). https://doi.org/10.1007/3-540-39200-9_31

6. Naor, M.: On cryptographic assumptions and challenges. In: Boneh, D. (ed.) CRYPTO 2003. LNCS, vol. 2729, pp. 96–109. Springer, Heidelberg (2003). https://doi.org/10.1007/978-3-540-45146-4_6

7. Groth, J., Sahai, A.: Efficient non-interactive proof systems for bilinear groups. In: Smart, N. (ed.) EUROCRYPT 2008. LNCS, vol. 4965, pp. 415–432. Springer, Heidelberg (2008). https://doi.org/10.1007/978-3-540-78967-3_24

8. Naor, M., Segev, G.: Public-key cryptosystems resilient to key leakage. In: Halevi, S. (ed.) CRYPTO 2009. LNCS, vol. 5677, pp. 18–35. Springer, Heidelberg (2009). https://doi.org/10.1007/978-3-642-03356-8_2

9. Dziembowski, S., Pietrzak, K., Wichs, D.: Non-malleable codes. In: Yao, A.C.-C. (ed.) ICS 2010, Beijing, China, 5–7 January 2010, pp. 434–452. Tsinghua University Press, Beijing (2010)

10. Bellare, M., Cash, D., Miller, R.: Cryptography secure against related-key attacks and tampering. In: Lee, D.H., Wang, X. (eds.) ASIACRYPT 2011. LNCS, vol. 7073, pp. 486–503. Springer, Heidelberg (2011). https://doi.org/10.1007/978-3-642-25385-0_26

11. Kalai, Y.T., Kanukurthi, B., Sahai, A.: Cryptography with tamperable and leaky memory. In: Rogaway, P. (ed.) CRYPTO 2011. LNCS, vol. 6841, pp. 373–390. Springer, Heidelberg (2011). https://doi.org/10.1007/978-3-642-22792-9_21

12. Liu, F.-H., Lysyanskaya, A.: Tamper and leakage resilience in the split-state model. In: Safavi-Naini, R., Canetti, R. (eds.) CRYPTO 2012. LNCS, vol. 7417, pp. 517–532. Springer, Heidelberg (2012). https://doi.org/10.1007/978-3-642-32009-5_30

13. Bellare, M., Paterson, K.G., Thomson, S.: RKA security beyond the linear barrier: IBE, encryption and signatures. In: Wang, X., Sako, K. (eds.) ASIACRYPT 2012. LNCS, vol. 7658, pp. 331–348. Springer, Heidelberg (2012). https://doi.org/10.1007/978-3-642-34961-4_21

14. Dziembowski, S., Kazana, T., Obremski, M.: Non-malleable codes from two-source extractors. In: Canetti, R., Garay, J.A. (eds.) CRYPTO 2013. LNCS, vol. 8043, pp. 239–257. Springer, Heidelberg (2013). https://doi.org/10.1007/978-3-642-40084-1_14

15. Damgård, I., Faust, S., Mukherjee, P., Venturi, D.: Bounded tamper resilience: how to go beyond the algebraic barrier. In: Sako, K., Sarkar, P. (eds.) ASIACRYPT 2013. LNCS, vol. 8270, pp. 140–160. Springer, Heidelberg (2013). https://doi.org/10.1007/978-3-642-42045-0_8

16. Aggarwal, D., Dodis, Y., Lovett, S.: Non-malleable codes from additive combinatorics. In: STOC, pp. 774–783 (2014)

17. Aggarwal, D., Dodis, Y., Kazana, T., Obremski, M.: Non-malleable reductions and applications. In: Proceedings of the Forty-Seventh Annual ACM on Symposium on Theory of Computing, pp. 459–468. ACM (2015)

18. Pereira, O., Standaert, F.X., Vivek, S.: Leakage-resilient authentication and encryption from symmetric cryptographic primitives. In: Ray, I., Li, N., Kruegel, C. (eds.) ACM CCS 2015, pp. 96–108. ACM Press (2015)

19. Kiayias, A., Liu, F.H., Tselekounis, Y.: Practical non-malleable codes from l-more extractable hash functions. In: Weippl, E.R., Katzenbeisser, S., Kruegel, C., Myers, A.C., Halevi, S. (eds.) ACM CCS 2016, pp. 1317–1328. ACM Press (2016)
20. Aggarwal, D., Agrawal, S., Gupta, D., Maji, H.K., Pandey, O., Prabhakaran, M.: Optimal computational split-state non-malleable codes. In: Kushilevitz, E., Malkin, T. (eds.) TCC 2016. LNCS, vol. 9563, pp. 393–417. Springer, Heidelberg (2016). https://doi.org/10.1007/978-3-662-49099-0_15
21. Fehr, S., Karpman, P., Mennink, B.: Short non-malleable codes from related-key secure block ciphers. IACR Trans. Symm. Cryptol., 336–352 (2018)

Cryptographic Role-Based Access Control, Reconsidered

Bin Liu[1]([✉])[iD], Antonis Michalas[1,2][iD], and Bogdan Warinschi[3,4][iD]

[1] Tampere University, Tampere, Finland
{bin.liu,antonios.michalas}@tuni.fi
[2] RISE Research Institutes of Sweden, Gothenburg, Sweden
[3] DFINITY, Zürich, Switzerland
[4] University of Bristol, Bristol, UK
csxbw@bristol.ac.uk

Abstract. In this paper, we follow the line of existing study on cryptographic enforcement of Role-Based Access Control (RBAC). Inspired by the study of the relation between the existing security definitions for such system, we identify two different types of attacks which cannot be captured by the existing ones. Therefore, we propose two new security definitions towards the goal of appropriately modelling cryptographic enforcement of Role-Based Access Control policies and study the relation between our new definitions and the existing ones. In addition, we show that the cost of supporting dynamic policy update is inherently expensive by presenting two lower bounds for such systems which guarantee correctness and secure access.

1 Introduction

A main concern in the existing studies of cryptographic access control is the gap between the specification of the access control policies being enforced and the implementation of the access control systems. In traditional monitor-based access control mechanisms, the correct enforcement of access control policies holds by design. But in cryptographic access control, the problem becomes more complicated. The enforcement not only relies on security guarantees of the underlying cryptographic primitives but also the appropriate key distribution/management. Even though some advanced cryptographic primitives are seemingly well-suited for cryptographic access control, their security guarantees cannot be directly translated to security guarantees of the whole system. It is widely accepted that there is often a gap between primitives and the applications motivating them.

This work was partially funded by the HARPOCRATES project, Horizon Europe and the Technology Innovation Institute (TII), Abu Dhabi, United Arab Emirates, for the project ARROWSMITH: Living (Securely) on the edge.
Due to the page limit, we leave out the preliminaries, some details of the results and the proofs of the theorems. A full version of this paper can be found on https://eprint.iacr.org/2022/1268.pdf.

C. Ge and F. Guo (Eds.): ProvSec 2022, LNCS 13600, pp. 282–289, 2022.
https://doi.org/10.1007/978-3-031-20917-8_19

The gap obscured by uses of similar terms and jargon at both application and primitive level. Once primitives are investigated, the step showing that they imply security of the motivating application is unfortunately often-omitted.

In order to bridge this gap, coming up with formal security definitions for cryptographic access control systems is crucially important. However, the study on formal security definitions is often neglected in the existing research on cryptographic access control. There have been some initial works in this area that focus on designing new primitives motivated by access control systems [2,7,13] and on designing access control systems based on those primitives [6,9,12,14].

Throughout the literature, rigorous definitions that look at the security of systems for access control have only been heuristically studied. Halevi et al. proposed a simulation-based security definition for access control on distributed file storage system in order to reason about the confinement problem [5]. Their result is for a particular system rather than a general one. Ferrara et al. defined a precise syntax for cryptographic role-based access control (cRBAC) systems and proposed a formal security definition with respect to secure read access in [4]. Later they extend their results in a setting which supports for write access [3] so that the need for the trusted monitors to mediate every write access request can be eliminated. Liu et al. studied security of cRBAC systems in the UC framework [10]. They proposed a UC security definition for such systems and also showed an impossibility result that such security cannot be achieved due to the commitment problem.

Garrison III et al. studied the practical implications of cryptographic access control systems that enforces RBAC policies [8]. They analysed the computational costs of two different constructions of cryptographic role-based access control systems via simulations with the use of real-world datasets. Their results indicate that supporting for dynamic access control policy enforcement may be prohibitively expensive, even under the assumption that write access is enforced with the minimum use of reference monitors.

NEW SECURITY DEFINITIONS. The results presented in [10] show a gap between the game-based and simulation-based security definitions for cRBAC systems, which raises a question here:

Do the existing security definitions appropriately capture the secure enforcement of access control policies?

Inspired by their results, we identify two different types of attacks which are overlooked in the existing works and propose two new security definitions in game-based setting: *past confidentiality* and *local correctness*. Our work can be considered as a step towards the goal of providing an appropriate and formal treatment for secure policy enforcement.

LOWER BOUNDS FOR SECURE cRBAC SYSTEMS. Motivated by Garrison III et al.'s work, we study lower bounds for secure cRBAC systems to find out where the inefficiency stems from. We show that the costs are inherent in secure cRBAC systems and also in those cryptographic access control systems that greatly or solely rely on cryptographic techniques to enforce access control on both read and write access. The main idea is, since the manager does not involve in any read and write operation to the file system, the local states of the users and also the file system should reflect the access control policy being enforced. Whenever the policy gets updated, the system might inevitably require re-keying and re-encryption in order to guarantee secure access and system correctness. We present two lower bounds for secure cRBAC systems. Our results can be valuable in the design of such systems for practical purposes.

2   Security Definitions

In this section, we present our formal security definitions of correctness, past confidentiality and local correctness for cRBAC systems.

2.1   Correctness

Correctness was first proposed by Ferrara et al. in [4], but it was omitted in their later work [3] where a new system model was introduced to support for write access. Therefore, we will need to reintroduce the definition of correctness.

Intuitively, a cryptographic access control system is said to be *correct* if every user in the system can get access to the resources to which it is authorised according to the symobilc state of the system.

Definition 1 (Correctness). *A cRBAC system Π defined by a cRBAC scheme for a fixed set of roles R is **correct** if for any probabilistic polynomial-time adversary $\mathcal{A}$, it holds that*

$$\mathbf{Adv}_{\Pi,\mathcal{A}}^{corr}(\lambda) := \Pr\left[\mathbf{Exp}_{\Pi,\mathcal{A}}^{corr}(\lambda) \to \mathbf{true}\right]$$

is 0, where the experiment $\mathbf{Exp}_{\Pi,\mathcal{A}}^{corr}$ is defined as follows:

$\mathbf{Exp}_{\Pi,\mathcal{A}}^{corr}(\lambda)$

    $T \leftarrow \emptyset;\ State \leftarrow (\emptyset, \emptyset, \emptyset, \emptyset, \emptyset)$
    $(st_M, fs, \{st_u\}_{u \in U}) \leftarrow\!\!\$\ \mathsf{Init}(1^\lambda, R)$
    $(u^*, o^*) \leftarrow\!\!\$\ \mathcal{A}(1^\lambda : \mathcal{O}_{corr})$
    if $\mathsf{HasAccess}(u^*, (o^*, \mathbf{read})) \wedge T[o^*] \neq \mathsf{Read}(st_{u^*}, o^*, fs)$ then
        return true
    else return false

The oracles $\mathcal{O}_{corr}$ that the adversary has access to are specified in Fig. 1.

2.2   Past Confidentiality

In the extended cRBAC system model, the enforcement of access control on write access is supported by employing a versioning file storage where users can append contents only. The versioning file storage allows users to have (quasi-) unrestricted read and write access to the file system, but it is also accompanied by some subtle security issues, even though the file system itself does not implement any access control mechanism. One of those security issues is unauthorised access

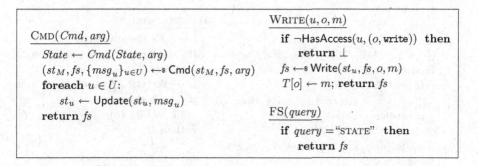

Fig. 1. $\mathcal{O}_{corr}$: Oracles for defining the experiment $\mathbf{Exp}^{\text{corr}}_{\Pi,\mathcal{A}}$.

to the previous contents, which is a severe security concern in cryptographic access control but not in the traditional mechanisms.

Unfortunately, such a security concern cannot be appropriately captured by the game-based security definitions of read security from the existing work [3,4]. In fact, the constructions proposed in their work cannot provide such a security guarantee. Interestingly, some recently proposed constructions of cryptographic access control systems have the similar security concern [1,8,11], even though they have been proven to securely enforce the corresponding access control policies within their individual frameworks.

We propose the following security definition called *past confidentiality* which is improved over the one presented in [3].

Definition 2 (Past Confidentiality). *A cRBAC system Π defined by a cRBAC scheme for a fixed set of roles R is said to preserve **past confidentiality** if for any probabilistic polynomial-time adversary $\mathcal{A}$, it holds that*

$$\mathbf{Adv}^{pc}_{\Pi,\mathcal{A}}(\lambda) := \big|\Pr[\mathbf{Exp}^{pc}_{\Pi,\mathcal{A}}(\lambda) \to \mathbf{true}] - \tfrac{1}{2}\big|$$

is negligible in λ, where the experiment $\mathbf{Exp}^{pc}_{\Pi,\mathcal{A}}$ is defined as follows:

$\underline{\mathbf{Exp}^{pc}_{\Pi,\mathcal{A}}(\lambda)}$

    $b \leftarrow_\$ \{0,1\};\ Cr, Ch, L, Ud \leftarrow \emptyset$

    $State \leftarrow (\emptyset, \emptyset, \emptyset, \emptyset, \emptyset)$

    $(st_M, fs, \{st_u\}_{u \in U}) \leftarrow_\$ \mathsf{Init}(1^\lambda, R)$

    $b' \leftarrow_\$ \mathcal{A}(1^\lambda : \mathcal{O}_{pc})$

    $\mathbf{return}\ (b' = b)$

The oracles $\mathcal{O}_{pc}$ that the adversary has access to are specified in Fig. 2.

Compared with the adversary in the game that defines read security of a cRBAC system, the adversary above is obviously more powerful since it has the ability to take over the users who can get read access to the challenged files under some restrictions. The following theorem confirms the implication between the two security definitions.

Theorem 1. *Past confidentiality is strictly stronger than secure read access.*

$\underline{\text{CMD}(Cmd, arg)}$
  $(U', O', P', UA', PA') \leftarrow Cmd(State, arg)$
  foreach $(u, o) \in Cr \times Ud$:
   if $\exists r \in R: (u, r) \in UA'$
          $\wedge ((o, \text{read}), r) \in PA'$ **then**
    return $\bot$
  $State \leftarrow (U', O', P', UA', PA')$
  $(st_M, fs, \{msg_u\}_{u \in U}) \leftarrow\!\!\text{\$} \ Cmd(st_M, fs, arg)$
  foreach $u \in U \setminus L$:
   if $\exists o \in Ud : \text{HasAccess}(u, (o, \text{read}))$ **then**
    $L \leftarrow L \cup \{u\}$
  foreach $u \in L$:
   if $\nexists o \in Ch : \text{HasAccess}(u, (o, \text{read}))$
         $\vee u \notin U$ **then**
    $L \leftarrow L \setminus \{u\}$
  foreach $o \in Ch$:
   if $o \notin O$ **then**
    $Ch \leftarrow Ch \setminus \{o\}; \ Ud \leftarrow Ud \setminus \{o\}$
  foreach $u \in U \setminus Cr$:
   $st_u \leftarrow \text{Update}(st_u, msg_u)$
  return $(fs, \{msg_u\}_{u \in Cr})$

$\underline{\text{CORRUPTU}(u)}$
  if $u \notin U \vee u \in L$ **then**
   return $\bot$
  $Cr \leftarrow Cr \cup \{u\};$ **return** st_u

$\underline{\text{WRITE}(u, o, m)}$
  If $u \in Cr$ **then return** $\bot$
  if $\neg\text{HasAccess}(u, (o, \text{write}))$ **then**
   return $\bot$
  $fs \leftarrow\!\!\text{\$} \ \text{Write}(st_u, fs, o, m)$
  if $o \in Ch$ **then**
   $Ud \leftarrow Ud \setminus \{o\}$
  return fs

$\underline{\text{CHALLENGE}(u, o, m_0, m_1)}$
  if $\neg\text{HasAccess}(u, (o, \text{write}))$ **then**
   return $\bot$
  if $|m_0| \neq |m_1|$ **then return** $\bot$
  foreach $u' \in Cr$:
   if $\text{HasAccess}(u', (o, \text{read}))$ **then**
    return $\bot$
  $fs \leftarrow\!\!\text{\$} \ \text{Write}(st_u, fs, o, m_b)$
  foreach $u' \in U$:
   if $\text{HasAccess}(u', (o, \text{read}))$ **then**
    $L \leftarrow L \cup \{u'\}$
  $Ch \leftarrow Ch \cup \{o\}; \ Ud \leftarrow Ud \cup \{o\}$
  return fs

$\underline{\text{FS}(query)}$
  if $query = \text{``STATE''}$ **then**
   return fs
  if $query = \text{``APPEND}(info)\text{''}$ **then**
   $fs \leftarrow fs\|info;$ **return** fs

Fig. 2. $\mathcal{O}_{pc}$: Oracles for defining the experiment $\mathbf{Exp}^{\text{pc}}_{CRBAC, \mathcal{A}}$.

2.3 Local Correctness

The *local correctness* captures the threat from "insiders" with respect to data availability. The append-only versioning file system allows users to get (quasi-)unrestricted write access to the files, but it also poses new security concern: a user who has the write permission of a file might be able to invalidate the file's future versions which are written by authorised users. Local correctness guarantees that such an attack is thwarted in such systems.

Definition 3 (Local Correctness). *A cRBAC system Π defined by a cRBAC scheme for a fixed set of roles R is said to preserve **local correctness** if for any probabilistic polynomial-time adversary $\mathcal{A}$, it holds that*

$$\mathbf{Adv}^{l\text{-}corr}_{\Pi, \mathcal{A}}(\lambda) := \Pr\left[\mathbf{Exp}^{l\text{-}corr}_{\Pi, \mathcal{A}}(\lambda) \rightarrow \text{true}\right]$$

is negligible in λ, *where* $\mathbf{Exp}_{\Pi,\mathcal{A}}^{l\text{-}corr}$ *is defined as follows:*

$\underline{\mathbf{Exp}_{\Pi,\mathcal{A}}^{l\text{-}corr}(\lambda)}$

   $T, Cr \leftarrow \emptyset; State \leftarrow (\emptyset, \emptyset, \emptyset, \emptyset, \emptyset)$

   $(st_M, fs, \{st_u\}_{u \in U}) \leftarrow_\$ \mathsf{Init}(1^\lambda, R)$

   $(u^*, o^*) \leftarrow_\$ \mathcal{A}(1^\lambda : \mathcal{O}_{l\text{-}corr})$

   if $T[o^*] \neq \mathsf{adv} \wedge T[o^*] \neq \mathsf{Read}(st_{u^*}, o^*, fs)$ then

      return true

   else return false

The oracles $\mathcal{O}_{l\text{-}corr}$ *that the adversary has access to are specified in Fig. 3.*

$\underline{\mathrm{CMD}(Cmd, arg)}$

   $State \leftarrow Cmd(State, arg)$

   $(st_M, fs, \{msg_u\}_{u \in U}) \leftarrow_\$ \mathsf{Cmd}(st_M, fs, arg)$

   foreach $u \in Cr$:

      if $u \notin U$ **then**

         $Cr \leftarrow Cr \setminus \{u\}$

   if $Cmd =$ "DELOBJECT" **then**

      Parse arg as o; $T[o] \leftarrow \emptyset$

   if $Cmd =$ "DELUSER" **then**

      Parse arg as u; $Cr \leftarrow Cr \setminus \{u\}$

   foreach $u \in U \setminus Cr$:

      $st_u \leftarrow \mathsf{Update}(st_u, msg_u)$

   return $(fs, \{st_u\}_{u \in Cr})$

$\underline{\mathrm{CORRUPTU}(u)}$

   if $u \notin U$ **then return** $\perp$

   $Cr \leftarrow Cr \cup \{u\}$; **return** st_u

$\underline{\mathrm{WRITE}(u, o, m)}$

   if $u \in Cr$ **then return** $\perp$

   if $\neg\mathsf{HasAccess}(u, (o, \mathsf{write}))$ **then**

      return $\perp$

   $fs \leftarrow_\$ \mathsf{Write}(st_u, fs, o, m)$

   $T[o] \leftarrow m$; **return** fs

$\underline{\mathrm{FS}(query)}$

   if $query =$ "STATE" **then**

      return fs

   if $query =$ "APPEND$(info)$" **then**

      Parse $info$ as (o, c)

      $T[o] \leftarrow \mathsf{adv}$; $fs \leftarrow fs \| info$

      return fs

Fig. 3. $\mathcal{O}_{l\text{-}corr}$: Oracles for defining the experiment $\mathbf{Exp}_{\Pi,\mathcal{A}}^{l\text{-}corr}$.

We further show that the cRBAC construction proposed by Ferrara et al. in [3] preserves this security property.

Theorem 2. *If both the predicate encryption scheme and the digital signature scheme are correct, the construction in [3] preserves local correctness.*

3 Lower Bounds for Secure cRBAC Systems

In this section, we present two lower bounds for secure cRBAC systems. By lower bounds, we mean the efficiency implications of secure cRBAC systems. To some extent, our results explain the reason why cRBAC systems that support dynamic policy updates may be prohibitively expensive: permission revocation can be costly.

Before we present our results, we introduce a technical term which is called *Permission Adjustment* for an RBAC system. Informally, permission adjustment is a sequence of administrative commands which changes the access rights of some users with respect to a set of permissions.

Definition 4 *(Permission Adjustment). Let $S_0 = (U, O, P, UA, PA)$ be the state of an RBAC system over a set of roles R. Given a set of users $\tilde{U} \subseteq U$ and a set of permissions $\tilde{P} \subseteq P$, where both $\tilde{U}$ and $\tilde{P}$ are non-empty, a sequence of RBAC administrative commands $q = (q_0, ..., q_n)$ is called a **permission adjustment** for S_0 with respect to $\tilde{U}$ and $\tilde{P}$:*

(1) *if $\forall u \in \tilde{U}, p \in \tilde{P} : \neg\mathsf{HasAccess}(u, p)$ holds for S_0 and after a sequence of transitions $S_0 \xrightarrow{q_0}_S S_1 \xrightarrow{q_1}_S, ..., \xrightarrow{q_{n-1}}_S S_n \xrightarrow{q_n}_S S_{n+1}, \forall u \in \tilde{U}, p \in \tilde{P} :$ $\mathsf{HasAccess}(u, p)$ holds for S_{n+1} or*
(2) *if $\forall u \in \tilde{U}, p \in \tilde{P} : \mathsf{HasAccess}(u, p)$ holds for S_0 and after a sequence of transitions $S_0 \xrightarrow{q_0}_S S_1 \xrightarrow{q_1}_S, ..., \xrightarrow{q_{n-1}}_S S_n \xrightarrow{q_n}_S S_{n+1}, \forall u \in \tilde{U}, p \in \tilde{P} :$ $\neg\mathsf{HasAccess}(u, p)$ holds for S_{n+1}.*

We denote the set of all possible q in case (1) by $\tilde{U}\uparrow\tilde{P}(S_0)$ and the set of all possible q in case (2) by $\tilde{U}\downarrow\tilde{P}(S_0)$.

In addition, we introduce two key properties with respect to efficiency.

Definition 5 *(File system preserving, informal). Let st_G be the global state of a cRBAC system, if after executing a sequence of RBAC administrative commands $q = (q_0, ..., q_n)$, the state of the file system remains unchanged, we call q **file system preserving** for st_G and it is reflected by the predicate $\mathsf{FSP}(q, st_G) = 1$.*

Definition 6 *(U-user local state preserving, informal). Let st_G be the global state of a cRBAC system, if after executing a sequence of RBAC administrative commands $q = (q_0, ..., q_n)$, the local states of the users in $\mathbb{U}$ remains unchanged, we call q **U-user local state preserving** for st_G and it is reflected by the predicate $\mathsf{LSP}(q, st_G, \mathbb{U}) = 1$.*

Finally, we introduce the concept of *non-trivial execution* for a cRBAC system. A non-trivial execution consists of a sequence of operations such that after executing every operation in order, for each file in the system, there should exist at least a user that has the read permission for it and also exist at least a user that has the write permission for it.

Now we present our lower bounds for cRBAC systems which are both correct and secure with respect to read (write, resp.) access.

Theorem 3. *For any cRBAC system which is **correct** and **secure with respect to** $\blacksquare \in \{\mathsf{read}, \mathsf{write}\}$ access, it holds that:*

$$\Pr\left[\begin{array}{c} st_G \leftarrow_\$ \mathsf{Init}(1^\lambda, R); st_G \xrightarrow{Q} st_G'; \forall q \in U\downarrow P(\phi(st_G')) : \\ \mathsf{FSP}(q, st_G') \wedge \mathsf{LSP}(q, st_G', U_c) \end{array} \right] \leq \epsilon,$$

where Q is any non-trivial execution for the system, $st_G' = (st_M', fs', \{st_u'\}_{u \in U'})$, $\phi(st_G') = (U', O', P', UA', PA'), U \subseteq U', P \subseteq \{(o, \blacksquare) | o \in O'\}, U_c = \{u | \forall (o, \blacksquare) \in P : \mathsf{HasAccess}(u, (o, \{\mathsf{read}, \mathsf{write}\} \setminus \blacksquare))\}$ and ϵ is a negligible function in λ.

References

1. Alderman, J., Crampton, J., Farley, N.: A framework for the cryptographic enforcement of information flow policies. In: Proceedings of the 22nd ACM on Symposium on Access Control Models and Technologies, SACMAT 2017, Indianapolis, IN, USA, 21–23 June 2017, pp. 143–154 (2017)
2. Clear, M., Hughes, A., Tewari, H.: Homomorphic encryption with access policies: characterization and new constructions. In: Youssef, A., Nitaj, A., Hassanien, A.E. (eds.) AFRICACRYPT 2013. LNCS, vol. 7918, pp. 61–87. Springer, Heidelberg (2013). https://doi.org/10.1007/978-3-642-38553-7_4
3. Ferrara, A.L., Fachsbauer, G., Liu, B., Warinschi, B.: Policy privacy in cryptographic access control. In: IEEE 28th Computer Security Foundations Symposium, CSF 2015, Verona, Italy, 13–17 July 2015, pp. 46–60 (2015)
4. Ferrara, A.L., Fuchsbauer, G., Warinschi, B.: Cryptographically enforced RBAC. In: 2013 IEEE 26th Computer Security Foundations Symposium, New Orleans, LA, USA, 26–28 June 2013, pp. 115–129 (2013)
5. Halevi, S., Karger, P.A., Naor, D.: Enforcing confinement in distributed storage and a cryptographic model for access control. IACR Cryptology ePrint Archive, 2005:169 (2005)
6. Huang, J., Sharaf, M.A., Huang, C.-T.: A hierarchical framework for secure and scalable EHR sharing and access control in multi-cloud. In: 41st International Conference on Parallel Processing Workshops, ICPPW 2012, Pittsburgh, PA, USA, 10–13 September 2012, pp. 279–287 (2012)
7. Ibraimi, L.: Cryptographically enforced distributed data access control. University of Twente (2011)
8. Garrison III, W.C., Shull, A., Lee, A.J., Myers, S.: Dynamic and private cryptographic access control for untrusted clouds: costs and constructions (extended version). CoRR, abs/1602.09069 (2016)
9. Jahid, S., Mittal, P., Borisov, N.: EASiER: encryption-based access control in social networks with efficient revocation. In: Proceedings of the 6th ACM Symposium on Information, Computer and Communications Security, ASIACCS 2011, Hong Kong, China, 22–24 March 2011, pp. 411–415 (2011)
10. Liu, B., Warinschi, B.: Universally composable cryptographic role-based access control. In: Chen, L., Han, J. (eds.) ProvSec 2016. LNCS, vol. 10005, pp. 61–80. Springer, Cham (2016). https://doi.org/10.1007/978-3-319-47422-9_4
11. Qi, S., Zheng, Y.: Crypt-DAC: cryptographically enforced dynamic access control in the cloud. IEEE Trans. Dependable Secur. Comput. 18(2), 765–779 (2021)
12. Wang, G., Liu, Q., Wu, J.: Hierarchical attribute-based encryption for fine-grained access control in cloud storage services. In: Proceedings of the 17th ACM Conference on Computer and Communications Security, CCS 2010, Chicago, Illinois, USA, 4–8 October 2010, pp. 735–737 (2010)
13. Weber, S.G.: Designing a hybrid attribute-based encryption scheme supporting dynamic attributes. IACR Cryptology ePrint Archive, 2013:219 (2013)
14. Zhu, Y., Ahn, G.-J., Hu, H., Wang, H.: Cryptographic role-based security mechanisms based on role-key hierarchy. In: Proceedings of the 5th ACM Symposium on Information, Computer and Communications Security, ASIACCS 2010, Beijing, China, 13–16 April 2010, pp. 314–319 (2010)

Author Index

Printed in the United States
by Baker & Taylor Publisher Services